THE CAMBRIDGE COMPANION TO

# THE TRINITY

How do Christians reconcile their belief in one God with the concept of three divine "persons"? This *Companion* provides an overview of how the Christian doctrine of the Trinity has been understood and articulated in the last two thousand years. The trinitarian theologies of key theologians, from the New Testament to the twenty-first century, are carefully examined, and the doctrine of the Trinity is brought into dialogue with non-Christian religions as well as with other Christian beliefs. Authors from a range of denominational backgrounds explore the importance of trinitarian thought, locating the Trinity within the wider context of systematic theology. Contemporary theology has seen a widespread revival of the doctrine of the Trinity, and this book incorporates the most recent developments in the scholarship.

Peter C. Phan holds the Ignacio Ellacuría Chair of Catholic Social Thought in the Department of Theology at Georgetown University. He is the author of numerous books including *Christianity with an Asian Face* (2003), *In Our Own Tongues: Asian Perspectives on Mission and Inculturation* (2004), and *Being Religious Interreligiously* (2004).

CAMBRIDGE COMPANIONS TO RELIGION

A series of companions to major topics and key figures in theology and religious studies. Each volume contains specially commissioned chapters by international scholars which provide an accessible and stimulating introduction to the subject for new readers and non-specialists.

*Other titles in the series*

THE CAMBRIDGE COMPANION TO CHRISTIAN DOCTRINE
edited by Colin Gunton (1997)
ISBN 0 521 47118 4 hardback ISBN 0 521 47695 x paperback

THE CAMBRIDGE COMPANION TO BIBLICAL INTERPRETATION
edited by John Barton (1998)
ISBN 0 521 48144 9 hardback ISBN 0 521 48593 2 paperback

THE CAMBRIDGE COMPANION TO DIETRICH BONHOEFFER
edited by John de Gruchy (1999)
ISBN 0 521 58258 x hardback ISBN 0 521 58781 6 paperback

THE CAMBRIDGE COMPANION TO KARL BARTH
edited by John Webster (2000)
ISBN 0 521 58476 0 hardback ISBN 0 521 58560 0 paperback

THE CAMBRIDGE COMPANION TO CHRISTIAN ETHICS
edited by Robin Gill (2001)
ISBN 0 521 77070 x hardback ISBN 0 521 77918 9 paperback

THE CAMBRIDGE COMPANION TO JESUS
edited by Markus Bockmuehl (2001)
ISBN 0 521 79261 4 hardback ISBN 0 521 79678 4 paperback

THE CAMBRIDGE COMPANION TO FEMINIST THEOLOGY
edited by Susan Frank Parsons (2002)
ISBN 0 521 66327 x hardback ISBN 0 521 66380 6 paperback

THE CAMBRIDGE COMPANION TO MARTIN LUTHER
edited by Donald K. McKim (2003)
ISBN 0 521 81648 3 hardback ISBN 0 521 01673 8 paperback

THE CAMBRIDGE COMPANION TO ST PAUL
edited by James D. G. Dunn (2003)
ISBN 0 521 78155 8 hardback ISBN 0 521 78694 0 paperback

THE CAMBRIDGE COMPANION TO POSTMODERN THEOLOGY
edited by Kevin J. Vanhoozer (2003)
ISBN 0 521 79062 x hardback ISBN 0 521 79395 5 paperback

THE CAMBRIDGE COMPANION TO JOHN CALVIN
edited by Donald K. McKim (2004)
ISBN 0 521 81647 5 hardback ISBN 0 521 01672 x paperback

THE CAMBRIDGE COMPANION TO HANS URS VON BALTHASAR
edited by Edward T. Oakes, SJ and David Moss (2004)
ISBN 0 521 81467 7 hardback ISBN 0 521 89147 7 paperback

THE CAMBRIDGE COMPANION TO REFORMATION THEOLOGY
edited by David Bagchi and David Steinmetz (2004)
ISBN 0 521 77224 9 hardback ISBN 0 521 77662 7 paperback

THE CAMBRIDGE COMPANION TO AMERICAN JUDAISM
edited by Dana Evan Kaplan (2005)
ISBN 0 521 82204 1 hardback ISBN 0 521 52951 4 paperback

THE CAMBRIDGE COMPANION TO KARL RAHNER
edited by Declan Marmion and Mary E. Hines (2005)
ISBN 0 521 83288 8 hardback ISBN 0 521 54045 3 paperback

THE CAMBRIDGE COMPANION TO FRIEDRICH SCHLEIERMACHER
edited by Jacqueline Mariña (2005)
ISBN 0 521 81448 0 hardback ISBN 0 521 89137 X paperback

THE CAMBRIDGE COMPANION TO THE GOSPELS
edited by Stephen C. Barton (2006)
ISBN 0 521 80766 2 hardback ISBN 0 521 00261 3 paperback

THE CAMBRIDGE COMPANION TO THE QUR'AN
edited by Jane Dammen McAuliffe (2006)
ISBN 0 521 83160 1 hardback ISBN 0 521 53934 X paperback

THE CAMBRIDGE COMPANION TO JONATHAN EDWARDS
edited by Stephen J. Stein (2007)
ISBN 0 521 85290 0 hardback ISBN 0 521 61805 3 paperback

THE CAMBRIDGE COMPANION TO EVANGELICAL THEOLOGY
edited by Timothy Larsen and Daniel J. Trier (2007)
ISBN 0 521 84698 6 hardback ISBN 0 521 60974 7 paperback

THE CAMBRIDGE COMPANION TO MODERN JEWISH PHILOSOPHY
edited by Michael L. Morgan and Peter Eli Gordon (2007)
ISBN 0 521 81312 3 hardback ISBN 0 521 01255 4 paperback

THE CAMBRIDGE COMPANION TO THE TALMUD AND RABBINIC LITERATURE
edited by Charlotte E. Fonrobert and Martin S. Jaffee (2007)
ISBN 0 521 84390 1 hardback ISBN 0 521 60508 3 paperback

THE CAMBRIDGE COMPANION TO LIBERATION THEOLOGY
second edition edited by Christopher Rowland (2007)
ISBN 9780521868839 hardback ISBN 9780521688932 paperback

THE CAMBRIDGE COMPANION TO THE JESUITS
edited by Thomas Worcester (2008)
ISBN 9780521857314 hardback ISBN 9780521673969 paperback

THE CAMBRIDGE COMPANION TO CLASSICAL ISLAMIC THEOLOGY
edited by Tim Winter (2008)
ISBN 9780521780582 hardback ISBN 9780521785495 paperback

THE CAMBRIDGE COMPANION TO PURITANISM
edited by John Coffey and Paul Lim (2008)
ISBN 9780521860888 hardback ISBN 9780521678001 paperback

THE CAMBRIDGE COMPANION TO ORTHODOX CHRISTIAN THEOLOGY
edited by Mary Cunningham and Elizabeth Theokritoff (2008)
ISBN 9780521864848 hardback ISBN 9780521683388 paperback

THE CAMBRIDGE COMPANION TO PAUL TILLICH
edited by Russell Re Manning (2009)
ISBN 9780521859899 hardback ISBN 9780521677356 paperback

THE CAMBRIDGE COMPANION TO JOHN HENRY NEWMAN
edited by Ian Ker and Terrence Merrigan (2009)
ISBN 9780521871860 hardback ISBN 9780521692724 paperback

THE CAMBRIDGE COMPANION TO JOHN WESLEY
edited by Randy L. Maddox and Jason E. Vickers (2010)
ISBN 9780521886536 hardback ISBN 9780521714037 paperback

THE CAMBRIDGE COMPANION TO CHRISTIAN PHILOSOPHICAL THEOLOGY
edited by Charles Taliaferro and Chad Meister (2010)
ISBN 9780521514330 hardback ISBN 9780521730372 paperback

THE CAMBRIDGE COMPANION TO MUHAMMAD
edited by Jonathan E. Brockopp (2010)
ISBN 9780521886079 hardback ISBN 9780521713726 paperback

THE CAMBRIDGE COMPANION TO SCIENCE AND RELIGION
edited by Peter Harrison (2010)
ISBN 9780521885386 hardback ISBN 9780521712514 paperback

THE CAMBRIDGE COMPANION TO GANDHI
edited by Judith Brown and Anthony Parel (2011)
ISBN 9780521116701 hardback ISBN 9780521133456 paperback

THE CAMBRIDGE COMPANION TO THOMAS MORE
edited by George Logan (2011)
ISBN 9780521888622 hardback ISBN 9780521716871 paperback

THE CAMBRIDGE COMPANION TO MIRACLES
edited by Graham H. Twelftree (2011)
ISBN 9780521899864 hardback ISBN 9780521728515 paperback

*Forthcoming*

THE CAMBRIDGE COMPANION TO FRANCIS OF ASSISI
edited by Michael J. P. Robson

THE CAMBRIDGE COMPANION TO NEW RELIGIOUS MOVEMENTS
edited by Olav Hammer and Mikael Rothstein

THE CAMBRIDGE COMPANION TO BLACK THEOLOGY
edited by Dwight Hopkins and Edward Antonio

THE CAMBRIDGE COMPANION TO

# THE TRINITY

Edited by Peter C. Phan

CAMBRIDGE UNIVERSITY PRESS
Cambridge, New York, Melbourne, Madrid, Cape Town,
Singapore, São Paulo, Delhi, Tokyo, Mexico City

Cambridge University Press
The Edinburgh Building, Cambridge CB2 8RU, UK

Published in the United States of America by Cambridge University Press, New York

www.cambridge.org
Information on this title: www.cambridge.org/9780521877398



First published 2011

Printed in the United Kingdom at the University Press, Cambridge

*A catalogue record for this publication is available from the British Library*

*Library of Congress Cataloguing in Publication data*
The Cambridge companion to the Trinity / edited by Peter C. Phan.
p. cm. – (Cambridge companions to religion)
Includes bibliographical references and index.
ISBN 978-0-521-87739-8 (hardback) – ISBN 978-0-521-70113-6 (pbk.)
1. Trinity – History of doctrines. I. Phan, Peter C., 1943–
BT111.3.C35 2011
231′.044 – dc22 2011015545

ISBN 978-0-521-87739-8 Hardback
ISBN 978-0-521-70113-6 Paperback

# Contents

# Notes on contributors

**Michel René Barnes** is Associate Professor of Historical Theology at Marquette University, Milwaukee, Wisconsin, USA. He received his doctorate from the University of St. Michael's College, Toronto, Ontario, Canada. Dr. Barnes is the author of many articles on Augustine's trinitarian theology and a monograph on Gregory of Nyssa's trinitarian theology, *The Power of God: Dunamis in Gregory of Nyssa's Trinitarian Theology*, and edited, with D. H. Williams, *Arianism after Arius*. He has recently published on Irenaeus' trinitarian theology, and has written a study of Christian pneumatology in the first two centuries.

**Young-Ho Chun,** Ph.D., is Professor of Systematic Theology at Saint Paul School of Theology, Kansas City. He was educated in South Korea, the USA, and Germany. He authored *Tillich and Religion: Toward a Theology of World Religions* and contributed numerous chapters to the Lit-Verlag series Tillich-Studien.

**Francis X. Clooney,** SJ, a Roman Catholic priest and a member of the Society of Jesus, joined Harvard Divinity School in 2005. His primary areas of scholarship are theological commentarial writings in the Sanskrit and Tamil traditions of Hindu India and comparative theology. Professor Clooney is the author of numerous articles and books, including *Hindu God, Christian God*; *Divine Mother, Blessed Mother: Hindu Goddesses and the Virgin Mary*; *Jesuit Postmodern: Scholarship, Vocation, and Identity in the 21st Century*; *Beyond Compare: St. Francis and Sri Vedanta Desika on Loving Surrender to God*; and *The Truth, the Way, the Life: Christian Commentary on the Three Holy Mantras of the Srivaisnava Hindus*.

**Miguel H. Díaz,** Ph.D., is currently US Ambassador to the Holy See. He was Professor of Systematic Theology at the College of Saint Benedict and Saint John's University in Collegeville, Minnesota. He has published a number of articles and is co-editor of the book *From the Heart of our People: Latino/a Explorations in Systematic Theology* and author of *On Being Human: U.S. Hispanic and Rahnerian Perspectives*.

**Patricia A. Fox** has studied systematic theology at Catholic Theological Union, Chicago, and at Flinders University, South Australia. She has been involved in secondary and tertiary education, as well as in formation, spiritual direction and retreat work. She has held leadership positions within the Institute of the

Sisters of Mercy of Australia and the Archdiocese of Adelaide. She is presently teaching at Flinders University and the Adelaide College of Divinity and is director of a ministry formation program for the Catholic archdiocese based on that campus.

**James L. Fredericks,** Ph.D., is a faculty member in the Department of Theological Studies at Loyola Marymount University. He is a specialist in interreligious dialogue, especially the dialogue between Buddhism and Christianity. In addition to publishing many articles, he is the author of *Faith among Faiths: Christian Theology and the Non-Christian Religions* and *Buddhists and Christians: Through Comparative Theology to a New Solidarity.*

**Christine Helmer** is Professor of Religious Studies and Adjunct Professor of German at Northwestern University. She is author of *The Trinity and Martin Luther* and is editor (or co-editor) of numerous volumes in the areas of Schleiermacher studies, philosophy of religion, and biblical theology. Her most recent publications are an edited volume, *The Global Luther: A Theologian for Modern Times*, an essay on Schleiermacher in *The Blackwell Companion to Nineteenth-Century Theology* (edited by David Fergusson), and an essay on theology's contribution to the contemporary study of religion in *The Cambridge Companion to Religious Studies* (edited by Robert A. Orsi).

**Peter Goodwin Heltzel** is Assistant Professor of Theology at New York Theological Seminary. An ordained minister in the Christian Church (Disciples of Christ), he is the author of *Jesus and Justice: Evangelicals, Race and Politics.* His edited volumes include *Chalice Introduction to Disciples Theology* and *Theology in Global Context.*

**Anne Hunt** is Dean of the Faculty of Theology and Philosophy at Australian Catholic University. In addition to her many publications on trinitarian theology, she has an interest in the visual arts as a powerful medium for communicating the mysteries of faith. Her latest book is *Trinity: Insights from the Mystics.*

**Dale T. Irvin** is President and Professor of World Christianity at New York Theological Seminary in New York City. A graduate of Princeton Theological Seminary and Union Theological Seminary in New York, he is the author of several books, including *History of the World Christian Movement*, with Scott W. Sunquist. Over the past several decades his articles have appeared in a number of journals such as *Christianity Today, Christian Century, The Ecumenical Review*, and *The Journal of Pentecostal Studies.* He is a founding editor of *The Journal of World Christianity* and serves on the editorial board of *The Living Pulpit.*

**Veli-Matti Kärkkäinen** (Dr. Theol. Habil., University of Helsinki) is Professor of Systematic Theology at Fuller Theological Seminary and Docent of Ecumenics at the University of Helsinki. A native of Finland, he has taught theology in Thailand. The author of a dozen scholarly books, among which are *Trinity and Religious Pluralism* and *The Trinity: Global Perspectives*, as well as more than one hundred articles, Dr. Kärkkäinen has participated widely in the theological, missiological, and interfaith work of the World Council of Churches and Faith and Order as well in several bilateral ecumenical dialogues.

**Karen Kilby** is an Associate Professor in Systematic Theology in the Department of Theology and Religious Studies in the University of Nottingham, where she also served as head of the department. She has previously written on the thought of Karl Rahner, on the relationship between Rahner and Balthasar, and on the doctrine of the Trinity. Her latest book is *Balthasar: A Very Critical Introduction*.

**Heup Young Kim** is Professor of Systematic Theology and a former Dean of the College of Humanities and the Graduate School of Theology, Kangnam University, Korea. He has published numerous works in the areas of interfaith dialogue, theology of religions, Asian theology, and theology and science, in both English and Korean, including *Wang Yang-ming and Karl Barth: A Confucian–Christian Dialogue*; *Toward a Theology of the Tao*; *Christ and the Tao*; and *Contemporary Natural Sciences and Christianity*.

**John A. McGuckin** is the Nielsen Professor of Patristic and Byzantine Thought at Union Theological Seminary and Columbia University New York. He has written extensively on New Testament and early Christian thought. He is a priest of the Romanian Orthodox Church.

**Anselm Kyongsuk Min** has been Professor of Philosophy of Religion and Theology at Claremont Graduate University in Southern California since 1992. He is the author of several books including *Paths to the Triune God: An Encounter between Aquinas and Recent Theologies*; *The Solidarity of Others in a Divided World: A Postmodern Theology After Postmodernism*; and *The Dialectic of Salvation: Issues in Theology of Liberation*, as well as of many articles on Hegel, postmodernism, liberation theology, pluralism, and Asian and Korean theologies.

**Kenan B. Osborne,** a Franciscan, has been a professor of systematic theology at the Franciscan School of Theology, part of the Graduate Theological Union, Berkeley, California, since 1968. He received his D.Theol. degree from Ludwig-Maximilians Universität, Munich, Germany, in 1967. He is a former president of the Catholic Theological Society of America. In 2002 he received the John Courtney Murray Award from this same society. He has written eighteen books and numerous articles on theological subjects. He is now an emeritus professor.

**Aristotle Papanikolaou** is Associate Professor of Theology in the Department of Theology and Co-Founding Director of the Orthodox Christian Studies Program at Fordham University, New York. He is the author of *Being with God: Trinity, Apophaticism, and Divine–Human Communion*, co-editor (with George Demacopoulos) of *Orthodox Readings of Augustine*, and co-editor (with Elizabeth Prodromou) of *Thinking through Faith: New Perspectives from Orthodox Christian Scholars*.

**Peter C. Phan** went to the USA as a refugee from Vietnam in 1975. Currently he is the holder of the Ignacio Ellacuría Chair of Catholic Social Thought at

Georgetown University. He has earned three doctorates and received two honorary doctorates. His fields of research include systematic theology, interreligious dialogue, and missiology. He has authored and edited over twenty books and published more than 300 articles. His book on Karl Rahner's eschatology won the Best Book Award from the College Theology Society in 1989, and his book on Alexandre de Rhodes was given the first place by the Catholic Publishers Association in 1999.

**Elaine M. Wainwright** is Inaugural Professor of Theology and Head of the School of Theology at the University of Auckland, New Zealand, a post she has held for the last six years. She is a New Testament scholar specializing in the gospel of Matthew, biblical hermeneutics, and feminist, postcolonial, and ecological interpretations of biblical texts. Her current research is an ecological reading of the gospel of Matthew. Among her recent publications are *Shall We Look for Another? A Feminist Rereading of the Matthean Jesus* and *Women Healing/Healing Women: The Genderization of Healing in Early Christianity.*

**Christian T. Collins Winn** is Associate Professor of Historical and Systematic Theology at Bethel University in St. Paul, Minnesota. He is the editor of *From the Margins: A Celebration of the Theological Work of Donald W. Dayton*; author of *"Jesus is Victor!" The Significance of the Blumhardts for the Theology of Karl Barth*; and the series editor of *The Blumhardts: Texts and Reception.*

**Susan K. Wood,** Ph.D., is professor and chair of the Department of Theology at Marquette University. She is an associate editor of *Pro ecclesia* and serves on the editorial advisory board of the journal *Ecclesiology*. Most of her writings explore the connections between ecclesiology and sacramental theology. In addition to numerous articles, she has published *Spiritual Exegesis and the Church in the Theology of Henri de Lubac*; *Sacramental Orders*; and *One Baptism: Ecumenical Dimensions of the Doctrine of Baptism*; and is the editor of *Ordering the Baptismal Priesthood.*

# Preface

The subject matter of this book is the Trinity, now widely acknowledged to be a mystery of salvation and the central Christian belief. That the Triune God is so now may be a commonplace, but that has not always been the case. One of the pleasant surprises in contemporary theology is the widespread revival of the doctrine of the Trinity. Long shunted to the wings, the Trinity is now occupying center stage. Karl Rahner's oft-quoted *bon mot* that Christians are, theologically speaking, "mere monotheists" (that is, unitarians) may have been true in the 1960s and earlier. Fortunately, it is no longer so. Recently, a spate of books and articles on the Trinity by Catholic, Orthodox, and Protestant theologians has restored this neglected Christian doctrine to its rightful place. These works have not only retrieved the classical teachings on the Trinity through serious historical research, but have also given the lie to the claim that the trinitarian dogma is nothing more than abstruse metaphysics and a conundrum of "higher mathematics" of one-equals-three and vice versa. They have shown how trinitarian theology is necessary for a full understanding of such burning issues as the nature of the human person, suffering, sexism, ecology, social and economic justice, interreligious dialogue, and so on.

The twists and turns through which the Triune God migrated from the center to the periphery of Christian consciousness and back to the center again are recounted in the following pages. These winding paths make a fascinating story in themselves, along which readers now are invited to travel. The only thing to be stressed here is that this volume is intended to be a "companion" to those who wish to understand what Christians mean by the Trinity. It is not a manual, a textbook, a digest, or (the Triune) God forbid, a CliffsNotes of trinitarian theology. Each contributor would like to be a fellow traveler with the reader, or better still, to invoke the etymology of "companion" (*com* + *panis*), someone who shares bread, the bread of knowledge and friendship, with the readers, be they students or scholars.

The volume itself has its own twists and turns of sorts. It began when Dr. Kate Brett, the senior editor at Cambridge University Press, approached me with the proposal to edit the *Companion*. Her thoughtfulness and gentleness persuaded me that it would be a worthwhile task. The book proposal went through the usual blind review process, and I am grateful to the anonymous reviewers for their helpful comments. Brett and I agreed that the contributors should not only represent a wide spectrum of theological views but also be balanced in terms of gender, ethnicity, and geography, to honor the global character of contemporary theology. Unfortunately, not every attempt to achieve these goals was successful, but the failure was not due to lack of will or occasional strong arm-twisting.

A number of administrative changes occurred at Cambridge University Press while the book was being worked on, and the hands overseeing the production of the volume changed several times. I am of course deeply grateful to Kate Brett for her gentle care and guidance. Gillian Dadd and, then, Aline Guillermet took over the editorial process with competence and diligence, and I am thankful to them for bringing the book to port.

Another person I would like to thank is Dr. Fiona Little. She is the copy editor any writer and publishing house can ever hope to have: detailed, sharp-eyed, timely, persistent, patient, kind. Shaping all these diverse essays into a consistent style and format was a colossal labor, and Fiona has achieved it with unparalleled professionalism and skills. However, any errors that may remain are my responsibility. I also thank Dr. Anh Tran for his help with indexing.

Of course, my deepest thanks go to the contributors themselves; without them the book would not have existed at all. In my correspondence with them I have always referred to it as "*our* Trinity book," and I meant it literally. Despite their busy writing schedules, they all have responded with generosity and alacrity to my request to write for the volume. No editor could have been more fortunate. May our friendship, and now our communion with our readers, be a sign, however feeble, of the *koinōnia* that unites the Three That Are One.

Peter C. Phan

# Part I

## *Introduction*

# 1 Developments of the doctrine of the Trinity

PETER C. PHAN

"All authority in heaven and on earth has been given to me. Go therefore and make disciples of all nations, baptizing them in the name of the Father and of the Son and of the Holy Spirit" (Mt 28:18–19, NRSV). So is Jesus reported to have said to his eleven disciples on a mountain in Galilee. While biblical scholars dispute whether these words are Jesus' *ipsissima verba* or a baptismal formula of the early church retroactively placed on Jesus' lips, the verse is an incontrovertible indication that faith in God who is Father, Son, and Holy Spirit, in whose name (note the singular "name" and not "names") baptism is administered, is already present in the New Testament itself.[1] It has been correctly pointed out that the Christian faith in the Trinity should not be understood to be based exclusively on explicitly triadic formulae such as the above-cited verse, 1 Corinthians 12:4–6, 2 Corinthians 13:14, 1 Peter 1:2, and so on. Rather, the trinitarian data of the New Testament include all the exceedingly numerous texts that speak of the relationship between Jesus and the Father, between Jesus and the Spirit, between the Father and the Spirit, and among the Father, Jesus, and the Spirit.[2] Indeed, the literary structure itself of most New Testament books is arguably trinitarian.[3] In addition, the reality of the Trinity is present not only in certain New Testament formulations but also in the events of Jesus' life and ministry, in particular his conception, baptism, transfiguration, and death and resurrection, and at the Pentecost. Finally, it can reasonably be claimed that there are already intimations or adumbrations of the Trinity in the Old Testament such as the many names used for God (e.g., Wisdom, Word, Spirit), the "angel of Yahweh" figure, and some theophanies (e.g., the three men in Gen 18:1–2 or the threefold Sanctus of Isaiah's vision in Isa 6:3).

While all these observations are correct, it does not mean that a full-fledged *doctrine* of the Trinity is already developed in the New Testament. As the various chapters of this book show, the road that leads from the New Testament embryonic affirmations on the Trinity to contemporary trinitarian theologies is a long, meandering, and tortuous one, at times disappearing and reappearing in the thicket of Christian doctrines. Despite the organic metaphors occasionally deployed for it that conjure a steady and accumulative growth (e.g., the acorn growing into an oak tree), doctrinal development has never been a linear evolution progressing from better to best. Rather, the history of Christian doctrines often exhibits a recurrent pattern of growth, decline, eclipse, retrieval, and possibly growth again, to which a variety of factors, including political pressure, have contributed. The intent of this introductory chapter is not to recount all and sundry developments in trinitarian theology but to outline some of the key forces and agencies that have provided the impetus for and shaped the developments of trinitarian theology, not all the stages of which constitute progress and advancement.

## FAITH SEEKING UNDERSTANDING

The first and perhaps the most fundamental of these forces and agencies is the very dynamics of faith itself. Though not rational, faith is a reasonable act and as such contains within itself an irresistible drive to understand itself, by determining precisely *what* it is to be believed, understanding its *meaning*, judging the grounds for its *truth*, and evaluating its moral *value* and *practical implications*. With regard to the doctrine of the Trinity, the early Christians face the task of reconciling in a conceptually coherent way their (Jewish) belief in the one God (monotheism) and their experience and consequent affirmation of the Father's, Jesus', and the Spirit's divine status and their distinct personal actions on their lives. To put it schematically, they believe that there is only one God (Deut 6:4), yet they experience – differently and distinctly – that the Father is God, that Jesus the Son is God, and that the Spirit is God. The effort to reconcile unity and plurality in God is not a matter of solving a mathematical conundrum or a metaphysical puzzle of how one is three and three is one. Rather, early Christians are compelled to account for the three distinct ways in which the one God is experienced as present and active in their lives and in the history of salvation – that God, who is the Father, the Son, and the Spirit, creates, saves, and sanctifies humans, not simply as three different and successive ways or roles in which God acts toward them but as three truly different personal "entities." These three "entities" however do not constitute three Gods but one God.

At the heart of this theological account is not a metaphysical speculation about the structure of the cosmos or the nature of the divine in the tradition of Greek philosophy but an attempt at holding together, for pastoral and spiritual purposes, two apparently contradictory *experiences*, namely, that God is one *and* that God is plural, insofar as the one God is perceived as acting in distinct modes as Father, Son, and Spirit. This is done primarily in narrative style, by telling the story of God's involvement with humanity and in the world as distinct agents. The word "person" is not yet used to designate these actors, even though they act with unmistakably personal characteristics such as understanding, freedom, and love. Rather, terms that are already familiar in the Old Testament discourse about God, such as "Father," "Son," "Word," "Wisdom," and "Spirit," are pressed into service to refer to these divine agents, not so much in their eternal mutual relationships (what theologians call the "immanent," "transcendental" Trinity) but in their relationships to and activities on behalf of humans (the "economic" Trinity). Later, a more technical terminology and conceptual apparatus will be adopted from Greek and Latin languages and philosophies to distinguish these three personal agents (*who* they are) from their nature (*what* they are) and from each other (their reciprocal *relations*). These terms and philosophies are not however used to discover new ideas about God but to express faithfully and accurately what experience has already taught Christians about *what* and *who* God is.

## HERESIES AND THE DEVELOPMENT OF DOCTRINE

In carrying out this task of "faith seeking understanding" – to use a definition of theology as *fides quaerens intellectum* by the eleventh-century theologian Anselm of Canterbury – it is inevitable that errors are committed, one-sided affirmations made, and inadequate perspectives adopted. To understand these errors it is helpful to remember that the theologians who are condemned as heresiarchs did not intentionally set out to innovate, itching for novelty and originality. Rather they were seriously concerned with the question of salvation and were engaged in the pastoral task of expressing the truths of faith in ways that would make sense to their contemporaries.[4] In so doing however they emphasized only one aspect rather maintaining the whole of the Christian faith. Faced with two apparently contradictory statements, they did not have a capacious enough analogical imagination to hold both of them in a creative and intellectually unresolvable tension of "both-and" but opted for the seductive clarity of "either-or," affirming one alternative and denying the other.

With regard to the Trinity, there are, theoretically speaking, two possibilities: either to affirm unity and deny plurality in God, and vice versa. All trinitarian heresies are but variations on these two "choices" (that is what the Greek *hairesis* means). *Tritheism*, which privileges God's plurality, while common among "pagans," was not a live option for early Christians, who adhered strictly to Jewish monotheism, even though it remains a constant danger in popular imagination, especially when the term "person" is used to refer to the Father, the Son, and the Spirit. Because of the heavily psychological connotation of the word "person" in contemporary usage, it is a natural temptation to imagine that the Father, the Son, and the Spirit constitute three distinct consciousnesses, three centers of activity, three concrete beings. That is why theologians as different as Augustine, Karl Barth, and Karl Rahner were reluctant to use the term "person" and coined other phrases such as *Seinsweise* (modes of being: Barth) or distinct *Subsistenzweise* (manners of subsisting: Rahner) to refer to the Father, the Son, and the Spirit.

The alternative option, that of privileging God's unity, known as *monarchianism*, arises in connection with the issue of the identity of Jesus. Confessing the Son as divine is seen by some as jeopardizing the godhead of the one God who is the Father. It takes two main forms. The first, attributed to Theodotus, Artemon, and Paul of Samosata, is called *dynamic monarchianism* or *adoptionism*, and according to this Jesus is a human being whom God adopts as his son at his incarnation or baptism. The second, attributed to Noetus, Praxeas, and Sabellius, is called *modalism*; according to this the Father, the Son, and the Spirit are three "ways" or "modes" or "faces" in which the one God acts in history but there is no real distinction among them. Another version of modalism is *patripassianism*, which holds that Jesus is God the Father who is incarnated and suffers as the Son.

The most (in)famous proponent of the oneness of God to the detriment of the divinity of the Son is the fourth-century Alexandrian presbyter Arius, according to whom the Son, being created, is inferior to the Father. For him God is an absolutely immaterial substance who cannot generate any son from his substance but only creates another being through an act of the will. The Son, though created, is however a perfect creature and is therefore superior to all other creatures. In fact, like Plato's demiurge, he is an intermediate being between the absolute, inaccessible, and unknowable one God and the material world.

Arius' trinitarian theology, later given an extreme form by Aetius and his disciple Eunomius and called *anomoean* (dissimilar), asserts a total dissimilarity between the Son and the Father.

Arianism is fiercely opposed by Athanasius of Alexandria and condemned by the Council of Nicaea (325), whose teaching affirms that the nature/substance/essence of the Son is the same as or identical to (*homoousios*) that of the Father and that therefore he is fully divine and equal to the Father. There is also the mediating position between Arius and Nicaea, espoused by Basil of Ancyra and several bishops friendly to the imperial court, which says that the Son is neither dissimilar nor identical in nature to the Father but only similar (*homoiousios*) to him.

However one judges these different trinitarian theologies, it is undeniable that heresies – in the early church and at any other stage of history – have played an important function in the development of the Christian doctrine of the Trinity. At the very least they compel the church to clarify its beliefs, provide them with scriptural warrants, elaborate arguments in their defense, show their connections with other doctrines, display their import for Christian living, and express them in a language appropriate for its contemporaries. These tasks lead us to the next factor in the development of the trinitarian doctrine.

## CRITICAL DIALOGUE WITH CONTEMPORARY CULTURES

In expounding the church's beliefs to their contemporaries, theologians necessarily enter into dialogue with the cultural resources of their times. These conversation partners normally include philosophy, but not exclusively; other disciplines have been brought into conversation with theology such as literature, psychology, sociology, religious studies, and the so-called hard sciences (e.g., biology, astrophysics, and medicine), especially today. This dialogue is known by various names such as "indigenization," "contextualization," "localization," or "inculturation." It is important to note that the gospel is not a divine message devoid of cultures, to be implanted in its pristine purity in other cultures. In fact, it is already laden with cultural elements (e.g., Jewish and Greek), so that the encounter between the gospel and other cultures is more properly viewed as an *intercultural* process. Furthermore, this intercultural encounter is not simply as a one-direction movement, from the gospel to cultures, as if the gospel only enriches other cultures and itself remains unaffected by them. On the contrary, both the gospel and the cultures enrich, complement, and even correct each other in the process.

In trinitarian theology, the first intercultural encounter is between the Christian faith and Greek and Latin languages and philosophy. Started already in the New Testament, it culminates at the Council of Nicaea, when the council decides to adopt the term *homoousios* to explain the divinity of Jesus, even though it is not a biblical term and has been used by Sabellius in a modalist sense. At other times, the church adopts a common term but modifies its meaning. For example, whereas *ousia* (being) and *hypostasis* (substance) are strictly speaking synonyms and are still used in this way by Nicaea, in the writings of the Cappadocians, that is, Basil of Caesarea, Gregory of Nyssa, and Gregory of Nazianzus, they are assigned totally different connotations, with *ousia* taken to mean what is common and abstract (Aristotle's "first substance"), and *hypostasis* what is proper and concrete (Aristotle's "second substance"). Eventually, the formula "*mia ousia* [one substance] *treis hypostaseis* [three persons]" is applied to the Trinity.[5] Another term, *prosopon*, literally meaning a face, mask, or role, is used (more frequently in Gregory of Nyssa) as equivalent to *hypostasis* but without any modalist undertone. In the East, the word *trias* is first used by Theophilus of Antioch. In the West, the third-century African theologian Tertullian coins the word *trinitas* and uses *substantia* and *persona* as equivalents of *ousia* and *prosopon* (or *hypostasis*) respectively.

Furthermore, trinitarian theology was developed not only with linguistic borrowings but also by adopting certain currents of philosophy. Early Apologists such as Justin and Theophilus of Antioch make use of Stoicism and Platonism, the latter as mediated by Philo, to explain how the Son as Word (*logos*) exists eternally with the Father as his "immanent Word" (*logos endiathetos*) and acts in time through creation and revelation as his "expressed Word" (*logos prophorikos*). Later, neo-Platonism, with its founder Plotinus, exerts a great influence on early Greek trinitarian theology, for instance, that of Origen and the Cappadocians.[6]

The use of philosophy to express the Christian understanding of the Trinity is not of course limited to the patristic era but continues throughout the subsequent history of Christianity. Thomas Aquinas makes use of Aristotle, and since the nineteenth century Kant, Hegel, Heidegger, Ernst Bloch, and Whitehead, just to mention a few, cast their long shadows over contemporary trinitarian theologies. Furthermore, as Christianity expands beyond its own Western habitat, it enters into dialogue with other cultures and religions such as Islam, Hinduism, Buddhism, and Chinese religions to enrich its trinitarian theologies.

Such use of linguistic conventions, philosophy, and religious thought to elaborate a theology of the Trinity has never been a wholesale, slavish adoption but is a critical and creative adaptation and transformation. Early theologians never simply transpose the trinitarian faith into the philosophical categories available in their days. In this intercultural encounter there has not been a Hellenization of Christianity, as Adolf Harnack charges. Rather the reverse is true, that is, there has been a Christianization of Greek thought. We have already mentioned the attribution of specifically Christian meanings to *ousia* and *hypostasis*. There is also a momentous transformation of the Greek understanding of "person" by the Cappadocians, especially Gregory of Nazianzus, who take "relation" not as a mere "accident" (that is, one of Aristotle's existing-in-a-substance categories) but as a self-subsisting and person-defining characteristic. (As Thomas later says, person is "subsisting relation.")

Neo-Platonism is modified by Athanasius, who rejects its notion of "unoriginate" as an essential attribute of God. Rather, for him, "unoriginate" is a personal and proper attribute of the Father alone, so that the Son, though originated (that is, begotten of the Father), is no less divine than the Father, and the Spirit, though "proceeding" from the Father through the Son (the West later added "*and* the Son"), is no less divine. Paradoxically, by using the non-biblical, Greek-sounding *homoousios* to affirm the Son's divinity, Nicaea rejects Arius' Hellenization-gone-too-far, in which the neo-Platonist concept of God is taken as the norm to judge the Christian understanding of who the Father of Jesus is.

## COUNCIL, CREED, WORSHIP

The mention of Nicaea brings us to another agency in the formation of the trinitarian doctrine. Nicaea and the subsequent councils demonstrate that theology, or better still theologizing or doing theology, is not a private enterprise where originality and novelty are the prized hallmarks of scholarship. Rather it is a communal, or, more precisely, ecclesial activity carried out in, with, for, and on behalf of the church, in faithfulness to God's self-revelation. It is an activity in which the corporate *sensus fidei* (the sense or instinct faith of the whole church) and the regulative teaching ministry of the bishops and councils play an indispensable role.

With regard to the Trinity, the divinity of the Son is affirmed by Nicaea (325) and that of the Holy Spirit by Constantinople (381). These teachings are set forth in "symbols" or creeds, later known as the Nicene creed and the Niceno-Constantinopolitan creed (the latter being a revised version of the symbol of Epiphanius of Salamis) respectively.

Subsequent councils in the West, local and general, adopt the practice of professing their faith in the Trinity by issuing creeds of their own, often incorporating the Niceno-Constantinopolitan creed, with the important addition "and the Son" (*filioque*) to the procession of the Spirit from the Father (e.g., the Eleventh Council of Toledo in 675, the Fourth Lateran Council in 1215, the Second Council of Lyons in 1274, and the Council of Basel-Ferrara-Florence-Rome in 1438–45).

These later Western creeds (including the so-called Athanasian creed *Quicumque vult*) tend to use a more technical language and function mainly as summary statements of the trinitarian faith. However, the early creeds or symbols of faith, especially the Niceno-Constantinopolitan creed and the so-called Apostles' creed, are used primarily in the context of worship, especially in the administration of baptism (where the form of a triple question-and-answer is used) and the celebration of the Eucharist (where it is sung on solemn occasions). Throughout history, the creed, whether recited in worship or used for didactic purposes, serves as the Christian community's profession of faith in and doxology of the Trinity and as the *regula fidei* (rule or canon of faith), ways of demarcating orthodoxy over against heresy and of distinguishing the Christian faith from other religious traditions.

In addition to being the proper context for the creeds, worship serves two other functions, namely faith-embodying and faith-generating. On the one hand, what the church believes, it celebrates, and vice versa: the church's beliefs regulate and shape its celebrations. Hence by observing what and how the church worships one can know what the church believes. The Latin phrase for this function is *lex credendi, lex orandi* (the law of belief [determines] the law of prayer). On the other hand, the liturgy also generates belief. At times, worship anticipates explicit formulations of belief; at others, it preserves beliefs that might have been forgotten or obscured. Hence, the liturgy is a source of faith, and the Latin phrase for this function is *lex orandi, lex credendi* (the law of prayer [determines] the law of belief). With regard to the Trinity, the feast of the Trinity was established in 1334 in the West to celebrate this central mystery of the Christian faith. It can also be argued that even if there has been a forgetfulness of the economic Trinity in theology, the memory of what God the Father, the Son, and the Spirit have done in the history of salvation is always kept alive in the consciousness of the church thanks to worship and prayer.

The development of the doctrine of the Trinity, as even a cursory perusal of the following pages will make clear, is a complex and tortuous

history. At times, especially to the theologically uninformed, the acrimonious quarrels and bitter church divisions that lead to exile (several times, as with Athanasius), excommunication (as with Arius and other heretics), and even burning at the stake (as in the case of Michael Servetus) seem to hinge on a different alphabet (as between *homousios* and *homoiousios*), a mathematical conundrum, or a petty struggle for power between rival sees and theological schools (e.g., Antioch vs. Alexandria) rather than on a matter of life and death. While power struggles, ecclesiastical and civil, were admittedly not absent, the parties involved in the trinitarian debates did believe that at stake was indeed something belonging to the *status confessionis* and not a matter of indifference (*adiaphora*), a metaphysical issue, or a mere question of semantics. Indeed, Athanasius and the Cappadocians were convinced that the denial of the divinity of Jesus and later, of the Holy Spirit, would jeopardize the very salvation of humanity. If Jesus is not divine, how could he have saved us, they argue, and if the Holy Spirit is not divine, how can he sanctify or divinize us? What is at stake then is nothing short of the very survival of the Christian faith.

This means that the Trinity lies at the heart and center of Christian life. This does not however mean that the doctrine of the Trinity has always been at the apex or the pivot of Christian theology. While the Trinity has always been at the center of the church's public prayer and worship, which is rendered to the Father in the Son and by the power of the Spirit – though not always in popular devotions – it has not always occupied a place of honor, at least in Western theology. Schleiermacher dedicates only a few pages to the Trinity at the end of his magnum opus *Der christliche Glaube* (*The Christian Faith*). In neo-scholastic manuals of Roman Catholic theology, God is treated in two separate treatises: *De Deo Uno* ("On the One God") and *De Deo Trino* ("On the Trine God"), with scarcely any connections between them. It took a Barth and a Rahner to make the Trinity not only the central doctrine of the Christian faith but also the structural principle of Christian theology.

The task of rediscovering the Trinity for faith, worship, and life is a constant challenge and need. It is an essential part of the *cogitatio fidei*, of thinking in faith about faith, to understand more deeply what God has revealed about Godself, to correct errors about God (and modernity and postmodernity are not devoid of them!), to retrieve what the Christian tradition has taught, to dialogue with contemporary cultures and religions, in communion with the Body of Christ. It is to contribute to this ongoing task that this *Companion* was conceived and realized.

## Notes

1. Allan Coppedge rightly argues that taking Mt 28:19 only as a baptismal formula misses the fact that its focus is on making disciples of the Triune God. See Allan Coppedge, *The God who is Triune: Revisioning the Christian Doctrine of God* (Downers Grove, IL: IVP Academic, 2007), 36–37. For a comprehensive study of the Trinity in the Bible, see Brian Edgar, *The Message of the Trinity* (Downers Grove, IL: InterVarsity Press, 2004).
2. See Coppedge, *The God who is Triune*, 26–34.
3. See ibid., 34–36.
4. That Arius, e.g., was thoroughly concerned with soteriology is shown by Robert C. Gregg and Dennis E. Groh, *Early Arianism: A View of Salvation* (Philadelphia: Fortress, 1981).
5. On this history of this formula, see Joseph T. Lienhard, "*Ousia* and *Hypostasis*: The Cappadocian Settlement and the Theology of 'One *Hypostasis*,'" in Stephen T. Davis, Daniel Kendall, and Gerald O'Collins, eds., *The Trinity: An Interdisciplinary Symposium on the Trinity* (Oxford University Press, 1999), 99–121.
6. Whether neo-Platonism has influenced Latin trinitarian theology, particularly that of Marius Victorinus (who composed the first Latin treatise on the Trinity) and Augustine, is much debated. Against a widespread reading of Augustine's theology as neo-Platonist, Michel René Barnes has vigorously argued that it is not. See his "Rereading Augustine's Theology of the Trinity," in Davis, Kendall, and O'Collins, eds., *The Trinity*, 145–76, and Chapter 5 below.

## Further reading

Farrelly, M. John, *The Trinity: Rediscovering the Central Christian Mystery* (Lanham, MD: Rowman & Littlefield, 2005).

Grenz, Stanley J., *Rediscovering the Triune God: The Trinity in Contemporary Theology* (Minneapolis: Fortress, 2004).

Herrich, Jennifer A., *Trinitarian Intelligibility: An Analysis of Contemporary Discussions* (Boca Raton, FL: Dissertation.com, 2006).

Leupp, Roderick T., *The Renewal of Trinitarian Theology: Themes, Patterns & Explorations* (Downers Grove, IL: IVP Academic, 2008).

Peters, Ted, *God as Trinity: Relationality and Temporality in Divine Life* (Louisville, KY: Westminster John Knox, 1993).

Thompson, John, *Modern Trinitarian Perspectives* (Oxford University Press, 1994).

Vanhoozer, Kevin J., ed., *The Trinity in a Pluralistic Age: Theological Essays on Culture and Religion* (Grand Rapids, MI: Eerdmans, 1997).

Volf, Miroslav, and Michael Welker, eds., *God's Life in Trinity* (Minneapolis: Fortress, 2006).

# 2 Systematic issues in trinitarian theology

PETER C. PHAN

About half a century ago, when the two arguably greatest theologians of the twentieth century, Karl Barth and Karl Rahner, first wrote on the Trinity, it was de rigueur to bemoan the marginalization of the Trinity from theology and spirituality and the dearth of works on the subject. Today writing on the Trinity has become something of a cottage industry, and the trinitarian mystery is unquestionably enthroned at the heart of Christian theology. But one of the drawbacks of the recent proliferation of trinitarian treatises is that with the rise of an enormous plethora of issues and views concerning the Trinity there is the danger of missing the forest for the trees. To obviate this pitfall, the following reflections are offered, not as a bibliographical survey but as a theological map to help readers identify the main issues, tenets, and directions in contemporary trinitarian theology.[1] Writing in 1993, Ted Peters identified twelve issues in contemporary trinitarian theology and various responses to them.[2] Since then other issues and answers have emerged. In a recent work Gerald O'Collins has also identified twelve issues in contemporary trinitarian theology, though his list is slightly different from that of Peters.[3] I will divide my own list into three categories: methodology, doctrine, and practice.

## METHODOLOGICAL ISSUES

Among the *loci theologici* of Christian doctrine, trininitarian theology has arguably, depending on where one stands, benefited or suffered the most from the use of metaphysics and analogies. To begin with analogies, they range from homespun images of the triangle or the shamrock or father, mother, and child to the so-called psychological models devised by Augustine[4] or Dorothy L. Sayers[5] to contemporary scientific models (e.g., particle, wave, and field).[6] Currently there is an excess of creativity in devising analogies for the Trinity, from the so-called *vestigia Trinitatis* so that any triad, however artificial and accidental, is harnessed for an illustration of the Trinity.[7] Furthermore, since all knowledge of and language for God, even that derived from the Bible, are by way of analogy, the question is raised as to whether there are criteria by which to judge the legitimacy and value of the analogies used for God, especially for the immanent Trinity. For example, are analogies derived from humans as *imago Dei* preferable to those taken from the material world? If so, what are the criteria to judge their usefulness and where are they to be found? Are they to be exclusively based on the Bible or to be determined philosophically?

With regard to the use of philosophy, from the historical standpoint, a variety of philosophical systems has been adopted, at times as mutually exclusive alternatives, to expound the Trinity, especially with regard to what is called the immanent Trinity. Among these philosophies neo-Platonic metaphysics, Stoic cosmology, Aristotelian substance metaphysics, Hegelian dialectical historicism, and, more recently, Whiteheadean process philosophy have occupied a prominent place, each with a long line of distinguished exponents and schools. Methodologically, the basic question is whether it is legitimate, let alone necessary, to have recourse to metaphysics in doing theology, especially in expounding the immanent Trinity. For instance, is it theologically permissible to begin the exposition of the Trinity with what reason can discover about God, for example God's existence, essence, and attributes, and only then to proceed to examine what God has revealed about Godself in the Bible, that is, God as Father, Son, and Spirit, their activities in history, and their mutual eternal relations? Is "natural theology" possible at all? Is all true knowledge of God obtained *exclusively* from God's self-revelation in Jesus (*sola scriptura*)?

Furthermore, granted that the use of metaphysics in trinitarian theology is legitimate and even necessary, and hence the indispensability of the *analogia entis* for theology (of course not all theologians, e.g., Karl Barth, would agree with this view), the question still remains as to *which* philosophical system is to be appropriated, albeit always critically. For example, should one use substance ontology,[8] or process philosophy,[9] or Hegel's philosophy of the Absolute Spirit,[10] or the Taoist yin-yang world-view,[11] or simply the metaphysics that is implicit in the Bible itself?[12]

In adopting a philosophy as the framework for trinitarian theology, what are the criteria for judging its appropriateness? For several contemporary theologians such philosophy must have at least two features, in accord with the nature of Christian revelation. First, it must be thoroughly historical and eschatological, since the Trinity has revealed itself in history as the world's future; and second, it must highlight the interpersonal and communitarian dimension of human existence, since the Trinity has revealed itself as a communion or *perichōrēsis* of Father, Son, and Spirit. In fact, among contemporary theologians, some would privilege the first, others the second, and still others both.[13]

Another methodological issue is how to structure trinitarian theology, or, more concretely, how one should begin the discussion of the Trinity. Should one start with the unity of the divine nature (the "essentialist" approach) or the plurality of the three divine persons (the "personalist" approach)? Arguably, either starting point can be justified biblically, since both the unity and the trinity of God are revealed, albeit through stages, as Gregory of Nazianzus has argued,[14] and provided that the understanding of both the oneness and the trinity of God is rooted in revelation.

After Théodore de Régnon's historical studies of trinitarian doctrines,[15] the essentialist approach is popularly identified with the Latin/Western theology and the personalist approach with the Greek/Eastern one. Such historical characterization however has been severely, and rightly, criticized, as a gross and misleading oversimplification, especially when Augustine and Aquinas are included among those accused of ontologizing the immanent Trinity with little or no attention to the economic Trinity.[16] While historically inaccurate if applied to great theologians such as Augustine and Aquinas, this criticism hits the target when aimed at neo-scholastic textbooks that were widely used in Roman Catholic seminaries prior to Vatican Council II (1962–65), with their treatment of God divided in two tracts, *De Deo Uno* and *De Deo Trino*. The former treatise generally adopts a philosophical orientation, though it often adduces proofs for its theses by citing texts from the Bible and church authorities. The latter is strictly biblical, though it also argues that Christian beliefs about the Trinity are harmonious with or at least not contradictory to reason.

Whatever the historical validity of Rahner's and other theologians' critique of the separation of the immanent Trinity from the economic Trinity in post-Augustinian theology, it has had an extremely salutary effect on the way the treatise on the Trinity is conceived and structured today. Rarely do contemporary theologians divide it into two parts, the first philosophical and the second theological. Even those who still preface the discussion of the Trinity with a presentation on the one God no longer can plausibly, from the Christian perspective, do so without taking God's self-revelation as the normative source for understanding the unity of God. Thus, for instance, it would be methodologically unacceptable for a Christian theologian to expound on God's immutability without taking into account the incarnation of the Logos and his death on the cross and exploring how these Christian "facts" should qualify whatever philosophers have to say about divine perfection and immutability. This is so because the one God is identified with God the Father of Jesus, whether this divine unity is seen to be rooted in the divine substance (in Latin theology), or in the Fatherhood of the First Person (in Greek theology) or in the *perichōrēsis* of the three divine persons (according to the proponents of social Trinitarianism).

## DOCTRINES

One of the much-debated doctrinal issues in trinitarian theology concerns the relationship between the economic Trinity and the immanent Trinity, with three interrelated questions.[17] First, is it possible and necessary to speak of the immanent, or transcendent, or ontological Trinity, that is, the eternal relations among Father, Son, and Spirit at all? Are not reflections on the economic Trinity, that is, on what God has revealed Godself to be, namely, Father, Son, and Spirit and their distinct activities in history, already sufficient? Is the God *in se* (in God's self) nothing more than the God *pro nobis* (for us)? If a discussion of the immanent Trinity is superfluous, how can believers reconcile theologically their distinct experiences of the presence and activities of the three divine persons with their belief in the one God? Does not the refusal to speak of the immanent Trinity leave the door open to tritheism, a lurking danger on the popular level?

Second, if a theology of the immanent Trinity is possible and even necessary, is the so-called psychological model that uses the human mind (Augustine's *mens* or *memoria*), with its twofold operation of knowing and loving (*intellegentia* and *amor*) as an analogy of the immanent Trinity, still valid and useful? On the one hand, does it not inevitably lead to modalism, and on the other, does it not produce ahistorical, spiritually sterile speculations, unmoored from God's activities in history? Does Augustine's account of the three divine persons as the Father knowing-*himself* (thereby generating the Son) and loving-*himself* (thereby originating the Spirit "through" and/or "and" the Son), while securing divine unity, not jeopardize the *interpersonal* relations in the Trinity, both immanent and economic?

Third, how are the economic Trinity and immanent Trinity related to each other? Is the immanent Trinity eternal, existing independently of its creative, redemptive, and sanctifying work in the world, or is it in the process of *being constituted* as Father, Son, and Spirit by their activities in history? If the former position is held, and hence the immanent Trinity is totally unaffected by the flow of history into which the Logos has really and truly entered and taken upon himself in Jesus of Nazareth, then the historicity of God's self-revelation, which is Christianity's distinctive teaching, is not taken in all its radical consequences. If the latter is espoused, and hence the history of Jesus and that of the world constitute and indeed *are* the history of God, divine freedom and autonomy will be compromised, since who God is in Godself is made dependent upon human actions in response to God's self-revelation.

Distinguished theologians can be found on both sides of the debate. Perhaps the best way to illustrate the stark differences in the theological stances on the relationship between the immanent Trinity and the economic Trinity is to examine how the so-called "Rahner's Rule" has been variously received.[18] In an effort to overcome the marginalization of the Trinity from Christian daily life, Rahner formulates as a fundamental axiom of trinitarian theology: "*The 'economic' Trinity is the 'immanent' Trinity and the 'immanent' Trinity is the 'economic' Trinity.*"[19] In one way or another the axiom involves the three questions outlined above. Interestingly it has been interpreted by both disciples and opponents alike as endorsing or rejecting *both* mutually contradictory answers to those three questions, depending on whether both parts of Rahner's Rule are accepted or only the first (i.e., the economic Trinity is the immanent Trinity) and not the second (i.e., the immanent is the economic Trinity). Today all theologians would likely subscribe to the first part of Rahner's Rule, agreeing that what humans encounter in history is nothing less than the immanent Trinity itself. Many however would reject its second part, on the ground that it would collapse the immanent Trinity into the economic Trinity, thereby compromising God's freedom and transcendence.

At least prima facie, Rahner posits a distinction (albeit also an identity) between the economic Trinity and the immanent Trinity. Theoretically then it is possible and even necessary to discourse on the immanent Trinity, as Rahner himself has done.[20] Those who favor this position can appeal to the authority of the Cappadocians, Augustine, Aquinas, and a long list of less illustrious theologians. On the other hand, one might argue that if the economic Trinity *is* the immanent Trinity, what we already know of the former is what we would know of the latter, and hence any subsequent discourse on the immanent Trinity would be at best superfluous and at worst a distraction from the spiritual and pastoral implications of the Trinity, or, as Catherine Mowry LaCugna puts it, a "defeat" of the Trinity.[21]

As for the usefulness of the psychological model, there are some who still make use of this analogy, though they are fully aware of its limitations, regarding it more as an *illustration* than as a properly theological interpretation. Others, while defending the necessity of a discourse about the immanent Trinity, would jettison the whole psychological conceptual apparatus and adopt a social model which favors interpersonal relationships.[22]

Finally, regarding the relationship between the economic Trinity and the immanent Trinity, the second part of Rahner's Rule is generally rejected by those who defend God's freedom and eternity and assert, appealing to the teaching of Athanasius against the Arians, that the Trinity would still be Father, Son, and Spirit even if God had not created. By contrast, those who accept the second part of Rahner's Rule without reservation would eliminate the eternal immanent Trinity altogether[23] or would hold that it is an eschatological reality, and hence on the way to becoming the Trinity of Father, Son, and Spirit in the fullness of history.[24] Still others, like Hans Urs von Balthasar, on the one hand hold on to the eternity and immutability of the immanent Trinity and on the other speak of the incarnation and death of Jesus on the cross as made possible by the "supra-temporal yet ever actual event" of the Father's self-emptying (kenosis) into the other, namely the Son (in other words, the divine "missions" in history are made possible by the intra-trinitarian eternal "processions").

However these three questions are answered, it is clear that the relationship between the immanent Trinity and the economic Trinity, that is, the issue of whether the former is eternal and ontologically prior to the latter or whether it is dissolved in and is historically constituted by the latter, though they are "identical" with each other, remains thorny and is a far from resolved issue in contemporary trinitarian theology. Currently, the consensus seems to be that the economic Trinity must be granted epistemological priority, that is, the only way to know God is by way of the activities of the Father through the Son and by the power of the Spirit, and that ontological priority must be given to the immanent Trinity to safeguard divine freedom and grace.

The second doctrinal issue concerns how to speak of the plurality of "actors" in the Trinity, both economic and immanent. As mentioned in Chapter 1, in developing a trinitarian theology the church has to make use of culturally available conceptual categories and terminology and at the same time modify them, ascribing new connotations to make them adequate expressions of its beliefs about the Trinity. More precisely, it has to find terms to express *what* God is, that is, God's being, nature, or essence, and *who* God is, that is, Father, Son, and Spirit. For the former, it uses *ousia* and *physis* (Greek) and *essentia* and *natura* (Latin) respectively. For the latter, it uses *hypostasis* and *prosopon* (Greek) and *substantia* and *persona* (Latin) respectively, even though *hypostasis* (literally, that which stands under) in secular usage is synonymous with *ousia* and even though its Latin equivalent *substantia* is not used to refer to *who* God is but to *what* God is, that is, as equivalent to *essentia* and *natura* and not to *hypostasis*.

As to the meaning of *hypostasis*, *prosopon*, and *persona* as applied to the Trinity, they do not mean that the Father, the Son, and the Spirit are three "individuals" belonging to the same species (as, for instance, Peter, Paul, and Mary are three individuals sharing the same human nature), for otherwise there would be three Gods. Rather they mean, as the Cappadocians put it, "modes of subsisting" (*tropoi hypaxeos*). These distinct modes are characterized by the three ways in which the numerically one and identical divine nature exists: as *ungenerated* or *unoriginated* in the Father (*agennesia*), as *generated* in the Son (*gennesis*), and as *proceeding* in the Spirit (*ekpempsis* or *ekporeusis*). Consequently, modalism is avoided. Thus "person" in the Trinity does not have the psychological connotation of self-consciousness with intellect, will, and freedom, as commonly understood today. Of course, God does have – or more exactly *is* – infinite intellect, will, and freedom, but this is not what is meant when Christians speak of the Father, the Son, and the Spirit as "persons." Given the widespread psychological connotation of "person" and given the fact the church cannot control the meaning of words in secular usage, there is a clear and present danger of tritheism, at least at the popular level, in using the word "person" for the Trinity.

The question is whether, in order to forestall this danger, new words should be coined to express what Christians mean by "person" in the Trinity. Barth suggests the phrase "mode of being" (*Seinsweise*), echoing the Cappadocians' *tropos hypaxeos*, while Rahner proposes a more extended one: "three modes of subsistence of the one God in his one sole nature," or more simply, "mode of subsistence" (*Subsistenzweise*). These new expressions, while theologically precise, are widely criticized as unsuitable for personal piety. However, the issue is much more than terminological. Both Barth and Rahner have been faulted, for example, by Moltmann, for continuing to conceive God as person in terms of the Hegelian absolute subject endowed with a single intellect and will and for denying as a consequence that there are interpersonal relations *within* God. That there are interpersonal relations among the three persons in the economic Trinity is arguably incontrovertible. Furthermore, if the economic Trinity is the immanent Trinity, as both Barth and Rahner maintain, then it must be inferred that there are interpersonal relations in the immanent Trinity as well.

The question therefore is how to conceive the "personhood" of God ("personhood" in the ontological sense, rather than "personality" in the psychological sense) in such a way as to both eschew tritheism and do justice to the reality of the interpersonal relations within the Trinity. One possible way is to derive our understanding of divine personhood not from the philosophical concept of person but from the relationships among the three divine persons. This will allow us to affirm, as Thomas Torrance, Hans Urs von Balthasar, Walter Kasper, and a host of proponents of social trinitarianism suggest, that while there cannot be three consciousnesses, and hence three intellects and three wills, in God (that would be tritheism), there are three "subjects" engaged in mutual knowing and loving, each conscious, in his proper and distinct way (that is, as Father, Son, and Spirit), of the one consciousness and hence also conscious of the others. In other words, each divine person has, as John Thompson puts it, "a three-way relationship and consciousness – a self-consciousness as divine, a consciousness of the other persons as of one divine being with them, and a consciousness of the others as persons in relation to them."[25]

The third doctrinal issue, which is related to the concept of person, concerns the theology of the Spirit (pneumatology). It is somewhat easy to understand the relations betwen God the Father and God the Son in terms of the Father being the unoriginated source (fatherhood) and the Son in terms of being generated from him (sonship), and consequently it is not difficult, partly thanks to their names, to imagine them as "person" (indeed, Christian art has often represented them as an older man and a younger man). The same thing can hardly be said of the Spirit, about whose personhood three issues are raised, namely, his mode of origination (and the *filioque* issue), the nature of his personhood, and his naming.

As to the Spirit's origination, appeal is often made to the New Testament texts that speak of the Spirit being "given" by the Father (e.g., Jn 14:16) or being "sent" "from (*para*) the Father" (Jn 15:26) by the risen Christ (Jn 16:7). The Spirit is also said to "proceed" (or "go out," *ekporeuestai*) from (*para*) the Father (Jn 15:26). From this "mission," that is, the sending of the Spirit *from* the Father as well as *by* Jesus in the economic Trinity, it is inferred that in the immanent Trinity the Spirit "proceeds" from the Father. The Council of Constantinople I (381), which affirms the divinity of the Spirit, professes faith "in the Holy Spirit, the Lord and Giver of life, who proceeds [*ekporeuomenon*] from [*ek*] the Father."

The Nicene-Constantinopolitan creed does not mention any role of the Son in the procession of the Spirit. Later, in the West, at the third Council of Toledo (589), the expression *filioque* (and the Son) was added to "from the Father" to ward off Arianizing and modalizing tendencies. Such innovation was vigorously rejected by the Greeks on both doctrinal and liturgical grounds. Greek trinitarian theology starts from the Father as the sole "principle" (*archē*) and "cause" (*aitia*) of divinity and denounces *filioque* as endangering monopatrism. Furthermore, the Latin addition is condemned as a violation of the prohibition of the councils of Ephesus (431) and Chalcedon (451) to modify the creed. Latin theologians respond that *filioque* is not lacking in biblical basis insofar as the Spirit is said to take or receive everything from the Son (Jn 16:14), to be sent by him, and to be the "Spirit of Christ." Furthermore, they point out that even Greek theology speaks of the Spirit proceeding from the Father "through" (*dia*) the Son or, as Maximus the Confessor puts it, "by means of the Word" (*dia mesou tou logou*). Today, thanks to historical research – especially on the unionizing councils of Lyons (1274) and Florence (1439) – and ecumenical dialogue, *filioque* is no longer seen as an unsurmountable obstacle for union between the Latin and Greek churches but as a legitimate theological development proper to the West, and it may be excised from the creed as long as its refutation of Arianizing and modalist errors is honored. One proposal to reconcile the Greek and Latin theologies of the Spirit is the use of two different words when speaking of his origination: *ekporeuesthai* (proceed) for his origin from the Father and *proïenai* (come forth) for his origin from or, better, through the Son from the Father.

Furthermore, granted the validity of *filioque*, a number of theologians propose that in line with the mutual indwelling or *perichōrēsis* among the three persons of the Trinity we conceive their relations in a fully triadic way, not simply in terms of origination but also in terms of reciprocal relations. Thus not only does the Spirit proceed from/through the Father and the Son (*ex patre filioque*) but also the Father is not Father except from/through the Son and the Spirit (*ex filio spirituque*).

Similarly, the Son is not Son except from/through the Spirit and the Father (*ex spiritu patreque*).[26] In this way, the relations among the divine persons are not marked by a linear and hierarchical descent but by a circular and inclusive movement or dance (*perichōrēsis*).

Concerning the personhood of the Spirit, even though the New Testament ascribes numerous personal activities and characteristics to the Spirit in the history of salvation, the various metaphors for the Spirit such as breath, wind, sound, fire, water, and dove – all taken from the material world – are admittedly not conducive to a personalistic conception of him within the immanent Trinity. Even when a psychological analogy such as Augustine's is used for the Trinity, speaking of the Spirit as the "mutual love" between the Father and the Son is hardly a significant advance in representing him as a "person" in the way the Father and the Son are. By contrast, Richard of St. Victor's model of supreme and perfect love as requiring a lover, another equal person to love, and a third equal person to share this love with – in trinitarian terms, the Father as the supreme lover, the Son as the beloved, and the Spirit as the one who issues from and shares in this perfect mutual love – makes a more persuasive case for the personhood of the Spirit.

One development in contemporary Christianity that provides useful clues to understand the personhood of the Spirit is the astonishing diffusion of Pentecostalism across all denominations throughout the globe, with thousands of movements, organizations, and names. Common to all these dizzying varieties of Pentecostalism is the personal encounter with the Holy Spirit, called baptism in (with) the Spirit. The Spirit is experienced as a divine personal power affecting the church and all Christians in all dimensions and aspects of life with his "gifts," such as healing, exorcism ("deliverance"), speaking in tongues, and prophecy. For Pentecostals the Spirit is a real person, speaking to them through the Bible and everyday events and transforming their lives from sickness to health, from poverty to prosperity, from oppression to liberation, from demonic possession to salvation. In this respect, Pentecostal pneumatology, despite its sometime individualist cast, ironically has close resonance with liberationist pneumatology, and makes a salutary contribution to the traditional theology of the Spirit.[27]

Lastly, there is the issue of naming the Spirit. Feminist theologians have pointed out how the Christian naming of the Trinity is lopsidedly in favor of masculinity, with two members of the Trinity given male "names," that is, Father and Son. While feminist critique of the Christian discourse about God goes much further and deeper than mere naming, as will be shown below, some theologians have noted that the gender of the Hebrew word for spirit (*ruach*) is feminine, and to counter the Christian overwhelmingly masculine speech about God, suggest that the Spirit is the feminine principle within the Trinity and that, at least in European languages, the feminine personal pronoun ("she" and "her") be used when referring to Spirit.[28] Most if not all theologians would not, for various reasons, endorse this approach, which brings us to the next issue in contemporary trinitarian theology.

All feminist theologies, despite their varied racial, ethnic, economic, socio-political, and cultural backgrounds (e.g., white – mostly North American and European, black, Latino, African, Asian, etc.), share in the same goal of liberating women from all forms of oppression, including (but not limited to) androcentrism and patriarchy, to achieve a full human flourishing, and the same task of doing theology that incorporates the voices and experiences of women. At first feminist theology focuses on biblical hermeneutics and Christology, but it soon turns to the question of God and more specifically the Trinity.

On trinitarian theology, the work of the Roman Catholic theologian Elizabeth Johnson is most significant.[29] Johnson rejects the attempt to restrict considerations of the femininity of God to the Spirit on the ground that it continues to perpetuate the cultural stereotypes about gender, with so-called male characteristics attributed to the Father and the Son and the female ones to the Spirit. Rather she proposes to reconceptualize the entire Trinity in terms of women's experiences, guided by three principles: the incomprehensibility of God, the necessity of analogical language in God-talk, and the validity of different ways of naming God.

Using the biblical image of God as *Sophia* (Wisdom) with its feminine overtones as the foundational analogy, Johnson reverses the traditional order of Father-Son-Spirit and starts with Spirit-Sophia, moves through Jesus-Sophia, and ends with Mother-Sophia. To each of these persons Johnson assigns certain activities that the Bible describes as belonging to the Spirit, the Son, and the Father and that seem to be more appropriate to women than to men. Johnson then moves on to present a theology of the immanent Trinity in which the divine relations are characterized as friendship that bespeaks relationality, mutuality, equality, and inclusiveness rather than autonomy, origination, hierarchy, and subordination.

Johnson does not intend to replace the biblical naming of God as Father, Son, and Spirit with her own feminist proposal of Spirit-Sophia, Jesus-Sophia, and Mother-Sophia but simply to subvert its patriarchal history and to bring to bear on it women's experience and perspective.

Her project however is rejected by both the right and the left. On the right are those (e.g., Robert Jensen, Wolfhart Pannenberg, Donald Bloesch, and Elizabeth Achtmeier) who hold that the biblical "proper names" of God as Father, Son, and Spirit cannot be replaced; on the left are those (e.g., Mary Daly) who believe that the Bible and therefore its naming of God are irretrievably sexist and therefore must be abandoned altogether and not tinkered with. In between are others who propose other triads. Some of these smack of modalism (e.g., Creator, Redeemer, Sanctifier); others of tritheism (e.g., Mother, Lover, Friend); still others of impersonalism (Source, Word, Spirit). The debate, at times vociferous, still rages on, not least because it has vast implications for church life and structures (e.g., the ordination of women).

The last issue in trinitarian theology is that of how to present it in the dialogue of Christianity with other religions and, more radically, how the doctrine of the Trinity can be a basis for developing a theology of religions. That Judaism and Islam reject the Christian doctrine of the Trinity as inimical to monotheism is well known. In this regard however some progress has been made. Through dialogue misunderstandings and caricatures of the Christian belief in the Trinity have been removed. Furthermore, while Jews and Muslims are of course not expected to acquiesce to the trinitarian doctrine, at least they do not see it as an outright absurdity or a heretical denial of the unicity of God.

Recently the doctrine of the Trinity has also received considerable attention in the Christian dialogues with Hinduism, Buddhism, and Confucianism. While there are no doubt triadic concepts in Hinduism (the Trimurti of Brahma, Vishnu, and Shiva), Buddhism (the doctrine of the Three Bodies of *Dharmakāya*, *Sambhogakāya*, and *Nirmānakāya*), and Confucianism (Heaven, Earth, and Humanity), they are generally not taken to be equivalent, much less identical, to the Christian understanding of God the Father, Son, and Spirit. Nevertheless, it has been suggested that the triadic structure of reality as expressed by these non-Christian teachings can at a minimum be regarded as *vestigia Trinitatis* and hence can furnish resources both for a dialogue with non-Christians on the Trinity and to help Christians themselves understand more deeply their own belief in the Trinity.[30]

## PRACTICE

Finally, contemporary theology, as elaborated especially by Jürgen Moltmann and Leonardo Boff, has shown that far from being an abstract speculation with no practical implications for Christian life, the doctrine of the Trinity reveals liberating and authentically human ways of worship (liturgy), living (spirituality), and socio-political practices. Of course it is not claimed that the doctrine of the Trinity provides a blueprint, much less a recipe, for worship and social and political organization. As far as liturgy and spirituality are concerned, it is claimed that Christian worship is not directed to a monistic or unitarian deity but rather to the Father in the Son and by the power of the Spirit. Similarly, Christian spirituality is not a way of life based on a normative ethics or some universalizable principles but one that is sustained by the Spirit, modeled on Jesus, and oriented toward the Father. Finally, the doctrine of the Trinity dictates that economic and political structures be organized not for profit and domination but according to the principles of equality and communion that characterize the relationships among the three divine Persons.

**Notes**

1. In addition to a list of systematic comprehensive, textbook-like treatises, there are many informative surveys of contemporary trinitarian theology among which the following stand out: Ted Peters, *God as Trinity: Relationality and Temporality in Divine Life* (Louisville, KY: Westminster John Knox, 1993); John Thompson, *Modern Trinitarian Perspectives* (Oxford University Press, 1994); Christoph Schwöbel, ed., *Trinitarian Theology Today: Essays on Divine Being and Act* (Edinburgh: T. & T. Clark, 1995); Kevin J. Vanhoozer, ed., *The Trinity in a Pluralistic Age: Theological Essays on Culture and Religion* (Grand Rapids, MI: Eerdmans, 1997); Stephen T. Davis, Daniel Kendall, and Gerald O'Collins, eds., *The Trinity: An Interdisciplinary Symposium on the Trinity* (Oxford University Press, 1999); Stanley J. Grenz, *Rediscovering the Triune God: The Trinity in Contemporary Theology* (Minneapolis: Fortress, 2004); James J. Buckley and David S. Yeago, eds., *Knowing the Triune God: The Work of the Spirit in the Practice of the Church* (Grand Rapids, MI: Eerdmans, 2001); M. John Farrelly, *The Trinity: Rediscovering the Central Christian Mystery* (Lanham, MD: Rowman & Littlefield, 2005); Miroslav Volf and Michael Welker, eds., *God's Life in the Trinity* (Minneapolis: Fortress, 2006); Jennifer Anne Herrick, *Trinitarian Intelligibility: An Analysis of Contemporary Discussions* (Boca Raton, FL: Dissertation.com, 2006); Veli-Matti Kärkkäinen, *The Trinity: Global Perspectives* (Louisville, KY: Westminster John Knox, 2007); and Roderick T. Leupp, *The Renewal of Trinitarian Theology: Themes, Patterns & Explorations* (Downers Grove, IL: IVP Academic, 2008). Comprehensive recent German works on the Trinity include Rudolf Weth, ed., *Der lebendige Gott: Auf den Spüren neueren trinitarischen Denkens* (Neukirche-Vluyn: Neukirchener, 2005), and Miroslav Volf and Michael

Welker, eds., *Der lebendige Gott als Trinität* (Gütersloh: Gütersloh Verlaghaus, 2006).

2. Ted Peters, *God as Trinity: Relationality and Temporality in Divine Life* (Louisville, KY: Westminster John Knox, 1993), 27–80.
3. See Gerald O'Collins, "The Holy Trinity: The State of the Questions," in Davis, Kendall, and O'Collins, eds., *The Trinity*, 1–25.
4. For an English translation of Augustine's *De Trinitate*, see *The Trinity*, trans. Stephen McKenna (Washington, DC: Catholic University Press, 1963).
5. See D. Sayers, *The Mind of the Maker* (New York: Harcourt, Brace, and Co., 1941).
6. For a helpful discussion of trinitarian analogies, see Allan Coppedge, *The God who is Triune: Revisioning the Christian Doctrine of God* (Downers Grove, IL: IVP Academic, 2007), 142–48. For scientific analogies, see John Polkinghorne, *Science and the Trinity: The Christian Encounter with Reality* (New Haven: Yale University Press, 2004). For a study of pneumatology in dialogue with Newton and Einstein, see Wolfgang Vondey, "The Holy Spirit and the Physical Universe: The Impact of Scientific Paradigm Shifts on Contemporary Pneumatology," *Theological Studies*, 70 (2009), 3–36.
7. For an excess of creativity in discerning the *vestigia Trinitatis*, see Leupp, *The Renewal of Trinitarian Theology*, 8–10, 173–78.
8. For a defense of the use of substance metaphysics in trinitarian theology, see William P. Alston, "Substance and the Trinity," in Davis, Kendall, and O'Collins, eds., *The Trinity*, 179–201.
9. For an elaboration of the Trinity in terms of process philosophy, see Joseph Bracken and Marjorie Hewitt Suchocki, eds., *Trinity in Process: A Relational Theology of God* (New York: Continuum, 1997), and Joseph Bracken, *The Triune Symbol: Persons, Process and Community* (Lanham, MD: University Press of America, 1985).
10. See the trinitarian works of Jürgen Moltmann, Wolfhart Pannenberg, and other proponents of social trinitarianism.
11. See Jung Young Lee, *The Trinity in Asian Perspective* (Nashville: Abingdon, 1996).
12. The Bible does of course present a "philosophy," albeit not a systematized one. Even theologians who deny the possibility of the use of metaphysics in theology must operate from some kind of metaphysics on the basis of which they can demonstrate the reasonableness or at least the non-absurdity of the Bible's teachings to those who do not accept them, unless they are prepared to assert them to be true simply because they are revealed.
13. See Grenz, *Discovering the Triune God*, 222. The historical and eschatological dimension is represented by J. Moltmann, W. Pannenberg, and Robert Johnson, and the communitarian dimension is represented by John Zizioulas and most contemporary theologians.
14. See his *Fifth Theological Oration*, 25–28; Eng. trans. in Edward R. Hardy, ed., *Christology of the Later Fathers* (Philadelphia: Westminster, 1954), 208–11.

15. Théodore de Régnon, *Études de théologie positive sur la sainte Trinité*, 4 vols. (Paris: Victor Retaux et Fils, 1892–98).
16. See Rahner's critique of Augustine and Thomas in Karl Rahner, *The Trinity*, trans. Joseph Donceel, introduction, index, and glossary by Catherine LaCugna (New York: Crossroad, 1997; original 1969), 15–20.
17. David Coffey suggests that a distinction is to be made between the biblical doctrine of the Trinity (the "biblical Trinity"), the immanent Trinity (the doctrine of the intra-trinitarian and eternal relations among Father, Son, and Spirit), and the economic Trinity (the doctrine of the saving activities of the three divine persons in history). For him, the New Testament offers only a functional theology of the Trinity, that is, there is no affirmation, not even in John 1:14, of an ontological incarnation ("becoming-human") of the Word of God but only of the descent into the realm of weakness (the "flesh") of the pre-existent divine "man" who had lived eternally in God. From here the first Apologists such as Justin Martyr derive the doctrine of the immanent Trinity, that is, speak of the incarnation of a divine being in metaphysical terms, which implies the divinity of Jesus. From here, Coffey suggests, theologians should move back to the biblical, purely functional data to develop a doctrine of the economic Trinity, which for him is the proper focus of trinitarian theology. See his *Deus Trinitas: The Doctrine of the Triune God* (Oxford University Press, 1999), 14–16. Obviously, the validity of Coffey's proposal depends on whether the New Testament does not have any metaphysical concept of the incarnation (and hence the divinity of Jesus), a highly controversial thesis. For a contrary view, with regard to Paul, see Gordon Fee, "Paul and the Trinity: The Experiences of Christ and the Spirit for Paul's Understanding of God," in Davis, Kendall, and O'Collins, eds., *The Trinity*, 49–72.
18. On Rahner's Rule and Karl Rahner's trinitarian theology in general, see Fred Sanders, *The Image of the Immanent Trinity: Rahner's Rule and the Theological Interpretation of Scripture* (New York: Peter Lang, 2005).
19. Rahner, *The Trinity*, 22 (italics in the original).
20. See ibid., 80–120.
21. See Catherine Mowry LaCugna, *God for Us: The Trinity and Christian Life* (San Francisco: HarperSanFrancisco, 1991). LaCugna rejects the concepts of "economic" and "immanent" Trinity and uses instead the Greek terms *oikonomia* (i.e., God's total plan of salvation in history from creation to consummation) and *theologia* (i.e., theological reflections on God's activities as Father, Son, and Spirit in this plan of salvation).
22. See the works of Leonardo Boff, John Zizioulas, and Catherine M. LaCugna among others. One contemporary theologian who basically accepts Aquinas' metaphysical model but strongly qualifies it by understanding God not as being itself (*ipsum esse*) but as *personal* being is M. John Farrelly. See his *The Trinity: Rediscovering the Central Christian Mystery* (Lanham, MD: Rowman & Littlefield, 2005).

23. While Catherine M. LaCugna's theology tends to lead her to eliminate the immanent Trinity, Piet Schoonenberg certainly has done so.
24. This position seems to be that of J. Moltmann.
25. Thompson, *Modern Trinitarian Perspectives*, 149.
26. See the work of the Orthodox theologian Paul Evdokimov, *L'Orthodoxie* (Neuchâtel-Paris: Delachaux et Niestlé, 1959), and Leonardo Boff, *Trinity and Society*, trans. Paul Burns (Maryknoll, NY: Orbis, 1988).
27. For an evangelical and Pentecostal trinitarian theology, see the works of Millard J. Erickson.
28. See Leonardo Boff, *The Maternal Face of God: The Feminine and its Religious Expressions*, trans. Robert R. Barr and John W. Diercksmeier (San Francisco: Harper & Row, 1987); Donald Gelpi, *The Divine Mother: A Trinitarian Theology of the Holy Spirit* (Lanham, MD: University Press of America, 1984); and Farrelly, *The Trinity*.
29. See Elizabeth A. Johnson, *She Who Is: The Mystery of God in Feminist Theological Discourse* (New York: Crossroad, 1992).
30. For study of the implication of trinitarian doctrine for religious pluralism and interreligious dialogue, see Raimundo Panikkar, *The Trinity and the Religious Experience of Man: Icon-Person-Mystery*, 2nd enlarged edn. (London: Darton, Longman & Todd; Maryknoll, NY: Orbis, 1975); Raimon Panikkar, *The Cosmotheandric Experience: Emerging Religious Consciousness* (Maryknoll, NY: Orbis, 1993); Jacques Dupuis, *Toward a Christian Theology of Religious Pluralism* (Maryknoll, NY: Orbis, 1997); Vanhoozer, ed., *The Trinity in a Pluralistic Age*; Gavin D'Costa, *The Meeting of Religions and the Trinity* (Maryknoll, NY: Orbis, 2000); and Veli-Matti Kärkkäinen, *Trinity and Religious Pluralism: The Doctrine of the Trinity in Christian Theology of Religions* (Aldershot, England: Ashgate, 2004).

## Further reading

Buckley, James, and David S. Yeago, eds., *Knowing the Triune God: The Work of the Spirit in the Practices of the Church* (Grand Rapids, MI: Eerdmans, 2001).

Coffey, David, *Deus Trinitas: The Doctrine of the Triune God* (Oxford University Press, 1999).

Coppedge, Alan, *The God who is Triune: Revisioning the Christian Doctrine of God* (Downers Grove, IL: IVP Academic, 2007).

Davis, Stephen T., Daniel Kendall, and Gerald O'Collins, eds., *The Trinity: An Interdisciplinary Symposium on the Trinity* (Oxford University Press, 1999).

D'Costa, Gavin, *The Meeting of Religions and the Trinity* (Maryknoll, NY: Orbis, 2000).

Hunt, Anne, *Trinity: The Nexus of the Mysteries of Christian Faith* (Maryknoll, NY: Orbis, 2005).

Kärkkäinen, Veli-Matti, *Trinity and Religious Pluralism: The Doctrine of the Trinity in Christian Theology of Religions* (Aldershot, England: Ashgate, 2004).

*The Trinity: Global Perspectives* (Louisville, KY: Westminster John Knox, 2007).

O'Collins, Gerald, *The Tripersonal God: Understanding and Interpreting the Trinity* (Mahwah, NJ: Paulist, 1999).
Placher, William, *The Triune God: An Essay in Postliberal Theology* (Louisville, KY: Westminster John Knox, 2007).
Torrance, Thomas F., *The Christian Doctrine of God: One Being, Three Persons* (Edinburgh: T. & T. Clark, 1996).

# Part II

## *Retrieving the sources*

# 3 Like a finger pointing to the moon: exploring the Trinity in/and the New Testament

ELAINE M. WAINWRIGHT

Exploring "Trinity in/and the New Testament" is a challenging task.[1] Francis Watson points to some of those challenges when he summarizes certain trends in recent New Testament scholarship in relation to Trinity:

> Modern biblical scholarship has no great love for the doctrine of the Trinity. It likes to warn its customers that, if they read a biblical text in the light of what was to become the orthodox Nicene theology of the fourth century, they will inevitably be committing the sin of anachronism. The doctrine of the Trinity should be left to church historians and systematic theologians: it has no place in "our" field.[2]

Addressing the question of Trinity in the New Testament could, therefore, be seen among some biblical scholars as a retrospective act, one which entails a looking back anachronistically at first-century texts through the lens of a fourth-century doctrine.[3] Such an approach can lead to survey articles which gather texts across the New Testament containing or hinting at "trinitarian formulae" or the naming of G*d[4] as Father, Son, and Spirit.[5] Recent scholarship has, however, challenged biblical scholars to undertake a more nuanced approach to the task. In this chapter, I propose to explore and lay out some of the contemporary hermeneutical and interpretive issues involved in the naming of G*d as Trinity and/in the New Testament, leading to an articulation of a multi-layered approach. The limitations of this chapter will, however, allow me the space to explore only the first layer of the approach, and I will do this through the gospel of Matthew. It is my hope that this limited beginning will encourage readers to explore further the rich and complex imaging of G*d in the New Testament, only some of which drew later theologians into naming G*d as triune.

## NAMING AND IMAGING OF G*D: ISSUES IN READING THE BIBLICAL TEXT

Turning to the critical issues for contemporary biblical scholars and the faith community when we name or image G*d, I want to address first the very nature of the task being undertaken. The metaphor of the "finger pointing to the moon," evoked in the title of this chapter, highlights the *metaphoric nature of the task of naming or imagining the Divine*.[6] All such attempts will be like a finger pointing toward the one who is beyond all our imagining but whose naming in our theologizing is limited to human language. G*d is always beyond our naming and imaging, hence the significance of the richness of our imagery as we strain toward divinity. Within the New Testament, the images of G*d and of Jesus are multiple. Focus on "father," "son," and "spirit," names or images which were drawn into later trinitarian theologizing, must be placed, therefore, within the context of this multitude of images and metaphors.[7]

Janet Martin Soskice defines metaphor as that "figure of speech whereby we speak about one thing in terms which are seen to be suggestive of another"[8] (we speak about G*d, about the ineffable one, in terms suggestive of human family structures and relationships – for instance, that of father and son). Mieke Bal addresses the classical "is"/"is not" aspect of metaphor (G*d is/is not father), noting that metaphor will carry traces of what has been suppressed, the "is not."[9] Most scholars seeking Trinity in the New Testament focus almost exclusively on the "is" aspect of the metaphors of father, son, and spirit, thereby obscuring the fact that what we are dealing with is *metaphoric language* straining toward a naming of the G*d whom early and emerging Christian communities had come to know anew in the advent of Jesus in human history and their later attempts to give meaning to this encounter.

A second aspect that needs attention is that the New Testament texts which give expression to the new metaphoric naming of G*d have a *context, both literary and socio-historical*, which will shape at least one layer of their meaning.[10] Soskice, whom I cited earlier, says further of metaphor that it cannot be limited simply to the combination of two terms such as G*d and "father," but that it will always have a context which will be both literary (a gospel narrative or an early Christian letter) and socio-cultural (first-century Syrian Antioch or Ephesus). This insight itself already points toward two layers of interpretation in a search for Trinity in the New Testament. The gospel of Matthew is not the gospel of John. Each must be read uniquely, attentive to the way/s in which the four evangelists, each in his own way, shape the genre of gospel to tell the story of Jesus and to theologize Jesus in relation to the G*d of Israel whom each knew and named as G*d within the context of the story. The metaphors and images used in this theologizing take their meaning not only from the context of the story but also from the socio-historical context of its construction. This points us, therefore, to the *first layer of interpretation* of a New Testament text, namely seeking to understand its theologizing in the literary and socio-historical context of the first century. The interpreter tries to stand with the first-century readers/hearers *behind the text,* as it were, or *in relation to the text* to hear, initially, the text in its context of origin and not through the lens of later theology.[11]

Over the first three to four centuries, the texts that we now know as the New Testament (gospels, letters, and others) moved from their unique contexts of origin to other contexts, both literary and socio-historical. They were assembled into the emerging collection of texts recognized as the scripture,[12] and they were interpreted in the context of the developing theology of the early church, Trinity being one example of the controversial aspects of that theologizing. This leads to a *second layer of interpretation,* which we might call the *canonical.* Frances Young's article "The Trinity and the New Testament" is an example of such an approach. She demonstrates that "Trinitarian theology is the product of exegesis of the biblical texts, refined by debate and argument, and rhetorically celebrated in liturgy."[13] She explores the monarchian and Arian controversies to demonstrate that "the doctrine of the Trinity is the outcome of reading the scriptural texts with particular questions generated by the socio-political context in which the Church Fathers found themselves. To that extent it is a conceptual superstructure built on the foundations of the New Testament."[14] Young concludes her excellent exploration with the claim that "there is no presuppositionless interpretation; and if the New Testament is to be read Christianly [or, we might add, *canonically*], we need to take seriously the hermeneutical principle that the future of the text is as significant as its past meaning."[15] This is a second layer of interpretation as the emerging understanding of G*d as triune becomes a lens through which early church theologians read the canonical biblical texts and through which contemporary interpreters read both those theologians and the biblical text.[16]

It can be seen from the above that the imaging of G*d as triune spirals out from the biblical text and its construction into the unfolding of the church's theologizing and back into the biblical text through the lens of the particular interpreter and the particular historical context with its socio-historical and religious perspectives. Interpretation will, therefore, always be shaped by the hermeneutical or interpretive perspectives of theologians and communities of faith. The *third layer of interpretation* is, therefore, what we might call the *contemporary*, or the *hermeneutical*, which recognizes the long history of trinitarian faith that has spiraled out over the life of the church and which has shaped the faith perspective of each interpreter in each new age. This perspective also takes cognizance of the fact that engagement with the biblical text and the history of trinitarian theology has been and continues to be informed by new questions rising up out of the contemporary context.[17] Liberation, gender and feminist concerns, ecological imperatives, and interreligious challenges are but some of the joys and hopes, griefs, and anxieties which will inform and open up new naming and imaging of a triune G*d in front of biblical and theological texts and traditions and will also spiral back into and inform the first-century biblical and later canonical layers of interpretation.

This returns me to my first and second layers with the question: how will we read a biblical text or tell the biblical story now? How will we hear its straining after G*d so that it can function for today's people seeking to name G*d in new ways? How will such hearing enable worship that leads to engagement in life in new ways that are of the G*d who is communion, incarnate in the flesh of the world, and encountered in the *koinōnia* of a community of faith that lives the righteousness, justice, and love of Matthew's gospel or the communion in the G*dhead of the Johannine gospel? As an initial step toward answering these questions, I turn now to a *first layer* reading of the Matthean naming and imaging of G*d with special attention to the images of "father," "son," and "spirit" but in the context of this literary work and its socio-historical context. Such a reading will, of necessity, be undertaken through my own contemporary hermeneutical lenses, which will both limit and enrich the task.

## READING WITH THE MATTHEAN COMMUNITY'S IMAGING AND NAMING OF G*D AND JESUS

The opening verse of the gospel of Matthew gives us an indication of the type of text that hearers/readers will encounter: it is the book of the genealogy, the origin, the birth of Jesus, the *Christos*.[18] This book will tell the story of Jesus, the human one who stands in the line of Abraham and David and generations of ancestors (Mt 1:1, 2–17). It will also capture an early gospel community's theologizing of Jesus – he is born of a spirit that is holy (1:18, 20), and in the birth of Jesus, G*d is said to be with G*d's people in a way which fulfills their prophetic yearnings (1:22–23; cf. Isa 7:14, 8:8). G*d can be encountered by and among the "us" of the narrative in and through Jesus, an endangered child of an endangered mother.[19] The G*d of the Matthean narrative is with G*d's people in radical discontinuity as well as expected continuity, and the tensive nature of the namings of this G*d and of Jesus who is born of Mary and of a spirit that is holy will continue into and through the unfolding gospel narrative.

It is within this literary and theological context that the G*d of the Matthean narrative is named and imaged: *kyrios*/lord (19 times), *pater*/father (41 times in 39 verses), and *theos*/G*d (50 times in 43 verses).[20] The titles *kyrios* and *theos* reflect the naming of G*d in the scriptures of the Matthean community.[21] *Pater*, on the other hand, is clearly characteristic of the Matthean community's story-telling and theologizing as its Markan source uses "father" as a form of address for G*d once only (Mk 14:36) and as a title three times (Mk 8:38, 13:32, 11:25). Further to this, of the Synoptic uses of *pater* to image G*d, 70 percent are unique to Matthew.[22] Also, *pater* is used only among the disciples and crowds and never among Jesus' adversaries or in scripture quotes,[23] occurring twice as often in Jesus' discourses as in the narrative.[24]

Closer examination of these Matthean names and images reveals a particular concentration of the metaphor *pater* in the Sermon on the Mount, namely 16 of the 28 occurrences in the discourses. In this sermon in particular, the reader is drawn into the ethos created by the pronoun "your" in relation to "father," which is repeated 14 times.[25] Only once is "our" used with "father," and it draws the listener into the particular prayer relationship with G*d that is characteristic of Jesus in this gospel (6:9). Similarly, the more exclusive pronoun "my" occurs with "father" only once on the lips of Jesus in 7:21.[26] Within the Matthean community's theologizing, *pater* becomes a central name and metaphor for G*d, drawing Jesus and the disciples of Jesus into the relationship it evokes.[27] This relational aspect of the construction of divinity can be retained today and explored through the lens of *koinōnia* and *perichōrēsis* that have characterized the history of trinitarian theologizing.[28] At the same time, for a contemporary interpreter, seeking to uncover the first-century meaning-making, it is important to critique the gender exclusivity effected in the gospel's construction of this relational metaphor.[29] The Matthean gospel, characterized as it is by discontinuity as well as continuity, contains the imperative of such a critical appraisal. "Father" or "head of the household" is omitted from Matthew 12:50 – "whoever does the will of my Father in heaven is my brother, and sister, and mother" – and from the injunction of 23:9: "call no man your father on earth." Further, Sheffield has demonstrated that the displacement and the discrediting of the earthly father within the narratives surrounding James and John and other texts points to a shift in the constitution of the new household or new fictive kinship.[30] This, in its turn, ought to inform critically a reconstitution or reconstruction of the "father" metaphor for G*d in third-layer contemporary theologizing.

Turning from literary to socio-historical and religio-cultural considerations, it has been well documented that, in Qumran prayers and Wisdom and Septuagint (LXX) texts, the term *pater* was used in prayer and as designation for G*d in Palestinian Judaism during the late Hellenistic and early imperial eras and that these may have informed the Matthean construction of its G*d image.[31] From her study of these uses of "father" as address to G*d and name of G*d, D'Angelo draws the conclusions that:

1. "father" designates G*d as "refuge of the afflicted and persecuted";
2. the title "accompanies a petition for or an assurance of forgiveness"; and
3. it "evokes the power and providence that govern the world."[32]

As such, it shares an ethos similar to that of *theos* and *kyrios* in the Jewish scriptures but it also evokes relational connotations as noted earlier, especially given its use with pronouns which seek to characterize the new fictive kinship or household.

The interchangeability of *kyrios* and *pater* evokes the conjoined powers in the imperial Roman world of the empire and the patriarchal family. Zeus was both father and king (Epictetus, *Diatribai* (*Dissertations*) 1.37–41), and emperors such as Augustus and Vespasian shared these titles (Seneca, *De clementia* 1.14.2–3).[33] Maleness and power were, therefore, co-terminous in these titles, and within the familial context of the household that was foundational in Matthew's Jewish Christianity,[34] they resided in the male head of that household, who had authority over the household's resources and personnel.

Examining the use of *pater* in Matthew's Sermon on the Mount, where it is initially concentrated, makes clear that it is a designation of divinity. In nine of its sixteen occurrences in the sermon, it is followed by the phrase "in the heavens," which Matthew distinguishes from the "earth" as the place of the human community, differentiating yet linking the two spatial designators. This fatherhood of G*d provides the ethos for the ethics which characterize the sermon. The one faithful to this father in the heavens does *kala erga* or good works (5:16); is *teleios*/perfect (5:48); gives alms in secret; prays and fasts in secret (6:1, 4, 6, 8, 18); and does what is the will of the *pater* in the heavens (7:21). As D'Angelo says of Dio Chrysostom's imperial theology, "God as father rationalizes the imperial rule and invites it to embrace an ethical code of clemency and responsibility,"[35] so too in Matthean theology, G*d as father invites the community to embrace an ethical code of righteousness or right ordering manifest in the ethics of the sermon.[36]

This is an ideal point at which to turn our attention to the naming of Jesus in the Matthean gospel and how this is drawn into the relational imaging of G*d and the evoking of the presence of a spirit that is holy. Such an exploration is, of course, much more complex than is possible to undertake here, given that the whole of the Matthean story narrates and images Jesus.[37] The focus of this chapter suggests that we begin with the designation *huios tou theou*/son of G*d, which links Jesus both relationally and by way of sharing of power with G*d. Some form of the title "son" occurs in 56 verses of the Matthean narrative. The title *huios tou anthōpou* ("son of man" or "son of the human one") dominates, occurring 26 times as the most often repeated title given to Jesus by the Matthean narrator, and hence challenges retrospective claims like that of Jack Kingsbury that "son of G*d" is the most central designation of Jesus in the Matthean text.[38] "Son of David" occurs 7 times.[39] Similarly, Jesus is named "son of G*d"/*huios tou theou* 7 times (4:3, 6, 8:29, 14:33, 16:16, 27:40, 54). A divine voice names Jesus as "my son" at his baptism and transfiguration (3:17, 17:5),[40] and three times *huios* is used with a definite article and no genitive – in 11:27, 24:36, and 28:19, verses in which *pater* also occurs with a definite article and without any genitive.

This naming of Jesus with titles occurs, however, in the context of story. To understand this naming more fully, it is important to retain its context in the gospel narrative. Turning first to the story of the baptism of Jesus, we find that there is a particular Matthean coloration of this story, namely that it is to fulfill all righteousness (3:15). *Dikaiosynē* is a concept that links two streams of tradition which come together in the Matthean characterization of Jesus, namely wisdom and prophetic traditions. Righteousness characterizes the preaching of the sages (Prov 1:3, 2:9, 20, 3:9) and the proclamation of the anointed prophet (Isa 61:3). Jesus' baptism by John takes its place within a world of rightly ordered conduct, and it participates in the right ordering of G*d, who is with Jesus and with G*d's people.

The actual baptism of Jesus is passed over very cursorily but is followed by the opening of the heavens and descent of the spirit and the voice from the heavens. Jesus, who was conceived of a spirit that was holy, now has that same spirit come down upon him from the open heavens, imagery which resonates intertextually with Isaiah 61:1, in which the prophet of post-exilic restoration claims that the divine spirit is upon him and that he has been anointed to bring the good news to the poor.[41] Jesus is confirmed as the anointed prophetic leader of a restored humanity.

The heavenly voice acclaims Jesus as "my son, the beloved" (3:17). Given the cosmic signs of the heavens opening and a voice speaking from the heavens, those communities of reception whose socio-cultural world was Graeco-Roman would have understood the words as indicating the divine favor given to this holy one so that he could be called a "son" or a "child" of G*d, as were other great leaders, sages, and philosophers. Among those for whom the heavenly one was imaged female as well as male,[42] Jesus may have been seen as the favored one of Sophia/Wisdom as well as of G*d imaged as father (Wis 2:12–20). Within the scribal communities, there may have been rich intertextual associations with Genesis 22:2, the image of the "beloved son" of Abraham, and with Psalm 2:7, the anointed son and king, as well as with the understanding of the nation of Israel as "son" (an interpretation which may have been more influential in the subsequent temptation narrative). Isaiah 42:1 links the one in whom G*d is well pleased with the sending of the spirit on the one who will bring forth justice to the nations. The intimacy of association of the Emmanuel/G*d-with-us imagery associated with Jesus unfolds in multiple ways which would have been understood by different households of the Matthean community in the context of first-century Palestinian Judaism and emerging Christianity within the Graeco-Roman world. Such naming, imaging, and story-telling continue through the gospel, taking us to its concluding verses.

From a mountain in Galilee, the crucified and risen Jesus, identified with no titles other than the name Jesus which parallels the Emmanuel/"G*d-with-us" of Matthew 1:21–23, proclaims: "All authority in heaven and earth has been given to me. Go, therefore, make disciples of all nations, baptizing them in the name of the [f]ather, and of the [s]on and of the [h]oly [s]pirit, teaching them to observe all that I have commanded you; and lo, I am with you always, to the close of the age" (28:18–20). It is this triadic formula associated with baptism that is often read as trinitarian, but, like all the other naming in the gospel at the first layer of interpretation, it needs to be read in its literary and socio-historical contexts.

In seeking to understand these final verses in such contexts, it should be noted that the command to baptize occurs only here in the final commissioning. Jesus himself did not baptize, even though John metaphorically characterized the ministry of the coming one as baptizing with the [h]oly [s]pirit and with fire (3:11). Nor did Jesus commission his disciples to baptize when he sent them on mission (10:8). Baptizing may, therefore, have been recognized by readers as the process of initiation that distinguished this particular group of Jewish-Christian households from other Jewish households in their context.[43] Baptizing in the name of the triadic formula authorizes the community's continuance within its Jewish story-telling context.

Baptism into father, son, and spirit would recall the baptism of Jesus that commissioned him for his *basileia* ministry (3:12–17, 4:17). His was an active ministry of preaching, teaching and healing, engaging him in a new fictive kinship (4:23//9:35, 4:18–22, 12:46–50). His commissioning of those who continue his work after him is likewise to a *basileia* ministry (all that he had taught or commanded). The triad of names into which disciples are to be baptized is not a name to be confessed according to the Matthean narrative. It is in the context of going and making disciples that baptism into this name will occur. The Matthean resurrection accounts are not confessional (28:1–10, 16–20), containing elements of stasis that seek to hold and solidify a fixed meaning-making from the past. Rather, both Matthean resurrection accounts associated with female and male disciples are characterized by commissionings. These point to the opening-up of new meaning-making potential into the future, the bringing out of the new and the old by each new scribe discipled for the *basileia*. This scribe is one who is taught and who receives, in many contexts, what Jesus has commanded, learning how to name and re-name the G*d who is with G*d's people in Jesus crucified and raised (13:52).

In the opening of the gospel and in the baptism of Jesus, and in the unfolding narrative, readers have encountered G*d, a spirit that is holy, and Jesus named "son" in relation to the heavenly one under a variety of rubrics as the community narrates and theologizes Jesus. The interrelationship of divine and human power is named in relation to Jesus in the unfolding story. It is into this named interrelationship of G*d – as father but also more than father, of Jesus named as son in myriad ways, and of a spirit that is holy – that those who hear and receive this gospel proclamation are to be baptized. As the gospel unfolding of this naming has been manifold, so too is the way in which it would have been received. I will look at just one further example of this below.

Jerome Murphy-O'Connor has shown that Matthew's account of the transfiguration of Jesus (17:2–8) in its gospel context can be understood intertextually with Daniel 10, in which "one in human form" interprets a divine vision and mission.[44] If Daniel is a significant intertext for the Matthean story-telling, Jane Schaberg's suggestion that Matthew 28:19 is basically Midrashic in relation to selected Danielic texts, particularly 7:13–14 and 12:13, is not surprising.[45] She concludes that:

> The triadic phrase in the context of the midrash is shorthand for the eschatological theophany, or for the event of exaltation... The figure of the exalted one, here named the Son, has been presented at the heavenly throne of the one called the Father... Both the power of the heavenly world and the power that brings one to the heavenly world may be captured in the phrase "the Holy Spirit."[46]

It is into this name that disciples are to be baptized. Just as I suggested earlier that commission undermines any tendency toward stasis, Schaberg claims that the Matthean addition of verse 20 does not allow the baptized to rest in a *theologia gloria*. Rather, she reminds her readers that baptism is also into a *theologia crucis* and a *theologia caritatis*.[47] The baptized will receive the teaching of Jesus, which will impel them to the mission of the *basileia*, the mission which brought Jesus to the cross and through death, by the power of the G*d who was with him, to resurrected life.

## CONCLUSION

This brief engagement with just one New Testament text through the lens of Trinity in/and the New Testament has shown, as will this volume of essays, that trinitarian theologizing is indeed multi-layered. I have undertaken a *first-layer* analysis of the gospel of Matthew in order to demonstrate that the naming of G*d in a particular New Testament text is complex and needs to be explored within a recognition of the metaphoric character of such naming and in the literary and sociohistorical first-century contexts of the text. What has emerged from the very limited nature of this focused analysis is the extraordinarily rich texture of the naming of the divine and of Jesus in relation to the G*d of Israel in the context of first-century Judaism. It is the story of G*d-with-us in Jesus which unfolds through the death of Jesus and his being resurrected by the power of G*d to commission the ongoing unfolding of his *basileia* ministry through the discipling of others into his teachings, authorized by baptism into the name of father, son, and spirit. Other New Testament authors and communities theologized G*d, Jesus, and spirit in very different ways. All these spiraled out into the second and fourth centuries, where Christian communities encountered new questions and issues. As a result, much more explicit and developed naming of G*d as triune emerged. The Matthean community and other New Testament theological communities pointed the Christian community in a new direction in their naming of the divine, reminding us in each new age that the G*d of many names always goes before us inviting us into new images evocative of new relationships, warning us not to confuse the pointing finger with the moon.

## Notes

1. The title "Like a finger pointing to the moon" takes up a metaphor from a Zen sutra cited by Phyllis Trible, *God and the Rhetoric of Sexuality*, Overtures to Biblical Theology (Philadelphia: Fortress, 1978), 16. She, in turn, acknowledges Philip Kapleau, *Three Pillars of Zen* (Boston: Beacon, 1965), 167, 174.

   The topic that I was asked to address in this chapter was "Trinity in the New Testament." In researching toward this, I encountered among many contemporary biblical scholars the questions and issues which I myself had in relation to the topic and which will be explored in the chapter. The title of Frances Young's article "The Trinity and the New Testament," in Christopher Rowland and Christopher Tuckett, eds., *The Nature of New Testament Theology: Essays in Honour of Robert Morgan* (Oxford: Blackwell, 2006), 286–305, offered a way of nuancing the topic so that the necessary issues and questions could be addressed in undertaking the task requested.
2. Francis Watson, "Trinity and Community: A Reading of John 17," *International Journal of Systematic Theology*, 1:2 (1999), 168. Note that Watson is summarizing what he believes to be a trend in New Testament scholarship. As his article proceeds, he provides reasons as to why he considers that "we should resist this scholarly anti-trinitarianism."
3. It should be noted here that Watson himself does not undertake his reading of John 17 anachronistically but, in his article, grapples with the difficult hermeneutical or interpretive issues which face biblical scholars who stand within the communities of theology and faith but seek to interpret biblical texts of the first century in their integrity.
4. One of the ways in which Elisabeth Schüssler Fiorenza has proposed to interrupt too easy a familiarity with our naming of the divine is to write

that name as G*d (see Elisabeth Schüssler Fiorenza, *Jesus – Miriam's Child, Sophia's Prophet: Critical Issues in Feminist Christology* (New York: Continuum, 1994), 191 n. 3). I will use this nomenclature throughout this paper to invite us to be or become deeply aware of the power and pervasiveness of the dominant male images of "Father" and "Son" in the naming of the Trinity.

5. Arthur Wainwright, *The Trinity in the New Testament* (London: SPCK, 1962), 237–67, who is aware of the problem and who concludes (242) that "there is no doctrine of the Trinity but there is material for the development of a doctrine"; and Edmund J. Fortman, *The Triune God: A Historical Study of the Doctrine of the Trinity* (London: Hutchinson, 1972), 3–33, who likewise recognizes (32) that "[t]here is no formal doctrine of the Trinity in the New Testament" but that what is there is given new expression by later theologians of the early church.
6. Sallie McFague, "Mother God," in Elisabeth Schüssler Fiorenza, ed., *The Power of Naming: A Concilium Reader in Feminist Liberation Theology* (Maryknoll, NY: Orbis, 1996), 324, says that "[w]e can speak of God only indirectly, using our world and ourselves as metaphors for expressing our relationship with the divine. One of the oldest and most powerful metaphors has been the parental one: however, in the Christian tradition only one parent – the father – has been allowed to image God."
7. Elizabeth A. Johnson, *She Who Is: The Mystery of God in Feminist Theological Discourse* (New York: Crossroad, 1992), 42–57, addresses this issue of multiple images, noting (56) that "[t]he mystery of God transcends all images."
8. Janet Martin Soskice, *Metaphor and Religious Language* (Oxford: Clarendon Press, 1985), 15.
9. Mieke Bal, "Metaphors He Lives By," *Semeia*, 61 (1993), 205. Miroslav Volf, *Exclusion and Embrace: A Theological Exploration of Identity, Otherness, and Reconciliation* (Nashville: Abingdon Press, 1996), 172, says in this regard, "God models our common humanity not our gender specificity . . . God does not model gender identity."
10. W. David Hall, "The Economy of the Gift: Paul Ricoeur's Poetic Redescription of Reality," *Literature and Theology*, 20:2 (2006), 195, acknowledges the significance of contextualizing metaphors in discourse or literature in order to understand them fully when he says that "[n]ames will indeed continue to play a role in our discourse about both our neighbor and our God, but names do not comport meaning in and of themselves, decontextualized from the stories that we tell about the entwined discourse and action that make up the fabric of our communicative praxis."
11. Contemporary hermeneutical theory recognizes that this is a difficult if not impossible task, especially if the search is for the intention of the original author. See Alan G. Padgett, "The Canonical Sense of Scripture: Trinitarian or Christocentric?," *Dialog*, 45:1 (2006), 37, who says that "we have no common access to the inner thoughts of the original biblical author and editors." The approach I suggest at this first layer is, however, socio-rhetorical. It recognizes the significance of what we

can reconstruct of the first-century worlds of texts and contexts that have left traces in the text. These point to possible first-century meanings available to the texts' original hearers and readers. See Vernon K. Robbins, *Exploring the Texture of Texts: A Guide to Socio-Rhetorical Interpretation* (Valley Forge, PA: Trinity Press International, 1996).

12. Padgett, "The Canonical Sense," 37–38.
13. Young, "Trinity and the New Testament," 288.
14. Ibid.
15. Ibid., 301 (parenthetical emphasis mine).
16. Alasdair Heron, "The Biblical Basis for the Doctrine of the Trinity," in Alasdair I. C. Heron, ed., *The Forgotten Trinity*, III*: A Selection of Papers Presented to the BCC Study Commission on Trinitarian Doctrine Today* (London: BCC/CCBI, 1991), 38, also highlights the hermeneutical issues being addressed here and articulates this second-layer interpretation in this way: "to relocate [the doctrine of Trinity] in its proper place as a *lens designed to focus for your eyes the nature of the God to which the Bible testifies as the God who has to do with us*. Its biblical basis is therefore to be looked for less in *proof-texts* than in *the whole sweep of the biblical message*" (emphasis in the original).
17. *Gaudium et spes*, §1, says that "[t]he joy and hope, the grief and anguish of the men [sic] of our time, especially those who are poor or afflicted in any way, are the joy and hope, the grief and anguish of the followers of Christ." See *Vatican Council II: The Conciliar and Post Conciliar Documents*, ed. Austin Flannery (Dublin: Dominican Publications, 1975), 903. It is this insight that authorizes the contemporary perspective on Christian tradition and life, interpreted and lived in engagement with these joys and hopes, grief and anguish.
18. This section of the chapter is informed by previous research published as "From Antiochean to Antipodean Naming of Divinity," in Winifred Wing Han Lamb and Ian Barns, eds., *God Down Under: Theology in the Antipodes*, ATF Series (Adelaide: ATF Press, 2003), 87–117, and drawn on with the permission of ATF Press. I also wish to acknowledge the invitation by the New Testament Society of South Africa to give a keynote address at its 2007 congress, which I entitled "Reflecting/Constructing God: A Dialogue with the Gospel of Matthew Today." This paper has likewise informed this section of the current chapter.
19. This aspect of the naming and characterizing of Jesus was first explored by Jane Schaberg, *The Illegitimacy of Jesus: A Feminist Theological Interpretation of the Infancy Narratives* (San Francisco: Harper & Row, 1987), 42–62. See also Elaine M. Wainwright, *Shall We Look for Another? A Feminist Rereading of the Matthean Jesus* (Maryknoll, NY: Orbis, 1998), 58–60.
20. See also Julian Sheffield, "The Father in the Gospel of Matthew," in Amy-Jill Levine, ed., *A Feminist Companion to Matthew*, Feminist Companion to the New Testament and Early Christian Writings, 1 (Sheffield: Sheffield Academic Press, 2001), 57, whose count differs slightly from mine.

21. I explored the titles *kyrios* and *theos* more fully in the paper entitled "Reflecting/Constructing God: A Dialogue with the Gospel of Matthew Today," referred to in n. 18, and hence can verify my very abbreviated conclusion but cannot lay it all out here.
22. Sheffield, "The Father," 53, who gives the figures: 44 in Matthew, 4 in Mark, and 17 in Luke. My own count of the Matthean usage is 41 in 39 verses, and Robert Hammerton-Kelly, *God the Father: Theology and Patriarchy in the Teaching of Jesus*, Overtures to Biblical Theology (Philadelphia: Fortress, 1979), 71, counts Matthean usage at 42, Mark at 4, and Luke at 15.
23. Sheffield, "The Father," 57, where it is noted that *kyrios* and *theos*, on the other hand, reflect scriptural usage and also that they are titles used by adversaries as well as disciples of Jesus.
24. Adele Reinhartz, "Introduction: 'Father' as Metaphor in the Fourth Gospel," in Adele Reinhartz, ed., *God the Father in the Gospel of John, Semeia*, 85 (Atlanta: Society of Biblical Literature, 1999), 1, shows that there is a similar pattern in the gospel of John, noting that it is the discourse material which develops "the Gospel's distinctive theology and Christology."
25. Mt 5:16, 45, 48, 6:1, 4, 6, 8, 14, 15, 18 (two references), 26, 32, 7:11.
26. In the Mission Discourse of chapter 10, *your* and *my* both occur twice with "father" in 10:20, 29, 32, and 33; *my* is used three times in the Community Discourse, at 18:10, 19, 35, and *your* just once, at 18:14; and in the final discourse *my* occurs once only, at 25:34. *My* also occurs with "father" seven times on the lips of Jesus in narrative sections (11:27, 12:50, 15:13, 16:17, 20:23, 26:29, 53) and twice in the prayer of Jesus in the garden (26:39, 42). All the uses of "father" in prayer in Matthew have sources in Mark and Q.
27. Mary Rose D'Angelo, "*Abba* and 'Father': Imperial Theology and the Jesus Traditions," *Journal of Biblical Literature*, 111:4 (1992), 622, says that "the title evoked the relation of humanity to God in terms of kindred and likeness."
28. Johnson, *She Who Is*, 220–22.
29. Watson, "Trinity and Community," 171–76, addresses the question "Is this community within the eternal divine life genuinely a community of men and of women?" After examining the presence of male and female within the community reflected in the Johannine gospel, Watson concludes that the divine metaphor *cannot* evoke a masculine relationship only because of the "is not" of the metaphor. What he fails to address is the complete absence of female metaphors or images in the naming of the divine as triune together with the power of the "is" aspect of the exclusive male metaphor in the theological and liturgical life of the church so that the female has been excluded from the imagining of G*d as triune until very recently.
30. Sheffield, "The Father," 58–63.
31. I draw particularly on D'Angelo, "*Abba* and 'Father'," 611–30; and her "Intimating Deity in the Gospel of John: Theology Language and 'Father' in 'Prayers of Jesus'," in Reinhartz, ed., *God the Father*, 83–104.

32. D'Angelo, "*Abba* and 'Father'," 621.
33. See Warren Carter, *Matthew and the Margins: A Sociopolitical and Religious Reading* (Maryknoll, NY: Orbis, 2000), 139.
34. See Michael H. Crosby, *House of Disciples: Church, Economics, and Justice in Matthew* (Maryknoll, NY: Orbis, 1988), who claims that "house" is the primary metaphor in Matthew's gospel.
35. D'Angelo, "*Abba* and 'Father'," 625. Note also that to use the language of the empire against the empire in one context may enable the community to use it for establishing itself as new empire in a new context. It is this which the church has done down through the ages.
36. See also the Matthean use of *dikaiosynē*/righteousness (5:6, 10, 20, 6:1, 33) and *basileia*/kingdom, empire, reign (5:3, 10, 19, 20, 6:10, 33, 7:21), both of which contribute to the ethical character of the sermon. Crosby, *House of Disciples*, 59–63, 179–95, suggests (181) that "Matthew arranged the main body of the Sermon around key passages related to justice."
37. See Wainwright, *Shall We Look for Another?* for a limited and yet much more extensive exploration of the narrative and metaphorical characterization of Jesus in the gospel story.
38. Jack Dean Kingsbury, "The Composition and Christology of Matt 28:16–20," *Journal of Biblical Literature*, 93 (1974), 573–84.
39. For an excellent treatment of this title in the Matthean gospel, see Dennis Duling, "Matthew's Plurisignificant 'Son of David' in Social Science Perspective: Kinship, Kingship, Magic, and Miracle," *Biblical Theology Bulletin*, 22 (1992), 99–116.
40. Some would consider the intertextual reference of 2:15, which draws into the text the words of Hosea "Out of Egypt I have called my son" (Hos 11:1), to be a third such reference, but it is a voice once removed from that of the narrator.
41. It seems that some manuscripts have added the definite article to *pneuma theou*, which may be indicative of later development of trinitarian thinking.
42. Leander E. Keck, "The Spirit and the Dove," *New Testament Studies*, 17 (1970–71), 41–67, points out that female deities like Ishtar, Astarte, and Aphrodite were often depicted with a dove.
43. J. Andrew Overman, *Community in Crisis: The Gospel According to Matthew* (Valley Forge, PA: Trinity Press International, 1996), argues for a Matthean context that is still within Judaism so that the gospel is read as a Jewish document.
44. Jerome Murphy-O'Connor, "What Really Happened at the Transfiguration: A Literary Critic Deepens our Understanding," *Bible Review*, 3:3 (1987), 8–21.
45. Jane Schaberg, *The Father, The Son and the Holy Spirit: The Triadic Phrase in Matthew 28:19b*, Society of Biblical Literature Dissertation Series, 61 (Chico, CA: Scholars Press, 1982).
46. Ibid., 327.
47. Ibid., 334.

## Further reading

D'Angelo, Mary Rose, "*Abba* and 'Father': Imperial Theology and the Jesus Traditions," *Journal of Biblical Literature*, 111:4 (1992), 611–30.

"Intimating Deity in the Gospel of John: Theology Language and 'Father' in 'Prayers of Jesus,'" in Adele Reinhartz, ed., *God the Father in the Gospel of John, Semeia*, 85 (Atlanta: Society of Biblical Literature, 1999), 83–104.

Johnson, Elizabeth A., *She Who Is: The Mystery of God in Feminist Theological Discourse* (New York: Crossroad, 1992).

Padgett, Alan G., "The Canonical Sense of Scripture: Trinitarian or Christocentric?," *Dialog*, 45:1 (2006), 36–43.

Reinhartz, Adele, ed., *God the Father in the Gospel of John, Semeia*, 85 (Atlanta: Society of Biblical Literature, 1999).

Schaberg, Jane, *The Father, The Son and the Holy Spirit: The Triadic Phrase in Matthew 28:19b*, Society of Biblical Literature Dissertation Series, 61 (Chico, CA: Scholars Press, 1982).

Schüssler Fiorenza, Elisabeth, *Jesus – Miriam's Child, Sophia's Prophet: Critical Issues in Feminist Christology* (New York: Continuum, 1994).

Sheffield, Julian, "The Father in the Gospel of Matthew," in Amy-Jill Levine, ed., *A Feminist Companion to Matthew*, Feminist Companion to the New Testament and Early Christian Writings, 1 (Sheffield: Sheffield Academic Press, 2001), 52–69.

Wainwright, Arthur, *The Trinity in the New Testament* (London: SPCK, 1962).

Watson, Francis, "Trinity and Community: A Reading of John 17," *International Journal of Systematic Theology*, 1:2 (1999), 168–84.

Young, Frances, "The Trinity and the New Testament," in Christopher Rowland and Christopher Tuckett, eds., *The Nature of New Testament Theology: Essays in Honour of Robert Morgan* (Oxford: Blackwell, 2006), 286–305.

# 4 The Trinity in the Greek Fathers

JOHN ANTHONY McGUCKIN

## IN SEARCH OF THE TRINITY

In terms of this overview of the Greek patristic theology of the Trinity, it might keep us from sinking into a welter of details to imagine five great acts of a play, each of which is differently weighted, to be sure, but which are all, in their own ways, progressive variations upon biblical premises, mediated through the lived experience of the church. The first is the sparse collection of second-century theologians. The second is the quickening of pace that occurred in the third-century Apologists. The third is the towering genius of Origen of Alexandria, whose work began a revolution. The fourth (a long-drawn-out scene) is the Nicene and post-Nicene reactions to Origen. Finally, Act Five – are we still in it? – is the bemused aftermath, a long quieting-down as the Trinity becomes a fixed dogma, a quieting that often lapses into silence.

This patristic period may be startling because of the speed and variety with which schools of thought during this time spun out new reflections on deeply mysterious ideas about God and his action in the cosmos. Yet it is also illuminating in that it shows how fluid and inter-reactive the early Christian theologians were. In general, for the Fathers, the scriptures and the liturgical mysteries of the church were always more immediately influential than anything else. Even their philosophy came to them, by and large, through the medium of rhetoric, as a form of "illustration of argument" – useful in the manner of argumentative method – rather than as the specific teachings of a school. This is true of the most philosophical of all the writers, Origen, and even more so of the Greek Fathers who followed him.

The Fathers clearly emerge as innovators in the long line of Late Antique syncretizers of the Second Sophistic Period. As philosophical innovators, however, their inspiration and drive comes from more discrete sources than eclectic readings of Plato and Pythagoras. They owe more to the community which acclaims Jesus as Lord and Saviour, as emissary of the unique God, and sender of the saving Spirit, master of the church. How they elaborate this good news to the world in which they lived is our heritage of trinitarian theology. Many centuries would have to pass before Christians could manage to sing a song of comparable richness on this theme.

## THE SECOND AND EARLY THIRD CENTURIES

The transition between the late New Testament era and the earliest Greek Fathers is a time when apocalypticism is still the church's preferred syntax of thought about the manner of God's relation with the world. Christ, the Father's own Son and messenger, and the Spirit, the gift of the Messiah to a renewed world (namely the church), are celebrated as the two primary means of the divine outreach of the Father. In this apocalyptic medium, the bringing of consonance between the heavenly reality (God's court where his will is perfectly fulfilled) and the earthly dominion (where evil regularly withstands God's overarching design) is the crux of all the theology of redemption. Nowhere is this summed up more succinctly than in the Lord's Prayer. The church's kerygma confesses that the Father has wrought reconciliation through the work of Jesus, his *adventus* to humankind, and inaugurated its extension on earth by the indwelling gift of the Spirit of holiness.

Because of this overarching perspective, the earliest level of Greek post-New Testamental theology is entirely dynamic, or "economic," in character. The Greek term *oikonomia* signifies how a household is brought into order. Sometimes it has been argued that this way of thinking is subservient to "metaphysical" reflection, as if metaphysical thinking were about realities, and economic thinking were about effects. Nothing could be more misleading. Early Christian economic theology is dynamic because it expresses the fundamental insight that God is one who saves his people. God is energy. God is not a thing. Economic theology is not some defective form of proto-trinitarianism; rather it is the first variation on the biblical doctrine of God's salvation in the form of acclamational theology, that is, theology that rises out of confessions of praise.

This confessionalism is found not only in early trinitarian prayers (doxologies), but also in patristic attempts to explain why God works so dramatically in this way (through Jesus) and not in any other way that could be posited as more "rational." This is also why the earliest of Christian patristic theologies is incidental, accidental almost. It does not arise out of precise and narrow controversies in the way the fourth-century arguments do. It comes out of the writers almost unconsciously; it is not offered as a "treatise on the nature of God" but rather as reflections on God's will for the present circumstances. In all of these apocalyptically charged patristic writings, the desire to conform to God's will is the theological axiom underlying all that may be called the "origins" of trinitarian theology.

## CLEMENT OF ROME

A prime example of this style is found in Clement of Rome (fl. c. 96), who wrote to the troubled Corinthian Christians to remind them of a threefold truth: that Christ is God's agent for redemption, that the Spirit is Christ's gift for reconciliation and insight, and that a peaceful church is the fruit of Christ's work. He writes: "It is to the humble that Christ belongs not to those who exalt themselves above his flock. The Lord Jesus, who is the scepter of God's own majesty, did not come in a show of arrogance and pride, but in humility, as the Holy Spirit spoke of him, saying: 'Lord, who has believed what we said... ?'" (Is 53:1–4).[1] And again: "For this is how Christ addresses us through his Holy Spirit: 'Come children and hear me that I may teach you the fear of the Lord...'" (Ps 34:11–14).[2]

The earliest references to the Trinity, therefore, are entirely made up of New Testament cloth (Clement's indebtedness to Paul is obvious in every line). The consonance of the heavenly court and the church on earth is at the forefront of Clement's mind. The Christ is the Lord who brings peace from the Father. And the Spirit of Holiness, who is the Messiah's gift, reveals the life-giving words of what is evidently Christ's own pre-existent revelation. It is Christ who speaks in Isaiah, in the Psalms, and so on. It is the Spirit who teaches Christ's heavenly and ineffable doctrine through the medium of the scriptures, which is one of the chief apocalyptic signs the church possesses. The church is the charter of truth that makes its earthly life consonant with the lifestyle of the heavenly court, where Christ and the Spirit attend the Father's throne of glory.

However "simple," or even "crude," Clement's trinitarian theology may be in the eyes of later readers, it is nonetheless fully formed and fairly impressive. It also gives the lie to any attempt to separate the economic Trinity from the immanent Trinity (long before Karl Rahner). We know God only by being conformed to his ways, Clement teaches, and this consonance is the eschatological gift of grace (reconciliation) which the Father has given to the world through the *adventus* of the Son, effected in the sanctifying and revelatory power of the Spirit. Clement's theology is that of a leader, and is stimulated by a crisis of governance in the important Corinthian church. He calls for the re-establishment of order, not for bourgeois reasons, but for fear that the church would endanger its reality of mirroring the heavenly court as the eschatological community of reconciliation and mercy.

## IGNATIUS OF ANTIOCH

Another theologian-bishop near Clement's time was put into a different form of crisis. For Ignatius Theophoros (Ignatius of Antioch, d. c. 107), the bitter persecution of the Christians that had caused his arrest and his long journey to Rome and his expected execution there was no less than a supreme eschatological sign. Bloody hatred of the church was not a political accident, but an apocalyptical "testing" of the church. His theology once more grows out of the eschatological environment, though unfortunately it has been quarried like a mountain ever since for what he had to say about the institution of bishops. Even this, however, was not a bourgeois development, but an eschatological expression of faith for the communities in the time of Ignatius. Bishops are icons of God the Father; priests are like Christ; deacons are the angels present in the churches. The threefold ministry is described as a living sign of the Trinity present in the eschatological mysteries of the Eucharist and baptism. Ignatius' voice as the inspired Spirit-bearer, he tells his readers, is the voice of God. It commands the Philadelphian church to obey the (earthly) hierarchy that is the icon of the heavenly harmony of God himself.[3]

This earliest level of patristic trinitarianism has often been dismissed as unformed, or pedestrian, largely because commentators are impatient to find signs or traces of the later formulae of the trinitarian doctrine in the early writers. But we will better appreciate the ancients if we lay aside that flawed methodology and remember that they are singing in a different key, or – to change metaphors – that they are working under a different light. Approach their dissonances on their own terms (as if looking under purple light instead of daylight) and we will see a wholly different set of facts. It is the eschatological dimension that explains many parts of the earliest theology when it speaks of Christ as the supreme pre-existent angel.[4]

It is because of this approach that the fourth-century church jettisoned the *Shepherd* from the proto-canon of scripture. By then the fluid terms had been co-opted into another agenda (which is very important to Arius) that divides beings into angelic (created) and divine (uncreated). What Hermas originally meant is that Christ is a pre-existent power at the throne of God, and one who bridges the eons, bringing the peace of the next age into this present world order. Three centuries after him, of course, the language no longer worked, and he had to go to the wall.

A similar tendency of pre-Nicene theology barely to differentiate the risen Christ from the Spirit equally confuses and troubles those later theologians who still read the ancients. For most of the "Apostolic Fathers,"[5] this intimate proximity of Christ and Spirit is presumed. "Spirit" is not merely "the Holy Spirit," but is also a synonym for "heavenly." The term was used for the very steps toward the throne of the divine being in an age when the simple ascription of the title "God" to Christ or the Holy Spirit would have seemed an abandonment of the heart of the Christian doctrine of God, namely, that the one and only Father has expressed his divine power *in* and *through* the Son and Spirit. This identification of Spirit with the "deity" continued into the age of the Apologists.[6] The apocalyptic language of "sending" and "emissary" conveys the aspect of the Father expressing his power *through* the Son and the Spirit quite brilliantly. The later patristic language of divine pre-existence will explicate it further, and will attempt to explain the other, more difficult aspect of the Father expressing his power *in* the Son and the Spirit.

Once again the overarching eschatological climate explains Ignatius' tendency of assimilating Son and Spirit, for "spirit" conveys the status of being an inhabitant of the heavenly court and an emissary of God. Talking of the "Spirit of God" was one of the few ways in which the writers of this era could articulate what theologians, after Origen, meant by the "pre-existence" of Christ (is he merely a man or does he have an eternal pre-existence in the heavenly court?). In the earlier eschatological idiom the question does not make sense, since apocalypticism works on the mainspring of the concept of outreach from the heavenly court to the earthly world in order to deliver a life-saving and urgent message. The theology of "pre-existence" that so carefully differentiated the Lord and the Spirit in the later centuries was working from the other direction, what we can crudely call upward from earth, or backward from human history to transcendence. A moment's thought shows that it is a straining of categories that cannot be sustained for long, and certainly does not make "better sense" than the earlier, and simpler, attempt. Christ's pre-existence is certainly "presumed" in such writings as Second Clement.[7] And the title "God" is also ascribed to Jesus in the second century,[8] along with a host of other acclamatory titles of extraordinary range and significance.[9]

## THE CHRISTIAN APOLOGISTS

A new intellectual ferment was in the making as the second century grew old. For the first time, Christians began attracting the attention of groups external to them, that is, the Jewish sages and religious philosophers. These groups were also formidable opponents to the Christians, who, by and large, did not then share their habit and culture of dialectical argument. In the face of the sharp logical process of the philosophers and the deep exegetical traditions of the rabbis, the Christians in the cities of the Empire, where interreligious discourse was a daily event, were sitting ducks. So it was that the era of the Christian Apologists commenced.[10] The Apologists at first were often Christians of a philosophical bent (it is difficult to call any one of them a serious philosopher as such) who tried to express fundamental Christian attitudes in ways with which a Hellenistic mind might resonate.

The early Apologists placed the doctrine of Trinity on a new footing by trying to explain for their audiences (curious seekers, whom the Christians regarded as potential catechumens) how they could claim to be continuing the monotheism of the Jews while worshiping Christ as God. At this period the *arcanum* of the Holy Spirit (that is the "secret" of his status and role and mission as sanctifying grace) was not communicated to the believer until the eve of his or her baptism, and then in the most simple fashion. Since Apologetic theology was addressed, in the main, to a "catechumenal" audience it was never regarded as a suitable place for discoursing about the work of the Spirit. This is partly why the doctrine of the person and role of the Spirit is shadowy in this literature, in comparison to the teachings about the person and work of Christ.

## THE APOLOGETIC USE OF LOGOS THEOLOGY

Among the Apologists the syntax of Logos theology became dominant very quickly. It was a term that is rooted in the holy scriptures and capable of many meanings. It may mean the plan of God's salvation, or the Father's spoken word which created the universe, or the divine Wisdom which held all things in order, or the supreme active Spirit of the transcendent God. All this semantic range had been elaborated long before the Apologists came onto the scene. But the genius of these thinkers was that they could presume it and subordinate its syntax to their own Christian agenda. "Logos" was a major term of reference among the Stoics. But it was Philo of Alexandria who had shown the Jewish and Christian communities its religious potentialities. He described the Logos as the pre-existent power of the supreme God who spoke and acted through all the theophanies of the Law and the *paideia* of the scripture.

Logos philosophy articulates how monotheism can be combined with confession of Jesus as divine power of the Father. Ancient polytheism was quite happy about using the title "God" and the term "divine" in a loose way. Judaism (and Christianity after it) was not. The God of the Bible was a jealous Lord who did not share divine honors as loosely as the cults of Late Antiquity would have it, or as the Hellenistic philosophers argued "should be" the case. For them the many deities were but different ways to the one truth. This form of pluralism, however, met with a frosty reception among Jews and Christians. Logos theology seemed a way around the problem of communication. The Logos could be divine without being the supreme God. It could be God of God, rather than God instead of God. The Apologists took this line of approach, using the Wisdom literature as an inspiration. Here the Wisdom of the Lord was his medium of creation and revelation. So too with the Logos. The Word was the creative medium of the unapproachable and transcendent Father, the face of God as turned out to the material world of creation, as it were. Christ was the earthly manifestation of the eternal Logos, the temporal expression of the Logos' eternal work of salvific economy for the human race. It was this movement of apologetic "bridging" that made the classic trinitarian development inevitable. In fact all later trinitarian thought, up to the eighth century, can be said to be the necessary elaboration and clarification of the terms of the Sophia-Logos theology that prioritized the Wisdom literature as a lens onto the issues of creation and redemption.

## THEOPHILUS OF ANTIOCH

Theophilus, a leader of the Antiochene Christians in the late second century, introduces to Christian discourse, from Hellenistic logic, the distinction between the *logos endiathetos* and the *logos prophorikos*.[11] The former refers to a conception as distinct from an elaborated argument or ideational activity as a prelude to rhetoric. Theophilus applies it to the issue of the relation of the Son and the Father, and goes on to use the idea to explain creation and redemption: how a historically conditioned Jesus can be understood as the same one who made the heavens and the earth, and who is older than the stars. A simple trope was now bearing a massive load. For Theophilus, the Father exists as the supreme monad in infinite transcendence. But when he decides to create the material world, he "utters" what he has hitherto kept secret within his own mind. In other words, the Father's Wisdom is always co-present and co-eternal, but at a specific moment (purely for the world's making) the Logos is "expressed," and becomes manifest in order to work. In this perspective it is the Logos' energy that makes all material reality. As such the creation cannot have an unmediated relationship with the unapproachable monad, but knows God only by means of its apprehension of the Logos, whose divine fashioning leaves spiritual seeds and traces in his earthly creations – especially in the mind of humans, his "image and likeness."

At one stroke Theophilus explains also why the Logos had to have charge of the redemption of the fallen world: it was *his* fallen world and he who made it came to repair it. Thus the incarnation of the invisible Logos is a logical outflow of his original mercy. The Logos' accepting of flesh is as economic as all his other expressions of salvific energy on behalf of the Father.

## JUSTIN MARTYR

The mid-second-century Samaritan Justin Martyr describes himself as a sage (he was remarked in the church as being the first one who had come into the ranks of Christians wearing the distinctive robe of the philosopher and still wishing to retain it after baptism). Justin takes the path of Theophilus further. Using Stoic ideas he theorizes that the Logos has left divine seeds (*logoi spermatikoi*) in all rational creatures. Applying Platonic ideas about the "recognition" of truth, he goes on to suggest that it is this aspect of human constitution that makes religious insight possible and Christianity the natural goal for all who wish to be wise. Before the coming of the Logos all human beings have "seedling" manifestations of the truth, which are authentic, but partial.[12] Now, after the incarnation, the church holds the power to bring all partial truths into focus. The Logos, Justin argues (in the context of possibly the first ever Jewish–Christian dialogue), is distinct from the supreme Father in name and number,[13] and yet the Logos is truly the Son of God issuing from God before all creatures.[14]

This divine origination makes the Logos authentically divine, worthy of the title "God," not a God alongside God but the Son of God from within the Father's bosom.[15] The Logos-Son is not a creature, issued from out of the Father's will, but, as the scriptures indicate, a true "offspring" produced from out of the Father, "by generation."[16] Thus the distinction between the concept of issuing by willed production and the concept of emanating by generation became an important theological construct of the later generation. It marks the difference between envisaging the Logos-Son as either made or begotten, as either the first of all the creatures or someone above the creation whose origin and status is "within the Deity." This notion will command the whole of the later fourth-century Christian dialectic.

This relation of the active Logos to the ineffable Father, in the hands of both Justin and Theophilus, articulates a way forward for what Christians at this period were told by their contemporaries was the most pressing religious question of the epoch. The question is: how can a religion that originates in folk tales (e.g., the quaint provincial stories of different Olympian gods, or even the tales of God's appearances to Jewish nomads as recounted in the Hebrew scriptures, indicating thus a sense of local deities) claim to be a universal way? If Roman religious philosophy at this period was ridiculing its own cults and arguing for a new awareness of universal divine transcendence, how could Christians possibly claim a meaningful new revelation which, on inspection, seems to be inescapably rooted in the material order? One of the most savage diatribes against the Christians for their religious provincialism was written at this period by the philosopher Celsus in a work entitled *Logos alethes* (*True Discourse*). Its charges would not be answered until the next century, when Origen turned his attention to it.

The Apologists, nevertheless, had begun sketching out an answer to the issue of universal salvation through the Logos theology. For the philosophy of the era, the problem is that of intellectual coherence: how can the sublime one relate to the vagaries of the many? This problem of the one and the many has infinite ramifications. For example, if God is by definition transcendent, how can any external thing be related to him? If God is infinitely benign, how can he be held responsible for this troubled world-order? There are many aspects to the problem, many of which have remained as religious issues of our own time. According to the Apologists, the world, strictly speaking, is not a work of the Father, but that of the Logos. The Father remains the supreme and transcendent one. The Logos is a reflection, an image, of the deity. It is, however, an icon, which is divine, of God, and is to be considered as being "within

God" rather than "without God," and as such worthy of worship by the church. The Apologists' arguments about the Logos made it clear that the title of Son is to be ascribed to Jesus on account of his pre-existent state as immanent Word and not merely as an honor applicable to his earthly ministry.

While not articulating, at many instances, an explicit theology of the Holy Spirit within this Logos theology[17] (it is oriented toward the work of revelation and creation rather than that of inspiration and sanctification), the very shape of the argument also spells out, implicitly, how the pneumatological aspects could be elaborated later. It would be the task of classical trinitarianism to extend the dyadic dynamic of the Logos theology (so beautifully adapted to the Father-Son analogy as found in the scriptures) into the triadic dynamic of the Father-Son-Spirit theology. This work was begun by Origen and perfected in the Nicene era. This elaboration, however, would not have been possible without the earlier foundations laid by the Apologists.

## IRENAEUS OF LYONS

Bridging the world of the Apologists and the next stage of Christian reflection is the work of perhaps the most influential among them, the late second-century theologian Irenaeus. Reacting against the theological currents swirling around him, Irenaeus composes a series of largely pastoral books, urging "caution" in theology, and elaborates a working doctrine of tradition, to serve as a canon, or criterion, of truth. Irenaeus' theological achievements as a whole are quite remarkable. He develops the Logos theology, gives an account of the process whereby the scriptures become canonical, and articulates the concepts of apostolic succession and *regula fidei* against the Gnostics (e.g., the use of simple confessions of faith such as baptismal creeds to withstand complicated theological speculations). All of Irenaeus' theological elaborations would acquire a large importance in the succeeding generations, and his work would be regarded as enduringly authoritative by later episcopal theologians. Origen was one of his later intellectual disciples. But in terms of trinitarian thought Irenaeus is of immense importance for being the first to position the Logos theology as the central pole in a great vista of cosmic redemption. In his hands it gives the first inkling that this is a scheme of thought that has truly cosmic soteriological dimensions.

Irenaeus perfects the concepts of the *logos endiathetos* and the *logos prophorikos*. He takes it away from an (implicit) presupposition that the

Logos is a stage in the life of God, and back toward the more biblically rooted sense of the Logos as the eternal Son of the Father's generation. Irenaeus reacts against the Gnostic scheme of a series of mediating lesser deities between the supreme God and the corrupted world, and robustly insists that the Logos is the supreme mediator of the sublime Father and is fully divine,[18] just as the Spirit of God is fully divine.[19] The immanent Logos and the emitted Logos are no longer seen as stages of creation, but as aspects of God's own being and as simultaneous with God, not his successive moments (which in an eternal being would be an impossibility). According to Irenaeus, the immanent Logos is to be understood as God existing in his intrinsic being, and the emitted Logos as God existing in relation and outreach to the world.[20] He is clear on this point: it is the same God existing in different modalities of relation. These three relations of Fatherhood (the one divine Being), sonship (the living Reason of the Father), and Spirit (the hypostatic Wisdom of the Father) exist from all eternity, but are fully manifested to the world only in the economy of salvation. It is from Irenaeus that the third-century church receives the principle of economic trinitarianism: namely that the Son and the Spirit, who are seen in the economy of salvation as being other than the Father, are, nevertheless, in the inner life of God, essentially one with him.

## THE EARLY THIRD-CENTURY THEOLOGIANS

The dawn of the third century witnesses Greek theologians such as Hippolytus and Novatian, who are deeply concerned with the trinitarian question and who want to marginalize the traditional (perhaps less intellectual) Christian leaders, such as Pope Callixtus,[21] whom they called "monarchians." These cling to the older and biblical phrases describing the Son's relation to the Father but are generally at a loss to explain the trinitarian relations except in terms of successive modalities of revelation. The attempts of these traditionalists to resist the onset of the Logos theologians were more or less doomed by the rise of a school of thought in Rome now known as "Modalism." The names of Theodotos the Banker, Asclepiodotus, Artemas, Noetus, and Sabellius are commonly associated with the movement, which tends to argue that the "names" of Father, Son, and Spirit are simply designations for different aspects of the same God working in different modes in the economy of salvation. Added on to the above theology is the Christological conclusion that the Spirit of God assumed and inhabited Jesus and therefore cannot be called divine, or God, in any personal way at all.

It was the latter thesis that ultimately scared off the traditionalists and drove a hesitant church into the arms of the Logos theologians. However, although the Logos theology had assumed a new international importance, the articulations of Hippolytus and Novatian about the trinitarian relations were still meager by comparison with what was soon to come. Hippolytus instinctively looks to the past. Novatian is a clearer thinker who (at a time when Tertullian is laying down major advances in Christian semantics concerning the Trinity) underlines the important principle that the Sonship of the Logos begins in eternity, and not with the creation.[22] He conceives the unity in the three divine persons as deriving from the will of the Father. This is a moral unity which, though it might appear as a weak notion in the relations of human beings, is, in terms of the power of God's sovereign will, far removed from fallibility and change. For Novatian, God's unicity is preserved since the Son is derived from the Father. As Son, he is truly divine; yet as Son, he is not the supreme Father.

There is thus a give-and-take in Novatian's conception of the eternal relations in the Trinity which will eventually be explicated and elaborated in terms of the trinitarian *perichōrēsis*. This view envisages the deity that the Father confers on the Son as ever returning to the source, while the Son is also said to have the divine attributes as "exclusively his."[23] Both Novatian and Hippolytus appear as highly sophisticated and educated theologians torn between an older and more poetical biblical idiom of theology and the growing demands for more clarification, as the church constantly faces a welter of alternative views about Jesus and his divine role. If there is a certain degree of confusion and uncertainty in their works, which are the first Christian treatises in Greek explicitly to face up to the trinitarian problem, it reflects their awareness that the church had come to a watershed in terms of its habits of confessional theology. Another level of genius was now required to make a breakthrough in the ranks of the Christian intellectuals. And the person who provides the impetus is Origen of Alexandria, the first Christian philosopher of any real standing, a literary interpreter whose acumen is the admiration of the outside world, and a powerhouse of devotion to the mystical beauty of Christ. For better or worse, Origen changes the face of trinitarian theology forever.

## ORIGEN OF ALEXANDRIA

Christoph Markschies rightly sums up Origen's importance: "The development of Trinitarian theology in all parts of the Church over the two centuries following him, did little other than develop the schema he himself had first sketched out, by clarifying the loose ends of his concept."[24] The speed at which the doctrine of the Trinity developed through the fourth century, reaching a plateau thereafter, is a direct reaction to Origen's scholarly agenda. Origen understands the problems facing the earlier Christian theologians in the doctrine of God and tries very hard to keep a balance between the Christian sense of the divine status of the Word (and the Spirit) and the sense of order that flows from the unique majesty of the one God, the Father. To emphasize the divine status of the Word and of the Spirit as if it were something "parallel" with that of the Father – equality in a static sense – would render the Trinity flat and lifeless. On the other hand, to emphasize the order (*taxis*) or process in the Trinity, that is, the mission of the Father as conveyed to the Son and the Spirit, as if it were a simple economy would imply the existence of inferiority in the Trinity, a subordinationist structure wherein the divinity of all the three hypostases cannot be sustained except as mythological symbols.

Origen comes to grasp the issues involved in the theology of the Trinity thanks to his study of the earlier writers and his deep knowledge of the scripture. He saw the Trinity as one of the key issues of all theology. This faith, he says, is the "triple woven rope" (Sir 4:12) "from which the whole Church hangs and by which it is sustained."[25] He explains that in the "time of the Law" the Trinity was not fully revealed since it was an economy of faith that had to wait for the pedagogy of the incarnated Logos.[26] Using the word *hypostasis* in the antique sense of "single concrete being" (which would cause problems for later centuries) Origen lays to rest the old monarchian theology once and for all, stating: "There are three hypostases; the Father, Son, and Holy Spirit. Only the Father is Unbegotten."[27] He goes on to denounce as "wrong faith" the equivalent of monotheism with its belief in a single hypostatic God.[28] On the other hand, while, contrary to what the monarchians affirm, the Father, the Son, and the Spirit are different *realia* of God, they "are one in terms of like-mindedness, and harmony, and identity of will."[29]

Famously, however (and it was to cost his reputation greatly), he rejects the concept of *homoousios* (consubstantiality) as being applicable to the Son and Father. Origen understands that word in the antique sense – as a Gnostic form of necessary emanation from one being to another and rejects it. He teaches instead that "the Son was made"[30] by an eternal generation from the Father.[31] His rejection of the *homoousion* is a deliberate rejection of the notion that the Son belongs to a "class" that could be described as "Godhead" containing different members.

Using Philo's terminology, for a similar end, he calls the Logos "a second God" (*deuteros theos*).[32]

Yet, as if to balance his subordinationist language, at other times Origen also insists that since the divine persons are essentially good and unwaveringly in harmony they can be regarded as being co-substantive,[33] saying: "nothing whatsoever in the Trinity can legitimately be regarded as major or minor."[34] And in his *Dialogue with Heracleides*, summing up this process of unity-in-diversity, he states: "To this extent our Saviour and Lord is, in his relation to the Father, but one single God."[35]

Origen's trinitarian theology is one in which the Father is the cause and origination of all, the Son the fashioner and pedagogue of the rational world, and the Spirit the sanctifier. The Spirit leads inexorably to the Word, and the Word to the Father. All the trinitarian energy is this movement from the Father to the world, through the Logos and the Spirit; and equally, the drawing of the redeemed world through the Spirit to the Logos, and in the Logos to the Father. There is no access to God the Father except by the Spirit and the Logos. The Spirit and the Logos are our access to God; they are all that we mean by "divine."

Origen's theology is a great step out of the ambivalences and obscurities of the earlier writers. At the same time it raises another set of problems by showing the great complexities inherent in the notions of differentiated and undifferentiated substance. Later generations will take his insights and suggestions in two different directions. On the one hand, the Arian party emphasizes the difference of the Son (*heteros theos*), being the supremely graced creature, from God. On the other, the Nicene theologians take up his insistence that the Son is eternally begotten from the Father and "one God" with him. To maintain this aspect of Origen's theology, however, they have to affirm the *homoousion*, in direct contradiction to his written legacy. For the Nicenes, Origen is a bane as much as a blessing.

## NICENE AND POST-NICENE REACTIONS

The older, more rambling pattern of Christian theology's progression met with difficulties in the early fourth century, when Arius, a priest of Alexandria, publicly denounced his bishop Alexander for misrepresenting the biblical tradition and claiming that the Logos is God of God. Alexander, according to Arius, ought to have taught that the Logos is inferior to God as God's servant. After Alexander dismissed him from office, Arius became a *cause célèbre.* For the next century, he turned the whole investigation of the Trinity into a series of public meetings of bishops modeled on the Roman Senate's law-making process.

The main landmarks on the road to trinitarianism are the Council of Nicaea in 325, the Synod of Alexandria in 362, and the Council of Constantinople I in 381.[36] The main theologians who form the Nicene and neo-Nicene parties and who bring Greek patristic trinitarian theology to its formal statement are Athanasius of Alexandria, Meletius of Antioch, and the Cappadocian Fathers (Basil the Great, Gregory of Nazianzus, and Gregory of Nyssa). The Nicene movement has been ably described, and at great length, elsewhere.[37] Suffice it to say here that a certain commonality can be found at the heart of these significantly different thinkers. It is partly, of course, an allegiance to the Council of Nicaea and its creed, in an era where all seemed to be in turmoil. The *homoousion*, or consubstantiality, of the Son and the Father has always been regarded as a pillar of this Nicene movement. It was widely felt that this word, for all its defects,[38] is the term of choice to bang the Arians on the head. It is unacceptable to the latter because the Nicenes claim that it explicitates the import of the old baptismal creed. According to the Nicenes, the belief "in one God, the Father, and in one Lord Jesus Christ" implies that there is unity between them and that the Son is divine, as he is confessed to be "God from God and Light from Light." The Arians counter that the Son could be called God in an honorific sense, but that he is more correctly understood as "a god from The God; a light from The Light."

The Nicenes press the issue, adding qualification after qualification to those baptismal confessions that become the Nicene creed so that there is no further possibility of eschewing the doctrine of the Son's divinity: "God of God, Light of Light, true God of true God, begotten not made, one in being with the Father." Athanasius, who took up the flag of Nicaea when it often seemed to have drooped in the East, had originally described the Son as having *tautotes tes ousias*, an identity of essence with the Father. But he was happy to use the Nicene formula as equivalent to his own phrase if it distinguished the opponents from the supporters of his overarching principle: is the Son divine in the full sense of the meaning of that term, or not?

By boiling the argument down to that (apparently) simple question, Athanasius brings a massive theological debate down to a pinpoint of brightness. Applying the old analogy of the sun and its radiance, Athanasius makes it clear that what is at issue here is singleness of being and distinction of person:

> The whole being of the Son belongs to the Father's substance, as radiance from light, and stream from source; so that he who sees the Son sees what belongs to the Father; and knows that the Son's being is in the Father just as it is from the Father. For the Father is in the Son as the sun is in its radiance, the thought in the word, the source in the stream.[39]

Once more, the relation of the Son to the Father occupies most of the debate. The discussion of the role of the Holy Spirit is deferred until later in the fourth century, and then resumed as a subset of the trinitarian arguments about the nature of the Son. Equality of stature in the deity is made by the Nicenes to be tantamount to a confession of the selfsame essence. Were it not so, the confession of two (or three) deities would be a polytheistic one. The traditional foggy language about Jesus' deity being simply honorific is seen by the Nicenes as an admission of mythological categories into the faith. If Jesus is divine, in a genuinely monotheist confession, his divinity must be the same as that of the Father in a single divinity.

This is what Athanasius means by *tautotes ousias*, that is, sameness of being. It is important to note that the Word and the Father have the selfsame being. They do not have generically the same kind of thing as if both belong to a same class. Rather they are exactly the selfsame being:[40] the Son possesses the being which is that of the Father himself (the Father's own being instantiated in the Son's). Basil the Great is not originally enthusiastic about the term *homoousion*, but with Gregory of Nazianzus' encouragement, he persuades the Eastern church to accept it[41] when he finally understands Athanasius' larger intent. Through the mediating work of Basil and the other Cappadocian Fathers, Athanasius' construct receives wide approval in the East toward the end of his career, and becomes the heart of the classical statement on the Trinity. Similarly, his theology of the Holy Spirit also receives wider attention.[42]

Moreover, if this central insight of the co-equality and selfsame essence in the Triune Godhead is to make sense, clearly another term in addition to "being" is needed to connote the distinctness of persons. At this time the word *hypostasis* moves to the fore and receives a new set of Christian resonances to give it the connotation of a "subsistent identity." Thus, there are three *hypostases* (persons) in the selfsame *ousia* (essence). *Hypostasis* evidently does not mean what is associated with the modern notion of person, such as separate volitional purpose and discrete autonomy, and to that extent it often is best left untranslated in discussing the ancient theology of the Trinity so as not to blunt the force of its meanings.

It is Gregory of Nazianzus who does most to clarify the theory of hypostatic relations in the affirmation of the *homoousion*. Gregory is a close student of Origenian thought, and remembers the old master's teaching about the need for balance. In his *Theological Orations* Gregory moves the debate toward a classical fixing of terminology. These five remarkable sermons will receive conciliar endorsement at Chalcedon, and their Latin version also makes them definitive for the Western church. Gregory teaches that the single selfsame *ousia* is differentiated in three *hypostases*. The Father possesses his own being, as cause (*aitia*) and principle (*archē*) of the divine Trinity; the Son and Spirit possess the being of the Father in differently instantiated forms and with different economic missions. Yet each person is God. The Son and Spirit are God of God, with the Son "begotten of the Father" and the Spirit "proceeding from the Father." These distinctions, Gregory says, are not open to mortal scrutiny to discover exactly what they connote, but they reveal their effects in salvation history.

> For us there is one God the Father, "from whom are all things; and one God the Son, through whom are all things";[43] and one Holy Spirit, "in whom are all things." The phrases "from whom," "through whom," "in whom," do not make a severance in the natures (if they did, there would never be an interchange of the prepositions, or of the order of the names) but they mark the personal distinctions within the unconfused nature.[44]

As Gregory is quite aware, this theology is difficult and is built on a paradox for human reason. Divine unity is a oneness that opens out into diversity, and this diversity is ever a concurrence into unity: "That single radiance of the single Godhead, personally distinct in a way that unites, and united together in a way that keeps its distinctions: all of which is a paradox. [1 Cor. 8.6.]"

## THE LATER AFTERMATH

Paradox is an important notion in Gregory's poetic hands. He explains its significance throughout his *First Theological Oration* as a dynamic of faith, rooted in worship and giving rise to mystical wonderment at the ineffable beauty of God. In less able hands than his, that mysterious paradox could degrade into a conundrum. Reading Gregory on the Trinity,[45] or Athanasius in many sections of the *Contra Arianos*, or Gregory of Nyssa in the *Contra Eunomium*, one senses immediately that one is following a professional philosopher of religion at the top of his game; one lapse in attention will require us to restart the whole page. These Fathers still make immensely difficult reading after all these centuries. The ancients too found them hard. What happened after the era of these great theologians is a certain degree of "fixing" in the doctrine. The emergence of classical trinitarianism had moved through the fire of the Arian controversy. It was the eager hope of the church of the fifth century never to repeat the experience of such division as it had known – some hope! By conciliar authority, backed by imperial law, Orthodoxy was more and more presented as a "synthesis" of the patristic writings, now used as proof texts.

One of the last creative theologians to stand in this line is John of Damascus in the eighth century. His contribution is as a systematizer, a synopsizer, a collator. His work becomes an authoritative reference book for all the East, and is later propagated more widely when Aquinas uses it as the reference node for his *Summa theologiae* (*The Summa of Theology*). John sums up the traditional trinitarian theology well when he retains Gregory of Nazianzus' insistence that the Trinity doctrine has a profound relevance to mystical worship: "The Trinity – one essence, one divinity, one power, one will, one energy, one beginning, one authority, one dominion, one sovereignty, made known in three perfect subsistences (*hypostases*) and adored with one single adoration; believed in and worshipped by all noetic creation."[46]

But not everyone approaches the Trinity in that way. Once it becomes loosed from its moorings as an expression of Christian faith and passion, with the "why of God" confessed as the "how of God's action" in life, then the patristic subtleties are in danger of becoming wooden dogmas, or worse, examples of pedantic obscurity, to subsequent generations. For this to happen, of course, one must either stop reading the Fathers altogether or read them in a naïve and wooden way. Sadly, down the ages there were many who would do both.

## Notes

1. Clement of Rome, *First Letter to the Corinthians* 16.
2. Ibid., 22.
3. Ignatius of Antioch, *Letter to the Philadelphians* 7.

4. Shepherd of Hermas, *Similitudes* 8.3.3, 9.1.1.
5. A collective term for the writings of Clement of Rome, Ignatius of Antioch, Hermas, Polycarp of Smyrna, and Papias of Hierapolis, the anonymous "Letter to Diognetus," the anonymous "Second Letter of Clement," and the Didache.
6. Athenagoras, *Supplication* 16; Tatian, *Oration to the Greeks* 4; Theophilus of Antioch, *Apologia to Autolycus* 2.10.
7. Second Letter of Clement 3.9.
8. Ignatius of Antioch, *Letter to the Ephesians* 18, 20.
9. Such as "Name," "Torah," "Light," "Principle." See J. Daniélou, *Histoire des doctrines chrétiennes avant Nicée*, I (Paris: Desclée, 1961), 195–96.
10. "Apologists" is a collective term for the writers of the late second and third centuries (excluding Origen). Those writing in Greek included Aristides, Justin Martyr, Athenagoras, Tatian, Theophilus of Antioch, Irenaeus, Hippolytus, and Clement of Alexandria.
11. Theophilus of Antioch, *Apologia to Autolycus* 22.
12. Justin Martyr, *First Apology* 32.8; *Second Apology* 8.1, 10.1–2.
13. Justin Martyr, *Dialogue with Trypho* 128.4.
14. Ibid., 62.4.
15. Ibid., 63.5; *First Apology* 63.15.
16. Justin Martyr, *Dialogue with Trypho* 62.105, 125; *First Apology* 21.
17. Justin discusses the triadic pattern of God's life in the context of baptismal and Eucharistic reflections in *First Apology* 61.3–12; Athenagoras calls the Spirit the "inspirer of prophets" in *Supplication* 7.2; and Theophilus identifies the Spirit with God's Wisdom, and the Logos with God's Word and creative energy in *Apologia to Autolycus* 1.7.
18. Irenaeus, *Demonstration of the Apostolic Preaching* 7.
19. Irenaeus, *Against the Heresies* 5.12.2.
20. Ibid., 2.30.9.
21. Possibly the "Busybody" (Praxeas) to whom Tertullian addressed his caustic attack on defective theology of the Trinity (*Adversus Praxean*).
22. Novatian, *On the Trinity* 16 (ibid., 31).
23. Ibid., 31.
24. Christopher Markschies, "Trinity," in J. A. McGuckin, ed., *The Westminster Handbook to Origen* (Louisville, KY, and London: Westminster John Knox, 2004), 207–09.
25. Origen of Alexandria, *Homilies on Exodus* 9.3.
26. Origen of Alexandria, *Commentary on John*, fragment 20; *Homilies on Joshua* 3.2.
27. Origen of Alexandria, *Commentary on John* 2.10.75, 2.2.16; *Dialogue with Heracleides*.
28. Origen of Alexandria, *Commentary on Matthew* 17.14; *Select Passages from Genesis*, in *Patrologiae cursus completus*, Series Graeca, ed. J.-P. Migne (Paris, 1857–66), XII, 109D.
29. Origen of Alexandria, *Against Celsus* 8.13; *On First Principles* 1.2.13; and *Commentary on John* 13.36.228–29.
30. Origen of Alexandria, *On First Principles* 4.4.1.

31. Ibid., 1.2.9.
32. Origen of Alexandria, *Against Celsus* 5.39.
33. That is *homoousios* in the broader sense, or devoid of internal distinctions: Origen of Alexandria, *On First Principles* 1.8.3, 1.6.2; and *Homilies on Numbers* 12.1.
34. Origen of Alexandria, *On First Principles* 1.3.7 (Greek text).
35. Origen of Alexandria, *Dialogue with Heracleides* 3 (alluding to Jn 10:30).
36. The first proclaiming the deity of the Son "of the being of the Father," the second laying down the authoritative terminology of "one *ousia* and three *hypostases*," and the third declaring the deity of the Holy Spirit, who is "worshiped with the Father and the Son." For more detail on the councils and their protagonists, see J. A. McGuckin, *The Westminster Handbook to Patristic Theology* (Louisville, KY, and London: Westminster John Knox, 2004).
37. Most notably in recent times by R. P. C. Hanson, *The Search for the Christian Doctrine of God* (Edinburgh: T. & T. Clark, 1988); Lewis Ayres, *Nicaea and its Legacy: An Approach to Fourth-Century Trinitarian Theology* (New York and Oxford: Oxford University Press, 2004); and John Behr, *The Nicene Faith* (Crestwood, NY: St. Vladimir's Seminary Press, 2004).
38. Theologians at the time complain that it is non-biblical, that it is excessively materialistic to describe the spiritual Godhead, and that it has already been synodically censured as a monarchian term (when used by Paul of Samosata).
39. Athanasius of Alexandria, *Against the Arians* 3.1–3.
40. "We are led perforce to say that the Son is entirely that which is 'of the substance of the Father.'" Ibid., 1.15–16.
41. Basil of Caesarea, Letter 52.1–3; *Against Eunomius* 1.19; Letter 361 to Apollinaris; Letter 9.3; *Homily* 24.3.
42. As begun in Athanasius' *Letters to Serapion*, where he argues that if the Spirit of God is said in the baptismal rites of the ancient church to make men and women into children of God (divinize them), then he has to be divine himself; and if divine, consubstantial with the Father just as the Son is. Basil the Great's *On the Holy Spirit* and Gregory of Nazianzus' *Fifth Theological Oration* take up these ideas and develop them to give the Holy Spirit the distinctive trinitarian roles of inspiration, sanctification, and illumination.
43. Gregory of Nazianzus, *Third Theological Oration* 2.
44. Ibid., 12.
45. See, for example, J. A. McGuckin, "Perceiving Light from Light in Light: The Trinitarian Theology of St. Gregory the Theologian," *Greek Orthodox Theological Review*, 39:1–2 (1994), 7–32.
46. John of Damascus, *On the Orthodox Faith* 1.8. Often badly translated as "rational," "noetic" really means the human capacity for "spiritual intelligence" (located in the *nous*) whereby the human creature has an inbuilt instinct from the Logos for the divine truth and therefore a mystical capacity for God that resonates with the truth of the Trinity.

## Further reading

Ayres, Lewis, *Nicaea and its Legacy: An Approach to Fourth-Century Trinitarian Theology* (New York and Oxford: Oxford University Press, 2004).

Behr, John, *The Nicene Faith* (Crestwood, NY: St. Vladimir's Seminary Press, 2004).

Bobrinskoy, Boris, *The Mystery of the Trinity* (Crestwood, NY: St. Vladimir's Seminary Press, 1999).

Hanson, Richard P. C., *The Search for the Christian Doctrine of God* (Edinburgh: T. & T. Clark, 1988).

Kelly, John N. D., *Early Christian Doctrines* (London: Harper & Row, 1980).

Rusch, William, *The Trinitarian Controversy* (Philadelphia: Fortress, 1980).

Wolfson, Harry D., *The Philosophy of the Church Fathers* (Cambridge, MA: Harvard University Press, 1976).

# 5 Latin trinitarian theology

MICHEL RENÉ BARNES

The first question that faces anyone writing on early Latin trinitarian theology is that of when or with whom to begin the account. The earliest Western Christian texts were written in Greek: should they be considered part of "Latin trinitarian theology"? Should some of these Greek writings be considered "Latin" on the basis of their origin in Rome (or Gaul)? The Greek work *Contra Noetum* (*Against Noetus*) attributed to Hippolytus and written in Rome is so like Tertullian's Latin *Adversus Praxean* (*Against Praxeas*) written in Carthage that the two works seem almost to originate from the same community.[1] I have opted for the straightforward criterion of language: if a text was originally written in Latin it falls within my brief. This decision allows one to discern continuities of vocabulary across texts, for example. Once this decision has been made, two important facts reveals themselves: the font of Latin trinitarian theology is Tertullian, and the internal disposition – the "logic" – of that theology originates in anti-monarchianism.

Latin-language trinitarian theology is born in the tumult of the fight against monarchianism (also known as patripassianism). In the late second century eloquent Christians with Eastern origins who resided in Rome and Carthage taught that the divinity in Jesus was the "Father," the one God, otherwise known as Spirit. The scriptural proofs that the divine in Jesus was the Father came from Jesus' own words in the gospel of John: "The Father and I are one" (Jn 10:30), "He who has seen me has seen the Father" (Jn 14:9), and especially "Do you not believe that I am in the Father and the Father is in me? The words I say to you I do not speak on my own authority; but the Father who dwells in me does his works" (Jn 14:10). These teachers differed among themselves as to what or who the name "Son" referred to, but they agreed with the equivalence of Father, Spirit, and divinity, and that the divinity *in* Jesus was the Father-*Spirit*. Those who spoke in this way also rejected the Logos theology of the Apologists (principally Justin and Theophilus): the "uttered" Word was not a separate being, but only words, as when

God "spoke" in Genesis 1.[2] The necessity of rebutting this predominantly Greek-language theology provides the setting for the beginning of Latin-language trinitarian theology.

In developing their arguments against the monarchians, Tertullian and Novatian first of all reaffirm two basic doctrines from the Apologists: that divinity is *from* the Father, not identical *with* the Father; and that the Father's Word (identified in the prologue to John) has a real and distinct existence. While the Apologists were concerned with the cosmological activity of the Word, the Latins focus attention on the second person's divine action within the context of the incarnation: what divine works did Jesus do?

Tertullian, Novatian, and the Latins thereafter articulate another basis for the unity of Father and Son, one that is based upon a commonality between Father and Son that is entirely free of topological descriptions, even as it preserves the Johannine language of "in." This basis of unity between Father and Son is "common power – common substance." While Latins strongly emphasize the Word as *the Spirit or divinity* who unites with flesh, "Word-Spirit" serves as the fulcrum not for demonstrating that Jesus and the Father were both divine, but for demonstrating that the divine being joined with flesh was not the Father. Tertullian's expression of the anti-monarchian argument is a paradigm for Latin trinitarian theology thereafter:

> Therefore the Father, abiding in the Son through works of power and words of doctrine, is seen through those things through which he abides, and through him in whom he abides: and from this very fact it is apparent that each Person is himself and none other, while he says, *I am in the Father and the Father in me.*

Latin theologies of the Trinity from Tertullian to Augustine follow this form: there is an explanation for how the Three are understood to be one, that is, *unity of works and power*; there is an explanation for how the Three are distinct from one another – that is, *causal relations*;[3] there is a statement that the Three are eternally irreducible and unconvertible – that is, *they are each always themselves and not another*; and there is a word for what is three in God – that is, *person* ("persona"). The content of "person" is not psychological, but ontological: "a substance [i.e., existent] which is himself," Tertullian says of "person," and, "Whatever therefore the substance [i.e., existent] of the Word was, that I call a Person, and for it [in this case] I claim the name of Son."[4] In short, the originating logic of Latin trinitarian theology is anti-monarchian (i.e., anti-modalist), and in that logic the grounds for real distinctions in the

Trinity are provided by causal relations and eternal irreducibility, not, as modern readers expect, by a logic built on the ontological difference between "person" and "essence" (or "nature").

While Tertullian builds his theology of the second person from the title "Word," Novatian – writing a generation later – builds from the title "Son."[5] Novatian develops a Christology of two "nativities" – the first nativity being the Son's spiritual birth from the Father, the second being his physical birth from Mary. This description of the Trinity and the incarnation is found in Cyprian and in Lactantius. The doctrine of "two nativities" is the foundation for the argument of Zeno of Verona (fl. 360 to late 370s) against both Arianism and Photinianism (modalism). Zeno is also a good example of the minor role that "Word" theology can play in Latin trinitarian theology: he never uses it.

## "HE WHO SEES ME SEES THE FATHER"

From its beginning Latin theology has an emphasis on "sight" in trinitarian theology: our sight of the Son, of the Father in the Son, and the Son's sight of the Father. The exegesis of John 14:9, which speaks of this sight, is linked to the exegesis of 14:10, and the meaning of the latter passage gives content to the former. (The point is also developed through exegesis of Phil 2:5–7, Col 1:15, and Heb 1:3.) The best-known example of the Latin interest in our sight of the Son is the recurring interest in theophanies, but there are other venues for developing theologies of the Son as visual object.

Faustinus (Rome, c.376–80) argues that scriptural descriptions of the Son's iconic or visual relationship to the Father establish the substantial unity between Father and Son, as when John 1:14 says, "And we beheld his glory, the glory as it were of the only begotten of the Father." The visual glory that is seen is in itself the mark of the only-begotten Son: glory attests to sonship. It should also be remembered that much of Augustine's *De Trinitate* (*On the Trinity*), not just books I to III, is concerned with the question of our sight – visual, symbolic, noetic, and eschatological – of the Son.

It is Tertullian who begins the Latin anti-monarchian emphasis on the theophanies as "proofs" for the separate existence of the Father and Son. For Tertullian, a doctrine of two divine persons, one invisible (the Father) and one visible (the Son or Word), is more true to scripture and makes better sense exegetically than the monarchian reading (that the Father enters the body of Jesus and that union is called the "Son"). Tertullian's reading preserves the reality of the Father who sent the

Son and the Son who was sent, which is the teaching of the *regula* and Scripture on the *oikonomia*. In Old Testament theophanies the Son reveals himself (i.e., the fact of his existence) and prophetically reveals his future incarnation; in the New Testament theophany, namely the incarnation, the Son is said to show the Father as well as to reveal his own divinity. The way in which the Son reveals the Father is the very same way in which the Son reveals his own divinity – by his works (*opera*).[6] This traditional Latin doctrine is the cornerstone of Latin trinitarian theology, and the basis for the West's sympathy for, and understanding of, theology associated with the Council of Nicaea (325). At the same time, Latins who reject "Nicene" theology likewise reject traditional Latin theology of "common works – common power."

## ONE POWER, COMMON WORKS

Tertullian also begins Latin trinitarian theology's argument that the divinity of the Son and his unity with the Father is shown by the character of his works or actions, and he lays down the basic understanding that the three individually manifest the same one power. In the Son's workings we perceive the operation of his power, and in recognizing the power we also recognize the substance to which it belongs. That substance is the same as the Father's, and insofar as any one recognizes Christ to be God in the power of his substance, he would thus come to know God the Father. This doctrine is not quite that of "common *operations*," because the conceptual emphasis is on the *common power* that causes, and is manifested in, the operations or works. The doctrine does not describe a direct parallelism between what the Father and Son do so much as describe the common cause manifested in what each does. The logic of the doctrine of common operations is easily adaptable to describing the Holy Spirit – but only insofar as there is a sense from one's reading of scripture (principally the Old Testament – Septuagint Version) that the Holy Spirit acts in divine ways. Augustine, for example, will later give extensive accounts of how the Father, Son, and Holy Spirit all *do the same thing*, such as create or bring about the incarnation (see his Sermon 52).

In Latin theology of the third and early fourth centuries the argument from *common power* continues to be applied almost exclusively for the sake of proving Jesus' divinity, to establish that the miraculous works that Jesus performed are of the same sort as the Father's works and that if the incarnate Son does them, he must have the same divine power (and substance) as the Father. When Latins of this period speak about the acts by the Son by which the Father is recognized, they are not speaking of cosmic acts by the Son or Word; they are speaking about the miracles performed by Jesus. The reality of those actions testifies to the presence of the divine power and substance in him. The divine substance is seen to be present in the works that only it could perform; the human substance is seen to be also present and intact in the works ("passions") typical of it. The flesh does not impede the operations or power of the spirit; the spirit does not expel or transmute the power and substance of the flesh. As Tertullian says: "And to such a degree did there remain unimpaired the proper being of each substance, that in him the Spirit [divine substance] carried out its own acts, that is, powers and works and signs, while the flesh accomplished its own passions."[7] In the late fourth century the "works indicate power" argument shifts from the incarnation to demonstrating the existence of common works and power among the pre-existent Word, the Holy Spirit, and the Father.

Tertullian's argument that "works indicate power" is ubiquitous in Latin trinitarian theology. "If Christ is only man," Novatian asks, "how is it that 'what the Father does, the Son also does in like manner'?"[8] Lactantius gives the same argument in more technical language: "The power of God appeared in him from the works he performed; the weakness of man from the passions which he endured."[9] In the first Latin work written against anti-Nicenes, Phoebadius' *Adversus Arianos* (*Against the Arians*, 359), the argument appears in a new context: the divine in the Son performed "its own activities in Him: namely powers, works, and signs. And the flesh exercised its own passions." In 378, Niceta of Remesciana argued that "If he [Christ] is seen as a man in his sufferings, in his divine works he is recognized as God." The common conceptual and exegetical ground in Latin theology between trinitarian and incarnational doctrines is evident. The same kind of logic applies to understanding the real humanity of Christ as to understanding his common divinity with God the Father: *by their works you shall know them.*

It is very important to understand that, in the main, Latin trinitarian theology of the fourth century does not pivot on the language of divine substance, but rather utilizes that language for polemical reasons (i.e., Nicaea used it; Sirmium, 357, tried to ban it). The most common language for describing trinitarian unity is "one *power*." In this regard Latins of the fourth century continue the doctrinal habits of Latins from Tertullian to Lactantius.[10] Phoebadius, for example, understands the attempt of Sirmium (357) to suppress essence/substance language as meaning in practice, "Let no one in the Church preach that there is one

Power of the Father and Son." Whenever Zeno of Verona speaks of the two or three as "one substance" he also says they are "one power";[11] and like Phoebadius, he will sometimes say "one power" without any mention of "one substance." Lucifer of Caligari, an unreconstructed Nicene, declares that the Father and Son have "one glory, one power and one majesty." Niceta of Remesciana (378) never says that the three have one substance, but he does say that the three have one power. Finally, typical among Damasus of Rome's formulae are the expressions "the Trinity of one power, one majesty, one divinity, and substance so that their power is inseparable" and "[the] Father, Son and Holy Spirit are of one deity, one power, one figure and one substance." Note the relative lack of emphasis on "one substance": the conclusion of Damasus' first list is a statement that the power among the three is inseparable. Clearly, this is not a trinitarian theology that pivots on the notion of substance, and in this Damasus is being consistent with the usual form of traditional Latin trinitarian theology.

There is indeed a fourth-century Latin tradition that strongly emphasizes substance language in its description of trinitarian unity: its primary representatives are Ossius of Cordoba, Marius Victorinus, and Potamius of Lisbon. Potamius and Ossius may represent an Iberian school influenced by Ossius' deacon, the Platonic philosopher Calcidius. Whenever Ossius attends a synod, substance language appears prominently in the bishops' proclamations (e.g., Nicaea, Western Serdica, and Second Sirmium). Victorinus' focus on substance language is indebted to the strong influence that the concept of *homoousios* exerted on his thought, as well as his own intimate familiarity with Porphyrian Platonism.

## SPIRIT CHRISTOLOGY AND THE THEOLOGY OF THE HOLY SPIRIT

The common assumption is that the result of Tertullian's Montanism would be a strong pneumatology, but such is not the case. If we compare Tertullian's understanding of what the Holy Spirit *does* with, for instance, the comparable understandings of Athenagoras, Theophilus, and Irenaeus, we find that Tertullian gives a diminished account of the Holy Spirit's activities. Montanism leads Tertullian to stress the continuing role of the Holy Spirit as the source of prophecy, inspiration, and ecstatic revelation, but unlike Athenagoras, Theophilus, and Irenaeus, Tertullian does not describe the Holy Spirit as co-creator, which is a very important omission. A second omission, inherited from Irenaeus, is a weak account of the generation of the Holy Spirit. From the late second century onward aetiological accounts play a fundamental role in Christian trinitarian theology, and the lack of a causal model for describing the Spirit's origin translates into a weak sense of the Holy Spirit's relationship to God the Father. (Conversely, the "high" pneumatologies of the late fourth century all articulate accounts of the Holy Spirit's origin.) A third reason for Tertullian's weak pneumatology is that in his account of the incarnation, "Spirit" names the second person who is joined with human flesh in Mary's womb. The exegetical result of this judgment is that any Old Testament "high" description of God's Spirit is taken to refer to the Son, and not, as we would expect, to the third person of the Trinity.

Spirit Christology may be found in the writings of Tertullian, Hippolytus, Novatian, Cyprian, Lactantius, the Council of Western Serdica (343), Phoebadius, and Hilary (the pre-exile *Commentarius in Evangelii Matthaei*, or *Commentary on the Gospel of Matthew*, as well as the post-exile *De Trinitate*, or *On the Trinity*.) The most self-conscious, developed, and exceedingly complicated account of the relationship among common Spirit, the Spirit "in" a Person, and the Holy Spirit occurs in Hilary's *On the Trinity* VIII; Augustine attempts to untangle Hilary and reconceive this relationship in his *On the Trinity* XV. After Hilary, Spirit Christology fades from Latin writings: if Potamius' writings are indicative, the change occurs in 360 or soon thereafter. Given that one important effect of Spirit Christology is a "low" pneumatology, the decline of Spirit Christology is an important factor in the resurgence of a "high" pneumatology. The remedy for the understandings that the Holy Spirit is not creator, and that he has an origin that is either unspecified or thinly conceived by Christians, comes exegetically when a Christocentric monopoly on Old Testament "spirit" references is overturned. Late fourth-century exegesis of key Old Testament Spirit passages (most notably, Ps 33/32) resembles the exegesis and conclusions of Athenagoras, Theophilus, and Irenaeus rather than Tertullian's and Novatian's. None of this is to say that Latin formulations of the Trinity in the third and early fourth centuries omit mention of the Holy Spirit: he is indeed included in summary statements of the Trinity, including Tertullian's key statement of criteria for what is one and what is three in God: there are the Father and Son and Spirit as three; three in sequence, aspect, and manifestation; one in substance, quality, and power. Aside from the problems with Latin pneumatology during this period that I outlined above, the functional binitarianism of Latin theology from 200 to 370 can be described most succinctly in the following way: the "logic" of

God's internal or natural relations worked with dynamics which successfully described a two-personed God, but which were unsuitable and ineffective as logics for a three-personed God.

It is true that Latins speak of the Holy Spirit as being "one in substance" with the Father and Son before Greeks do. Potamius of Lisbon says, around 360, that "the substance of the Father, the Son and the Holy Spirit is one." One cannot find a Greek who says in 360 that the Holy Spirit is *homoousios* with the Father and the Son – because, at least in significant part, of the particular understanding Greeks have of *homoousios* that has no parallel in the West. For Athanasius and the Greeks he influenced, *homoousios* was a unique and one-way predicate statement: one could and should say "the Son is *homoousios* with the Father" but one could not meaningfully or piously say "the Father is *homoousios* with the Son." Ignorant of this technicality, Latins were free to say that the Father and the Son – and the Holy Spirit – were of one single substance.

The first Latin Nicene descriptions of the Holy Spirit in terms of the interior life of the Trinity[12] occur in the writings of Marius Victorinus and Hilary of Poitiers, both of whom thus contribute significantly to Augustine's mature pneumatology.[13] It is Hilary who offers a description of the Holy Spirit as interior or intra-trinitarian "gift." Ambrose of Milan is often treated as the first Latin theologian to articulate a theology of the full divinity of the Holy Spirit, and certainly his *De Spiritu sancto* (*On the Holy Spirit*) is the first lengthy Latin treatise on the third person. In fact, however, Ambrose's pneumatology follows in the footsteps of the earlier accomplishments of the Latin theologian Niceta of Remesciana (as well as owing heavily to the Alexandrian Didymus the Blind). It is Niceta who first articulates a Latin theology of the Holy Spirit that fully redresses the limitations of Latin pneumatology since Tertullian.

Niceta describes in detail the works that the Holy Spirit performs in common with the Father and the Son, which exhibit the one power that they all share in common, and which is the sign of their common divinity. Niceta explicitly criticizes Spirit Christology for the effect it has had through exegesis in undermining pneumatology. He is emphatic that it is the Holy Spirit who overshadowed Mary and not the Word himself.[14] The weakness of Niceta's pneumatology that results in the historical occlusion of his contribution to late Nicene doctrines of the Holy Spirit is that it lacks any account of the internal (intra-trinitarian) relationship of the Spirit to the Father and Son. In this regard Niceta offers less than Victorinus and Hilary, and thus it is with the aid of these latter two authors that Augustine develops his doctrine of the Holy Spirit's procession from the Father and the Son. Augustine recognizes that of all the terms we use for God (e.g., "spirit," "good," "wise," "eternal," etc.) it is "spirit" alone that initially seems to be substance, but he declines to continue the Latin "common substance of God is spirit" approach.[15] Augustine does accept from previous Latins the judgment that the Spirit is the Spirit *of God* and *of the Son*, and restates it as the doctrine that the Holy Spirit is the intra-trinitarian love. Augustine's principal concern, however, is in articulating an aetiology of the Holy Spirit (i.e., procession) that is logically parallel to and as dense as the traditional aetiology of the Son's generation.[16]

## AUGUSTINE

Several of the doctrinal *topoi* I have described as fundamental to Latin trinitarian theology do not appear as such in Augustine's *On the Trinity* although these *topoi* do appear in other writings by Augustine in which he speaks about the Trinity (and there are many). The question arises as to why *topoi* fundamental to Latin trinitarian theology for 200 years are not fundamental in any explicit way in *On the Trinity*. The answer lies in recognizing the true subject of *On the Trinity*. The work is not an exposition on the doctrine of the Trinity *per se*: it is a study of the problematic of knowing God who is Trinity. In *On the Trinity* Augustine is writing on trinitarian hermeneutics or epistemology. His concern is, therefore, with all the types and cases of revelation and our specific capacities for being revealed to, ranging from scripture to scriptural episodes of divine revelation (the theophanies, the incarnation), to signs, to doctrines, to the image and likeness of God (the human mind), to the perfect "form" of God (the Word) as wisdom and knowledge, and to the necessity of faith and purity for the mind to advance in any understanding of the Trinity. Or, to describe *On the Trinity* along another axis, the book is concerned with created signs (primarily but not exclusively material) that range from word to text to theophany to our mind (as image and likeness) to the incarnation (the Word uniting with created human nature); with the relationship between these signs to the uncreated that they signify; and with the tension between material signs and their immaterial referent.

Knowing that Augustine's trinitarian theology does not remain unchanged throughout his writing career, nevertheless, I seek to outline those foundational features that remain consistent throughout Augustine's Trinitarian writings. There are three concepts that are foundational to Augustine's thinking on the Trinity: first is the doctrine of

God's immaterial nature; second is the doctrine of common operations in the Trinity; and third is the doctrine that theological language is meant to purify our thoughts about God as a necessary precondition to thinking about God (as well as, for the greater end, seeing God).

In the first case, the role that the doctrine of divine immateriality plays in Augustine's trinitarian theology is without antecedents in Latin or Greek Christianity, and the significance of the doctrine seems to arise out of the intellectual pilgrimage that is uniquely Augustine's. From our perspective we can recognize precedents for Augustine's interest in the issue of divine immateriality, but we cannot find other Latin patristic theologians who are quite so interested in the question and indeed for whom the doctrine becomes a touchstone for the proper understanding of God. While a strong judgment on God's immateriality may be found in the stages of Nicene theology, such statements are typically made in the context of a proper understanding of the generation of the Son – that it is not emanation or a partition or sexual reproduction – but such a concern over divine immateriality does not figure with any emphasis in Augustine's theology. The related theological attention to the question of God's simplicity, which one finds among some trinitarian theologians of the second half of the fourth century such as Hilary of Poitiers, Gregory of Nyssa, and Gregory of Nazianzus, does figure in Augustine's trinitarian theology, and on this question one can see precedents and even possible sources or influences for Augustine's thought among Latin authors concerned with divine simplicity.

Augustine articulates the late Nicene emphasis on God's distinction from creation through a strong emphasis on divine immateriality. The goal of clearly delineating the difference between the divine nature and all other natures is something that Augustine shares with all other late Nicene trinitarian theologians. Indeed, one accomplishment of Nicene theologies was to establish that the distinction between divine nature and all other natures was nothing other than the distinction between divine nature and created nature – that there was no intermediate or middle, "third kind" of nature. What is distinctive to Augustine's theology, compared with the theologies of other late Nicenes, is the emphasis he places on divine immateriality to anchor the distinction between uncreated and created natures.

The key move comes when Augustine understands that the perfect immateriality of divine existence makes possible a degree of common operation that is otherwise impossible, and that to the degree that one removes a materialist way of thinking about the Trinity from one's theology then the perfectly common operations of the Trinity becomes a meaningful way of speaking about divine unity. The beginning of understanding Augustine's treatment of trinitarian theology in *On the Trinity*, and indeed in everything he wrote about the Trinity, is to look at it from the perspective of the transformation of our way of thinking about the divine life from a material hermeneutic to an immaterial hermeneutic. Augustine's "immaterial hermeneutic of doctrine" brings a critique to any example of a theology, testing whether its epistemological structure restates a material hermeneutic.

The second concept foundational to Augustine's thinking on the Trinity is the doctrine of common operations in the Trinity; by the last quarter of the fourth century, this doctrine is the central one in Nicene trinitarian theology. The duration of Augustine's engagement with the doctrine of common operations, which spans his entire career, and the characteristically profound thought he brought to the doctrine, give him a special place as an epitome of the late Nicene tradition. However, while earlier Latins articulated a doctrine of common operations through exegesis of John 14:10, Augustine's articulation turns upon John 5:19. While John 5:19 is not unknown among Latins as a statement of common operations, it takes on a significant role only beginning with Hilary and Ambrose, who probably take it over from Greek sources. Augustine's interest in and understanding of the full depth of "common operations" theology develops in significant ways over a period of twenty-plus years.

Augustine's use of the noetic triad – the "psychological analogy" – represents an attempt by Augustine to understand the unity of the Trinity as articulated in the doctrine of common operations. Augustine brings to bear the insights gained from a rigorous thinking through of divine immateriality, and joins them to his rhetorician's concern for a teaching similitude. When Augustine introduces the similitude he typically starts by pointing out that every operation that we do is done by our memory, intelligence, and will together, and that whatever is done by one of the three (e.g., speaking is "by" intelligence) is also done with the other two. Similarly, the operations which pertain not only to all three persons but also those assigned to one person are done inseparably or in common. We cannot know what it means for three to act inseparably and in common, but we can imagine something of it on the basis of our own experience. For Augustine, the doctrine of "common operations" becomes the thought-experiment for developing and testing the progress of the mind in thinking immaterially about the Trinity.

Augustine's understanding of the intricacies and significance of common operations is more developed in his *In Johannis evangelium tractatus* (*Twentieth Tractate on John*) than in *On the Trinity*. *On the Trinity* may give us Augustine's theology as no other single text of his on the Trinity does, but it does not give us his most developed articulation of his own trinitarian theology. It is, quite literally, not his last word on the Trinity. The triad memory-intelligence-will makes a brief appearance in *Confessiones* (*Confessions*), it figures in Sermon 52 and *Epistola* (Letter) 160, and, of course, it has a role in certain books of *On the Trinity*. However, the noetic triad of memory, intelligence, and will makes no appearance when Augustine treats trinitarian theology in his other writings.

The third fundamental concept that is foundational to Augustine's thinking on the Trinity is his understanding that true theological language must be the instrument of the elevation and purification of the soul. Theological language has no other ultimate purpose than to strip from the mind the material form and content of its thinking about God and to shape the heart in love for God; together these actions constitute the purification of the heart. For Augustine, the distinctive characteristics of each person of the Trinity are not articulated through an ontological analysis but through an analysis of the epistemological or soteriological prerequisite for human knowledge of the reality of the unity of the common operations of the Trinity. There is no neutral theological discourse: every proper genre of theological discourse – scripture, creeds, liturgy, sermons, exegesis and commentary, letters, dialogues and studies – has the goal of building a proper love for God that is correctly directed to the true God, or God as he truly is. *On the Trinity* VIII begins by announcing that "a flesh-bound habit of thought cannot grasp" that the persons of the Trinity are all equal. Augustine continues, "since we desire to understand as far as it is given us the eternity and equality and unity of the Trinity, and since we must believe before we can understand, we must take care that our faith is not fabricated. [There is the true]... trinity we are to enjoy in order to live in bliss; but if we have false beliefs about it our hope is vain and our charity is not chaste."[17] Augustine understands that all theological language shapes our thinking about God. Hence, if the discourse about God remains focused upon a God still conceived in a material fashion, and if our love remains directed at a "God" who is an idol, then our "God" is noetically composed of constructs derived from a materialist way of thinking. The resource that has been given to us to overturn these materialist constructs is the discipline of faith, which trains our mind and forms our heart and thus enables us to think properly about God the Trinity.

## CONCLUSION

Latin trinitarian theology begins, historically and logically, as anti-modalist. The logic of anti-modalism does not distinguish God-as-Trinity from God-as-unity on the basis of an opposition between person and essence: persons are not "that which is not essence" but "that which has the Father as cause" and "that which is always itself" – the Father is always Father, the Son from the Father is always Son. Even when scripture says that the Son is "in" the Father, or the Father is "in" the Son, the Father is never the Son, and the Son is never the Father.

Similarly, given its anti-monarchian origins, from the beginning Latin trinitarian theology is concerned with how the Father is seen in the Son, and how the Son is seen to be divine. The basic Latin account of these "sights" is that the works of the Son reveal the Father as they also reveal the Son's own divinity. This concern never falls out of Latin patristic theology. A tradition of trinitarian theology whose origins lay in a disposition against monarchianism will logically find Christology to be its necessary point of departure. It is, however, a general truth that little of what is necessary or fundamental in any system of thought is displayed first or conspicuously to any reader.

## Notes

1. The best English translation of Tertullian's *Against Praxeas* is by Ernest Evans, *Tertullian's Treatise against Praxeas* (London: SPCK, 1948); it includes a Latin text and extensive notes. *Against Noetus*, attributed to Hippolytus, appears in English translation by Robert Butterworth, with Greek text facing: *Hippolytus of Rome – Contra Noetum* (London: Heythrop Monographs, 1977).
2. See Jean Daniélou, *Gospel Message and Hellenistic Culture*, trans. John Austin Baker (London: Darton, Longman & Todd, 1973), 345–86, and Ronald Heine, "The Christology of Callistus," *Journal of Theological Studies*, 49 (1998), 56–91.
3. It is the traditionally strong role of aetiological models in Latin trinitarian theology that provides a basis for the Western understanding of the Creed of Nicaea's "God from God, Light from Light, true God from true God" language.
4. Tertullian, *Against Praxeas*, trans. Evans, 138.

5. It is Novatian who coins the term *incarnatus* – incarnation.
6. As Tertullian puts it, the Father "becomes visible in the Son, in consequence of acts of power, and not in consequence of actual manifestation of his person." *Against Praxeas*, trans. Evans, 168.
7. Ibid., 174.
8. Novatian, *De Trinitate* 11.4, 9; see R. J. De Simone, *The Treatise of Novatian the Roman Presbyter on the Trinity* (Rome: Institutum Patristicum Augustinianum, 1970).
9. Lactantius, *Divinae institutiones* 4.13; trans. M. F. McDonald as *The Divine Institutes* (Washington, DC: Catholic University of America Press, 1964).
10. Novatian, for example, used substance language only to talk about the incarnation, i.e., the two "substances" in Jesus.
11. See Zeno of Verona, *Tractatus* I.7.30, I.37.11–12, II.5.84.
12. That is, the Holy Spirit existing or arising between the Father and the Son. Most accounts of the Holy Spirit's origin seem to fail the test of logical density, and the advantage of Augustine's *filioque* theology was, historically, that it was a stronger description of the Spirit's causal origins than alternative accounts.
13. See Nello Cipriani, "La presenza di Mario Victorino nella riflessione trinitaria di Agostino," *Augustinianum*, 42 (2002), 261–313.
14. It is worth noting that Niceta's own creed, a variant of the Roman creed, contains the clause "born of the Holy Spirit and the Virgin Mary," while the creed of Nicaea contains no such clause and indeed does not mention Mary or anything remotely related to Luke 1:35–36 at all. The creed of Constantinople, 381, says that the Son was "incarnate[d] from the Holy Spirit and the Virgin Mary." (The now familiar "Niceno-Constantinopolitan" liturgical creed contains the clause, "By the power of the Holy Spirit," which is a pleasant echo of Luke 1:5, but which seems to originate in some modern translation of Constantinople by some anonymous liturgical committee, because the clause is not in the original creed.)
15. Augustine, *De Trinitate* XV.8; see *Saint Augustine: The Trinity*, trans. Edmund Hill (Brooklyn, NY: New City Press, 1991).
16. Augustine, *De Trinitate* XV.37, 47–48.
17. Ibid., VIII.2 and VIII.8.

## Further reading

Ayres, Lewis, *Nicaea and its Legacy: An Approach to Fourth-Century Trinitarian Theology* (Oxford University Press, 2004).

Barnes, Michel René, "The Use of Augustine in Contemporary Trinitarian Theology," *Theological Studies*, 56 (1995), 237–51.

Bavel, T. J. van, *Recherches sur la christologie de saint Augustin*, Paradosis, 10 (Fribourg: Éditions Universaires Fribourg Suisse, 1954).

D'Alès, A., *Novatien: Étude sur la theólogie romaine au milieu du III siècle* (Paris: Gabriel Beauchesne, 1925).

Daley, Brian, "The Giant's Twin Substance: Ambrose and the Christology of Augustine's *Contra sermonem Arianorum,*" in Joseph Lienhard, Earl Muller, and Roland Teske, eds., *Collectanea Augustiniana* (New York: Peter Lang, 1993), 477–95.

Daniélou, Jean, *The Origins of Latin Christianity*, trans. David Smith and John Austin Baker, ed. and with a postscript by John Austin Baker (London: Darton, Longman & Todd; Philadelphia: Westminster, 1977).

Meslin, Michel, *Les ariens d'Occident 335–430* (Paris: Éditions du Seuil, 1967).

Weedman, Mark, *The Trinitarian Theology of Hilary of Poitiers* (Leiden and Boston: Brill, 2007).

Williams, Daniel H., *Ambrose of Milan and the End of the Nicene–Arian Conflicts* (Oxford: Clarendon Press, 1995).

# Part III

*Renewing the tradition*

# 6 God as the mystery of sharing and shared love: Thomas Aquinas on the Trinity

ANSELM KYONGSUK MIN

No trinitarian theology has exercised as much influence on Catholic theology as has that of St. Thomas Aquinas, yet no trinitarian theology has proven as difficult to comprehend either. In this chapter I begin with the ontological constitution of the Trinity in terms of processions, relations, and persons. I then go on to discuss the personal characteristics of Father, Son, and Holy Spirit, and the logic of the immanent processions as the grammar of God's action in the world. I will end with a brief reflection on his relation to the patristic tradition, East and West, and on his challenges to our contemporary reconstructive tasks. My presentation is largely based on his *Summa theologiae* (*The Summa of Theology*) I, qq. 27–43, and *Summa contra gentiles* (known in English as *On the Truth of the Catholic Faith*) IV, 1–26.[1]

## THE ONTOLOGICAL CONSTITUTION OF THE TRINITY: PROCESSIONS, RELATIONS, PERSONS

The most important systematic question of all trinitarian theology is perhaps the question concerning the origin of plurality or threeness in God, a being whose very essence is so uniquely "one" as to be "simple" in the sense of having no internal ontological composition in the way that finite entities do. How can there be three persons in the one God whose very essence is identical with his existence? How does one show the possibility of this plurality without falling into tritheism or modalism, the two extremes that an orthodox trinitarian theology must avoid? Aquinas takes on this question in the most orderly, systematic way. There are many steps to his answer.

The first question is how the three persons originate or proceed at all. Procession presupposes action, and the nature of procession depends on the nature of the action involved. Here Aquinas distinguishes between two kinds of action, transient and immanent. Transient action is an action proceeding from an agent and leading to an effect different from and external to the agent. All causal relations among material things are based on transient action. Immanent action, on the other hand, does not proceed to anything outside the agent but remains within the agent. This applies especially to the action of the intellect, which proceeds within the intellect and terminates in the concept or word of the thing understood.

For Aquinas it is crucial that we take the model of procession from the immanent activity of the intellect, the highest creature we know, and not from the transient activity of material things. While transient activity necessarily assumes an ontological difference between agent and effect because they are mutually external, immanent activity does not. Intellectual activities, the best example of immanent activity, proceed within the same entity, and the more perfect they are, the more closely are they united with their source. The more perfectly a thing is understood, the more intimately is its concept joined and united to the intellect, as there is unity between the intelligible in act and the intellect in act. To know a thing is to become one with the thing known, and the unity and intimacy of the knower and the known are in direct proportion to the degree of the perfection of that knowledge. As the divine intellect is the very supreme perfection of God, the divine Word or Concept in which God's self-understanding terminates is necessarily perfectly united with the source from which it proceeds without any kind of diversity (*diversitas*), that is, difference between two substances. The procession in God must be understood on the model of intellectual emanation as the best example of immanent activity (*Summa theologiae* I, q. 27, a. 1).

Can this intellectual emanation as Word be called "generation"? For Aquinas, the procession of the Word cannot be called generation if by generation is meant the change from non-existence to existence as in the case of the generation of corruptible beings. The true meaning (*ratio*) of generation, however, consists in the origination of a living being from a conjoined living principle by way of similitude in the same specific nature. The intellectual procession of the Word fulfills this meaning and does so in the most perfect way: understanding in God is God's operation as a living being, and the Word shares the similitude of God because the concept of the intellect is the likeness of the object conceived, and exists in the same nature as God because in God there is identity between his act of understanding, his essence, and his existence. In human beings, their act of understanding is not identical with the substance of their intellect, and their words, therefore, are not of the same nature as their intellect, which means that the idea of generation cannot properly and fully apply to human intellectual operations. In God, however, the act of understanding is identical with God's very substance, and the Word proceeds as subsisting in the same divine nature. The procession of the Word, then, is generation, and the Word is the Son, in the most eminent and paradigmatic sense. No biological generation involves, between parents and children, the perfect similitude of Father and Son, and it involves only the communication of the "specifically" identical nature of the parents, never the "numerically" identical nature of the divine Father (*Summa theologiae* I, q. 27, a. 2; *Summa contra gentiles* IV, 11).

In addition to the procession of the Word, there is in God another procession, that of love, whereby the object loved is in the lover as the object of the intellect is in the intellect. The intellect and will are not two different things (*diversi*) in God, but there is a distinction of order or relationship between them in the sense that nothing can be loved by the will unless first conceived by the intellect. Furthermore, "all that exists in God is God," and "the divine nature is communicated by every procession which is not outward" (*Summa theologiae* I, q. 27, a. 3 ad 2), and the person proceeding as love also receives the divine nature. This procession of love, however, cannot be called generation. The procession of the intellect is by way of its similitude to the object understood and can be called generation, whereas the procession of the will is by way of its inclination, impulse, and movement to the object willed. What proceeds in God by way of love, then, does not proceed as begotten or as Son but as Spirit, which expresses a certain impulse and movement inherent in the driving power of love. As we can name God only from creatures, and as generation is the only principle of communication of nature in created beings, so generation has been the name given to the procession of the intellect in God, while the procession of the will has remained without an appropriate name. However, this procession can be called "spiration," as it is the procession of the Holy Spirit (I, q. 27, aa. 3 and 4; *Summa contra gentiles* IV, 19).

How can there be three persons within the unity of the divine essence? Unable to introduce plurality into the divine essence itself, Aquinas is noted for placing the plurality in the relations outside the divine essence and calling the persons "subsisting relations." It is crucial here to understand the fine points of his analyses and arguments in order to appreciate the doctrine of subsisting relations. In particular, we have to note the peculiarity of the category of "relation" among the nine categories of accidents, the distinctive notion of "relative" opposition, the distinction between the divine essence and the divine relations, which is only logical, and the distinction between the relations that is real.

In Christian faith the Father is really different from the Son, and both are really different from the Holy Spirit. The three persons are not merely the modalities in which the divine essence or the Father manifests himself in finite creation which human reason merely perceives to be different, even though they are not really different in themselves. They are really different in who they are as persons, although they share the same divine essence. These real differences cannot be located in the divine essence itself without destroying the unity and simplicity of that essence. Given the ten Aristotelian categories, the category of substance and the nine categories of accidents – and it is important to remember that Aquinas is utilizing these categories although "analogically" – the only locus in which he can locate divine plurality is the accidental category of relations. Why only in relations?

For Aquinas, there are two aspects to the nature of accidents. The first aspect is the existential aspect that belongs to all accidents insofar as they are accidents. As accidents their existence is to be in (*inesse*) or inhere in a subject; their being, therefore, is accidental being (*esse accidentale*), not substantial being (*esse substantiale*). The second aspect is the formal aspect, the proper meaning (*propria ratio*), of each accident. Here Aquinas points out that in the case of all accidents except relation, the formal aspect necessarily includes a respect or reference to the subject in which they inhere; for example, quantity is essentially the measure of the substance whose quantity it is, as quality is unthinkable except as the quality or disposition of the substance in which it exists. The formal meaning of these accidents is intrinsically dependent on the substance in which they inhere. In contrast, the proper meaning of relation does not lie in its reference or respect to the subject in which it inheres but in its respect or order to something other than itself (*respectus, habitudo, ordo ad alterum*). What is at stake in relation is not primarily its relation to the substance in which it inheres but its relation to an other to which it refers beyond itself, that is, its order, reference, or respect to an other, its being-toward-an-other (*esse ad alterum*). The nature of relation does not depend primarily on the nature of the substance in which it inheres and which it expresses, as do all other accidents, but on the nature of the other to which it refers. This *pure referentiality* to an other is the unique character of relation.

In God, of course, there are no accidents, and all that is in God is her essence. We cannot introduce accidents in their accidental, dependent being into the divine essence, but we can apply relation to

God analogically, that is, by negating its accidental being and elevating its formal meaning as pure relationality to God. It is true that in God relation is identical with the divine essence in reality and distinct from the divine essence only in its intelligible meaning, so that the being (*esse*) of relation in God is that of the divine essence itself in which it subsists. Relation in God is possible only as subsisting relation. However, taken in its proper meaning, relation does not signify a reference to the divine essence as such but only a respect to an other. We can apply relation to God, then, not according to the mode of its inherence but according to the mode of its pure relationality while also fully recognizing the divine being (*esse*) of such a relation. Ignoring relationality reduces the triune to a unitarian God, and ignoring the unity of its divine being invites tritheism. We need both (*Summa theologiae* I, q. 28, aa. 1 and 2; *Summa contra gentiles* IV, 14, 12).

The source of distinction and plurality in God, however, is not just any relation but only a relation of opposition or relative opposition of a certain kind. For Aquinas, things that are not opposed but merely different can belong to the same thing. Goodness, wisdom, power, and simplicity are not opposed and can all belong to and be predicated of the same divine nature. If there are real distinctions in God, they must be based on real opposition, not mere difference. However, some oppositions are unsuited to be predicated of God: the opposition of being and non-being or affirmation and negation, of the perfect and the imperfect or possession and privation, which are "absolute" oppositions, which cannot coexist in God. The only suitable opposition, then, is "relative" or relational opposition, in which one is referred to an other without being negated or contradicted by the other. Relative oppositions may in turn be founded on quantity, action, or passion. If the opposition is based on a diversity of quantity (e.g., greater or less), it will not be predicable of God without destroying the equality of persons. If it is based on action and passion (e.g., mover and moved, master and slave, parent and child), this is not predicable of God either because it originates from transient actions involving differences of power.

The only source of distinction in God, then, must be relative opposition based on something that does not destroy either the equality of persons as sharers in the unity of the divine essence, by introducing absolute oppositions and differences of nature and power, or the real differences of persons, by removing all multiplicities. That is to say, the only source of distinction in God is the two immanent intellectual operations or processions discussed earlier, in which the Father generates the Son and spirates the Holy Spirit by communicating his numerically identical divine nature, which opposes the three persons only relationally as Father and Son, Father and the Holy Spirit, not absolutely as three different kinds of beings. In other words, the three divine persons are distinguished only by relations of relative opposition based on origin, which truly distinguishes the persons as Father, Son, and Holy Spirit, but also unites them in the transcendent intimacy of the numerically identical divine nature perfectly and totally shared (*Summa theologiae* I, q. 36, a. 2; *Summa contra gentiles* IV, 24, 7).

Now, for Aquinas, the relations that distinguish the persons are real, not logical, relations. Relations are real if regard to an other exists in the nature of things so that things are by their own very nature ordered and inclined to each other, as in the relation between a heavy body and the center. Relations are logical or rational if regard to an other exists not in the nature of reality but only in the apprehending and comparing activity of reason, as in the relation between a human being and an animal interpreted as a relation between the species and the genus. The relations among the divine persons are real because they are based on the necessary immanent processions of the divine nature and the mutual ordering they produce. In contrast to these real immanent relations, God's relation to creatures is logical, not real. God exists outside the whole order of creation, and does not produce creatures by any necessity of her nature but only by the freedom of her intellect and will. God does not depend on creatures, which makes her relation to creatures only logical, whereas creatures by their very nature depend on God, which makes their relation to God real. The divine processions, on the other hand, occur in an identity of nature, and on the basis of real processions, which, therefore, produce real relations. Thus paternity and filiation are real, not just logical, relations. The Father is not the Son, as the Son is not the Father, but the Father is constituted as Father by his paternal relation to the Son, as the Son is constituted as Son by his filial relation to the Father. Relation is both intrinsic and constitutive for the persons. God is truly Father and Son, not merely in our understanding of him (*Summa theologiae* I, q. 28, a. 1).

What does Aquinas mean by "person"? Following Boethius, he defines "person" as an individual substance of a rational nature. In this metaphysical sense – not to be confused with the psychological or phenomenological sense – person is the most perfect thing we know in all of nature. Since God contains every perfection in her essence, and since we can name God only from creatures, it is "fitting" (*conveniens*) to attribute personhood to God. We may do so, however, only analogically, not univocally, by purifying it of all modes of its signification in finite beings (*modus significandi*) and affirming only its signified content (*res significata*) of God in the "more excellent mode" (*excellentiori modo*). In defining person as "individual substance of a rational nature" and applying person to God, we have to deny it all association with the "mask" worn by actors in ancient Greece, the accidents that finite substances underlie, the discursive nature of human understanding, and individuation by matter, and apply to God only the pure meaning of the dignity of a rational being, subsistence, intellectual nature, and incommunicability. Once thus purified, "person" is a perfection that pertains to God in the most eminent sense (*Summa theologiae* I, q. 29, a. 3).

Is this definition of person as an individual "substance" of a rational nature consistent with the claim that divine persons are "relations"? Person in itself does not seem to have any reference to an other. Without denying the difficulties here involved, Aquinas begins by distinguishing the general meaning of "person" from its specific meaning when it is applied to God, just as it is legitimate to distinguish the general meaning of "animal" from its specific meaning when applied to a human being. As an individual, "person" in itself simply means something "undivided," but it also means something "distinct from others," something relational. Even in its general sense, therefore, "person" does signify something "distinct" in that nature. In its specific human sense, the person as an individual contains "this flesh," "these bones," and "this soul," the individuating principles of human persons, although they do not pertain to the general concept of person.

Applying this distinction between the general and the specific uses of the term "person," Aquinas claims that what is distinct in God is based on relations of origin as we saw, while relations are not accidents in God but identical with the divine essence itself that subsists. Relations in God, then, are not opposed to "substance" but identical with substance in the sense of subsistence: divine relations are subsisting relations or persons. A divine person signifies a relation as subsisting or relation by way of substance. Divine paternity is God the Father. Thus we can say that "person" signifies (subsisting) relation directly and the divine essence indirectly. In another sense we can say that it signifies the essence directly and the relation indirectly insofar as the essence is the same as the *hypostasis* or person, and insofar as the divine person is made distinct by the relation, which therefore indirectly enters into the notion of the person. There is no incompatibility, then, between person and relation. Because of the peculiarity of divine persons, "person" means relation not only by custom and stipulation but also by its own proper meaning. Only it means relation not by way of relation but by way of substance or *hypostasis*, that is, relation as subsisting in the divine nature (*Summa theologiae* I, q. 29, a. 4).

## FATHER, SON, AND HOLY SPIRIT: DIFFERENCE IN IDENTITY

What are the differentiating characteristics of these persons thus constituted by relations of origin? Here Aquinas works out an impressive synthesis of the various biblical names given to the three persons such as Father, Son, Word, Image, Holy Spirit, Love, and Gift on the one hand and their ontological analyses and interpretations on the other. In the process he is also concerned to show how these names are thoroughly relational or personal and proper to each.

### The Father

For Aquinas, the Father is not just one of the three persons but first and foremost the origin or "principle of the whole Godhead" (*principium totius divinitatis*) (*Summa theologiae* I, q. 39, a. 5). As such, the Father is the source of all things, both divine and created, without himself deriving from another, and in this sense the "unbegotten" "principle not from a principle" (*principium non de principio*), in contrast to the Son, who is referred to as the "principle from a principle" (I, q. 33, a. 4). In distinction from "cause," which denotes diversity of substance and the dependence of one thing on another, Aquinas here prefers "principle" as more fitting to apply to God because this means only that from which something proceeds in any way whatsoever, that is, only a certain order of relation to each other (e.g., the point as the principle of a line), and origin without implying (temporal) priority, and is more comprehensive than "cause" (I, q. 33, a. 1).

For Aquinas, "Father" is the "proper" name of the person of the Father in the sense that it signifies paternity, which distinguishes the Father from the other persons and which is unique or proper to him. In fact, paternity, like generation, is predicated of God before creatures as regards its pure signified reality, although not as regards its finite mode of signification. In this regard, it is important to note that Aquinas does not locate the fatherhood of the Father in some moral qualities such as love and care independent of the act of generation, as do John D. Zizioulas and Thomas F. Torrance, but precisely in the generation of the Son, as does the entire patristic tradition.[2] The essence of generation lies in the communication of the same nature to another, and the perfection of generation lies in the nearness and similitude of the generated to the form of the generator. The Father's generation of the Son is an infinitely perfect generation because the Father communicates to the Son the totality of his divine nature which is identical "numerically," not just "specifically" as in creatures, rendering the Father and the Son totally identical and equal in *what* they are, their essence as God, and mutually immanent, while distinguishing them only in their mutual relations as Father and Son. In this sense, paternity applies most properly, not metaphorically, to the Father, from whom all human fatherhood derives, as Ephesians 3:15 asserts (*Summa theologiae* I, q. 33, a. 2).

Fatherhood is not only the "proper" name of the Father but also his "personal" name in the sense that it defines his relation to the Son that constitutes the person of the Father, although it can also secondarily be an "essential" name referring to the divine essence as such and applying to God's relationship to his creatures. A name applies primarily to that which perfectly preserves the essential meaning (*ratio*) of the word and secondarily to that which does so in a partial way and in similarity to the former. Because of the oneness of the nature and glory that belong to the Father and the Son, the meaning of fatherhood is paradigmatically realized in the Father's relation to the Son. Thus the name applies primarily to the personal relation between the two, and only secondarily to the relation between God and creatures where the two parties do not share the same nature, where creatures acquire a certain likeness to the creator only in proportion as they are "conformed" to the Son by participating in his likeness to the Father. In this sense fatherhood is primarily a personal name defining the Father's constitutive relation to the Son and only secondarily an essential name describing God's relationship to his creatures (*Summa theologiae* I, q. 33, a. 3).

### The Son

If the Father is above all the "unbegotten" origin of the divinity of the Son and the Holy Spirit, for Aquinas the Son is primarily the "begotten" of the Father born of the ineffable communication of the Father's numerically identical divine nature and thus totally "consubstantial" (*homoousios*) with the Father. The Son proceeds from the "substance" of the Father, as creatures do not (*Summa contra gentiles* IV, 7, 5). This Son has two other names, Word and Image. Are these also personal and proper names of the second person, not essential names that apply to the divine essence as such? Do they both constitutively relate the Son to other persons ("personal") and distinguish him from them ("proper") as authentic trinitarianism would require?

For Aquinas, the Word in God, taken properly, is a personal, not essential, name. "Word" can mean three related things, the external sound, the concept of the intellect that constitutes the signification of the sound, and the external sound as imagined. Of these, of course, only the concept of the intellect can apply to the Word in God. "Word" in the sense of the internal concept, however, refers to something that proceeds from something other than itself, that is, from the knowledge of the Father understanding himself, and contains in its very nature a reference to another from which it proceeds, that is, a relation of origin, which makes it personal, not essential. Just as Word in God is personal, not essential, so is speaking in God. There are not three speakers, the Father, Son, and Holy Spirit, as Anselm says. For Aquinas, as the Word is not common to the three persons, so speaking is not common to them either. To speak is to utter a word and implies a habitude or relation to the thing conceived and understood. As a relational name, speaking belongs only to the Father who utters the Word, and being spoken as a word is spoken belongs only to the Word. Insofar as being spoken also includes being understood in the word, it also belongs to each person to be spoken. As Aquinas succinctly puts it: "the Father, by understanding Himself, the Son, and the Holy Spirit, and all other things comprised in this knowledge, conceives the Word; so that thus the whole Trinity is spoken in the Word; and likewise also all creatures" (*Summa theologiae* I, q. 34, a. 1 ad 3).

Word is not only the personal but also the proper name of the Son. As an emanation of the intellect, Word is distinctive of the Son and belongs to him alone because the intellectual procession or emanation in God fulfills the meaning of generation in the most perfect way because of the numerical identity of the divine nature shared between the intellect and the intelligible in God, justifying and necessitating the name Son for the Word in which God's self-understanding terminates. Word is the proper name of the Son as Son. In fact, Word is one of the many ways of expressing the perfections of the Son. In relation to the Father, the Son is called "the Son" to express his sharing of the same nature (*connaturalis*), "the Splendor" to show his co-eternity, "the Image" to manifest his total likeness (*omnino similis*), and "the Word" to express his being immaterially begotten. No one name can exhaustively express the richness of these divine truths.

The third name that Aquinas attributes to the Son is Image. Image is likewise both personal and proper to the Son. It is a personal name insofar as it implies origination or procession from something similar to itself in nature or form. The Son is the perfect Image of the

Father because he receives the numerically identical divine nature of the Father, an imitation of the Father implying only assimiliation, not posteriority (*Summa theologiae* I, q. 35, a. 1). It is also a name proper to the Son, not to the Holy Spirit. It is true that both the Son and the Holy Spirit receive the nature of the Father through their respective processions. Still, the Holy Spirit is not said to be "born," which makes it improper to call the Spirit the Image. The Son proceeds as Word, and it is essential to the Word to be of like nature or form with that from which it originates, but this is not the proper meaning of love, whose essence lies in the movement to the object loved, not similarity with it, although this similarity does obtain in the divine kind of love which is the Holy Spirit. Human beings are also called the image of God in the way that the image of a king may be found in something of a different nature like a coin, but the Son is the perfect Image of the Father in the way that the image of a king may be found in his son sharing the same nature (I, q. 35, a. 2).

### The Holy Spirit

The third divine person, like the second, has three names, Holy Spirit, Love, and Gift, which are also both personal and proper names. Unlike the procession of the Son, which has the name of generation, the procession of the Holy Spirit does not have an appropriate name, nor therefore do the relations that follow from this procession. "Holy Spirit" does not seem of itself to indicate a relation like "Father" and "Son." In order to meet this embarrassment, tradition has accommodated terms like "procession" and "spiration" to refer to relations, although they properly express originating acts more than relations. Nevertheless, Aquinas argues for the appropriateness of "Holy Spirit" in two ways. First, it is appropriate for the Holy Spirit, who is common to the Father and the Son as their bond, to be called by a name that is also common to both. Both the Father and the Son are holy, and both are also spirits. Second, "spirit" in corporeal things signifies impulse and movement, as in the case of breath and wind, and appropriately represents the property of love whereby love moves and impels the will of the lover toward the object loved, while "holy" refers to whatever is ordered to God. The Holy Spirit, therefore, is a proper name of the third person, who proceeds by way of the love whereby God is loved (*Summa theologiae* I, q. 36, a. 1).

Now, to touch upon an ecumenically sensitive issue, Aquinas argues that the Holy Spirit does also proceed from the Son, not only from the Father, that the Holy Spirit proceeds from the Father through the Son, and that the Father and the Son are one principle of the Holy Spirit. Aquinas makes a number of arguments for this thesis. First, the only distinction in God is due to relative opposition based on origin, as we saw earlier, which means that the Holy Spirit cannot be distinguished from the Son unless he is related and opposed to him either as that which proceeds to the principle from which it proceeds or as the principle to that which proceeds from that principle. Since we cannot say that the Son proceeds from the Holy Spirit, we must say that the Holy Spirit proceeds from the Son. Second, love must proceed from the Word because nothing can be loved unless it is first conceived and known. Third, if two persons proceed from the one person of the Father, there must be some order or relation between the two, and this order within the same nature can be based only on origin. Fourth, the Father shares everything with the Son except what distinguishes each from the other, which means that one power belongs to both the Father and the Son, and whatever is from the Father must also be from the Son.

Insofar as the Son receives from the Father that the Holy Spirit proceed from the Son, we can say that the Holy Spirit proceeds from the Father through the Son, or immediately from the Father and mediately from the Son. This does not make the Son either a secondary source of the Holy Spirit independent of the Father, as Jürgen Moltmann might fear,[3] or an instrumental cause of the Holy Spirit, because the power that the Son receives from the Father to spirate the Holy Spirit is not a numerically distinct but a numerically identical power. Because of the numerically identical divine nature totally shared between the Father and the Son, these are one in everything except where they are relationally opposed as Father and Son. Since there is no relative opposition in the matter of the spiration of the Holy Spirit, the Father and the Son constitute "one" principle of the Holy Spirit. Furthermore, the Father loves himself and the Son with one love, and the Father and the Son love each other, and it is from this mutual love that the Holy Spirit proceeds as their bond, as the "unitive love" (*amor unitivus*) of both (*Summa theologiae* I, q. 36, aa. 2–4; I, q. 37, a. I ad 3).

Can we predicate Love of the Holy Spirit? Can love be a personal name when it is also an essential name that applies to the divine essence as such and therefore to the whole Trinity? Is love not more a reference to an action than to a subsistent person? Here again we touch upon a certain linguistic peculiarity in naming the Holy Spirit. Just as "Father" can be taken both essentially and personally, so "Love," if taken properly, can be taken both essentially as an attribute of the divine essence as such (*Summa theologiae* I, 20) and personally as the distinguishing attribute of the Holy Spirit. For Aquinas, we are more familiar with the procession of the Word by way of the intellect than with the procession of Love by way of the will, and have been able to come up with more fitting names to describe the former than the latter. As a result, we are obliged to make do with circumlocutions such as "procession" and "spiration," which are accommodated to refer to relations, although they refer to acts of origin in their proper meaning.

The Holy Spirit is not only Love but also Gift, which is a relational and therefore personal name. Gift implies an aptitude for being given and a relation to both the giver and the recipient to whom it is given. It is related to the giver, whose it is and who alone can give it to others, and to the recipient, who must be able to receive and possess it. The Holy Spirit and the Son belong to the Father by origin, who can therefore give them as gifts to others. Non-rational creatures, however, cannot truly receive and possess anything because they are not free to use and enjoy what they possess; they can be moved by a divine person but not enjoy him. As creatures capable of freely knowing and loving, rational creatures meet the necessary condition for receiving and possessing the divine gifts, but not the sufficient condition. Receiving, enjoying, and partaking of the divine Word and the divine Love so as to freely know and love God truly and rightly is not within their own natural power. The power to do so must come from above, that is, must be given to them by God and thus as a gift. A divine person can be given and be a gift only by divine grace. The Holy Spirit is given to creatures only in time, but the aptitude to be given is eternal. The Holy Spirit is Gift from all eternity (*Summa theologiae* I, q. 38, a. 1).

Gift is not only a personal name but also a proper name of the Holy Spirit. A gift in the proper sense is something gratuitously given without the expectation of a return. The reason for gratuitous donation is love whereby we wish the recipient well. All true gifts are possible only through love, which therefore constitutes the first or primordial gift as condition of all genuine giving. Since the Holy Spirit proceeds as Love, he is also the first gift. The Son too is given, but given precisely from the Father's love. Gift, therefore, is also the proper name of the Holy Spirit, as is Love (*Summa theologiae* I, q. 38, a. 2).

### Mutual equality and indwelling

The same divine nature subsists in the three persons, making them alike, and does so in indivisible, perfect equality. We cannot say that the divine essence belongs more to the Father than to the Son. We can say, therefore, not only against Eunomius, that the Son is like to the

Father, but also, against Arius, that he is equal to the Father. By the same token, two divine persons do not mean more than one person, although two human persons mean more than one person. All the relations and persons are numerically one in essence and being. In a most profound statement of the trinitarian mystery of infinite sharing among the persons, Aquinas says that "all the relations together are not greater than only one; nor are all the persons something greater than only one; because the whole perfection of the divine nature [*tota perfectio divinae naturae*] exists in each person" (*Summa theologiae* 1, q. 42, a. 4 ad 3).

Contemporary trinitarian theology is fond of the idea of *perichōrēsis* or the co-inherence of the divine persons in one another as an indication of the interpersonal communion that constitutes the life of the Triune God. The Father is in the Son, and the Son is in the Father (Jn 14:10). What is the basis of this co-inherence? Aquinas gives three reasons based on essence, relation, and origin. First, the Father exists in the Son by his essence insofar as the Father is his essence and generates the Son by communicating that essence in its totality. The Father's essence, that is, the Father himself, exists in the Son, who too is his own essence and is in the Father in whom he has his essence. Second, relations constitute the persons, who are subsisting relations to one another. The Father exists in the Son and the Son exists in the Father as mutually constituting opposites. Third, the procession of the intellectual word, as an immanent activity, occurs within, not outside, the speaker of the word. The same applies to the Holy Spirit (*Summa theologiae* 1, q. 42, a. 5).

## THE LOGIC OF THE IMMANENT PROCESSIONS AS THE GRAMMAR OF GOD'S ACTION IN THE WORLD

One last important issue I want to discuss is the relation between the essential and the personal in the immanent and the economic Trinity. Ever since Augustine, one axiom in trinitarian theology has been that the action of the Trinity *ad extra* or in creation is undivided and common to the three persons. Aquinas echoes this by saying that action follows essence and that it is by her divine essence that God acts in the world. This idea is reinforced by his thesis that we can argue to the existence and attributes of the one God from creation but not to the Trinity of divine persons, which is strictly a mystery of revelation. This has given rise to the suspicion that Aquinas' God may be trinitarian in the immanent Trinity but remains thoroughly unitarian in her action on the world except by way of the "appropriation" of the common essential attributes to particular persons, which is not trinitarian enough.[4] I argue that this is not the case at all. Aquinas is thoroughly trinitarian not only in the immanent but also in the economic Trinity: God acts according to the specific properties of each person in the economic Trinity, while the concept of appropriation, which is itself based on the "logic" of the immanent processions, is simply a way of "manifesting" precisely the trinitarian content of faith by means of something better known to us. The doctrine of appropriation is not meant to be a denial of God's trinitarian action in the world or a reduction of God's action to the one divine essence without intrinsic personal differentiation.

Let me begin with a reminder of the nature of the divine person. The concept of divine person always simultaneously includes the divine nature in which he subsists and the relationally distinguishing attributes proper to each person with which each subsists as God. In this sense the Father is God as existing in the particular mode of the unbegotten or underived principle of the total divinity of the two other persons. The Son is God as existing in the mode of the one begotten of the total self-communication of the Father in his divine nature in a procession of the intellect and therefore as Word and Image of the Father as well. The Holy Spirit is God as existing in the mode of one proceeding from the Father through the Son in a procession of the will and therefore also as Love and Gift between the Father and the Son. The divine nature always exists in these three mutually irreducible, intrinsically differentiated ways, which is why Aquinas insists that they are personal and proper attributes of each person, not essential attributes. The divine nature always belongs to the persons in an order of mutual relation originating in the immanent processions.

This trinitarian character of the immanent life of God does not change in her relation to creation. Even in the immanent Trinity God posits and gives herself an eternal relation to her creation precisely as Triune God. It is true that a divine person, simply as person, who is thoroughly relational, refers only to each other, not to creatures, but as divine, he can and does refer to them. Just as it is proper for the Son to be Son, so it is proper for the Son to be God begotten and as such also Creator begotten, which implies a relation to creatures. For Aquinas, the Word has a relation to creatures (*respectus ad creaturam*) in the sense that "all things were made through him" (Jn 1:3). What kind of a relation is this? Words represent things understood, and human beings need different acts of understanding and different words for different things understood. God, on the other hand, needs only one act to understand himself and all other things, which he knows by knowing himself or his own essence, and needs only one Word to express his knowledge. It is important, however, to distinguish between God's knowledge of things divine, which is only cognitive, and God's knowledge of things created, which is both cognitive and operative. Likewise, the Word of God that expresses this knowledge is only expressive as regards what is in God but both expressive and operative as regards creatures. The Word contains the operative idea or model (*ratio factiva*) of all things that God makes (*Summa theologiae* I, q. 34, a. 3).

There are, however, two kinds of God's relation to creation. One kind of relation follows upon God's transient activity such as creating, governing, and saving, which applies to God only in time, but there is another kind of relation that follows from God's immanent activity such as knowing and willing, which does not apply to God in time but in eternity, and it is this second kind of relation that is entailed in the Word as the operative idea or exemplar of all creatures. Although the Word primarily connotes a relation to the Speaker or the Father, it secondarily implies a relation to creatures insofar as God eternally understands every creature by understanding himself in the one Word, the primordial Image of the Father and as such also the primordial Exemplar of all things the Father creates through his Word (*Summa theologiae* I, q. 34, a. 3; I, q. 13, a. 7 ad 3; *Summa contra gentiles* IV, 13). In a way parallel to the Word, the Holy Spirit as Gift likewise implies an eternal reference or relation to creatures to which it will be given. A gift is not called a gift because it is actually given but because it has the aptitude for being given. The Holy Spirit is called Gift from eternity although actually given only in time.

This relation is not an expression of God's dependence on creatures but an expression of God's eternal and eternally prevenient knowledge (the Word) and love (the Holy Spirit) of the things God creates in time (*Summa theologiae* I, q. 38, a. 1 ad 4). Just as the Father speaks himself and every creature by his begotten Word, insofar as the Word begotten adequately represents the Father and every creature, so he loves himself and every creature by the Holy Spirit, insofar as the Holy Spirit "proceeds as the love of the primal goodness whereby the Father loves himself and every creature" (I, q. 37, a. 2).

In addition to these thoroughly personal, trinitarian relations to creation posited by God from all eternity, Aquinas' discussion of the work of creation in time also reveals the thoroughly trinitarian character of the economic Trinity. To create is to produce the very being (*esse*) of things out of nothing, which therefore belongs to God's essence common to the three persons. It does not belong to a single person. However, this does not mean that creation is the work of God simply in her undifferentiated essence. The divine persons as such, "according to the logic [*ratio*] of their processions, have causality with regard to the creation of things" (*Summa theologiae* I, q. 45, a. 6). God causes things according to her intellect and will. As artisans make things through the word conceived in their intellect and through the love of their will for them, so "God the Father made the creature through his Word, which is the Son, and through his love, which is the Holy Spirit. And accordingly, processions of the persons are the reasons (*rationes*) for the production of creatures, insofar as they include the essential attributes, knowledge and will" (I, q. 45, a. 6). It is not just the divine essence that creates; the processions of the divine persons are "also in some way the cause and reason [*ratio*] of creation" (I, q. 45, a. 7 ad 3).

The power to create belongs to all three persons, but each person exercises that power according to his own personal mode. Thus the Father exercises that power in the way proper to him as one who is the unbegotten source of that power, the Son as one to whom that power is given from another and therefore as the primordial model through whom all things are made, and the Holy Spirit as one who receives the power from both and therefore as one who governs and gives life to those created by the Father through the Son (*Summa theologiae* I, q. 45, a. 6). Just as the creative causality of God is exercised in a thoroughly trinitarian way, so the created effects also reveal the trinitarian character of that causality. The (relatively) independent subsistence of the creature in its own being with a causal power of its own is the trace of the Father as the primordial principle, and its possession of a form or essence of its own shows the trace of the Word, the divine Exemplar of all things, while its teleological relation of order to things other than itself and to God manifests the trace of the Holy Spirit as Love. Substantiality, form, and relations of order in created things are the traces of the Trinity, not merely of the divine nature (I, q. 45, a. 7).

The doctrine of appropriation, which consists in the appropriation of essential names to the persons, does not deny but reinforces this trinitarian nature of God's work in creation. This becomes clear from the three presuppositions that govern appropriation. The first presupposition is that appropriation should not be misinterpreted to imply that the names appropriated belong exclusively to the person to whom they are appropriated, which is fair enough. After all, we are dealing with essential names, those that by definition belong to the divine essence as such and belong equally to all persons. The second rule is that the essential attributes are gathered from creation and better known to us than the personal attributes, and that it is "fitting" to use things better known to us in order to manifest or clarify the revealed content of faith. The purpose of appropriation is to help us better understand the content of personal names, not to ignore them and fall into unitarianism. The third assumption is that appropriation must be governed precisely according to the "logic" (*ratio*) of the eternal trinitarian processions, that is, according to similitude to each person in his personal character, not arbitrarily; it involves the personalization of the essential names, not the essentialization of personal names (*Summa theologiae* I, q. 39, a. 7).

It is for these reasons that after the thoroughly trinitarian explanation of creation, Aquinas goes on to say that such trinitarian explanation can "also" (*etiam*) be helped by the common logic of appropriation. Being the creator is appropriated to the Father because power, especially the power to create, is especially fitting to the Father as the unbegotten principle of all things, and wisdom is appropriated to the Son because wisdom is that through which intellectual agents act and therefore especially fitting to the Word, the primordial exemplar "through whom all things were created," while goodness is appropriated to the Holy Spirit because government, which brings all things to their proper end, and the giving of life in their internal teleology belong to goodness, which is especially fitting to the Holy Spirit as the primordial goodness with which the Father loves himself, the Son, and all created things (*Summa theologiae* I, q. 45, a. 6 ad 2).[5]

## AQUINAS' CHALLENGE TO CONTEMPORARY TRINITARIAN THEOLOGY

Aquinas' trinitarian theology has been subjected to many criticisms during the last half century, and I tried to respond to some of them elsewhere.[6] By way of conclusion I would make two brief observations, one on Aquinas' relationship to the patristic tradition, and the other on the many challenges he throws at contemporary trinitarian theology.

As an orthodox theologian Aquinas fully recognizes his indebtedness to the entire patristic tradition, both East and West. He accepts the idea of generation as the communication of the same divine nature, the location of all personal differences in relationality and the subsequent relational definition of the divine person, the necessity of distinguishing between relative and essential predications, and the doctrine of mutual *perichōrēsis* based on the sharing of the identical divine nature. Aquinas also inherits from Augustine the model of the mind as the paradigm for talking about the three divine persons and a relatively developed doctrine of appropriation. The genius of Aquinas lies in elaborating, developing, and expanding these inherited teachings into a theology of the Trinity with a comprehensiveness of treatment, a systematic thoroughness, a conceptual coherence, and a metaphysical sophistication yet to be surpassed.

If Aquinas inherited the classical tradition, he has also left contemporary theologians with a legacy of challenges and questions that any trinitarian reconstruction must address. Substantively, there are three questions. The first concerns the ontological constitution of the Trinity: how do we conceptualize the process in which three divine persons emerge or originate in such a way as to distinguish each as a distinct person but without denying their common divine nature, while also guaranteeing their equality, co-eternity, and mutual coinherence? The second concerns the relation between the essential and the personal in God: do we have a conception of the divine "person" adequate enough to avoid tritheism and modalism by including in itself both the divine essence as God and the distinguishing traits proper to each person? By what criteria do we assign certain attributes to the common essence and certain others to the personal distinctions? The third concerns the relation of the immanent and economic Trinity: what is there in the immanent Trinity that moves God to create, redeem, and govern the world? How does the life and structure of the immanent trinity serve as the ontological *ratio* of the economic Trinity?

There are also two methodological questions which Aquinas did ask and which remain pertinent today. The first concerns the method and criteria of predicating divine names: do we have a developed theory that will justify the use of the only language we know in talking about God, our human language derived from the material world, yet also does justice to the ontological difference between God and creatures and protects our language from the idolatry of anthropomorphism and the abusiveness of ideology? The second concerns the model we use for talking about the Trinity: is the model adequate to indicate something of the infinity of God, the immanence of divine life, and sufficient freedom from our created world while also suggesting an eternal love for creation? Are the models supple enough to accommodate coherently the many aspects of trinitiarian theology such as processions, relations, persons, the difference between the relational and the essential, the immanent and the economic, and capable of promoting the coherent, theological appropriation of biblical names (e.g., Father, Son, Word, Gift, etc.)?

## Notes

1. References to the *Summa theologiae* of St. Thomas Aquinas are by part, question (q.), and article (a.), and those to the *Summa contra gentiles* are by book, chapter, and paragraph. All quotations are from the Leonine editions, available online at www.unav.es/filosofia/alarcon/amicis/ctopera.html.
2. John D. Zizioulas, "The Doctrine of the Holy Trinity: The Significance of the Cappadocian Contribution," in Christoph Schwöbel, ed., *Trinitarian Theology Today: Essays on Divine Being and Act* (Edinburgh: T. & T. Clark, 1995), 60; Thomas F. Torrance, *The Christian Doctrine of God: One Being, Three Persons* (Edinburgh: T. & T. Clark, 1996), 137–41, 157–61, 193.
3. Jürgen Moltmann, *The Trinity and the Kingdom of God: The Doctrine of God* (San Francisco: Harper Row; London: SCM Press, 1981), 167.
4. See Catherine Mowry LaCugna, *God for Us: The Trinity and Christian Life* (San Francisco: HarperSanFrancisco, 1991), 165–66; Robert W. Jenson, *The Triune Identity: God According to the Gospel* (Philadelphia: Fortress, 1982), 126; and Wolfhart Pannenberg, *Systematic Theology*, trans. Geoffrey W. Bromiley, II (Grand Rapids, MI: Eerdmans, 1994), 26.
5. For an elaborate, insightful, and persuasive defense of Aquinas against the common charge that he does not do justice to the truly trinitarian character of divine action in the world, see Gilles Emery, *Trinity in Aquinas* (Naples, FL: Sapientia Press of Ave Maria University, 2003), 165–208, and his article "The Personal Mode of Trinitarian Action in Saint Thomas Aquinas," *The Thomist*, 69 (2005), 31–77.
6. For a further discussion of Aquinas' trinitarian theology, possible Thomistic responses to certain critiques of Aquinas, and a relatively thorough critique of three contemporary trinitarian theologians, Jürgen Moltmann, Wolfhart Pannenberg, and Cornelius Plantinga, in light of Aquinas' trinitarian theology, see the relevant sections of my book *Paths to the Triune God: An Encounter between Aquinas and Recent Theologies* (University of Notre Dame Press, 2005).

## Further reading

Coffey, David, *Deus Trinitas: The Doctrine of the Triune God* (Oxford University Press, 1999).

Cunningham, Francis L. B., *The Indwelling of the Trinity: A Historico-Doctrinal Study of the Theory of St. Thomas Aquinas* (Eugene, OR: Wipf & Stock, 2008).

Davis, Stephen T., Daniel Kendall, and Gerald O'Collins, eds., *The Trinity: An Interdisciplinary Symposium on the Trinity* (Oxford University Press, 1999).

Emery, Gilles, *The Trinitarian Theology of St. Thomas Aquinas* (Oxford University Press, 2007).

*Trinity, Church and the Human Person* (Naples, FL: Sapientia Press of Ave Maria University, 2007).

Hill, William J., *The Three-Personed God: The Trinity as a Mystery of Salvation* (Washington, DC: Catholic University of America Press, 1982).
Merriell, D. Juvenal, *To the Image of the Trinity: A Study in the Development of Aquinas' Teaching* (Toronto: Pontifical Institute of Medieval Studies, 1990).
Min, Anselm K., *Paths to the Triune God: An Encounter between Aquinas and Recent Theologies* (University of Notre Dame Press, 2005).
Nieuwenhove, Rick Van, and Joseph Wawrikow, eds., *The Theology of Thomas Aquinas* (University of Notre Dame Press, 2005).
Pinto de Oliveira, Carlos Josephat, ed., *Ordo sapientiae et amoris* (Fribourg: Éditions Universitaires, 1993).

# 7 The Trinity in Bonaventure

KENAN B. OSBORNE

From 1248 to 1257, Bonaventure of Bagnoregio (1217–1274) taught theology at the University of Paris, offering courses on Peter Lombard's *Sententiae in IV libris diotinctae* (commonly known as the *Sentences*). His lectures eventually became the four-volume *Commentarium in libros sententiarum* (*Commentary on the Books of Sentences*), a critical edition of which was published by the Collegium S. Bonaventurae.[1] In 1257, when he was elected Minister General of the Franciscan Order, his university teaching career for all practical purposes came to an end.[2]

## TEXTUAL, CONTEXTUAL, AND HERMENEUTICAL ISSUES

Several preliminary hermeneutical issues need to be considered to assure a correct reading of Bonaventure's texts on the Trinity. Each issue has major implications for interpreting Bonaventure's theological works. From 1900 on, numerous publications on the theology of Bonaventure were published. Because they propose differing interpretations of Bonaventure's theology and exert varying degrees of influence, let us begin by considering the major contextual and hermeneutical issues involved in the interpretation of Bonaventure's theology.

### Bonaventure's writings on the Trinity

Bonaventure's writings on the Trinity include five major and two minor texts. First is the *Commentary on Book 1 of the Sentences*, which offers Bonaventure's most complete trinitarian theology;[3] second is, the *Quaestiones disputatae de mysterio Trinitatis* (*Disputed Questions on the Mystery of the Trinity*), commonly dated from late 1256 to early 1257.[4] The *Disputed Questions* focuses on eight issues:[5]

Concerning the certitude with which the existence of God is known and concerning the faith by which the Trinity of the same God is believed.

Whether a Trinity of persons can exist with unity of nature.
Whether the Trinity can exist together with the highest simplicity.
Whether the Trinity can exist with highest infinity.
Whether the Trinity of persons can exist together with highest eternity.
Whether the Trinity can exist together with supreme immutability.
Whether the Trinity can exist together with necessity.
Whether the Trinity can exist together with supreme primacy.

The third text is the *Breviloquium* (*Brief Discourse*), written shortly after the two above texts.[6] The material on the Trinity in the *Brief Discourse* is a summary of Bonaventure's trinitarian theology expressed in his *Commentary*. However, its context is different. According to J. Guy Bougerol, "now he [Bonaventure] is free from the pattern of the Schools, and has been able during these two years to develop and control even more fully the theological synthesis already elaborated: assimilating it both by reflection and by experience."[7]

The fourth text is the *Itinerarium mentis in Deum* (*Journey of the Mind to God*), which is dated at 1259.[8] In chapter 6, "De speculatione beatissimae Trinitatis in eius nomine quod est bonum" ("Reflections on the Name of Goodness of the Blessed Trinity"), Bonaventure speaks of contuition (*contuitio*), not intuition, of God as Trinity.[9] He describes the relational essence of God. "For as PURE BEING is the root and basis for the contemplation of God's essential oneness, and the name through which the other attributes come to be known, so PURE GOODNESS is the absolutely first foundation for the contemplation of the divine emanations."[10] The highest good is that which is most simple, and nothing better can be thought as being or existing than the best, "since to be is absolutely better than not to be." He concludes: "It cannot rightly be conceived except as both triune and one" inasmuch as "Good is said to be self-diffusive."[11]

Supreme self-diffusion happens only if there is a being "intrinsic yet actual, substantial yet personal, essential yet voluntary, necessary yet free, perfect yet incessant."[12] For Bonaventure, divine *ens*, *essentia*, and *esse* are simultaneously relational.

The fifth text is the *Collationes in Hexaëmeron* (*Lectures on the Hexaemeron*), Bonaventure's last theological writing.[13] The *Collationes* were lectures delivered in Paris between April 9 and May 28, 1273. In a detailed way, lectures IX, X, and XI discuss the Trinity, although trinitarian overtones pervade the entire work. Bougerol states: "When, in 1273, at the height of the doctrinal dispute (between seculars and

Mendicants), Bonaventure gave his famous lectures on the *Hexaëmeron*, the whole university attended."[14]

Two minor texts of Bonaventure's trinitarian theology are his sermons on the Trinity: *Sermo 1: De triplici testimonio sanctissimae Trinitatis* (*Sermon 1: On the Triple Witness to the Most Holy Trinity*), and *Sermo de Trinitate* (*Sermon on the Trinity*).[15] All the above-mentioned primary sources are necessary for understanding Bonaventure's trinitarian theology.

**Contemporary hermeneutics and medieval texts**

According to Maurice de Wulf (1867–1947) and Fernand van Steenberghen (1904–1993), the Renaissance and the Reformation sounded the death-knell for medieval scholasticism.[16] However, current research indicates that scholasticism remained very much alive during the sixteenth, seventeenth, and eighteenth centuries in the universities of Europe. Not until 1800 did the European universities completely reject the study of scholasticism. Antonie Vos states that "the first quarter of the nineteenth century had simply forgotten what scholastic thought consisted of."[17]

Théodore de Régnon (1831–1893), in his *Études de théologie positive sur la sainte Trinité*,[18] claimed that there were only two scholastic approaches to the Trinity: Thomas' interpretation, based on Augustine, Anselm of Canterbury, Peter Lombard, and Albert the Great; and Bonaventure's interpretation, rooted in Dionysius, Richard of St. Victor, William of Auvergne, William of Auxerre, and Alexander of Hales. In 1966, Olegario González de Cardedal argued in his book on Bonaventure's trinitarian theology that Bonaventure constructed a third theology of the Trinity radically different from those of both Augustine and Richard of St. Victor.[19] His work has changed current interpretation of Bonaventure.

**Bonaventure's understanding of God**

Bonaventure was a scholar of exceptional intellectual abilities. He was also a deeply committed Christian. As a Christian, Bonaventure acknowledged only the Christian God, the trinitarian God. Whenever he wrote the word "God," he meant, either implicitly or explicitly, the trinitarian God.

Bonaventure begins his lengthy discussion on God in the first book of his *Commentary on the Sentences* (d. 2, a. 1, q. 1).[20] The first question reads: "Whether there is only one God." In his two-page response, he states: "If the word 'God' is correctly understood, it [the plurality of Gods] is not only impossible but also unintelligible."[21] This position remains constant throughout Bonaventure's writings. Every human mind can and should recognize the existence of one God.[22]

Bonaventure then asks the second question: "Whether a plurality of persons must be affirmed in God."[23] For Bonaventure God's existence and unicity are self-evident (he spends only two pages on them), whereas the important question is the Trinity, to which he devotes 806 pages.[24]

Today, we must emphasize Bonaventure's historical condition.[25] We can interpret Bonaventure's understanding of God only from his historical context and not from our contemporary context, in which the term "God" has different meanings for different religious groups.[26]

## SOURCES OF BONAVENTURE'S THEOLOGY

Bonaventure draws from several sources to develop his trinitarian theology.

### Holy scripture, the foundational source of Bonaventure's theology

The primary source of Bonaventure's theology is sacred scripture. His text was the Latin Vulgate. At the time of Bonaventure no full-fledged concordance of the Bible existed.[27] Contemporary scholars, such as Dominic Monti, Thomas Reist, Hans-Joseph Klauck, Robert Karris, Jacques Guy Bougerol, and Hans Mercker, have explained Bonaventure's use of scripture.[28] In the *Prologus* of the *Brief Discourse*, Bonaventure wrote: "Since it [scripture] hides several meanings under a single text, the expositor must bring hidden things to light (Job 28:11). Once a meaning has been brought forth, it is necessary to clarify it further through another, more evident, scriptural passage."[29] Bonaventure then describes the breadth, length, height, and depth of scriptural passages.

At the end of his discussion, he mentions four meanings of scripture: the *literal* (what we read), the *tropological* (what we should do), the *allegorical* (what we should believe), and the *anagogical* (what we should desire).[30] In the *Lectures on the Hexaemeron*, Bonaventure uses a metaphor to describe this multiple hermeneutics of the Bible. He writes: "All of scripture is like a single zither. And the lesser string does not produce the harmony by itself, but in union with others. Likewise, one passage of scripture depends upon another. Indeed, a thousand passages are related to a single passage."[31] Medieval interpretation of scripture must be honored. Contemporary biblical hermeneutics cannot be superimposed on medieval texts.

**Francis of Assisi**

The second most important source of Bonaventure's theology is Francis of Assisi, whose influence on Bonaventure surpasses that of Augustine. Francis' gospel vision influenced Bonaventure from his childhood onward. This vision, expressed in Francis' life and writings, is a spiritual one. Bonaventure, along with other university-oriented Franciscans, provides an intellectual and theological program which draws its inspiration from the gospel and from the way Francis interprets it. Unless one has some knowledge of the Franciscan vision, the impact of Bonaventure's philosophical theology will be misinterpreted. Unfortunately, at times his "Franciscan" character has been used by some authors to make Bonaventure a mystical and spiritual writer rather than an academic scholar.[32]

**Augustine**

The theological foundation of scholasticism is Augustine. From the eleventh century onward, all Western theologians began with the Augustinian legacy as they constructed their own theological approaches. From the thirteenth century to the present, two new approaches became significant for the Catholic Church: the Dominican or Thomistic tradition and the Franciscan tradition. These two traditions did not eliminate the Augustinian approach. In the theological world of the Roman Catholic Church, from the thirteenth century onward, there have been three major intellectual traditions: the Augustinian, the Thomistic, and the Franciscan. Bonaventure is a major creator of the Franciscan tradition.

Bonaventure's writings indicate his debt to Augustine. He calls Augustine the "Greatest of the Latin Fathers"[33] and the "Supereminent Doctor."[34] Bonaventure cites Augustine over 3,000 times. From Augustine, Bonaventure accepts the primacy of faith over reason, his interconnection of faith and reason, his teaching on exemplarism, and many of his neo-Platonic positions.[35] Hayes mentions a major area in which Bonaventure and Augustine parted company: "While it is true that Bonaventure owed a great debt to the work of Augustine, it has long been known that this so-called great Augustinian departed from the African master profoundly in what has to count as a central area of his teaching: the doctrine on the trinity."[36] In discussing

Bonaventure's theology of the Trinity, it must be kept in mind that Bonaventure deliberately departs from Augustine's *De Trinitate* (*On the Trinity*).

### John Damascene and Dionysius

Bonaventure's citations of the early Fathers of the church other than Augustine are limited. The same is true of almost all the twelfth-century authors. Pre-Nicene Fathers were rarely cited at that time;[37] among the post-Nicene Greek Fathers, Basil, Gregory of Nazianzus, and John Chrysostom were more frequently cited, because Latin translations of their works were available.[38]

Two Greek writers frequently quoted by Bonaventure are John Damascene (700–754), cited over 200 times, and Dionysius the Pseudo-Areopagite, cited 239 times.[39] Dionysius provided Bonaventure with three things: a viewpoint, a method, and a basic principle. Dionysian neo-Platonism influenced Bonaventure's viewpoint, as did Dionysius' *Celestial Hierarchy*.[40] In the *Lectures on the Hexaemeron*, Bonaventure makes two statements which have strong Dionysian methodical overtones: "This is the whole of our metaphysics: It is about emanation, exemplarity, and consummation: that is, to be illumined by spiritual rays and to be led back to the supreme Being."[41] "For any person who is unable to consider how things originate, how they are led back to their end, and how God shines forth in them, is incapable of achieving true wisdom."[42] The Dionysian theme, "good diffuses itself," became a basic principle for Bonaventure.[43]

### Anselm

The writings of Anselm (1033–1109) were rarely cited during the twelfth century. Around 1240, Alexander of Hales, Bonaventure, and Thomas Aquinas took an interest in Anselm's writings, and his theology began to exert a strong influence on scholasticism. Bonaventure cites Anselm 249 times, although Bonaventure, like his contemporaries, modifies many of Anselm's ideas to suit his theological approach.

### Hugh and Richard of St. Victor

In 1113 a group of Augustinian canons formed the abbey of St. Victor in Paris. Three leading scholars in this Victorine community were Hugh of St. Victor (d. 1141), Adam of St. Victor (d. 1143), and Richard of St. Victor (d. 1173). Two works of Hugh, *Eruditio didascalia* and *De sacramentis christianae fidei tractatus*, deeply influenced Bonaventure in the way they presented Christianity as a spiritual journey. For

Bonaventure, not only Christians but all people are on a journey to God.[44]

Richard caught Bonaventure's interest with his treatises *De Trinitate* and *De quattuor gradibus violentae caritatis*. Although in his *De Trinitate* Richard selected Augustine's mention of human love as his primary analog for trinitarian theology, Augustine selected the intellectual life as his primary analog. The consensus of scholars since 1965 indicates that Richard is radically Augustinian and that Bonaventure did not derive his Dionysian inspiration from Richard.[45]

### Alexander of Hales and the *Summa alexandrina*

It was the *Summa alexandrina* which provided the fundamental source for Bonaventure's interest in Dionysius. Two key features of the *Summa* strongly influenced Bonaventure's understanding of the Trinity. First, it stresses the Dionysian phrase *bonum est sui diffusivum* and its connection to the Trinity. Second, it affirms the Aristotelian principle, correlating intellect and will. Bonaventure, however, developed a trinitarian theology which "transcends that of the *Summa* in unity and coherence of thought."[46]

Alexander was one of Bonaventure's teachers. In 1236 or 1237 Alexander became a Franciscan, and since Bonaventure had come to Paris in 1235, he knew Alexander mainly as a Franciscan confrère. He speaks of Alexander as *patris et magistri bonae memoriae fratris Alexandri* ("Brother Alexander, father and teacher of holy memory");[47] *verumtamen pater et magister noster bonae memoriae frater Alexander* ("Brother Alexander, truly our father and teacher of holy memory") and *et fratris Alexandri de Hales, patris et magistri nostri* ("and Brother Alexander of Hales, our father and teacher").[48] Alexander's interconnection of Trinity and incarnation and his understanding of the image of God in the human person[49] are central to Bonaventure's own theology.

## BONAVENTURE'S TRINITARIAN THEOLOGY

We now focus specifically on Bonaventure's trinitarian theology. My presentation follows the *Commentary* and utilizes the *Disputed Questions, Brief Discourse, Journey of the Mind to God*, and *Lectures on the Hexaemeron* when they add to the *Commentary*.

Bonaventure offers only a two-page response to the question *Utrum sit unus tantum Deus*, in which he affirms the existence of only one

God on the basis that God is "absolutely the highest" and "nothing greater than God can be thought of." For him, the existence of God is an indubitable truth, and this truth is impressed on all rational minds.

In *Disputed Questions*, Bonaventure presents a fuller explanation. Instead of listing only six points in favor of his position (as in the *Commentary*) he lists twenty-nine. Instead of only four objections against his thesis (as in the *Commentary*), he lists fourteen. After these lengthy lists, Bonaventure states: "That God exists cannot be doubted if 'dubitable' is understood as a truth for which evidence is lacking in itself, or in its proof, or in the intellect that apprehends it."[50] No other arguments are made. For Bonaventure, the existence of God is a given. If someone doubts that God exists, this doubt arises "from the viewpoint of the knower, namely, by reason of a deficiency in the act of apprehending, judging, and reducing."[51]

In the *Commentary* Bonaventure begins his exposition of the Trinity with the question "Whether a plurality of persons must be affirmed in God."[52] In the *respondeo*, he uses four specific terms: *simplicitas* (simplicity), *primitas* (primacy), *perfectio* (perfection), and *beatitudo et caritas* (beatitude and charity). Simplicity, he says, is a communicable essence. Primacy is an innate ability to produce, which he calls *innascibilitas* (innascibility) and *fontalis plenitudo ad omnem emanationem* (source of fullness for all emanations). Perfection entails an immediate (*prompta*) and readily available (*apta*) presence to another. Beatitude and charity connote the will (*voluntaria*). These four terms form the foundation of Bonaventure's trinitarian theology.

The very nature of God is "communicable" and "powerful," for it produces another person "from itself" and is the "source" of fullness for all emanations. God's communication, power, productivity, and fontal fullness occur voluntarily, that is, from God's infinitely free will. One might ask: must God *necessarily* be a Trinity? Bonaventure would shy away from any mechanistic necessitarianism. Rather, he would ask: must God be loving? Love comes from free will, and infinite love comes from an infinite *free* will. That God must be God may imply a necessity, but the essence of God in Bonaventure is infinitely free love, which moves the discourse beyond any necessitarian stance. In the Franciscan tradition, the will and the intellect dance together, but in the trinitarian relationality it is infinite free love (will) which is paramount.[53] Let us consider each of Bonaventure's terms in his *respondeo*, since it is in and through them that Bonaventure elaborates his theology of Trinity.

### *Primitas* and *innascibilitas*

Bonaventure considers *primitas* and *innascibilitas* as synonyms.[54] In *distinctio* XXVIII, he presents his position in detail.[55] In the first *quaestio*, he asks "Whether the term 'unborn' or 'innascibility' is used substantially or relatively." The very wording of this question should be noted. The substance of God is the essence or nature of God. If this substance of God is non-relational there can be no Trinity, but God *is* relational.[56]

In Bonaventurian theology, two important theses are made. First, relationship is the basis for a trinitarian theology of God, not vice versa. God is not first trinitarian and then relational. Rather, God is relational, and therefore we can speak of God as trinitarian. Second, the very nature of God in itself is relational. Were one to exclude any and all relational aspects from God, the theology of a trinitarian God would be meaningless.

Bonaventure argues that *innascibilitas* means "in no way being from another."[57] Even though this is stated in a negative way, the *primitas* aspect of *innascibilitas* is positive, since it is *plenitudo fontalis*.[58] Bonaventure concludes: "Therefore, it primarily connotes relationship, though negatively, but positively by implication, and therefore it does not mean a negation which says nothing."[59] What a masterful way of describing *primitas-innascibilitas*!

Since there is no *principium*, one might argue that the relationship is merely negative, that is, not begotten. However, since the unbegottenness is also *primitas* or *plenitudo fontalis*, there is and continues to be an overwhelming positivity. If *innascibilitas* were only backward-looking – such an expression is unintelligible for an eternal principle – there would be only negativity. But if one looks forward to what this primal fountain of fullness produces, there is divine positivity.

This forward-looking view of productivity goes far beyond any form of causality. Bonaventure discusses the threefold causality (i.e., efficient, exemplary, and final), but, as Hayes notes, "Bonaventure's reflection on the structure of created realities searches out trinitarian reflections at ever deeper levels."[60] This deeper level is due to the very nature of God as relational.[61]

In *quaestio* II, Bonaventure compares the naming of Father to innascibility: "Whether innascibility and paternity refer to the same relation." His focus is on the relational nature of God. He does not view *innascibilitas* and *paternitas* as synonyms. *Innascibilitas* looks backward and asserts something negative, namely that there is no beginning (*principium*). On the other hand, *paternitas* looks forward and affirms something positive, that is, generation (*filiatio*).[62]

### *Simplicitas*

For Bonaventure, the essence of simplicity is communicability (*communicabilis*) and power (*potens*).[63] In *distinctio* XXXI, *quaestio* 2, Bonaventure asks "Whether equality and similitude in God refer to God's nature or God's relation."[64] Once again, he raises the issue of relationality. In the *Respondeo* he notes that *similitudo* and *aequalitas* refer to God's nature, and yet they are relational. He writes: "Properly and principally, the three divine Persons are similar in virtue of their relations, and causally, they are equal, according to their nature."[65]

This dual aspect, Bonaventures notes, has been presented by theologians in different ways. Bonaventure concludes that God is more than the first efficient or final cause, or the first principle, because God the Father does not "cause" either the Son or the Spirit. Non-causal productivity in God indicates something far more than causality. Nor does production refer only to creation, which is finite, contingent, and temporal. Relationality is intrinsic to God's nature in ways that cannot be explained by causality, but it can be described through the infinite *fontalis plenitudo* of the *summum ens* (highest being).

In the response of *distinctio* VIII, Bonaventure simply states: "Supreme simplicity must be affirmed of God." However, in answer to the objections, he adds: "Where supreme simplicity is affirmed, it is necessary to affirm supreme actuality, if there is supreme nobility. And where there is supreme actuality, there supreme diffusion and communication must be affirmed."[66] Simplicity, for Bonaventure, means supreme actuality, and supreme actuality includes diffusion and communication, which are relational terms. He concludes, therefore: "Therefore divine nature cannot be understood as supreme simplicity unless it is affirmed of the three divine persons of whom one is from another."[67]

### *Perfectio prompta et apta*

Like other thirteenth-century theologians, Bonaventure writes about God as the most perfect being. He notes that in Aristotle's *Metaphysics* the philosopher states: "The perfection of the intellect is the intelligible."[68] Whenever the mind understands something, it is perfected. However, Bonaventure argues that Aristotle is thinking of something outside the human intellect. A finite creature is perfected by something beyond its finiteness. In God perfection does not come from anything outside of God.[69] God is perfect, *a se* not *ab alio*.[70] Elsewhere, Bonaventure cites John Damascene: "God is as it were an infinite sea [*pelagus*] of substance."[71] The word *pelagus* means "sea," and for Bonaventure, this sea is a *fons perfectionis*.

Love is Bonaventure's primary description of God. God is an infinite sea of love, and this is infinite perfection. Divine love is immediately present (*prompta*) and readily available (*apta*). In God, this immediacy is an eternal and never-failing relationship of trinitarian love. The very being of God is a perfect relationship of trinitarian love.

### *Beatitudo et caritas*

Although Bonaventure's theology of the Trinity revolves around divine simplicity, primacy-innascibility, and perfection, it is his explanation of divine *beatitudo et caritas* that makes his approach to the Trinity radically new. In Bonaventure's understanding of God as love, we see most clearly how he moves away from Augustine's and Richard's trinitarian theology and also parts company with Thomas Aquinas.[72] In his trinitarian theology, "love" is not a noun but a verb: God loves eternally, infinitely, and relationally.[73] Causality *ad extra* in God, he writes, is attributed to God's will, because of *bonitas* (goodness), namely, *bonum est sui diffusivum*.[74] The divine will is not only powerful but also *universalissima* (supremely universal) and *actualissima* (supremely actual).[75]

## UNITY AND RELATIONALITY IN THE TRINITY

In sum, the following statements can be affirmed of Bonaventure's theology of the Trinity.

First, the Trinity is the foundation of Bonaventure's entire theological program. According to Hayes, there are two texts which indicate the starting point of Bonaventure's theology. In the first, *Disputed Questions*, "Bonaventure speaks of the entire edifice of Christian faith. This foundation, he argues, is the mystery of the trinity."[76] In the second, *Lectures on the Hexaemeron*, "We are to begin at the center of reality; and the center is Christ."[77] Both are foundational, and for Bonaventure there is a dialectical relationship between them, which he calls the "two roots of faith."[78] Bonaventure's theology is neither exclusively theocentric nor exclusively Christocentric. It maintains that the Trinity is the more profound foundation, and that Christ is intelligible as the center only on the basis of a trinitarian God.

Second, the unity of the divine essence must be understood with divine relationality. In Bonaventure's description of simplicity, primacy, perfection, and love, two sets of terms are joined together. On the one hand, Bonaventure speaks of the oneness, uniqueness, and unity of God, using essentialistic terms such as the following: one, only one, one nature, one essence, one substance, immutable, and *summe simplex*.[79] On the other hand, he uses the following relational expressions to describe the same nature of God: ability to produce, eternal production, emanation, communicability, powerful, fontal fullness, infinitely free love, positive relationship, primal fountain, greater than primary/final causality, non-causal productivity, highest actuality which includes *summa diffusio et communicatio*, and *caritas*.

What is remarkable is Bonaventure's interconnection of essential terms and relational terms. In the Aristotelian framework, an essence or substance is non-relational.[80] An essence or primary substance is that which can be defined without any relationship to another being. In Plotinian neo-Platonism, the One is also non-relational. From the One there may be emanations to many other beings, but in itself the One is an isolated unity.

Bonaventure places before us a very different understanding of the divine *ens*, *essentia*, and *esse*. God is essentially relational and relationally essential. God cannot be understood only through the essentialistic terms listed above: one, only one, one nature, one essence, one substance, immutable. Simultaneously and *ad intra*, the one and unique *Summum Ens* involves the other set of terms: ability to produce, eternal production, emanation, communicability, powerful, fontal fullness, infinitely free love, positive relationship, and so on.

For Bonaventure, God is in essence communicable, fontal, able to produce, and so on. *Summe simplex* is not a description of God to which a trinitarian relational reality is subsequently attached. An infinite being is a being without any *principium*. God's essentiality and relationality are also infinite and without any *principium*. In this context, "infinite" means not only durational infinity, but also essential infinity. Every aspect of God is not at only one and unique but also relational and communicable. For God, "to be" means to be a fountain of plenitude and to be communicable. Such a being moves beyond mere causal productivity.

Bonaventure never claims that his understanding of being differs from that of Aristotle. Rather, he attributes to God both essentialistic qualities and relational qualities. Only one conclusion, however, can be drawn from this juxtaposition: for Bonaventure, being itself (*Summum Ens*) is relational.

Third, Bonaventure formulates a third trinitarian theology, different from that of Augustine, Thomas Aquinas, and Richard of St. Victor. In Bonaventure's view, Richard of St. Victor's position on the Trinity is inadequate because it lacks the Dionysian element of *bonum est sui diffusivum*. Likewise, Augustine's *On the Trinity* is inadequate since it lacks the same Dionysian principle. Bonaventure, building on Alexander of Hales and the *Summa alexandrina*, envisions a radically new Western approach to a theology of Trinity. It is through the findings of contemporary scholars, such as González, Bougerol, and Hayes, that the radical newness of Bonaventure's trinitarian theology has come to light.[81]

## SUMMARY

The foregoing pages have established the context of Bonaventure's thought and the basis of his trinitarian theology through an analysis of the four aspects of God's relationality. God's very being is inner-relational being, inner-relational goodness, which is therefore intrinsically *sui diffusivum* and inner-relational freedom. A deeper meditation on this inner-relationality indicates that a relationship involves more than an "A" and a "B." A may relate to B and B may relate to A, but how deeply does A relate to B and B relate to A? The intensity of a relationship involves C. Every relationship is a triad of A, B, and C.

Bonaventure frequently uses the terms "Father," "Son," and "Spirit," but he does not base his theological argument for a trinity on a definition of person, whether the definition comes from Boethius, Richard of St. Victor, or Alexander of Hales. Nor does he base his theological argument for a trinity only on an analysis of paternity, filiation, and spiration. What is amazing and unique is his constant return to the relational nature of God and to the four divine characteristics of *primitas* or *innascibilitas, simplicitas, perfectio prompta et apta*, and *beatitudo et caritas*.

The main point of Bonaventure's trinitarian theology is that the very nature of God is relational, and that it is only in and through meditation on this basic relational nature of God that one can formulate the Trinity of Father, Son, and Spirit. God is not first of all one God to which a Trinity is added. God is relational *sine principio*.

So far we have considered the Trinity *ad intra*. There are, however, trinitarian actions *ad extra*. A complete understanding of Bonaventure's theology of Trinity needs to show how he unites the Trinity's *actiones ad intra* with its *actiones ad extra*. To grasp Bonaventure's understanding of this relationship, a review of his teaching on vestige, image, and similitude of the Trinity in creation is central.

## THE "BOOK OF CREATION": *VESTIGIUM, SIMILITUDO* AND *IMAGO DEI*

The *Brief Discourse* explains Bonaventure's creational theology as reflecting the trinitarian God as follows:

> The created world is like a book in which its Maker, the trinity, shines forth, is represented, and can be read at three levels of expression: namely, as a vestige, as an image, and as a similitude. The reality of the vestige is found in all creatures; that of the image is found only in intellectual beings or rational spirits; and that of the similitude is found only in those creatures which have become conformed to God.[82]

It is the trinitarian God, not simply the "one God," that Bonaventure finds reflected in creation. An argument based solely on efficient and final causes of finite reality leads to the conclusion that for all created beings there must be a first cause or a first principle, and that this first cause or principle can be given the name God. For Bonaventure, this way of thinking is not adequate to the Christian faith since the only God Christians believe in is the trinitarian God. Therefore, the God reflected in the "Book of Creation" is the trinitarian God.[83]

*Vestigium* is often translated as "footprint," and footprints can at times be traced back to their source. Bonaventure does not say that the *vestigium* is the same as a "footprint-reflection" of God in creation caused by the causality in God. A "first cause" argument is not what he has in mind. For him, there is in the *vestigium* itself a personal reflection of the trinitarian God. This deeper reflection is that of a God who is not simply the first cause but the trinitarian first cause, since trinitarian goodness is *diffusivum sui*. This trinitarian God is personally present in all of creation.

*Imago* is a more radiant reflection of the trinitarian God, since for an intellectual being or rational spirit, there is a relationship of mutual love. The trinitarian God is recognized as truth, beauty, and love. Rocks and trees may reflect the truth, beauty, and love of the Triune God, but these creatures do not intellectually and voluntarily respond to God's truth, beauty, and love. In the *imago*-reflection Bonaventure emphasizes the role of the human will. This is seen in his insistence that there must be a willing response to the loving presence of God.

*Similitudo* is reserved for those who are God-conformed. *Similitudo* is not simply a prerogative of the blessed in heaven; it is present in all holy people. In the *Brief Discourse, similitudo* is said to be achieved in the unitive way.[84] In the *Lectures on the Hexaemeron*, this realization is present in the community of God's holy people. Actually, one should not say "God-conformed," but "Trinity-conformed," for *similitudo* includes an indwelling within the Trinity's relational life itself.

## THE CONNECTION OF CREATION TO FATHER, LOGOS, AND SPIRIT

Another central theme of Bonaventure's trinitarian theology is the role of Jesus as the center of all creation and the role of the Holy Spirit in all of creation.[85] In the first book of the *Sentences, distinctiones* I–XV, Peter Lombard discussed the Trinity *ad intra*. However, in *distinctiones* XV–XVIII, he focused on the *missio* and *manifestatio* of the Logos and the Spirit *ad extra*.[86] In other words, Bonaventure moves from the Trinity *ad intra* to the Trinity *ad extra*. Included in the one divine action *ad extra* are three realities: the creation of the entire universe, the sending and manifesting of the Logos (incarnation), and the sending and manifestation of the Spirit. Both Bonaventure and Scotus stress the radical interconnection of these three *actiones ad extra*. In the Franciscan theological tradition, the theology of creation cannot be developed apart from the theology of incarnation and the sending of the Spirit.

Peter Lombard, Bonaventure, and Scotus defer a detailed analysis of the incarnational *actio ad extra* (the sending of the Logos) to *Liber* II of the *Sentences*. Consequently, the sending of the Spirit receives considerable attention in *distinctiones* XV–XVIII. Bonaventure affirms: *Missio Filii et Spiritus sancti sunt indivisae* ("The mission of the Son and that of the Spirit are undivided").[87] When creation is connected to a theology of these two sendings, the incarnation cannot be seen as "caused" or "motivated" by the sin of Adam.

Contemporary Western theologians have begun to acknowledge the tremendous contribution of Bonaventure, namely Jürgen Moltmann, Wolfhart Pannenberg, Karl Barth, Leonardo Boff, Catherine Mowry LaCugna, Karl Rahner, Anselm Min, Anne Hunt, Ted Peters, Thomas Torrance, Elizabeth Johnson, and Raimon Panikkar. Too often, however, these authors give only a limited treatment of Bonaventure's trinitarian vision. Other theologians such as Zachary Hayes, Konrad Fischer, Olegario González, Robert Karris, Johannes Freyer, A. Van Si

Nguyen, Blanco Chavero, Tito Szabó, and Giovanni Iammarrone have made the study of Bonaventure's unique trinitarian theology a contemporary imperative.

**Notes**

1. Bonaventure, *Commentarium in libros sententiarum*, in *S. Bonaventurae opera omnia*, I–IV (Quarrachi: Typographia Collegii S. Bonaventurae, 1882–89), cited henceforth as *Commentarium*.
2. From 1248 to 1254, Bonaventure taught at the Franciscan house of studies in Paris, the Convent des Cordeliers. In 1254 he became regent-master at the University of Paris.
3. Unlike other theologians of the thirteenth century, Bonaventure never wrote a volume or a long essay on *De Deo Uno* ("On the One God"). In his *Summa theologiae*, Thomas Aquinas devotes about a hundred pages to *De Deo Uno* (questions 2–26). Only with question 27 does he begin his elaboration of *De Deo Trino* ("On the Trine God"). See *Summa theologiae* I, qq. 2–27; Eng. trans., Blackfriars edn. (New York: McGraw-Hill, 1966–80).
4. Bonaventure, *Quaestiones disputatae de mysterio trinitatis*, in *Opera omnia*, V (Quarrachi: Typographia Collegii S. Bonaventurae, 1891), 45–115; trans. Zachary Hayes as *Disputed Questions on the Mystery of the Trinity* (St. Bonaventure, NY: Franciscan Institute, 1979).
5. Bonaventure, *Disputed Questions*, 26.
6. Bonaventure, *Breviloquium*, in *Opera omnia*, V, 199–313.
7. Jacques Guy Bougerol, *Introduction à l'étude de Saint Bonaventure* (Tournai: Desclée, 1961); trans. José de Vinck as *Introduction to the Works of Bonaventure* (Paterson, NJ: St. Anthony's Guild Press, 1964), 123.
8. Bonaventure, *Itinerarium mentis in Deum*, in *Opera omnia*, V, 297–313.
9. Bonaventure, *Itinerarium*, c. 6, 1.
10. Ibid.
11. Ibid., c. 6, 2.
12. Ibid.
13. Bonaventure, *Collationes in Hexaëmeron*, in *Opera omnia*, V, 327–449.
14. Bougerol, *Introduction*, 19.
15. The faculty of arts at the University of Paris had by this time become a stronghold of "Latin Averröism." For the *Sermones de Trinitate*, see Bonaventure, *Disputed Questions*, 26.
16. Maurice de Wulf, *Histoire de la philosophie médiévale*, I–III (Louvain: Publications universitaires, 1934, 1936, 1947); Fernand van Steenberghen, *La philosophie au XIII siècle* (Louvain: Publications universitaires, 1966) and *Introduction à l'étude de la philosophie médiévale* (Louvain: Publications universitaires, 1974).
17. Antonie Vos, *The Philosophy of John Duns Scotus* (Edinburgh University Press, 2006), 542. The Dutch De Rijk School under Cornelia Johanna de Vogel (1905–1986) and Lambertus Marie de Rijk (b. 1924)

has developed a new approach to historical hermeneutics during the scholastic period.

18. Vos, *Philosophy of John Duns Scotus*, 5. For a Bonaventure lexicon, see Bougerol, *Introduction*, 55–56. See also Mary Beth Ingham, "Letting Scotus Speak for Himself," *Medieval Philosophy and Theology*, 10:2 (2001), 173–216, and Théodore de Régnon, *Études de théologie positive sur la sainte Trinité*, 4 vols. (Paris: Victor Retaux et Fils, 1892–98).
19. Olegario González de Cardedal, *Misterio trinitario y existencia humana: estudio histórico teológico en torno a san Buenaventura* (Madrid: Ediciones Rialp, 1966).
20. Two other passages in Bonaventure focus on God's being and our knowledge of God: *Commentarium*, L. 1, d. 8, p. 1, a. 1, q. 2, *conclusio*; and *Quaestiones disputatae*, q. 1, a. 1, *conclusio* (in these references, L. = *lectio*, d. = *distinctio*, p. = *pars*, a. = *ad*, q. = *quaestio*). In both passages, Bonaventure argues that God is readily known by men and women when they use their faculties of intellect and will correctly.
21. Ibid., L. 1, d. 2, a. 1, q. 1, *respondeo*.
22. While Bonaventure categorically states that every human person can intellectually conclude that there is a God, Thomas Aquinas maintains both the possibility and the limits of the human intellect *vis-à-vis* the knowledge of God. See John Wippel, *The Metaphysical Thought of Thomas Aquinas* (Washington, DC: Catholic University of America Press, 2000), 501–75.
23. *Commentarium*, L. 1, d. 2, a. 1, q. 1, *respondeo*; L. 1, d. 2, a. 1, q. 2. The *quaestio* is only two pages in length.
24. Bonaventure's formal treatment of the Trinity begins in *Commentarium*, on p. 53 and ends on p. 859. See *Quaestiones disputatae*, q. 1, a. 1, *respondeo* ad 9; *Disputed Questions*, 121–37.
25. Bonaventure, *Quaestiones disputatae*, q. 1, a. 1, *respondeo* ad 9; *Disputed Questions*, 121–37.
26. Cf. John P. Dourley, "The Relationship between Knowledge of God and Knowledge of the Trinity in Bonaventure's *De mysterio Trinitatis*," *San Bonaventura maestro di vita francescana e di sapienza cristiana*, II (Rome: Pontificia Facoltà Teologica "San Bonaventura," 1976), 41–48.
27. See R. H. Rouse and M. A. Rouse, "The Verbal Concordance of the Scriptures," *Archivum Fratrum Praedicatorum*, 44 (1974), 5–30. In this article the authors convincingly show that there was no full-fledged biblical concordance until the end of the thirteenth century.
28. See Dominic Monti, "Bonaventure's Use of 'The Divine Word' in Academic Theology," in Michael Cusato and Edward Coughlin, eds., *That Others may Know and Love* (St. Bonaventure, NY: Franciscan Institute, 1997), 65–88; Thomas Reist, *Saint Bonaventure as a Biblical Commentator* (Lanham, MD: University Press of America, 1985); Hans-Joseph Klauck, "Theorie der Exegese bei Bonaventura," *S. Bonaventura 1274–1974*, IV: *Theologica* (Grottaferrata: Collegio S. Bonaventura, 1974), 71–128; Robert Karris, "Introduction," in *The Works of Bonaventure: Commentary on the Gospel of Luke* (St. Bonaventure, NY: Franciscan Institute, 2001), vi–xxxvii; Jacques Guy Bougerol, "Doctor Scripturae

Evangelicae," in *Introduction to the Works of Bonaventure*, 85–98; Hans Mercker, *Schriftauslegung als Weltauslegung: Untersuchungen zur Stellung der Schrift in der Theologie Bonaventuras* (Munich: Ferdinand Schöningh, 1971).

29. Bonaventure, *Breviloquium*, Prologus, n. 6. Eng. trans. by Dominic Monti as cited in Timothy Johnson's *Bonaventure: Mystic of God's Word* (Hyde Park, NY: New City Press, 1999), 43.
30. Bonaventure, *Breviloquium*, Prologus, n. 4.
31. Bonaventure, *Collationes in Hexaëmeron*, n. 7; trans. Karris, in *Commentary on the Gospel of Luke*, xxi.
32. See Andreas Speer, "Bonaventure and the Question of Medieval Philosophy," *Medieval Philosophy and Theology*, 6:1 (1997), 26–29.
33. Bonaventure, *Commentarium*, L. 3, d. 3, p. 2, a. 2, q. 1.
34. Bonaventure, *Breviloquium*, p. 3, c. 8. See also his accolades of Augustine in *Commentarium*, L. 3, d. 38, a. 1, q. 4, and L. 4, d. 44, p. 2, a. 2, q. 1.
35. Bonaventure, however, was very explicit on his non-acceptance of the Platonic positions of Avicenna and Avicebron.
36. Hayes, "Bonaventure: Mystery of the Triune God," in K. Osborne, ed., *The History of Franciscan Theology* (St. Bonaventure, NY: Franciscan Institute, 2007), 43.
37. J. de Ghellinck, *Le mouvement théologique du 12 siècle* (Louvain: Publications universitaires, 1948), 233.
38. Latin citations of these Greek Fathers are found in the writings of Peter Lombard, Gratian, and Walfrid Strabo.
39. For a reference to the importance of Dionysius, see González, *Misterio trinitario*, 197–211.
40. Paul G. Kuntz, "The Hierarchical Vision of St. Bonaventure," *San Bonaventura maestro di vita francescana e di sapienza cristiana*, II (Rome: Pontificia Facoltà Teologica "San Bonaventura," 1976), 233–48.
41. *Hexaëmeron, Collatio* 1, ad 17.
42. Ibid., *Collatio* 3, ad 2.
43. See González, *Misterio trinitario*, 212–33.
44. John F. Quinn, *The Historical Constitution of St. Bonaventure's Philosophy* (Toronto: Institute of Mediaeval Studies, 1973), 881–82; Scott Matthews, "Arguments, Texts and Contexts: Anselm's Argument and the Friars," *Medieval Philosophy and Theology*, 8:1 (1999), 84; Bonaventure, *Commentarium*, L. 1, d. 8, a. 1, q. 2, *conclusio*; *Quaestiones disputatae*, q. a. 1, *conclusio* and *solutio*, 1, 1, 3. The issue is also treated in the *Itinerarium*, cc. 1, 2, 5, 6, and 7. See Matthews, "Arguments, Texts and Contexts," 84–93, 102–03.
45. On this radical change regarding Richard's sources, see González, *Misterio trinitario*.
46. Bonaventure, *Disputed Questions*, 21–23, at 22.
47. Bonaventure, *Commentarium*, L. 2, *praelocutio*.
48. Ibid., L. 2, d. 23, a. 2, q. 3. The *Summa alexandrina* was a work in which Alexander played a leading role. Other major authors of this work were John de la Rochelle and Bonaventure.

49. Alexander, "De verbo incarnato," *Quaestiones disputatae antequam esset frater*, q. 9 (Quarrachi: Collegium S. Bonaventurae, 1960), I, 80–141. Cf. Johannes Freyer, *Homo viator: Der Mensch im Lichte der Heilsgeschichte. Eine theologische Anthropologie aus franziskaner Perspective* (Kevelaer: Butzon und Bercker, 2001), 79–81.
50. Bonaventure, *Questiones disputatae*, q. 1, a. 1, *conclusio*; *Disputed Questions*, 115.
51. Ibid.
52. Bonaventure, *Commentarium*, L. 1, d. 2, a. 1, q. 2.
53. Both Aristotle and Augustine accepted human intellect and will as correlative. Thomas Aquinas stressed the intellect over the will.
54. Bonaventure, *Commentarium*, L. I, d. 2, a. 1, q. 2, *respondeo.*
55. Ibid., L. 1, d. 28, a. 1, *titulus.*
56. Ibid., q. 1, *titulus.*
57. Ibid., *respondeo*, final paragraph.
58. Cf. Hayes, "Bonaventure: Mystery of the Triune God," 57. In this section Hayes speaks of the internal emanations which are all positive.
59. Bonaventure, *Commentarium*, L. 1, d. 28, a. 1, q. 1, *respondeo*, final paragraph.
60. Hayes, "Bonaventure: Mystery of the Triune God," 75. See Bonaventure, *Quaestiones disputatae*, q. 8, ad 7.
61. Bonaventure, *Commentarium*, L. 1, d. 28, a. 1, q. 1.
62. Ibid., L. 1, d. 28, a. 1, q. 2.
63. Ibid., L. 1, d. 2, a. 1, q. 2.
64. Ibid., L. 1, d. 31, a. 1, q. 2.
65. Ibid., L. 1, d. 31, a. 1, q. 2, *conclusio.*
66. Ibid., L. 1, d. 8, p. 2, q. 1, *respondeo* ad 1.
67. Ibid., *respondeo* ad 1.
68. Aristotle, *Metaphysics*, XI, 9.
69. Bonaventure, *Commentarium*, L. 1, d. 39, a. 1, q. 1, *respondeo.*
70. Ibid., in *respondeo.*
71. John Damascene, *Liber I De fide orthodoxa: Versions of Burgundio and Cornabus*, ed. Eligius M. Buytaert (St. Bonaventure, NY: Franciscan Institute, 1955), c. 9; Bonaventure, *Commentarium*, L. 1, d. 43, a. 1, q. 2, *respondeo*. He repeats the reference to *pelagus* in d. 45, a. 2, q. 1, *respondeo.*
72. For the relationship of Aquinas to Augustine, see Anselm Min, *Paths to the Triune God: An Encounter Between Aquinas and Recent Theologies* (University of Notre Dame Press, 2005), 125, 126, 170, 171, 174. See also Anne Hunt, *Trinity: Nexus of the Mysteries of Christian Faith* (Maryknoll, NY: Orbis, 2005), 20–23.
73. See Bonaventure, *Commentarium*, L. 1, d. 45, a. 1, q. 1; see also L. 1, d. 45, a. 1, q. 2, *respondeo.*
74. Ibid., L. 1, d. 45, a. 2, q. 1, *respondeo.*
75. Ibid., L. 1, d. 45, a. 2, q. 2, *respondeo*. The generation of the Son involves both *ratio* and *voluntas*; see ibid., L. 1, d. 6, a. 1, qq. 1–3.
76. Hayes, "Bonaventure: Mystery of the Triune God," 49, citing *Quaestiones disputatae*, q. 1, a. 2, 131.

77. Ibid., citing Bonaventure, *Hexaëmeron, Collatio* 1, 1.
78. Bonaventure, *Hexaëmeron, Collatio* 8, ad 9: "Isti sunt duae radices fidei."
79. See, for example, Bonaventure, *Commentarium*, L. 1, d. 21, a. 1, q. 2; also L. 1, d. 23, a. 1, qq. 2 and 3.
80. See Aristotle, *Categoriae*, c. 5.
81. Étienne Gilson's *The Philosophy of St. Bonaventure*, trans. Illtyd Trethowan and Frank Sheed (Paterson, NJ: St. Anthony's Guild Press, 1965), has tended to dominate the contemporary interpretation of Bonaventure, an interpretation which is now dated.
82. Bonaventure, *Breviloquium*, 2, 12.
83. See the above section on "Bonaventure's understanding of God."
84. Bonaventure, *Itinerarium*, c. 7, n. 5.
85. Bonaventure, *Commentary*, L. 1, dd. XV–XVIII.
86. I have analyzed this same distinction on the basis of John Duns Scotus in "A Scotistic Foundation for Christian Spirituality," in M. Cusato and J. F. Godet-Calogeras, eds., *Vita evangelica* (St. Bonaventure, NY: Franciscan Institute, 2006), 363–405.
87. Bonaventure, *Commentary*, L. 1, d. 15, a. 1, q. 2.

## Further reading

Bougerol, Jacques Guy, *Introduction to the Works of Bonaventure*, trans. José de Vinck (Paterson, NJ: St. Anthony's Guild Press, 1964).

Freyer, Johannes, *Homo viator: Der Mensch im Lichte der Heilsgeschite. Eine theologische Anthropologie aus franziskanischer Perspective* (Kevelaer: Butzon und Bercker, 2001).

Gilson, Étienne, *The Philosophy of St. Bonaventure*, trans. Illtyd Trethowan and Frank Sheed (Paterson, NJ: St. Anthony's Guild Press, 1965).

González de Cardedal, Olegario, *Misterio trinitario y existencia humana: studio histórico teológico en torno a san Buenaventura* (Madrid: Ediciones Rialp, 1966).

Hayes, Zachary, "Bonaventure: Mystery of the Triune God," in K. Osborne, ed., *The History of Franciscan Theology* (St. Bonaventure, NY: Franciscan Institute, 2007), 39–125.

Hellmann, Wayne, *Divine and Created Order in Bonaventure's Theology* (St. Bonaventure, NY: Franciscan Institute, 2001).

Osborne, Kenan, *A Theology of the Church for the New Millennium: A Franciscan Approach* (Leiden: Brill, 2009).

"Trinitarian Doctrine: 500 to 1500 AD," in Joseph R. Strayer, ed., *Dictionary of the Middle Ages* (New York: C. Scribner's Sons, 1989).

# 8 The Trinity in the Protestant Reformation: continuity within discontinuity

YOUNG-HO CHUN

## THE BIBLE AS THE "EXCLUSIVE" SOURCE OF REVELATION AND THE "ONLY" AUTHORITY

The sixteenth-century Protestant Reformation, which is considered by many to be one of the most important events in the history of Christianity, was much indebted to the Renaissance. There is a wisecrack that Erasmus laid the egg and Luther hatched it. In the view of many of the most ardent Reformers, this humorous saying, however, may be an overstatement. There is a sizable consensus that the Reformation was connected to the Renaissance only to the extent that it restricted the Renaissance's call to return to the ancient sources (*ad fontes*) to an acceptance of the Bible as the exclusive source of faith (*sola scriptura*). This principle solidified the normative authority of the Bible for all things theological and liturgical in the life of the church. The power of the Word was directly related to the power of the message of the Bible. According to the Reformers, the gospel message had to be emancipated from the oppressive authority of the Roman Catholic Church and its tradition, and thereby was set free to work directly on human hearts.

October 31, 1517 is commemorated by various Protestant churches as "Reformation Day." This is the day when Martin Luther (1483–1546) posted the Ninety-Five Theses (propositions for debate) in Wittenberg. The first of these propositions reads: "When our Lord and Master Jesus Christ said 'Repent,' he willed the entire life of believers to be one of repentance." The subtext of this thesis was the abuse of the sacrament of penance in the Roman Catholic Church through the selling of indulgences. The proposition appealed to the higher authority of scripture – the message of Jesus as recorded in the gospels – against the long-standing sacramental and penitential practices of the Roman Catholic Church.

According to the Reformers, no practice or teaching of the church could claim to possess divine authority unless it had the word of the holy Bible to back it up. The holy Bible became the exclusive principle for everything ecclesial: dogma, liturgy, catechism, the pastoral care for the dead, the content of the preaching, including the episcopacy and the papacy. Accordingly, Reformation theologians identified themselves as *biblical* theologians.[1]

What exactly does "biblical" mean? Something such as a word or concept is biblical if it is actually present in the Bible and, as a consequence, authoritative.[2] The issue is not merely semantics, but rather it has to do with God's self-revelation and how the Bible narrates this divine self-disclosure. For Calvin, any church practice not commanded by the Bible had to be forbidden.[3] This presupposition shaped the Protestant Reformation's approach to the theological curriculum for clergy formation. A learned member of the clergy was defined as one who was well trained in the biblical languages and equipped to preach expository sermons of the Bible on the basis of a thorough knowledge of both Testaments. The Bible became what it had not been before, that is, "a doctrine in its own right."[4] "The sole authority of the Bible stood as the line of demarcation between Protestantism and Roman Catholicism."[5]

But if the doctrine of *sola scriptura* defined and delimited the scope of what was properly theological and ecclesial, then how could a fundamental theological concept, such as the Trinity, which is in important respects extra-biblical, become not only accepted by Luther and Calvin, but central and essential to their faith? The doctrine of the Trinity developed by Luther and Calvin shows that they plumbed the wisdom and theological insights of the previous generation of theologians as they developed their own distinctive views. This sheds some light on non-exclusive adherence to the "exclusive principle" of *sola scriptura* in the Reformation doctrine of the Trinity.

Because of the limited space available here, we will discuss only the trinitarian theology of John Calvin, whose theological work has had a definitive influence on Reformed theologians, and that of Martin Luther, the founder of the Lutheran tradition. The principal task is to show the main characteristics, styles, perspectives, and tendencies in Luther's and Calvin's writings on the Trinity. What is presented here is by no means exhaustive and does not claim to do justice to the richness of their contributions.

## LUTHER'S THEOLOGY OF THE TRINITY

We begin by pointing out two interesting facts about Luther's theological development. First, he was not a systematic theologian, as such. Oswald Bayer notes that Martin Luther did not write any systematic theological work like Philipp Melanchthon's *Loci communes* or Thomas Aquinas' *Summa theologiae* (*The Summa of Theology*). Systematic thinking was alien (*fremd*) to him.[6] Second, his theology arose out of a deep engagement with scripture, especially with the Old Testament. In fact, Luther began his teaching career by lecturing on the Psalms.[7] A biblical scholar, he translated the Bible into German in a mere eleven weeks while he was confined in Wartburg Castle. The primary rhythms of Luther's life as an Augustinian monk were provided by spiritual practices, especially daily prayers using the Psalms. Consequently, he paid scholarly attention to the Psalms in a special way; it was only natural that his first lecture course was on the Psalms, and this marked the beginning of his lifelong fascination with the Old Testament. These proclivities provide an important clue to the unique character of his theology, which linked closely the pulpit of the church and the academic lectern of a university lecture hall. He preached as both a monk and a professor till the end of his life, whenever opportunities were offered, especially in the castle church of Wittenberg.

According to Christine Helmer, biblical engagement shaped Luther's theological contribution, most importantly for our purposes "his discovery of the Old Testament for trinitarian theology."[8] As Kendall Soulen points out, Christian trinitarian theology tends to pass over God's identity as the God of Israel in order to emphasize the trinitarian God as Father, Son, and Holy Spirit. But the Old Testament, with its doctrine of the dynamic presence of YHWH as "speaker," has profound implications for trinitarian theology. Where there is a speaker, there emerge triadic relations: the speaker, the hearer, and the message. Helmer reminds us of the important fact that Luther was greatly influenced by the Hebraic approach to discourse on God, not only as it appears in the Old Testament narratives but also as it is manifested in the Hebrew language itself.

The exclusive principle of *sola scriptura* led Luther to reject as unbiblical the medieval doctrine of the sacraments, and to deny any authority to the pope and the councils. But, as shown in his tract *Von den Conciliis und Kirchen* (*On the Councils and Churches*, 1539) and the three symbols (creeds) of 1538, Luther's attitude toward the ancient dogmas was a positive one. He acknowledged and frequently reiterated Nicene doctrine of the Trinity and the Chalcedonian Christology. He regarded them with great respect, especially the Apostles' creed, which, he declared, contains all the principal articles of faith. At first, Luther objected to the word "Trinity," declaring that it "sounds cold" and was "discovered and invented" by human beings.[9] Luther's position was that dogmas are true only insofar as they agree with the holy scriptures; otherwise they have no authority. His insistence on the exclusive principle of *sola scriptura* may have contributed to him making his hermeneutics of the creeds dependent upon scripture, rather than acknowledging that creeds do help us frame and understand scripture.

The last academic disputation of which Luther was in charge took place on July 3, 1545. Luther prepared the theses for this event. Theses 1 to 17 are about the doctrine of the Trinity,[10] and they show that Luther retains much of the medieval theological heritage. The theme of these theses is Christ as "the Wisdom of the Father." The question of the nature of the Son as *sapientia patris* was often discussed in medieval theology, because Augustine had found it problematic and dealt with it in detail in *De Trinitate* (*On the Trinity*), VI.1–7 and VII.1–6.[11] The issue at hand here has to do with whether this is an essential predication or an indicative of a relational expression between the Father and the Son. According to thesis 16, "Father," "Son," and "Spirit" are relative concepts, from which the presence of a real "other" can be inferred. They are terms that signify a relation of two different members. The Father is Father because he generates; he does not generate because he is Father. The distinct things indicate the relations between them (thesis 14).

What are the sources for Luther's theses? Of course, Luther knew Augustine's *On the Trinity*, the *Sententiae in IV libris distinctae* (commonly known as the *Sentences*) of Peter Lombard, and Gabriel Biel's commentary on the *Sentences*.[12] And as noted above, he accepted the three symbols of the Christian faith: the Apostles' creed, the creed of St. Athanasius, and "the Nicene Symbol."[13] In questions of trinitarian theology, Biel closely followed William of Ockham's commentary on the *Sentences*, in which Aquinas and Henry of Ghent were frequently criticized. Thus Luther knew the trinitarian theologies of Ockham, Henry of Ghent, and Aquinas, at least by way of Biel. It is likely that he had also studied Ockham and Aquinas at first hand. As a professor of theology, he must also have been acquainted with the trinitarian teachings of important synods and councils.[14]

Luther's *De servo arbitrio* (*The Bondage of the Will*, 1525) is significant.[15] It was this book, along with the 1535 *Galatervorlesungen* (*Lectures on Galatians*), that Luther himself treasured most highly. More important, this work most clearly exemplifies Luther's approach to God in terms of relational power. At the outset (prologue), Luther associates the concept of power with that of freedom. Erasmus uses this association to argue that if man has no effective freedom, that is, no power to do good before God, then God's will must be in part evil, since sin exists in the world. Luther's response contains a subtle nuance: man is not free to contribute to his salvation. It is God who has the power, that is, freedom to act with complete effectiveness in this world, and it is man's will that is evil, that is unfree and in bondage to sinful human nature. God's power is to be understood not as a speculated quality in God Godself, but as an *active relation* to the human, as understood in Hebrew thought.

Luther's functional understanding of God indicates that *God is in himself what God does in us*. In this sense God *is* active power. Luther understood the divine essence in terms of God's active presence.[16] We see this most clearly in Luther's works on the Lord's Supper (1527–28), in which he identifies God's essence with power. God's omnipotence is identified with God's active omnipresence. It is on the basis of God's active omnipresence (that is, omnipotence) that, in Christ, God can be essentially present and powerfully active in the Lord's Supper.[17] In his various writings, the systematic assumption of God as *act* – as free presence and power – seems to dominate Luther's thinking. For Luther, the power and presence of God are manifest in and through the Son and the Spirit, although in different ways. The Son represents the "formal" or "wisdom" *dimension*, while the Spirit represents the "love" or "goodness" *dimension* of the Trinity. It is the Christ who is our teacher (the formal or wisdom function), and it is the Holy Spirit who is the new energy living in us (the love or goodness function). The Son represents wisdom, and the Spirit love.

Thus in Luther the functions of Christ and the Spirit become rather sharply differentiated. Luther insists that Jesus Christ is the only means of access to the knowledge of God and that Christ is "the only God there is" ("for us," to be precise). A comparable attribution occurs with regard to the work of the Holy Spirit. Luther normally holds that the Spirit instills the love of Christ in our hearts (Rom 5:5). But against "spiritual" opponents, Luther also stresses the work of the Holy Spirit in terms of order. He says that the true function of the Holy Spirit is to stir up an internal conflict between the corrupt peace of the "old man" and the true peace which is the indwelling Christ. The true function of the Holy Spirit is to bring God's kingdom, God's peace and order, out of humanity's disorder.[18] In his commentary on Galatians 3 Luther says that the Holy Spirit is given only through the hearing of the Word or gospel. The Holy Spirit is the *gift* brought by means of the *preached and heard Word* of God. The Holy Spirit is what the Word brings. It brings with it certain knowledge of God and of oneself, which entails the forgiveness of sins.[19] Forgiveness of sins means that the proper order between the human being and God is restored. It means that the disordered, false relation to God in terms of works-righteousness is replaced by God's order: overcoming the desires of the flesh by the Spirit.[20] For example, commenting on Galatians 5:10, Luther picks up the theme of the Holy Spirit as the love of God, but develops it in terms of the Christian love of neighbor.[21] The basic theme in Luther is that the Holy Spirit, operating wholly in and through the preached Word, certifies forgiveness of sins – the love of God – in our hearts, and in so doing insures the ordered harmony of God's love among the community of her people.

Luther repeatedly affirms that *God is present for us*, and that God's nature and will are made known only in Christ the Word. He is so deeply taken up with this notion that he unguardedly overstates: "Apart from Christ, there is no God" – even "no Godhead."[22] Knowledge of the Triune God is thus possible not just through the "second Person," the form, wisdom, or logos of the Trinity, but through the *incarnate* Christ. For Luther, Christ is not just the disembodied Word, the second person of the Trinity, but the incarnate, suffering Christ of Galilee. It is because this Christ is both hidden and revealed, both physical and spiritual, that Luther is able to speak of God in similar fashion. Because of their consubstantiality, what is true of Christ is true of God. Thanks to this concentration on the incarnate Christ, Luther's theology is inclined toward fusing the transcendence of God and the natural (immanent) world without abrogating the boundary line between them. This results in de-emphasizing the metaphysical distinctions of God from the world. It is the unity of the God–world relationship, as seen in Christ's incarnation, that provides a basic clue to understanding Luther's theological epistemology, doxology, and soteriology.

This perspective on consubstantiality most clearly appears in Luther's discussion of the Lord's Supper and the gift or application to us of Christ's atoning work. He understands the nature of God the Father, God the Son, and God the Spirit in terms of activity. It is in Christ's body *broken for us* that God personally reveals Godself. The God revealed there is the Triune God. Thus for Luther, human beings are connected to God in Christ only through the mediating work of the Holy Spirit, that is, through the reception of faith, the hearing of the Word, and participation in the sacraments. Not only is Christ the only "place" where the transcendent Triune God is immanently present for us, but God is present for us only where and when there exists the community of faith, formed by Christ's Word and ordered by the Holy Spirit to receive God in the church.

A special characteristic of Luther's theology is the distinction he makes between "a theology of glory" and "a theology of the cross."[23] The thesis of the theology of the cross is that "God can be found only in suffering and the cross," so that "he who does not know Christ does not know God hidden in suffering."[24] Luther's theology of the cross is a polemic against a theology of glory as well as against the prevalent theological method of scholasticism, which is accused of treating the truths of the Christian faith as objects of intellectual curiosity, without reference to the cross and benefits of Christ. Specifically, for Luther, the dogmas of the Trinity and the person of Christ are not exercises in logical inquiry or metaphysical speculation. In the same vein, Melanchthon declares, "to know Christ is to know his benefits."[25] For Luther, God the Redeemer is clearly and definitively manifested in Christ the Word. God has no other form in which to be found than the form of God's Word, that is, Christ, who thus reveals the justice, the righteousness, and the glory of God. But the glory of God is anything but obvious; Christ is the emptied form of God, now taking the form of a slave or servant, without losing his divine connaturality with God the Father and God the Spirit.

Divine glory is unlike human glory. It appears hidden under its opposite. Christ's divinity manifests itself in his self-differentiation from, not withstanding his union with, God the Father, who begets him in love. God is power and freedom, yet acts through weakness and bondage, so that we human beings can experience his redemptive power and liberating grace (forgiveness) in faith, even while we are still enmeshed in suffering, guilt, and bondage to sin. God is always *pro nobis* and, hence, *pro me*. This "I" is an old "I." The old "I" is sinful, curved in upon itself, existing in a hellish, distanceless self-conversation – entirely *incommunicative*. In the being of Jesus Christ, God gives Godself entirely to us. God gives Godself with everything that God is and does, what God has, and what lies in God's power, without condition and reservation. In union with the being of Christ who eternally communicates with the other persons of the Trinity in a *perichoretic* relationship, the new "I" becomes and lives as an entirely *communicative* being. We are incorporated into God's community through God's self-gift to us.[26]

For Luther, God's very being is self-giving. This self-giving is not an automatic expression of the divine nature, but rather an attentive "response" of God's *hearing* of the wretched human condition. God's hearing means salvation, which takes place historically in the incarnation, death, and resurrection of Jesus. The doctrine of the Trinity contains nothing other than the gospel. The gospel is the event of salvation and liberation. It is the freedom that Christ has won for us and has brought to us. Christ continues to promise and to communicate this freedom to us by his presence as God's Word in the Holy Spirit.

Here is an important challenge of Luther's teaching. As Oswald Bayer puts it: "*It is absolutely important to distinguish between the doctrine of the Trinity and a 'general' doctrine of God linked to anthropology*. The two distinct doctrines cannot be collapsed into each other."[27] In concluding his interpretation of the Christian faith in the *Grosser Katechismus* (*Large Catechism*), Luther makes this distinction: "Although the whole world has sought painstakingly to learn what God is and what he thinks and does, yet it has never succeeded in the least . . . even though [monotheists] believe in and worship only the one, true God, nevertheless, [they] do not know what his attitude is toward them. They cannot be confident of his love and blessing." Even the Ten Commandments, Luther goes on to say,

> do not by themselves make us Christians. . . . But here, you have everything in richest measure. In these three articles God himself has revealed and opened to us the most profound depths of his fatherly heart, his sheer, unutterable love. He created us for this very purpose, to redeem and sanctify us. Moreover, having bestowed upon us everything in heaven and on earth, he has given us his Son and his Holy Spirit, through whom he brings us to himself. As we explained before, we could never come to recognize the Father's favor and grace were it not for the Lord Christ, who is a mirror of the Father's heart. Apart from him we see nothing but an angry and terrible Judge. But neither could we know anything of Christ, had it not been revealed by the Holy Spirit.[28]

Luther adds: "Apart from him [Christ] we see nothing but an angry and terrible Judge." This is the God outside the Triune God who is entirely love. "To look for God outside of Jesus is to encounter the devil."[29] The general doctrine of God, distinguished from the doctrine of the Trinity, thematizes the human being prior to encountering Christ. The general doctrine of God is linked to the experience of the Law that accuses and kills. It finally reaches beyond the accusing Law to the experience of the incomprehensible, terrible hiddenness of God. Luther's challenge to contemporary theologians is how not to turn the doctrine of the Trinity into a general doctrine of God derived from anthropology.

Although self-consciously stringent in applying his exclusive principle of *sola scriptura* to his theological and ecclesial agenda of reforming the church, Luther reached back into the theological and spiritual treasures of the church's teaching as he formulated his view of the Trinity. He embraced "continuity" of theological wisdom even in his reformative "discontinuity."

## CALVIN'S TRINITARIAN THEOLOGY

John Calvin's reform has generally been acknowledged to represent a more radical break from the medieval Roman Catholic Church in worship, polity and theology. John Calvin (1509–1564) first wrote his *Christianae religionis institutio* (*Institutes of the Christian Religion*) as a small catechism for lay people. Eventually, through numerous revisions, it grew considerably larger and its contribution to the trinitarian theology became distinctive.

The 1559 edition of the *Institutes* is considered to be the definitive one. Anyone acquainted with the scholastic treatises on the Trinity, especially that of Thomas Aquinas, would be struck by the departure from their style. Rather than making a logically rigorous argument for a particular doctrine, for instance, asking how the one God can also be three persons, Calvin presents a biblically based exposition that largely avoids philosophical terminologies, even though he did not reject traditional terms such as *ousia*, *hypostasis*, *essentia*, *substantia*, and *homoousios*.

Scholars disagree as to how different Calvin's theology of the Trinity is from the traditional view. Robert Reymond argues that Calvin departs from "Nicenetrinitarianism."[30] Edward Dowey, Jr., argues that Calvin's view of the Trinity adheres to the principle of *sola scriptura* because it is "exclusively biblical in origin."[31] In contrast, others maintain that Calvin's trinitarian theology is traditional: that is to say, it is grounded in certain extra-biblical traditions that assist his appropriation of the biblical witness. François Wendel regards Calvin as "carefully avoiding anything that could have been considered an innovation," because the traditional teaching on the Trinity is an essential part of his theology.[32] Wilhelm Niesel says that Calvin "took over from the early church fathers the doctrine of the Trinity with all the theological equipment that accompanied it" and that his whole purpose in this doctrine was to secure the biblical message.[33] Michael O'Carroll finds Calvin, of all Protestants, to have formed "the fullest, most evidently traditional and orthodox Trinitarian theology."[34] T. H. L. Parker agrees that, from as early as 1536, Calvin was "perfectly orthodox" and further reports that, as he matured, Calvin found that "the orthodox doctrine of the Trinity said precisely what he himself wanted to say."[35]

We take the 1559 edition of the *Institutes* as the basis of our discussion of Calvin's trinitarian theology.[36] The table of contents of this definitive edition reveals four basic parts, which appear to follow roughly the order of the Apostles' creed (I: Father, II: Son, III: Holy Spirit, IV: church).[37] Though the Trinity cannot be comprehended apart from Christ's revelation and the work of the Holy Spirit, the doctrine is fully worked out in book I, while the treatment of Christ is located in book II and that of the Holy Spirit in book III. This suggests that Calvin may not have intended the *Institutes* to be a *systematic* treatise of all the Christian doctrines in relation to one another in a manner reminiscent of Thomas Aquinas. It may not be called a *summa theologiae*, but a *summa pietatis*.[38] This is an important key in evaluating Calvin's thought on the Trinity.

Robert Letham makes a strong claim that from this edition it is clear that "the Trinity is [Calvin's] doctrine of God."[39] This may be an overstatement, but it definitely points to a significant departure from Aquinas' separation of his treatment of the one God from his discussion of the Trinity. There is no detailed discussion in the *Institutes* of the existence, nature, or attributes of God, which the teaching of the Christian tradition on God presupposes. Nevertheless, it may be said that the trinitarian doctrine is so integral to Calvin's understanding of God that the whole *Institutes* has a trinitarian structure. In fact, the Apostles' creed provides, as noted above, the structure of the *Institutes*.[40] Although Calvin's basic tendency is to emphasize the unity of God, he devotes much space in his treatment of God to the divinity of the Son[41] and the Holy Spirit.[42] Calvin's focus on the three divine persons does not, however, undermine the unity of God, for he takes it as axiomatic that God's being is one. The three divine persons are distinct, not divided from each other.[43]

In his discussion of the three divine persons, Calvin refers to a wide range of biblical passages from both Testaments in support of the divinity of the Son. He also draws much support from the Fathers. According to the mature Calvin, there is no gradation in the Godhead, though earlier he had been charged as "Arian" by Pierre Caroli in 1537 (on the basis of the 1536 edition) and challenged in various ways by Michael Servetus after 1531.

In keeping with patristic and medieval teaching, Calvin regards God the Father as the *principium*. "To the Father as the fountain and well-spring of all things is attributed the beginning of activity; to the Son, wisdom, counsel, and the ordered disposition of all things; to the Holy Spirit, the power and efficacy of that activity." In all God's works, the three act together in concert.[44] But in these activities there is a clear order. It is a relational order. The Father is first; from him is the Son; and from both is the Spirit. For this reason, "the Son is said to come forth from the Father alone; the Holy Spirit, from the Father and the Son at the same time."[45] Thus, it is permissible to state that "in respect to order and degree, the beginning of divinity is in the Father." "The Father is first in order . . . the beginning and fountainhead of the whole of divinity."[46] Of course, this order is relational, not temporal.

Because Calvin's theology of the Son was developed in the heat of his disputes with the Italian anti-Nicenes Michael Servetus and Valentine Gentile,[47] it is quite complex. In his *Expositio impietatis Valentini Gentilis* (*Exposition of the Impiety of the Pagan Valentinus*), he frequently refers to the Son as *autotheos* ("God of himself").[48] This strongly signals his opposition to any idea that the Son receives his divinity from the Father. Calvin holds that the Son has his divinity from himself, just as the Father does. This is in opposition to Gentile's teaching in 1558 that the Father alone is *autotheos*, so that the Son and the Holy Spirit are of a different essence from the Father. Such a view[49] is vulnerable to the Sabellian heresy as well as to Manichaeism. But Calvin clearly teaches that the Son is of himself in respect of essence, not of person. On this point, Calvin even received support and sympathy from Robert Bellarmine, a Roman Catholic theologian, who argued that the reason why Calvin said that the Son is *autotheos* was that he was driven to it by Gentile.[50]

What did Calvin mean by this term? On the premise that God is one and indivisible, it follows that all three persons share in the one identical and undivided being of God. Thus the Son cannot be said to derive his divinity from the Father. Where does that leave the classic notion that the Son is eternally begotten of the Father? And the notion of the eternal procession of the Holy Spirit? Gentile's criticism was that Calvin cannot maintain his notion of *autotheos* together with the affirmation of the Niceno-Constantinopolitan creed. The eternal generation of the Son and the procession of the Holy Spirit are incompatible with Calvin's notion of *autotheos* of the Son and the Holy Spirit. To this criticism, Calvin states:

> Indeed, if we hold fast to what has been sufficiently shown above from Scripture – that the essence of the one God is simple

> and undivided, and that it belongs to the Father, the Son and the Spirit; and on the other hand that by a certain characteristic the Father differs from the Son, and the Son from the Spirit – the gate will be closed not only to Arius and Sabellius but to other ancient authors of errors.[51]

According to Calvin, in the Son, "with respect to his divinity, his being is from himself." The anti-Nicenes held that the Father alone has the being of God and imparts this essence to the Son. But Calvin says, with respect to the essence, that there is no distinction between the Father and the Son.[52] Yet he says that we can still hold to the distinct, eternal relations among the persons, since we do not separate the persons from the essence, but rather distinguish them while they remain within it. Calvin concludes:

> Therefore we say that deity in an absolute sense exists of itself; whence likewise we confess that the Son, since he is God, exists of himself, but not in respect of his Person; indeed, since he is the Son, we say that he exists from the Father. Thus his essence is without beginning; while the beginning of his person is God himself.[53]

The Word was eternally hidden in God before he was revealed in the creation of the world, but his *hypostasis* is distinct from the Father while he is of the same essence as the Father, "concealed in God."[54] Christ the Son is also distinct from the Holy Spirit.[55] Consequently there is a distinction of persons in God. Calvin holds that the incarnate Son is "the only-begotten 'in the bosom of the Father.'"[56] The notion of a "continuous act of begetting" as found in Origen was taken by Calvin as "foolish," since the relation is eternal.

Calvin accepts the eternal procession of the Holy Spirit from the Father and the Son, a teaching which he anchors in chapter 8 of Paul's letter to the Romans.[57] With regard to the full divinity of the Holy Spirit,[58] it is relatively underdeveloped in comparison to that of the Son. When it comes to the question of the *filioque*, Calvin was clearly Western and Augustinian. Gerald Bray argues that this is at the heart of Calvin's theology and central to evangelical Protestantism.[59]

Both Christ and the Holy Spirit are called by the same name, *paracletos* ("comforter"), for it is their common task to comfort, exhort, and guard us by their patronage. As long as he lived in the world, Christ was our patron. Then he committed us to the patronage of the Holy Spirit.

Christ, however, is still our patron. After all, it is Christ who communicates, as the mediator, his life to us "by the power of his Spirit."

The whole divine nature is possessed by each divine *hypostasis*.[60] Referring to John 14:10, Calvin states that "the Father is wholly in the Son, the Son wholly in the Father."[61] The same is expressed in Calvin's commentary on John 17:3. Calvin uses the phrase *in solidum* to attest the three persons' sharing completely and equally in the one being of God. This entails their mutual indwelling.[62] The Holy Spirit is the bond of the Father and the Son.[63]

Although Calvin insisted that all doctrines must be founded on the teaching of the Bible, he did not break with the Catholic doctrine of the Trinity in any fundamental way. He supports the church Fathers' use of terms such as *hypostasis* and *ousia*, in order to defend the biblical teaching.[64] He is far from rejecting the Nicene creed, which expresses the consubstantiality of the Son with the Father through the *homoousion* clause, and accepts the eternal generation of the Son before all time. Thomas F. Torrance argues that Calvin has a close theological kinship to Augustine, Gregory of Nazianzus, and Athanasius.[65] Letham contends that if there is any innovation in Calvin's trinitarian theology, it may have to do with the *form* of the expression, not the *content*. Guided by the church Fathers and specific luminaries of the Roman tradition, Calvin restores a more biblical expression to trinitarian doctrine and reduces speculative abstraction.

After all is said and done, Calvin's focus is on the economic activity of the divine persons. His basic question is: what does this teaching on the Trinity have to do with our "righteousness"? Calvin makes it clear that our righteousness is brought about by Christ: "You see that our righteousness is not in us but in Christ, that we possess it only because we are partakers in Christ: indeed, with him we possess all its riches."[66] What do we receive when we are joined to Christ (*unio cum Christo*)? We receive a form of his *filial relationship*[67] with the Father and all that it includes. Christ's perfection lies in the unbroken relationship he maintained with the Father. It is to Christ's relationship to the Father that we are united; by it we are justified, for the justified life is the *filial* life in relation to the Father.

Calvin's theological thinking reflects his Christian piety. The latter frames his arguments for the divinity of the Son and the Holy Spirit, which appeal primarily to their exhibited works or powers.[68] This is a typical mark of all Reformation theology; that is to say, proper evangelical theology concerns itself only with God who is *pro nobis* (for us), God who acts with regard to his world and people.[69] God is discussed only in his actions in relation to his people. Thus biblical and theological thinking is essentially relational.

This *pro nobis* character of God should not be taken as a permission to domesticate the transcendent nature of the Triune God who loves us in freedom.[70] It does not allow us to project onto God what we most desire concerning the character and nature of God who "works" for our salvation. This may be a challenge to certain contemporary theological movements which at times tend to articulate the divine character and nature from the standpoint of sociological and psychological findings and hypotheses.

European Protestantism was divided into three main families.[71] Of these Lutheranism and Calvinism represent the two main traditions in early Protestantism. Calvinism, as we have noted, claimed to be a more thorough and consistently biblical reformation than Lutheranism. Ironically, however, Calvinism has produced more splits, often over insignificant differences and issues. It spawned varieties of theological liberalism such as unitarianism and antitrinitarianism. By contrast, Lutheranism has produced relatively few heresies. The Reformation claimed as its *raison d'être* a greater fidelity than traditional Roman Catholicism to the biblical message and historical Christianity. Nevertheless, ironically, the Reformation produced far more doctrinal chaos than the church had experienced since the second century.

## SUMMING UP

In the history of theological reflection on the Trinity, one encounters time and again problems related to the theology and philosophy of language. These problems are inevitable in any attempt to translate the ancient terminology such as *ousia* and *hypostasis* into contemporary language. While this focus on linguistic issues is still significant for contemporary trinitarian theology, it may divert our attention from its fundamental connection with the biblical revelation and lead to an impoverished understanding of the relevance of the Trinity for worship, the theology of the sacraments, and moral theology.

Neither Calvin nor Luther, by virtue of their fundamentally biblical orientation and grounding, engaged in the scholastic method of theological reflection on the Trinity. Rather they were predominantly biblical in their approach to this doctrine. Consequently, their theologies of the Trinity are cast in a soteriological framework. What differentiates one from the other is that Calvin's lens is *theo*logical whereas Luther's is *Christo*logical. What unites them is their existential (soteriological) rather than metaphysical approach.

Oswald Bayer distinguishes two types of theology.[72] He calls the first type, which is geared toward proclamation, "the monastic model." The second type, "the scholastic model," has an emphasis on thinking. Proclaiming God and thinking of God should not of course be divorced from each other, nor should they be collapsed into each other. A viable articulation of the Trinity requires a close dialogue between the two. The monastic type of theology, which is appropriate for worship, needs the rational structure of scholastic theology in order to remain true. On the other hand, the scholastic type of theology would be sterile if it were not linked to the worshiping community where the Trinity is adored and celebrated in the liturgy, the sacraments, and hymns. Both types of theology need each other, so that, in Bayer's words, "the monastic theology will not become blind and the scholastic theology empty."[73] Both Calvin and Luther demonstrate a balance between these two types of theological reflection, perhaps with a bias toward the monastic model, compared with their predecessors' predilection for the scholastic approach. Since then Protestant reflection on the Trinity has made a conscious effort to anchor it in Christology and soteriology.

Another lesson from the Reformers' theologies of the Trinity has to do with their (at times unarticulated) method. In doing theology they take into account its double demand, namely, faithfulness to the biblical sources and relevance to the human condition. This balance between the two poles is an important mark of an evangelical theology that is rooted in the Reformation tradition. This is still a viable guide and a useful criterion by which contemporary theologians can evaluate their own constructive theological endeavors in claiming, naming, and renaming the Trinity.

## Notes

1. *Luther's Works*, American Edition, ed. Jaroslav Pelikan and Helmut T. Lehman, 55 vols. (St. Louis: Concordia Publishing House, 1955–). Thirty volumes, more than half of the entire set, are devoted to Luther's commentaries on the Bible, twenty to the Old Testament and ten to the New Testament. Luther also wrote many other biblical works that are not included in this edition. Similarly John Calvin composed commentaries on every book of the Bible except the book of Revelation. He regarded his *Christianae religionis institutio (Institutes of the Christian Religion*), which first appeared in 1536, as a biblical exposition of the Apostles' creed.

2. K. Greene-McCreight, "When I Say God, I Mean Father, Son and Holy Spirit: On the Ecumenical Baptismal Formula," *Pro ecclesia*, 6:3 (1997), 296.
3. For Luther, however, any church practice not commanded by the Bible may be permitted but may not be required.
4. Jaroslav Pelikan, *Whose Bible is it? A History of the Scriptures through the Ages* (New York: Penguin Group, 2005), 166.
5. Ibid.
6. Oswald Bayer, *Martin Luthers Theologie*, 3rd edn. (Tübingen: Mohr Siebeck, 2007), vii.
7. *D. Martin Luthers Werke: Kritische Gesamtausgabe*, ed. J. R. F. Knaake et al., 69 vols. (Weimar: Hermann Böhlaus Nachfolger, 1883–1999), and *Luther's Works*, American Edition. These two resources are cited depending upon each text's availability and preferability. See *Luthers Werke*, III, 11–652, and IV, 1–526 (*Dictata super Psalterium*, 1513–16); *Luthers Werke*, V, 19–673 (*Operationes in Psalmos*, 1519–21); *Luthers Werke*, XL/2, 193–312 (*Enarratio Psalmi II*, 1532–46); *Luthers Werke*, XL/2, 315–470 (*Enarratio Psalmi LI*, 1521/38); *Luthers Werke*, XL/2, 472–610 (*Praelectio in Psalmum 45*, 1532/33); *Luthers Werke*, XL/3, 9–475 (*Vorlesung über die Stufenpsalmen*, 120–34, 1532–33/40); *Luthers Werke*, XL/3, 484–594 (*Enarratio Psalmi XC*, 1534–35/41).
8. Christine Helmer, "Luther's Trinitarian Hermeneutic and the Old Testament," *Modern Theology*, 18:1 (January 2002), 60. See also R. Kendall Soulen, "YHWH the Triune God," *Modern Theology*, 15:1 (January 1999), 25–54. Soulen diagnosed the supersessionist trinitarian model where "the God of Israel is made ultimately dispensable for the purpose of articulating God's eternal identity and God's enduring and universal purposes for creation" (47).
9. Luther's works, Erlangen edn., VI, 230, and XII, 378, cited in Reinhold Seeburg, *The History of Doctrines*, trans. Charles E. Hay, 2 vols. (Grand Rapids, MI: Baker, 1977), II, 303.
10. *Luthers Werke*, XXXIX/2, 339–40.
11. Augustine, *De Trinitate*, ed. W. J. Mountain and F. Glorie, Corpus Christianorum, Series Latina, 50 (Turnhout: Brepols, 1968). For a detailed treatment of this, see Simo Knuuttila and Risto Saarinen, "Innertrinitarische Theologie in der Scholastik und bei Luther," in O. Bayer et al., eds., *Caritas Dei: Festschrift für Tuomo Mannermaa zum 60. Geburtstag* (Helsinki: Luther-Agricola-Society, 1997), 243–64.
12. Gabriel Biel, *Collectorium in quattuor libros Sententiarum*, ed. W. Werbeck and U. Hofmann (Tübingen: J. C. B. Mohr, 1973–79).
13. *Luther's Works*, XXXIV/4, 197–229.
14. For a perspective on the medieval background of Luther's trinitarian theology, see Simo Knuuttila and Risto Saarinen, "Luther's Trinitarian Theology and its Medieval Background," *Studia theologica*, 53 (1999), 3–12.
15. Martin Luther and Desiderius Erasmus, *Luther and Erasmus: Free Will and Salvation*, ed. and trans. E. Gordon Rupp and Philip S. Watson, Library of Christian Classics, 17 (Philadelphia: Westminster, 1969).

16. This is apparent in his writings *The Bondage of the Will* (1525), *The Exposition of Jonah* (1526), and the works on the Lord's Supper (1527 and 1528).
17. *Luther's Works*, XXIII, 133–49.
18. Cf. ibid., XXVI, 202–26, 374, XXVII, 3 ff., 97 ff.; *Lectures on Galatians* (1535), chs. 3.2–5, 4.6, 5.16, and 5.25. Here one can see Luther's own full and systematic presentation of the work of the Holy Spirit in relation to Christ. See also Regin Prenter, *Spiritus creator*, trans. John Jensen (Philadelphia: Muhlenberg, 1953) for a detailed discussion of Luther's doctrine of the Holy Spirit.
19. *Luther's Works*, XXVI, 213.
20. Ibid., XXVI, 215.
21. Ibid., XXVII, 65 ff.
22. Ibid., XXXVII, LVI and LXI.
23. Luther, *Heidelberg Disputation*, 19–21 (*Luthers Werke*, I, 354).
24. Luther, *Heidelberg Disputation*, 21 (*Luthers Werke*, I, 362).
25. Philipp Melanchthon, *The Loci communes of Philipp Melanchthon (1521)*, trans. Charles Leander-Hill (Boston: Meador, 1944), 63.
26. Luther, *Confession concerning Christ's Supper* (1528), *Luther's Works*, XXXVII, 366 (*Luthers Werke*, XXVI, 505): The Triune God "has given himself to us all wholly and completely, with all he is and has" ("such uns allen selbst ganz und gar gegeben hat mit allem, was er ist und hat").
27. Oswald Bayer, "Poetologische Trinitätslehre," in Joachim Heubach, ed., *Zur Trinitätslehre in der lutherischen Kirche*, Veröffentlichungen der Luther-Akademie Sondershausen Ratzeburg 26 (Erlangen: Martin Luther Verlag, 1996), 67–79; Eng. text in *Lutheran Quarterly*, 15 (2001), 43–58.
28. Luther, *Large Catechism*, in *The Book of Concord: The Confessions of the Evangelical Lutheran Church*, trans. and ed. Theodore G. Tappert (Philadelphia: Fortress, 1959), 419–20; German text in *Die Bekenntnisschriften der evangelisch-lutherischen Kirche*, 11th edn. (Göttingen: Vandenhoeck & Ruprecht, 1992), §660, lines 23–27; §661, lines 30–33, 36–42 respectively.
29. Commentary on Ps 130:1 (1532/33), *Luthers Werke*, XL/3, 337, 1: "Extra Iesum deum quaerere est diabolus."
30. Robert L. Reymond, *A New Systematic Theology of the Christian Faith* (New York: Nelson, 1998), but in the second edition he corrects this claim. See a critical article of Paul Owen, "Calvin and Catholic Trinitarianism: An Examination of Robert Reymond's Understanding of the Trinity and his Appeal to John Calvin," *Calvin Theological Journal*, 35 (2000), 262–81.
31. Edward A. Dowey, Jr., *The Knowledge of God in Calvin's Theology* (Grand Rapids, MI: Eerdmans, 1994), 125–26, 146.
32. François Wendel, *Calvin: The Origin and Development of his Religious Thought*, trans. Philip Mairet (London: Collins, 1987), 168–69.
33. Wilhelm Niesel, *The Theology of Calvin*, trans. Harold Knight (Grand Rapids, MI: Baker, 1980), 54–57.

34. Michael O'Carroll, *Trinitas: A Theological Encyclopedia of the Holy Trinity* (Collegeville, MN: Liturgical Press, 1987), 194.
35. T. H. L. Parker, *The Doctrine of the Knowledge of God: A Study in the Theology of John Calvin* (Edinburgh: Oliver and Boyd, 1952), 61–62. See also Jan Koopmans, *Das altkirchliche Dogma in der Reformation* (Munich: Chr. Kaiser Verlag, 1955), 66–75; Benjamin Breckinridge Warfield, "Calvin's Doctrine of the Trinity," in Samuel G. Craig, ed., *Calvin and Augustine* (Philadelphia: Presbyterian and Reformed, 1974), 187–284; Philip Walker Butin, *Revelation, Redemption, and Response: Calvin's Trinitarian Understanding of the Divine–Human Relationship* (New York: Oxford University Press, 1995).
36. John Calvin, *Institutes of the Christian Religion*, ed. John T. McNeill, trans. Ford Lewis Battles, 2 vols., Library of Christian Classics, 20–21 (Philadelphia: Westminster, 1960). For a proper approach to Calvin's *magnum opus*, see Elsie Anne McKee, "Exegesis, Theology, and Development in Calvin's *Institutio*: A Methodological Suggestion," in Brian G. Armstrong, ed., *Probing the Reformed Tradition: Historical Studies in Honor of Edward A Dowey, Jr.* (Louisville, KY: Westminster John Knox, 1989), 154–72.
37. Paul Jacobs, *Praedestination und Verantwortlichkeit bei Calvin* (Neukirchen: Buchhandlung des Erziehungsvereins, 1937), is organized I: Trinity; II–III: soteriology; IV: ecclesiology. The four divisions are more readily visible in his French Catechism of 1541.
38. A. M. Hunter, *The Teaching of Calvin* (London: James Clarke and Co., 1950), 296, suggests that we should evaluate *Institutes* as a work of piety.
39. Robert Letham, *The Holy Trinity: In Scripture, History, Theology, and Worship* (Phillipsburg, NJ: P. & R., 2004), 253.
40. The Apostles' creed is patterned on the Trinity. Parker outlines the growth of a pervasively Trinitarian cast to Calvin's theology which was based on the Apostles' creed. See Parker, *The Doctrine of the Knowledge of God*, 61–69.
41. Calvin, *Institutes*, I.13.7–13.
42. Ibid., I.13.14–15.
43. Ibid., I.13.17.
44. This echoes Augustine's perspective. Augustine's first achievement was to stress that the activity of the Trinitarian persons, flowing from their unity, was inseparable. Cf. Augustine, *Letters*, 169, in *Nicene and Post-Nicene Fathers*, ed. Philip Schaffand Henry Wace (repr. Peabody, MA: Hendrickson, 1994), I, 541 (*Patrologia latina*, XXXIII, 740–41). This text shows how the persons of the Trinity are distinct, and particular actions are attributable to particular persons, while, at the same time, the being (and work) of the Trinity is indivisible.
45. Calvin, *Institutes*, I.13.18.
46. Ibid., I.13.24–25. This is very clear in Calvin's catechetical work *Le catechisme de l'église de Genève* (Latin version, *Catechismus ecclesiae Genevensis*) published in 1545, in question 19. He is speaking here of the relations of the persons, not of the one divine essence or being.

47. John Calvin, *Opera quae superunt omnia*, ed. William Baum, Edward Cunitz, and Edward Reiss, 59 vols., Corpus Reformatorum, 29–87 (Brunswick: C. A. Schwetschke, 1863–1900), IX: 368–70.
48. I am much indebted to Letham, *The Holy Trinity*, 256–57.
49. Calvin, *Institutes*, 1.13.19, 23.
50. Robert Bellarmine, "Secunda controversia generalis de Christo," in *Disputationes de controversiis Christianae fidei adversus haereticos* (Rome: Ex Typographia Bonarum Artium, 1833–40), I, 307–08, 10. Bellarmine recognized that, in the terms of classic trinitarian dogma, Calvin was orthodox. Calvin's novelty was in his terminology, his manner of speech (*modus loquendi*).
51. Calvin, *Institutes*, 1.13.22.
52. Ibid., 1.13.23.
53. Ibid., 1.13.25. Calvin cites here Augustine in support, from his commentary on Psalm 109:13. See *Nicene and Post-Nicene Fathers*, VIII, 542 ff. (*Patrologia latina*, XXXVII, 1457), and also Augustine, *De Trinitate*, trans. Edmund Hill (Brooklyn, NY: New City Press, 1991), book V.
54. John Calvin, *Calvin's Commentaries: The Gospel According to St. John 1–10*, trans. T. H. L. Parker, ed. David W. Torrance and Thomas F. Torrance (Edinburgh: Oliver and Boyd, 1959), on Jn 1:1–3.
55. Ibid., on John 14:16.
56. Calvin, *Institutes*, 1.13.17, 23–25.
57. Ibid., 1.13.18.
58. Ibid., 1.13.14–15.
59. Gerald Bray, "The *filioque* Clause in History and Theology," *Tyndale Bulletin*, 34 (1983), 91–144.
60. Calvin, *The Gospel According to St. John 11–21*, on Jn 17:21.
61. Calvin, *Institutes*, 1.13.19.
62. Thomas F. Torrance, *The Christian Doctrine of God: One Being, Three Persons* (Edinburgh: T. & T. Clark, 1996), 194–202. See also Nonna Verna Harrison, "*Perichoresis* in the Greek Fathers," *St. Vladimir's Theological Quarterly*, 35 (1991), 53–65. The Greek word *perichōrēsis* has often been rendered in Latin as either *circumincessio* or *circuminsessio*, which in turn translated into English as "co-inherence," "mutual indwelling," or "mutual containment," etc. The doctrine of "co-inherence," or "circumincession," means that each of the *hypostaseis* is a complete manifestation of the divine essence. It also implies that every divine attribute applies equally to all three *hypostaseis*, i.e., all are omnipotent, omniscient, omnipresent/eternal.
63. Calvin, *Institutes*, 1.13.19; cf. 23.
64. Calvin, *The Gospel According to St. John 1–10*, on Jn 1:1.
65. Thomas F. Torrance, "The Doctrine of the Holy Trinity in Gregory Nazianzen and John Calvin," in *Trinitarian Perspectives: Toward Doctrinal Agreement* (Edinburgh: T. & T. Clark, 1994), 21–40. Cf. Gregory of Nazianzus, *Orations*, 40, 41, cited by Calvin in *Institutes*, 1.13.17. Anthony N. S. Lane, *John Calvin: Student of the Church Fathers* (Grand Rapids, MI: Baker, 1999), 1–13, 83–86, dampened this thesis by producing evidence that Calvin hardly read Gregory of Nazianzus. Lane's

distance from Torrance's thesis seems to be dictated by his stringent rule of a direct citation.

See Owen, "Calvin and Catholic Trinitarianism," 271. For a more balanced assessment, see Johannes van Oort, "John Calvin and the Church Fathers," in Irena Backus, ed., *The Reception of the Church Fathers in the West: From the Carolingians to the Maurists* (Leiden: Brill, 1997), II, 661–700.

66. Calvin, *Institutes*, 3.1.1 and also 3.11.23.
67. This notion of "filial relationship" has been appropriated by many Chinese and Korean theologians who aim for indigenous Christian constructive theology with Confucian heritage. Confucianism grounds a sound perspective on life in the society (in the cosmos) on the five basic relationships. A "filial relationship to one's father" is one of the fundamental ways of being in the world. See, for instance, Tu Wei-ming, *Confucian Thought: Selfhood as Creative Transformation* (Albany: State University of New York Press, 1990).
68. Calvin, *Institutes*, 1.13.9–15.
69. Ibid., 1.13.21.
70. Karl Barth helps us to make a wonderfully apt characterization of God as "One who loves in freedom." See Karl Barth, "The Being of God as the One who Loves in Freedom," in *Church Dogmatics*, II/1: *The Doctrine of God*, trans. G. W. Bromiley (Edinburgh: T. & T. Clark International, 2004), 257, and also Karl Barth, *God Here and Now*, trans. Paul M. van Buren (London and New York: Routledge, 2003), 4.
71. "The lines of division and the distinctions between them are often vague and somewhat arbitrary, but it is convenient to group the early Protestants into two main 'magisterial' branches and to divide the 'radicals' into two groups. The magisterial Reformation falls into Lutheran and Reformed (or Calvinist) branches. It may be possible to call Anglicanism a third branch, but inasmuch as it was theologically influenced by the Calvinist Reformation, especially at the beginning, and was rather different from Lutheranism, we may place the early Anglicans among the Reformed.... The radical Reformation involved a tremendous variety of doctrinal and disciplinary positions, but it makes sense to subdivide it into those groups that were radical in their life-style and discipleship, but conservative in their doctrine – such as the Mennonites and Baptists – and those who embraced antitrinitarianism or other marked heresies." See Harold J. Brown, *Heresies: The Image of Christ in the Mirror of Heresy and Orthodoxy from the Apostles to the Present* (New York: Doubleday, 1984), 340–41.
72. Oswald Bayer, *Theologie: Handbuch systematischer Theologie*, ed. Carl Heinz Ratschow, I (Gütersloh: Gütersloher Verlaghaus, 1994), 27–31.
73. Ibid., 28.

## Further reading

Barth, Karl, *Church Dogmatics*, I/1: *The Doctrine of the Word of God*, trans. G. W. Bromiley (Edinburgh: T. & T. Clark, 1975).

Bayer, Oswald, *Martin Luther's Theology: A Contemporary Interpretation*, trans. Thomas H. Trapp from *Martin Luthers Theologie*, 3rd edn., 2007 (Grand Rapids, MI: Eerdmans, 2008).

Bielfeldt, Denis, et al., *The Substance of the Faith: Luther's Doctrinal Theology for Today*, ed. and intro. Paul R. Hinlicky (Minneapolis: Fortress, 2008).

*The Book of Concord: The Confessions of the Evangelical Lutheran Church*, trans. and ed. Theodore G. Tappert (Philadelphia: Fortress, 1959).

Calvin, John, *Institutes of the Christian Religion*, ed. John T. McNeill, trans. Ford Lewis Battles, 2 vols., Library of Christian Classics, 20–21 (Philadelphia: Westminster Press, 1960).

Dowey, Edward A., Jr., *The Knowledge of God in Calvin's Theology* (Grand Rapids, MI: Eerdmans, 1994).

Helmer, Christine, *The Trinity and Martin Luther: A Study on the Relationship between Genre, Language and the Trinity in Luther's Works (1523–1546)*, Veröffentlichungen des Instituts für Europäische Geschichte, Abteilung Abendländische Religionsgeschichte, 174 (Mainz: Philipp von Zabern, 1999).

Heubach, Joachim, ed., *Zur Trinitätslehre in der lutherischen Kirche*, Veröffentlichungen der Luther-Akademie Sondershausen-Ratzeburg, 26 (Erlangen: Martin Luther Verlag, 1996).

Letham, Robert, *The Holy Trinity: In Scripture, History, Theology, and Worship* (Phillipsburg, NJ: P. & R., 2004).

Luther, Martin, *Luther's Works*, American Edition, ed. Jaroslav Pelikan and Helmut T. Lehman, 55 vols. (St. Louis: Concordia, 1955–), esp. III, XXVI, XXVII, XXXVII, XXXVIII.

Melanchthon, Philipp, *The Loci communes of Philipp Melanchthon (1521)*, trans. Charles Leander Hill (Boston: Meador, 1944).

Moltmann, Jürgen, *The Trinity and the Kingdom of God: The Doctrine of God*, trans. Margaret Kohl (San Francisco: Harper & Row; London: SCM Press, 1981).

Niesel, Wilhelm, *The Theology of Calvin*, trans. Harold Knight (Grand Rapids, MI: Baker, 1980).

Torrance, Thomas F., *The Christian Doctrine of God: One Being, Three Persons* (Edinburgh: T. & T. Clark, 1996).

# 9 Between history and speculation: Christian trinitarian thinking after the Reformation

CHRISTINE HELMER

That the Christian dogma of the Trinity has a history, meaning that it was not given entirely, once and for all, by revelation, was one of the most profoundly transformative and consequential claims for Christian theology in the post-Reformation period. But contemporary theology has recast this history of the dogma of the Trinity in a way that is at variance with the development of post-Reformation thought. The "ditch" between history and revelation has been reopened, to put this briefly. In the words of the Orthodox theologian Pavel Florensky: "the single word *homoousios* expressed not only a Christological dogma but also a spiritual evaluation of the rational laws of thought. Here rationality was given a death blow."[1] Now, as Florensky and others propose, the Trinity's story is plotted as the death of "rationality." The specific concepts employed to articulate how three things can be one thing (*tres res sunt una res*, the classic medieval proposition for the Trinity) are seen as having been, from the very origins of the doctrine's development, a defiance of human reason. In this account, revelation wins the battle with reason, and faith is victorious over history.

One term – contextualized exclusively by the Christian dogma of the Son's eternal co-equality with the Father – subverts the entire semantic field of language's capacity to refer to reality and the logic underlying this referential capacity. The interruption of reason by language used theologically creates a new system for relating language, thought, and reality, and in this way, the trinitarian axiom of a Christian theological system is pitted against the psychological, anthropological, and philosophical constituents of any human rational system.

I will refer to this historical narrative, with its theological authorizations, that pits revelation against its binary opposite, reason, as the "received" story. Much is at stake in seeing the history of the doctrine of the Trinity as conceptually constructed by binary opposites, namely Christian orthodoxy as a received single tradition. Hence it is told in the drama of historical protagonists fighting to establish the boundaries of Christian orthodoxy and heresy against their opponents, in polemical relationship to each other. To put the matter of stakes another way, the Trinity is taken to be the dogma by which Christianity, or one normative account of Christianity, stands or falls.

Challenges to the received story have recently come from history (as indeed they have done since the eighteenth century). New historiographies are calling the struggle between orthodoxy and heresy into historical question. Recent studies in New Testament and ancient Christianity, in particular, see the initial development of Christianity in social, religious, political, and gender perspectives that effectively challenge a simple theological either-or.[2] Already in the early nineteenth century Friedrich Schleiermacher was plumbing the second and third centuries CE for an interpretation of developing trinitarian thinking that ran alongside what would later become the dominant Athanasian doctrine of the Trinity.[3] Schleiermacher's fate, alas, was sealed in the history of Christianity by his suspect trinitarian view. Yet his call to historical-critical examination of Christian origins remains. We have arrived back at a Schleiermacherian moment: the traditional boundaries of orthodoxy and heresy are being complicated by new historical visions that will inevitably have radical implications for the designation of trinitarian orthodoxy in the future. It may even be that trinitarian theologies will see new aspects to God's infinite being, which is always more interesting than a dominant theology can define.

I intend in this chapter to develop another story about the Trinity in the history of post-Reformation thought. The received story that sees the Trinity as a triumph of orthodoxy represents the Enlightenment as eroding the fundamental doctrinal pillars of Christianity. Yet this caricature of the Enlightenment (singular, whereas historians have recently shown the multiplicity over time and space of the protean movement), with its concomitant demand among cultured despisers of modernity that Christians resist it, must be questioned as to its representation of what happened. While this is an undertaking beyond the scope of this chapter, my goal here is to adumbrate another story, messier than the received history of binary opposition. This alternative story, rather than demarcating the boundary between revelation and reason in antithesis, considers the far-reaching and exciting contributions of the Trinity to modern thinking. This entails a reinterpretation of Trinity in relation to Enlightenment.

I develop this alternative history chronologically, beginning with its anticipations in Luther and turning next to the interaction between history and system in eighteenth-century Protestant Orthodoxy and

Pietism. I end with the trinitarian systems of Georg Wilhelm Friedrich Hegel and Friedrich Schleiermacher. I argue that these paved the way for the Trinitarian "renaissance" in twentieth-century theology. The culmination of this revised story is the Trinity as the fundamental axiom of theological systems; trinitarian theology free from the rejection of modernity is the result of post-Reformation efforts to think creatively through the Trinity between history and speculation.

## HISTORICAL SEMANTICS: LUTHER'S EXAMPLE OF THE *HOMOOUSIOS*

My starting point is the sixteenth-century Reformation, in particular an incident in Martin Luther's later life that indicates his increasing awareness of the historicity of trinitarian-theological terms. Although a similar story can also be found in John Calvin's dealings with Michael Servetus, I use Luther to detect the beginnings of a historical semantics in the Reformation, anticipating new possibilities of relating Trinity to its history.

Toward the end of his life, between 1542 and 1545, Luther held four disputations on a topic unusual for him. The Trinity, a doctrine that the Reformer contended was never implicated in his conflict with Rome, was under attack, Luther averred. The disputation of 1543 records how Luther himself conceptualizes the Trinity in such a way as to open up, on historical grounds, the diversity of terms available to refer to the Trinity. His immediate historical context gives evidence of emerging differences in how the Trinity of the Christian God was coming to be interpreted. Luther writes, "Our adversaries . . . are fanatics about words, because they want us to demonstrate the truth of the trinitarian article to them, just as they wanted the Arians to do, by asking us to assent to the term *homoousios*."[4] Luther articulates here surprising flexibility about a precise technical trinitarian term. *Homoousios* cannot be taken as the transhistorical guarantor at the linguistic level about the intra-trinitarian relations. Rather the term is used adequately only when it is understood to convey the co-equality of the subjects Father and Son to which it refers. For Luther the *res* has priority over its corresponding *verbum*.

This disputational record illustrates how Luther situates theological articulation in a broader philosophical theory about language, which is meaning, and referent. The privileging of *res* over *verbum* represents Luther's theory about language, particularly explicit in his semantic theory. A term's meaning is designated by its interrelations with other terms; this meaning renders the term's capacity to refer to a subject that is experienced, understood, and known. The theological contextualization of the language–subject relation is of particular concern to Luther in relation to the Trinity. The primary challenge presented by trinitarian terms is their referent in eternity. Trinitarian terms, such as *homoousios*, are for Luther a "stammering" and "babbling." The terms refer to a subject in eternity, but are unable to convey any meaning beyond the most minimal determination. The semantics of eternity and co-equality are oddly introduced as the meaning of terms that are inevitably tensed and differentiated as separate "things." Luther's response to this theological case of a philosophical problem is not to create an entirely new theo-logic that would explain the trinitarian relations. Rather Luther makes use of the disputations to clarify an adequate meaning of the doctrine and to separate true from false interpretations by appealing to philosophical tools, logic, semantics, and metaphysics. Trinitarian terms, even terms taken as referring to an eternal subject, are not ahistorical foils to rationality, but are articulated in history in order that their meanings can be explored, determined to some extent, and understood, at least a bit.

The issue of semantics would turn on the historical meanings of trinitarian terms and conceptions in Bible, creed, and theological tradition. Although Luther and Calvin appealed to semantics in order to come up with arguments for the Trinity's truth, they did not go as far in pressing a historical semantics as some of their contemporaries and later theologians did. The Reformers still assumed that the normative texts of Bible, both Old Testament and New Testament, and creeds, equivocated between their trinitarian referent. Different terms in Hebrew, Greek, and Latin were still taken in the same sense of the *homoousios* dogma.

The equivocation was increasingly questioned. The divine referent described in the Hebrew Bible, the "God of Israel," could not be seen on historical grounds as semantically identical with either the "proto-trinitarian" God of the New Testament (e.g., the trinitarian benediction in 2 Cor 13:13 and the baptismal formula of the Great Commissioning in Mt 28:28) or the explicitly articulated Trinity of the fourth-century Niceno-Constantinopolitan creed. The breakdown of semantic unity had to do with the growing awareness that a historicized semantics was required in order to understand the Trinity in relation to its history. The development of unitarian views of the Christian God are implied by these Reformation and early post-Reformation developments in contextualizing the historical-cultural meanings of trinitarian conceptions.[5] This historicized semantics opened up new metaphysical possibilities of conceiving the eternal distinctions in God and their relations to world history. If meanings of trinitarian concepts differed in history, then their accompanying metaphysic would require revision. History and speculation would become the two interwoven story lines of the Trinity's post-Reformation history.

## SYSTEM AND SALVATION: PROTESTANT ORTHODOXY AND PIETISM

New views of empiricism and rationalism drove the search for knowledge in the seventeenth and eighteenth centuries, in the protean "Enlightenment," in Berlin and Paris, Edinburgh and Boston. A consensus of the received story of Christian ideas pits reason against revelation. Whether or not doctrinal content is deemed "above reason," maybe even "contrary to reason," Christian mystery is trumped by reason. The question is not whether but the extent to which accommodation must occur; not whether it must, but how fierce the resistance.

But another story can be told about the Trinity in the Enlightenment. By studying two ecumenically representative Christian theologies in the seventeenth and eighteenth centuries, we can see how the idea of Trinity was developed under the cultural conditions of deepening methodological consciousness about speculation and experience. I begin this section by showing how Protestant theologians articulated the Trinity as a function of their doctrinal systems. The theological task in post-Reformation orthodoxies, Lutheran, Reformed, and Roman Catholic, was shaped by, as it contributed to, the developing requirements for academic (*wissenschaftlich*) rationality as system, and the Trinity's place in these systems was integral to a broader cultural-philosophical effort to set up the system as the paradigm of scientific knowledge. I conclude this section by showing how Pietist traditions pressed historical and experiential dimensions of Christianity in ways that were expressive of cultural-philosophical efforts to secure the limits and possibilities of reason in relation to experience. Sometimes the doctrine of the Trinity challenged these limits; sometimes the limits were applied to trinitarian claims. Nevertheless, this alternative story explores how the Trinity was creatively integrated into ways of thinking and experiencing congruent to modernity's development.

### Trinity and system in Protestant orthodoxy

The idea of "system" is immensely important for understanding how the Trinity is contextualized in post-Reformation thinking. This importance is, first of all, historical. The genre in which Protestant orthodox theologians conceived their theologies was the system. Their systems were the immediate blueprint for Friedrich Schleiermacher's *Der christliche Glaube* (*The Christian Faith*, 1820 and 1830–31), recognized as the foundational text of modern theology. Consensus still continues to claim system's advantage for presenting theological knowledge, although in recent theology, system's capacity for comprehensiveness is called into question on experiential grounds. The historical significance of system, moreover, immediately implies a constructive-theological impact. Although Protestant orthodoxy is commonly seen as a "systematizing" movement, organizing the occasional and literarily diverse writings of the Protestant Reformers, its connection to the cultural-philosophical emergence of system casts its theological development in the light of seventeenth-century academic (*wissenschaftlich*) thinking.

The sixteenth-century Reformer Philipp Melanchthon was the first link to subsequent systematization. His *Loci communes*, begun in 1521 and emendated until as late as 1543, organized the main theological topics (*loci*) as they are treated in Paul's letter to the Romans. Subsequent theological construction leaves this exegetical format behind: post-Reformation theologies are self-consciously constructed as systems that explicitly follow rules of formal construction. This systematization of theological truths was predicated on the broader philosophical consensus that system fulfills the requirements for knowledge (*scientia* in Latin; *Wissenschaft* in German). From the earliest geometric systems constructed as strict logical deductions from axioms, to the later systems that adapted deductive demonstration to the subject matter of history, such as religion, systematization represented the Western academic form for organizing ideas. Its culmination was achieved by Gottfried Wilhelm Leibniz, the founder of the Prussian Academy of Sciences, who pronounced "C'est là, mon système" upon completion of his *Monadologie*. From this point on, "scientific" means "systematic," and for theology, this identification is no exception.

The systematic assignment of the Trinity in Protestant orthodox systems is connected to the crucial question regarding the Bible and the Trinity that was opened in the sixteenth century.[6] The system gave theology a solution to the terminological discrepancies that Luther had already encountered. The prolegomena to the system, itself an idiosyncratic outcome of the Reformation, circumscribed theology's nature and task, particularly as the task's requirements and sources were determined by scripture. Although this circumscription is commonly assumed to be determined by confessional polemics between Lutheran,

Reformed, and Roman Catholic traditions, its contextualization in cultural-philosophical questions of systematic construction is of even greater significance. System as the developing form of scientific thinking implied adaptation by different disciplines defining their respective subject matters, particularly if that subject matter could not be strictly deduced from axioms, as was the case with any discipline relying on the interpretation of historical texts. A significant and long-lasting achievement of Protestant orthodoxy is the highly developed doctrine of scripture. The scriptures were the "given" foundations of theology, and their implications for distinct theological methods therefore required clarification.

Theology's subject matter was considered a reality, given in scripture, and explicated by the doctrines of God and the Trinity. These two doctrines were located in part I of orthodox systems, right after the prolegomena in the section entitled "Doctrine of God, the goal [*finis*] of theology." Prolegomena and part I were intimately connected by the realist preoccupation with theology's subject matter. Theology's final goal is the divine *res*, God, and as such this goal establishes the rationale for integrating Bible and doctrine. Hence the fundamental structural unity between Bible and theology is established by their consistent subject matter; the problem of disparate historical semantics between Bible and Trinity is solved conceptually by identity in the subject. Further, the structuring principle of God as final cause attributes to theology its scientific status as a practical discipline, aligned with the natural sciences by their justification in experience.[7] All practical disciplines require the analytic method to study the discrete parts implied by and contained in the overarching unity for the discipline.[8] In the case of theology, the use of philosophical tools, particularly logic and dialectic, is oriented theologically toward theology's final cause.

The way in which the doctrine of God was intricately related to the Trinity in these systems demonstrates how theologians used reason to fit the explication of revelation's content. Metaphysical understanding of God, primarily causality, and metaphysical attributes, for example unity and infinity, were discussed first under the doctrine of God. These metaphysical determinations were then explicitly connected in the subsequent section on the Trinity to the divine essence constituting the Trinity. Furthermore, the works of God, primarily creation and providence, were located after an explication of the Trinity. By this systematic link theologians showed that the works reveal the unity of the essence that is itself constituted by the three persons. In this way, the divine essence was not divorced from the Trinity, and the three persons were not separated from the works they performed in consort. Metaphysical reason served as the handmaid of theological reason.

Leibniz definitively moved Protestant orthodoxy's commitment to system to its academic apex. A recent excellent work by Maria Rosa Antognazza discusses Leibniz, a lifelong Lutheran, and his work on the Trinity, which was articulated from a systematic perspective. The methodological distinction between explanation and comprehension gave Leibniz the theological room he needed to investigate the trinitarian mystery, freeing him to explain the meanings of terms that in and of themselves were ambiguous.[9] His writings were often occasioned by numerous dialogues with advocates of unitarian or non-trinitarian understandings of God,[10] and they demonstrated his adaptation of philosophical reason to explain the Trinity theologically. His responses took the form of clarifying the connection of a metaphysical distinction between divine intellect and will to the three persons as they were commonly acknowledged by the psychological trinitarian model from the church Fathers: as power, wisdom, and love.[11] When his nephew Friedrich Löffler attempted to deduce the Trinity according to a strict geometrical model, Leibniz reworked the model to account for the revealed truths of scripture as they were interpreted by church teaching.[12] Leibniz held together Bible and trinitarian tradition by contextualizing both in a system that adjusted reason in view of revelation and used the Trinity to integrate historical elements into the system.

The trinitarian story so far shows how Protestant orthodox systems carefully connected historical and revealed elements with metaphysical claims in order to explain, not comprehend, the Trinity. Later theological development, particularly beginning with Schleiermacher, sought to distinguish between historical and rationalist claims, thereby limiting the extent to which metaphysical reason could be adapted for theology. I treat Pietism in the next section to show how the use of critical reason opened the possibility for understanding the Trinity in history.

### Trinity and history in Pietism

The history of the doctrine of the Trinity that I am developing here necessarily includes Pietism, the ecumenical Christian movement that transgressed confessional boundaries in the seventeenth and eighteenth centuries. Pietism's aim was to establish Christianity as a transformation of the heart, and to this end it incorporated mystical and devotional strands from the Reformation as well as classic texts from Christian history in order to precipitate the "warming of the heart" felt by Christians experiencing the immediacy of a living relationship with Christ. Yet its theology is often viewed as the "anti-intellectual" antidote or alternative to the rationalist systems of Protestant orthodoxy. This misconception is slowly being revised as scholarship takes note of the deep connections between Pietism and the Enlightenment's focus on individuality.[13] If the Enlightenment is synonymous with the development of modern subjectivity, then Pietism must be said to contribute in a significant way toward understanding the person, both human and divine.

Subjectivity is the hallmark of Western modernity, and its primary distinguishing characteristic is individualism; Pietism's employment of the Bible's metaphor of the heart appropriated (as it contributed to the development of) this crucial dimension of modern Western culture for Christianity. Pietist theologians, from the earlier Johann Arndt to the later "father" of Pietism, Philipp Jakob Spener, took the cultivation of a true and living personal Christian faith as an essential component of the reform of Christian communities. Deeper Christian commitment follows the transformation of the individual by his or her personal relationship with Christ, a relationship cultivated through personal piety and education. Within Pietism, the motto of the Reformation, *sola scriptura*, was understood as endorsement of the capacity of persons to discover biblical truths; from this came the practice of *Losungen*, biblical passages selected at random and interpreted to speak God's will directly into the personal circumstances of individual lives. The cultivated Pietist heart was to be transformed in this way by immediate contact with the subject matter of scripture. Personal engagement with the scriptures was experience with the text's *res*, that is, God and the divine will. The Trinity would be framed from this experiential perspective.

Modern notions of subjectivity rely on the distinction between inner and outer, which is likewise the key distinction in the modern historicist paradigm: in this latter instance between the outer change of history and its inner metaphysical constancy. This is Lessing's "ugly ditch" between the historical and the rational. Immanuel Kant's work arises in the context of Pietism that opened up the historical as the realm of religious experience. This problem facing Pietism and later taken up by Kant is the problem of the historical as related to the principle of unity or self-sameness through time, which is the realm of the speculative. How do you relate the historical to the speculative?

The way Pietism responded to this challenge was to follow Luther's sacramental understanding that the outer conveys the inner; the word, however limited, conveys the thing. The philosophical problem of Lessing's "ugly ditch" becomes less of an issue for Christian theology in its Pietist expression, which saw the inner core of subjectivity tied closely to its outer appearances. This is so for human and for divine subjectivity: the inner core of subjectivity is accessed by outer "works" or functions. One result of this scheme is that the outer is privileged as a legitimate and necessary area of study. Pietism's great contribution to modern reason is that the experience of redemption opens up the historical as the subject of intellectual study. The encounter with Jesus is constitutive of Pietist interiority, and the outpouring of the Spirit is responsible for historical transformations; and so the study of church history, scripture, and ancient devotional and mystical texts becomes a vehicle for understanding the way of God in history. Historical criticism was launched by Pietism, beginning with Johann Albrecht Bengel's critical edition of the New Testament (1734) and his influential *Gnomon Novi Testamenti* (*Exegetical Annotations of the New Testament*) of 1742. Pietism thus contributed to the appreciation of Christianity as a historical religion, for the application of historical methods to Christian truth (although these methods were devised with "historical" as a theological term relating to experience as transformative encounter, whereas history in positivist terms would subtract the human component and turn history into a study of the past).

Yet the terms of "system" require bringing unity to historical change. Pietism's own speculative tendency has had implications for creative trinitarian thinking. The preoccupation with history as the realm of divine agency, available to individual access, frees the "inner" from "outer" biblical and doctrinal constraints and opens it to mystical and visionary experience. Count Nicolas von Zinzendorf had a Jesus-centered piety that did not detract from a "doctrinal novelty" to see the Spirit as Mother, thereby implying a marital relation between Father and Spirit.[14] Two later figures, Jakob Boehme and Friedrich Christof Oetinger, moved even further in speculation, both preceding and influencing the early nineteenth-century thought of G. W. F. Hegel and F. W. J. von Schelling. Boehme moved speculation in the controversial direction of theogonic narrative. Oetinger, like Bengel, a Pietist from Swabia in southwest Germany, was on a lifelong quest for truth of the Bible that led in a speculative direction integrating kabbala with Trinity.[15] Such visionary strands emerged from Pietism, a broad idiom that moves between tempering speculation by rooting it in scripture on the one hand, and a speculative creativity not stymied by fixation on correct orthodox formulation on the other.

Post-Reformation Pietism and Protestant orthodoxy contributed to the fundamental shaping of speculation and history in particular relationship, with implications for the Trinity. Protestant orthodoxy oriented Bible, metaphysics, and theology to the trinitarian *res*, and articulated these relations by system. Pietism, oriented by the question of subjectivity, led to a preoccupation with history, developed by parameters of critical reason that limited speculative doctrines of the Trinity, but also opened up creative visions by virtue of individual inspiration without doctrinal constraint. Western reason subsequently, down to the present, would be experimenting with system and science, history and critical reason, so that the history of trinitarian reflection is a history of the articulation of a mystery that opens up possibilities of language and thinking, in distinct cultural and philosophical forms.

## SPECULATION AND HISTORY IN POST-KANTIAN SYSTEMS

In post-Kantian systems, the trinitarian question, problematized by the question of the relation of language to reality, is extended into the quest for system-building. This was in explicit engagement with emerging historical consciousness, in terms of psychological individuality, national consciousness, and world history. History in this post-Kantian context emerged as the new metaphysic; any system now was held to the requirement of conceptualizing the reality of historical change in relation to speculative factors determining the constancy of agency in history, whether human, political, or divine.

The two major exemplars of the modern system are Georg Wilhelm Friedrich Hegel and Friedrich Schleiermacher, who dominate the ways in which modern philosophical and theological thought are conceived as system. It is customary to see the two in conflict, and indeed they were hostile colleagues at the University of Berlin. They represent two different ways of constructing a system as the integration of speculation and history by assigning to the Trinity both metaphysical and epistemological functions.

### Hegel's speculative trinitarian thought

Post-Kantian system sought to bring together the two realms of nature and spirit, two metaphysically distinct realms (in Kant's formulation), one determined by the laws of natural causality, the other by the laws of freedom. The post-Kantians were looking for a system to integrate one with the other, for a metaphysical system that would unite them while still accounting for their difference. This quest for systematic integration in German Idealism and its outcomes had the greatest repercussions for understanding the Trinity.

Leibniz helped in this context by proposing his solution of the metaphysic of power and appearance, with power providing the underlying unity of distinct appearances of a *res* in time. This metaphysic functioned for Hegel (as it did for Schleiermacher too) as the means of integrating the system of thought (Idealism or the concept) with the system of being (Realism or history). Unity, for Hegel, is based on the assumption of an ontological point of indifference between both binary opposites, the point where nature is indifferent to freedom; by this assumption, the construction of system follows by reconstructing the route that the concept, or underlying unity, takes as it emerges into its opposite, the appearances, and as it returns to its origin. In Hegel's understanding of Christianity as the religion that most adequately measures up to the systematic requirement of correspondence of thought and being (in Hegel's terms, "the consummate religion"), the Trinity is seen as the primary ontological structure that can explain the reason for the concept's necessary emergence into the history of appearances.

Hegel's Trinity is constitutive of system. Two studies of Hegel's Trinity, by Cyril O'Regan and Peter Hodgson, agree in this regard, particularly with respect to Hegel's speculative philosophy, which transposes temporal representation into the speculative concept.[16] By this move, the speculative concept, which is the metaphysical power underlying all reality, integrates history into a speculative narrative that is able to integrate time and infinity as reciprocally determining. Hegel accomplished this unity by appealing to his Lutheran orthodox theological commitment that the finite is capable of circumscribing the infinite (the motto *finitum capax infiniti* was one of the defining Lutheran theological issues in the late eighteenth century), most particularly in the incarnation, which united the two realms. History becomes constitutive of the eternal Trinity.

Hegel's allusion to Joachim of Fiore, the thirteenth-century Calabrian abbot, is decisive here. Fiore's trinitarian dispensationalism gave Hegel the conceptual tool to relate Trinity intimately to world history.[17] The starting point in Hegel's account of Trinity and history is the inchoate Trinity, or the un-self-differentiated Trinity, which Hegel correlates with the first trinitarian moment of the Father. The second moment, of the Son, extends the Trinity into history, under the rubric of creation and redemption. These trinitarian works are necessary to explicate the differentiating moment of Father and Son in the reality of history. The final moment of the Spirit is constituted by the Trinity's full explication in the realm of reality, as that moment is integrated back into the divine life. The historically actual is returned to its eternal destination in Spirit.

The building of Hegel's system required a conceptual vehicle that distinguished between the immanent and the economic Trinity. God's relationship to the world is determined by the self-differentiation of God from the world, by the creation of the world. To use Hegelian logical categories, universality requires differentiation from particularity. Yet through this original self-differentiation, the Trinity emerges in redemption, a process that entails the differentiation of the Trinity into the moment of the Son. The return is subsumed under the rubric of Spirit, whereby the Spirit of love unites particularity with universality in order to reach the actuality of concrete universality or individuality. At the end of the process, individuality is assigned its distinct metaphysical status in the universal. Furthermore, at the end of the process, the explication of the Trinity as self-differentiated has become actual; by this, Hegel sees the economic Trinity's manifestation as necessary to the process by which both God and world become actual through history. God becomes explicitly trinitarian through differentiation from and in relation to the world. The economic Trinity reveals the immanent Trinity as its inchoate presupposition and fully explicit goal.

The brilliance of Hegel's systematic proposal is that trinitarian speculation is a legitimate tool of reason for comprehending God's relation to the world. Yet Hegel's speculation is decisively modern; it is justified by epistemology. The model of self-consciousness that serves the psychological basis for Hegel's epistemology is in earnest continuity with the Augustinian tradition that sees the human mind as a trinitarian trace (*vestigium Trinitatis*). Although Hegel is more optimistic than Augustine about the epistemological power of the human mind to grasp the Trinity – Augustine's *De Trinitate* (*On the Trinity*) should be read as a failure rather than as the success of mind to approach the Trinity – he is nonetheless indebted to this early Christian proposal. The transparency between human thinking and trinitarian processions of wisdom and love is a decisively Hegelian contribution to the Trinity. This contribution is achieved on the basis of the model of self-consciousness that Hegel adopts, in which appearance is transparent to its underlying unity. The human mind is capable of achieving speculative knowledge of its ground because it is caught up at the intersection of God's work in creation. And this metaphysical relation justifies an epistemology that would declare the processions revelatory in both directions – in human and divine thinking. Whether transparency is called into question on psychological grounds – as is the case with Schleiermacher – or on epistemological grounds – as is the case with critical reason – Hegel's powerful model succeeds in establishing the Trinity as system's cornerstone: in the human mind as it is part of the world, and in the explicit immanent Trinity, which includes the totality of history.

## Schleiermacher's historical trinitarian thought

The Trinity is often regarded as a glaringly heterodox problem in Schleiermacher's system. Schleiermacher locates the doctrine at the conclusion of *The Christian Faith*, which then results in the criticism that the Trinity is not the central doctrinal factor of his theology. Yet the mere fact that it occurs at the end is no warrant for such a charge. Schleiermacher entertained the notion of relocating it at the beginning, as he wrote in his famous second letter to Friedrich Lücke.[18] But this systematic reordering begs the important question that Schleiermacher poses in his *Christian Faith*, one that he answers by constructing an entire system culminating with the Trinity as a combination of historical expressions of Christianity.[19]

The relation between language and *res* is the key determinant in Schleiermacher's thinking. He understood language as the "form" or "outer" that conveys the "inner" or meaning, which is always distinct yet also always connected to outer form on a continuum. The distinct theological problem of language is posed on the philosophical self-consciousness model of a continuum between thought and language, whereby thought is the inner constituting identity or unity of language that is necessarily linear on grammatical and syntactical principles. Schleiermacher's main theological concern for "outer" language is to preserve its link to its "inner" power.[20] In Christian theological terms, the "inner" is the redemptive power emanating from Jesus, constant in the history of Christianity. Language evolves from its immediate biblical forms of poetry and rhetoric and becomes explicitly conceptual in theology. At all points along this continuum, the inner dimension of constancy must be traced back to Jesus' redeeming power. Theological language inevitably expresses this soteriological succession.

The soteriological focus exhibits Schleiermacher's Pietist and Kantian preoccupation with experience as well as his wariness of epistemologically unjustified claims of inner essences. Language appropriate to theology's subject matter must be derived from the historical experience of redemption, and hence any speculation that does not have an experiential connection is not permissible. Here Schleiermacher decisively rejects the commingling of metaphysical and historical claims, turning away from Leibniz and Hegel for confusing two sources of knowledge about God. The only claims made about self, world, and God are on experiential terms expressed in language. (Yet paradoxically, this insistence on history as the place of seeking the Trinity ends up in accusations that he has rejected orthodox trinitarianism!)

The issue of language has, as is characteristic of post-Reformation trinitarian thought, serious implications for the construal of the doctrine. Schleiermacher famously excludes the legitimacy of claiming the "eternal" distinctions in the concluding passages of *The Christian Faith*.[21] This exclusion should not be read as a rejection of "trinitarian orthodoxy." Rather, it must be read in light of a theory of language that admits into theology only expressions derived from experience of Jesus of Nazareth. The linguistic issue is for Schleiermacher ultimately soteriological. If the Trinity is to be construed within such limits (a legitimate enterprise, to be sure, thus cleansing theological claims from non-experientially derived accretions), then only those statements can be used to construct an understanding of the Trinity. For Schleiermacher, any Old Testament passages used classically as warrants for the eternal distinctions must be rejected as well.[22] He argues this dangerous biblical-theological claim on the soteriological grounds that any statements issued historically prior to the appearance of Jesus of Nazareth in Galilee are, in his opinion, pre-Christian, and thereby inadmissible as expressions of redemption attributed to Jesus.

What this does to the Trinity is remarkable: Schleiermacher's own very detailed study of second- and third-century trinitarianism in the persons of Praxeas and Noetus demonstrates the care and concern he devotes to constructing a doctrine from soteriological statements.[23] Critics have deemed this study to represent the Sabellian heresy. Although this charge is perhaps more accurately reflected in Schleiermacher's own admission of an alternative Sabellianism, which he proposes as an alternative to the classic Athanasian Trinity (meaning the *homoousios* doctrine), it must be interpreted in the conceptual light of Schleiermacher's overarching philosophical question of system and his theological commitment to soteriological utterances. If history is the realm of God-world experience, and if statements can be derived only from this realm of experience, then metaphysical speculation on eternal distinctions falls outside the bounds of critical theological reason on the grounds of both rationalist criticism and soteriological principles. Hence history for Schleiermacher becomes the defining metaphysic: reality is historical, and that reality as determined by God's causality is a historical reality.

At this point Schleiermacher appeals to Leibniz in order to justify these epistemological claims on metaphysical grounds. Appearance is the realm of history; what we can know about God's interaction with the world is derived from expressions of Christian self-consciousness. Power is the metaphysical unity of causality, which is, of course, Schleiermacher's concept of God as it is famously derived from the most immediate reflection in immediate self-consciousness on the "whence" of absolute dependence.[24] Knowledge of the Trinity is not metaphysically presupposed as the point of indifference at the beginning of the "narrative" in Hegelian terms, but is cumulative – the culmination of God's causality, experienced in the redemptive terms of Christ and the Spirit as the historical working-out of God's power in the world as wisdom and love.[25] Hence Schleiermacher's Sabellianism is modified by his distinct appeal to Fiorean periodization to resolve the (modern) problem of history and speculation. Periodization is relevant only after the historical appearance of Jesus. Classic Sabellianism sees modes of God as interchangeable, whereas Schleiermacher sees Son and then Spirit as historically non-reducible to each other and, once introduced historically, as irrevocable constituents of the Trinity. By this restriction of trinitarian claims to the experience of redemption, the soteriological core of Christianity is preserved throughout its developing history. Finally for Schleiermacher, Christianity's history is the culmination of the Trinity's history in the world when all creation has been redeemed by the work of Christ and the Spirit.

## Self-consciousness and history: Schleiermacher and Georg W. F. Hegel

Like Hegel, Schleiermacher constructs his trinitarian system on the psychological basis of self-consciousness. Unlike Hegel's, Schleiermacher's psychological model is one of immediate self-consciousness, meaning that the self-relation constituting individuality is never available as such in discursive thought. Immediate self-consciousness renders a discursive religion only as it is inevitably contextualized in a historical religion. As an unmediated self-relation sustaining the self's constancy through time, immediate self-consciousness never serves as source of a religious idea or action. It is linked to God as divine causality, yet the link is indirect, formed as a non-discursive inference in feeling from the denial of absolute freedom to the affirmation of absolute dependence. God as cause of all existence is related to immediate self-consciousness in the indirect terms of the feeling of a lack in immediate self-consciousness of its own ground. This designation of

God is determined theologically as God is rendered historically in the Christian religion. Schleiermacher's modified Sabellianism results from a systematic conception of this specific psychological model in the historical terms of a divine causality that proceeds through wisdom and love with a decisive universal outreach. Yet Schleiermacher uses this psychological model to underline importantly the opacity of reality to reason on both sides; the limits of critical reason disallow speculation as to the "ground" because there is no immediate inference or access to it. The principle of revelation used by Hegel's transparent model of self-consciousness is blocked, leading to a Trinity that is much more hidden than revealed.

Speculation is restricted to the limits provided by the divine causality in redemptive history. Schleiermacher implies a very precise Trinitarian metaphysic and language by this restriction. Christian dogma is not about knowledge, nor even about the "knowledge of true doctrine," but rather about salvation that must be experienced before it is thought or acted. This restriction undercuts rationalist principles, even the principle of revelation used to legitimate trinitarian orthodoxy, and opens the way for developing a trinitarian understanding that is tightly connected to God's loving work in creation. Schleiermacher accurately concludes his system with the Trinity as its culmination, the Trinity's revelation at the end of history. What is "lost" by Schleiermacher's conception is also an important matter of discussion. Perhaps new work needs to be done to understand precisely how metaphysics may make use of speculation on soteriological grounds, rather than rejecting it entirely.

Both Hegel and Schleiermacher offer paradigmatic ways of wrestling with system requirements with the discrepant attractions of history and speculation. Perhaps even more pressing in the nineteenth century than during the Enlightenment was the question of construing history as a metaphysical reality. The problem of identity and change required a model uniting both so that Lessing's "ugly ditch" could be crossed. Both Hegel and Schleiermacher conceptualized their respective systems by making powerful uses of the Trinity. Hegel situated the Trinity at the two end points of his "metanarrative" system; the Trinity was his system's ground and goal, and it historically traversed dispensations of Father, Son, and Spirit before culminating in a fully explicit immanent Trinity. Schleiermacher's system used the metaphysic of power/appearance to explain historical change through time; the Trinity was a culmination of faith statements expressing the redemptive effects of Jesus and of the Spirit in the church, and ultimately through the church in the world. Both demonstrated how seriously the Trinity was to be taken in Western thought. The Trinity challenged Western thinking to conceive change as a function of a trinitarian metaphysic that could account for constancy through time. The Trinity was also challenged by Western thinking to explain history's integration with speculation. The result was Trinity as system.

## THEOLOGICAL OUTCOME

The history that I have developed in this chapter, which is an alternative to the received version, has centered on the integral place of the doctrine of the Trinity in the structures of Western thought and culture, during the three centuries following the sixteenth-century Reformation. In my account the Trinity, far from dealing a "death blow" to "rationality" (to quote Florensky again), decisively probed and stretched Western thinking by contributing to its development. As new paradigms arose in the post-Reformation period for scientific (*wissenschaftlich*) reasoning, Christian theology inevitably participated in the academic inquiry into truth and the search for knowledge. History and the natural world were opened up by the arts and sciences; inquiries into reason and rationality opened up the speculative dimensions of the world and its history. Christian theological development took hold of the academic idioms of its day. History and speculation became the two distinct areas of theological inquiry. The Trinity gradually emerged as the central defining doctrine for Christianity by the end of this epoch because its ultimate systematic conceptualization satisfied the dual idioms of history and speculation that had been established by academic consensus. The Trinity was not given this right by revelation. It earned this place by actively participating in the development of rationality. The story of how the Trinity achieved this result has been the preoccupation of this chapter.

The Christian theological outcome of this story in the twentieth century is what the "received" story has designated a "trinitarian renaissance." Rather than being portrayed as a time when a trinitarian phoenix arose from the ashes of Enlightenment reason, the twentieth century and its fascination with the Trinity should be regarded as the product of Western reason's three-hundred-year enterprise of absorbing, answering to, and bending around the challenges of cultural-philosophical history. The Trinity came to the twentieth century already in service as the systematic axiom of Hegel's philosophical-theological system and the historical culmination of Schleiermacher's dogmatic-theological system.

Its systematic privileging was the result of a development that had conceptualized the Trinity according to academic questions of history and speculation. Although Christian theology had always assented to the Trinity as a revealed truth, it seized as its task during the Enlightenment to explore doctrinal content in light of academic reason and conversely to present questions to reason on the basis of the Trinity in order to see new possibilities for thinking and action. From experience to system, from economic to immanent, the Trinity was conceived together with the parameters of modern thought. History and eternity were conceived together in Christian thought to bring system to trinitarian-theological completion. Rather than tolling the death-knell of reason, the *homoousios* has inspired new ways to think the life of the triune God.

**Notes**

1. Pavel Florensky, *The Pillar and Ground of the Truth: An Essay in Orthodox Theodicy in Twelve Letters*, trans. Boris Jakim (Princeton University Press, 1997), 41.
2. See, for example, Karen L. King's *What is Gnosticism?* (Cambridge, MA: Belknap Press of Harvard University Press, 2005).
3. See pp. 162–66 above for my discussion of Schleiermacher on the Trinity.
4. Martin Luther, "Doctoral Disputation of Georg Major (1543)," in *D. Martin Luthers Werke: Kritische Gesantausgabe*, 69 vols. (Weimar: Hermann Böhlaus Nachfolger, 1883–1999), XXXIX/2, 305A, 1–3 (my translation).
5. Still a valuable resource for issues of Bible and philosophy in sixteenth-century trinitarian controversies: Roland Bainton, *Hunted Heretic: The Life and Death of Michael Servetus 1511–1533* (Boston: Beacon, 1953).
6. Ratschow's study of the prolegomena and part 1 of Protestant orthodox theological systems is an exceptional resource as it decisively corrects the structural and substantive errors of the authoritative anthologies of Lutheran and Reformed orthodoxies. Unfortunately Ratschow was unable to complete his study, leaving the investigation of all parts of the system following the doctrines of God and the Trinity to posterity. See Carl Heinz Ratschow, *Lutherische Dogmatik zwischen Reformation und Aufklärung*, 2 vols. (Gütersloh: Gerd Mohn, 1964, 1966).
7. Ibid., 1, 35.
8. Ibid.
9. Maria Rosa Antognazza, *Leibniz on the Trinity and the Incarnation: Reason and Revelation in the Seventeenth Century*, trans. Gerald Parks (New Haven: Yale University Press, 2007), 105–06.

10. Antognazza describes these discussions with exceptional detail in ibid., 16–33, 120–60.
11. Ibid., 167.
12. Ibid., 111–13.
13. See the learned research of Johannes Wallman, most recently collected in his *Pietismus-Studien* (Tübingen: Mohr Siebeck, 2008).
14. See Samuel M. Powell, *The Trinity in German Thought* (Cambridge University Press, 2001), 40.
15. See Friedrich Christof Oetinger, *Die Lehrtafel der Prinzessin Antonia*, ed. Reinhard Breymayer and Friedrich Häußerman (Berlin: de Gruyter, 1997).
16. Cyril O'Regan, *The Heterodox Hegel*, SUNY Series in Hegelian Studies (Albany, NY: State University of New York Press, 1994); Peter C. Hodgson, *Hegel & Christian Theology: A Reading of the Lectures on the Philosophy of Religion* (Oxford University Press, 2005).
17. See Georg Wilhelm Friedrich Hegel, *Lectures on the Philosophy of Religion*, ed. Peter C. Hodgson, trans. R. F. Brown, P. C. Hodgson, and J. M. Stewart with the assistance of H. S. Harris, 3 vols. (Berkeley and Los Angeles: University of California Press, 1984, 1985, 1987; Oxford University Press, 2006).
18. Friedrich Schleiermacher, *On the Glaubenslehre: Two Letters to Dr. Lücke*, trans. James O. Duke and Francis Fiorenza, American Academy of Religion Texts and Translations Series, 3 (Chico, CA: Scholars Press, 1981), 32.
19. "a combination of utterances from our Christian self-consciousness" (my translation): Friedrich Schleiermacher, *The Christian Faith*, trans. D. M. Baillie et al. from 2nd German edn. (1830–31), ed. H. R. Mackintosh and J. S. Stewart (Edinburgh: T. & T. Clark, 1999), §170.3.
20. Ibid., §16.
21. Ibid., §171.
22. Ibid., §170.3.
23. Friedrich Schleiermacher, "Über den Gegensatz zwischen der Sabellianischen und der Athanasianischen Vorstellung von der Trinität," in *Kritische Gesamtausgabe*, I/10, ed. Hans-Friedrich Traulsen (Berlin: de Gruyter, 1990); trans. Moses Stuart as "On the Discrepancy between the Sabellian and Athanasian Method of Representing the Doctrine of the Trinity (1822)," *Biblical Repository and Quarterly Observer*, 5 (April 1835), 31–33; 6 (July 1835), 1–116.
24. Schleiermacher, *The Christian Faith*, §4.4.
25. An insightful study of Schleiermacher's Trinity in relation to the doctrine of God, culminating in the processions of wisdom and love, is Francis Schüssler Fiorenza's "Schleiermacher's Understanding of God as Triune," in *The Cambridge Companion to Friedrich Schleiermacher*, ed. Jacqueline Mariña, Cambridge Companions to Religion (Cambridge University Press, 2005), 171–88.

## Further reading

Antognazza, Maria Rosa, *Leibniz on the Trinity and the Incarnation: Reason and Revelation in the Seventeenth Century*, trans. Gerald Parks (New Haven: Yale University Press, 2007).

Fiorenza, Francis Schüssler, "Schleiermacher's Understanding of God as Triune," in Jacqueline Mariña, ed., *The Cambridge Companion to Friedrich Schleiermacher*, Cambridge Companions to Religion (Cambridge University Press, 2005), 171–88.

Hegel, Georg Wilhelm Friedrich, *Lectures on the Philosophy of Religion*, ed. Peter C. Hodgson, trans. R. F. Brown, P. C. Hodgson, and J. M. Stewart with the assistance of H. S. Harris, 3 vols. (Berkeley and Los Angeles: University of California Press, 1984, 1985, 1987; Oxford University Press, 2006); single-vol. edn.: *The Lectures of 1827* (Berkeley and Los Angeles: University of California Press, 1988; Oxford: Clarendon Press, 2006).

Helmer, Christine, *The Trinity and Martin Luther: A Study on the Relationship between Genre, Language and the Trinity in Luther's Works (1523–1546)*, Veröffentlichungen des Instituts für Europäische Geschichte, Abteilung Abendländische Religionsgeschichte, 174 (Mainz: Philipp von Zabern, 1999).

Hodgson, Peter C., *Hegel & Christian Theology: A Reading of the Lectures on the Philosophy of Religion* (Oxford University Press, 2005).

O'Regan, Cyril J., *The Heterodox Hegel*, SUNY Series in Hegelian Studies (Albany, NY: State University of New York Press, 1994).

Powell, Samuel M., *The Trinity in German Thought* (Cambridge University Press, 2001).

Ratschow, Carl Heinz, *Lutherische Dogmatik zwischen Reformation und Aufklärung*, 2 vols. (Gütersloh: Gerd Mohn, 1964, 1966).

Schleiermacher, Friedrich, *The Christian Faith*, trans. D. M. Baillie et al. from 2nd German edn., 1830–31, ed. H. R. Mackintosh and J. S. Stewart (Edinburgh: T. & T. Clark, 1999).

# Part IV

## *Contemporary theologians*

# 10 Karl Barth, reconciliation, and the Triune God

PETER GOODWIN HELTZEL AND
CHRISTIAN T. COLLINS WINN

It has become commonplace to attribute the twentieth-century recovery of the doctrine of the Trinity to the Swiss theologian Karl Barth (1886–1968).[1] Barth, though not alone, was indeed a major figure in the modern trinitarian renaissance. In his massive *Kirchliche Dogmatik* (*Church Dogmatics*),[2] published in fourteen volumes from 1932 to 1967, Barth developed and expounded the thesis that the doctrine of the Trinity was foundational for Christian theological discourse. In the inaugural volume, he argued, "The doctrine of the Trinity is what basically distinguishes the Christian doctrine of God as Christian, and therefore what already distinguishes the Christian concept of revelation as Christian, in contrast to all other possible doctrines of God and concepts of revelation" (*Church Dogmatics*, I/1, 301). These words are emblematic of Barth's effort to place the doctrine of the Trinity back in the center of Christian theology. Indeed, following his own advice, Barth placed the doctrine of the Trinity at the very beginning of the *Church Dogmatics*, arguing that it constituted the internal dynamic of God's speech to humanity and as such functioned as the basic grammar of Christian discourse.

Much ink has been spilt over Barth's theological intervention; however, until recently, few commentators have attended to the question of how Barth's early "revelational trinitarianism" developed and matured over the course of the *Church Dogmatics*.[3] The most important commentator to take up this question has undoubtedly been Bruce McCormack, though his own interpretative and constructive efforts have created some controversy among Barth interpreters.[4] While briefly discussing the controversy over McCormack's interpretation of Barth, we will not seek to adjudicate between the emerging positions within the debate. Rather, our concern will be to consider how Barth's trinitarian theology was further developed in his doctrine of reconciliation.

In the early volumes of the *Church Dogmatics* (specifically I/1), Barth developed the doctrine of the Trinity in relation to the doctrine of revelation, seeking to articulate how humanity comes to a knowledge of God through the Word of God. Barth argued that God's address to humanity in the life, death, and resurrection of Jesus Christ as witnessed to in holy scripture is trinitarian in form and content. His primary concern then was theo-epistemic (though his coordination of reconciliation and revelation even at this early stage shows a concern with genuine material transformation) – that is to say, it was focused on the question: how do we know God? Without leaving behind these theo-epistemic concerns, Barth's later theology further elaborates the contours of the revelation of the Triune God within the space–time manifold of human history. Barth's concern with God's triune action in the travail of history becomes especially manifest in the *theologumenon* "Jesus is Victor" in his discussion of reconciliation (See *Church Dogmatics* IV/3.1, 165–274). "Jesus is Victor" functions there as a theological complex which draws together the event of reconciliation enacted in Jesus Christ, the eloquent manifestation of that event in the resurrection of Jesus Christ and the outpouring of the Holy Spirit, and the ongoing history of humanity and the church which, though marked with suffering and uncertainty, is nonetheless called and empowered to hope in the provisional and final manifestation of God's kingdom on earth.

When reflecting on Barth's doctrine of the Trinity our guiding problematic, then, is not how the life history of Jesus Christ is seen as the historical fulfillment of God's eternal being, a concern receiving a great amount of attention at the present time, but rather how humanity comes to participate in the drama of the life history of Jesus in the promise of the Spirit. Through turning our focus to Barth's theology and ethic of reconciliation, we are interested in recovering a "political" reading of Barth, building on earlier studies by Friedrich-Wilhelm Marquardt, George Hunsinger, and Timothy Gorringe.[5] Social ethics was an animating concern throughout Barth's tenure as the "red pastor of Safenwil."[6] Thus a latent question that drives our approach is: in what ways does Barth's doctrine of the Trinity ground his radical politics? When Barth's doctrine of the Trinity is interpreted through the doctrine of reconciliation, an eschatological horizon is opened through which we can deepen our understanding of God's triune action in and for the world amid the tragicomedy of history. In sum, the most expansive implications of Barth's doctrine of the economic Trinity come to fullest expression in the doctrine of reconciliation, where Christ's victory is manifest in a parabolic fashion through the power of the Spirit in signs of the kingdom of God.

## THE TRINITY AND REVELATION

Though Barth's early theology is not bereft of trinitarian assumptions, it is in the first two volumes of the *Church Dogmatics* that Barth offers what is considered his most coherent exposition of the doctrine of the Trinity.[7] For Barth, "We arrive at the doctrine of the Trinity by no other way than that of an analysis of the concept of revelation" (*Church Dogmatics*, I/I, 312). The doctrine of the Trinity, then, is an attempt to both analyze and elaborate the biblically derived truth that "God reveals Himself as the Lord." As such, the doctrine of the Trinity, as a faithful description of the singular and particular lordship of the God revealed in scripture,[8] is both an epistemological and an ontological inference of "the promulgation of the *basilea tou theou* of the lordship of God" (I/I, 306). The revelation of God's lordship (i.e., *basilea tou theou*) is associated especially with Jesus Christ.

Barth's argument begins with the theo-epistemic concern of what it means that God reveals himself as Lord. Of singular importance for Barth is to stress that that which we encounter, or are encountered by, in revelation is none other than God, that there is no God behind the back of the God who presents himself in Jesus Christ. Barth defines revelation as "the self-unveiling, imparted to men, of the God who by nature cannot be unveiled to men . . . self-unveiling means that God does what men themselves cannot do in any sense or in any way: He makes himself present, known, and significant to them as God" (*Church Dogmatics*, I/I, 315).[9]

Because it is *God* who reveals himself, and because *God* reveals himself as *Lord*, Barth argues that lordship characterizes not only the content of revelation, but also its very happening. The lordship that characterizes the form and content of revelation is God's inalienable subjectivity (*Church Dogmatics*, I/I, 381). Because revelation is by grace alone, it must be grounded in God's own actuality – God is really and truly present in revelation and thus *God* is the one who reveals, *God* is the one who is revealed, and *God* is the effect of that revelation. Or in Barth's language,. "God in unimpaired unity yet also in unimpaired distinction is Revealer, Revelation, and Revealedness" (I/I, 295). These are not three moments behind which stands the real God, a hidden divine fourth. Rather, the three "moments" are God as "He is in Himself," in the actuality of the divine life, because the distinctions are rooted in the very essence or being of God (I/I, 382–83). Thus Barth synthesizes the event of revelation and the doctrine of the Trinity by correlating the three forms of revelation with the three persons of the Trinity: God the

Father is the revealer, the Son is the revelation, and the Holy Spirit is revelation's revealedness (I/1, 296 ff.).

This triadic conception of God understood as Revealer, Revelation, and Revealedness mirrors patristic notions in which revelation is understood to proceed from the Father, through the Son, and in the Spirit.[10] Each person of the Trinity plays an active role in the process of unveiling God's gracious love for the whole of the good creation. Barth writes,

> And in this very event God is who He is. God is He who in this event is subject, predicate and object; the revealer, the act of revelation, the revealed; Father, Son and Holy Spirit. God is the Lord active in this event. We say "active" in this event, and therefore for our salvation and for His glory, but in any case active . . . To its very deepest depths God's Godhead consists in the fact that it is an event – not any event, not events in general, but the event of His action, in which we have a share in God's revelation.
>
> (*Church Dogmatics*, II/1, 262–63)

As mentioned above, of great import for Barth is the implication that the event of revelation has for our understanding of God's own immanent being. If God "Himself" has truly come to speech in the event of revelation, so to speak, then the God who differentiates "Himself" in order to speak "Himself" is none other than *God*, as "He is in Himself" apart from and prior to the event of revelation. Thus the economic Trinity *is* the immanent Trinity, with the caveat that this is the case only by the grace of God and not by necessity (I/1, 172–73).[11]

To fill out and explicate the contours of the immanent life of the triune God, Barth utilizes the patristic concepts of *homoousia* and *perichōrēsis*. Barth declares that "The Son and the Spirit are of one essence with the Father" (*Church Dogmatics*, I/1, 393). Likewise, the mutual indwelling denoted by the doctrine of *perichōrēsis* characterizes the nature of the divine relations, and therefore the divine life (I/1, 370–71). God is a communion of love in which the Father, Son, and Holy Spirit subsist in their mutual indwelling relations. Thus the being of God is relational in nature, and *perichōrēsis* becomes shorthand for the "dialectical union and distinction" of the one God who in intimate communion is irreducibly three (I/1, 369).

"Mode of being" (*Seinsweise*) was Barth's preferred phrase for translating *hypostasis*, the term used to describe the three "persons" of the Trinity (*Church Dogmatics*, I/1, 358–68). Because of his use of the discourse of "modes of being," some interpreters have wrongly accused

Barth of modalism.[12] Critics have often failed to realize, however, that Barth was commandeering the grammar of an ancient Eastern theological tradition rooted in Cappadocian theology (Basil, Gregory of Nazianzus, and Gregory of Nyssa).[13] Barth argued that "mode of being" is a more accurate descriptor for the "persons" of the Trinity because it clarified the unity of divine action between the three "modes of being" while simultaneously avoiding the perceived excesses and pitfalls of existential theologians who used the language of personhood (I/I, 349 ff.; II/I, 287–97). In anticipation of the charges of modalism, Barth argued that the three *hypostases* are intrinsic to the divine *ousia*, such that the "modes of being" within the Trinity are not the "masks" of modalism concealing a primordial oneness, but are rather three distinct *hypostases* that together are a dynamic communion throughout eternity.[14]

It is fair to say that while each of the three "modes of being" are co-equal, the center is decidedly Christological. In keeping with Barth's own convictions about the center of the New Testament message and his emphasis on the need for theology to be a kind of *Nachdenken* ("thinking after") of the biblical witness, pride of place is given to God's revelation, which is identified with the second person of the Trinity.[15] At the same time, however, it is the communion of the threefold God which is enacted in the life history of Jesus of Nazareth and mediated through the Holy Spirit (*Church Dogmatics*, I/2, 33–35). Thus, though pride of place is given to the second person of the Trinity epistemologically, the living reality that encounters, transforms, and thereby draws our humanity into new life in the event of revelation is none other than the threefold God who lives in eternal communion.[16]

The lordship of God is revealed through God's dynamic action ("the event of His action") in history as a communion of love. God is revealed as the loving Lord who actively seeks and creates fellowship with humanity and all creation.[17] God is

> Father, Son and Holy Spirit and therefore alive in His unique being with and for and in another. The unbroken unity of his being, knowledge and will is at the same time an act of deliberation, decision and intercourse. He does not exist in solitude but in fellowship. Therefore what He seeks and creates between Himself and us is in fact nothing else but what He wills and completes and therefore is in Himself.
>
> (*Church Dogmatics*, II/I, 275)

The divine character of self-giving love is expressed in the unique tri-*hypostatic* being of God that is "with and for and in another" both in the immanent Trinity and in the economy of salvation (II/1, 275). In revelation, *God* is unveiled as the one who loves in freedom and as the one whose love and freedom creates communion among humanity as a reflection of the self-giving love of the triune communion.

Because *this* is the God who is unveiled in revelation, reconciliation is necessarily constitutive of revelation.[18] In other words, reconciliation, as rooted in God's own harmonious communion, is both the content (i.e., the life, death, and resurrection of Jesus) and the effect (i.e., the outpouring of the Holy Spirit, on the church and then the whole world) of the event of revelation. By coordinating revelation and reconciliation in this way, Barth secures the event of revelation from being understood as simply the neutral conveyance of a knowledge which can be held at arm's length or ideologically manipulated. He also obviates the question of how and in what way the reconciliation of God is actualized in the individual, as there is no gap between the reception of revelation and the event of reconciliation in its subjective dimension. Furthermore, the pairing of revelation and reconciliation also inoculates Barth's construal of the Trinity, which is decidedly abstract in *Church Dogmatics*, I/1, from being misunderstood. That is, the event of reconciliation which is enacted in the life history of Jesus of Nazareth *is* the second person of the Trinity in his act of self-affirmation. That which is revealed in Jesus, in the history of his life and suffering, is not an aspect of God's character, but is the very heart of God.[19] The more abstract discussion of the Trinity is quickly supplemented by lengthy discussions of Christology, pneumatology and ecclesiology in I/2. But Barth's insistence that Christian theology ought not to be concerned with divinity in general receives further deepening and radicalization in his discussion of the doctrine of election.

## TRINITY AND ELECTION

The reformulation of the doctrine of election found in *Church Dogmatics*, II/2 is considered by many as one of the most radical and far-reaching contributions to Christian theology made by Karl Barth.[20] For Barth, Jesus Christ is both the subject and object of the divine election. That is, Jesus Christ is both the electing God and elect humanity. This simple formula has serious implications, and has recently produced a heated debate within Barth studies about how those implications do or do not impinge on his understanding of the Trinity.

Barth's commitment to a Christocentric doctrine of revelation leads him to identify the electing God with Jesus Christ, proclaiming that

"Jesus Christ is the electing God. We must begin with this assertion because by its content it has the character and dignity of a basic principle, and because the other assertion, that Jesus Christ is elected man, can be understood only in the light of it" (*Church Dogmatics*, II/2, 103). Because we know God only in the person of Jesus Christ, it is inconceivable to postulate a God "behind the back of Jesus Christ" to whom we assign the eternal decision of election. The God who elects from all eternity is no *Deus absconditus*, but the God revealed in Jesus Christ.

Since the Son of God is the subject who animates the person Jesus Christ, and because the Son of God is fully God and therefore participates fully in the eternal divine will of the Father, Son, and Holy Spirit, it can be said that Jesus Christ is the subject of election – God in his "second mode of being" determining and determined to be *pro nobis*.[21] In other words, as the second person of the Trinity, the Son of God determines "himself," and therefore God determines Godself, to be not only the eternal triune communion, but also with and for humanity.

To make sense of the language of "divine self-determination" it is helpful to point out that Barth was fully committed to a permutation of what is known as ontological actualism, a notion of "being" or "essence" in which a particular "being" is constituted, realized, and known as such only in its own act. In reference to the being of God, then, "the word 'event' or 'act' is *final*, and cannot be surpassed or compromised. To its very deepest depths God's Godhead consists in the fact that it is an event" (*Church Dogmatics*, II/1, 263). That is, the being of God *is* and *is known* only in God's own self-defining act. To clarify further, the actualization of God's own being for Barth is not in the hands of "being" as such. Rather, because God is free, the act in which the being of God is determined is God's own and no other. In other words, God is Lord over God's own being.[22]

To draw the thread back to its Christological and trinitarian focus, Barth is quick to note that God determines to be God in a very specific fashion. That is, God determines Godself in a very particular way and no other: "*Actus purus* is not sufficient as a description of God. To it there must be added at least '*et singularis*.' . . . His being, is not actuality in general and as such, but that in His revelation and in eternity it is a specific act with a definite content" (*Church Dogmatics*, II/1, 264, 272). To be sure, the very "specific act with a definite content" to which Barth is referring is trinitarian in nature. "But God's act is God's love . . . 'God is' means 'God loves'" (II/1, 283), and the love, which is the being of God, is the love of the Father, Son, and Holy Spirit, whose ever dynamic and mutual subsisting relations constitute the concrete being of God

(II/1, 297). Thus the triune life of God as Father, Son, and Holy Spirit is the eternal and self-consistent decision of God.

In light of Barth's reformulation of the doctrine of election, however, divine ontology, election, and the doctrine of revelation are now coordinated, such that God's decision to be *God* is understood to be concurrent with God's decision to be *pro nobis*. That is, God determines Godself in the eternal decision of election. Or, put differently, because Jesus Christ is the electing God, not only is God the subject of election,[23] but God is also its primary object. God determines something about Godself in the eternal decision of election.[24]

But to what *extent* and in what *way* does God determine Godself in the eternal decision of election? Is this a decision that is decisive and therefore constitutive of the triune being of God, *or* is it a decision that confirms the antecedent triune being of God? If the former, how does the doctrine of God not collapse into the doctrine of reconciliation? If the latter, how are we to speak about a God who precedes the God we know in the gracious election of Jesus Christ? These are some of the questions fueling a vigorous debate over how to interpret Barth's understanding of divine self-determination and his reformulation of the doctrine of election. Ultimately the questions revolve around whether or not the ground of election is to be found in the immanent Trinity or the ground of the Trinity is to be found in God's electing decision. Or, put more succinctly, is the triune being of God constituted *or* confirmed in the eternal decision to elect?

Two different approaches to this question have emerged with modest attempts to bridge the divide. Bruce McCormack has argued that God's self-determination to be triune and the divine act of electing humanity should be considered as one and the same act.[25] That is, the divine decision in which God constitutes God's own being (i.e., the decision in which God is eternally self-existent as Father, Son, and Holy Spirit) is one and the same act in which God determines to be "God with us."[26] In contrast, Paul Molnar has argued that election confirms the pre-existence of the eternal triune communion of love.[27] Much of this debate hinges on the relationship of being and will within God, the status of the so-called *logos asarkos* (i.e., the pre-existent "logos without flesh"), and the function of the immanent Trinity in Barth's theology. While this debate is in some measure concerned with the way in which the experience of the worldly space–time manifold may or may not affect the divine being, we want to delineate further the developments in Barth's economic trinitarian thought that will help to reorient this debate. Instead of thinking about Barth's doctrine of the Trinity through the lens of the divine election, we propose thinking about Barth's doctrine of the Trinity through the lenses of history and social ethics. When reflecting on Barth's doctrine of the Trinity, our guiding problematic is not how the life history of Jesus Christ is seen as the historical fulfillment of God's eternal being, but rather how humanity participates in the reconciliation of the world in the ongoing history of Jesus the Victor, through the promise of the Holy Spirit manifest in the church's struggle for justice.

## "JESUS IS VICTOR": A TRINITARIAN THEOLOGY OF HISTORY

In the early section of *Church Dogmatics*, Barth identifies the kingdom of God with the lordship of God manifest in Jesus Christ (I/1, 306), an identification that lays the foundation for his exposition of the doctrine of the Trinity. In the context of reconciliation, Barth moves in the opposite direction, from lordship back toward the concrete manifestation of the kingdom in the life history of Jesus and the outpouring of the Holy Spirit. In both cases, Jesus Christ is at the center. In the doctrine of reconciliation, however, Barth includes the added dimension of ongoing history so that the triune lordship of God – identified directly with the presence of the resurrected Christ, the embodied kingdom of God – is indirectly identified with pneumatologically empowered "parables of the kingdom." This finds its crystallization point in Barth's development of the prophetic work of Christ, and more specifically on his discussion of "Jesus is Victor," a motif drawn from the writings of the Blumhardts – the elder Johann Christoph (1805–1880) and his son Christoph Friedrich (1842–1919).[28]

In Barth's novel appropriation of this motif, "Jesus is Victor" bears multiple meanings. It refers to the outcome of the life history of Jesus as lived and recounted in the gospels in all of its tragedy. It describes Jesus' triumph over the limitation of death by his resurrection, which points both to the illumination of his life as well as to its further promulgation in history. It also describes ongoing history, which now lives in the light of the resurrected Jesus and the Spirit of Pentecost. And finally, it refers to the end toward which the whole of the cosmos is moving: the transformation of all things. As such, "Jesus is Victor" summarizes the will of God, and therefore is a concise description of God's determining decision of election as well as the promulgation or revelation of that decision.[29] This decision is not an abstract decision, but rather is a trans-temporal determination which is embodied in the conflictual life history of Jesus the Victor.

In the watchword "Jesus is Victor", a theological drama is denoted in the "is" which links "the life with the light, the covenant with the Word of God, the reconciliation with revelation, Jesus Christ the High-priest and King with Jesus Christ the Prophet" (*Church Dogmatics*, IV/3.1, 165).[30] Christ's prophetic work illumines the meaning of his life and death: Jesus suffers so that humanity may be healed; Jesus embodies the "weakness" of divine power which unveils the lesser strength of the "powers and principalities"; through his self-sacrificial life and death, all of creation finds eternal life.[31]

For Barth, the historical context in which "Jesus is Victor" was first uttered illumines the dynamic the phrase is meant to denote (*Church Dogmatics*, IV/3.1, 168–71). In the small village of Möttlingen, the elder Blumhardt was engaged in what he came to view as a case of demonic possession.[32] The case involved Gottliebin and Katharina Dittus, two sisters, the former of whom was the more severely affected. After a two-year saga, the demonic power was exorcized on December 28, 1843. At the climax of this event the cry "Jesus is Victor!" was heard to come from the lips of Katharina,

> not as a saying of her sister, but as a cry of despair – Blumhardt refers to a shriek "which is almost inconceivable on human lips" – which the demonic power uttered through her lips at the very moment when a superior opponent forced it to yield its control over Gottliebin – this power being cautiously described by Blumhardt as . . . "an angel of Satan."
>
> (IV/3.1, 169)

The cry "Jesus is Victor" was the cry of a demonic power, howling in the face of the superior strength of the Triune God. It was a confession that occurred at the end of a genuine struggle in which Jesus Christ's divine healing power shined through to the community in a singular act of individual healing and liberation, but which disclosed universally God's gracious triune activity in history.

Though Barth allowed for multiple interpretations of these events, he was most especially taken by Blumhardt's "discovery" of the lordship of Jesus Christ and his association of that lordship with the kingdom. Barth writes,

> Nor did he meet with anything new – except the new thing of the New Testament – at the crisis of the battle. Yet the fact remains that this well-known truth was then much more to him than the confirmation of an existing conviction or the success of

> his pastoral venture in the strength of his conviction. It came as a new thing and in an unexpected way when he heard that simple statement: "Jesus is Victor," at the beginning of the healing of the afflicted in demonstration of the power of Jesus.
> (*Church Dogmatics*, IV/3.1, 170)

The expression "new thing of the New Testament" refers to the concrete history of Jesus Christ, the expression of the lordship of God enacted in history. In the demonic power's confession "Jesus is Victor," Blumhardt experienced the faithful, healing power of God definitively embodied in Jesus, but present now in the midst of the struggle involving the Dittus sisters. What makes this intervention "trinitarian" is the fact that Christ's inbreaking is conducted through the power of the Holy Spirit.

Barth notes that Blumhardt interpreted the event as a fresh outpouring of God's Spirit, "in new intercession with the unquenchable expectation and indestructible hope that there will be fresh declarations of this lordship and a fresh outpouring of the Holy Ghost on all flesh (of which Blumhardt saw the beginning in this event and the utterance of this cry)" (*Church Dogmatics*, IV/3.1, 170). For Blumhardt this episode was akin to Pentecost. In concert with Blumhardt, Barth argued that the inbreaking of Jesus the Victor in ongoing history was to be understood under the banner of the "promise of the Spirit," revealing that God's work of reclamation, which gives shape to ongoing history, is trinitarian in nature (IV/3.1, 191, 193).

In his reflections on the promise of the Holy Spirit (*Church Dogmatics*, IV/3.1, 274–367), Barth interprets the Spirit as a co-equal partner in the implementation of Jesus Christ's prophetic work – a work of reconciliation in and for the world. In this section he introduces his idea of the threefold *parousia*: the resurrection of Jesus Christ, the outpouring of the Holy Spirit, and the second coming of Jesus Christ (IV/3.1, 296), echoing the threefold form of Hebrews 13:8, "Jesus Christ is the same, yesterday and today and for ever." As the middle term in this threefold temporality, it is the Holy Spirit who links the particular resurrection of Jesus of Nazareth with the universal resurrection of all flesh at the end of days (IV/3.1, 359). It is through the communion of the Holy Spirit that Christians actually participate in the *parousia* here and now. The Holy Spirit brings the ministry of Jesus the prophet, the head of the church, alive in the present through its sanctifying and active energies, what Barth calls the Spirit's "gifts and lights and powers" (IV/3.1, 353). The ongoing presence of Jesus the Victor in the power of the Holy Spirit is none other than the person and presence of the crucified and risen one, through his humiliation as the Son of God and exaltation as the Son of Man (IV/3.1, 389). As the Spirit of Pentecost was poured out on all flesh, Christ, too, in the kenotic, incarnational logic of Philippians 2 is poured out again and again. The Christ of the suffering of "Gethsemane and Golgotha" (IV/3.1, 390) is the only form that the triumphant Christ takes and therefore the victory of Jesus is the victory of the Crucified.

## LONGING FOR THE TRIUNE GOD

The revelation of God's lordship (i.e., kingdom of God) manifest in the person of Jesus Christ is now present in ongoing history as the pneumatological presence of "Jesus the Victor." As such, ongoing history is determined and given its substance under the impress of the trinitarian work of "Jesus the Victor." However, this does not preclude human action. Rather, in the "time between the times," the living Jesus and His Spirit elicit from humanity "parables of the kingdom."

"Parables of the kingdom" are living *human* correspondences to the one kingdom of God, Jesus Christ. When God's righteous reign of love and justice breaks into a world of sin and evil, we have a taste of the victory of Jesus in a penultimate dimension. "Jesus is Victor" as the sign of the victory of God is extended into history not only through the pneumatological presence of the risen Christ, but also by eliciting parabolic correspondences in human history like the Blumhardt exorcism.

The Blumhardt exorcism was a moment where God's reign and triune transcendence broke forth in the immanent space of human history, but not to the exclusion of human action. Rather, it elicited the prayer and righteous action of the faithful human community. Barth was quite explicit in pointing out that Blumhardt had a role to play in the conflict in which he was engaged, and that by extension so does any person or community who lives in the "time between the times" (*Church Dogmatics*, IV/3.1, 176). It is in these moments of faithful prayer and righteous action that we see a manifestation of the *Totus Christus* (IV/3.1, 216) – Christ in his totality graciously embracing and reconciling the whole of creation, because the action of God does not exclude, but includes faithful human action.

It is through the Son and the Spirit that God reconciles creation in triune majesty, and thus the character of God's triune love for the world and God's desire to see this reign of justice manifest "on earth as it is in heaven" becomes increasingly clear. In a very real sense, it is in human vulnerability and suffering that humanity comes face to face with the full humanity of Jesus. Though Barth is careful not to offer any guarantees, nonetheless, it is in the midst of tragedy, pain, suffering, and despair that the cry for God becomes a moment of participation in the kingdom of God. For as recounted in the Blumhardt story, the cry "Jesus is Victor!" was simultaneously the humiliated cry of acquiescence, the longing sigh for healing, and the shout of victory.

"Jesus is Victor," then, reminds us of the depths of the cry of despair, the groans of creation, and the call for the coming Christ. It is also a reassurance that Christ is and will be victorious over the forces of darkness, and a summons to join in the struggle. The victory of God in Christ and our participation in that struggle are both sealed by the promise of the Spirit. The victory of Jesus is a victory of the Holy Spirit. Put another way, it is in and through the Spirit that the person and work of Christ are present to us here and now, both reconciling and calling us to participate in the reconciling work of God. Humanity is to wait and hasten, with "Thy kingdom come!" as the quintessential prayer – which is also understood by Barth as *concrete social action* – which is to be prayed from a kingdom heart that is "zealous and brave."[33] The act of God in Christ calls forth something in us; divine grace elicits a concrete human response. In all of this, the Spirit manifests its divinity through helping to empower all Christians to express the love and justice of God through their own humble yet substantive witness to God's righteous reign on earth. Through the death and resurrection of the Son and the outpouring of the Holy Spirit, the eternal fullness of God's triune revelation is unveiled to the whole creation.

## CONCLUSION

In conclusion, to understand Barth's doctrine of the Trinity fully we must understand the ways in which the three persons of the Trinity work together in the economy of reconciliation. Recent discussions of the Trinity and election in Barth's theology have placed new attention on God's triune activity in the space–time manifold of history. This "turn to history" has helped us to see with new eyes the way in which Barth "historicized" the doctrine of God. However, much of the recent scholarship has focused on the ways in which election affects the divine nature. In this chapter we have sought to dislocate the debate on Trinity and election, and relocate it in a discussion of Trinity, history, and ethics.

From the *Römerbrief* (*Letter to the Romans*) to the doctrine of reconciliation, Barth's theology has been inextricably linked with ethics and tends toward a trinitarian ethic of reconciliation. When it is viewed as a "reconciliational trinitarianism," a new horizon is opened up to pull together key threads in Barth's thought, including the Trinity, the victory of Jesus, the promise of the Holy Spirit, and the kingdom of God. Barth's doctrine of the economic Trinity comes to its fullest expression in the doctrine of reconciliation, where Christ's victory is manifest in a parabolic fashion through pneumatologically empowered signs of the kingdom of God.

Barth makes an innovative contribution to the twentieth-century trinitarian renaissance through his trinitarian cartography of God's gracious activity in the economy of redemption. As his theology matures, the economic Trinity's narrative drama of reconciling action becomes increasingly clear. The triune acts of God in redemptive history shed light on God's being, a communion of love that is truly for and with the world. The victory of Jesus Christ, unveiled in the resurrection, and the power of the Holy Spirit, disclosed in the outpouring on all human flesh, becomes paradigmatic to this mature doctrine of the economic Trinity. The victory of Jesus and the outpouring of the Spirit at Pentecost become the two ways through which the Triune God lavishly pours out the divine love to reconcile and redeem humanity and the whole creation. In these two divine acts, humanity is included as the living Christ and the Spirit of Pentecost elicit true and faithful human response embodied in prayer and righteous action.

Barth's trinitarian doctrine deployed in the doctrine of reconciliation is trinitarian reflection at its best. It not only provides a new horizon for uniting creation, reconciliation, and eschatology for Christian theology, but it also presses for the proclamation and embodiment of a prophetic social ethic in an age of "lordless powers."[34]

## Notes

1. For a recent example, see Veli-Matti Kärkkäinen, *The Trinity: Global Perspectives* (Louisville, KY: Westminster John Knox, 2007), xx, 67.
2. Karl Barth, *Kirchliche Dogmatik* (Zürich: Evangelischer Verlag, 1932–67); trans. G. W. Bromiley as *Church Dogmatics*, 4 vols. (Edinburgh: T. & T. Clark, 1936–69). All citations are given in the text according to volume and part (e.g., I/1).
3. Some of the most significant studies of Barth's trinitarian theology as found in the early volumes of the *Church Dogmatics* include: Colin E. Gunton, *Becoming and Being: The Doctrine of God in Charles Hartshorne and Karl Barth* (Oxford University Press, 1978); Rowan Williams, "Barth on the Triune God," in S. W. Sykes, ed., *Karl Barth:*

*Studies of his Theological Method* (Oxford: Clarendon Press, 1979), 147–93; Eberhard Jüngel, *Gottes Sein ist im Werden* (Tübingen: J. C. B. Mohr, 1976); rev. trans. John Webster as *God's Being is in Becoming: The Trinitarian Being of God in the Theology of Karl Barth* (Grand Rapids, MI: Eerdmans, 2001); Alan Torrance, "The Trinity," in John Webster, ed., *The Cambridge Companion to Karl Barth* (Cambridge University Press, 2000), 72–91. For the phrase "revelational trinitarianism" see Stanley J. Grenz, *The Social God and the Relational Self: A Trinitarian Theology of the Imago Dei* (Louisville, KY: Westminster John Knox, 2001), 34.

4. McCormack's interpretation is concerned with the relationship between the novel formulation of Barth's doctrine of election – elaborated only after his groundbreaking work on the Trinity – and the doctrine of Trinity. The first fruits of McCormack's interpretive work appeared in his essay "Grace and Being: The Role of God's Gracious Election in Karl Barth's Theological Ontology," in Webster, ed., *The Cambridge Companion to Karl Barth*, 92–110.
5. Friedrich-Wilhelm Marquardt, *Theologie und Sozialismus: Das Beispiel Karl Barths* (Munich: Chr. Kaiser Verlag, 1985); George Hunsinger, ed., *Karl Barth and Radical Politics* (Philadelphia: Westminster, 1976); Peter Winzeler, *Widerstehende Theologie: Karl Barth 1920–1935* (Stuttgart: Alektor, 1982); George Hunsinger, "Part I: Political Theology," in *Disruptive Grace: Studies in the Theology of Karl Barth* (Grand Rapids, MI: Eerdmans, 2000), 21–130; and Timothy Gorringe, *Karl Barth: Against Hegemony* (New York: Oxford University Press, 1999).

   Our understanding of Barth's ethics of reconciliation has been shaped by John Webster; however, we seek to expand Webster's account of Barth's ethics of reconciliation through giving greater dogmatic prominence to the doctrine of the Trinity and greater historical prominence to the influence of the Blumhardts on Barth's doctrine of reconciliation. See John Webster, *Barth's Ethics of Reconciliation* (Cambridge University Press, 1995); and John Webster, *Barth's Moral Theology: Human Action in Barth's Thought* (Grand Rapids, MI: Eerdmans, 1998).
6. For a concise introduction to Barth's prophetic ministry, with a sensitivity to the ways in which a radical socialist vision animated his own public engagements, see Frank Jehle, *Ever against the Stream: The Politics of Karl Barth, 1906–1968* (Grand Rapids, MI: Eerdmans, 2002).
7. Standing between the second edition of the *Römerbrief* (*Epistle to the Romans*) and the *Church Dogmatics* are two other lecture cycles, the so-called Göttingen dogmatics (1924–25) and *Christliche Dogmatik* (*Christian Dogmatics*, 1927), in which Barth laid the groundwork for his construction of the doctrine of the Trinity as found in the later *Church Dogmatics*. We do not tarry over these explications because, as Bruce McCormack has noted, "The truth is that a systematic comparison, section by section, of *all three versions* of the prolegomena (the Göttingen and Münster versions together with the *Church Dogmatics*, I/1 and I/2) makes evident the extent to which the fundamental dogmatic decisions

which control even *Church Dogmatics* I/1 and I/2 were already made in 1924/5 in Göttingen." Bruce McCormack, *Karl Barth's Critically Realistic Dialectical Theology: Its Genesis and Development, 1909–1936* (Oxford: Clarendon Press, 1997), 375.

See also Karl Barth, *The Göttingen Dogmatics: Instruction in the Christian Religion*, trans. G. W. Bromiley (Edinburgh: T. & T. Clark, 1991), 87–130; and Karl Barth, *Die christliche Dogmatik im Entwurf* (Munich: Chr. Kaiser, 1927), 126–214.

8. "The doctrine of the Trinity is not itself a text of revelation but only a commentary upon it" (*Church Dogmatics*, I/2, 35).
9. Revelation is the "self-unveiling" of God through which God graciously makes Godself fully known to humanity in Jesus Christ. Barth understands revelation primarily as a divine act, a disclosure that humanity "cannot do in any sense or in any way." For us to have knowledge of God, then, we must necessarily be encountered by God, which means that revelation itself is an event which God initiates, inhabits, and brings to fulfillment. Revelation is and must necessarily be the self-unveiling or "self-interpretation of this God" (*Church Dogmatics*, I/1, 311). Barth's doctrine of revelation is an explicit critique of a tradition of liberal theology with roots in the theology of F. D. E. Schleiermacher (1768–1834) that emphasized an innate human capacity for knowledge of God.
10. On the broad and substantive imprint of patristic thought on the trinitarian architecture of Barth's theology see T. F. Torrance, "Karl Barth and Patristic Theology," in John Thompson, ed., *Theology beyond Christendom: Essays on the Centenary of the Birth of Karl Barth May 10, 1986* (Allison Park, PA: Pickwick, 1986), 215–39.
11. The correspondence of the economic and immanent Trinity is not framed according to the logic of ontic identity as articulated by Rahner, but is rather one of dialectical correspondence. As George Hunsinger has argued, for Barth there is only one Holy Trinity, subsisting in two different forms: the one immanent, the other economic. Barth's dialectic pertains to them both, and their relation is governed by, among other things, the Chalcedonian pattern, the dialectical correspondence of Jesus Christ's full divinity and full humanity, which are both present in the personhood of Jesus the Jew from Nazareth. See George Hunsinger, "Election and the Trinity: Twenty-Five Theses on the Theology of Karl Barth," *Modern Theology*, 24:2 (April 2008), 179–198; and George Hunsinger, "Karl Barth's Christology: Its Basic Chalcedonian Character," in *Disruptive Grace*, 131–47.
12. For example, William Hill calls Barth a "trinitarian modalist," a trinitarian because there is no fourth divine essence that unites the three and a modalist because there is but one seat of divine subjectivity. See William J. Hill, *The Three-Personed God: The Trinity as a Mystery of Salvation* (Washington, DC: Catholic University of America, 1982), 113–24.
13. See Jüngel, *God's Being is in Becoming*, 37.

14. For a helpful historical and systematic discussion of Barth's use of "modes of being" (*Seinsweise*) across his dogmatic *oeuvre*, see Iain Taylor, "In Defense of Karl Barth's Doctrine of the Trinity," *International Journal of Systematic Theology*, 5:1 (March 2003), 33–46.
15. "Similarly the doctrine of the Trinity, when considered historically in its origin and development, is not equally interested in the Father, the Son and the Holy Ghost. Here too the theme is primarily the second person of the Trinity, God the Son, the deity of Christ" (*Church Dogmatics*, I/1, 315).
16. For a helpful discussion of this see Alan J. Torrance, "The Trinity," 81–83.
17. See *Church Dogmatics*, I/1, 139 ff.; cf. II/1, 275; II/2, 121.
18. e.g., ibid., I/1, 415, 424–26, 430, 442.
19. "The love of God is not an abstract quality of God's; it is an act: God takes to heart our misery. In Jesus Christ, He declares His mercy unto us and puts this mercy to work, and there is no mercy towards us outside Jesus Christ.... He is the mercy of God, he is the love of God, he is the open heart of God." Karl Barth, *The Faith of the Church: A Commentary on the Apostles' Creed According to Calvin's Catechism* (New York: Meridian, 1959), 37–38.
20. "When the history of theology in the twentieth century is written from the vantage point of, let us say, one hundred years from now, I am confident that the greatest contribution of Karl Barth to the development of church doctrine will be located in his doctrine of election." McCormack, "Grace and Being," 92.
21. "It is also true that He does not elect alone, but in company with the electing of the Father and the Holy Spirit. But He does elect. The obedience which He renders as the Son of God is, as genuine obedience, His own decision and electing, a decision and electing no less divinely free than the electing and decision of the Father and the Holy Spirit... In the harmony of the triune God He is no less the original Subject of this electing than He is its original object" (*Church Dogmatics*, II/2, 105).
22. As Eberhard Jüngel phrases it, "God's being-in-act was understood to mean that God is his decision." *God's Being is in Becoming*, 83.
23. Barth develops the point that Jesus Christ is the subject of election such that not only is the divine Son understood to be the "Elector" but so also is the human will which is included in the one person of Jesus. On this point, see the illuminating work of Paul Dafydd Jones, *The Humanity of Christ: Christology in Karl Barth's* Church Dogmatics (Edinburgh: T. & T. Clark, 2008), 60–116.
24. See *Church Dogmatics*, II/2, 9–10.
25. McCormack, "Grace and Being"; Bruce McCormack, "'Seek God Where He may be Found': A Response to Edwin Chr. van Driel," *Scottish Journal of Theology*, 60 (2007), 62–79. Cf. Matthias Gockel, *Barth and Schleiermacher on the Doctrine of Election: A Systematic-Theological Comparison* (Oxford University Press, 2006); and Adam Eitel, "The

Resurrection of Jesus Christ: Karl Barth and the Historicization of God's Being," *International Journal of Systematic Theology*, 10:1 (2007), 36–53.

Two recent attempts to adjudicate between McCormack and Molnar are: Kevin W. Hector, "God's Triunity and Self-Determination: A Conversation with Karl Barth, Bruce McCormack and Paul Molnar," *International Journal of Systematic Theology*, 7:3 (2005), 246–61; and Aaron T. Smith, "God's Self-Specification: His Being is his Electing," *Scottish Journal of Theology*, 62 (2009), 1–25.

26. For McCormack, God's eternal act of self-determination to be God as Father, Son, and Holy Spirit and God's eternal act of self-determination to be "God for us" are one and the same act. Thus God's triunity is a function of the divine election. Though election does not precede the divine triunity chronologically, it does precede it logically, for it is God's eternal act of determining himself to be God for us that constitutes God as triune. Election is an eternal decision, revealed to humanity in the revelation of Jesus Christ, which is the revelation of the electing and elected God. It is in light of this that McCormack is led to argue that humanity cannot know of a God prior to, or other than the one revealed in, this decision. Therefore, there is no eternal Logos *in abstraction* (no *logos asarkos*), but only the Logos manifest eternally in the incarnation of Jesus Christ (i.e., *logos ensarkos*).
27. Paul Molnar, *Divine Freedom and the Doctrine of the Immanent Trinity: In Dialogue with Karl Barth and Contemporary Theology* (Edinburgh: T. & T. Clark, 2005); Paul Molnar, "The Trinity, Election and God's Ontological Freedom: A Response to Kevin W. Hector," *International Journal of Systematic Theology*, 8 (2006), 294–306; Paul Molnar, "Can the Electing God be God Without Us? Some Implications of Bruce McCormack's Understanding of Barth's Doctrine of Election for the Doctrine of the Trinity," *Neue Zeitschrift für Systematische Theologie und Religionsphilosophie*, 49:2 (2008), 199–222; Paul Molnar, "What Does it Mean to Say that Jesus Christ is Indispensable to a Properly Conceived Doctrine of the Immanent Trinity? A Response to Jeffrey Hensley," *Scottish Journal of Theology*, 61 (February 2008), 96–106. Cf. Edwin Chr. van Driel, "Karl Barth on the Eternal Existence of Jesus Christ," *Scottish Journal of Theology*, 60 (2007), 45–61; and Hunsinger, "Election and the Trinity."
28. Barth is quite clear that this phrase and the multiple dynamics it names come from the "underground stream of the insight" of the Blumhardts. See *Church Dogmatics*, IV/3.1, 169–71. See also Christian T. Collins Winn, *"Jesus is Victor!" The Significance of the Blumhardts for the Theology of Karl Barth* (Eugene, OR: Pickwick, 2008).
29. Adam Eitel shows how Barth begins his doctrine of reconciliation through advancing the connection between the Trinity and the resurrection. See his "The Resurrection of Jesus Christ."
30. Clearly Barth is working within the Reformed tradition and especially Calvin's construal of the *munus triplex* ("threefold office") in the *Institutes of the Christian Religion*; cf. Philip Walker Butin, "Two

Early Reformed Catechisms, the Threefold Office, and the Shape of Karl Barth's Christology," *Scottish Journal of Theology*, 44 (1991), 195–214.

31. Barth interprets Jesus' prophetic office as a dramatic narrative: "Hence in this third form too, as a doctrine of Jesus Christ the true light, Word and Revealer, as a doctrine of His prophetic office, Christology is a narration of His history, and specifically of the shining of His light, the real speaking of the covenant, the revelation of reconciliation, the action of the Prophet Jesus Christ . . . It is a drama which can only be followed, or rather experienced and recounted" (Barth, *Church Dogmatics*, IV/3.1, 166).
32. For a discussion of these events see, Collins Winn, *"Jesus is Victor!,"* 83–91.
33. Karl Barth, *The Christian Life: Church Dogmatics* IV/4, *Lecture Fragments*, trans. G. W. Bromiley (Grand Rapids, MI: Eerdmans, 1981), 263.
34. This chapter was helped by comments from our colleagues and friends John L. Drury, George Hunsinger, Adam Eitel, and Paul Molnar.

## Further reading

Barth, Karl, *Church Dogmatics*, I/1: *The Doctrine of the Word of God*, trans. G. W. Bromiley and F. W. Torrance (Edinburgh: T. & T. Clark, 1975).

Collins Winn, Christian T., *"Jesus is Victor!": The Significance of the Blumhardts for the Theology of Karl Barth* (Eugene, OR: Pickwick, 2008).

Gunton, Colin E., *Becoming and Being: The Doctrine of God in Charles Hartshorne and Karl Barth* (Oxford University Press, 1978).

Hunsinger, George, "Election and the Trinity: Twenty-Five Theses on the Theology of Karl Barth," *Modern Theology*, 24:2 (April 2008), 179–98.

Jüngel, Eberhard, *God's Being is in Becoming: The Trinitarian Being of God in the Theology of Karl Barth*, rev. trans. John Webster (Grand Rapids, MI: Eerdmans, 2001).

McCormack, Bruce L., "Grace and Being: The Role of God's Gracious Election in Karl Barth's Theological Ontology," in J. Webster, ed., *The Cambridge Companion to Karl Barth* (Cambridge University Press, 2000), 92–110.

Molnar, Paul D., *Divine Freedom and the Doctrine of the Immanent Trinity*: In Dialogue with Karl Barth and Contemporary Theology (Edinburgh: T. & T. Clark, 2005).

Torrance, Alan, "The Trinity," in J. Webster, ed., *The Cambridge Companion to Karl Barth* (Cambridge University Press, 2000), 72–91.

Williams, Rowan, "Barth on the Triune God," in S. W. Sykes, ed., *Karl Barth: Studies of his Theological Method* (Oxford: Clarendon Press, 1979), 147–93.

# 11 Mystery of grace and salvation: Karl Rahner's theology of the Trinity

PETER C. PHAN

Anyone familiar with the gargantuan theological output of the German Jesuit theologian Karl Rahner (1904–1984) can hardly miss the irony that for someone who is universally hailed as the most influential contributor to the renaissance of trinitarian theology in the twentieth century, at least in the Catholic Church, and who vigorously insists that the Trinity be the center of theology and Christian life, the bulk of his explicit writings on the Trinity is minuscule. His synthetic magnum opus *Grundkurs des Glauben* (*Foundations of Christian Faith*) contains barely four pages on the Trinity, entitled "Towards an Understanding of the Doctrine of the Trinity."[1] Apart from a handful of pieces in his *Schriften zur Theologie* (*Theological Investigations*)[2] and two entries in the encyclopedia *Sacramentum mundi*,[3] Rahner's longest writing on the Trinity is a booklet-length contribution to a handbook of theology.[4]

Why, then, in spite of the paucity of his writings on the Trinity, is Rahner celebrated as the initiator of the rediscovery of the Trinity in Catholic theology? Does this paucity reflect a lack of consistency between Rahner's theory and praxis? Or could it be argued that it is precisely because the Trinity so thoroughly informs the structure and contents of *Foundations of Christian Faith* that a lengthy treatment of it is unnecessary? What is so significant about his trinitarian theology, and in which ways has it renewed the Christian theology of the Trinity? To answer these questions would require, first, situating Rahner's trinitarian theology in the context of the Catholic neo-scholastic or manualistic theology which was the staple fare in Catholic seminaries until the 1960s and, second, examining in detail, albeit within a very limited space, its major tenets.[5]

## HISTORICAL AND THEOLOGICAL CONTEXTS

Another irony in Rahner's academic career is that he was at first destined by his superiors to be a professor of philosophy and not of theology.

It was only after his doctoral dissertation in philosophy, a commentary on Thomas Aquinas' *Summa theologiae* (*The Summa of Theology*), 1, q. 84, a. 7, later published as *Geist in Welt* (*Spirit in the World*),[6] had been rejected by his advisor, the Dominican Martin Honecker, for being insufficiently Thomistic, that his superiors sent him to the University of Innsbruck to earn a doctorate in theology, which he completed in a couple of months and which enabled him to pursue a career in theology. Nevertheless, his philosophical background stood Rahner in good stead, especially his philosophical anthropology, which he claims is rooted in Aquinas' epistemology and which he elaborates further in his *Hörer des Wortes* (*Hearers of the Word*).[7]

### The human person as "spirit in world"

Although Rahner's trinitarian theology is rooted primarily in the Bible, the Greek Fathers, and Christian spirituality, it finds deep echoes in his metaphysics of knowledge[8] and philosophical anthropology.[9] According to Rahner, the human person is *Geist in Welt*, literally, "spirit in world" (not "spirit in *the* world"). Insofar as humans are "spirit," they necessarily transcend themselves, in acts of knowledge and freedom, toward the infinite and ever-regressive horizon of truth and love, whom Rahner calls Holy Mystery, or God.[10] This act, termed *Vorgriff* ("reaching out"), an anticipatory reaching out for the Absolute Being without ever grasping it as an object, reveals humans as possessing a *potentia obedientialis* (ability to hear) for divine revelation, that is, an existential disposition and innate capacity in all humans to receive a word or self-communication from God, *if* God chooses to speak to them.

However, insofar as they are "in world," humans can perform this act of self-transcendence of knowledge and love only in history, within time and space, so that, should God *freely* elect to speak to them at all, God cannot but do so in and through historical events. If and when God does so, God, the ever-receding horizon and the asymptotic goal of human knowing and loving, will reveal himself not as a distant deity but as Emmanuel, God-with-us, dwelling in human history.

### The world of all-embracing Grace

It is only from the standpoint of faith that Christians, Rahner points out, can assert that God has *in fact* come near to humanity, assumed a historical existence as "Word," and given himself to us as "Grace." Indeed, Christian faith calls this act of God's self-gift to us in knowledge and love the incarnation of the Son and the grace of the Spirit respectively. Thus, ironically, albeit highly critical of Augustine's so-called psychological analogy of the Trinity, Rahner does invoke the human acts of knowing and love as intimations of the Trinity, though, as we will see, with an all-important difference, namely that, for Rahner, it is not the mind knowing and loving *itself* that is the analogy of life in the Trinity but our knowing and loving *others*, and ultimately God, in *the world* and in *history*, that points to the plural reality of God's inner life. In this sense, Rahner's trinitarian theology is an ascending or "from below" theology as it were, that is, starting from our concrete and historical experiences of God's self-gift in the threefold modality of Father, Son, and Spirit.

Methodologically, according to Rahner, it is exclusively from the vantage point of the events of God the Father's self-communication in Word and Spirit in history (what is termed the "economic Trinity") that a theology of the Trinity can and should be constructed in order to arrive at some understanding of who God is in God's intra-trinitarian life (the "immanent Trinity"). To this point we will return below.

Because of this self-gift of God, in contrast to other theologians, such as Karl Barth and Hans Urs von Balthasar, who emphasize the universal sinfulness of humanity and therefore God's redemption through Jesus' death on the cross, Rahner tends to view human history as being permeated through and through by God's self-communication, which is manifested in the incarnation of the Logos and in the bestowal of the Spirit. The world, though marred by sin, is truly and really a world of grace in which humanity's *potentia obedientialis* has been transformed in *each and every* human person, Christian or not, prior to his or her personal decision, into what Rahner terms the "supernatural existential" – that is, a constitutive and intrinsic (albeit not "essential," since it is gratuitous) dimension of human existence, affecting human consciousness. Being graced, at least in the fundamental mode of God's self-offer, is what defines human beings, and not the putative "human nature." The latter is a philosophically deduced reality, which for Rahner is but a residual or remainder concept (*Restbegriff*), that is, whatever remains left over after the human person is understood as intrinsically graced.

This grace, Rahner insists, is God's self-gift bestowed to all humans through Christ and in the power of the Spirit. All grace is Christological and pneumatological. Hence, humans can be said to possess a trinitarian constitution, and, since grace is given through Christ, *all* persons can be said to be, in Rahner's celebrated and controversial phrase, "anonymous Christians." By this Rahner does not mean that we can be certain that all humans will de facto accept God's offer of grace. He only means that God wills all humans to be saved and to come to a knowledge of the truth

(1 Tim 2:4) through Christ and by the power of the Spirit, and that God's universal will of salvation is something that transforms all humans ontologically and consciously. Grace, for Rahner, is not primarily some *thing*, a quality (or, as the manualist tradition puts it, an "accident") created in us by God by way of efficient causality ("created grace"), but the Triune God dwelling in us in God's threefold reality of Father, Son, and Spirit, by way of quasi-formal causality ("Uncreated Grace").

## God: one and/or trine?

If the Trinity is the central reality in human life and forms the heart of Christian theology, how on earth has there been a massive and long-standing forgetfulness of it in both spirituality and theology, at least in Latin theology? Or, as Rahner pus it somewhat hyperbolically, "Christians are, in their practical life, almost mere 'monotheists,'" (*The Trinity*, 10) or, more accurately, unitarian or deist. Rahner traces this eclipse of the Trinity in the West to the influence of Augustine and Aquinas on the way the treatise on God was structured. In neo-scholastic manuals, the treatise on God was usually divided in two tractates: "On the One God" (*De Deo Uno*), based mainly on the metaphysics of being, and "On the Trine God" (*De Deo Trino*), based exclusively on revelation, with little if any connection between the two parts.[11]

Rahner's historical account has been widely – and rightly – disputed. Whether one agrees with Augustine's or Aquinas' theologies of the Trinity or not, it is incontrovertible that their understanding of the one God is rooted in the Bible and not in Greek philosophy, either Platonic or Aristotelian. Rather, the eclipse of the Trinity in Western theology is, in the view of many, to be laid at the door of modern theology. In reacting to the deistic and, later, atheistic challenges of the Enlightenment, Christian theology suffered a loss of nerve and was co-opted into elaborating philosophical counter-arguments for the existence of an Absolute Being and its essence rather than expounding what Christian revelation affirms *who* (and not *what*) God is and God's *behavior* and *character* (and not God's "attributes"). In such an approach, *De Deo Uno* unavoidably gets the upper if not exclusive hand, and as a consequence, the Christian God who is Father, Son, and Spirit and who acts in history vanishes from sight.

Whatever the accuracy of Rahner's historical reconstruction of the roots of the separation between the *De Deo Uno* and the *De Deo Trino*, and whether or not the Trinity has ever been totally marginalized from Christian theology and spirituality in the West, there is no gainsaying that the eclipse of the Trinity did produce a defective understanding of key Christian doctrines. Rahner claims that as a result of what he calls "anti-trinitarian timidity" (*The Trinity*, 13), creation has been viewed only as an *ad extra* operation common to all the three divine persons by way of efficient causality and not also as the distinct work of each person of the Trinity by way of exemplary causality; prayer is often addressed to God in general or the divine nature rather than to the Father, in the Son, and by the power of the Spirit; the sacrifice of the Mass is understood as being offered by Jesus to a generic deity rather than by the Son to God the Father; the incarnation is seen as an act that in principle any person of the Trinity could have performed indifferently and not as an act that is exclusively appropriate to the Word; grace is seen primarily as a created reality and not as the indwelling of the Trinity; and beatific vision is taken to be a vision of the divine essence and not a specifically distinct relation of the human person to each of the divine persons.[12]

For Rahner then there are two issues in developing a theology of the Trinity, one methodological, the other substantive. First, how is the treatise on God to be structured? Is it to be divided into two tractates, that is, "On the One God" and "On the Trine God"? If such a division is adopted, how is the "oneness" of God to be understood? Does this oneness consist in the "unicity" of God (the numerically one God) or in the "unity" of Father, Son, and Spirit (unity as the communion among the three divine persons)? Furthermore, what does "God" refer to? The divine nature or the Father, the source of the Son and the Spirit? For Rahner, the correct answers to these two questions are the second alternatives, that is, the oneness of God consists in the communion or *perichōrēsis* among the three divine persons, and "God" refers to the Father, the unoriginate origin of the Son and the Spirit. However, with these presuppositions, the division of the treatise on God into *De Deo Uno* and *De Deo Trino* is no longer justified or helpful.

Second, the most fundamental issue is the relationship between the "economic" Trinity (who God is and what God does in history) and the "immanent" Trinity (who God is as Father, Son, and Spirit in their eternal relations). For Rahner, this is the crux of trinitarian theology determining whether the Trinity is seen as *the* mystery of salvation lying at the heart of the Christian life and the center unifying all the other Christian doctrines, or is treated as a theological conundrum, to be expounded through various kinds of analogies but bereft of any connection with and impact upon theology and spirituality. It is here that Rahner's approach has left a permanent legacy, and to his proposal, which constitutes Rahner's most significant contribution to the theology of the Trinity, we now turn.

## "RAHNER'S RULE": ECONOMIC AND IMMANENT TRINITY

### "Rahner's Rule"

To the question of the relationship between the economic (or historical) and immanent (or transcendent) Trinity, Rahner gives a terse answer in an axiom which is now dubbed "Rahner's Rule": *"The 'economic' Trinity is the 'immanent' Trinity and the 'immanent' Trinity is the 'economic' Trinity"* (*The Trinity*, 22).[13] The rule is composed of two assertions which categorically affirm the "identity" between the economic Trinity and the immanent Trinity. What is meant by "economic" and "immanent" Trinity has been noted above, and will be explained further. What is not clear is what Rahner means by the identity between the economic and immanent Trinity, which the copula "is" implies. Does identity mean numerical unicity (that is, there is only one Trinity, either economic or immanent or both), or does it mean essential sameness (there are two Trinities but they are the same in nature, though different in some non-essential respects, like a pair of identical twins)? Furthermore, if the economic Trinity is (identical with) the immanent Trinity, by implication the immanent Trinity is (identical with) the economic Trinity. Why does Rahner feel it necessary to add the second assertion that the immanent Trinity is the economic Trinity? Is such an assertion redundant? If not, what is its import?[14] Should one make only the first assertion and not the second? Different answers to these questions bring Rahner's Rule into theological positions that he may not have anticipated or agreed with.

### The purpose of Rahner's Rule

To understand Rahner's Rule correctly, it is necessary to recall to mind what Rahner intends to achieve with it. By identifying the economic Trinity with the immanent Trinity, Rahner's basic intention is to make the Trinity the central and primordial mystery of salvation. First, Rahner wants to restore the Trinity as a *mystery of salvation*, because he claims that neo-scholastic, manualistic theology of the Trinity, which he terms *Schultheologie* (school, i.e., Roman Catholic seminary, theology), has turned it into an object of psychological and metaphysical speculation totally divorced from the history of God's self-communication. In this way, Rahner wants to affirm that God's self-revelation and self-gift to us in history (the economic Trinity) is *no other than* or *exactly the same* as the Trinity of Father, Son, and Spirit in their eternal mutual relations (the immanent Trinity).

Let it be noted that by using the two expressions "economic Trinity" and "immanent Trinity" Rahner does not mean that there are *two* Trinities that happen to be identical with each other, the one acting in history and given to us to know and love in time, the other in eternity with its three "persons" wholly inaccessible to us, the former a copy or a partial duplication or a representation of the latter. Rahner's point is that there is not an immanent Trinity hidden lying behind or above the Trinity that we encounter in history. On the contrary, there is only *one* Trinity who gives itself to us as Father, Son, and Spirit, exactly as they are related to each other in themselves. The question of whether for Rahner this one Trinity is changed or, more radically, is temporally constituted as Trinity so that God is not eternally trinitarian but is now in the process of becoming Father, Son, and Spirit in and through its self-communication to humanity in history will be taken up later.

Second, by retrieving the Trinity as a mystery of salvation Rahner also achieves his other goal of making it the *central and primordial mystery* which illumines and shapes our understanding of the other Christian doctrines. As mentioned above, Rahner hints at how the Trinity should influence our theology of creation, incarnation, redemption, grace, prayer, and eschatology. This is not the place to elaborate how Rahner has developed these various aspects of the Christian faith and to what extent they are shaped by his trinitarian theology. Suffice it to note that for Rahner, "no adequate distinction can be made between the doctrine of the Trinity and the doctrine of the economy of salvation" (*The Trinity*, 24).[15] Thus, for Rahner, to discuss the theological themes listed above in the context of the history of salvation is ipso facto speaking, at least indirectly, of the Trinity.

### The theological foundation of Rahner's Rule

From the length to which Rahner goes to defend his axiom it is clear that he does not think he is stating the obvious. On the contrary, he is well aware that his thesis is going against the grain of traditional theology. The arguments he marshals in its favor are of two types. The first type is by way of *reductio ad absurdum*. If the economic Trinity is not the immanent Trinity, and if the immanent Trinity is something other than the economic Trinity, then divine revelation has not told us anything reliable and true about God. At the most, it has conveyed *something* about God but it would not be God's *self*-communication to us, and consequently, revelation would not have reached its eschatological consummation. Similarly, grace would be simply a created grace and not the Uncreated Grace, that is, the indwelling of the Trinity in us. All this, Rahner contends, would be contrary to what Christian faith says about revelation and grace.

Rahner's second type of argumentation consists in refuting three possible objections against his axiom. The first is based on a common opinion in neo-scholastic theology that since the incarnation is a divine operation *ad extra* that is done by way of efficient causality, it is a common act of the Trinity and therefore it could be done by *any* divine person equally effectively. At best it may be argued that the hypostatic union is *appropriate* to the Logos but not specific to him. If this is the case, then the incarnation of the Logos does not by itself say anything specific about the person of the Logos, and as a consequence, the economic Trinity need not be the same as the immanent Trinity. Against this opinion Rahner argues that it unjustifiably assumes that the concept of "person" as implicated in the notion of "hypostatic union" is the same when applied to the Logos and to the other two divine persons, which would make the incarnation equally appropriate to any of the divine persons. Must we not, Rahner suggests, entertain the possibility that "person" as applied to the Logos is so distinctive of him that *only* he can become incarnated, just as "person" as applied to the Father and Spirit is so distinctive of each of them that they cannot enter into history as incarnated but only under another modality? In this case, the economic Trinity is identical with the immanent Trinity, with the hypostatic union of the Logos being an "instance" of this axiom (see *The Trinity*, 24–28).

The second objection, closely related to the first, argues that although we know through revelation that the Word has been made flesh, our experience of God would not have been different if another divine person had been incarnated since that person could still reveal to us what and who God is by means of *words*, and not by who he is, that is, his person. Hence the economic Trinity need not be the immanent Trinity. Rahner responds that Christian tradition before Augustine has never entertained this possibility; on the contrary, it has always maintained that God the Father reveals himself through his Word, who therefore manifests the Father in both the immanent and the economic Trinity. Furthermore, Rahner points out, the objection is false because it presupposes that what is true of one divine person is also true of another since it takes the concept of "person" as applied to the three members of the Trinity to be univocal, which, as has been mentioned above, is at best loosely analogical (see *The Trinity*, 28–30). Hence this objection does not invalidate Rahner's axiom that the economic Trinity is the immanent Trinity and vice versa.

The third objection is more directly Christological. It argues that the human nature that the Logos assumes in his incarnation does not, in and by itself, say anything specific about the Logos. It is simply a neutral instrument by which the Logos is present and active in the world. Its relation to the Logos is no different from that of any other created reality to the Logos. This relation is merely something *added* to what human nature already is and is not *constitutive* of it. Consequently, it cannot be said that the human nature that the Logos assumes is that *in* and *through* which the Logos manifests who he is, and hence, the economic Trinity is not necessarily identical with the immanent Trinity. Rahner rejects the thesis that the human nature that is assumed by the Logos is just any creature possessing only a general, external relation to the Logos. Rather, its relation to the Logos is much more like that between the reality symbolized (i.e., the Logos) and the symbol (i.e., human nature). Rahner calls human nature the *Realsymbol* (the "real symbol") of the Logos.[16] It is that *in* and *through* which the Logos expresses himself and becomes present in the world. Human nature comes to be because the Logos expresses himself in something other than himself. Rahner puts it tersely: "Man is possible because the exteriorization of the Logos is possible" (*The Trinity*, 33). Consequently, the economic Trinity (in which the Logos becomes human) can and should be said to be the immanent Trinity.

## Corollaries of Rahner's Rule

Rahner's Rule, if accepted, would have ample and profound ramifications for Christian theology. We have already mentioned above the several areas of theology in which according to Rahner theological elaborations should be guided by the doctrine of the Trinity. Rahner himself focuses on the doctrine of grace, which is the heart of his theology. From Rahner's Rule it follows that the opinion common in neo-scholastic theology that in grace humans are related to God only in a general way and that at best this relation may be *appropriated* to each of the divine persons is no longer tenable. Rather, if the economic Trinity is the immanent Trinity, that is, if the three divine persons of the immanent Trinity communicate themselves in the economic Trinity in their specific differences in virtue of their eternal mutual relations, then graced human beings are related to each of the divine persons in a distinct and specific way, in accordance with how each of the divine persons communicates himself in history. As Rahner puts it concisely: "Each one of the three divine persons communicates himself to man in gratuitous grace in his own personal particularity and diversity" (*The Trinity*, 34–35). In the following rather dense paragraph we have Rahner's theology of the Trinity and grace in a nutshell:

> [The] three self-communications are the self-communication of the one God in the three relative ways in which God subsists. The Father gives himself to us too as *Father*, that is, precisely because and insofar as he himself, being essentially with *himself*, utters himself and *in this way* communicates the Son, as his own, personal self-manifestation; and because and insofar as the Father and the Son (receiving from the Father), welcoming each other in love, drawn and returning to each other, communicate themselves *in this way*, as received in mutual love, that is, as Holy Spirit. God relates to us in a threefold manner, and this threefold, free, gratuitous relation to us *is* not merely a copy or an analogy of the inner Trinity, but this Trinity itself, albeit as freely and gratuitously communicated.
>
> (*The Trinity*, 35)

Rahner invokes two kinds of causality to explain how this *self*-communication of the immanent Trinity in the economic Trinity makes the latter identical with the former and enables human beings who receive this divine self-communication to have specifically distinct relations with each of the divine persons. This divine self-communication occurs not only by means of efficient causality creating something new in us (i.e., sanctifying grace) but also by means of formal, or more precisely, "quasi-formal" causality in which the three divine persons give *themselves* to us in their threefold and really distinct ways of subsisting (that is, persons) in the immanent Trinity: the Father as that which is given but remaining the ever-incomprehensible Mystery, the Son as the uttered Word of Truth of this Mystery, and the Spirit as the Love of this Mystery and his Word enabling us to welcome this divine self-gift.

Another corollary of Rahner's Rule is theological methodology. If the economic Trinity is the immanent Trinity, then the only starting point for developing a theology of an immanent Trinity is not some speculative analogy, psychological or metaphysical, but our historical experiences of God the Father as manifested in the twofold modality of Word and Spirit. As Rahner affirms: "We can really grasp the content of the doctrine of the Trinity only by going back to the history of salvation and of grace, to our experience of Jesus and of the Spirit of God, who operates in us, because in them we really already possess the Trinity itself as such" (*The Trinity*, 40).

## GOD THE FATHER'S SELF-COMMUNICATION IN TWO DISTINCT MODALITIES OF WORD AND SPIRIT

### God the Father's free act of self-communication in two necessary modalities of Word and Spirit in history

Following the biblical and Greek patristics tradition, Rahner takes "God" to refer to the Father and not the divine essence. The Father communicates *himself* in history as Word and Spirit while himself remaining the unoriginate source of divinity or the Absolute Mystery. The theological challenge, as Rahner sees it, is how to understand these two self-communicating modalities as intrinsically related, yet distinct, moments of the *one* act of the Father's self-communication. These two modalities, experienced in history as two distinct events, should not be viewed as two mere, accidental, and unrelated facts, as if they could be mutually interchangeable, that is, as if the Spirit could be incarnated as Word, and the Word could be given as Spirit. If that were the case, the economic Trinity would not tell us anything really true about the immanent Trinity. Rather, according to Rahner,

> when God freely steps outside of himself in *self*-communication (not merely through creation, positing other realities which are not himself), it is and must be the Son who appears historically in the flesh as man. And it is and must be the Spirit who brings about the acceptance by the world (as creation) in faith, hope, and love of this self-communication.
>
> (*The Trinity*, 86)

It is to be noted that the Father's act of self-communication is free but its modalities are necessary. These two modalities are not simply two interchangeable "functions" of the Father, but together with the Father, they constitute the economic Trinity that is identical with the immanent Trinity.

### Four aspects of God the Father's self-communication

God the Father's self-communication in the two distinct modalities of Word and Spirit does not of course occur in the void but presupposes the creation of a recipient appropriate to and capable of accepting this self-communication. Such a recipient, for Rahner, can only and must be "spirit-in-world," that is, the human person. On the basis of the nature of the human person Rahner elaborates four, albeit not exhaustive, double aspects of God the Father's self-communication: (1) origin-future; (2) history-transcendence; (3) offer-acceptance; and (4) knowledge-love (see *The Trinity*, 88). It is to be noted that these four pairs characterize both God's self-communication and the human person as its addressee. For Rahner, theology implicates anthropology and vice versa. To understand the economic Trinity requires an examination of the structure of the human person that receives this Trinity, and this anthropological structure is in turn illuminated by the two modalities in which God communicates Godself to humans.

The first pair of aspects of this divine self-communication that correspond to the human person is (a) "origin," insofar as God's self-communication creates and constitutes the human person as its addressee, and (b) "future," insofar as this self-communication as received by the human person tends toward its fullness to be realized in the future, though not deterministically but through the history of freedom. The second pair of aspects is (a) "history," insofar as God's self-communication takes place necessarily in the world of space and time, and (b) "transcendence," insofar as God's self-communication is the horizon toward which the human person is oriented when receiving this divine self-communication through acts of knowing and loving particular objects. The third pair is (a) "offer" insofar as God's self-communication engages the human person to accept it in freedom, and (b) "acceptance" insofar as God's self-communication cannot be accepted by the human person except by the power it gives to the human person to do so. The fourth pair is (a) "knowledge" (that is, actuation of truth in bodily action) insofar as God's self-communication presents itself to the human person as the absolute truth to be known and not just particular truths, and (b) "love" insofar as God's self-communication presents itself to the human person as the absolute good to be loved, and not just particular goods (see *The Trinity*, 88–94).

### The unity of the different aspects of God's self-communication in its two modalities

Rahner's next step is to argue that these four pairs of aspects of God's self-communication to humans are not random theological musings but are organically linked and intrinsically connected, though some of these links and connections are more obvious than others. Rahner's goal is to show that there is unity among the four pairs and that "there are *two* and only two basic manners of the self-communication of God, which are distinct *and* condition each other in such a way that the specific character of each may be grasped conceptually and distinguished from the other" (*The Trinity*, 94).

That there is unity among the first three aspects, namely, origin-history-offer, Rahner notes, is somewhat obvious. On the one hand, "origin" and "offer" are constituted by God's will to communicate himself to humans. On the other, "history" unfolds as the divine self-communication is freely accepted (or refused) by human recipients. It is less obvious how "knowledge" (or "truth") is intrinsically connected with the triad of origin-history-offer. Rahner argues that the connection will be easily seen if truth is understood not primarily as a grasping of a true state of affairs in a judgment (truth as correspondence between mind and reality) but as an act of truly revealing one's true nature (truth as manifestation). Understood as faithfulness – the biblical *emet* – truth can be seen as connected with origin-history-offer insofar as it is within this triad that God's truth is seen as God's fidelity to his promises to humanity.

About the other quaternity of future-transcendence-acceptance-love, it is, Rahner argues, relatively easy to see the unity between future and transcendence. "Future" here refers to God himself, whose self-communication is presented as the consummation of humanity. On the other hand, God as future calls forth human "transcendence" as both openness to the *possible* absolute future (insofar as humans are spirit) and the *actual* self-communication of this absolute future already present in history. Furthermore, because this divine self-communication of God is unconditionally willed by God, it carries with it "acceptance" as an act posited by God's power, though without detriment to human freedom. Finally, future-transcendence-acceptance is characterized as "love" insofar as this absolute future, to which humans transcend, creates itself the possibility and the actuality of acceptance, freely offered to humans (see *The Trinity*, 96–98).

The point of Rahner's reflections here is twofold. On the one hand, he wants to show the unity of the first group of four aspects, namely, origin-history-offer-knowledge, as well as the unity of the second group of four aspects, namely, future-transcendence-acceptance-love. On the other hand, he also wants to show that these two sets of aspects of God's self-communication are distinct yet not separate and that they mutually condition each other. At bottom, then, God's self-communication takes place with two sets of aspects. The first group of four can be summarized as "history" or "truth," and the second group of four as "spirit" or "love." Rahner suggests that we say: "*The divine self-communication occurs in unity and distinction in history (of the truth) and in the spirit (of love)*" (*The Trinity*, 99).

**From the economic Trinity to the immanent Trinity**

So far Rahner has been describing the Trinity as we experience it in history, that is, the economic Trinity of God the Father self-communicating in the two modalities of truth and love, or Word and Spirit. The question is whether this economic Trinity is identical to the immanent Trinity. The point is not, Rahner reminds us, to prove the immanent Trinity by rational arguments. Rather, it is to ask about the possibility of a transcendental deduction, that is, starting from a posteriori experience one asks about the a priori condition of possibility for such an experience. Here, Rahner argues that, given the fact of God's self-communication in two modes, which we experience a posteriori in history and is made known to us through revelation, it is possible and necessary to "deduce" from the economic Trinity to the immanent Trinity, for otherwise God's self-communication would not be a *self*-communication.

## Notes

1. Karl Rahner, *Foundations of Christian Faith: An Introduction to the Idea of Christianity*, trans. William V. Dych (New York: Seabury, 1978; original 1976).
2. The German sixteen-volume collection of Rahner's essays has been translated by various translators and published by various publishers in twenty-three volumes under the title *Theological Investigations*. In England: London: Darton, Longman & Todd, 1961–84. In the USA: vols. I–VI (Baltimore: Helicon); VII–X (New York: Herder & Herder); XI–XVI (New York: Seabury); and XVII–XXIII (New York: Crossroad). A projected thirty-two volume collection, *Karl Rahner: Sämtliche Werke*, ed. Karl Lehmann, Johann-Baptist Metz, Karl-Heinz Neufeldt, and Herbert Vorgrimmler, is being published by Herder (Freiburg, 1995–). There are four immediately relevant essays: "*Theos* in the New Testament," *Theological Investigations*, I, 79–148; "Remarks on the Dogmatic Treatise '*De Trinitate*,'" ibid., IV, 77–102; "Observations on the Doctrine of God in Catholic Dogmatics," ibid., IX, 127–44; and "Oneness and Threefoldness in Discussion with Islam," ibid., XVIII, 105–21.
3. Karl Rahner, Anton Darlap et al., eds., *Sacramentum mundi: An Encyclopedia of Theology*, 6 vols. (New York: Herder & Herder, 1968–70). The two entries are "Trinity, Divine" and "Trinity in Theology" in vol. VI.
4. The German work is *Mysterium salutis: Grundriss heilsgeschichtlicher Dogmatik*, ed. Johannes Feiner and Magnus Löhrer (Einsiedeln: Benziger Verlag, 1967). Rahner's contribution, titled "Der dreifältige Gott als transzendenter Urgrund der Heilsgechichte," constitutes ch. 5 of vol. II, *Die Heilsgeschichte vor Christus*. An English translation by

Joseph Donceel was issued as *The Trinity* in 1969 by the Seabury Press, New York, and reissued in 1997 by Crossroad (New York), with introduction, index, and glossary by Catherine LaCugna.

5. Readers interested in primary and secondary bibliographies on Rahner, which run into several thousands of items, can consult the Karl Rahner Archive at the University of Innsbruck (http://theol.uibk.ac.at/). One very helpful study is Declan Marmion and Mary E. Hines, eds., *The Cambridge Companion to Karl Rahner* (Cambridge University Press, 2005).
6. Karl Rahner, *Geist in Welt: Zur Metaphysik der endlichen Erkenntnis bei Thomas von Aquin*, 2nd edn., rev. J. B. Metz (Munich: Kösel, 1957; original Innsbruck: F. Rauch, 1939); trans. William Dych as *Spirit in the World* (New York: Herder & Herder, 1968), 2nd edn. (New York: Continuum, 1994).
7. Karl Rahner, *Hörer des Wortes: Grundlegung einer Religionsphilosophie*, 2nd edn., rev. J. B. Metz (Freiburg: Herderbücherei, 1971; original 1941); trans. Joseph Donceel as *Hearers of the Word* (New York: Continuum, 1994).
8. For Rahner's metaphysics of knowledge, see his brief but dense exposition in *Foundations of Christian Faith*, 14–23.
9. For Rahner's philosophical anthropology, see ibid., 26–43.
10. See ibid., 65.
11. For Rahner's critique of Augustine and Aquinas, see his *The Trinity*, 15–17.
12. For Rahner's brief elaborations of these points, see ibid., 10–15.
13. Italics in the original.
14. Rahner gives a preliminary explanation of this rule in the first part of *The Trinity*, which discusses the method and structure of the treatise on the Trinity. He will explain it in greater detail in the third part of the book, in which he attempts a systematic outline of his theology of the Trinity.
15. Rahner makes this statement fully aware that according to scholastic theology, there is no "real" relation in God vis-à-vis the world, though the reverse is true. Rahner does not subscribe to the first part of this teaching. He maintains that his statement is valid as long as we have to affirm of the Logos *himself* (and only he, not the Father and the Spirit) that he has really and truly become human. At least in this one instance, the statement about the economy of salvation is also true of the immanent Trinity.
16. On Rahner's theology of the symbol, see his "The Theology of the Symbol," in *Theological Investigations*, IV, 221–52.

## Further reading

Burke, Patrick, *Reinterpreting Rahner: A Critical Study of his Major Themes* (New York: Fordham University Press, 2002).

Crowley, Paul D., ed., *Rahner beyond Rahner: A Great Theologian Encounters the Pacific Rim* (Lanham, MD: Rowman & Littlefield, 2005).

Marmion, Declan, and Mary E. Hines, eds., *The Cambridge Companion to Karl Rahner* (Cambridge University Press, 2005).

Phan, Peter C., *Eternity in Time: A Study of Karl Rahner's Eschatology* (Selinsgrove: Susquehanna University Press, 1988).

Rahner, Karl, *Foundations of Christian Faith: An Introduction to the Idea of Christianity*, trans. William V. Dych (New York: Seabury, 1978; original 1976).

*The Trinity*, trans. Joseph Donceel, introduction, index, and glossary by Catherine LaCugna (New York: Crossroad, 1997; original 1969).

Sanders, Fred, *The Image of the Immanent Trinity: Rahner's Rule and the Theological Interpretation of Scripture* (New York: Peter Lang, 2005).

Vorgrimmler, Herbert, *Understanding Karl Rahner: An Introduction to his Life and Thought*, trans. John Bowden (New York: Crossroad, 1986).

# 12 Hans Urs von Balthasar on the Trinity

KAREN KILBY

One of the striking aspects of Hans Urs von Balthasar's work is the integration of his reflections on the Trinity – on the eternal, inner life of the Trinity, in particular – into the fabric of his thought as a whole.[1] A good deal of recent theology has been preoccupied with the question of what *to do* with the Trinity: how to make clear the relevance of a doctrine which surely ought to be central, but which, with its "substance" and *hypostasis*, its "processions" and "relations," can seem like nothing but a series of technicalities and intellectual difficulties. In the context of Balthasar's theology, such questions simply do not need to be raised. One finds in his work, that is to say, both a very vivid depiction of the inner life of the Trinity and one which is genuinely *integral* to his presentation of the story of salvation. Whether ultimately he has the right to such a vivid picture of the eternal life of God is a question we shall ask below, as is also whether the integration he achieves requires too resolved a vision – too positive a vision, indeed – of suffering and evil.[2] But we will begin by examining some of the ways in which Balthasar interweaves (to use the usual terms) economic and immanent Trinity.

## MISSION CHRISTOLOGY AND THE TRINITY

In his "Outline of Christology" in the third volume of the *Theodramatik* (*Theo-Drama*), Balthasar highlights as the central, defining feature of Jesus' existence his consciousness of *mission*. This, especially when coupled with an insistence on his absolute identification with this mission, allows for a striking integration of a reading of the life of Jesus with classic formulations of the Son's eternal procession from the Father.

Jesus' mission is central to him: this is something Balthasar takes to stand out particularly clearly in the gospel of John, but also to be attested in the synoptic gospels and indeed throughout the New Testament. Both the language of being sent and the language of coming or having come point to this, and without it, Balthasar argues, we cannot understand Jesus' apocalyptic sayings. And this mission is linked with who Jesus is: indeed, Balthasar does not stop with the claim that he has a very strong sense of mission, or that this sense of mission is particularly central to him, but in fact *identifies* Jesus with his mission. Jesus does not just have a mission – he *is* the mission.

What does this mean? Some light can be shed from a consideration of Balthasar's broader[3] reflections on the notion of "person." There is, he proposes, a difference between the question of *what* we are and the question of *who* we are. We all share the same "what," as human beings, but how is one to know *who* one is? This matter of being a "who," of being someone distinct, Balthasar identifies with being a person. He rejects the possibility of working out the "who" by compiling a list of distinguishing features – this would take us no further than "an accumulation of chance details" – and also the possibility that we can learn it from other people's valuation of us: the regard of others can be withdrawn, and in any case we could only ever learn who we are *for those* who love us. Ultimately, the guarantee of who one is can only come from God: "It is when God addresses a conscious subject, tells him who he is and what he means to the eternal God of truth and shows him the purpose of his existence – that is, imparts a distinctive and divinely authorized mission – that we can say of a conscious subject that he is a 'person.'"[4] Being a "who" (having, that is, a distinct identity), being a person, and being given a purpose, a mission, by God are all then, on this account, the same thing.

This connection between person and mission, which is true in general, is also true in Christ.[5] But there is a difference. In other cases, one is first a conscious subject, and then at some stage one may be "called" to a mission, and so struggle to become, to grow into, the person one already is in God's sight: we undergo a process of "bringing our innate nonidentity into an ever-closer approximation to perfect identity," of assimilating "our own 'I' more and more completely to our God-given mission."[6] In the case of Christ, however, the one archetypal case, there is, from the beginning, an absolute identity. He is, at all times, fully identified with his sense of mission. So whereas we may have a mission, and strive to let our identities be conformed to it, Christ *is* his mission.

In classic formulations of the doctrine of the Trinity, the Father is described as the "unoriginate origin," and the Son (as also the Spirit) as coming out from, proceeding from, him. In presenting mission as central to the New Testament portrayals of Jesus and to Jesus' self-consciousness, then, Balthasar develops a portrait of Jesus which is already integrated into an account of the immanent Trinity: the centrality for Jesus of mission, of being *sent* by the Father, reflects, or is the incarnate working-out of, the Son's eternal *proceeding* from the Father.

In actually identifying Jesus' person with his mission, Balthasar offers a still more striking integration. In an account such as one finds, for instance, in Thomas Aquinas, not only are the relations of the persons of the Trinity described in terms of processions – the Son is generated by the Father, the Spirit spirated from Father and Son – but the persons simply *are* these relations. This is ordinarily one of the more baffling aspects of trinitarian thought. But in his Christology Balthasar offers a very concrete working-out of it: Jesus is the person who so completely accepts, lives out, and identifies himself with his mission that whereas others may have a mission, he simply *is* his mission. If one follows Balthasar to the point of saying that Jesus is the one "in whom Person and mission are identical,"[7] then it may not seem such a conundrum to say that the eternal Son just *is* his proceeding from the Father.

Balthasar's development of a mission Christology, then, manages to unite what can seem one of the most odd and intractable features of trinitarian theology with a textually concrete reading of the life of Jesus, and, incidentally, to do this in a way which is connected to his larger *dramatic* scheme (for one's mission is one's divinely given role) and which allows him to integrate anthropology into his Christology (for he maintains that all others find both their mission and their existence as persons through inclusion in Christ).

## TRINITY AND CROSS

In the previous section, we remained at a formal level in speaking of Christ's "mission": what in fact stands at the heart of this mission, as Balthasar understands it, is Jesus' passion and death. And here too we find a particular understanding of the life of the immanent Trinity integrated into the heart of Balthasar's theology. The doctrine of the Trinity, he writes, is the "backdrop of the entire action": it provides "the ever-present, inner presupposition of the doctrine of the Cross."[8] Closely bound up with Balthasar's understanding of the events of Christ's death and descent into hell, then, is what turns out to be a distinctive conception of the eternal relations between the persons of the Trinity, relations which he characterizes not only in familiar language of love and gift, but also in terms of distance (indeed, infinite distance), otherness, risk, and kenosis.

The language of the Father giving everything, giving indeed himself, to the Son, is a very common theme in traditional trinitarian reflection; what is far less familiar is the way Balthasar glosses this giving as a giving *up*, giving *away*, a self-stripping: "the Father strips himself, without remainder, of his Godhead and hands it over to the Son"; the Father "can give his divinity away"; the Father "lets go of his divinity"; this is an "original self-surrender" in which the Father "must go to the very extreme of self-lessness."[9]

Where classic treatments of the Trinity tend to emphasize the closeness, the inseparability, of the persons, Balthasar writes repeatedly of distance between them (in his more cautious moments, of "something like distance"), of otherness and separation. The Son is "infinitely Other" than the Father; there is "an absolute, infinite 'distance'" between them, "a unique and incomprehensible 'separation' of God from himself."[10] Interestingly, where in classic treatments the closeness, the inseparability, of the persons tends to be conceived as linked to the fullness of the Father's self-gift – because the Father gives everything he is to the Son, there can be no distance between them – in Balthasar's thought this same self-gift of the Father leads in precisely the opposite direction: Balthasar's assertion of the infinite difference or separation of the persons regularly follows references to the Father giving himself away completely to the Son.

Kenosis, then, begins not with the cross or the incarnation, but in the Father's generation of the Son. The Father does not exactly do away with himself in this kenosis – "the Father, in uttering and surrendering himself without reserve, does not lose himself. He does not extinguish himself by self-giving."[11] Nevertheless, Balthasar is keen to preserve something like a sense of risk, something vulnerable and dangerous, in this giving-away.

Such an understanding of the inner relations of the eternal divine persons allows Balthasar both to develop a trinitarian understanding of the meaning of the cross and to maintain that the cross marks no breach or change in the eternal intra-trinitarian relations. He is able, that is, to present the cross as the enactment of a drama between the Father and the Son, while at the same time insisting, with the tradition, that God is not somehow altered through an engagement with history.

The cross should not be understood, Balthasar thinks, simply as God incarnate, in his human nature, undergoing suffering and death on behalf of or in place of sinners. Such a statement may not be false, but it does not go far enough, does not get to the most profound level of what is at stake. It is not just God incarnate who undergoes the cross, but *the*

*Son*, and what is undergone is not just suffering and death, but more profoundly forsakenness, abandonment, rejection, by the Father. On the cross we see God rejected by and alienated from God. On the cross the relationship between God's wrath and sin is played out between the Father and the Son, and therefore taken over *into* God, into the relationship between the Father and the Son. But because of the infinite distance, the "incomprehensible separation" which all along, so to speak, characterizes the Father–Son relations, this is not the introduction of something *new* into the Trinity. The alienation between the sinner and the holy God can be taken into the Trinity because infinite distance and something like alienation were always already there. The Trinity, one could say, is "big enough" to encompass and so overcome even the terrible distance between the righteous and holy God and the lost sinner.

Balthasar's much-debated proposal concerning Holy Saturday is in fact really little more than the working-out of this same idea. What happens in the time between Christ's death and his resurrection, between Good Friday and Easter Sunday? There is biblical reference to Christ's preaching to the dead, and traditionally this has been developed into a notion of a victorious descent. Balthasar proposes by contrast that Christ is utterly passive on Holy Saturday, that he can no longer act, that he is genuinely dead in solidarity with the dead, and indeed that, having become identified with sin itself, he experiences the full horror of it, which is to say hell, utter rejection and abandonment by the Father.

Balthasar's soteriology is powerful and vivid. It seems to take seriously the gravity of sin, and the recurrent biblical theme of divine wrath against sin, while presenting a drama in which the overwhelming theme is still that of love. We find here traditional themes of Christ's substitution for us, even of something like Christ bearing punishment for us, but because of the thoroughly trinitarian way in which Balthasar sets out the drama, the usual difficulty of these themes – that a requirement for a perfectly just man to be killed for the iniquities of the unjust is repellent, arbitrary, unfair – is, if not entirely eliminated, at least reduced. The dominant sense one is left with is not of God insisting on punishing one party rather than another, but of God taking into and overcoming within his own life the conflict between sin and love.

Our main concern here, of course, is not with his soteriology for its own sake, but with his treatment of the Trinity, and particularly the way he interweaves reflections on the Trinity with soteriology. To appreciate the distinctiveness of this integration, it is useful to compare it with what has become in recent years the more typical pattern of trinitarian reflection. Many contemporary theologians, as we mentioned at the outset, feel the need to restore to the doctrine of the Trinity its relevance. One very common strategy is to reject the traditional Western "psychological analogy" and introduce in its place a social analogy: the Trinity is to be modeled not on the multiple faculties or activities of a single mind, but on a small community bound together by love. Its relevance is then found in the way it becomes itself a model for community, and in the quality of the relationships within it, relationships so profound that they can make the three genuinely one. If the doctrine of the Trinity portrays the divine in its innermost reality as persons-in-relation, then it must have something to say about how we think about family, about church, about society at all levels, and about ourselves.

Social theories are of course varied, but many share in a common pattern – a pattern of abstraction followed by application. At some stage in the discussion one moves away from the complexities of the biblical texts, away from discussions of creation, incarnation, cross, resurrection, ascension, Pentecost, to rest one's focus on a set of abstract concepts – concepts of persons, relations, and *perichōrēsis* – and then, taking these to be the heart of the doctrine of the Trinity, one looks to find application for the concepts, to give the abstractions relevance. So one can find a Colin Gunton, for instance, writing enthusiastically about the applications of the notion of *perichōrēsis* in metaphysics or in conceiving of the interpenetration of different academic disciplines, or a Jürgen Moltmann drawing on the eternal relations of the Trinity as a way to provide a model for church polity and to move beyond the impasse between Western individualism and Eastern communitarianism.

On some points Balthasar is at one with such social theorists. He too envisages the "persons" of the Trinity functioning as something not too far from "persons" in our ordinary sense of the term,[12] and so imagines the Trinity as closer to a small family than to differing aspects of a single psyche. But here the ways part, for Balthasar does not engage in the abstraction so characteristic of most social theories of the Trinity. The Trinity is never, in Balthasar's theology, a doctrine in search of a meaning, and he does not need to propose for it some extra "relevance" of its own: it is rather, as he presents it, intimately concerned with, and necessary for an understanding of, the life of Jesus and particularly the cross. So although Balthasar, like the social theorists, is concerned with the eternal relations of the Trinity, he leads us not into musings over a general concept of relation that can also find useful application elsewhere, but into a reflection very specifically on the relation of the

Father to the Son (and to some extent of the Holy Spirit to both). We have in Balthasar as vivid and gripping a presentation of the inner life of the Trinity as any social theorist could wish for, then, but one which maintains at every stage vital links with the drama of salvation.

## TOO VIVID?

Balthasar portrays the immanent Trinity in a way which is lively and powerful. There is eternal kenosis, infinite difference, distance, otherness which is nevertheless united in love, a "primal drama." But does he have a right to be so vivid? We turn now to the question of how Balthasar can know what he appears to know about the Trinity.[13]

Insofar as he provides an *explicit* account of a method of trinitarian reflection, there seems little to which one might object. Like most theologians, Balthasar maintains that we learn of the Trinity not through philosophical reflection on God and the world, but through Christ. More than other theologians perhaps, he lays particular emphasis on the *cross* as revelatory of the Trinity, but there seems little reason to object to this, given the centrality of the cross in the gospel accounts and indeed in Christian belief and practice. At certain points Balthasar makes explicit gestures in the direction of epistemological humility, writing of our need to "feel our way back into the mystery" and of the process of doing so as "walk[ing] on a knife edge."[14]

The problem, then, lies not in what Balthasar *says* about how one should reflect on the Trinity but in how he in fact *does* it. Consider, for instance, the language of distance in the Trinity. Between the Father and the Son, united though they are in love, Balthasar maintains, there is an infinite distance. This is, as we have already suggested, a relatively novel claim. How, then, does Balthasar think we know of this infinite distance, separation, otherness, in the Trinity? There are two routes. One has to do with the avoidance of modalism: Balthasar seems to suggest that something like distance, or "infinite space," must be necessary for the distinction between the trinitarian persons to be real. The second route, more frequently stressed, is by way of the cross: we do not, he thinks, know of this intra-trinitarian distance *only* from the cross, but we somehow know it better, know of its full seriousness, from the cross.

But, of course, it is not the case that one has only to look at the passion narratives to come to the conclusion that there must, in eternity, be an infinite distance between Father and Son: certainly this is not something that most of the tradition has in fact concluded from these narratives. At least two things are required in order to "learn" about distance in the Trinity from the cross. The first is a particular construal of the cross itself; the second is a more speculative move from the cross (thus construed) to what one could call the eternal conditions of its possibility.

First, then, one must construe Christ's passion and death as most fundamentally a drama of abandonment of Christ by the Father. While Balthasar is not alone in interpreting it thus (for all the differences at other points, here he is fundamentally in accord with Moltmann), this cannot pose as an obvious or unquestionable reading of the New Testament. There is, for instance, considerable debate over how to interpret Jesus' cry "My God, my God, why have you forsaken me?" as recorded in Mark and Matthew: is this an expression of a sense of abandonment, or, as a quotation of the first line of Psalm 22, an affirmation of faith? And there is a further step – one needs to hold not only that Jesus is portrayed as *feeling* abandoned, but that fundamentally he *is* abandoned. A sense of abandonment, in other words, needs to be seen not just as part of the experience of Jesus as a suffering and dying human being, but as pointing to the underlying truth, indeed the central underlying truth, of the cross.

In addition to reading the cross as a drama of God's abandonment by God, the Father's rejection of the Son, the second thing one must do to arrive at the notion of distance in the Trinity is to suppose that this abandonment on the cross (and during Holy Saturday) is possible *only if* the eternal trinitarian relations are characterized by infinite, "absolute" distance, radical otherness, separation. This is not a matter of reasoning from an effect back to its cause, exactly, but rather from a historical (or quasi-historical[15]) drama of the economic Trinity to its eternal ground. What must have always been the case in the relations between Father and Son if they can on the cross be expressed in terms of abandonment of the latter by the former? To be able to answer this question, it is worth noting, one has to suppose one knows how to do a certain kind of sifting, considering the various elements of the drama of the cross and distinguishing between those which do and those which do not reveal something of the eternal life of the Trinity. One does not, for instance, directly impute rejection and forsakenness to the immanent Trinity, but one does learn of distance and separation.

To move from the cross to the affirmation of an infinite distance in the eternal life of God, then, requires both that one adopt a particular, contestable reading of the significance of the death of Jesus, and that one make a deduction from the cross thus construed to the eternal conditions of its possibility. None of this need be illegitimate. But what emerges is that this notion of infinite, "absolute" distance in the Trinity cannot be put forward as a self-evident starting point for further argument or reflection, but is at most the rather precarious conclusion to a train of reflection.

One can see this precariousness also if one turns to the question of what exactly it might *mean* to speak of infinite distance in the Trinity. It is certainly a suggestive, an evocative notion, but not on the face of it a particularly clear one. Balthasar does not, of course, propose that the trinitarian persons have bodies which could be located at particular points in space, and between which one could therefore measure physical distance. But if it is not as physical or spatial, how then are we in fact to think of this distance? Rowan Williams suggests interpreting *Abstand*, the word Balthasar uses here, as "difference," so would we perhaps make more headway if we asked what might be meant by the infinite, absolute *difference* between Father and Son? This too is, prima facie, difficult to grasp, given that the persons are consubstantial. That everything the Father is, he gives to the Son, is a traditional claim, and one reaffirmed by Balthasar. The difference cannot lie in the "what" that is given, then; the only place left to locate the interval between them would seem to be in the fact that in one instance something is given, in the other received. The Father is the one who gives everything to the Son, the Son the one who receives everything from the Father. Can this distance, this separation of which Balthasar speaks – this *infinite* and absolute difference, distance, separateness – be a matter of the difference between total gift and total reception? Perhaps. But there is room for questions.

Reflection on more familiar instances of giving may give rise to hesitation. In general, we do not think of giving, and in particular giving of oneself, as creating distance between giver and receiver – not unless the giving goes wrong. Even if we suppose that giving and receiving are radically different in the sphere of the divine, or that in light of the cross and the Trinity we must reconceive all giving, there are other difficulties. The Father, according to Balthasar, empties himself, strips himself, in the originally kenotic act of giving himself to the Son, and we are exploring the possibility that it is in the difference between such kenosis and the Son's reception that infinite distance or difference is to be found. But then the Son of course is also engaged in kenosis: as the image of the Father, the Son too completely gives himself away. So how can this, the difference between giving and receiving, actually constitute the otherness, the distance, between Father and Son, if self-giving is one of the things in which the Son precisely images the Father?

Again, here too perhaps answers can be found. Perhaps it is not in giving and receiving as such that one is to find the locus for the infinite, absolute distance, but in the very particular relations between Father and Son that involve the one always giving and the other always receiving. Perhaps it is then *this* act of giving and receiving that somehow sets the two in a relation of infinite difference. The "somehow," though, needs to be distinctly stressed here.

I do not mean to suggest that we should say that language of distance and separateness in the eternal life of the Trinity is senseless, that it can in principle have no meaning. But certainly it seems that we find ourselves in rather difficult waters if we try to imagine what exactly is envisaged. Ultimately it seems that the position is something like this: if the cross is conceived as God abandoning God, and if we are not, like Moltmann, to think of it as introducing something *new*, something previously unexperienced, into the life of the Trinity, then we are bound to suppose that there is *something* eternally present in the life of the Trinity which anticipates it, something to which it gives expression. Balthasar calls this whatever-it-is that anticipates the cross "distance," *Abstand*, but as the explorations above suggest, that really gets us no further toward imagining what it might be than would the phrase "that inexplicable, incomprehensible X in the eternal life of the Trinity, whatever it may be, which is a condition of the possibility of the cross."

What is striking in Balthasar's trinitarian discussions, however, is that in a great many cases they are *not* marked by the tentativeness, the sense of precariousness, that ought to follow both from the way such notions as absolute distance are derived, and from the questions surrounding what they might mean. Instead we find confidence, expansiveness, fluency. We find in him not someone driven to stutter uncertainly, somehow, in light of the cross, about the Trinity, but rather a theologian who seems very well to know his way around, to have a view – sometimes something that seems remarkably like an insider's view – of what happens in the inner life of the Trinity.

Balthasar is expansive on a number of fronts. He seems to know quite a bit about what one might call the mechanism of the trinitarian processions, affirming, for instance, not only that the Father begets the Son, but that the Son "antecedently consents" to being begotten. He also seems to know in some detail about what one might call the intra-trinitarian dispositions: he tells us that the Father is *grateful* to the Son for allowing himself to be begotten, who in turn is grateful to the Father for *wanting* to beget him. Balthasar also tells us that surprise, "eternal amazement," is an element of the life of the Trinity, so that for instance "It is as if the Son... 'from the outset surpasses the Father's wildest expectations,'"[16] while the Son himself is always beholding the Father from new angles. The eternal life of the Trinity is, he seems somehow to know, characterized by thanksgiving, by worship, and by petitionary prayer.

Balthasar is even able to describe what one might call the Trinity's decision-making processes.

> If the Father has a (primary) intention – perhaps with regard to the shape of the creation he has planned – he communicates this intention to the Son in begetting him, giving him "preludes, beginnings taken up by the Son to be realized"; thus he leaves it to the Son to "promote the fatherly purposes". In begetting the Son, the Father, as it were, addresses a request to him, and the Son in turn wishes nothing other than to employ his entire filial freedom in fulfilling the Father's will. So "the Father is the first to ask: and he asks the Son, in order to give him the joy of granting his request... Even before the Son asks him" (for instance, to be entrusted with the task of saving the world through the Cross), "the Father wants to make his request, as if to give the Son precedence in the delight of granting."[17]

The Father, then, has the broad ideas, but he leaves it to the Son (out of "consideration," a desire to give the Son a certain precedence) to work out the finer points of implementation.[18]

At times, as we have seen, Balthasar makes gestures of epistemic humility. At times he points to a scriptural basis, or a process of reasoning, by which he arrives at his claims about the inner life of God. But in general, he does not write like a theologian who is "feeling his way back" into a mystery, on the basis of Christ and the cross; he writes more like a novelist[19] who, with a particular vision of the climactic scene (the cross) as starting point, freely fills out background, adds character details, and constructs prior scenes.

## TOO INTEGRATED?

The previous section was focused on *how* Balthasar knows all that he seems to know, how any theologian could be in a position to make the claims he does. There are also questions to raise concerning *what* he says. Balthasar does not, quite, attribute suffering to the eternal persons of the Trinity, but he does introduce something very *like* suffering and loss into the Godhead. Whether this leads to a problematic picture of the divine life is difficult to say because it is so hard to know what "supra-suffering" or eternal kenosis might be. But what it does lead to, I would suggest, is a problematic understanding of suffering and loss.

A proclivity in general to cast suffering in a positive light, and to link faith, love, and obedience with self-loss, self-abasement, even something like annihilation of the self, in fact frequently makes itself felt in Balthasar's writings. Thus his treatment of the cross and its extension into Holy Saturday is marked by a distinct dwelling on Jesus' agony, a concern to bring out the unbearable, unthinkable (and eternal) enormity of Christ's suffering of the betrayal and abandonment of the Father; and his characterization of the Christian life constantly places surrender, loss of self, sacrifice of the self, to the fore. Mary's *fiat* he takes to be the perfect and archetypal response of faith, and interprets very much in terms of self-abnegation. At almost every turn in his writings the sense that suffering, self-abnegation, and indeed humiliation carry a fundamentally positive valuation is confirmed. In a single volume of essays on the church, for instance, we find references to the church in its sinful members as "borne by the suffering members," to the "inner mystery of suffering" that the Constantinian church of glory hid, to the true Christian spirit as "the will to poverty, abasement and humility," to the "real, fruitful humiliation" of Peter, which was not a "mere exercise in humiliation," to a humility which, because we are sinners, must be "instilled into us by humiliation," to "self-abnegation in the service of Christ" as the only way to reveal Christ's own self-abnegation, to a self-abnegation that liturgical piety requires (one which indeed Balthasar describes as "this violent, this often 'crucifying' sacrifice of the pious subject to the ecclesial object"), and to "complete self-abnegation and obedience to the hierarchy" as something that Charles de Foucauld rightly commended.[20]

Should we be troubled by such a persistent alignment between love and suffering, love and (self-)loss, in Balthasar's understanding of faith and the church? Opinion may divide over whether it represents a distortion of Christianity or a necessary resistance to the optimism and activism of our culture. But there is less room for debate, it seems to me, when this general alignment of love and loss turns out to have its apex in Balthasar's depiction of the divine life.

As already indicated, Balthasar does not – quite – bring suffering into the Trinity,[21] but he does speak of something in the Trinity which can develop into suffering, of a "supra-suffering" in God, and of risk, of distance, and of something "dark" in the eternal trinitarian drama. And as we have seen, he consistently construes the *giving* internal to the Trinity in terms of giving *away*, giving up – in terms suggestive of loss – so that the Father's role, for instance, is one of letting go of his divinity, giving it away, surrendering himself, going "to the very extreme of self-lessness."

By bringing together in his depiction of God self-loss, self-abnegation, something that comes very close to self-annihilation on the one hand and love on the other, or again by bringing bliss together with something described either as "supra-suffering" or as that which can develop into suffering, Balthasar seems in clear danger of fundamentally blurring the distinction between love and loss, joy and suffering, in themselves. It is not then just that in this broken world suffering is mysteriously redemptive and loss required by love. If love and renunciation, suffering (or something like it) and joy, are linked, not just in the Christian life and the economy of salvation, but eternally in God, it is hard to escape the conclusion that suffering and loss are given an *intrinsically* positive valuation: suffering and loss really are, ultimately, mysteriously good. And if at the heart of Christianity lies the message that suffering and loss are ultimately good, it is hard to see how Christianity itself can be "good news."

**Notes**

1. Hans Urs von Balthasar (1905–1988) was a prolific Swiss Roman Catholic theologian who has emerged as one of the most influential of the twentieth century. His largest work is a trilogy, composed of *Herrlichkeit: Eine theologische Ästhetik* (*The Glory of the Lord: A Theological Aesthetics*), *Theodramatik* (*Theo-Drama*), and *Theologik* (*Theo-Logic*) and running (in English) to fifteen volumes altogether.
2. In pursuing such matters, I will be offering an approach to Balthasar's trinitarian thought that is as much critical as it is expository. I engage in questioning Balthasar more heavily than one might expect in a volume such as this in part because there already exists, in the Cambridge Companion series, a largely commendatory essay on the topic. See Rowan Williams, "Balthasar and the Trinity," in Edward T. Oakes and David Moss, eds., *The Cambridge Companion to Hans Urs von Balthasar* (Cambridge University Press, 2004), 37–50. See Williams' essay also for a discussion of the way Balthasar uses categories of *gender* in the Trinity, something not dealt with here.
3. "Broader" here should not be taken to imply "prior" – Balthasar holds that only from Christ do we learn what it is to be a person.
4. Hans Urs von Balthasar, *Theo-Drama: Theological Dramatic Theory*, III: *Dramatis Personae: Persons in Christ* (San Francisco: Ignatius, 1990), 201.

5. It is in fact because of Christ, on Balthasar's account, that it is true in general.
6. Balthasar, *Theo-Drama*, III, 270, 271.
7. Ibid., III, 157.
8. Balthasar, *Theo-Drama: Theological Dramatic Theory*, IV: *The Action* (San Francisco: Ignatius, 1994), 318, 319.
9. It should be said that such language, though unusual, is not entirely unprecedented: Balthasar is influenced by the Russian thinker Sergii Bulgakov in this notion of an intra-trinitarian kenosis.
10. All the phrases quoted in this and the previous paragraph are from *Theo-Drama*, IV, 323–25.
11. Ibid., IV, 325.
12. Cf. Karen Kilby, "Perichoresis and Projection: Problems with Social Doctrines of the Trinity," *New Blackfriars*, 81 (2000), 432–45, for a discussion of this as a distinguishing feature of social trinitarians.
13. One question that I will not attempt to deal with here is whether Balthasar is in fact propounding tritheism. This is a concern to which his theology, like that of the social theorists discussed above, can give rise. In both cases the persons of the Trinity seem to be presented as three centers of consciousness, three "I"s with three wills which are, in principle at least, distinct: in Balthasar there are passages suggesting that the persons of the Trinity "arrive" at an agreement about what to do.

    The reason I will not take up this issue here is that it seems to me that trinitarian theology of the last century and this has arrived at a kind of stand-off in this area. One finds a sharp divide between those, like Barth and Rahner, who think that the term "person" has become misleading in a trinitarian context and reach for some other technical term to discuss what is threefold in God, and those who take there to be real continuity between our contemporary understanding of "person" and the trinitarian persons. And on each side of this divide there is suspicion of the orthodoxy of the other: if there is a question about whether the social theorists and Balthasar are advocating tritheism, there can also be a question as to whether the other side is in fact modalist.
14. Balthasar, *Theo-Drama*, IV, 324.
15. Balthasar's characterization of Christ's experience of hell on Holy Saturday as "timeless" raises a question about the term "historical."
16. Balthasar, *Theo-Drama: Theological Dramatic Theory*, V: *The Last Act* (San Francisco: Ignatius, 1998), 79, quoting from Adrienne von Speyer.
17. Ibid., 88–89. Balthasar is here again quoting from the works of Adrienne von Speyer. In general he emphasized the close relationship of his theology to hers, and also credited her with a range of mystical experiences. In this volume he draws particularly heavily on her work. One explanation for how such a vivid knowledge of the Trinity is possible is that it can be derived directly from von Speyer's experience. Although the frequency of citation (in *Theo-Drama*, V in particular) and the absolute confidence that Balthasar elsewhere displays in her extraordinary experiences might seem to point in such a direction,

it would be fundamentally uncharitable to read Balthasar's trinitarian writing in this way.

18. Just how concretely and seriously this division of labor is meant becomes clear in a further quote from Adrienne von Speyer that Balthasar introduces in a footnote: "Perhaps the Father would have had other suggestions, other ideas pertaining to redemption that would not have made the abandonment of the Cross necessary. But he does not express them; he leaves redemption up to the Son. In love, what is best is always what the other wishes." *Theo-Drama*, v, 89.
19. I suggest a novelist rather than a dramatist, though the latter might seem the obvious analogy to reach for, because like a novelist Balthasar takes us *inside* his characters, informing us directly about their feelings and dispositions.
20. Balthasar, *Explorations in Theology*, II: *Spouse of the Word* (San Francisco: Ignatius, 1991), 179, 16, 14, 114, 188, 27, 30, 25.
21. See Gerard O'Hanlon, *The Immutability of God in the Theology of Hans Urs von Balthasar* (Cambridge University Press, 1990) for a careful discussion of the issue.

## Further reading

Mongrain, Kevin, *The Systematic Thought of Hans Urs von Balthasar: An Irenaean Retrieval* (New York: Crossroad and Herder & Herder, 2002).

Oakes, Edward T., *Pattern of Redemption: The Theology of Hans Urs von Balthasar* (New York: Continuum, 2002).

O'Donnell, John, *Hans Urs von Balthasar* (London and New York: Continuum, 1991).

O'Hanlon, Gerard, *The Immutability of God in the Theology of Hans Urs von Balthasar* (Cambridge University Press, 1990).

Quash, Ben, *Theology and the Drama of History* (Cambridge University Press, 2005).

Williams, Rowan, "Balthasar and the Trinity," in Edward T. Oakes and David Moss, eds., *The Cambridge Companion to Hans Urs von Balthasar* (Cambridge University Press, 2004), 37–50.

# 13 The trinitarian doctrines of Jürgen Moltmann and Wolfhart Pannenberg in the context of contemporary discussion

VELI-MATTI KÄRKKÄINEN

The purpose of this chapter is to discuss the contributions to trinitarian thought of the Reformed theologian Jürgen Moltmann and the Lutheran Wolfhart Pannenberg. To treat them together with regard to the content of their trinitarian theologies is justifiable because in spite of all their differences, these two German theologians both echo and have shaped nearly all the key themes of the doctrine of the Trinity in contemporary theology.

In order to orient the reader to the context and background of these two trinitarian theologies as well as the state of current discussion, a list of key themes follows here:

1. Following Barth and Rahner, both Moltmann and Pannenberg seek to ground the Trinity in revelation and salvation history rather than in abstract speculation.
2. Therefore, Rahner's Rule – beginning with *oikonomia* (God's actions in history) to speak of *theologia* (who and what God is) – has become a standard principle.
3. Again, following both Rahner and Barth, the "turn to history" has become one of the contemporary canons of trinitarian reflection.
4. The "turn to history" has made reflection on the relationship between the economic and immanent Trinity a focal issue.
5. Contrary to tradition, threeness is taken for granted, while the unity of God becomes the challenge.
6. Consequently, eschatology has risen to a new position of appreciation in trinitarian theology.
7. Because of the turn to the social analogy under the leadership of Moltmann, the "practical" implications of Trinity are being discussed in a fresh way.

With these current developments in mind, let me first examine Moltmann's and Pannenberg's contributions separately. I will then subject both of them to critical discussion. The final section will briefly offer some further questions and challenges.

## MOLTMANN: TRINITARIAN PANENTHEISM

### Trinity: a distinctively Christian understanding of God

It took Moltmann almost two decades to produce a major monograph on the topic of the Trinity, *Trinität und Reich Gottes* (*The Trinity and the Kingdom of God*, 1981),[1] although he had already started to incorporate trinitarian insights into his theology in one of his earlier major works, *Der gekreuzigte Gott* (*The Crucified God*)[2]. Since then, he has continued to refine and expand his views.[3]

Moltmann joins Rahner and other contemporary theologians who have lamented the neglect of the doctrine in theology and ethics (Moltmann, *Trinity*, 1). One of the main reasons for Moltmann's complaint is the doctrine's perceived lack of practicability (2–9). Over against two traditional – and, in Moltmann's estimation, mistaken – approaches to God in Christian theology, namely, the idea of God as supreme substance and as absolute subject, both of which build on a monotheistic and thus non-trinitarian conception of God, Moltmann advocates the understanding of God as "triunity, the three-in-one" (10–16, at 10). "Trinity" means nothing less than "the Christianization of the concept of God" (132).

Methodologically and theologically, then, for Moltmann the threeness of God is given: "We are beginning with the trinity of the Persons and shall then go on to ask about the unity." As a result, a "social doctrine of the Trinity" emerges. Rather than focusing on one divine substance, it focuses on "relationships and communities," reflecting the general turn from "subject" to relationality (*Trinity*, 19).

While building on Barth's and Rahner's legacy, Moltmann is also very much concerned to overcome what he perceives as strong modalistic implications in their approaches.[4] One of the key issues – if not *the* issue – in contemporary trinitarian reflection has to do with the way in which the eternal God can be related to human life and history and to the world.[5]

### The cross of Jesus Christ as the beginning of the doctrine of the Trinity

For Moltmann, "the cross of the Son stands from eternity in the center of the Trinity" (*Trinity*, xvi).[6] In *The Crucified God*, he focuses on not only the suffering *of* God but even more the suffering *in* God. In *The*

*Trinity and the Kingdom of God*, Moltmann takes up this theme again and radicalizes it in the Christological and trinitarian context by pushing aside what he sees as the mainstream of tradition, pejoratively called the "apathy axiom" (22).[7] "How can Christian faith understand Christ's passion as being the revelation of God, if the deity cannot suffer?" he asks (21). Borrowing from Luther, some Jewish scholars, and the Japanese theologian K. Kitamori, Moltmann purposes the doctrine of *theopathy* (25). The God of the Bible, the Father of Jesus Christ, is different from the passionless God of Greek metaphysical notions (esp. 22). God's passion can be called "active passion," since it is a voluntary identification with the suffering of the world and is based on love (23).

The God of the dying Son Jesus Christ does not shy away from the suffering either of his Son or of the world but rather makes the suffering his own and so overcomes it in hope. All suffering becomes God's so that God may overcome it (Moltmann, *Crucified God*, 246). Moltmann takes the words of Psalm 22 on the lips of the dying Jesus, "My God, my God, why have you forsaken me?" not only as an expression of the utmost suffering and anguish of the innocent victim (146–47), but also as a cry of the Father who deserts his Son: "The grief of the Father is here as important as the death of the Son" (243). The Son suffers the pain of being cut off from the life of the Father, and the Father suffers the pain of giving up his Son. By doing so, God "also accepts and adopts [suffering] in himself, making it part of his own eternal life" (119). Therefore the cross is not only an event between God and humanity. In addition, "What happened on the cross was an event between God and God. It was a deep division in God himself, in so far as God abandoned God and contradicted himself, and at the same time a unity in God, in so far as God was at one with God and corresponded to himself" (244). Thus the cross belongs to the inner life of God (249). "God's being is in suffering and suffering in God's being itself," because God is love (72).[8]

Here is the reason for God's willingness to suffer, namely, love. Rather than being a neutral observer of world events, God is "pathetic" in that "he suffers from the love which is the superabundance and overflowing of his being" (Moltmann, *Trinity*, 23). This is reciprocal love; God is truly affected by the objects of his love: "A God who cannot suffer is poorer than any man. For a God who is incapable of suffering is a being who cannot be involved. Suffering and injustice do not affect him.... But the one who cannot suffer cannot love either. So he is also a loveless being" (Moltmann, *Crucified God*, 222).

What about God's freedom? Tradition and, for example, Barth have been keen on defending God's freedom, even at the expense of casting doubt on his love (Moltmann, *Trinity*, 52–55). The concept of "freedom" which posits a solitary God, however, is based on the idea of lordship and domination. For Moltmann, "God's freedom can never contradict the truth he himself is," namely love. Love can never exist alone, love shares, love gives (53, 99, among others). In other words, there is reciprocal relationship between the world and God (98, among others), a topic which is expanded in Moltmann's doctrine of creation.

**The constitution of the Trinity**

Similarly to Pannenberg, Moltmann starts from the salvation history of the Bible: "The New Testament talks about God by proclaiming in narrative the relationships of the Father, the Son and the Spirit, which are relationships of fellowship and are open to the world" (*Trinity*, 64).[9] The cross, as mentioned above, belongs to the intra-trinitarian life and thus is constitutive of the persons of the Trinity in unity-in-diversity, or presence-in-absence (80).[10] This paradox becomes more understandable in light of Moltmann's idea of the oneness of Father and Son to the point at which they "represent a single surrendering movement" (*Trinity*, 82).[11]

Furthermore, the cross is also the way to connect the Spirit to Father and Son. The Spirit proceeds "from this event [of the cross] between the Father and the Son" and thus is the "boundless love which proceeds from the grief of the Father and the dying of the Son" and reaches out to humanity (Moltmann, *Crucified God*, 245). The Spirit also opens up the Trinity to creation. In the sending of the Spirit, the Trinity is an open Trinity; in this act the trinitarian history of God becomes open to the world as well as the future. Men and women are thus integrated into the history of the Trinity (Moltmann, *Trinity*, 89–90).

Having established the threeness of the Christian God, Moltmann faces two major issues: the question of the mutuality of the three persons and the problem of unity. Moltmann believes that mutuality can be established, first, with the reference to the eschatological "movement" of the kingdom from one trinitarian person to another. Quite similarly to Pannenberg, he argues for the mutual constitution of three trinitarian members. Speaking of the eschatological history of the Son, Moltmann says:

> Here we must particularly note the mutual workings of the Father and the Son: the Father subjects everything to the Son, the Son subjects himself to the Father. Through "the power of the resurrection" the Son destroys all other powers and death itself, then transferring the consummated kingdom of life and the love that is free of violence to the Father. The kingdom of God is therefore transferred from one divine subject to the other; and its form is changed in the process. So *God's triunity precedes the divine lordship.*
>
> (*Trinity*, 92–93)[12]

The second way in which Moltmann advocates the idea of mutuality has to do with the understanding of "person" in the context of relationships: "The three divine Persons exist in their particular, unique natures as Father, Son and Spirit in their relationships to one another, and are determined through these relationships. It is in these relationships that they are persons. Being as persons in this respect means existing-in-relationship" (145). Following the contemporary understanding of personhood relationally, Moltmann says that persons "ex-ist totally in the other: the Father ex-ists by virtue of his love, as himself entirely in the Son; the Son, by virtue of his self-surrender, ex-ists as himself totally in the Father; and so on" (173–74).[13]

In combining these two ideas of the eschatological shifting of the kingdom from one divine person to the other and the social constitution of the persons, Moltmann believes he has succeeded in reaching a major goal of his trinitarian theology, which he summarizes in this way: "Only when we are capable of thinking of Persons, relations, and changes in the relations *together* does the idea of the Trinity lose its usual static, rigid quality. Then not only does the eternal life of the triune God become conceivable; its eternal *vitality* becomes conceivable too" (*Trinity*, 174).[14]

There is a surprising move, however, in Moltmann's thinking here, and that has to do with his desire to lift up the Father as the "source" of the divinity, yet in a different way from typical Eastern Orthodox theology. Taking his clue from naming of God as "Father" in the Apostles' creed, Moltmann surmises that rather than being "the Father of the Universe," an idea which supports a hierarchical and oppressive view of God (*Trinity*, 162–63), the Father is exclusively "the Father of the Son," Jesus Christ. No patriarchal connotations can be found in this Father of the Son (163). Acknowledging the implications of this idea for his insistence on the mutuality, Moltmann makes the distinction between the intra-trinitarian and economic constitution of the Trinity, claiming that the "monarchy of the Father" thus defined applies only to the immanent Trinity.

**Unity as *perichōrēsis***

Critical of the tradition's ways of establishing the unity of God, whether based on the unity of the divine substance or on one divine subject (*Trinity*, 149), Moltmann represents a radical social trinitarian approach which begins with three persons and works from that toward unity (19). The eschatological consummation is both the key to the unity of the Trinity and the way of reconciling the relationship between the economic and immanent Trinity. There is an eschatological movement to the unity: "The unity of the Father, the Son and the Spirit is then the eschatological question about the consummation of the trinitarian history of God" (149).

Since the trinitarian members as "three divine subjects are co-active in this history," there is no way to define the unity in terms of "monadic unity." The unity spoken of here rather "lies in the *union* of the Father, the Son and the Spirit. It lies in their *fellowship*" (Moltmann, *Trinity*, 95).[15] Being a dynamic concept, it is also "*communicable* unity and... an *open, inviting unity, capable of interaction,*" over against the traditional exclusive ways of establishing unity that build on the ideas of the oneness of the substance or the sameness of the absolute subject (149–50, at 149).[16] Moltmann utilizes the ancient concept of *perichōrēsis* to elaborate on his view: it is the mutual indwelling of trinitarian persons in each other, "the unitedness, the at-oneness of the three Persons with one another, or: the unitedness, at-oneness of the triune God." This unity "must be perceived in the *perichoresis* of the divine Persons" (150).

This *perichōrēsis* will be consummated in the eschaton in the coming union of God and of God and the world in the eschaton. Moltmann thus "link[s] the consummation of salvation history in eschatology with the consummation of the Trinitarian life of God in itself."[17] This finally takes us to the culmination of Moltmann's theological vision and shows the way in which he believes we can reconcile the distinction between the economic and the immanent Trinity: "The economic Trinity completes and perfects itself to immanent Trinity when the history and experience of salvation are completed and perfected. When everything is 'in God' and 'God is in all,' then the economic Trinity is raised into and transcended in the immanent Trinity" (*Trinity*, 161). Divine unity exists as a result: "the trinitarian persons form their unity by themselves in the circulation of the divine life" (175). This theme is further developed in his eschatology.

Is there any place then for the distinction between the immanent and economic Trinity? The only legitimate way of continuing the distinction is to relegate it to doxology, the human response to the experience of salvation and anticipation of the coming kingdom (Moltmann, *Trinity*, 152, 161). "Doxological response" means participation in and transformation into God rather than an attempt to know God *in se* (152).

### The function of the doctrine of the Trinity: the kingdom of freedom

One of Moltmann's major contributions to contemporary trinitarian theology is the way in which he utilizes the Trinity as a critical theological, social, and political criterion.[18] His thesis is simple and bold: human societies, including the church, should reflect the principle of egalitarianism and mutual "indwelling" evident in the Trinity. Moltmann is critical of all kinds of notions of hierarchy and dominion in the Triune God. God's fatherhood does not imply any notions of power. Even more, in light of the Son proceeding from the Father, there is an idea of begetting and birth related to the deity, which inspires Moltmann to speak of "motherly Father" and "fatherly Mother."[19] Rejecting both monotheism, the religion of the patriarchy, and pantheism, the religion of matriarchy, Moltmann advocates the concept of the Triune God that leads to an equal fellowship of men and women (*Trinity*, 164–65).

## PANNENBERG: TRINITY AS "PUBLIC THEOLOGY"

### Revising the canons of trinitarian theology

Pannenberg's choice of title for the first chapter of the first volume of his *Systematische Theologie* (*Systematic Theology*) reveals the basic agenda of all of his theology: "The Truth of Christian Doctrine as the Theme of Systematic Theology" (I, 1).[20] The task of systematic theology is the exposition of Christian doctrine in a way that leads to a coherent presentation in correlation with what we know of God and reality as a whole.[21] Pannenberg's three-volume *summa* gave him finally an opportunity to flesh out the intimations given earlier; this systematic theology is "more thoroughly Trinitarian than any example I know of."[22] For Pannenberg, all systematic theology is but expansion of the doctrine of the Triune God, and therefore it is only with the consummation of the world with the eschatological coming of the kingdom that the doctrine of God finally reaches its final goal (I, 447–48).[23]

The moment it appears that the one God can be better understood without rather than with the doctrine of the Trinity, that doctrine appears to be a superfluous addition to the concept of the one God, even though it is reverently treated as a mystery of revelation. Even worse, it is bound to seem incompatible with the divine unity (Pannenberg, *Systematic Theology*, I, 291).

In keeping with his basic methodological choice, Pannenberg reverses the order of traditional systematic treatment, beginning with the doctrine of the Trinity and only after that moving to the question of the unity and attributes of God.[24] This is "concrete monotheism" (*Systematic Theology*, I, 335). Why begin with threeness when speaking of one God? Pannenberg sees the order and content of his trinitarian doctrine as built on revelation (I, 299),[25] yet with a significant departure from what he sees as the main weakness in Barth, namely, basing the doctrine on a *formal* principle rather than on concrete salvation history as it unfolds in scripture.[26] Because Pannenberg wants to go beyond the formal, logical principle drawn from scriptural teaching, he takes as his point of departure for the doctrine of the Trinity the coming of Jesus as the announcer and inaugurator of his Father's kingdom. Submission to his heavenly Father as "Son" forms the concrete basis for the trinitarian self-distinction;[27] this is of course also the beginning point for early Christology, and it will also involve the self-distinction of the Spirit from and unity with Father and Son.[28]

### The threeness of the one God of revelation

As Son, Jesus both distinguished himself from the Father, in submitting himself to his Father and the service of the coming of the kingdom (Pannenberg, *Systematic Theology*, I, 263),[29] and "also realized that he was very closely linked to the Father in his work" (I, 263–64). That the Son is the eternal counterpart of the Father was seen only in light of the resurrection, which serves as the divine confirmation of Jesus' claim to the sonship (I, 264–65).

The third member of the Trinity, the Spirit, is understood – in keeping with tradition – as the medium of the communion of Jesus with the Father as well as the medium of our participation in Christ (Pannenberg, *Systematic Theology*, I, 266–67). Otherwise, "the Christian doctrine of the deity of the Spirit would be a purely external addition to the confession of the relation of the Son to the deity of the Father" (I, 268).[30]

Starting with the concrete salvation history as revealed in scripture and building on the idea of self-distinction and relationality, Pannenberg offers an alternative to traditional ways of deriving the trinitarian persons from the concept of God as one being, either as love (Augustine, Richard of St. Victor) or as spirit (Hegel and German Idealism) (*Systematic Theology*, I, 296, 298). Pannenberg clarifies and sharpens his starting point by a careful systematic-philosophical construction, borrowing the idea of self-distinction from Hegel.[31] According to this idea, "person" is a relational, correlative term: one gains one's personality by giving oneself to one's counterpart; thus identity is gained in separation from, yet also in dependence on, the other. Fittingly enough, that section of trinitarian discussion is titled "The Reciprocal Self-Distinction of Father, Son, and Spirit as the Concrete Form of Trinitarian Relations" (*Systematic Theology*, I, 308).

## Self-distinction and mutual dependency in the Trinity

By subjecting himself as creature to his heavenly Father, Jesus shows himself to be the Son, and so at one with the Father from eternity as the Father's counterpart: "The eternal God cannot be directly thought of as from eternity related to a temporal and creaturely reality unless this is itself eternal, as a correlate of the eternal God" (Pannenberg, *Systematic Theology*, I, 311). What about the Father's relation to the Son? And furthermore: how is the idea of self-distinction to be applied to the Spirit's relation to the Father and Son and vice versa?

Differently from tradition, which assigns the Father the status of being without origin (and, conversely, the origin of the deity of Son and Spirit), Pannenberg argues for a genuine mutuality, appropriately labeled by Ted Peters the principle of "dependent divinity."[32] While the relations between the Father and Son are irreversible (the Father is not begotten by the Son), the Father's fatherhood is dependent on the Son. As the holder of lordship and position of rule given by him by the Father (Mt 11:27, 28:18; Lk 10:22; Phil 2:9 ff.), the Son destroys "every rule and every authority and power" and "must reign until he has put all his enemies under his feet" (1 Cor 15:24–25), in order to hand it finally back to the Father in the eschatological consummation. In keeping with Rahner's Rule (while that is not mentioned here), the intra-trinitarian relations can be inferred from the mutual relations between the historical person of Jesus and the Father (*Systematic Theology*, I, 312).[33] Consequently:

> In the handing over of lordship from the Father to the Son, and its handing back from the Son to the Father, we see *a mutuality in their relationship* that we do not see in the begetting. By handing over lordship to the Son the Father makes his kingship *dependent* on whether the Son glorifies him and fulfils his lordship by fulfilling his mission... The rule of the kingdom of the Father is not so external to his deity that he might be God without his kingdom.
>
> (I, 313)[34]

Going in the same direction as Moltmann but not quite as far, Pannenberg agrees that "in the death of Jesus the deity of his God and Father was at issue" and that therefore it is an event that does "affect eternal placidity of the Trinitarian life of God." Yet to speak of the "death of God" or even "directly of the death of God in the Son" is not acceptable. Rather, the ultimate humiliation and acceptance of death are the ultimate consequence of the Son's self-distinction from his Father. At the same time, the Father's deity is questioned and thus the Father shares the suffering of the Son in his "sym-pathy with the passion" (*Systematic Theology*, I, 314).

As in Moltmann, the cross also highlights the role of the Spirit. For Pannenberg, however, that comes to the fore in the act of the Spirit as the one who raises the Son from death (Rom 1:4, 8:11; 1 Cor 15:44 ff.; 1 Tim 3:16b), yet does so together with the Father (Acts 2:24 among others). As a consequence, here is then "a self-distinction which constitutes the Spirit a separate person from the Father and the Son and relates him to both" (*Systematic Theology*, I, 314–15).[35]

In keeping with the principle of mutual self-distinction and dependency among trinitarian members, Pannenberg critiques the idea of Father, Son, and Spirit as different modes of one divine subject and regards them rather as "living realizations of separate centers of action" (*Systematic Theology*, I, 319). If self-distinctions are the key to affirming the personhood of Father, Son, and Spirit in the one God (I, 320), they mean also that "the relations between the persons are constitutive not merely for their distinctions but also for their deity" (I, 323). This, however, does not mean that the monarchy of the Father is set aside. On the contrary, "By their work the Son and Spirit serve the monarchy of the Father. Yet the Father does not have his kingdom or monarchy without the Son and Spirit, but only through them" (I, 324). Nor does this mean that the subordination of the Son to his Father would imply ontological inferiority. By subjecting himself to the Father, the Son is "himself in eternity the locus of the monarchy of the Father" and so one with the

Father and Spirit. The monarchy of the Father is not a presupposition but the result of the working together of three persons, and as such then "the seal of their unity" (I, 325).

The idea of self-distinction and resulting dependency among three persons leads Pannenberg to revisit traditional terminology as it relates to the coming of the Son and the Spirit. Instead of the "generation" of the Son and the "procession" of the Spirit, Pannenberg uses terms that suggest self-distinction and mutuality such as "handing over," "giving back," "glorification," "(voluntary) submission," and so forth.

**The unity of God as the challenge for Christian theology**

For Pannenberg, as for Moltmann, the threeness is a given, and the establishment of God's unity is the challenge. Yet, unlike that of Moltmann and many other social trinitarians, Pannenberg's trinitarian doctrine also bears a similarity with traditional approaches, in that he affirms a single divine essence, as indicated in one of the chapter titles in *Systematic Theology*, "The Unity and Attributes of the Divine Essence."[36] "Thus, the doctrine of the Trinity is in fact concrete monotheism in contrast to the notions of an abstract transcendence of the one God and abstract notions of a divine unity that leaves no place for plurality" (I, 335–36).

Not surprisingly, Pannenberg finds earlier ways of affirming unity less than satisfactory,[37] whether the traditional way of establishing unity on the basis of the person of the Father as deity (*Systematic Theology*, I, 311–12, 314)[38] or the idea of God as the divine subject affirmed in various ways in tradition.[39] Pannenberg even finds wanting the efforts to base unity on *perichōrēsis*, as Moltmann and many who followed him, such as L. Boff, have done. Pannenberg criticizes this approach because *perichōrēsis* was never used in tradition, not even by John the Damascene, as a means of establishing unity, but was used rather as a way of illustrating unity-in-diversity (I, 334).[40] Nor is the idea of establishing unity with the help of the Father's monarchy totally satisfactory, even though Pannenberg speaks of the Father's monarchy in mutual terms (I, esp. 324–26).

Summarizing Pannenberg's complex and ambiguous discussion of unity is challenging. Yet the outline is quite clear. Agreeing with tradition that the concept of "essence" is needed to affirm the unity of the three persons, Pannenberg also revises this concept radically in order to move beyond the now-disputed substance ontology of the past. He conceives "the divine essence as the epitome of the personal relations among Father, Son, and Spirit" (*Systematic Theology*, I, 334). "This requires a concept of essence that is not external to the category of relations" (I, 334–35, 366–67). Relationality not only helps us to move beyond the outdated substance ontology but ties the discussion of the unity to the economy of salvation, including the coming of the kingdom.

### "The unity and attributes of the divine essence"

In order to establish the link between God's essence, unity-in-threeness, and economy of salvation, Pannenberg corrects the traditional view according to which God's existence and essence can be gleaned from the work of creation whereas only revelation gives knowledge of the Trinity (*Systematic Theology*, I, 341–42).[41] In Pannenberg's view "the solution to this problem lies in viewing the divine attributes as arising out of the activity of God in the world, for God's essence (the divine 'whatness') is bound up with God's existence (the divine 'thereness'), and this existence is found only in the trinitarian persons."[42] To speak of the acts of God in the world and thus of God's essence from eternity to eternity, however, only doxological language (rather than analogical, as tradition has had it) is available to human beings, because God is incomprehensible.[43]

A key concept here for Pannenberg is that of infinity, which he finds most helpfully developed by Descartes. While everything finite is limited by the infinite, infinity not only transcends but also embraces all that is finite (otherwise, there would be no infinity) (*Systematic Theology*, I, 349–51). In the Bible, the idea of infinity is described with the help of the idea of (God as) spirit and love. Divine essence, thus, is understood by Pannenberg as the "incomprehensible [force] field," and God's presence in creation as "a comprehensive field of force that releases event after event into finite existence."[44] This "field," spirit, is not only the impersonal presence of God but also the manifestation of the three trinitarian persons. "The deity as field can find equal manifestation in all three persons" (I, 383).

Combining the idea of relationality of the essence and divine essence as infinite spirit gives Pannenberg the resources he needs for affirming the unity of the Godhead. These insights "now permit us . . . to understand the trinitarian persons, *without derivation* from a divine essence that differs from them, as centers of action of the one movement which embraces and permeates all of them – the movement of the divine Spirit who has his existence only in them" (*Systematic Theology*, I, 385).[45] Anticipating the charge that this *perichōrēsis* is only secondary, he continues: "The persons are not first constituted in their distinction, by derivation from the Father, and only then united in *perichōrēsis* and common action. As modes of being of the one divine life they are always permeated by its dynamic through their mutual relations" (I, 385).

The common activity of the three divine persons – as against the traditional view[46] – is not enough to affirm unity. Pannenberg elaborates on this in his discussion of the attributes and works of God and how they relate to unity.

The other main biblical "definition" of God is love (1 Jn 4:8).[47] Pannenberg sees all the basic elements of affirming unity as connected in the notion of love: "the statement that God is love will prove to be the concrete form of the divine essence that is initially described as Spirit and in terms of the concept of the Infinite" (*Systematic Theology*, I, 396).

Finally, Pannenberg sets forth his understanding of the economic–immanent distinction: "Because God is love, having once created a world in his freedom, he finally does not have his own existence without this world, but over against it and in it in the process of its ongoing consummation" (*Systematic Theology*, I, 447). In the final analysis, then, the establishment of divine unity is "bound up with the work of the three persons in the world (the economic Trinity), which work – and hence which unity – is completed only eschatologically and is linked to the relations found in the eternal life of the trinitarian persons (the immanent Trinity)."[48]

## CRITICAL REFLECTIONS

### Shared views

Moltmann and Pannenberg share several key affirmations. Both ground the Trinity in revelation and thus attempt to avoid abstract speculation. While for Pannenberg the coming of the Son of the Father is the key, for Moltmann the Father's suffering in his Son is the focus. Thus both begin with *oikonomia* and proceed to *theologia*.

Both theologians include history in the divine life, Moltmann more liberally because of his panentheism. Moltmann's doctrines of creation and eschatology reap the harvest of his emerging panentheism and envision at the end a mutual indwelling of not only God and his people, as tradition, based on the vision of Revelation 21–22, has maintained, but also of God and the renewed creation. Pannenberg is more keen to affirm the distinction if not separation between God and world. For both theologians, threeness is given, while the unity is the challenge.

Both theologians introduce the person of the Spirit in relation to the coming of Jesus; yet I find Pannenberg's way more satisfactory, for I am not quite sure exactly what Moltmann's idea of the Spirit "emerging" from the event of the cross means.

While emphasizing mutuality and relationality, neither theologian is willing to make any member of the deity the "source." Yet Pannenberg – in my opinion, rightly – still speaks of the "monarchy" of the Father, yet not separately from the mutuality.

Having briefly outlined the main similarities between Moltmann and Pannenberg, let me now highlight two key challenges in their theologies: the question of the unity of the Triune God and the economic–immanent distinction. These two questions not only stand at the heart of contemporary discussion in general but also are related to other issues mentioned in the introductory paragraphs of this chapter.

### The unity of the Triune God

Moltmann's proposal has raised serious concerns about tritheism;[49] some critics have even leveled the charge of tritheism.[50] Moltmann's key concept in defense of the unity – *perichōrēsis* – has been found wanting.[51] Alongside *perichōrēsis*, for Moltmann the most important way of safeguarding the unity of the Triune God is to refer to the eschatological consummation. While that may help establish the unity of God, it also at the same time raises the serious question of the economic–immanent distinction, to be taken up in the following section.

Overall, Moltmann himself has not appeared to be too much concerned about these criticisms since for him, as already mentioned, tritheism has never been a real problem in Christian theology; rather, "monotheism," as he calls it, and modalism have been.

The main reason for raising the question about Pannenberg's capacity to establish the unity of the Triune God has to do with his novel idea of three divine persons as distinct centers of consciousness and action.[52] Pannenberg is of course not a tritheist,[53] nor does his "idea of mutual reciprocity between the persons drive . . . him *in the direction of tritheism*," as some have surmised.[54] I do not see much danger of tritheism in Pannenberg, for many reasons, and especially because of his relentless insistence on the need to speak of divine essence as well as the idea of God as spirit and love.[55]

That said, it is true that the *way* in which Pannenberg attempts to establish unity is ambiguous at best and frail at worst – even when it is granted that it may be "the most nuanced"[56] among contemporary luminaries. It all boils down to the plurality of methods he employs in defending unity, without really clarifying their inner relationships: from divine essence to attributes to the idea of God as spirit to God as love to *perichōrēsis* to the kingdom of God! The question naturally arises as to whether "Pannenberg's many descriptions of the divine essence can coherently and meaningfully refer to a single reality."[57]

## The economic–immanent distinction

Many commentators believe that Moltmann has taken Rahner's Rule to its logical end, that is, finally conflating the immanent Trinity with the economic.[58] Moltmann's own statements have given rise to this concern: "In order to grasp the death of the Son in its significance for God himself, I found myself bound to surrender the traditional distinction between the immanent and the economic Trinity, according to which the cross comes to stand only in the economy of salvation, but not within the immanent Trinity" (*Trinity*, 160). Furthermore, Moltmann argues not only that the economic Trinity reveals the immanent Trinity but that it has a retroactive effect on the immanent Trinity. "The pain of the cross determines the inner life of the triune God from eternity to eternity," similarly to the responsive love in glorification through the Spirit (160–61, at 161).[59]

It seems to me the only respect in which Moltmann still holds onto the distinction is with reference to doxology. Remarking that while doxology is based on and derives from the experience of salvation, he states that it also "grow[s] up out of the conclusion drawn from this experience about the *transcendent conditions which make the experience possible*," which leads to "that experiences' *transcendent ground*" (*Trinity*, 153).[60] Not all are convinced, however, that this indirect "defense" of the distinction suffices.

Pannenberg is well aware of the danger, since "the equation of the two means the absorption of the immanent Trinity in the economic Trinity." Consequently, "This steals from the Trinity of the salvation history all sense and significance. For this Trinity has sense and significance only if God is the same in salvation history as he is from eternity" (*Systematic Theology*, I, 331). While Pannenberg certainly sees the need to correct the traditional view of history and the divine life as more or less independent (I, 332–33), he is also critical of some contemporary revisions, which for him seem to blur the distinction completely (mentioning as examples both Moltmann and process theology). Pannenberg's idea of dependency does not make God prisoner to world happenings but rather speaks of "the dependence of the trinitarian persons upon one another as the kingdom is handed over and handed back in connection with the economy of salvation" (I, 329).[61]

Clearly, Pannenberg takes Rahner's Rule as his basis but expands and reformulates it in a significant way. For him, the rule "means that the doctrine of the Trinity does not merely begin with the revelation of God in Jesus Christ and then work to a trinity in the eternal essence of God, but that it must constantly link the trinity in the eternal essence of God to his historical revelation, since revelation cannot be viewed as extraneous to his deity" (*Systematic Theology*, 1, 328). This means that for Pannenberg the unity of the economic and immanent Trinity occurs in relation to history and finds its culmination in the eschaton.

## IN LIEU OF CONCLUSIONS: QUESTIONS FOR THE FUTURE

Other questions in need of further clarification include the following:

1. While beginning with the threeness of God serves the purposes of correcting the modalistic tendencies of tradition, is not the movement from the unity to Trinity also justified in light of the developing biblical revelation, which begins with the unity (Deut 6:4) and moves to threeness only with the coming of Jesus?
2. Does not Moltmann's continued pejorative charge of "monotheism" ironically compromise his willingness to dialogue with Judaism (and Islam, with which he has not engaged)?
3. Should not the use of the Trinity to critique social inequalities be checked against the incommensurability of the divine and human communities?
4. Furthermore, is all talk about power and hierarchy in itself anti-trinitarian? If so, what should be done with the rich scriptural language that seems to imply hierarchy?

### Notes

1. Jürgen Moltmann, *The Trinity and the Kingdom of God: The Doctrine of God*, trans. Margaret Kohl (San Francisco: Harper & Row; London: SCM Press, 1981).
2. Jürgen Moltmann, *The Crucified God: The Cross of Christ as the Foundation and Criticism of Christian Theology*, trans. Margaret Kohl (London: SCM Press, 1974).
3. Stanley J. Grenz names Moltmann's view "Trinitarian eschatological panentheism" (and traces the label back to R. Bauckham, *The Theology of Jürgen Moltmann* (Edinburgh: T. & T. Clark, 1995), 17). Stanley

J. Grenz, *The Social God and the Relational Self: A Trinitarian Theology of the Imago Dei* (Louisville, KY: Westminster John Knox, 2001), 41.

4. For his dialogue with Barth and Rahner, see Moltmann, *Trinity*, 139–48. See also Jayne H. Davis, "Opening Dialogue: Jürgen Moltmann's Interaction with the Thought of Karl Barth," *Review and Expositor*, 100:4 (Fall 2003), 695–711.
5. Ted Peters, *God as Trinity: Relationality and Temporality in Divine Life* (Louisville, KY: Westminster John Knox, 1993), 102.
6. See also Moltmann, *Trinity*, 78.
7. A helpful discussion can be found in Bauckham, *The Theology of Jürgen Moltmann*, ch. 3.
8. See further, Geiko Müller-Fahrenholz, *The Kingdom and the Power: The Theology of Jürgen Moltmann* (Minneapolis: Fortress, 2001), 72–73.
9. In the original, the whole text is in italics.
10. See also Moltmann, *Crucified God*, 244.
11. See also Moltmann, *Crucified God*, 244.
12. Ibid. Emphases in the original. See also Wolfhart Pannenberg, *Systematic Theology*, I, trans. Geoffrey W. Bromiley (Grand Rapids, MI: Eerdmans, 1991), esp. 313.
13. For the Augustinian reference, see Moltmann, *Trinity*, 172.
14. First emphasis in the original, second mine.
15. Emphases in the original. See also *Trinity*, 96.
16. Emphases in the original.
17. Pannenberg, *Systematic Theology*, I, 330, with reference to Moltmann, *Trinity*, esp. 126.
18. While a profound thinker, Moltmann declares that the practical implications of the theology are high on his agenda. See further Jürgen Moltmann, "An Autobiographical Note," in A. J. Conyers, *God, Hope, and History: Jürgen Moltmann and the Christian Concept of History* (Macon, GA: Mercer University Press, 1988), 204.
19. Moltmann refers to the statement of the Eleventh Council of Toledo (675) about the Son having been begotten out of the Father's womb. Moltmann, *Trinity*, 165.
20. For a succinct discussion of Pannenberg's method in light of his overall theology, see Stanley J. Grenz, *Reason for Hope: The Systematic Theology of Wolfhart Pannenberg* (Oxford and New York: Oxford University Press, 1990), ch. 1.
21. For his definition of theology along these lines, see Pannenberg, *Systematic Theology*, I, 59–60.
22. Pannenberg, "God's Presence in History," *Christian Century*, 11 (March 1981), 263. Many commentators have acknowledged this: Roger E. Olson, "Wolfhart Pannenberg's Doctrine of the Trinity," *Scottish Journal of Theology*, 43 (1990), 175–76; Grenz, *Reason for Hope*, 44.
23. See also Pannenberg, *Systematic Theology*, I, 59–61, 335.

24. Ch. 5 in ibid., Vol. 1, is titled "The Trinitarian God," and ch. 6 "The Unity and Attributes of the Divine Essence."
25. See also ibid., 1, 304, among others.
26. On criticism of Barth in this respect, see ibid., 1, 296, 303, and the discussion in my critical reflections on Barth earlier in this chapter.
27. The first section in ch. 5, "The Trinitarian God," is appropriately titled "The God of Jesus and the Beginning of the Doctrine of the Trinity." See Pannenberg, *Systematic Theology*, 1, 259.
28. See especially ibid., 1, 263.
29. See also ibid., 1, 309, among others.
30. See also ibid., 1, 304–05.
31. W. Pannenberg, *Jesus – God and Man*, trans. Lewis L. Wilkins and Duane A. Priebe, 2nd edn. (Philadelphia: Westminster, 1977), 181–83, 340.
32. Peters, *God as Trinity*, 135.
33. The biblical passage is quoted in *Systematic Theology*, 1, 312.
34. Emphases mine.
35. All quotations at 1, 315.
36. Ch. 6 of *Systematic Theology*, 1, is titled "The Unity and Attributes of the Divine Essence."
37. For summary statements, see ibid., 1, 334, 342.
38. See also 1, 279.
39. W. Pannenberg, "Problems of a Trinitarian Doctrine of God," *Dialog*, 26, 4 (Fall 1987), 251.
40. This is argued in more detail in Michael L. Chiavone, "The Unity of God as Understood by Four Twentieth Century Trinitarian Theologians: Karl Rahner, Millard Erickson, John Zizioulas, and Wolfhart Pannenberg," Ph.D. dissertation, Southeastern Baptist Theological Seminary, Wake Forest, NC, 2005, 125–27. The structure of John's discussion confirms this judgment. He begins the discussion of Trinity with the oneness of God and then proceeds from there to considering Trinity, thus – ironically – anticipating the standard Western tradition.
41. The heading of this section is taken from Pannenberg, *Systematic Theology*, 1, ch. 6.
42. Stanley J. Grenz, *Rediscovering the Triune God: The Trinity in Contemporary Theology* (Minneapolis: Fortress, 2004), 99.
43. This argumentation is developed in the first three sections of ch. 6 of Pannenberg's *Systematic Theology*, 1.
44. W. Pannenberg, *Introduction to Systematic Theology* (Grand Rapids, MI: Eerdmans, 1991), 194.
45. Emphases in the original.
46. See further Pannenberg, *Systematic Theology*, 1, 278.
47. For the connection between these concepts, see ibid., 1, 395; for the discussion between love and Trinity, see 422–32.
48. Grenz, *Rediscovering the Triune God*, 100; Pannenberg, *Systematic Theology*, 1, 447.

49. Peters, *God as Trinity*, 109; Thomas F. Torrance, *The Christian Doctrine of God: One Being, Three Persons* (Edinburgh: T. & T. Clark, 1996), 247 n. 39; Gerald O'Collins, *The Tripersonal God: Understanding and Interpreting the Trinity* (Mahwah, NJ: Paulist, 1999), 158, among others.
50. Paul D. Molnar, *Divine Freedom and the Doctrine of the Immanent Trinity: In Dialogue with Karl Barth and Contemporary Theology* (Edinburgh: T. & T. Clark, 2005), 201–02, with references to many others; Robert Letham, *The Holy Trinity: In Scripture, History, Theology, and Worship* (Phillipsburg, NJ: P. & R., 2004), 307–09.
51. A helpful discussion can be found in Randall E. Otto, "The Use and Abuse of Perichoresis in Recent Theology," *Scottish Journal of Theology*, 54 (2001), 366–84.
52. See, e.g., John L. Gresham, Jr., "The Social Model of the Trinity and Its Critics," *Scottish Journal of Theology*, 46 (1993), 330, 342; William J. Hill, *The Three-Personed God: The Trinity as a Mystery of Salvation* (Washington, DC: Catholic University of America Press, 1982), 254.
53. Contra Henri Blocher, "Immanence and Transcendence in Trinitarian Theology," in Kevin J. Vanhoozer, ed., *The Trinity in a Pluralistic Age: Theological Essays on Culture and Religion* (Grand Rapids, MI: Eerdmans, 1997), 107.
54. Letham, *The Holy Trinity*, 316 (emphases mine).
55. See here the helpful comment by Chiavone, "The Unity of God," 243.
56. Ibid., 224.
57. Ibid., 234; see also Olson, "Pannenberg's Doctrine," 206.
58. Even the most sympathetic and moderate critics have expressed this opinion, such as R. Bauckham, "Jürgen Moltmann," in David F. Ford, ed., *The Modern Theologians: An Introduction to Christian Theology in the Twentieth Century*, 2 vols. (New York: Blackwell, 1989), I, 304; Samuel M. Powell, *The Trinity in German Thought* (Cambridge University Press, 2001), 201–02.
59. See also Roger Olson, "Trinity and Eschatology: The Historical Being of God in Jürgen Moltmann and Wolfhart Pannenberg," *Scottish Journal of Theology*, 36 (1983), 217–18.
60. Emphases mine.
61. See also *Systematic Theology*, I, 331.

## Further reading

Davis, Stephen T., Daniel Kendall, and Gerald O'Collins, eds., *The Trinity* (Oxford University Press, 1999).

Grenz, Stanley J., *Rediscovering the Triune God: The Trinity in Contemporary Theology* (Minneapolis: Fortress, 2004).

Gunton, Colin, *The Promise of Trinitarian Theology*, 2nd edn. (Edinburgh: T. & T. Clark, 1997).

Kärkkäinen, Veli-Matti, *The Trinity: Global Perspectives* (Louisville, KY: Westminster John Knox, 2007).
LaCugna, Catherine Mowry, *God for Us: The Trinity and Christian Life* (San Francisco: HarperSanFrancisco, 1991).
O'Collins, Gerald, *The Tripersonal God: Understanding and Interpreting the Trinity* (Mahwah, NJ: Paulist, 1999).
Moltmann, Jürgen, *The Trinity and the Kingdom: The Doctrine of God*, trans. Margaret Kohl (San Francisco: Harper & Row; London: SCM Press, 1981).
Pannenberg, Wolfhart, *Systematic Theology*, vol. 1, trans. Geoffrey W. Bromiley (Grand Rapids, MI: Eerdmans, 1991).
Peters, Ted, *God as Trinity: Relationality and Temporality in Divine Life.* (Louisville, KY: Westminster John Knox, 1993).
Volf, Miroslav, and Michael Welker, eds., *God's Life in Trinity* (Minneapolis: Fortress, 2006).

# 14 Sophia, apophasis, and communion: the Trinity in contemporary Orthodox theology

ARISTOTLE PAPANIKOLAOU

In 1453, Orthodox Christianity experienced not only the fall of Constantinople, but the beginning of the hibernation of a once-vibrant intellectual tradition: for nearly 400 years, most of the Orthodox world would suffer under Ottoman oppression. In the nineteenth century, the Orthodox Christian intellectual tradition would awaken from its slumber when Russian thinkers would begin responding to the flood of modern ideas and philosophies being imported from the West as a result of the reforms of Tsar Peter the Great. What is remarkable about this theological awakening is its consistency with the Byzantine intellectual tradition silenced by the Ottomans, most especially on the principle of divine–human communion as the core of Orthodox thought. Contemporary Orthodox theologians of the nineteenth and twentieth centuries would share a consensus that divine–human communion constitutes the very heart of Orthodox theology – it is where all theology thinking must begin and end. In addition to this consensus, the doctrine of the Trinity was considered, again in continuity with the Byzantine intellectual tradition, indispensable for conceptualizing the God–world relation in terms of divine–human communion. These points of agreement, however, did not preclude the development of three distinctive and, in part, mutually incompatible trajectories in contemporary Orthodox trinitarian theology. In this chapter, I will offer an analysis of the three most influential: the sophiology of Sergius Bulgakov, the apophaticism of Vladimir Lossky, and the communion ontology of John Zizioulas.

## SERGIUS BULGAKOV

One of the most profound and controversial Orthodox theologians of the twentieth century is Sergei Nikolaevich Bulgakov (1871–1944).[1] Bulgakov is known for offering the most sophisticated systematization and, hence, culmination of a philosophical and theological intellectual tradition within Russia known as "sophiology," whose roots can be traced back to Vladimir Sergeevich Soloviev (1853–1900). Toward the end of his life, he published a three-volume sophiological systematic theology entitled *O bogochelovechestve* (*On Divine Humanity*, 1933–45). The first volume of this trilogy, *The Lamb of God*, sparked a controversy which became known as the "Sophia Affair" and in which Bulgakov had to defend himself against accusations of heresy by the Moscow Patriarchate and the rival émigré synod of the Russian Orthodox Church.[2] Bulgakov's trilogy contains his most developed formulation of his sophiological understanding of the doctrine of the Trinity.

For Bulgakov, Sophia is the "self-revelation of the Holy Trinity."[3] The Father is the principle of the Holy Trinity, and as such, the Father is the self-revealing *hypostasis*. Bulgakov refers to the Father as the "Divine Depth and Mystery, the Divine Subject of self-revelation,"[4] the apophatic face of God's trinitarian life. The self-revelation of the Father is the Son and the Holy Spirit. The Father reveals himself[5] in the Son, who is the content of the self-revelation of the Father. The self-revelation of the Father in the Son is completed by the third *hypostasis*, the Holy Spirit. In the self-revelation of the Father in the Son, the Father breathes forth the Spirit, who proceeds from the Father as the hypostatic love of the Father for the Son; the Holy Spirit returns to the Father "through the Son" as the loving answer to the self-revelation of the Father in the Son. The Holy Spirit is the hypostatic love that unites the Father and the Son and completes the self-revelation of the Father in the Son and the Holy Spirit. The Son is identified with the content of this revelation and, hence, is the Truth of the Father's self-revelation; the Holy Spirit manifests and realizes the Truth of this self-revelation and, hence, is identified with Beauty. The Holy Trinity is an event of self-revelation of Love, Truth, and Beauty, all of which are entailed in the name of names for the Holy Trinity – Sophia.

The self-revelation of the Holy Trinity as an event of love between the Father, the Son, and the Holy Spirit is, thus, an event of *kenosis*, which Bulgakov defines as a movement of mutual self-giving, sacrifice, effacement, and reception. This trinitarian kenotic love is the ground for the kenosis of the Son in the incarnation: "in the cross of the earthly path is realized the cross of the heavenly kenosis."[6] It also constitutes God as Creator insofar as the intra-trinitarian kenosis of mutual self-giving and reception *is* God's freedom to give God's life, Sophia, kenotically to created existence.

Although the understanding of the Holy Trinity in terms of the self-revealing God bears the stamp of German Idealism, Bulgakov's primary motivation is an understanding of the God–world relation in terms of divine–human communion. "This revelation of the Absolute in the *world*, however, is such that it presupposes the self-revelation of the Absolute in itself, which in turn is included in the revelation of the Absolute to the world."[7] The idea of God as self-positing absolute subject begins, for Bulgakov, with an understanding of human beings as persons, which he defines as "consciousness of self."[8] If human persons are created in God's image, and if personal self-consciousness exists only as a self-positing to what is other than the self, then God's being as person is also a self-consciousness as self-positing to another. God's personal self-consciousness, however, must be understood without the limitations of space and time inherent in created spirit.[9] The others in relation to which the self-positing of absolute subjectivity finds its completion are themselves God, who are not "not-I" but their own personal centers, together constituting the "we" of the divine Trinity: "in the Divine Absolute subject . . . all altero-positings of I cannot be actualized outside of it, because of the absence of all 'outside,' but must be contained in it itself, so that it itself is for itself simultaneously I, though, he, and therefore we and you."[10] For Bulgakov, if the self-positing of the subject is the condition for the possibility of relating to what is other than the "I," God is free to commune with what is not God because God's life is one of self-positing as self-revelation. In this "deduction of the trinity as the triune absolute subject,"[11] Bulgakov's main concern is not a rational defense of how God is one and three; rather, he is attempting to understand how God can commune with what is not God, specifically with a humanity whose existence is personal self-consciousness. Bulgakov is ultimately attempting to understand how humans were created to receive what transcends them and, conversely, how God exists so as to commune with what is not God. The question of divine–human communion is central to theology, which is why "it must be emancipated from formal verbal dialectic and raised to the higher principles of theo-anthropology: How is divine-humanity possible? What are its general preconditions?"[12]

This understanding of divine–human communion in terms of the self-revelation of personal self-consciousness would not be complete without discussion of the aspect of Bulgakov's theology that is most distinctive – Sophia. Sophia is the *ousia* (nature) of God, but the *ousia* of God *as* revealed. Bulgakov talks of God's Sophia, the *ousia* of God as Glory, that is, as revealed, as if it is a fourth "thing" in God, but he is very clear that Sophia is not another *hypostasis* (person), nor some "thing" in addition to the *ousia* and *hypostases* of the Trinity.[13] Sophia is not reducible to *ousia*, nor to the divine *hypostasis*, even though each divine *hypostasis* is Sophia: Father-Sophia, Son-Sophia, Holy Spirit-Sophia; Sophia is the result of *ousia* hypostatized, the divine predicate of the absolute subject. The Holy Trinity is God's life as Truth, Beauty, and Love; it is a manifestation of the Glory of God, which Bulgakov feels compelled to name Sophia.

The naming of God's very life as Trinity as Sophia is best understood in light of Bulgakov's understanding of the God–world relation. For Bulgakov, since God is eternal, God exists such that God is eternally relating to the world, even if the world does not eternally exist as created, that is, in time. Sophia is God's self-revelation, and this revelation contains all that God *is*, including God, out of kenotic love, creating and relating to what is not God: "Sophia is the Pelorma, the Divine world . . . [a]nd in itself this Divine world contains all that the Holy Trinity reveals about itself in itself."[14] God is eternally the God for the other-than-God, and, for Bulgakov, there can be no consideration of the Holy Trinity *in itself* and, hence, no separation between the immanent and the economic Trinity. God's very being as Truth, Beauty, and Love, that is, as Sophia, is *as* Creator of the not-God, that is, the world: "Not only does He act in the world, but He is also defined on the basis of the world."[15] Sophia as the divine world is the divine-humanity (*bogochelovechestvo*), the being of God as relating eternally to the not-God. This divine-humanity is the ground for the creation in time, the creaturely Sophia, and for the incarnation of the God-man. Creation in time is creaturely Sophia's movement toward union with heavenly Sophia. As from all eternity, the kenosis of the Son and the Spirit in relation to creation in time accomplishes the self-revelation of the Father, which is the realization of Sophia: *"One and the same Sophia is revealed in God and in creation."*[16]

Why is the concept of Sophia necessary for trinitarian theology? What is at stake for Bulgakov with the concept of Sophia is the very realism of divine–human communion. For Bulgakov, there is no option for conceptualizing the God–world relation other than in terms of divine–human communion. He further argues that the bridge between Creator and creation is inconceivable without this particular understanding of the Holy Trinity in terms of Sophia. For Bulgakov, if the development of the doctrine of God as Trinity is simultaneously the Christian conceptualization of the God–world relation in terms of divine–human communion, then the latter cannot make sense without a category in addition to *ousia*, *hypostasis*, and energy, that is, without Sophia:

> the hypostasis of the Logos cannot provide such a unifying principle between God and the world... The principle we require is not to be sought in the person of God at all, but in his Nature, considered first as his intimate self-revelation, and second as his revelation in the world. And here we have at once Sophia in both its aspects, divine and creaturely. Sophia unites God with the world as the one common principle, the divine ground of creaturely existence.[17]

## VLADIMIR LOSSKY

Like Bulgakov, Vladimir Nikolaeivich Lossky (1903–1958), the son of the philosopher Nicholas Lossky, was exiled from Russia and eventually settled in Paris.[18] Lossky, however, was never affiliated with the Institut de Théologie Orthodoxe Saint Serge, largely because of his involvement in the Sophia Affair. Lossky contributed a short pamphlet to the Sophia Affair, *Spor o Sofii* (*The Debate on Sophia*), which he produced for the brotherhood of St. Photius.

Both Lossky and Georges Florovsky, the well-known patristics scholar who was the one-time professor at St. Sergius, self-identified with the "neo-patristic" trajectory of contemporary Orthodox theology, a phrase coined by Florovsky. This neo-patristic school has affinities with the *nouvelle théologie* movement within twentieth-century Roman Catholic theology, which is not surprising given the commingling of many Russian émigré and Roman Catholic theologians in Paris from the 1930s through the 1950s.[19] In addition to their call to return to the Fathers, the neo-patristic and *nouvelle théologie* schools share in common the rejection of neo-Thomism. Both Lossky and Florovsky, however, also saw the return to the Fathers as a response to the philosophical theology of Bulgakov. It would be a mistake to interpret the debate between Bulgakov on the one hand and Lossky and Florovsky on the other as simply one over the relation of Orthodoxy to modernity, or over the relation between theology and philosophy.[20] In the end, they all held the position that divine–human communion is at the heart of Orthodox theology. Behind the disagreements on the relation of philosophy to theology or about the adequacy of patristic thought lies a more fundamental debate over the implications and the conceptualization of the divine–human communion realized in Jesus Christ.

For Lossky, God as Trinity is revealed in the event of the incarnation, which is the beginning of all theology. God as Trinity is simply revealed as a "primordial fact,"[21] and there is no need for a Bulgakovian "deduction of the Trinity." Lossky interprets Eastern Christian thought not as a history of the development of the doctrine of the Trinity as a more coherent conceptualization of the God–world relation, but as a groping for the proper categories to express what is essentially an antinomy, which Lossky defines as the "non-opposition of opposites," that is, the opposition "of contrary but equally true propositions."[22] The doctrine of the Trinity affirms that God is simultaneously one and three, and the goal of theology is not to justify rationally what is essentially unjustifiable within the bounds of philosophical logic, but to find the proper categories that prevent either pole of the antinomy from collapsing into the other.

Lossky credits the Cappadocian Fathers, Basil of Caesarea, Gregory the Theologian (Gregory of Nazianzus), and Gregory of Nyssa, for discerning the categories of *hypostasis* and *ousia* as most adequate for expressing the trinitarian antinomy of unity and plurality, sameness and irreducibility. The genius of the Cappadocians was in their choice of two categories that were synonymous, which allowed them to rework the category of *hypostasis* by deconceptualizing it so that it could express the irreducibility of the Father, the Son, and the Holy Spirit. When thinking, thus, about the divine *ousia* one also brings to mind the divine *hypostases*, which are the *ousia* of God, and in thinking of the divine *ousia* one also brings to mind the divine *hypostases*. It is, thus, not quite accurate to accuse Lossky, as Michel René Barnes does, of appropriating uncritically Théodore de Régnon's interpretation that "Latin philosophy envisages first the nature in itself and then proceeds to the expression; Greek philosophy envisages first the expression and then penetrates it to find the nature."[23] Although Lossky, together with virtually every Orthodox theologian of the twentieth century, is guilty of reducing Western trinitarian theology to the simplistic notion of beginning with the essence,[24] Lossky is clear that what is important is not where one begins but maintaining the antinomy: "Nevertheless, the two ways were both equally legitimate so long as the first did not attribute to the essence a supremacy over the three persons, nor the second to the three persons a supremacy over the common nature."[25]

As a revealed "fact" of the revelation, the trinitarian antinomy, for Lossky, is rooted in the antinomy of divine–human communion in the incarnation, which is the union of two ontological others – the uncreated and the created. The antinomy of the union of the uncreated and the created demands that theology be apophatic, which has a much more complex meaning for Lossky than simply defining God in terms of what God is not, or declaring that the being of God exceeds language. Apophaticism is the affirmation that God's very being is antinomic insofar as God is simultaneously transcendent to and immanent in the other of God, the not-God, that is, creation. Such an understanding of God is the basis for the Greek patristic distinction between the essence and the energies of God. The essence of God refers to that which is incomprehensible in God, while the energies signify the life of God in which creation participates. The essence–energies distinction is central to most contemporary Orthodox theologians,[26] which is why Orthodox theology is often described as neo-Palamite. Though it is often criticized as nonsensical,[27] its non-opposition of opposites is what renders it adequate, according to Lossky, for expressing the transcendence and immanence of God. There is, however, a lack of integration between Lossky's trinitarian theology and his conceptualizing divine–human communion in terms of the essence–energies distinction, which can be summed up in the question: if God relates to the world with God's energies, why is God's being as Trinity? Lossky may respond that God as Trinity is simply revealed as fact, but the strength of Bulgakov's trinitarian theology, and, as we shall see, Zizioulas', rests in attempting to demonstrate the inseparable link between divine–human communion and conceptualizing God as Trinity. If Lossky's response might be that such an approach attempts to justify the unjustifiable, the danger of Lossky's own apophaticism is that it may render the doctrine of the Trinity superfluous.[28]

Apophaticism ultimately affirms that true knowledge of God is union with God, that is, it is not cognitive but realized in ascetical practice. Antinomic theological expressions serve the ascetical practice, insofar as they are meant to resist theological complacency that may result from rational justifications of Christian dogmas. Theological apophaticism is an attempt to conceptualize divine–human communion not simply for understanding, but so as to propel the ascetic movement toward union with God. It is this understanding of union with God that undergirds Lossky's virulent critique of the *filioque*, especially in its Thomistic form. Lossky interprets the latter to be the attempt at rationally justifying how the one God is triune, of which the *filioque* is the natural result. Lossky's attack is against the understanding of theology behind the *filioque*, whose definition of knowledge of God is propositional rather than mystical. According to Lossky, "by the dogma of the *Filioque*, the God of the philosophers and savants is introduced into the heart of the Living God."[29]

Lossky's trinitarian theology forms the basis for a theology of personhood that would have considerable influence in contemporary Orthodox theology, but exists in some tension with his own understanding of theology as apophatic. Although he argues that *hypostasis* and *ousia* are functional categories insofar as they are adequate for expressing the trinitarian antinomy of sameness and irreducibility, Lossky also develops, especially in his later writings, a more ontological understanding of these categories. The trinitarian distinction between *hypostasis* and *ousia* intimates a theology of person defined in terms of irreducibility and freedom. To *be* person is not simply to be reduced to *ousia*, but to be more than simply the *ousia*. In terms of human personhood, this translates into a uniqueness as irreducibility to the common human nature. This uniqueness as irreducibility is also an event of freedom (*ecstasis*) from human nature insofar as the human person is not determined by the necessity of nature.[30] Personhood as irreducibility and freedom is not so much what humans are as much as what they can become in union with God. It is also grounded in the very life of God as Trinity, which is an event of irreducibility and freedom. This less antinomic and more ontological unpacking of the trinitarian categories of *hypostasis* and *ousia* is evident in Lossky's discussion of the monarchy of the Father. The Father is the "cause" of the Son and the Spirit and, hence, of God's being as Trinity, *as* Father, that is, as the person of the Father irreducible to the divine *ousia* so as to give the divine *ousia* freely to the Son and the Spirit.[31] The Father does so out of love, which means that personal uniqueness and freedom are realized in relations of love. This trinitarian understanding of personhood would have a lasting impact on Orthodox theology, and particularly on the Greek theologians Christos Yannaras and John Zizioulas.

## JOHN ZIZIOULAS

The neo-patristic school left an indelible mark on contemporary Orthodox theology and, in particular, on a group of young Greek theologians of the 1950s who were looking to break away from what they perceived to be an imitative manual-style theology that dominated the Greek universities.[32] One of those Greek theologians was Christos Yannaras, who admits that "he started with Lossky."[33] In what remains Yannaras' most important work, *Person and Eros*, Lossky's apophaticism, the essence–energies distinction, and the theology of personhood are evident throughout.[34] Zizioulas studied with Georges Florovsky at Harvard in the early 1960s, and his early work in his Eucharistic ecclesiology would become foundational for his trinitarian theology and his relational theology of personhood.[35] Although his theology of personhood is strikingly similar to that of Lossky, Zizioulas disavows any Losskian influence, and is especially critical of Lossky's apophaticism throughout his writings.[36] Zizioulas does admit, however, that he was influenced by Yannaras' *Person and Eros*; it is, thus, likely that Lossky may have influenced Zizioulas' thought, albeit indirectly.[37]

For Zizioulas, the Christian doctrine of the Trinity, especially as formulated by the Cappadocian Fathers, amounts to an ontological revolution.[38] With the doctrine of the Trinity, for the first time in ontology, being is attributed to person rather than to essence. The ontological revolution is for Zizioulas an understanding of God's trinitarian life such that God is free to be in communion with what is not-God. If in traditional substance ontology notions such as person, relation, communion, difference lacked ontological import, in a trinitarian ontology they are constitutive of being. Such an ontological revolution required two "leavenings" of Greek ontology. The first is the uncreated–created distinction, which rejects the notion of an eternally existing creation. The distinction allows for conceptualizing the relation between God and creation in terms of a communion of freedom as love between two ontological others.

Such a revolution in ontology, that is, one that allows for communion between the uncreated and the created, requires an additional leavening, one that introduces freedom into the very being of God by attributing God's being to a person. The latter was accomplished, according to Zizioulas, by the Cappadocians in two moves. The first was to unite the concepts of *hypostasis* (literally, substance) and *prosopon* (literally, mask). In an interpretation that differs from Lossky's, Zizioulas argues that the synonymy between *hypostasis* and *ousia* made the former unsuitable for trinitarian theology. As such, *hypostasis* would not imply God as Trinity but three gods. The Greek category of *prosopon* was a relational category, but equally unsuitable since it lacked ontological content and would lead to Sabellianism, a denial of the hypostatic irreducibility in the life of God. The Cappadocian solution was to unite the two concepts in such a way as to affirm the unique and irreducible existence of the three *hypostases*, Father, Son, and Holy Spirit, but also to preserve the non-negotiable axiom of the One God.[39]

The importance of the unity of the two categories is clearly seen in the second Cappadocian move – the emphasis on the monarchy of the Father. The Father is not simply a *hypostasis*, that is, but a *prosopon* insofar as the Father *as* Father is constitutive of and constituted by the life of the Trinity. Trinitarian personhood is, thus, relational in that the uniqueness and irreducibility (*hypostasis*) of each of the persons of the Trinity are constituted in relations of love and freedom to the other persons. For Zizioulas, it is critical that this trinitarian movement be understood as having its origin in the person of the Father. In one of his more controversial claims, Zizioulas argues that "God, as Father and not as substance, perpetually confirms through 'being' His *free* will to exist. And it is precisely His trinitarian existence that constitutes this confirmation: the Father out of love – that is, freely – begets the Son and brings forth the Spirit."[40] The Father *as* Father, that is, as person, is not only *hypostatic*, unique and irreducible, but also *ecstatic*, by which Zizioulas means freedom from the necessity of nature. As person, the Father is not simply the divine essence, but through a personal freedom as love constitutes the very life of God as trinitarian. To *be* person, thus, for Zizioulas, is to *be* constituted as unique and irreducible in relations of freedom and love.

More is at stake in Zizioulas' insistence on the monarchy of the Father than simply the conceptualization of the unity of God; without the monarchy of the Father, divine–human communion is inconceivable. Zizioulas' logic is as follows: human existence is one of longing for uniqueness and irreducibility, which is evident in the examination of the creation of art,[41] in the birth of a child,[42] or in the analysis of the question "who am I?"[43] Such a longing is fundamentally tragic since death reduces all human existence to an indistinguishable sameness.[44] The only hope for fulfillment of the human longing for uniqueness and irreducibility is a communion with what is other than finite existence, namely a divine–human communion. In such a communion, however, the very being of God must be constituted in freedom: since human uniqueness and particularity are constituted in a freedom from the "given," that is, a freedom from the necessity of death inherent in finite existence, in order for such a freedom to be realized in a communion with the divine, God's being must itself be free from necessity, even the necessity of God's essence. Otherwise, God cannot give what God does not have.[45] Put another way, God's existence is freely constituted so as to be free to give God's life of freedom as love to what is not God.

Unlike Lossky, Zizioulas does not conceptualize divine–human communion in terms of the divine energies. Divine–human communion is an hypostatic event that is realized in the *hypostasis* of Christ. It is in the person of Christ that one enters into a relation that the Son has from all eternity with the Father, and that one is, thus, constituted as a unique and irreducible child of the Father in a relation of freedom as love.[46] This unity in Christ is a Eucharistic event: it is in the Eucharist that the Holy Spirit constitutes the community literally as the Body of Christ; Christ becomes the one and the many, the one in whom the many are united through Christ to each other and to God the Father in relations of freedom and love.[47] In this sense, there is no strict, apophatic divide between the economic and immanent Trinity for Zizioulas; while not completely rejecting apophaticism, Zizioulas does affirm that the Eucharist is the experience of the immanent life of God's trinitarian being.[48] Union with Christ is a communion with the *hopos esti* (the how of being) of God's trinitarian existence, the *tropos hyparxeos* (the manner of subsisting), which Zizioulas identifies with the divine *hypostases*.[49] In the end, the trinitarian ontology of relational personhood is an articulation of the experience of divine–human communion in the Eucharist. This trinitarian ontology becomes the lens through which Zizioulas interprets all other aspects of theology, including ecclesiology and ecotheology.

## FUTURE ISSUES

In spite of their shared consensus on the principle of divine–human communion as the fundamental axiom for theology, and on their understanding of the doctrine of the Trinity as the conceptualization of God's being in relation to the world in terms of divine–human communion, deep differences exist between Bulgakov, Lossky, and Zizioulas on the details of trinitarian theology. These differences are not surprising in light of the fact that the theology of Lossky was constructed, in part, in opposition to Bulgakov, and that of Zizioulas in opposition to Lossky. One could argue that contemporary Orthodox theology is a tradition of debate over the implications of divine–human communion for trinitarian theology.

One of the most glaring differences is over their understanding of the relation of the immanent Trinity and the economic Trinity. For Lossky, apophaticism as grounded in the divine–human communion in Christ demands a strict division between the immanent Trinity and the economic Trinity. Lossky's apophaticism, however, does not allow him to relate the principle of divine communion to God's being *as* Trinity, which results in the conceptualization of divine–human communion in terms of the essence–energies distinction. The irony is that Lossky injects the more philosophical apophatic understanding of God-beyond-being into trinitarian theology; the question remains, however, in what way apophaticism and trinitarian theology are compatible.

Both Bulgakov and Zizioulas interpret the development of the doctrine of the Trinity as the Christian conceptualization of the God–world relation in terms of divine–human communion. Whereas Lossky resorts to the essence–energies distinction, the categories adequate for conceptualizing divine–human communion are the trinitarian categories. For Bulgakov, Sophia is a trinitarian category, one required to give a full accounting of the understanding of the trinitarian God who communes with creation.

Lossky's distinctive contribution to trinitarian theology is his theology of personhood, which he grounds in the trinitarian category of *hypostasis*. Although Bulgakov argues for an analogous relation between absolute and created subjectivity and understands subjectivity in terms of *hypostasis*, it would be Lossky who would claim that the trinitarian categories used to express God's being antinomically as Trinity also imply an understanding of personhood in terms of irreducibility and freedom. This Losskian understanding of personhood would become the core of Zizioulas' trinitarian ontology of communion, minus Lossky's apophaticism.

This trinitarian understanding of personhood has come under fire by patristic scholars, both Orthodox and non-Orthodox, who argue that such a notion of personhood does not exist in the Cappadocians and is a modern Orthodox theological construction.[50] Such a criticism keeps to the fore in Orthodox theology the perennial question of patristic hermeneutics, especially in relation to trinitarian theology. Orthodox theologians also face the challenge of making more explicit the practical implications of the doctrine of the Trinity and, hence, of the principle of divine–human communion, especially in relation to issues of gender, race, and politics. It is not a question of how trinitarian theology can be both mystical *and* prophetic, but of how the mystical *is* the prophetic, since, as Bulgakov himself implied, there is nothing but the mystical.

## Notes

1. For biographies of Bulgakov, see Michael Plekon, *Living Icons: Persons of Faith in the Eastern Church* (University of Notre Dame Press, 2002), 29–58, and Catherine Evtuhov, *The Cross and the Sickle: Sergei Bulgakov and the Fate of Russian Religious Philosophy: 1890–1920* (Ithaca, NY: Cornell University Press, 1997).
2. Eventually known as the Russian Orthodox Church Outside Russia, or ROCOR, which recently reunited with the Moscow Patriarchate. For details of the "Sophia Affair," see the special volume devoted to Bulgakov by *St. Vladimir's Theological Quarterly*, 49:1–2 (2005).
3. Sergius Bulgakov, *The Bride of the Lamb*, trans. Boris Jakim (Grand Rapids, MI: Eerdmans, 2002), 26.

4. Sergius Bulgakov, *The Comforter*, trans. Boris Jakim (Grand Rapids, MI: Eerdmans, 2004), 364.
5. I am following Bulgakov's own practice of referring to God in gender-specific pronouns, which is not unimportant to his theology, since he consistently refers to Sophia in feminine pronouns.
6. Sergius Bulgakov, *The Lamb of God*, trans. Boris Jakim (Grand Rapids, MI: Eerdmans, 2008), 217. See also *The Comforter*, 180–81, 384.
7. Bulgakov, *The Comforter*, 361.
8. Bulgakov, *The Lamb of God*, 89.
9. For a fuller elaboration of the analogy between created and divine subjectivity, see ibid., 89–101.
10. Bulgakov, *The Comforter*, 54–55.
11. Ibid., 56.
12. Bulgakov, *The Lamb of God*, 48.
13. Ibid., 105, and Bulgakov, *The Comforter*, 141.
14. Bulgakov, *The Lamb of God*, 103.
15. Ibid., 133.
16. Ibid., 126.
17. Sergei Bulgakov, *Sophia the Wisdom of God: An Outline of Sophiology* (Hudson, NY: Lindisfarne, 1993), 74.
18. For a biography of Lossky, see Rowan D. Williams, "The Theology of Vladimir Nikolaeivich Lossky: An Exposition and Critique," D.Phil. dissertation, University of Oxford, 1975.
19. On this commingling, see Antoine Arjakovsky, *La génération des penseurs religieux de l'émigration russe* (Kiev and Paris: L'Esprit et la Lettre, 2002); Eng. trans. (University of Notre Dame Press, in press).
20. As Paul Valliere maintains in *Modern Russian Theology: Bukharev, Soloviev, Bulgakov: Orthodox Theology in a New Key* (Grand Rapids, MI: Eerdmans, 2000). Valliere offers the best account of the "Russian School" of the late nineteenth and early twentieth centuries.
21. Vladimir Lossky, *The Mystical Theology of the Eastern Church* (Crestwood, NY: St. Vladimir's Seminary Press, 1976; original 1944), 64.
22. Vladimir Lossky, "Apophasis and Trinitarian Theology," in *In the Image and Likeness of God*, ed. John H. Erickson and Thomas E. Bird (Crestwood, NY: St. Vladimir's Seminary Press, 1974), 26, 51.
23. As quoted in Lossky's "Procession of the Holy Spirit," in *In the Image and Likeness*, 78 n. 10. See Théodore de Régnon's *Études de théologie positive sur la Sainte Trinité*, I (Paris, 1892), 309. Michel René Barnes' accusation is in his "De Régnon Reconsidered," *Augustinian Studies*, 26:2 (1995), 51–79. For a fuller response to Barnes, see my *Being with God: Trinity, Apophaticism and Divine–Human Communion* (University of Notre Dame Press, 2006), 181 n. 101.
24. For a critique of interpreting Augustine in this way, see Lewis Ayres, "*Sempiterne Spiritus Donum*: Augustine's Pneumatology and the Metaphysics of Spirit," in George Demacopoulos and Aristotle Papanikolaou, eds., *Orthodox Readings of Augustine* (Grand Rapids, MI: Eerdmans; Crestwood, NY: St. Vladimir's Seminary Press, 2008).
25. Lossky, *The Mystical Theology*, 56.

26. With the exception of Bulgakov and Zizioulas.
27. For a good overview of the contemporary debate on the essence–energies distinction, see David Bradshaw, *Aristotle East and West: Metaphysics and the Division of Christendom* (Cambridge University Press, 2004), 263–77.
28. For more on this tension, see Papanikolaou, *Being with God*, 119–27.
29. Lossky, "Procession of the Holy Spirit," 88.
30. Lossky, "The Theological Notion of Person," in *In the Image and Likeness*, 120. See also Lossky, *Mystical Theology*, 122–23.
31. Vladimir Lossky, *Orthodox Theology: An Introduction*, trans. Ian and Ihita Kesarcodi-Watson (Crestwood, NY: St. Vladimir's Seminary Press, 1978), 46–47.
32. For more on theology in Greece during this period, see Christos Yannaras, "Theology in Present-Day Greece," *St. Vladimir's Theological Quarterly*, 16 (1972), 195–214, and Christos Yannaras, *Orthodoxy and the West*, trans. Peter Chamberas and Norman Russell (Brookline, MA: Holy Cross Orthodox Press, 2006).
33. Private conversation, spring 1996. For Lossky's influence on Yannaras and on Greek theologians in general, see Basilio Petrà, "Personalist Thought in Greek in the Twentieth Century: A First Tentative Synthesis," *Greek Orthodox Theological Review*, 50 (2005), and Yannaras, *Orthodoxy and the West*.
34. Christos Yannaras, *Person and Eros*, trans. Norman Russell from 4th edn. (Brookline, MA: Holy Cross Orthodox Press, 2007; original 1970).
35. For a thorough biography of Zizioulas, see Patricia A. Fox, *God as Communion: John Zizioulas, Elizabeth Johnson, and the Retrieval of the Symbol of the Triune God* (Collegeville, MI: Liturgical Press, 2001).
36. For more on Zizioulas' criticism of Lossky's apophaticism, see Papanikolaou, *Being with God*.
37. For more on the theology of personhood in contemporary Orthodox theology, see Papanikolaou, "Personhood and its exponents in Twentieth-Century Orthodox Theology," in Elizabeth Theokritoff and Mary Cunningham, eds., *The Cambridge Companion to Christian Orthodox Theology* (Cambridge University Press, 2008), 232–45.
38. John Zizioulas, *Being as Communion: Studies in Personhood and the Church* (Crestwood, NY: St. Vladimir's Seminary Press, 1985), 27–49.
39. For criticism of the notion of a "Cappadocian solution," see Joseph T. Lienhard, "*Ousia* and *Hypostasis*: The Cappadocian Settlement and the Theology of 'One *Hypostasis*,'" in Stephen T. Davis, Daniel Kendall, and Gerald O'Collins, eds., *The Trinity: An Interdisciplinary Symposium on the Trinity* (Oxford University Press, 1999), 99–121.
40. Zizioulas, *Being as Communion*, 210. See also Zizioulas, *Communion and Otherness: Further Studies in Personhood and the Church*, ed. Paul McPartlan (London and New York: T. & T. Clark, 2006), 113–54. The latter book contains a collection of some of Zizioulas' most important articles on the Trinity, together with some new writing.
41. Zizioulas, *Communion and Otherness*, 206–49.

42. Zizioulas, *Being as Communion*, 49–53.
43. Zizioulas, *Communion and Otherness*, 99–112.
44. John Zizioulas, "Preserving God's Creation: Lecture Three," *King's Theological Review*, 13 (1990), 2.
45. Zizioulas, *Being as Communion*, 43.
46. Zizioulas, *Communion and Otherness*, 109.
47. On the early Christian experience of the Eucharist as divine–human communion in Christ, see John Zizioulas, "The Early Christian Community," in Bernard McGinn and John Meyendorff in collaboration with Jean Leclerq, eds., *Christian Spirituality: Origins to the Twelfth Century* (New York: Crossroad, 1989), 23–43. For Zizioulas' pneumatological Christology, see his *Being as Communion*, 123–42.
48. Zizioulas, *Communion and Otherness*, 189.
49. For more on *hopos esti* and *tropos hyparxeos* in Zizioulas, see Papanikolaou, *Being with God*, 91–106.
50. In addition to the Lienhard reference in n. 39 above, see the work of the dean of St. Vladimir's Orthodox theological Seminary in Crestwood, NY, John Behr, *The Nicene Faith* (Crestwood, NY: St. Vladimir's Seminary Press, 2004). For a response to Behr, see Alan Brown, "On the Criticism of *Being as Communion* in Anglophone Orthodox Theology," in Douglas H. Knight, ed., *The Theology of John Zizioulas* (Burlington, VI: Ashgate, 2007), 35–78.

## Further reading


Behr, John, *The Nicene Faith* (Crestwood, NY: St. Vladimir's Seminary Press, 2004).

Bulgakov, Sergius, *On Divine Humanity*, trans. Boris Jakin, I: *The Lamb of God*; II: *The Comforter*; III: *The Bride of the Lamb* (Grand Rapids, MI: Eerdmans, 2008, 2004, 2002).

Lossky, Vladimir, *In the Image and Likeness of God*, ed. John H. Erickson and Thomas E. Bird (Crestwood, NY: St. Vladimir's Seminary Press, 1974).

*The Mystical Theology of the Eastern Church* (Crestwood, NY: St. Vladimir's Seminary Press, 1976; original 1944).

*Orthodox Theology: An Introduction*, trans. Ian and Ihita Kesarcodi-Watson (Crestwood, NY: St. Vladimir's Seminary Press, 1978).

Papanikolaou, Aristotle, *Being with God: Trinity, Apophaticism and Divine–Human Communion* (University of Notre Dame Press, 2006).

"Personhood and its Exponents in Twentieth-Century Orthodox Theology," in Mary B. Cunningham and Elizabeth Theokritoff, eds., *The Cambridge Companion to Orthodox Christian Theology* (Cambridge University Press, 2008), 232–45.

Staniloae, Dumitru, *The Experience of God*, trans. and ed. Ioan Ionita and Robert Barringer, 6 vols. (Brookline, MA: Holy Cross Orthodox Press, 1994, 2000).

Valliere, Paul, *Modern Russian Theology: Bukharev, Soloviev, Bulgakov: Orthodox Theology in a New Key* (Grand Rapids, MI: Eerdmanns, 2000).

Zizioulas, John, *Being as Communion: Studies in Personhood and the Church* (Crestwood, NY: St. Vladimir's Seminary Press, 1985).

*Communion and Otherness: Further Studies in Personhood and the Church*, ed. Paul McPartlan (London and New York: T. & T. Clark, 2006).

*Remembering the Future: An Eschatological Ontology* (New York: T. & T Clark, 2008).

# 15 The life-giving reality of God from black, Latin American, and US Hispanic theological perspectives

MIGUEL H. DÍAZ

The doctrine of the Trinity is a signpost that points to God's mystery as a life-giving triune presence in history.[1] God's life has been shared in history for the sake of human salvation. Thus wherever the question of creaturely life arises, the reality of God emerges as its answer.[2] As the Latin American theologian Ignacio Ellacuría underscores, it is not so much that "God is in all things" but that "all things, each in its own way, have been grafted with the triune life and refer essentially to that life."[3] In this sense, trinitarian theology probes within manifold creaturely experiences "the triune life itself, however mediated, incarnated, and historicized."[4]

This chapter probes the triune life of God from black, Latin American, and US Hispanic perspectives. The first part of the chapter explores the fundamental relationship between God and salvation history. It underscores how black, Latin American, and US Hispanic theologies understand racial, socio-economic, and cultural marginalization as loci for understanding the life-giving manifestation of God's reality. I draw primarily from the writings of James Cone, Gustavo Gutíerrez, and Virgilio Elizondo. Each of these theologians provides distinct building-blocks in black, Latin American, and US Hispanic trinitarian reflections.

The second part of this chapter names God's reality from the perspective of black theologies of liberation. Black theology in the USA emerged in the late 1960s, independently of Latin American and US Hispanic theologies (Latin American theologies emerged in the late 1960s and US Hispanic theologies in the early 1970s). Although black theology addresses issues of race primarily within the US landscape, the dehumanization of black persons elsewhere is also within its scope of interest. As Cone has argued, it is impossible to develop "Black Theology in isolation from Blacks in other parts of the world."[5] I would also underscore that because blackness is essential to understanding Latin American and US Hispanic historical realities, it is impossible to theologize from these perspectives without considering the contributions of black theologies of liberation.

The third and fourth parts of this chapter explore God's reality from Latin American and US Hispanic theologies respectively.[6] The relationship between Latin American theology and US Hispanic theology originates in the early 1970s, and can be characterized as a sibling relationship. Although these theologies have much in common, as is often the case with siblings, each is also very distinct. These distinctions can be traced to human experiences, social conditions, geographical locations, theological methodologies, and theological sources.[7] For instance, while the preferential option for the poor, characteristic of Latin American theologies, emerges from socio-economic marginalization in Latin America, the preferential option for culture, characteristic of US Hispanic theologies, reflects socio-cultural and religious marginalization within the US landscape.[8]

The methodological choice in this chapter to highlight various forms of human marginalization in order to probe God's life-giving presence does not mean that marginalization is to be understood univocally or that God's offer of "life" always takes the same form within manifold human experiences. The God of Jesus Christ is the God of life but, surely, the kind of life that God bestows varies in accordance with the particularity and diversity of human needs. Furthermore, the choice to address in separate sections how the life of God relates to issues of socio-economic, racial, and cultural forms of oppression to some extent violates the interdependence of these human experiences. This decision is simply intended to highlight the particular human experience that provides the central lens for looking into each of the liberation theologies under consideration in this chapter. In the end, embracing the contribution and interdependence of all three of these trinitarian liberation perspectives is essential in the process of deepening the ties that already bind these perspectives.[9]

## GOD'S REALITY IN HISTORY

God's life does not belong to God alone, but it belongs to humans as well.[10] This is the main reason why liberation and salvation are so closely connected in theologies of liberation. For Cone, God "always encounters us in a situation of historical liberation."[11] Cone maintains that in accordance with biblical tradition, God is to be sought as being "involved in the concrete affairs of human history, liberating the oppressed."[12] To raise the question of the reality of God is, according to Cone, to focus on God's actions. In turn, to consider God's actions is "to center on human events as they pertain to the liberation of suffering humanity."[13] God always remains more than any human life-giving experience – liberation is not the fullness of salvation – but the encounter with God comes through nothing less than the human liberation that overcomes oppressive and death-like experiences.[14]

"God liberates because God is the God of life."[15] Like Cone, Gutíerrez rejects the separation between God's life and human life. In Chalcedonian-like manner, Gutíerrez distinguishes the radical offer of God's life (salvation) from human life-giving actions that bring about the liberation of the oppressed. Salvation and liberation are not juxtaposed orders that have little or no connection to each other.[16] Rather, relying on biblical sources (e.g., the Exodus narrative) and recent developments in theological anthropology such as Rahner's notion of the "supernatural existential,"[17] Gutíerrez underscores that the life-giving action of God underlies all human existence.[18]

In a similar way, Virgilio Elizondo echoes the arguments of black and Latin American liberation theologies. However, while Cone primarily relates God's life to the liberation of racially oppressed black communities, and Gutíerrez relates God's life to the death caused by poverty in Latin America, Elizondo associates "the historical meaning of God's saving way" with the liberation of US Hispanics who suffer socio-cultural marginalization. The incarnation, argues Elizondo, does not simply entail the history of God becoming flesh. The incarnation highlights the history of God becoming a marginalized Galilean Jew.[19] The Galilean reality of Jesus reveals God's life-giving option for and empowerment of socio-culturally marginalized human realities:

> As a Galilean he demonstrates the role of a marginal person who by reason of being marginal is *both* an insider *and* an outsider – partly both, yet fully neither. And he is not just trying to get into the structures, but to change the structures in such a way that no one will be kept out, segregated, dehumanized, or exploited.[20]

All three of these theologies of liberation embrace the "oneness" of history with respect to the communion between divine and human life. This one history neither "hyper-inflates" human realities nor focuses on the "immanent" reality of God to the detriment of God's historical mediations.[21] History, especially the history of liberation from racial, socio-economic, and cultural oppressive human experiences, is the exterior manifestation of the triune life of grace, just as conversely this triune life is the intrinsic presupposition and perfection of that history (that for the sake of which history exists).[22] History is that human reality that exists concretely from, through, and in the reality of God. Taking the latter premise as my point of departure, the following reflections name the reality of God from black, Latin American, and US Hispanic theological perspectives.

## THE BLACK GOD AS BELOVED COMMUNITY

"God is black."[23] Like all true metaphors, the expression "God is black" creates a tension by relating two seemingly unrelated realities: God and blackness.[24] The expression is not intended to be taken literally, for God is outside the boundary of color. Yet as Cone argues, metaphorical conjugations such as these are necessary to protect the word "God" from ontological and linguistic trivialization.[25] More specifically, Cone argues that unless God-talk is directed at the liberation of oppressed communities, theological language becomes an idol that must be destroyed.

In arguing for the blackness of God, Cone situates the reality of God within oppressed communal experiences. The blackness of God means that God elects, becomes one with, and continues to accompany oppressed communities for the sake of their liberation. Thus life-giving liberation becomes the hallmark that defines the innermost nature of God. Cone writes:

> The blackness of God implies that essence of the nature of God is to be found in the concept of liberation. Taking seriously the Trinitarian view of the Godhead, black theology says that as Creator, God identified with oppressed Israel, participating in the bringing into being of this people; as Redeemer, God became the Oppressed One in order that all may be free from oppression; as Holy Spirit, God continues the work of liberation. The Holy Spirit is the Spirit of the Creator and the Redeemer at work in the forces of liberation in our society today.[26]

The blackness of God reveals a "beloved triune community" at work in the liberation of the oppressed.[27] "God comes to us in God's blackness, which is wholly unlike whiteness."[28] The interpretation of the triune life of God as black establishes an analogical connection (in the Catholic sense of the term) between oppressed human persons and the beloved triune community. God's triune community identifies with oppressed persons and becomes present in their history as a liberating force that raises the oppressed to life. Cone's focus on God's wholly otherness with respect to sinful humanity (e.g., "white" or racist humanity) maintains the more traditional dialectical Protestant understanding to relating human and divine life.

God is partial to and identifies with black persons because God cannot stand on the side of oppression. "What could love possibly mean," asks Cone, "in a racist society except the righteous condemnation of everything racist?"[29] Thus God's self-giving in Christ and the Spirit necessarily implies that God is a righteous and just God. The blackness of God is the key to understanding that God gives Godself away in righteousness, that is, for the sake of overcoming oppression and fostering life. Simply stated, God's trinitarian self-giving is God's just self-giving (and vice versa). Were this not to be the case, self-giving could be demanded of oppressed persons with respect to their oppressors as if it were iconic of God's life.[30]

Black theologians also argue that the survival of black humanity and the preservation of black culture reflect the life-giving presence of God. As Dolores Williams highlights, "God's response of survival and quality of life to Hagar is God's response of survival and quality of life to African American women and mothers of slave descent struggling to sustain their families with God's help."[31] Thus whether we speak of liberation from oppressive communal relationships or the struggle to sustain communal identity, black theology affirms the human encounter of God's life-giving presence.

As beloved triune community, God "dances" to birth human communities torn by suffering, hatred, and division. God empathizes with the oppressed in "blues-filled" experiences and directs their anger creatively and constructively for the sake of justice.[32] In particular, the Spirit who hovered in creation from the beginning of the world is the creative and "life-inspiring relation of God" that makes "a way out of no way possible."[33] "She" is the relational action of God sent "to create beauty out of ugliness, celebrate life in the midst of suffering, and walk in love in the midst of hate."[34] As the life-giving relation, the Spirit prophetically seeks to realize human societies in the image of God.

## GOD AS INCLUSIVE SOCIETY (COMMUNION)

God is an inclusive society.[35] God is a communion of divine persons who act in history on behalf of oppressed persons to liberate them from socio-economic injustices.[36] In the image of the divine society, Latin American theologians challenge human societies to reorder history so as to achieve a more equitable and just sharing of resources. Because "Each of the divine persons is for the others, with the others, and in the others," Boff argues, "the only category capable of expressing this reality is *communion*."[37] Communion is the life-giving reality of God, which challenges a Latin American context of profuse socio-economic poverty.[38] Communion responds to "the deepest needs of the poor," who seek active participation and a "more active co-existence, maintained in respect for differences."[39]

Latin American trinitarian theologies respond to oppressive human conditions in which the earth's resources are in the hands of the powerfully few (rich).[40] These theologies turn to the communal life of God and God's self-sharing in salvation history as the foundation for re-visioning a new social order where the marginalized many (masses of the poor, especially women and children) can be empowered to participate fully in society (in a socio-economic, political, and cultural sense). The absence of this social order reveals the sinful condition of humanity and its failure to image the divine society.

In efforts to moor the reality of God within human society, Latin American liberation theologians underscore the radical communion of the divine persons. They point out that the notion of communion carries enormous social implications for any given society.[41] For instance, as a result of communion, sharing is the rule of God's household. Because God rules in the company of others, a society that mirrors God's household must be structured around the sharing of power and resources.[42]

The "proof" that God's life is shared life for the sake of social life lies with the incarnation and deification. Christ and the Spirit extend God's social life into history. In this sense the oft-cited aphorism *mi casa es tu casa* ("my household is your household") can be used to describe God's invitation to human societies to enter into and participate in the reality of God's inclusive social order.

Latin American liberation theology associates God's life not only with the liberation of marginalized persons but also with the life of all oppressed creatures. As Ivone Gerbara argues, while "the Trinity is the expression of the Mystery, both one and multiple, that envelops us, that has made us what we are, and in which we participate ceaselessly,"[43] participation in this existential experience is not confined to the realm of human relationships. The "trinitarian structure" of oneness as diversity permeates the cosmos, all living creatures of the earth, all cultures and peoples, and every living human being.[44] Latin American liberation theology therefore underscores the interdependence among all forms of life and their dependence on and expression of God's triune life.

In the midst of socio-economic conditions that sentence the masses to death, Latin American liberation theology prophetically proclaims the mystery of God as life-giving mystery. *Rachamin* (Hebrew "mercy"), *ruach* (Hebrew "wind," "spirit"), and *Sophia* (Greek "wisdom") are all liberating expressions to characterize the God of life. The God of Latin American liberation theology is the merciful, creative, and wise "Maternal-Father" who sends forth Jesus to gather oppressed chicks under his wings (Lk 13:34).[45] This is the God of Jesus Christ who brings down the mighty from their thrones and lifts up the poor (Lk 1:46–55). In lifting the poor from all that oppresses them God is revealed as the God of life. Thus Gutiérrez writes:

> Liberation embodies a will to life. The action of liberation is directed against oppression, servitude, and death; against a situation that has at its root the breaking of friendship with God and others – that is, sin. Hence the essential importance of the liberation from sin that brings us into new communion with the Lord and others. Liberation expresses a will to life; consequently, by liberating us God is shown to be a liberating God, a living God, and the friend of life.[46]

## *EL DIOS DE NOSOTROS*

Whereas black and Latin American liberation theologies turn to the life-giving reality of God as an answer to racial and socio-economic oppressions, US Hispanic trinitarian theology has emerged in response to ecclesial and socio-political contexts where the practice of "melting away" differences and assimilation is the norm to effect communal unity. US Hispanic theology points to the reality of God, the one who exists in threefold differentiation, as the life-giving and prophetic alternative to this false sense of community. It sees personal differences and particularity as indispensable in building authentic community.[47]

The history of intercultural relationships that birthed communal identity as a result of the Spanish conquest of the Americas (*mestizaje*) and the enslavement of black persons (*mulatez*), as well as the ongoing intercultural relationships within US landscapes, provides vestiges of the life-giving communal otherness of God. As is the case with any human history, this history of communal relationships has been marked by sin. When properly understood, however, *mestizaje* and *mulatez* offer a life-giving sign of how human beings and all creatures have been called to exist in the image of God.

*Mestizos* and *mulattos* are persons who have been born from living "in between" two cultures (e.g., Spanish-Amerindian, Spanish-African, Mexican-American, Afro-Cuban, etc.). This reality of being-with, being-for, and being-from others has been embodied and expressed in a wide range of cultural and religious experiences. Apart from this orientation to another, this communal otherness, *mestizos* and *mulattos* cannot exist. The following remarks, though not explicitly trinitarian, offer some important insights into the life-giving significance of this culturally situated human experience: "the theology I envision is a theology that, because of its roots, cannot hide or disguise or reject mixture, for it finds that *mezcolanza* is life and gives life; a theology that given its very reality and experience, cannot bypass, assimilate, or annihilate the other, for again it finds itself that *otredad* also is life and gives life."[48]

The Spanish word *nosotros* best names the reality of God from the US Hispanic experiences of "life on hyphen."[49] The word *nosotros* "literally means 'we others,' a community of *otros*, or others."[50] The word suggests that communal unity cannot come about without affirming distinct others. Seen from a trinitarian perspective, it affirms that otherness is essential to God's life and thereby essential to human life as well.[51]

To live is to be born and be sustained in communal otherness. God does not marginalize personal differences, but rather personal differences constitute the life of God (Father, Son, and Spirit). God is essentially the *one* who is *otredad* (otherness). God is a community of distinct others where life is given and received. Analogously, "Created out of God's for-otherness, our humanity is expressed in our own for-otherness for God as well as for creation and for other human beings."[52]

To name God as *El Dios de Nosotros* (the God who is for us) is to claim that God lives as a community of others. Simply put, God "exists" in and through others. Life for God is necessarily a life with others. In accordance with Christian tradition, this name suggests that God offers Godself in God's otherness for our sake and our salvation. The otherness of God, which is for humans and not God alone, is a life-giving reality. Conversely, marginalizing otherness, "melting away" creaturely differences, brings about death.

The otherness of God implies that God is distinctly *pro nobis* in God's twofold self-expression in history. Among other things, mooring this "for us" of God within US Hispanic experiences means attending to life-risking and life-seeking experiences of exile, migration, and immigration: in Jesus, God undertakes a life-seeking migration (salvation) and life-threatening exile (cross). In Jesus, God bestows life to those exiled out of community, and offers life to those who risk their lives "dying to live" in the deserts and seas that surround US borders. In Jesus, God's migrant fieldworker, God labors to cultivate an inclusive community of others. And as an immigrant presence among us, the Spirit continues to challenge the "walls" that separate humans from being for one another.[53]

This re-visioning of God's two hands as migrant worker and permanent immigrant presence suggests that US Hispanic trinitarian theology addresses not only questions of theological content but also questions that concern the forms of God's self-manifestation.[54] With respect to the forms of revelation that reveal the trinitarian life of God, US Hispanic popular Catholicism offers an indispensable source. Deeply tied to human identity, this popular expression of Catholicism puts a socio-cultural face to the Trinity. Two popular religious forms deserve brief discussion: the symbol of the crucified Christ and the Marys of US Hispanic popular Catholicism (e.g., Our Lady of Guadalupe, Our Lady of Charity, Our Lady of Montserrat, etc.).

US Hispanic celebrations of the Triduum mediate the encounter with the first of these forms. In these celebrations US Hispanics re-enact Jesus' way of the cross. "Caminemos con Jesús" ("Let us walk with Jesus") is the cry of contemporary "Galileans" who publicly proclaim while accompanying Jesus during Triduum celebrations that life is *acompañamiento* (accompaniment). Just as Jesus lives through communal relationships, so do human persons find life in and through relationships. Suggesting the trinitarian referent of the human person, Roberto S. Goizueta argues:

> The human person is defined, above all, by his or her character as a relational being. Yet this relationality is not merely some static "essence" of the person, but an *active* relating in and through which the person defines him or herself, in interaction with others. Relationship is not something that "happens to" someone, something one "experiences" in a passive way, or something one "possesses"; it is something one *does*, the most basic form of human action since, through relationship, we discover and live out our identity as intrinsically relational beings.[55]

The second of these aesthetic forms closely links Marian devotions with the presence of the Spirit. The Marys of US Hispanic Catholicism put socio-cultural faces to the Spirit. In Mary, US Hispanic communities faithfully sense the Spirit as advocate and protector of the poor. In the

Spirit, who is always "pregnant" with life, the "Juan Diegos" and the "Juan Morenos" of this world find protection (the former is the nahua Amerindian in the Mexican story of Our Lady of Guadalupe, and the latter is the black slave boy in the Cuban narrative of Our Lady of Charity). As giver and sustainer of life, the Spirit labors to birth inclusive communal relationships, especially for the sake of offering the marginalized life-giving relationships.[56]

## CONCLUSION

*Gloria Dei, vivens homo.* God's glory, argues Irenaeus, is the living human being. This chapter has examined the Trinity as the story of God's life, shared in history for the sake of the life of the oppressed. Each of the liberation perspectives that I have addressed tells the story of God's life-giving presence from particular oppressed human experiences. Black theologians tell the story from the struggle to overcome racism, Latin Americans tell the story from the struggle to overcome socio-economic poverty, and US Hispanics tell the story from the struggle to overcome socio-cultural and religious homogenization.

Each of these perspectives affirms that the reality of God is a life-giving reality. Liberation concerns the totality of creaturely existence. It is a life-giving process that among other things overcomes socio-economic, racial, and cultural forms of oppression. To overcome death with life as a result of overcoming these oppressions is not the whole of salvation. At the same time, however, God's trinitarian life is always and necessarily "mediated, incarnated, and historicized." Thus the distinct liberation perspectives discussed in this chapter offer vestiges of God's life-giving presence in history from black, Latin American, and US Hispanic perspectives.

"Must God Remain Greek?"[57] These trinitarian reflections from Latin American, US Hispanic, and black theological perspectives hint at an answer to this question in their attempts to pour "new wine into new wineskins." As exemplified in these three theologies of liberation, even if it may seem that the old is being poured into new wineskins (using classical terms and ideas in new contexts), classical terms always acquire new meaning in the process of reinterpretation and re-appropriation.

God is not only Greek or Latin, but must also be black, red, Asian, Latin American, and US Hispanic, to point to a few human possibilities that name the human and divine encounter. The import of liberation theologies, however, is that the poor and marginalized are the primary addressees of God's abundant life. In this sense, a theology of God that does not attend to issues of human liberation, a trinitarian theology unable to challenge oppressive human experiences that cause death, does not reveal the life-giving mystery of God. As Karl Rahner rightly concludes, "The Trinity is a mystery of *salvation*, otherwise it would never have been revealed."[58] Perhaps one of the central contributions of liberation theologies is to remind us of the non-negotiable connection between God's life (immanent Trinity) and the "for us" of this life (economic Trinity). The glory of God is truly the human being "fully" alive.

The God who identifies with oppressed black persons, the God who seeks to build inclusive society from the body of the poor, and the God whose life is existence with others is Emmanuel. God who is for us (Father), from us (Son), and permanently among us (Holy Spirit) is *mysterium liberationis*. This mystery that was made known in the fullness of time liberates us "*from* oppressive divisions in the human community" and liberates us "*for* a new or beloved community that embraces all into one communion under God."[59]

### Notes

1. On the notion of the doctrine of the Trinity as a signpost, see Catherine M. LaCugna, "The Practical Trinity," *The Christian Century*, 109 (1992), 682.
2. See Walter Kasper, who argues that "the Christian's concern is not with God in himself but with God-for-us, the God of Jesus Christ, who is the God of human beings (Heb. 11.16)." See Walter Kasper, *The God of Jesus Christ*, trans. Matthew J. O'Connell (New York: Crossroad, 1989), 158.
3. Ignacio Ellacuría, "Historicity of Christian Salvation," in Ignacio Ellacuría and Jon Sobrino, eds., *Mysterium liberationis: Fundamental Concepts of Liberation Theology* (Maryknoll, NY: Orbis, 1993), 277.
4. Ibid.
5. See James H. Cone and Gayraud S. Wilmore, *Black Theology: A Documentary History*, I: *1966–1979* (Maryknoll, NY: Orbis, 1993), 432.
6. In this chapter I will consistently use the term "US Hispanic" in reference to communities of persons that reside permanently in the USA and whose humanity has been primarily shaped by the Spanish-speaking Latin American context (including its indigenous and African heritage).
7. On the distinction between Latin American and US Hispanic theologies, see María Pilar Aquino, "Theological Method in U.S. Latino/a Theology," in Orlando Espín and Miguel H. Díaz, eds., *From the Heart of Our People: Latino/a Explorations in Catholic Systematic Theology*

(Maryknoll, NY: Orbis, 1999), 15–17; Gilbert R. Cadena, "The Social Location of Liberation Theology: From Latin America to the United States," in Ada María Isasi-Díaz and Fernando F. Segovia, eds., *Hispanic/Latino Theology: Challenge and Promise* (Minneapolis: Fortress, 1996), 167–82.

8. Orlando O. Espín and I coined this phrase back in 1999. See the "Introduction," in our *From the Heart of Our People*, 3.
9. On the relationship between Latin American and black theologies of liberation, see Dwight N. Hopkins, *Black Theology of Liberation* (Maryknoll, NY: Orbis, 1999), 167–72; on the relationship between black and US Hispanic theologies, see Anthony B. Pinn and Benjamin Valentin, eds., *The Ties that Bind: African American and Hispanic American/Latino/a Theologies in Dialogue* (New York: Continuum, 2001).
10. Catherine Mowry LaCugna, *God for Us: The Trinity and Christian Life* (San Francisco: HarperSanFrancisco, 1991), 228.
11. James Cone, *A Black Theology of Liberation* (Maryknoll, NY: Orbis, 1990), 76.
12. Ibid.
13. Ibid.
14. Ibid., 78.
15. See Gustavo Gutíerrez, *The God of Life*, trans. Matthew J. O'Connell (Maryknoll, NY: Orbis, 1991), 3.
16. See Gustavo Gutíerrez, *A Theology of Liberation* (Maryknoll, NY: Orbis, 1988), 104.
17. Ibid., 43–46. On the supernaturally elevated condition of humanity see Karl Rahner's essay "Nature and Grace," in *Theological Investigations*, IV, trans. Kevin Smyth (New York: Crossroad, 1982), 165–88. On the historical transformation of this notion see, Ignacio Ellacuría, "Historia de la salvación," in his *Escritos teológicos* (San Salvador: UCA Editores, 2000), 604.
18. Gutíerrez, *A Theology of Liberation*, 86.
19. See Virgilio Elizondo, "*Mestizaje* as a Locus of Theological Reflection," in Timothy Matovina, ed., *Beyond Borders: Writings of Virgilio Elizondo* (Maryknoll, NY: Orbis, 2000), 168; Virgilio Elizondo, *Galilean Journey: The Mexican-American Promise* (Maryknoll, NY: Orbis, 2000).
20. Elizondo, *Galilean Journey*, 107 (emphasis mine).
21. Note that Bonino, a Latin American Protestant liberation theologian, has voiced the concern that Latin American liberation theologies must uphold ontological primacy of the "immanent Trinity." His concerns appear to reflect the desire to safeguard the primacy of grace that characterizes much of Protestant thought.
22. This is a trinitarian restatement of the classical Thomistic axiom that affirms that "grace presupposes nature" (*gratia supponit naturam*). In this trinitarian re-visioning of Thomas Aquinas' axiom, I follow and paraphrase Kasper's excellent discussion of this Thomistic affirmation in *God of Jesus Christ*, 73.
23. James Cone, "God is Black," in Susan Brooks Thistlethwaite and Mary Potter Engel, eds., *Lift Every Voice: Constructing Christian Theologies*

*from the Underside* (Maryknoll, NY: Orbis, 2001), 101–14. This piece is basically a reprint of ch. 4 of Cone's *A Black Theology of Liberation.*

24. On Cone's metaphorical use of "blackness" see Diana L. Hayes, "James Cone's Hermeneutic of Language and Black Theology," *Theological Studies*, 61:4 (2000), 619–22.
25. Note that in the revised version of his earlier piece that appears in *Lift Every Voice*, "God is Black," Cone names other metaphors: "God is mother," "God is rice," and "God is red." See Thistlethwaite and Engel, eds., *Lift Every Voice*, 103.
26. Cone, "God is Black," 105.
27. The expression "beloved community" was coined in the early twentieth century by Josiah Royce.
28. Cone, "God is Black," 107.
29. Ibid., 108.
30. Ibid., 110.
31. Cited in Hopkins, *Black Theology of Liberation*, 146–47.
32. See Karen Baker-Fletcher, *Dancing with God: The Trinity from a Womanist Perspective* (St. Louis: Chalice Press, 2006), 146–69.
33. Ibid., 62, 160, 166.
34. Ibid., 163.
35. See Leonardo Boff, *Trinity and Society*, trans. Paul Burns (Maryknoll, NY: Orbis, 1988), 118–20; Juan Luis Segundo, *Our Idea of God* (Maryknoll, NY: Orbis, 1974), 63–66; Veli-Matti Kärkkäinen, *The Trinity: Global Perspectives* (Louisville, KY: Westminster John Knox, 2007), 267–91.
36. Note that while most Latin American liberation theologians focus on socio-economic liberation, some feminist liberation theologians have cautioned that this focus on historical efficacy and activity can "easily degenerate into desire for power and obsessive pragmatism." See María Clara Bingemer, "Reflections on the Trinity," in Elsa Tamez, ed., *Through her Eyes: Women's Theology from Latin America* (Maryknoll, NY: Orbis, 1989), 80.
37. Leonardo Boff, "Trinity," in Jon Sobrino and Ignacio Ellacuría, eds., *Systematic Theology: Perspectives from Liberation Theology* (Maryknoll, NY: Orbis, 1996), 84 (emphasis in the original).
38. See María Pilar Aquino, *Our Cry for Life: Feminist Reflection from Latin America* (Maryknoll, NY: Orbis, 1993), 37–38.
39. See Boff, "Trinity," 83–84.
40. Ibid., 85.
41. As María Bingemer writes: "A society in which women have an inferior status and are not partners with men in the struggle for justice and in the attempt to live as friends is far from representing the mystery of God." "Reflections on the Trinity," 79. See also Aquino, *Our Cry for Life*, 17.
42. See Boff, *Trinity and Society*, 20–23, 134–45.
43. Ivone Gebara, *Longing for Running Water: Ecofeminism and Liberation* (Minneapolis: Fortress, 1999), 153.
44. Ibid.

45. Bingemer, "Reflections on the Trinity," 61–68, 70–78; Aquino, *Our Cry for Life*, 134–38; Boff, *Trinity and Society*, 170, 182, 196.
46. Gutíerrez, *God of Life*, 19.
47. Miguel Díaz, "A Trinitarian Approach to the Community-Building Process of Tradition: Oneness *as* Diversity in Christian Traditioning," in Orlando O. Espín and Gary Macy, eds., *Futuring our Past: Explorations into the Theology of Tradition* (Maryknoll, NY: Orbis, 2006), 157–79.
48. Fernando Segovia, "Two Places and No Place on Which to Stand: Mixture and Otherness in Hispanic American Theology," *Listening: Journal of Religion and Culture*, 27:1 (1992), 37.
49. For an exploration of hyphenated existence from the perspective of Cuban-Americans, see Gustavo Pérez Firmat, *Life on the Hyphen: The Cuban-American* Way (Austin: University of Texas Press, 1994).
50. See Roberto S. Goizueta, "*Nosotros*: Toward a U.S. Hispanic Anthropology," *Listening: Journal of Religion and Culture*, 27:1 (1992), 57.
51. For an insightful metaphysical approach to otherness, see Zizioulas, *Communion and Otherness*, 13–98.
52. Teresa Chavez Sauceda, "Love in the Crossroads: Stepping-Stones to a Doctrine of God in Hispanic/Latino Theology," José David Rodríguez and Loida I. Martell-Otero, eds., *Teología en conjunto: A Collaborative Hispanic Protestant Theology* (Louisville, KY: Westminster John Knox, 1997), 27.
53. See Miguel Díaz, "Life-Giving Migrations: Revisioning the Mystery of God through U.S. Hispanic Eyes," *e-Journal of Hispanic/Latino Theology*, www.latinotheology.org/ (accessed December 19, 2010).
54. See Sixto J. García, "U.S. Hispanic and Mainstream Trinitarian Theologies," in Allan Figueroa Deck, ed., *Frontiers of Hispanic Theology in the United States* (Maryknoll, NY: Orbis, 1992), 93–101; Alejandro García-Rivera, *The Community of the Beautiful: A Theological Aesthetics* (Collegeville, MN: Liturgical Press, 1999), 7–38; Michelle A. Gonzalez, *Sor Juana: Beauty and Justice in the Americas* (Maryknoll, NY: Orbis, 2003), 153–89.
55. Roberto S. Goizueta, *Caminemos con Jesús: Toward a Hispanic/Latino Theology of Accompaniment* (Maryknoll, NY: Orbis, 1995), 72.
56. Orlando O. Espín, *The Faith of The People: Theological Reflections on Popular Catholicism* (Maryknoll, NY: Orbis, 1997), esp. 11–90; Goizueta, *Caminemos con Jesús*, 18–46; Jeanette Rodriguez, "God is Always Pregnant," in Theresa King, ed., *The Divine Mosaic: Women's Images of the Sacred Other* (St. Paul, MN: Yes International Publishers, 1994), 112–26.
57. Robert E. Hood, *Must God Remain Greek? Afro Cultures and God-Talk* (Minneapolis: Fortress Press, 1990).
58. See Karl Rahner, *The Trinity*, trans. Joseph Donceel, introduction, index, and glossary by Catherine LaCugna (New York: Crossroad, 1997), 21.
59. Jamie T. Phelps, "Communion Ecclesiology and Black Liberation Theology," *Theological Studies*, 61:4 (2000), 694.

## Further reading

Baker-Fletcher, Karen, *Dancing with God: The Trinity from a Womanist Perspective* (St. Louis: Chalice, 2006).

Bingemer, María Clara, "Reflections on the Trinity," in Elsa Tanez, ed., *Through her Eyes: Women's Theology from Latin America*, Eng. trans. (Maryknoll, NY: Orbis, 1989).

Boff, Leonardo, *Trinity and Society*, trans. Paul Burns (Maryknoll, NY: Orbis, 1988).

Chavez Sauceda, Teresa, "Love in the Crossroads: Stepping-Stones to a Doctrine of God in Hispanic/Latino Theology," in José David Rodríguez and Loida I. Martell-Otero, eds., *Teología en conjunto: A Collaborative Hispanic Protestant Theology* (Louisville, KY: Westminster John Knox, 1997).

Cone, James, *God of the Oppressed* (Maryknoll, NY: Orbis, 1997).

Díaz, Miguel, "Human Beings at the Crossroads of Divine Self-Disclosure: Otherness in Black Catholic and Latino/a Catholic Theologies and the Otherness of God," *e-Journal of Hispanic/Latino Theology*, www.latinotheology.org/ (accessed December 19, 2010).

"Life-Giving Migrations: Revisioning the Mystery of God through U.S. Hispanic Eyes," *e-Journal of Hispanic/Latino Theology*, www.latinotheology.org/ (accessed December 19, 2010).

"A Trinitarian Approach to the Community-Building Process of Tradition: Oneness *as* Diversity in Christian Traditioning," in Orlando O. Espín and Gary Macy, eds., *Futuring our Past: Explorations into the Theology of Tradition* (Maryknoll, NY: Orbis, 2006), 157–79.

Gebara, Ivone, *Longing for Running Water: Ecofeminism and Liberation* (Minneapolis: Fortress, 1999).

Gutíerrez, Gustavo, *The God of Life*, trans. Matthew J. O'Connell (Maryknoll, NY: Orbis, 1991).

# 16 Feminist theologies and the Trinity

PATRICIA A. FOX

The title of James Alison's publication *Undergoing God: Dispatches from the Scene of a Break-in*[1] provides one way of thinking about the significance of feminist theologies within the recent widespread revival of the doctrine of the Trinity. The image of a "break-in" communicates something of the disruptive and unexpected. At times the effects of a break-in are immediate and obvious, at other times they are only discovered gradually. A break-in can also cause dismay and anger, which need to be dealt with as quickly as possible so that life can proceed as before. However, in terms of the spiritual life, a break-in has a positive connotation: an in-breaking of the Spirit heralds conversion and transformation. The systematic theologian Anne Carr uses the term "transforming grace" to describe the gift of feminist theology to the church.[2] It is in this sense that I will use "break-in" in this chapter.

In order to explore the contribution of feminist theologies to the evolving reception of the mystery of God as Trinity, I have taken account of the work of feminist theologians from various cultures and perspectives, including womanist, *mujerista*, and Asian theologians, and then examined the mosaic that came to light. To communicate the essential elements of the patterns that emerged, I will use Alison's evocative image and describe dispatches from five scenes of a feminist break-in on trinitarian discourse. These dispatches will use the theologians' own voices as directly as possible. I will then summarize the various strands of the collective picture.

## FROM ASIA

The experience of a major exhibition at the Art Gallery of New South Wales in Sydney, Australia, in early 2007 entitled "Goddess: Divine Energy" alerted me, a white Western middle-class, Christian feminist theologian, to a way of interpreting what had previously seemed to be only the slightest suggestion of a break-in from Asian women upon trinitarian theology. This exhibition explored the many manifestations of the divine female in Hindu and Buddhist art. The works of beauty depicted were rich with symbols and had been created as a focus for veneration and meditation. They engaged those who gazed at them attentively, and as the brochure promised, conveyed "lessons and insights that the Goddess provides as she guides towards attainment and ultimate bliss."[3]

Trinitarian theology has not yet become a popular focus of feminist theologians from Africa and Asia, and there is very little published on the subject. One of the reasons for this may be that these cultures, assisted by the structure of their languages,[4] have maintained inclusive representations of the divine. With the coming of Christianity into many Asian cultures there was therefore a dissonance created by the introduction of a monotheistic and male-centered symbolic order. Kwok Pui-lan, originally from Hong Kong, describes it in this way:

> Among the Asian religious traditions, the worship of the goddesses and the feminine images of the divine have a long history, dating back to the prehistoric period. Worshipped by women and men, the prevalent goddesses of Ina, Guanyin, Durga, Kali, and Sita, as mothers, consorts, daughters, and protectors, had not been superseded by the male gods as they were in Mesopotamia and prehistoric Europe. Thus, the propagation of a monotheistic, Christian God imaged as a male being, modeled after the father, king, lord, introduced gender asymmetry into religious symbolic system and reinforced male domination.[5]

Engaging with the sheer abundance, color, and diversity of the "Goddess" exhibition provided me with a glimpse into what it would be like to be raised in a culture permeated by the myths and practices associated with female divine presence and power. The effect was inclusive of the beholder, energizing and dynamic. I could thus appreciate that while the symbol of the Trinity introduced through prayer and liturgy was able to find a place within eclectic Asian religious imagery and practice, it was the confining and dogmatic limits of the doctrine of the Trinity, always represented as Father, Son, and Holy Spirit, that presented problems.

Most Asian religious traditions are profoundly cosmological without the dualisms separating male and female, life and death, divine and human, or the divine and the created world. In such a context, the purpose of theology "is not to *define* God, but rather to express a sense of wonder, awe and grace in the presence of the living power and energy of the divine."[6] As the Korean feminist theologian Chung Hyun Kyung emphasizes: "Theology as vision quest . . . is remembering the original wholeness of creation and activating the dangerous memory of the future."[7] It is a vision that is often intrinsic to survival and one which places more importance on what one practices in life than on what one believes.

The Indonesian theologian Marianne Katoppo, for example, reflects on Durga, the Hindu goddess of death:

> The oldest temple in Bali is perched on a steep promontory hundreds of metres over the Indonesian Ocean of which she is believed to be the queen. Durga's statue, which must be over a thousand years old, is almost worn smooth. How can people worship a goddess of death with such devotion? Because she is also the goddess of life, activity, energy, power. Life and death are one.[8]

It is in this context that Katoppo goes on to observe bluntly that "[f]orcing people to relate to an all-male Trinity is oppression. In the context of Asian cosmic religion and meta-cosmic soteriologies, it is also ridiculous."[9] Exposure to the creatively curated "Goddess" exhibition illustrated for me how, given the way in which the Trinity is often communicated within Western theological discourse, it could indeed appear to be ridiculous. The rich, salvific, relational, divine presence afforded by access to a panoply of female gods discloses dimensions of God's trinitarian being that many treatises on the subject from the West do not.

Understanding God as a community, however, is congruent with Asian religious thought.[10] Reflecting on Genesis 1:26, Elizabeth Dominguez from the Philippines claims: "To be in the image of God is to be in community. It is not simply a man or a woman who can reflect God, but it is the community in relationship." Chung Hyun Kyung, referring to this, comments: "Where there is no mutual relationship, there is no human experience of God. Asian women emphasize the importance of community in their theologies because only in community can humanity reflect God and fulfill the image of God in which we were created for mutual relationship."[11]

The editors of the series "Introductions in Feminist Theologies" offer a crucial caution to those seeking to take account of Asian feminist voices engaging with key Christian doctrines: "What the West has defined as Asia includes more than half the world's population and contains seven major languages and innumerable dialects. The racial and cultural mix under this broad title is immense... Asian feminist theologians, if they are Christian, are part of a 3 per cent population."[12] To attempt a meaningful dialogue between the religious diversity of Asia and a doctrine born of biblical Christianity and Greek ontology, which until recently has been deeply codified into male European thought, is too complex a task to be approached in a direct manner. The conceptual worlds are too far apart. This provides a stark reminder that the definitive fourth-century doctrinal expression of the God revealed by Jesus, which was adopted by a communion of Christian churches on the Mediterranean rim, is simply not able to convey all that can be known of the mystery of God so revealed.

Christian theology teaches that God's revelatory Spirit continues to break in upon creation and humanity within all living cultures, including those that inhabit more than half the world's population in Asia. Without doubt, it was something of God's trinitarian self that I glimpsed at the "Goddess" exhibition in Sydney. And it alerted me to how the work of Asian feminist theologians who are shaped by Hinduism, Buddhism, Taoism, Confucianism, and other Asian religions are providing a "break-in" to the diverse experiences and manifold expressions of ultimate mystery. While there are not yet trinitarian theologies published, there is a rich vein of discourse emerging which opens into the personal, the relational, to God as Wisdom and Compassion, to the God known as the One and the Many, who will not be limited by any religious systems.

## FROM LATIN AMERICA

By contrast with the situation in Asia, the thick overlay of Christendom that arrived with the might of the conquistadores in Latin America ensured that in spite of the religious diversity of the indigenous peoples, the iconography of the Trinity took a strong hold. It pervaded catechesis, liturgy, and popular devotions, including the ubiquitous practice of making the sign of the cross, and it cast an ironclad structure of maleness on the experience and worship of God. Doing theology from the point of view of Latin American women, especially poor women, has therefore meant challenging the overwhelmingly androcentric character of the understanding of God.

In 1986 a volume of essays by Latin American women theologians edited by Elsa Tamez was published in Costa Rica. This work was based within the liberation theology that had emerged within the continent, but with a firm basis from within women's experience. One of the contributors, the Brazilian theologian Ivone Gebara, stated in her chapter "Women Doing Theology in Latin America":

> There is a way of doing theology that starts with shared experience from oral transmission, from the simple fact of sharing life... It is as though the aim were to bridge the gap between speech and reality, the distance that the formal and idealist discourse of religion has imposed on us for a long time. It is as though we were discovering, very powerfully, and starting from our own situation, the mystery of the incarnation, of the divine in the human, not just because "we have been told," but because we experience it in the confines of our lives as women.[13]

A decade later Gebara, still writing from northeastern Brazil, was specifically addressing the issue of God, this time within the context of ecofeminism as well as liberation.[14] She writes of the Trinity: "Thinking about the Trinity would appear to be superfluous, hardly worth spending time on in the light of the anguished cries of so many, many people threatened by hunger, disease, unemployment, war, and meaninglessness."[15] Nevertheless, she sets out to discover the Trinity's relevance beyond "eternal substances and essences." She describes "Father, Son, and Holy Spirit" as symbols that refer to life experiences, but whose symbolism "has grown hazy and been absolutized within a closed, eminently masculine and more or less arcane theoretical system." She claims that this naming and ordering "need to be decoded. They must be continually re-interpreted so their great richness and meaning can manifest themselves."[16] To address this, Gebara does not choose to engage with what she calls "the formal theological tradition"[17] but rather adopts a methodology that holds much in common with the philosophy of religion. She sets out to explore what in human experience is related to trinitarian language, examines religious language and its crystallization in religious institutions, and reconstructs trinitarian meanings. She wants the methodology she uses to demonstrate that the experience of God as Trinity is about celebrating life.[18]

Gebara's work emanates from a strong connection to the sufferings of the poor, especially the women among whom she lives, and from a heightened awareness of the interconnectedness of the abuse of women, of the environment, and of the planet as a whole. She bemoans the fact that throughout Christian history the Trinity has been presented as "the absolute, the totally different, the altogether superior, independent, and perfect Being."[19] She rejects what she calls the petrified language of patriarchal religion: "We are slaves to language, and, above all consecrated language. We behave as if it were the only one all people should adhere to in order to be faithful to God's will . . . we drift far from the dynamic meaning of the Trinity. We fall into a kind of coded monism . . ."[20] It is because of her solidarity with the experience of "plurality in pain, in interior division, in fear, in suffering, and in the precariousness of joy" that she wants to "look for one God who is above the multiplicity that marks us, a God who unifies in one single being all the diversity that is essential to our nature . . . [The Trinity] is a communion to which we aspire in the midst of tears, in the midst of pain and suffering."[21] Gebara suggests that in order to recover the dynamism of the Trinity, there is a need to recover the dynamism of our own existence, even at the risk of the insecurity involved. She is aware that organized religion fears the true relativity of things, their fragility, their finiteness, and the transformations inherent in all life processes. She believes that a renewed reception of the meaning of the trinitarian symbol will provide the insight and courage needed for such risk: "we need to reaffirm that the Trinity is the expression of the Mystery, both one and multiple, that envelops us, that has made us what we are, and in which we participate ceaselessly . . . the Trinity is relationship, after all; an existential experience in ourselves and in the world."[22]

Gebara's theological work comes from what she believes is a new moment in human and cosmic history. It comes from a lifelong commitment to the following of Jesus, which has profoundly shaped the choices of her life and which in turn has created in her a passion for justice for the poor and the planet. Her writing communicates awe and wonder before the infinite mystery of the three persons of the Trinity, who are so close to the fragility of our lives. It is within the particularity of this context that God as Trinity has opened up for her a new way of living. Her dispatches from this Latino break-in of renewed trinitarian awareness provide an ethic that is at once deeply personal and political.

## FROM BRITAIN

The work of Sarah Coakley, a British-born Anglican priest who is now Norris-Hulse Professor of Divinity at the University of Cambridge, springs from a different kind of earthing. Coakley holds that "an 'earthed' sense of the meaningfulness and truth of the doctrine of the Trinity, most naturally arises out of a simultaneous renewal of a commitment to prayer, and especially prayer of a relatively wordless kind."

She traces the links between the Trinity, prayer, and sexuality, claiming that "the close analysis of such prayer and its implicitly trinitarian structure, make the confrontation of a particular range of fundamental issues about sexuality unavoidable." She argues that "enacted sexual desire and desire for God" can no longer be set in mutual enmity but must be looked at together.[23]

Coakley identifies the "third" in God as the entry point for her trinitarian theology.[24] Speaking experientially, Coakley claims the Spirit as *primary* and believes "that leaving non-cluttered space for the Spirit is the absolute precondition for the unimpeded flowing of this divine exchange in us."[25] She argues tartly that the Spirit must no longer be seen "as in so much Western medieval iconography of the Trinity – as the wafting 'feminine' adjunct to an all male negotiation of salvation." A foundational text for her work on the Trinity is Romans 8, where Paul speaks "simultaneously of prayer divinely done *in us* in the Spirit 'with sighs too deep for words' (Rom. 8:26), and yet also forging us . . . into the very likeness of Christ, into 'the glorious liberty of the children of God' (Rom. 8:21)." Drawing further from the Pauline vision within Galatians 3:28, "neither male and female," she argues that maleness and femaleness are rendered spiritually insignificant in the face of the Spirit's work and our transformations into Christ's body.[26]

Coakley thinks of the Trinity "not as a set of perfect mutual relations into which the (known) gender binary somehow has been imposed in a cleansed form, but rather as an irreducible threeness that always *refuses* a mere mutuality of two." As in prayer, she suggests, "we step into a circle of divine desire (the 'sighs too deep for words' that signal the Spirit's loving gift of plenitude drawing us to the 'Father') which is necessarily beyond our comprehension and categorization, but is drawing us by degrees into the 'likeness' of the 'Son.'"[27]

Coakley's re-reading of patristic sources is a major strength in her work. In a particular way, she values the apophatic tradition as she examines the capacity of patristic sources to hold the contradictions and ambiguities of language necessary for appreciating the mystery of both God and self. She focuses on Gregory of Nyssa, demonstrating that the process of human transformation is the Trinity's very point of intersection with our lives. She suggests that such transformation requires "profound, even alarming shifts in our gender perceptions, shifts which have bearing as much on our thinking about God as about our understanding of ourselves."[28] She refers to Gregory's late work, *In canticum canticorum* (*Commentary on the Song of Songs*), where he "charts in the highly imagistic and eroticized language, the ascent of the soul into the intimacy of the Trinity." Coakley observes that the message that Gregory wishes to convey is that if the soul is to advance to supreme intimacy with the trinitarian God, "gender stereotypes must be reversed, undermined, and transcended; and that the language of sexuality and gender, far from being an optional aside or mere rhetorical flourish in the process, is somehow necessary and intrinsic to the epistemological deepening that Gregory seeks to describe."[29] She thus demonstrates that Gregory has the mystic's clarity that trinitarian doctrine does not strictly speaking *describe* God.[30]

Through such patristic evidence, Coakley attempts to illuminate an "alternative" approach to the Trinity which gives experiential priority to the Spirit and to prayer. In so doing she uncovers what she believes are the false divisions between "theology" and "spirituality."[31] Further, she speculates that from patristic times until now the church has had politico-ecclesiastical reasons for preventing this vision of emphasis on the Spirit. Such a vision could release the Christian from the rational constraints of the Logos.

Coakley's work on the Trinity, combined as it is with the experiential, has been episodic thus far, but is a significant break-in. It harnesses a re-reading of patristic sources in a way that is fresh and powerful. With a four-volume systematic theology from a feminist perspective in train, of which the first volume will be on the Trinity, there will no doubt be further invigorating dispatches forthcoming.[32]

## FROM THE USA

The above dispatches from scenes of a break-in provide a glimpse of patterns that emerge within the broader discourse between feminist theology and trinitarian theology. They also give some sense of the global, multicultural consciousness that began to be present within women's theology toward the end of the last century. It is within such a context that substantive contributions from two North American theologians, Catherine Mowry LaCugna and Elizabeth Johnson, were published. Their primary publications on the Trinity are respectively *God for Us: The Trinity and Christian Life* (1991) and *SHE WHO IS: The Mystery of God in Feminist Theological Discourse* (1992).

The work of Catherine Mowry LaCugna, Professor of Systematic Theology at Notre Dame University from 1981 until her death at the age of forty-four in 1997, is primarily that of a trinitarian theologian. At the time of her death LaCugna was working on a book on the Holy Spirit in sequel to *God for Us*.

The work of Elizabeth Johnson, CSJ, Distinguished Professor of Theology at Fordham University, is primarily that of a feminist theologian who places the full humanity of women at the center of her theological agenda. The main areas of Johnson's research are the theology of God, Jesus Christ, Mary, the communion of saints, science and religion, the problem of suffering, and ecological ethics. Both of these theologians communicate powerful insights into the practical implications and radical consequences of our understandings of the Christian doctrine of God. Both trace how several conventional assumptions about the Christian faith play out destructively in their embodiment within the structures of the church. Both have made major contributions to the present revival of the Trinity.

### Catherine Mowry LaCugna

In 1993 Catherine LaCugna edited *Freeing Theology: The Essentials of Theology in Feminist Perspective*, a collection of essays of Catholic feminist scholarship which set out to "demonstrate what it means to recover, challenge and indeed, create tradition through reinterpretation."[33] In her own contribution to the volume, "God in Communion with Us – the Trinity," LaCugna identifies that the doctrine of the Trinity has been seen to compromise the feminist concern for the equality of women and men, primarily because of the perceived hierarchical relationship between the divine persons and because of the solely male images for God. She addresses these directly by applying the weight of her own work in historical analysis and theological retrieval.

Key to LaCugna's work of retrieving the doctrine of the Trinity is the communion between God and humanity and all of creation. She focuses on the two affirmations at the center of the Christian doctrine of God: God has given Godself to us in Jesus Christ and the Spirit (*oikonomia*), and this self-revelation is nothing less than what God is as God (*theologia*). God's actions reveal who and what God is, in one dynamic movement. By returning to this biblical pattern of thought, LaCugna recognizes that the distinction between "God" and "God-for-us" remains essential since the mystery of God is more than "God-for-us." She also emphasizes that trinitarian life is our life, that the doctrine of the Trinity is not ultimately a teaching about God but a teaching about God's life with us and our life with each other.

Focusing on the work of the Cappadocians, who made person rather than substance the primary ontological category, she argues that this principle "not only made the doctrine of the Trinity possible in the first place, [but] it also stands in direct contradiction to the patriarchal idea of God as essentially unrelated." She writes:

> In other words, the radical move of the Cappadocians was to assert that divinity or Godhead originates with personhood (someone toward another) not with substance (something in and of itself). Love for and relationship with another is primary over autonomy, ecstasis over stasis, fecundity over self-sufficiency. Thus personhood, being-in-relation-to-another, was secured as the ultimate originating principle of all reality.[34]

LaCugna emphasizes that this new way of conceiving God – that "God by nature is out-going love and self-donation" – radically affected previously held assumptions about God.[35] She argues further that Gregory of Nazianzus' reconception of God as monarch to a shared divine *archē* contained the seeds of a radical social order: "The divine unity was no longer located in the Father-God who was prior to or greater than everyone and everything else. Instead the divine unity and divine life were located in the communion among equal though unique persons, not in the primacy of one person over another."[36] She notes that a trinitarian monotheism so described preserved the principle of shared rule while, at least in principle, removing the idea that any person is subordinate to another. And she argues that this "is the kernel of the radical theological and political proposal of the Cappadocians that is relevant to the program of feminism today."[37]

Mutual relationship stands at the very center of an understanding of God as Trinity, and in spite of what she describes as the "defeat" of the Trinity, LaCugna notes that a living sense of the three persons of the Trinity was kept alive over the centuries within the liturgy and in spirituality. The focus of her work of retrieval is "to reunite doctrine and practice and restore the doctrine of the Trinity to its rightful place at the centre of Christian faith and practice."[38] Following the principles of the Cappadocian doctrine of the Trinity, she argues that "living as persons in communion, in right relationship is the *meaning of salvation*." She asserts that "clarification of personhood must always be referred to Jesus Christ, who is the communion of the divine and human, and to the Holy Spirit, who transfigures and deifies human beings, uniting all persons, divine and human in communion."[39] She concludes that "Person not substance is the ultimate ontological category and God's to-be is to-be-in-relation and to-be-in-communion."[40]

Such an ontology of relation locates the trinitarian mystery and the process of "deification" within the practical life of the Christian now. It recognizes both that personhood, relationship, and communion have their origin and destiny in God's personal existence and that they are the modality of all existence. LaCugna brings these concepts into dialogue with the fruits of contemporary philosophies, theologies of person, and theologies of communion,[41] and determines that the doctrine of the Trinity is the "*sine qua non* for preserving the essential relational character of God, the relational character of human existence and the interdependent quality of the entire universe."[42]

LaCugna's work has been described as constituting a paradigm shift within trinitarian theology – from an economic and immanent axis to an understanding of *theologia* and *oikonomia* as distinct but inseparable dimensions of trinitarian theology.[43] In achieving this she is emphatic that "every trinitarian theology is ineluctably both christological and pneumatological."[44] She affirms spirituality as the entry point to this central mystery of God and that trinitarian theology can draw the reader to doxology, to praise. Above all, Catherine LaCugna communicates a lived conviction that the doctrine of the Trinity is of immense practical importance with radical consequences for Christian life and mission.

**Elizabeth Johnson**

Johnson's contribution to the doctrine of the Trinity is of equal significance but from a very different perspective. Like LaCugna, Johnson addresses the issue of why the doctrine of the Trinity became irrelevant to Christian life. Her focus on the practical impact of the symbol of God uncovers how this central symbol of God as Trinity has functioned for millennia "to support an imaginative and structural world that excludes or subordinates women" and how, in turn, this "undermines women's human dignity as equally created in the image of God."[45] She shows how patriarchal religious culture has both confined women to an inferior place and limited speech about God to male images. The seriousness of this situation is emphasized early in *SHE WHO IS* when she repeats in mantric fashion, "The symbol of God functions."[46] She uses this sentence like a red flashing light to alert the reader that "what is at stake is the truth about God, inseparable from the situations of human beings, and the identity and mission of the faith community itself."[47]

From this perspective, a reconsideration of the imagery of the Trinity takes on a particular urgency. Johnson's method evaluates the effects of sexism within society and theological discourse and addresses the debilitating patriarchal effects of the names, imagery, and structure of the Trinity, on the Christian community, and on women's lives in particular. She draws attention to a fact that has been steadfastly ignored by theologians for centuries: that exclusively male imagery for God has been used in an uncritically literal way, leading to a form of idolatry. This has occurred in spite of key theological principles for language about God commonly accepted at the heart of the tradition.[48] Further, she shows that while affirming and promoting the equality of the divine persons and their mutual interrelation, the classic doctrine subverts this by maintaining the rigid hierarchical ordering as Father, Son, and Holy Spirit.

Johnson's constructive feminist theology of the Trinity addresses the challenge posed by the names, imagery, and structure of the Trinity. She is aware that naming the three persons must be congruent with the biblical witness and communicate their relation of origin with each other. In her work of retrieval of this symbol, Johnson draws from three major sources within the tradition: Christology, Mariology, and the Wisdom tradition in the scriptures.[49] She mines the biblical sources of Wisdom/Sophia within both testaments and shows biblical Sophia to be one who creates, redeems, and sustains in different times and in different cultures and comes to speak about God as Sophia. In contrast to classical theology, she chooses an inductive approach in speaking about the Triune God. She begins with God experienced here and now in the person of the Spirit, God's continuing creative action and presence in the world. She renames the divine persons as Spirit-Sophia, Jesus-Sophia, and Mother-Sophia.

By beginning her retrieval of the trinitarian doctrine with Spirit-Sophia, God actively present in the world, the "first person" of the Trinity that we experience, Johnson makes a case for a more fully developed pneumatology. She retells the story of Jesus as the preaching, ingathering, confronting, dying, and rising of Jesus-Sophia. She reclaims the inclusive intent of the original formulation of the Christological doctrine and brings out the inclusive meaning of the whole Christ and of the eschatological character of the risen Christ. Then she seeks to moderate the exclusive use of Father imaging by introducing Mother-Sophia as the name for the one who is the source of all being. In arguing for the benefits of alternative female imaging, Johnson suggests that "speaking about God as mother fixes as bedrock the idea that relationship is a constitutive way in which divine freedom enacts itself."[50]

By choosing an ordering that begins with the Spirit, Johnson also ensures that the structure used for naming the Trinity does not impede the prophetic teaching on the equal and mutual relationships within the *koinōnia* of the Triune God. She proposes the model of mutual friendship[51] as a way of understanding these relationships and, like LaCugna, appeals to the ancient concept of *perichōrēsis* or mutual indwelling of the divine persons. Further, tuning directly into the power of Aquinas' thought, she suggests that the language of being can communicate that "all things are on fire with existence by participation in God's holy being which is unquenchable." When applying the language of being to God, Johnson reminds the reader that "the being of God that we are speaking of is essentially love. God's being is identical with an act of communion."[52]

It is through this lens of understanding being that Johnson focuses on the powerful story of encounter between Moses and God described in the book of Exodus (3:7–8) and on the self-identifying name that God gives on this occasion, "I AM WHO I AM." Following Aquinas' name "Qui Est" for God,[53] Johnson argues that since God is not intrinsically male and that if the referent became Sophia-God, this highly influential text that carries the meaning of a divine relational being could be translated with a feminist gloss as SHE WHO IS. Moreover, because this name is suggestive of the God revealed in the narrative of the burning bush, she argues that it can convey the mystery of a God who is dynamically present to the needy and active to free all that is bound. Naming God SHE WHO IS also conveys a call to humanity for mutuality with her in the task of saving a suffering world. While the classical tradition has rejected the idea of divine suffering, Johnson embraces it. To speak of a suffering God totally subverts the patriarchal image of perfection and the consequent ideal of unilateral power. The power of Sophia-God is "the liberating power of connectedness that is effective in compassionate love."[54] This leads her to a redefinition of omnipotence and to propose a further name for the trinitarian God as "Suffering God: Compassion Poured Out."[55]

Elizabeth Johnson's passion is to speak rightly about God as Holy Mystery. She is profoundly conscious of the power of the symbol of God to undermine women as *imago Dei*. Drawing from the wisdom of the apophatic tradition, as well as from classic theological and biblical sources, she is concerned to communicate that God is finally beyond all names and that there is a need to use many names for God, including female as well as male.[56] Johnson's vibrant work of retrieval provides a vision that both motivates and sustains action toward creating a world in which the whole of humanity lives in kinship with its own multiple diversities and with creation.

## CONTRIBUTIONS FROM FEMINIST THEOLOGIES: A DEEPER RECEPTION OF THE DOCTRINE OF THE TRINITY

The reception of the doctrine of the Trinity, like that of every doctrine, is a work in progress. A full reception requires that all peoples and cultures can engage with the God revealed by Jesus the Christ and the Holy Spirit. The advent of feminist theologies has begun to redress an imbalance of two thousand years. It also assists in the process of opening a space for a work of a more sustained inculturation of this central doctrine of Christian faith.

This chapter finishes with seven contributions that have emerged from soundings taken from a broad reading of feminist theologies and which have been focused in particular ways in the "break-ins" described above. All are to do with "undergoing" God.

1. Recognizing the significance of the full humanity of all women and men if the truth about God is to be told in trinitarian theology, especially by paying attention to women's voices and experiences.
2. Ensuring that many names, images, metaphors, and models for God from all peoples and cultures can be accessed, including female imaging.
3. Valuing the cognitive dissonance and destabilization of set paradigms created by the interplay of contradictory images from multiple sources.
4. Beginning trinitarian discourse with the Spirit and seeking to restore pneumatology to its proper place. Making connections between the neglect of nature, women, and the Spirit, and between trinitarian theology and ecofeminism and ecotheology.
5. Re-reading creatively patristic, scholastic, and medieval sources for trinitarian discourse in the light of the accrued wisdom and contemporary research.
6. Basing trinitarian theology firmly within the spiritual and liturgical.
7. Broadening trinitarian discourse to include East and West, North and South in geographical and cultural as well as ecclesial terms.

Finally, the image evoked by the title *Undergoing God: Dispatches from the Scene of a Break-in* brings to mind the challenge of Catherine Mowry LaCugna. I would like her to have the last word: "Perhaps in no area of theology is it more important to keep in mind than in trinitarian theology that the 'object' upon which we reflect is another 'subject' or 'self,' namely, the God who relentlessly pursues us to become partners in communion."[57]

## Notes

1. James Alison, *Undergoing God: Dispatches from the Scene of a Break-in* (London: Darton, Longman & Todd, 2006).
2. Anne E. Carr, *Transforming Grace: Christian Tradition and Women's Experience* (San Francisco: Harper & Row, 1988).
3. "Goddess: Divine Energy Exhibition," Art Gallery of New South Wales, Sydney, October 13, 2006 to January 28, 2007.
4. In classical Chinese, for example, personal pronouns are not gender-specific.
5. Kwok Pui-lan, "Feminist Theology, Southern," in Peter Scott and William T. Kavanagh, eds., *The Blackwell Companion to Political Theology* (Oxford: Blackwell, 2004), 198.
6. Kwok Pui-lan, *Introducing Asian Feminist Theology* (Cleveland, OH: Pilgrim, 2000), 68.
7. Chung Hyun Kyung, *Struggle to be the Sun Again: Introducing Asian Women's Theology* (Maryknoll, NY: Orbis, 1991), 101.
8. Marianne Katoppo, "The Concept of God and the Spirit from the Feminist Perspective," in Ursula King, ed., *Feminist Theology from the Third World* (London: SPCK, 1994), 247.
9. Ibid.
10. Central also to African and many other indigenous cultures, including Australian, is the social communal focus. See John S. Mbiti, *African Religions and Philosophy* (London: Heinemann, 1969), 108.
11. Chung Hyun Kyung, "To be Human is to be Created in God's Image," in King, ed., *Feminist Theology*, 253–54.
12. See "Editor's Preface," in Kwok Pui-lan, ed., *Introducing Asian Feminist Theology*, 7.
13. Ivone Gebara, "Women Doing Theology in Latin America," in Elsa Tamez, ed., *Through her Eyes: Women's Theology from Latin America*, Eng. trans. (Maryknoll, NY: Orbis, 1989), 39–42.
14. Ivone Gebara, *Longing for Running Water: Ecofeminism and Liberation* (Minneapolis: Fortress, 1999).
15. Ibid., 138.
16. Ibid., 144.
17. See ibid., 139, where Gebara recommends the North American theologian Elizabeth Johnson for her work in this mode.
18. Ibid.
19. Ibid., 152.
20. Ibid.
21. Ibid., 148.
22. Ibid., 153.
23. Sarah Coakley, "Living into the Mystery of the Holy Trinity: The Trinity, Prayer, and Sexuality," in Janet Martin Soskice and Diana Lipton, eds., *Feminism & Theology*, Oxford Readings in Feminism (Oxford University Press, 2003), 258.
24. Note that Coakley's emphasis differs from that of other exponents of this model (e.g., Congar) in that she does not want to end with "the

remaining strain of neoplatonic subordinationism which proceeds 'up' the divine hierarchy back to the Father." See Sarah Coakley, "Why Three? Some Further Reflections on the Origins of the Doctrine of the Trinity," in Sarah Coakley and David A. Pailin, eds., *The Making and Remaking of Christian Doctrine: Essays in Honour of Maurice Wiles* (Oxford University Press, 1993), 39.

25. Coakley, "Living into the Mystery," 261.
26. Sarah Coakley, "The Trinity and Gender Reconsidered," in Miroslav Volf and Michael Welker, eds., *God's Life in the Trinity* (Minneapolis: Fortress, 2006), 140.
27. Ibid.
28. Coakley, "'Persons' in the 'Social' Doctrine of the Trinity: A Critique of Current Analytic Discussion," in Stephen T. Davis, Daniel Kendall, and Gerald O'Collins, eds., *The Trinity: An Interdisciplinary Symposium on the Trinity* (Oxford University Press, 1999), 125.
29. Ibid., 142.
30. Coakley, "Why Three?," 47.
31. Ibid.
32. See Mark Oppenheimer, "Sarah Coakley Reconstructs Feminism," *The Christian Century* (June 28, 2003), 25–31.
33. Catherine Mowry LaCugna, ed., *Freeing Theology: The Essentials of Theology in Feminist Perspective* (San Francisco: HarperCollins, 1993), 1.
34. Ibid., 86–87.
35. Ibid., 87.
36. Ibid., 87–88.
37. Ibid., 88.
38. Ibid.
39. Catherine Mowry LaCugna, *God for Us: The Trinity and Christian Life* (San Francisco: HarperSanFrancisco, 1991), 292.
40. Ibid., 14 and 250.
41. See ibid., 255–88.
42. Ibid., 289.
43. See Elizabeth T. Groppe, "Catherine Mowry LaCugna's Contribution to Trinitarian Theology," *Theological Studies*, 63 (2002), 730–63.
44. LaCugna, *Freeing Theology*, 92.
45. Elizabeth A. Johnson, *SHE WHO IS: The Mystery of God in Feminist Theological Discourse* (New York: Crossroad, 1993), 5.
46. Ibid., 4–6.
47. Ibid., 6.
48. Johnson refers to the testimony in scripture and later tradition re the incomprehensibility of God, to the centrality of the teaching on analogy within the Roman Catholic tradition, to the need for many names of God, to the apophatic tradition within Christianity. See ibid., 104–20.
49. See Patricia A. Fox, *God as Communion: John Zizioulas, Elizabeth Johnson and the Retrieval of the Symbol of the Triune God* (Collegeville, MN: Liturgical Press, 2001), 110–33, where I draw on a wider base of Johnson's work than *SHE WHO IS*.

50. Johnson, *SHE WHO IS*, 185.
51. See also Sallie McFague, *Models of God: Theology for an Ecological, Nuclear Age* (Philadelphia: Fortress, 1987).
52. Johnson, *SHE WHO IS*, 238.
53. See Thomas Aquinas, *Summa theologiae* I, q. 13, a. 11; Eng. trans., Blackfriars edn. (New York: McGraw-Hill, 1966–80).
54. Johnson, *SHE WHO IS*, 270.
55. See ibid., 246–72. For an example of how Johnson's work has acted as a catalyst for other theologians, see a development of a model of the creative suffering of the Triune God in Gloria Schaab, "A Procreative Paradigm of the Creative Suffering of the Triune God: Implications of Arthur Peacocke's Evolutionary Theology," *Theological Studies*, 67 (2006), 542–66.
56. In order to restore some balance she makes a strong case for privileging the use of female names in the immediate future.
57. LaCugna, *God for Us*, 332.

## Further reading

Fabella, Virginia, and Mercy Amba Oduyoye, eds., *With Passion and Compassion: Third World Women Doing Theology* (Maryknoll, NY: Orbis, 1988).

Johnson, Elizabeth A., *Women, Earth and Creator Spirit* (New York: Paulist, 1993).

King, Ursula, ed., *Feminist Theology from the Third World* (London: SPCK, 1994).

Ruether, Rosemary Radford, *Feminist Theologies: Legacy and Prospect* (Minneapolis: Fortress, 2007).

# Part V

*In dialogue with other religions*

# 17 The Tao in Confucianism and Taoism: the Trinity in East Asian perspective

HEUP YOUNG KIM

## THE "EASTERNIZATION" OF THE TRINITY

Since its renaissance initiated by Karl Barth and Karl Rahner, the doctrine of the Trinity has regained its status as the center of Christian theology. The doctrinal restoration of the Trinity has received widespread support from such ecumenically diverse theologians. In this chapter, the fascinating story of the rediscovery of the Trinity in contemporary theology will not be pursued, being presumed to be the task of other authors. However, one observation may be in order. As an East Asian theologian, I am intrigued by the fact that in this impressive retrieval of the trinitarian doctrine there has been a rediscovery of the East and a turn of Christian theology to the East.

In this restoration of the trinitarian center, the pendulum of Christian theology seems to have swung toward the East. At first, Western trinitarian theology appeared to have reached a climax with "Rahner's Rule" and "Pannenberg's Principle."[1] The former identifies the immanent Trinity with the economic Trinity and vice versa, while the latter underscores the history of divine rule over the world. Then, at its next stage, trinitarian theology turned to the East. Moving to the Near East, it rediscovered the significance of Eastern Orthodox trinitarian theology, embodied in "Zizioulas' Dictum," according to which the divine being is the communion of the three trinitarian persons.[2] This encounter brought about the recovery and reconstruction of ontology in the doctrine of the Trinity, especially that of relationship, personhood, or "personal relatedness." This discovery also shows how essentialism and the reduction of the person to self-consciousness constitute the root cause of the modern impasse in trinitarian theology. Moving to South Asia, especially India, trinitarian theology encountered religious plurality and gave rise to the "Panikkar Project."[3] Since the Trinity constitutes an archetypical structure for world religions, Panikkar argues, it is an ideal locus for inter-religious and intra-religious dialogue.

This trajectory of the development of contemporary trinitarian theology already reveals an Easternizing movement. However, it should not stop at India but should move further to East Asia. My contribution is an East Asian Christian interpretation of the Trinity in light of Confucianism and Taoism. Specifically, I will discuss how the Trinity can be understood in the religio-cultural matrix of East Asia, which is heavily influenced by Confucianism and Taoism. My goal is not to replace Western interpretations of the Trinity with this East Asian approach, which may at first appear strange to some. Rather my hope is that an East Asian interpretation of the Trinity will enrich the contemporary theology of Trinity and situate it in the global context. Furthermore, such Easternization of trinitarian doctrine in light of Confucian and Taoist insights may offer valuable clues to resolve some of the long-standing problems in trinitarian theology.

## CONFUCIAN AND TAOIST INSIGHTS

### Confucianism and Taoism (Neo-Confucianism): the third great religious river system

Hans Küng makes an important correction to the geography of world religions. Rather than adopting the generally accepted dipolar view of Middle Eastern and Indian religions, he argues for a tripolar view that includes East Asian religions such as Confucianism and Taoism. He claims that Confucianism and Taoism are "a third independent religious river system" of sapiential character, comparable to the other two great river systems, the first being of Semitic origin and prophetic character (Judaism, Christianity, and Islam) and the second of Indian origin and mystical character (Hinduism, Buddhism, etc.).[4]

Although often neglected by the dominant bipolar view of world religions, Confucianism and Taoism represent a most distinctive feature of the East Asian religio-cultural matrix. More precisely, Neo-Confucianism, a reformed Confucianism in synthesis with Taoism, is recognized as "the common background of the peoples of East Asia" and "the most plausible rationale" in attempts to understand the attitude of "the inward-looking civilization of East Asia" (referring to Korea, China, Japan, Taiwan, Vietnam, and Singapore).[5] Tu Wei-ming states, "East Asians may profess themselves to be Shintoists, Taoists, Buddhists, Muslims, or Christians, but by announcing their religious affiliations seldom do they cease to be Confucians."[6] Consequently, "doing East Asian theology necessarily involves the study of Confucianism as a theological task."[7] Confucianism and Taoism are broad and complex religio-cultural traditions with a history longer than that of Christianity. In the following I will present only some basic concepts relevant to the theology of the Trinity.

**Anthropocosmic vision and inclusive humanism**

One axiomatic pillar of Confucianism is what has been termed the "anthropocosmic vision," inherent in the Confucian belief in the "mutual dependence and organic unity" of Heaven and Humanity.[8] *The Doctrine of the Mean*, one of the Confucian Four Books, begins, "What Heaven imparts to man is called human nature. To follow our nature is called the Way (Tao). Cultivating the Way is called education."[9] In this anthropocosmic vision, humanity (anthropology) is not only inseparable from Heaven (cosmology), but is also conceived as its microcosm. This approach to anthropology is different from the anthropocentric approach to cosmology prevalent in the West.[10]

Cheng Chung-ying called this view "inclusive humanism," in contrast to the "exclusive humanism" dominant in the West since Descartes' dualistic rationalism. Whereas exclusive humanism "exalts the human species, placing it in a position of mastery of and domination over the universe," inclusive humanism "stresses the coordinating powers of humanity as the very reason for its existence." He points out that "humanism in the modern West is nothing more than a secular will for power or a striving for domination, with rationalistic science at its disposal." And he continues: "Humanism in this exclusive sense is a disguise for the individualistic entrepreneurship of modern man armed with science and technology as tools of conquest and devastation." In contrast, the inclusive humanism that is rooted in Confucianism "focuses on the human person as an agency of both self-transformation and transformation of reality at large. As the self-transformation of a person is rooted in reality and the transformation of reality is rooted in the person, there is no dichotomy or bifurcation between the human and reality."[11]

This point, albeit controversial, is important not only to demonstrate the relevance of Confucianism for our age of ecological crisis, but also to clarify the confusion in the modern concept of person as applied to the Trinity. In retrieving the Eastern Orthodox tradition, contemporary Western theologies of the Trinity to some extent rehabilitate the ontology of personhood beyond Barthian modalism (*Seinsweise*, modes of being). However, they still seem not to have been completely liberated from the modern notion of person as an isolated self-conscious ego, and are still prone to exclusive humanism, which Barth vehemently resisted.

This exclusive anthropology perpetuates the long-standing trinitarian dilemma between modalism and tritheism. Inclusive humanism may help solve this problem by showing how exclusive humanism, which underwrites individualism and essentialism, is the root cause of many problems in the modern theology of the Trinity. Over against the essentialist and exclusivist view of human person, inclusive humanism stresses the "between-ness" or "among-ness" of the person. (The Chinese character for the human being 人間 connotes "in-between-ness.") In inclusive humanism, a person is not so much a static substance as a network of relationships in constant change (*I*).[12] This relational vision of being in continual change is called "ontocosmology."[13]

## Confucian and Taoist ontocosmology: the Great Ultimate (T'ai-chi)

The Confucian and Taoist ontocosmology basically originates from the notion of T'ai-chi (which incidentally is the main symbol on the Korean national flag). In *An Explanation of the Diagram of the Great Ultimate*, Chou Tun-i states:

> The Ultimate of Non-being and also the Great Ultimate! The Great Ultimate through movement generates yang. When its activity reaches its limit, it becomes tranquil. Through tranquility the Great Ultimate generates yin. When tranquility reaches its limit, activity begins again. So movement and tranquility alternate and become the root of each other, giving rise to the distinction of yin and yang, and the two modes are thus established.[14]

T'ai-chi, symbolized by a circle enclosing yin and yang, denotes the complementarity of opposites. The circle signifies "an inexhaustible source of creativity, which is one and undifferentiated," and the dynamic process of yin-yang interaction is "always ready to be differentiated into concrete and individual things." It is "the constant fountainhead amidst all things and provides the integrative and purposive unity of any type or any individual token while, at the same time, it also serves as the impetus for the diversity of things as types of tokens."[15] T'ai-chi so conceived entails precisely unity in multiplicity or diversity in unity, which is a crucial principle for trinitarian theology.

The ontocosmology of T'ai-chi is pertinent not only to Confucianism but also to Taoism. Lao-tzu states:

> Tao [the Way] produced the One.
> The One produced the two.
> The two produced the three.
> And the three produced the ten thousand things.
> The ten thousand things carry the yin and embrace the yang, and through the blending of the material force (ch'i) they achieve harmony.
>
> (*Tao-te Ching* 42)[16]

This statement refers to the dynamic creative process of T'ai-chi or Tao, which produces the One, which produces the Two (yin-yang), which produce the Three (offspring of yin-yang), all of which, as will be shown, have profound implications for understanding the Trinity. "The whole is both absolute and relative, it is both one (singularity) and two (plurality) at the same time."[17] The creativity of Tao is the creative process of T'ai-chi through the dynamic yin-yang interaction and always in the process of change. It stipulates the dialogical paradigm of harmony or equilibrium in East Asian thought, in contrast to the dialectical paradigm of strife or conflict in Western thought. T'ai-chi "signifies both a process and world *qua* the totality of things in which there is a profound equilibrium from the beginning and a pervasive accord or harmony among all things at any time."[18]

### Confucian ontology of relation: the yin-yang complementary opposites

The yin-yang relationship is a key to understanding the Tao in East Asian thought. In the yin-yang relationship, the two opposites are not in conflict but complement each other in order to attain harmony and equilibrium. In the Western model of strife (conflicting dualism), we must choose one of the two alternatives and eliminate the other (an "either-or" paradigm). In the East Asian model of harmony (complementary dualism), the two opposites are complementary and belong to each other (a "both-and" paradigm). It is analogous to the relationship between a male and a female who, though opposite in gender, become one couple through marriage (and bring forth the child, which is the third).

The East Asian holistic way of yin-yang thinking is more allied with the both-and paradigm, whereas the modern critical method is more allied with the either-or paradigm. Wilfred Cantwell Smith states: "We in the West presume that an intelligent man must choose *either* this *or* that . . . [But] In all ultimate matters, truth lies not in an either-or, but in a both-and."[19] Since the doctrine of the Trinity pertains to the ultimate reality of the whole, it is to be envisaged with the both-and paradigm rather than with the either-or mode of thinking that is more pertinent to penultimate matters.

### The ontology of change

Furthermore, the yin-yang mode of thinking entails the ontology of change in contrast to the ontology of substance that is dominant in the West. The yin-yang relationship is characterized by continuous change; change is primary and prior to ontic being or substance. In this ontocosmology of T'ai-chi, change is not a function of being, as Western ontology generally assumes. On the contrary, change is the ultimate itself, whereas being or substance is a penultimate manifestation of change. The ontology of change where only change is changeless calls for a paradigm shift in the philosophy of being.

### The Confucian Trinity: Heaven, Earth, and Humanity

Inclusive humanism rooted in the Neo-Confucian ontocosmology is luminously expressed in the *Western Inscription* of Chang Tsai, as the Confucian Trinity of Heaven, Earth, and Humanity:

> Heaven is my father and Earth is my mother, and even such a small creature as I finds an intimate place in their midst. Therefore, that which fills the universe I regard as my body and that which directs the universe I consider as my nature. All people are my brothers and sisters, and all things are my companions.[20]

The universe is visualized as a cosmic triune family, and a human being as a cosmic person, a member of the cosmic Trinity. From this vantage point, a Confucian-Christian idea of the Trinity has been suggested: "We might see God the Son as the ideal human, God the Father would be heaven (the creative spirit), and God the Holy Spirit the earth (the receptive co-spirit), or agent of the world which testifies to the accomplishment of the divinity."[21]

## A CONFUCIAN AND TAOIST INTERPRETATION OF THE TRINITY

Jung Young Lee is a pioneer in developing an East Asian Christian theology of the Trinity, particularly through the yin-yang paradigm. Although his project is not yet widely known, his challenging insights deserve careful consideration in articulating a contemporary trinitarian theology.

### One and three

Because of the dominant either-or paradigm of substance metaphysics, the trinitarian paradox of one nature (*una substantia*) and three persons (*tres hypostaseis*) has been a vexing problem to Western theology. In light of the yin-yang way of complementary opposites, however, this one-and-three paradox is no longer a problem but can be reconciled within the both-and paradigm of relational thinking. The "one and two" and the "one and three" principles are the foundation of the ontocosmology of Tao (*Tao-te Ching* 42). The ontocosmology of T'ai-chi replaces the essentialist ontology of being with the relational ontology of change. Pursuing this line of thought, Lee proposes a Trinity of change, namely, God the Father as "change itself," God the Holy Spirit as "the power of change," and God the Son as "the perfect manifestation of change."[22]

### *Perichōrēsis*

In the diagram of T'ai-chi, there is an eye (a small circle of yang) inside yin, and another eye (a small circle of yin) inside yang. They symbolize the "in-ness" (inclusion) of yang "in" yin and of yin "in" yang, or the existence of "the inner connecting principle" between yin and yang (when yin reaches its limit, it becomes yang, and vice versa). This insight of in-ness or the inner connecting principle in yin and yang illuminates the meaning of *perichōrēsis* (co-inherence) in Jesus' saying "Believe me that I am *in* the Father and the Father is *in* me" (Jn 14:11).

Furthermore, from this vantage point of in-ness, Rahner's Rule, that the immanent Trinity *is* the economic Trinity and vice versa, can be made more precise by maintaining their distinction. Thus Lee writes: "Just as yin and yang always coexist without losing their distinctive identity, the economic Trinity and the immanent Trinity always coexist, but they are different." Hence Lee revises Rahner's Rule: "In this inclusive rather than identical relationship, we can revise Rahner's rule: The immanent Trinity is *in* the economic Trinity and the economic Trinity is *in* the immanent Trinity. This rule will help us retain their distinctiveness as well as their unity."[23]

### The cosmic family analogy

This ontocosmology always in the process of change is also conceived as "a procreative process" (*Tao-te Ching* 42). As we have seen in the *Western Inscription*, this trinitarian process culminates in the expression of a cosmic family of Trinity (Heaven, Earth, and Humanity). Lee further develops a family analogy of the Trinity, identifying the Father as the "heavenly Father," the Holy Spirit as the "sustainer" of the earth in the feminine symbol of "mother," and the Son as the "child" of the father and the mother. From the vantage point of a cosmic vestige of the trinitarian family, the Holy Spirit is conceived of as feminine, as mother, just as "spirit" is feminine in Hebrew (*ruach*). Lee claims that "the gender balance between mother and father is possible."[24] Furthermore, in the both-and paradigm of the cosmic Trinity, God is not only both male (yang) and female (yin), but also both personal and non-personal, and ultimately transcends all of these categories as the ineffable Tao.

**God the Son: the connecting principle (Tao Christology)**

In developing his theology of the Trinity, Lee starts from the Son rather than from the Father. Lee argues that it is through the Son that we know the Father and that the idea of two (i.e., divinity and humanity in Christ) is a prerequisite to understand the three. Furthermore, in light of East Asian cosmo-anthropology, the incarnation can be understood in a closer connection with creation. The Son (anthropology) is "a fulfillment of Trinitarian process in creation" (cosmology), and Christ (the prototype of cosmo-anthropology) is "the perfect manifestation of change in the world."[25] Lee formulates a trinitarian interpretation of creation: the Son as the act of creation, the Father as the source of creation, and the Spirit as the power of creation.

Just as the Christ is identified as the Logos (Word) in the first-century Graeco-Roman milieu (Jn 1), he can be understood as the Tao (Way) in the East Asian context. Christ as the Word as well as the Way is not so much "a form of structure" as "the act of creativity."[26] The ineffable Tao that transcends verbal limitations is the ultimate reality and the power of all creativities. As *Tao-te Ching* says about the "supra-essential" Tao:

> The Tao that can be told is not the eternal Tao.
> The Nameless is the origin of Heaven and Earth.
> The Named is the mother of all things.[27]

The Taoist complementary paradox of fullness (yang) and emptiness (yin) is comparable to the Christological paradox of kenosis (self-emptying) and exaltation in the letter to the Philippians (2:5–9). "The Word as the Tao, which is also known as *I* or change, is a ceaseless act of emptying and fulfilling process." From the cosmo-anthropological perspective, "death is inseparable from life, just as life cannot exist independently from death."[28] When yin reaches its maximum, yang begins to arise (like the wax and wane of the moon), and vice versa. Likewise, if the death of Jesus refers to the maximum expansion or the perfection of yin, then the resurrection of Christ is regarded as the yang that begins to expand toward perfection.

The obedience of the Son to the Father until the death on the cross can be well understood within the context of filial piety, a cardinal virtue serving as the gate to attain the supreme Confucian goal of human relatedness, *jen* (benevolence or co-humanity). The Son's filial piety becomes a clue to understanding salvation as the restoration of the harmonious relationship in creation. Thus "it was not the divine substance of the Son but his filial piety that saved us."[29] Hence salvation is not so much substantial as relational, and sin is a disruption of this harmonious relationship not only among creatures but also between humans and the divine Trinity.

**God the Holy Spirit: the Mother and the material principle**

In light of the East Asian Trinity of Cosmic Family, the Spirit can be understood as the feminine member of the Trinity, "she," the Mother (Yin), who complements the Father (Yang). Furthermore, this vision embraces the intriguing East Asian notion of *ch'i*, "the vital energy," the material principle. The concept of *ch'i* (*ki* in Korean) is very much similar to the biblical notion of spirit, *ruach* in Hebrew and *pneuma* in Greek, both of which have a double meaning of wind and breath. "While wind brings nature to life, breath makes the living alive," as God-breathing is a life-giving power (Gen 2:7).[30]

In the T'ai-chi diagram, *ch'i* is the embodiment and materialization of the Great Ultimate through the complementary actualization of tranquility and activity (yin and yang). While the Father is transcendent as the heavenly principle (*li*), the Spirit, the Mother, is immanent as the material principle (*ch'i*). And the Son is both transcendent and immanent in the unity of the heaven (*li*) and the earth (*ch'i*). In this context of Trinity as cosmic family, the doctrine of *filioque* is unacceptable, in Lee's view: "In this respect, it is not the Spirit which proceeds from the Father and the Son, but the Son which proceeds from the Spirit and the Father." The *Tao-te Ching* describes the Tao basically with feminine metaphors such as the female spirit or the womb of the "mystical mother" which is the root or the ground of being, Heaven and Earth:

The spirit of valley never dies.
This is called the mysterious female [or mother].
The gateway [or womb] of the mysterious female [mother]
Is called the root of Heaven and Earth.
Dimly visible, it seems as if it were there,
Yet use will never drain it.[31]

(*Tao-te Ching* 6)

**God the Father: the unifying principle**

*Li*, generally translated as "principle," is the key concept in Neo-Confucianism. It is usually discussed in association with *ch'i*, usually translated as "material force." If the T'ai-chi refers to *li* as the ontological principle, yin and yang signify the movement of *ch'i* (the material embodiment). The relationship between *li* and *ch'i*, particularly as to which of them is prior to the other, was hotly debated in the history of Korean Neo-Confucianism. Lee introduces this discussion into the trinitarian discourse, identifying the Father with *li* and the Holy Spirit with *ch'i* respectively. In light of the relationship between *li* and *ch'i*, Lee understands the trinitarian relationships as follows: "God as the Father is analogous to a universal principle (*li*), while the Spirit as the Mother is analogous to a material principle (*ch'i*). In the Son both *li* and *ch'i* are united, for the Son serves as a connecting principle in the relationship between the Father and the Mother."[32]

Romanticism toward the patriarchal family in the context of East Asian ontocosmology is certainly a defect in Lee's otherwise splendid theology of the Trinity. Siding with Chu Hsi's orthodoxy, he insists on justifying the priority of the Father, which is highly controversial in this age of post-feminist revolution. "It belongs to the Tao of *li*, 'above-shaped,' while all others belong to *ch'i*, 'within-shaped.' Even though the 'above-shaped' and 'within-shaped' are inseparable, the former seems to take priority." In this interpretation, the Father – the masculine (yang) member of the Trinity – represents "the transcendent moral and spiritual Principle of Heaven," whereas the Spirit – the feminine (yin) member – represents "the immanent Principle of the Earth."

Burdened with memories of his father, however, Lee seems to have forgotten that the Tao is primarily feminine and focuses exclusively on the paradoxical reversal of weakness (which he terms the "margin"). As he states: "Here we notice that the center becomes the margin, and the margin becomes the center, in the process of creativity and change. In trinitarian thinking, the centrality of the Father is marginalized by the Spirit, and the marginality of the Spirit is recentered in the Son."[33]

## REVIEW AND CONCLUSION

These East Asian interpretations of the Trinity, especially that of Jung Young Lee, may seem odd to readers accustomed to the analytical thinking associated with substantialism, individualism, and exclusive humanism. They require a radical rethinking of the fundamental worldview, ontology, anthropology, and pneumatology that incorporate the anthropocosmic vision, the notion of change, inclusive humanism, and *ch'i*. Of course, all these concepts should be subject to a rigorous scrutiny before their adoption to the Christian doctrine of the Trinity. In conclusion, I will highlight four issues that seem to be significant for a future trinitarian theology.

### Decentering Western theology

East Asian interpretations of Trinity welcome the direction of contemporary trinitarian theology, which I have called "Easternization." The East Asian notion of inclusive humanism enriches the concept of person in trinitarian theology and shows that the root cause of the impasse in contemporary trinitarian theology lies in the Western anthropology of exclusive humanism. Furthermore, the yin-yang paradigm promotes the "triumph of relationship" in contemporary theology of the Trinity, replacing the ontology of substance with the ontology of relations.[34] The ontocosmology of T'ai-chi endorses the Cappadocian Fathers' privileging of relation over substance and the "Zizioulas Rule" of *Being as Communion*.[35]

Lee and Zizioulas converge at this point in saying, "God is not first one and then three, but *simultaneously* One and Three," on the basis of East Asian ontocosmology of change (*I*) and the Eastern onto-*personality* of communion (*koinōnia*) respectively.[36] Lee's explication of "in-ness" in the T'ai-chi (yang in yin and yin in yang) is in line with Leonardo Boff's affirmation of *perichōrēsis* as "the structural axis" of an "open" trinitarian theology,[37] thus modifying Rahner's Rule to the effect that "the immanent Trinity is *in* the economic Trinity and the economic Trinity is *in* the immanent Trinity." In this movement of Trinity from the West toward the Middle East and the Far East, the process of decentering Western theology is advanced further.

### Relation with feminist theology

Lee's patriarchal bias undermines the efficacy of his project. In contrast to Lee's, the Confucian and Taoist interpretation of the Trinity has a lot in common with feminist theology. In the both-and paradigm of yin-yang, God is not only both female and male, but also both personal and non-personal, and ultimately transcends those categories. The cosmic Trinity rooted in the ontocosmology of T'ai-chi definitely includes a feminine personhood and encourages the view of the Holy Spirit as God-Mother. Like Sophia, the Tao refers to Wisdom primarily in feminine metaphors. The *Tao-te ching* notes how the seemingly weak feminine (yin) exerts power over the apparently strong masculine (yang). Primordially, the ultimate reality (the Tao) lies in the yin rather than in the yang. The Tao is also depicted as the Mysterious Female or Mother who is the root of Heaven and Earth.

Although Lee criticizes the Christocentric focus of Western theology, he himself unfortunately falls into the same pitfall by making Christology the starting point for trinitarian discourse. Since the notion of *ch'i* offers great pneumatological possibilities and since Lao-tzu gives more power to yin and "the feminine spirit" ("the Spirit of Valley"), East Asian theology of the Trinity can endorse the feminist "methodological shift to the Spirit" (Elizabeth Johnson) as the point of departure for trinitarian theology.[38]

From an East Asian perspective, however, feminist theologies in general have not yet been fully freed from exclusive humanism, even though they radically oppose essentialism or substantialism. This is due perhaps to the lack of an alternative ontology in the West. In this regard, the Confucian and Taoist ontology of change or nothingness can offer a viable alternative.

### The ontology of nothingness

The *Tao-te ching* is the book for the empowerment (*te*) of the ineffable Tao. The foundation of the ontocosmology of T'ai-chi is *Wu-chi* (the Ultimate Non-Being). Together, *Wu-chi* (Non-Being) and T'ai-chi (Being) constitute the ultimate complementary paradox of opposites. In this ultimate paradox, Nothing-ness (Non-Being) is primordial and prior to Thing-ness (Being). "All things are born of being. Being is born of non-being . . . The Tao is nowhere to be found. Yet it nourishes and completes all things" (*Tao-te Ching* 40, 41).

The notion of the ineffable Tao as the Non-Being is akin to that of "supra-essential Trinity." Here, again, the East Asian Taoist ontology of nothingness converges with the Eastern apophatic theology. Reminiscent of the opening lines of the *Tao-te Ching*, John of Damascus states, "The Deity being incomprehensible is also assuredly nameless. Therefore since we know not His essence, let us not seek for a name for his essence."[39] The supra-essential ontology of nothingness and emptiness is a subject requiring further discussion in contemporary theology of the Trinity. Eastern apophatic theology and East Asian theology of the Tao (which I call "theo-tao," in contrast to traditional theology's "theo-logos" and liberation theology's "theo-praxis") have a lot in common and deserve further discussion.[40]

### The power of kenotic return

Lao-tzu enthusiastically speaks of the Tao's "super-*kenosis*."[41] The ontocosmology of T'ai-chi and the superkenotic Tao endorse a "perichoresic kenotic trinitarian ontology."[42] However, they do not imply an abstract, powerless metaphysics of the Trinity. On the contrary, they reveal the concrete trajectory of the revolutionary and subversive life force (the *ch'i* of great yin). Like the divine breath, this cosmogonic energy makes all things alive.

A clue to understanding the mystery of the hidden but unquenchable power of the Tao is the principle of "reversal" and the power of radical return. Jesus occasionally speaks of the principle of reversal: "Blessed are you that are hungry now, for you will be filled . . . Woe to you who are full now, for you will be hungry" (Lk 6:21, 25). St. Paul also says: "Whenever I am weak, then I am strong" (2 Cor 12:10).

A vivid symbol of the Tao's power of radical return is a feeble fish's jumping up against the mighty river current to return to its origin.[43] With its preferential option for the yin, the Non-Being, the powerless (*minjung*), and the margin, East Asian trinitarian theology of the Tao is not just a romantic hankering after past things East Asian. Rather it is a serious reinterpretation of the Christian mystery of the crucifixion as Non-Being and the resurrection as Being, the ultimate paradox of apophatic reversal and superkenotic return. The Korean theologian Ryu Young-mo offers the intriguing insight that Christ is "the Being-in-Non-Being," that is to say, the great cosmogonic Trinity (T'ai-chi in *Wu-chi*).[44] Jesus Christ is therefore also a or the supreme Tao of the East Asian Trinity. These insights into the supra-essential Tao of superkenotic return provide rich resources for developing a global trinitarian theology in the third millennium. Lao-tzu presents a tantalizing hint:

Attain complete vacuity [emptiness],
Maintain steadfast quietude.
All things come into being,
And I see thereby their return.
All things flourish,
But each one returns to its root.
This return to its root means tranquility.
It is called returning to its destiny.
To return to destiny is called the eternal (Tao).
To know the eternal is called enlightenment.

(*Tao-te Ching* 16)[45]

**Notes**

1. Karl Rahner, *The Trinity*, trans. Joseph Donceel, introduction, index, and glossary by Catherine LaCugna (New York: Crossroad, 1997), 22; Wolfhart Pannenberg, *Theology and the Kingdom of God* (Philadelphia: Westminster, 1969), 55–56, cited in Stanley J. Grenz, *Rediscovering the Trinity in Contemporary Theology: The Triune God* (Minneapolis: Fortress, 2004), 96.
2. See Grenz, *Rediscovering the Trinity*, 134–35, 141–43, 134.
3. Raymond Panikkar, *The Trinity and the Religious Experience of Man: Icon, Person, Mystery* (Maryknoll, NY: Orbis; London: Darton, Longman & Todd, 1973).
4. Hans Küng and Julia Ching, *Christianity and Chinese Religions*, trans. Peter Beyer (New York: Doubleday, 1989), xi–xv.
5. W. Theodore de Bary, *East Asian Civilizations: A Dialogue in Five Stages* (Cambridge, MA: Harvard University Press, 1989), 44.
6. Tu Wei-ming, *Confucianism in a Historical Perspective* (Singapore: Institute of East Asian Philosophies, 1989), 3.
7. Heup Young Kim, *Wang Yang-ming and Karl Barth: A Confucian–Christian Dialogue* (Lanham, MD, and London: University Press of America, 1996), 1.
8. Tu Wei-ming, *Centrality and Commonality: An Essay on Confucian Religiousness* (Albany, NY: State University of New York Press, 1989), 107.
9. Wing-tsit Chan, trans., *A Source Book in Chinese Philosophy* (Princeton University Press, 1963), 98.
10. See Jung Young Lee, *The Trinity in Asian Perspective* (Nashville: Abingdon Press, 1996), 18.
11. Cheng Chung-ying, "The Trinity of Cosmology, Ecology, and Ethics in the Confucian Personhood," in Mary Evelyn Tucker and John Berthrong, eds., *Confucianism and Ecology: The Interrelation of Heaven, Earth, and Humans* (Cambridge, MA: Harvard University Press, 1998), 213–15.

12. This key Confucian and Taoist notion is presented in *I Ching*, one of the Five Confucian Classics. See *The I Ching or Book of Changes*, trans. Richard Wilhelm, 3rd edn. (Princeton University Press, 1967).
13. Cheng, "The Trinity," 216.
14. Chan, trans., *A Source Book*, 463.
15. Cheng, "The Trinity," 219.
16. Chan, trans., *A Source Book*, 160–61.
17. Lee, *The Trinity*, 30.
18. Cheng, "The Trinity," 291.
19. Wilfred Cantwell Smith, *The Faith of Other Men* (New York: New American Library, 1963), 72.
20. Chan, trans., *A Source Book*, 497.
21. Cheng, "The Trinity," 225.
22. Lee, *The Trinity*, 66.
23. Ibid., 58, 67–68.
24. Ibid., 63–65.
25. Ibid., 71.
26. Ibid., 72. The Hebrew word *dabhar* (Word) means the creative act.
27. Chan, trans., *A Source Book*, 144.
28. Lee, *The Trinity*, 73, 83.
29. Ibid., 89.
30. Ibid., 96, 97.
31. *Lao Tzu: Tao Te Ching*, trans. D. C. Lau (Harmondsworth: Penguin, 1963), 62.
32. Lee, *The Trinity*, 112.
33. Ibid., 150.
34. Grenz, *Rediscovering the Trinity*, 5.
35. See John D. Zizioulas, *Being as Communion: Studies in Personhood and the Church* (Crestwood, NY: St. Vladimir's Seminary Press, 1985).
36. John D. Zizioulas, "Communion and Otherness," *St. Vladimir's Theological Quarterly*, 38:4 (1994), 353 (italics mine); cf. Lee, *The Trinity*, 63.
37. Leonardo Boff, *Trinity and Society*, trans. Paul Burns (Maryknoll, NY: Orbis, 1988), 119–20.
38. Grenz, *Rediscovering the Trinity*, 173.
39. John of Damascus, *On the Orthodox Faith*, 1.12, cited from Thomas Hopko, "Apophatic Theology and the Naming of God in Eastern Orthodox Tradition," in Alvin Kimel, Jr., ed., *Speaking the Christian God: the Holy Trinity and the Challenge of Feminism* (Grand Rapids, MI: Eerdmans, 1992), 157.
40. See Heup Young Kim, *Christ and the Tao* (Hong Kong: Christian Conference of Asia, 2003), 135–82; see also Heup Young Kim, "A Tao of Asian Theology in the Twenty First Century," *Asia Journal of Theology*, 13:2 (1999), 276–93.
41. Grenz, *Rediscovering the Trinity*, 221.
42. Robert Kess, "Unity in Diversity and Diversity in Unity: Toward an Ecumenical Perichoresic Kenotic Trinitarian Ontology," *Dialogue & Alliance*, 4:3 (1990), 66–70.

43. For this subversive power of return, see Heup Young Kim, *Christ and the Tao* (Hong Kong: Christian Conference of Asia, 2003), esp. 138–44.
44. See Heup Young Kim, "The Word Made Flesh: Ryu Young-mo's Christotao, A Korean Perspective," in Mercy Amba Oduyoye and Handrik M. Vroom, eds., *One Gospel and Many Cultures: Case Studies and Reflections on Cross-Cultural Theology* (Amsterdam and New York: Rodopi, 2003), 129–48, esp. 143–44.
45. Chan, trans., *A Source Book*, 147.

## Further reading

Boff, Leonardo, *Trinity and Society*, trans. Paul Burns (Maryknoll, NY: Orbis, 1988).

Chan, Wing-tsit, *A Source Book in Chinese Philosophy* (Princeton University Press, 1963).

Grenz, Stanley J., *Rediscovering the Trinity in Contemporary Theology: The Triune God* (Minneapolis: Fortress, 2004).

*The I Ching or Book of Changes*, trans. Richard Wilhelm, 3rd edn. (Princeton University Press, 1967).

Kim, Heup Young, *Christ and the Tao* (Hong Kong: Christian Conference of Asia, 2003; reprint Eugene, OR: Wipf and Stock, 2010).

*Wang Yang-ming and Karl Barth: A Confucian–Christian Dialogue* (Lanham, MD, and London: University Press of America, 1996).

Küng, Hans, and Julia Ching, *Christianity and Chinese Religions*, trans. Peter Beyer (New York: Doubleday, 1989).

*Lao Tzu: Tao Te Ching*, trans. D. C. Lau (Harmondsworth: Penguin, 1963).

Lee, Jung Young, *The Trinity in Asian Perspective* (Nashville: Abingdon, 1996).

Panikkar, Raimundo, *The Trinity and the Religious Experience of Man: Icon-Person-Mystery* (Maryknoll, NY: Orbis; London: Darton, Longman & Todd, 1973).

Pannenberg, Wolfhart, *Theology and the Kingdom of God* (Philadelphia: Westminster, 1969).

Rahner, Karl, *The Trinity*, trans. Joseph Donceel, introduction, index, and glossary by Catherine LaCugna (New York: Crossroad, 1997).

Smith, Wilfred Cantwell, *The Faith of Other Men* (New York: New American Library, 1963).

Tu Wei-ming, *Confucianism in a Historical Perspective* (Singapore: Institute of East Asian Philosophies, 1989).

Zizioulas, John D., *Being as Communion: Studies in Personhood and the Church* (Crestwood, NY: St. Vladimir's Seminary Press, 1985).

# 18 Trinity and Hinduism

FRANCIS X. CLOONEY, SJ

This chapter shares the recognition presupposed in this volume of the Trinity's place at the core of Christian reflection on a very wide range of topics of theological and spiritual import. It is no surprise that Christians consider world religions, in general and also in their particular forms, in light of the reality and theology of Trinity, and we can expect that trinitarian theology will inform how we construct Christian theology, even in its interreligious form. What is true in general remains pertinent in particular cases, among which Hindu traditions (henceforth "Hinduism") are a particularly interesting case. Given the specific nature of the Hindu–Christian relationship – long and varied, surprising in its instances of common ground, yet far less foundational or developed than Christian relations with Judaism and Islam – reflection on the Trinity in relation to Hinduism enables us to see the possibilities and drawbacks of using a trinitarian hermeneutic in encounter with a tradition so interestingly like yet unlike the Christian. In this brief chapter, I explore some older Christian uses of trinitarian imagery in understanding and judging Hinduism, Hindu reactions to and appropriations of the Trinity, the contemporary use of trinitarian theology with particular reference to Hinduism, and the larger problem of the reality and theology of Trinity in Hinduism. Given the breadth of possibilities, I limit my reflections to topics that highlight the trinitarian dimension, thus forgoing topics such as creation, incarnation, and inspiration that in other contexts would naturally be considered from a trinitarian perspective.

## IN THE MISSIONARY ERA AND THEREAFTER: FASCINATION WITH THE TRIMURTI

Missionaries who went to India seeking initial points of contact were often enchanted by parallels to Christian truths that they discovered in the beliefs and practices of Brahmins and other Hindus. Triads caught their notice, often being respected as imperfect but honest human efforts, aided by a mysterious divine grace, to capture the fundamental (and Christian) structure of reality.

**Discovering Trinity in India: the Trimurti**

Most important is the long tradition of parallels between the Trinity and the Trimurti. This belief in the *Tri-murti* ("the Three-Forms") refers to the three deities, Brahma, Vishnu, and Shiva, who respectively undertake three primary cosmic functions: creation, preservation, and dissolution. Bailey traces the early history of the Trimurti concept, beginning with the *Maitri Upanisad* and the parallelism of the deities to the three constituents of nature, the lucid, passionate, and lethargic. Later, Puranic texts also correlate the three deities with the three letters of the sacred syllable *aum*. In the course of his erudite review of the history of the concept, Jan Gonda also notices early Christian reflection on the Trimurti, a venerable comparative experiment perhaps beginning with Duarte Barbosa in the sixteenth century.

The Jesuit Thomas Stephens (1549–1619) was one of the first to express in writing a parallel between Christian and Hindu trinities. Stephens (as Jaaware tells us) uses the term *traikya* – "the oneness of the three" – for the former while reserving Trimurti for the latter, thus indicating his determination to highlight differences. Roberto de Nobili (1577–1656), another pioneering Jesuit missionary and scholar, finds a hidden representation of the Trinity in the ancient *Taittiriya Upanisad*, by the grace of

> the most gracious and most high God who without a doubt vouchsafes even to these far distant lands some inkling of the most hidden secret of our faith, by the teaching of some sage living among these people, in much the same way as by a rather mysterious inspiration he deigned to illuminate the Sybils, Trismegistus, and certain other masters of human wisdom in our part of the world.[1]

But in addition to this rather obscure insight, we also have his sober dismissal of the Trimurti in his *Catechism*, where he sees the Trinity as a unique, revealed truth, which should never be hastily expounded to pagans or new converts, but only to maturing new Christians, along with other precious truths such as the divinity of Christ and his Eucharistic presence. Indeed, he adds, the Trimurti as concept is a confusion disseminated by Satan, a reminder of the errors to which those not guided by revelation are prone. In the *Akkiyana Nivaranam* (*Dispelling of Ignorance*), attributed to de Nobili, a series of dialogues vigorously argue the imperfection of each deity, Brahma, Vishnu, and Shiva, so as to pre-empt the idea that Trimurti indicates a higher, integral divine being like the Christian God. While de Nobili seems to have found in the trinitarian analogy a reason for hope in communicating with Indians, he also uses it as a tool for criticizing Hindu conceptions of God.

Jean Venance Bouchet (1655–1732), a founder of the French Jesuit mission in south India, follows de Nobili's thinking. In a 1710 letter he observes that the Indians retain an inkling of the mystery of the Trinity, which had in ancient times been preached to them. Acknowledging that Trimurti theology can be sophisticated and indicative of a nuanced concept of God, Bouchet concludes that such ideas show that inklings of the truth were preserved in India, even if the human mind by itself cannot properly express so great a mystery as the Trinity.

Bartholomaeus Ziegenbalg (1682–1719), an erudite scholar who was one of the first Protestant missionaries in India, wrote *Thirty Four Conferences between the Danish Missionaries and the Malabarian Brahmins (or Heathen Priests) in the East Indies*. In the eleventh conversation in this work, showing "the falseness of the heathen gods" and answering "objections against the Trinity," the missionary's exposition of the supreme God revealed in his Son Jesus prompts the Brahmin interlocutor to ask whether Christians thus believe in two Gods. Confused by a further elaboration of divine unity and trinity, the Brahmin asks for corresponding patience in hearing his explanation of the Indian plurality and unity of deities. But the missionary refuses, arguing that the textual contradictions and moral offensiveness of Indian teachings already show that these cannot be anything like the mystery of trinitarian teaching.

### Theorizing Trinity in India

Around 1760, at the end of the early period of Jesuit missionary exploration and scholarship, G.-L. Coeurdoux wrote a large work entitled *Moeurs et coutumes des Indiens*. In it he notes an indigenous explanation of the three deities as symbolic of the interconnected evolution of water, earth, and fire; the three deities, like the elements, flourish in conjunction and not apart from one another. He observes that this kind of religious and natural observation had precedent in the early church, when Fathers such as Justin, Clement, Theodoret, and Augustine used Greek philosophy to show the mystery of the Trinity. Pointing to a lack of clarity in Indian mythology and obscurity regarding the origins of various beliefs, he is skeptical about the possibility of illuminating historical or theoretical comparisons.[2] J. A. Dubois' *Hindu Manners, Customs and Ceremonies*, largely an adaptation of Coeurdoux's work, speculates on the derivation of the Trimurti. After discussing possible derivations of the Trimurti theory in Indian observation of nature and philosophical theory, and noting parallels in Indo-European mythology and patristic usage, Dubois concludes that whatever the origins of Trimurti, over time even simple natural and philosophical insights became confused, ending in the "extravagant and barbarous idolatry which forms the religious system of the Hindus."[3]

J. Lockman, editor of the 1743 English translation of selected letters from the *Lettres édifiantes et curieuses des Jésuites*, was, in numerous footnotes, skeptical about the Catholic and Jesuit missionary enterprise and reading of India. His comment on the project of trinitarian comparisons[4] such as those we find in Bouchet and Coeurdoux captures the inevitable ambiguities. Citing the views of François Bernier (1620–1688), a writer and traveler to India, Lockman writes:

> With respect to these three Beings (of the Trimurti), I have met (says he [Bernier]) with some European missionaries, who pretend that the Heathens have some Idea of the Mystery of the Trinity; and say that it is expressly declared in their Books, that they are three Persons in one God. I myself (says Bernier) have frequently discoursed with the Brahmins on this Subject, but they expressed themselves so confusedly, that I never could understand their Meaning perfectly.

Lockman concludes that discoveries of Trinity are over-enthusiastic: some Hindus portray the three divinities as individual deities, while others hold that they are "really but one and the same God, considered in three Respects, viz., as Creator, Preserver, and Destroyer of Things." But Trinity is nowhere to be found, since "they did not observe anything of three distinct Persons in one sole God."[5]

In the nineteenth century, Brahmabandhab Upadhyay (1861–1907), a famed convert to Catholicism, argued that the Trimurti is not the same as the Trinity, because it is only a phenomenal aspect of the divine: at cosmic dissolution, the Trimurti dissolves and is no more; by contrast, the Christian Trinity is God's own inner identity, eternal and unchanging.[6] In a similar vein, he sharply criticizes Annie Besant, a leading Theosophist and proponent of the deeper unity of religions, for the superficiality of her comparison of Trinity and Trimurti. Contrary to her views, he argues that the three deities are material, imperfect, and even sinful, far from the mystery of the God who knows himself (as the Son known by the Father) and loves himself (as the Spirit, the love of

Father and Son). Moreover, Upadhyay adds, even the trinitarian notion of person, having to do with a rational *individuum*, "a being endowed with reason and free will," is distant from the Indian mythic masks of the divine.[7]

At the end of the nineteenth century, theologians in Europe were also assessing the legacy of comparisons involving the Trinity and Hindu thought. In 1894, for instance, Merwin-Marie Snell argued for the positive meeting points of Hindu and trinitarian thought, such that Christian trinitarians should welcome the discovery of common ground, as the triads of Brahma, Vishnu, and Shiva, and of Sat, Cit, and Ananda, are brought into close comparison with the Christian triads of Divine Being, Wisdom, and Love, and of Father, Son, and Spirit. He concluded that the honest reader "must at least admit that there is in the Hindu mind not only a strong sense of the personality of God, but a traditional tendency to a line of thought that would seem to have its legitimate outcome in the doctrine of the Trinity."[8] In 1910, a more cautious Ernest Hull offered another perspective on "the Hindu Trinity." While believing that Trimurti might have been derived from the Christian Trinity, he thinks it probably was not. Rather, the doctrine served an indigenous need internal to Hinduism, with respect to the coherent worship of multiple deities. He observes that the problem facing the early church – "How can there be *processiones reales ad intra*, or a triplicity of really distinct hypostases in an infinitely simple substance?" – was not an issue in ancient India, with its own different ontology and theology. He adds that Christians and Hindus do not even think of their deities the same way: for the Christian, the Trinity is a deep mystery of faith, while Hindus see all multiplicities, even of deities, as "the delusions of Maya."[9]

## Trinity in the study of religions

The emerging field of comparative religion also took up the issue of similarities and their meaning. In *The Bible in India: Hindoo Origin of Hebrew and Christian Revelation*, Louis Jacolliot (1837–1890) concluded his reflection on the Trimurti with the judgment that this doctrine was more reasonable than that of Trinity, and probably the source of the latter: "The Trinity in Unity, rejected by Moses, became afterwards the foundation of Christian theology, which incontestably acquired it from India."[10] More dispassionately, Levi Leonard Paine's *The Ethnic Trinities and their Relations to the Christian Trinity* (1901) looked to the "primary sources [of trinitarianism] as well as its historical evolution through the various Ethnic trinities until it enters its

Christian stage," in order "to compare with each other these different stages of religious thought and draw from such comparison its historical conclusions."[11] Paine's attention to India focuses on "the Hindoo Brahmanic Trinity" (with Buddhism taken as a form of Hindu thought, and paired with Zoroastrian and Greek trinities). For Paine, the Hindu trinity and Hindu notion of mediation are stopping points on the path from polytheism to monotheism, and also wonderful intimations of truths made clear only in Christ.

In still more recent theorizations of comparative religion, complex (triadic or other) structures remain of great interest, and the Trinity is taken as a way of presenting a transcendent divinity who is nonetheless engaged in the world. For example, Geoffrey Parrinder, in his entry on "Triads" for the *Encyclopedia of Religion*, surveys ancient Indian, Hindu, Buddhist, Chinese, and ancient Mediterranean and Greek uses of triadic imagery, as well as Jewish and Islamic ambivalence toward triadic imagery. In concluding he alludes to the Christian doctrine of the Trinity (treated in a separate entry) in a way that invites additional, more unpredictable comparisons:

> Christian doctrine developed, against an Old Testament background, from devotion to Christ, but as it developed it came into contact with triadic concepts of the divine from Egypt and the Near East. Belief in a divine family emerged, for the concepts of Father and Son were in Christianity from the beginning. The Holy Spirit was regarded as the third hypostasis in the Trinity, but it was often a vague or neglected notion.

Tantalizing possibilities are not allowed to develop: "With the growth of the cult of the Virgin and Mother the female side of a triad seemed guaranteed . . . In popular religion that might have happened, but Trinitarian theology was anchored in the Bible, and Christian teachings developed from those scriptures that gave a threefold baptismal formula and a triadic blessing." In conclusion, though, he cautions against enthusiasm in comparative studies: "As with other religions, the threefold doctrine is best understood in its historical context, however attractive seeming cultural parallels may be."[12]

## HINDU VIEWS OF THE TRINITY

Before moving into the modern era and modern Christian theological reflections on world religions in light of the Trinity, we must take a "detour" into Hindu views of Trinity. In light of Christian and related

Western views of Trinity and Trimurti, it is worthwhile also to notice how Hindus themselves interpreted the Christian Trinity; here too we must be very selective.

### Rejecting the Trimurti

We must first note that Hindus themselves were sober in their assessment of Trimurti, which was never a universally accepted doctrine. For instance, in the Tamil devotional tradition of the medieval Vaisnava saints known as the alvars, we find ambivalence toward "the three." Their hymns both recognize the Trimurti and downplay its importance. The famous Vaisnava saint Satakopan (ninth century), for instance, clearly knew of the Trimurti and chose to praise Vishnu as the supreme God, over Brahma and Shiva. Later Vaisnavas have adhered to this view; Vedanta Desika (thirteenth to fourteenth centuries), for instance, was at pains to clarify right thinking about God's unity and distinction. In his *Srimadrahasyatrayasara* (*Auspicious Essence of the Three Mysteries*) he rejects the Trimurti, and insists on the subordination of Shiva and Brahma to Vishnu. Similarly, for Saivas, it is Shiva who reigns, while Vishnu and Brahma are his servants; here, we might look at the *Sivajnanasiddhiyar* (*Confirmation of the Knowledge of Siva*) of Arul Nanti (thirteenth century), which expounds Saiva views of the three great gods, and the subordination of all lesser gods to the supreme Shiva. And while we cannot point to instances of the supremacy of Brahma, in Nondualist (Advaita) Vedanta, the ideal principle of Brahman is often held up as beyond the Trimurti.

### Hindu apologetics in rejection of Trinity

While we cannot take the characterization of Brahminical views in missionary reports at face value, we can at least infer Hindu responses to the views of de Nobili, Ziegenbalg, and later missionaries. Hindus may well have sympathetically received the notion of Trinity – the one personified in several forms – but were less enthusiastic when it was proposed as qualitatively superior to Hindu representations of the divine, and as an exclusive alternative. In *Resistant Hinduism* (1981) Richard Young recounts debates in which the Trinity is argued by missionaries and Hindu scholars of the eighteenth and nineteenth centuries. For instance, the pandit Somanatha argues that the doctrine of Trinity indicates that Christians too believe that the one God can have multiple names.[13] In another debate, an unnamed Hindu intellectual observes that those holding so complicated a view of God as Trinity should be more sympathetic to the complexities of Hindu thought: "Those who favor these doctrines [such as Trinity, incarnation] maintain that . . . the unity of God is undestroyed . . . If, then, these three divinities occasion no bewilderment of mind . . . how can the worship of Rama, Krishna, and other gods, occasion an over-growing bewilderment to us?"[14]

### Ram Mohun Roy, Hindu reformer and founder of the Brahmo Samaj (1772–1833)

A "Hindu Unitarian," Ram Mohun Roy was deeply engaged in communication with missionaries, and in arguments as well. While firm in his intention to reform and purify Hinduism, he resisted the implication that Christian views were somehow more evident, sensible, or beyond critique. In "Reasons of a Hindoo for Rejecting the Doctrines of Christianity" he criticizes trinitarian doctrine.[15] The notion of three distinct persons in one God does not make sense, while the allocation of qualities such as justice, mercy, and inspiration to different divine persons is puzzling. In one section of his essay, he lists the explanations of Trinity given by ten Protestant theologians, observing that if these scholars cannot agree among themselves, they can hardly hope to convince Hindus. Christianity is actually more impressive in its practice than in its arcane theories, he suggests, and so moral practices are the better meeting point for Hindus and Christians; doctrines such as Trinity should be treated as internal affairs. Elsewhere he reaffirms that faith in the Trinity is hardly more satisfying than faith in the multiplicity of Hindu deities:

> After I have long relinquished every idea of a plurality of Gods, or of the persons of the Godhead, taught under different systems of modern Hindooism, I cannot conscientiously and consistently embrace one of a similar nature, though greatly refined by the religious reformations of modern times; since whatever arguments can be adduced against a plurality of persons of the God; and, on the other hand, whatever excuse may be pleaded in favour of a plurality of persons of the Deity, can be offered with equal propriety in defence of Polytheism.[16]

### *Sat, cit, ananda*

Keshab Chunder Sen (1838–1884), founder of the Church of the New Dispensation, and writing in the same "unitarian" Brahmo Samaj tradition, offered a more constructive link – and alternative – to the Trinitarian tradition in his famous lecture "That Marvellous Mystery – the Trinity." The Trinity signals the divinization of the world: "Divinity coming down to humanity is the Son; Divinity carrying up humanity to heaven is the Holy Ghost."[17] All three persons are necessary: it would be idolatry, he says, to replace the Father with the Son; it would leave humans outside God were we to forget the Spirit, God's power enabling us to respond to God: "Whether alone or manifest in the Son, or quickening humanity as the Holy Spirit, it is the same God, the same identical Deity, whose unity continues indivisible amid multiplicity of manifestations."[18] Most famously, Sen may have been the first, in the same speech, to correlate the Father, Son, and Spirit with *sat*, *cit*, and *ananda*, which he explains as "the True, the Good, the Beautiful." Elsewhere, referring to the "three great ideas" of true Christianity – Father, Son, Spirit – Sen complains that Christians have failed to comprehend the unity of the divine and would do well to retrieve the earlier Jewish sense of the unity and grandeur of God.[19] Instead of dividing up the mystery of God in subservience to logic and dogma, Christians would do better to appreciate the deep, universal meaning of Trinity: "the spirit of Christ is the spirit of truth in humanity, not Christ as God, but Christ as manifesting God – not another God, but God's spirit, working practically in the human heart."[20] We can note here that Brahmabandhab Upadhyay, mentioned above, draws on Thomistic thought in venturing to correct Sen's *Saccidananda* analogy with more proper understandings of "person" and "nature." His theology is most famously expressed in his famous hymn *Vande Saccidanandam*:

> I adore the *Sat* (Being), *Cit* (Intelligence) and *Ananda* (Bliss), the highest goal . . . the Father, Begetter, the Highest Lord, unbegotten, the rootless principle of the tree of existence . . . the increate, infinite Logos or Word, supremely great, the Image of the Father, one whose form is intelligence, the giver of the highest freedom, the one who proceeds from the union of *Sat* and *Cit*, the blessed Spirit (breath), intense bliss.[21]

In *The Light of Truth*, a largely constructive work of reformed Hindu theology, Dayananda Sarasvati (1824–1883) took a strikingly unsympathetic stance toward trinitarian theology. In a particularly polemical section that turns missionary arguments against Christians, he argues the implausibility of multiple images of God in the Bible, including the view that Jesus as presented in the Bible could possibly be God: "When [the Father] is the only true God, it is absurd for the Christians to talk about three Gods (The Father, the Son, and the Holy Ghost)."[22]

### The Trinity as self-realization

In his monumental *The Second Coming of Christ*, Paramahansa Yogananda (1893–1952) offered a more positive insight, in keeping with

Sen's constructive perspective. In this lengthy (and posthumously published) "revelatory commentary on the original teachings of Jesus," Yogananda offers numerous reflections on gospel texts, and in that context occasionally reflects on the primordial Spirit that manifests itself as Trinity. For Yogananda, the Father "becomes manifest within the Holy Ghost vibration as the Son – the Christ Consciousness, God's intelligence in all vibratory creation."[23] "The Father (*Sat*) is God as the Creator existing beyond creation (Cosmic Consciousness). The Son (*Tat*) is God's omnipresent intelligence existing in creation (Christ Consciousness . . . ). The Holy Ghost (*Aum*) is the vibratory power of God that objectifies and becomes creation." But these are provisional, since "at the time of cosmic dissolution, the Trinity and all other relativities of creation resolve into the Absolute Spirit."[24] The importance of contact with saints is that they open the way to the experience of this "trifold Unity," the triple consciousness of Spirit, Son, and Father. In Yogavatar Lahiri Mahasaya's self-realization teachings, Yogananda says, devotees most deeply contact "the Holy Ghost Cosmic Vibration, and are filled with its eternal electrifying bliss, are indeed real witnesses of the Spirit of Truth and knowers of the Infinite Christ."[25]

Bringing trinitarian thought to India, however, also has an additional price that we must be willing to pay: a successful introduction of Trinity into Hindu discourse has meant that the language of three persons in one God has become a resource for Hindu reflection, to be interpreted in accord with Hindu theological discourse. None of these Hindu views matches a proper and orthodox Christian understanding of the Trinity, but it was inevitable that missionary success itself would lead to such unpredicted results. Once the doctrine of Trinity crossed religious lines, it had a new life among Hindu thinkers, and as such could no longer be fixed entirely in accord with Christian expectations. Such constructions of Trinity may diverge from the doctrines of Christian tradition, but must nevertheless be respected, even if leading to conclusions we did not anticipate. As we shall now see by way of just one example, some Christian thinkers have indeed responded fruitfully to these new directions.

## REDISCOVERING THE TRINITY IN INDIA: MEDITATIONS ON SACCIDANANDA

Jules Monchanin (1895–1957) and Henri Le Saux (1910–1973; commonly known as Swami Abhishiktananda) were co-founders of a famed ashram which they dedicated to the Trinity and accordingly named

Saccidananda Ashram. Inspired by the example of Upadhyay, Monchanin saw India as "the land of the Trinity."[26] His theological claim is strong: "Only the mystery of the Trinity is capable of resolving the antimonies which cause Hindu thought to swing endlessly between monism and pluralism, between a personal and an impersonal God."[27] Le Saux reflects at length on the Trinity in writings such as *Saccidananda: A Christian Approach to Advaitic Experience* (1974), particularly in relation to Nondualist (Advaita) Vedanta. The Trinity fully illumines the Reality already powerfully manifest in Nondualism. This truth is also a matter of experience. In the depths of the experience of the Trinity we find a Christian opening into the depths of the Nondualist Vedanta experience; theologically and in faith, the supreme truth of the Trinity and the deepest Nondualist experience manifest the Saccidananda of Trinity. As he writes in the hymn near the end of *Saccidananda*, "I sing *Saccidananda* to the Father through the Son in the Spirit. I sing the Glory of *Saccidananda* to the Father through the Son in the Spirit. I am myself the glory of *Saccidananda* – in being called to be by the Father in the Son through the Spirit."[28] Sr. Elizabeth Trinity, summarizing Le Saux's position, suggests that it is "part of the advaitic experience that a Christian can realize the Trinitarian God as *Saccidananda* in his personal experience."[29] His experience is both Nondualist and trinitarian, a "losing of oneself in the infinite reality of the absolute... From the bosom of Being itself he will contemplate Being and Truth, Wisdom and the Word, beholding what he is with an ineffable awareness of being in the bliss of the Spirit, *sat-cit-ananda*."[30]

In *A Benedictine Ashram*, the founding document of their monastic experiment, Monchanin and Le Saux make clear their trinitarian vision when they recommend to Christians to pray with *sat, cit*, and *ananda*, the Father as *sat*, the "principleless Principle," the Son as *cit*, the "intellectual Image of the Existent," and the Spirit as *ananda*, unifying Father and Son: "Just as AUM is one sound out of three elements (A, U, M), so also the mystery of the one identical essence in three 'hypostases' may be expressed by that pregnant utterance."[31] Mattam sums up the position shared by Monchanin and Le Saux this way:

> The Christian when thinking of the Father, the origin without origin, the Source and End of the "expansion" and the "recollection" of the divine life, can say *Sat*, Being; in the same way, he can say *Cit*, thought, when considering the Logos, the consubstantial Image of the Existent; and *Ananda*, Bliss, Joy

> when meditating on the Spirit, the "non-duality" of Father and Son. These words are not used as attributes of God, but they express what He is: *Sat, Cit, Ananda*.[32]

We can expect that this century will see fresh reflection on the Trinity in India, by younger generations of Indian Christian thinkers.

## THE TRINITY IN INDIA: THE LIMIT OF OUR EXPECTATIONS

In conclusion, what then of the Trinity within Hinduism? The preceding reflections make clear the fruitful yet ambiguous role of reflection on the Trinity in the Indian context. By expecting trinitarian parallels, missionaries found ways to be open to the new religions they encountered. By the finding of similarities, however these might be explained, new light was shed on Christian and Hindu doctrines, new insights into each tradition coming to the fore. Both traditions value the unity and diversity of divine identity and action, and both expect humans to be able to appreciate distinction without separation, and unity without sameness. The standard analogies – Trinity and Trimurti, Trinity as Saccidananda, the interpenetration of Trinity and Nondualism – have over the centuries been beneficial, prompting conversation and mutual learning, and yet all of them have been in some way deficient as well.

That the record is mixed should not surprise us. We know that the rich, deep Christian tradition of trinitarian theology, so nuanced and difficult, did not come together easily or suddenly in the earliest church; rather, it took centuries to put together right insights into the three persons of God with right vocabulary that could hold in place distinctions about those persons. As the history outlined in the earlier part of this chapter suggests, it was very hard indeed to explain in India the fine points of trinitarian thought, and as a result many did not see a great difference between Christian ideas of God and Hindu ideas.

However we might imagine the reality of the Trinity in India, it would be unreasonable to expect a neatly parallel language in Hinduism, such as could be easily adopted to Christian uses. This is not because Indians would be incapable of such thinking, or because Hinduism is bereft of comparably subtle technical discourses about God, but because it makes little sense to expect that the language about God, as substantial theology, that developed in the Christian context would also have developed in India. This is obviously true regarding the overall complex of ideas that contributed to the doctrine of Trinity, but it is also true of each individual aspect. Basic ideas about God differ in small ways; the concept of person does not translate easily into Sanskrit, as Paul Hacker showed in his 1963 article on the topic;[33] divine embodiment is not thought out in precisely the same way in Hinduism and Christianity, as Steven Tsoukalas has shown; the "Spirit of God" is a powerful evocation in both Hindu and Christian discourse, but each has its own tradition of ways of making sense of this Spirit in relation to God.

In any of these theological ventures, we do well to keep reminding ourselves of the history of Christian and Hindu exchanges on Trinity, examining how missionary scholars translated the technical language of Christianity into Indian languages, how Hindus received and translated Trinity into their own terms, and, finally, how contemporary Christian theologians have hopes to ground a better understanding of Hinduism and other religions in trinitarian theology. But in light of the difficulties of this history and its long series of mutual misunderstandings, there seems to be little point in expecting an exact parallel to trinitarian language in Hindu theology, or some final point of adequate contact, verification, or even symmetrical mutual understanding. We do better to admit that talk (by Christians as well as Hindus) of "the Trinity within Hinduism" will always fall short of the exactitude that would make it entirely compelling.

We can also clarify the situation by broadening our perspective, since here, too, the Trinity is best understood in light of other doctrines. If we wish to say that the reality of Trinity is present everywhere, and has been in some way known to Hindus throughout the millennia, we will do better to examine analogous cases, wherein Hindu theologians fashioned a unity-in-difference language for divine persons: as when Srivaisnava Hindus seek a way to speak of the distinction-and-unity of Lord Narayana with the goddess Sri, or when Saiva theologians articulate their understanding of Lord Shiva with Sakti, his divine female energy. While such reflection will not contribute directly to a Hindu reading of Trinity or a vindication of the presence of the Trinity in India, it will at least indicate that we are dealing with similar problems of human language about divine realities. Claims about the uniqueness of a Christian trinitarian perspective, or simpler faith claims about the presence of the Trinity in India, will have to be grounded elsewhere, justified without expectation of discernible exact parallels. Even when comparisons are fruitful, their limitations must be remembered, lest the subtleties of

Trinity, Trimurti, and Saccidananda be lost in an overly enthusiastic embrace of what is similar.

We can of course still move beyond issues of historical understanding and theological technicality to a more fundamental faith conviction that the substantive reality of the Trinity must somehow be manifest in the realities of Hindu faith, piety, theology, and life. If indeed India (though not only India) is "the land of the Trinity," we can expect that explorations of the Trinity with respect to Indian thought – albeit as exploratory, experimental, intuitive ventures – will continue to draw together, enrich, and probably also problematize our understanding of the Hindu and Christian traditions. We must therefore proceed by faith, allowing critical and interreligious perspectives to purify the theologies arising from that faith before we speak confidently on the mysteries of God at home or abroad.

## Notes

1. Roberto de Nobili, "Report on Indian Customs," in *Preaching Wisdom to the Wise*, ed. and trans. Anand Amaladass and Francis X. Clooney (St. Louis: Institute of Jesuit Sources, 2000; reprinted Chennai: Satya Nilayam Publications, 2005).
2. G.-L. Coeurdoux, *Moeurs et coutumes des Indiens* (1777), rev. N.-J. Desvaulx, VI/1, ed. Sylvie Murr (Paris: École Française d'Extrême Orient, 1987), 137–38.
3. J. A. Dubois, *Hindu Manners, Customs and Ceremonies*, trans. Henry K. Beauchamp (Oxford: Clarendon Press, 1906), 555.
4. J. Lockman, *Travels of the Jesuits into Various Parts of the World* (London: John Noon, 1743), II, 246.
5. Ibid., 246–47.
6. Brahmabandhab Upadhyay, *The Writings of Brahmabandhab Upadhyay*, ed. Julius Lipner and George Gispert-Sauch, 2 vols. (Bangalore: United Theological College, 1991, 2002), I, 79.
7. Ibid., II, 397.
8. Merwin-Marie Snell, "Hinduism's Points of Contact with Christianity," *The Biblical World*, 3:3 (March 1894), 197.
9. Ernest Hull, "Hinduism," in C. C. Martindale, ed., *The History of Religions*, 4 vols. (London: Catholic Truth Society, 1910), I, 15–17.
10. Louis Jacolliot, *The Bible in India*, Eng. trans. (New York: G. W. Dillingham and Co., 1868), 194.
11. Levi L. Paine, *The Ethnic Trinities and their Relations to the Christian Trinity* (Boston: Houghton, Mifflin and Company, 1901), v–vi.
12. Geoffrey Parrinder, "Triads," in Lindsay Jones, ed., *The Encyclopedia of Religion*, 2nd edn., 15 vols. (Detroit: Macmillan Reference USA, 2005), XIV, 3951.

13. Richard Fox Young, *Resistant Hinduism*, De Nobili Research Library, 8 (Vienna: Institute for Indology of the University of Vienna, 1981), 119.
14. Ibid., 27.
15. Ram Mohun Roy, "Reasons for a Hindoo for Rejecting the Doctrines of Christianity," in *The Missionary and the Brahmun: Being a Vindication of the Hindoo Religion against the Attacks of Christian Missionaries* (Calcutta: Brahmunical Magazine, 1821), 187–98; *The English Works of Raja Rammohun Roy* (Allahabad: Panini Office, 1906; reprinted New York: AMS Press, 1978), 143–98.
16. Ibid., 874.
17. Keshub Chunder Sen, *Keshub Chunder Sen*, ed. David C. Scott (Bangalore: Christian Literature Society, 1979), 228.
18. Ibid., 228.
19. Keshub Chunder Sen, *Keshub Chunder Sen in England*, ed. P. Lal (Calcutta: Writers Workshop, 1980; original 1871), 455 ff.
20. Ibid., 459.
21. Upadhyay, *The Writings*, I, 66.
22. Dayananda Sarasvati, *Light of Truth (Satyarth Prakash)*, trans. Chiranjiva Bharadwaja (Allahabad: K. C. Bhalla, 1906), 632.
23. Paramahansa Yogananda, *The Second Coming of Christ: The Resurrection of the Christ within You: A Revelatory Commentary on the Original Teachings of Jesus*, 2 vols. (Los Angeles: Self-Realization Fellowship, 2004), I, 11.
24. Ibid., II, 1594.
25. Ibid., I, 1407.
26. Joseph Mattam, *Land of the Trinity* (Bangalore: TPI, 1975), 162.
27. Robin Boyd, *An Introduction to Indian Christian Theology* (Madras: Christian Literature Society, 1969), 219.
28. Henri Le Saux, *Saccidananda: A Christian Approach to Advaitic Experience* (Delhi: ISPCK, 1974), 191.
29. Elizabeth Trinity, "The Trinity according to Abhishiktananda," *Indian Journal of* Spirituality, 7:3 (1994), 306.
30. Ibid., 309.
31. Henri Le Saux and Jules Monchanin, *A Benedictine Ashram* (Douglas, Isle of Man: Times Press, 1964; original 1951), 77–78.
32. Mattam, *Land of the Trinity*, 169.
33. Paul Hacker, "The Idea of the Person in the Thinking of Vedanta Philosophers," in Wilhelm Halbfass, ed., *Philology and Confrontation: Paul Hacker on Traditional and Modern Vedanta* (Albany: State University of New York Press, 1995), 153–75.

## Further reading

Bailey, G. M., "Traditional Elements in the Mythology of the Hindu Trimurti," *Numen*, 26:2 (1979), 152–63.

Boyd, Robin, *An Introduction to Indian Christian Theology* (Madras: Christian Literature Society, 1969).

Clooney, Francis X., *Fr. Bouchet's India* (Chennai: Satya Nilayam Publications, 2006).

Falcao, Nelson, *Kristapurana* (Anand: Gujarat Sahitya Prakash, 2003).

Gonda, Jan, "The Hindu Trinity," *Anthropos*, 63 (1968), 212–25.

Hacker, Paul, "The Idea of the Person in the Thinking of Vedanta Philosophers," in Wilhelm Halbfass, ed., *Philology and Confrontation: Paul Hacker on Traditional and Modern Vedanta* (Albany, NY: State University of New York Press, 1995), 153–75.

Mattam, Joseph, *Land of the Trinity* (Bangalore: TPI, 1975).

Nobili, Roberto de, *Report on Indian Customs*, in *Preaching Wisdom to the Wise*, ed. and trans. Anand Amaladass and Francis X. Clooney (St. Louis: Institute of Jesuit Sources, 2000; reprinted Chennai: Satya Nilayam Publications, 2005).

Parrinder, Geoffrey, "Triads," in Lindsay Jones, ed., *The Encyclopedia of Religion*, 2nd edn., 15 vols. (Detroit: Macmillan Reference USA, 2005), XIV, 9345–50.

Tsoukalas, Steven, *Krsna and Christ: Body–Divine Relation in the Thought of Sankara, Ramanuja, and Classical Christian Orthodoxy* (Milton Keynes, UK: Paternoster Theological Monographs, 2006).

Young, Richard Fox, *Resistant Hinduism*, De Nobili Research Library, 8 (Vienna: Institute for Indology of the University of Vienna, 1981).

# 19 Primordial Vow: reflections on the Holy Trinity in light of dialogue with Pure Land Buddhism

JAMES L. FREDERICKS

Noriaki Ito is the Rinban (a kind of abbot or pastor) of the Higashi Hongan-ji Betsuin, a century-old Buddhist community in the Little Tokyo neighborhood of Los Angeles. He is a Pure Land Buddhist of the Jodōshinshū sect. Nori has been my friend for many years. He is also my teacher in matters of Buddhist faith, as I am his in matters of Christian faith. We have spent many happy hours sharing our respective faiths and learning from one another important truths. In this chapter, I want to reflect on certain aspects of the doctrine of the Holy Trinity in light of what I have learned from Nori and other Pure Land Buddhists, both in Los Angeles and in Japan. Especially, I want to reflect on the Trinity in light of the Pure Land Buddhist teaching of the "Primordial Vow" (*hongan*), in which the ultimate character of all reality is affirmed as utterly selfless compassion. Nori may be my teacher, but the errors in this chapter, regarding both Buddhism and Christianity, are my own. Therefore I am the one "to be beaten with his own stick," as the Japanese proverb has it. I shall consider this chapter a huge success if these preliminary reflections lead to more Christian thinking about the Trinity in light of the teachings of Buddhism.

## THE "DEFEAT" OF THE TRINITY

In a short but influential essay on the Trinity, Karl Rahner noted that Christians, "despite their orthodox confession of the Trinity," have become, in their practical lives, "almost mere 'monotheists.'" Should the church decide to abandon the doctrine of the Holy Trinity, "the major part of religious literature could well remain virtually unchanged."[1] The core of this pastoral problem, in Rahner's view, lies in the alienation of the doctrine from our witness in faith to the economy of salvation. The connection between what God has done in creating, redeeming, and sanctifying the world (*oikonomia*) and what God is in

God's intra-trinitarian life (*theologia*) has largely been lost. Catherine LaCugna, in her magisterial work on the Trinity, *God for Us*, sees in this separation of *theologia* and *oikonomia* the "defeat" of the doctrine of the Trinity.[2]

The specifically Christian understanding of God lies in the intuition that the eternal God is revealed in the economy of creation, redemption, and sanctification, not metaphysical speculation *per se*. Yet when, early in Christian tradition, the relationship between the Father and the Son (and eventually the Spirit) became an obdurate problem because of Arianism, the Council of Nicaea turned to a Greek metaphysics of substance in order to clarify theological understanding, acknowledging that, in the witness of scripture and the rule of liturgy, the Son is subordinate to the Father, but in the inner life of God, the Son was "of one substance" with the Father. Thus began a long process in which it became possible to think of God *in se* (the immanent Trinity) apart from God-for-us (the economic Trinity). The end result of this process is what Catherine LaCugna sees as "a one-sided theology that had little to do with the economy of Christ and the Spirit, with the themes of incarnation and grace, and therefore little to do with Christian life."[3]

My dialogue with Buddhists has helped me to recognize that a metaphysics of substance (ancient and modern) has contributed in no small way to the defeat of the doctrine. Buddhism offers Christians a tradition of some twenty-five centuries of metaphysical reflection aimed at deconstructing the notion of substance. Moreover, Buddhist metaphysical reflection is deeply rooted in Buddhist religious life and practice. The concern for integrating theory and practice also recommends dialogue with Buddhists to Christians concerned about the defeat of their doctrine of God. This is what I hope to demonstrate in this chapter. Of course, I am not alone among Christian theologians in my dissatisfaction with substance metaphysics. Catherine LaCugna argues that Christian trinitarian faith calls for a "relational ontology," in which relatedness, not substance, is the primary ontological category.[4] I want to show how our dialogue with Buddhists contributes to the development of such an ontology and, thus, how the dialogue helps Christians to address the defeat of the doctrine.

According to Jaroslav Pelikan, the roots of this problem can be seen in the failure of the Cappadocians to give a full speculative treatment of the relation between the one divine substance and the three hypostases. Cappadocian theology was occasioned largely by the need to respond to the neo-Arianism of Eunomius in the late fourth century. The Cappadocians defended Nicaea by claiming that God was three different persons united by a single substance: *mia ousia, treis hypostaseis* (one being, three persons). Never resolved was the relationship between the one divine substance and the three *hypostases*. Sometimes, the Cappadocians held that the *hypostases* were "modes of being" (*tropoi hyparxeōs*) of the one divine substance. In this case, the one substance or "Godhead" (*theotēs*) functions as a Platonic universal (*to koinon*). This line of thinking, however, could suggest a kind of modalism in which the Godhead (the one divine *ousia*) transcended the three *hypostases*. The Cappadocians were quite aware of this problem and took pains to draw attention to the limitations of their language. I would argue that the problem lay in having no alternative to the category "substance" as a way of construing the unity of the three persons. One indication that this is the case is the fact that the Cappadocians also argued that the unity of the three hypostases rested in the *monarchia* of the Father, not the divine substance. The unity of the Trinity is not to be found in a pre-personal substance, but rather in the *hypostasis* of the Father as the one source (*monas archē*) of the Son and Spirit. The subordinationist leanings of this approach must be juxtaposed to the modalist tendency of establishing the unity of the three *hypostases* in one substance of the Godhead.[5]

The inability of the Cappadocians to resolve this problem became a lasting legacy for the entire tradition that contributed to the defeat of the doctrine. In both Latin and Greek theology, the unsuitability of the Greek metaphysics of substance to the demands of trinitarian faith helped to maintain the separation of immanent Trinity from the economy of salvation. We have been left with a theology which is attentive to the demands of philosophical reason, while remaining largely unrelated to the economy of creating, redeeming, and sanctifying.

Are there alternatives to "substance" as the primary ontological category? How might we go about reflecting on the Trinity in light of LaCugna's call for an "ontology of relation"? Here I suggest that we turn to Christianity's ongoing dialogue with Buddhists. I wish to focus attention on a specific teaching of Mahayana Buddhism, the doctrine of the "three bodies of the Buddha" (*Trikāya*) as understood by Noriaki Ito's Japanese denomination, the True Pure Land Sect.

## THE THREE BODIES OF THE BUDDHA

The True Pure Land Sect (Jōdōshinshū) is a form of Mahayana Buddhism whose sole religious practice is "faith" (*shinjin*) in the saving power of Amida Buddha. According to the sacred narrative of Nori's Buddhist community, Amida Buddha vows to save all those who call out his name in faith, breaking the chains of karma that bind them to rebirth into *samsāra* and leading them instead to a final birth in his "Pure Land in the West" where all will reach final enlightenment. The nature of Amida Buddha as an object of devotion and the ways in which Pure Land Buddhists reconcile their practice of faith in Amida with Mahayana Buddhism's non-theistic understanding of ultimate reality are of specific interest to our inquiry into the Holy Trinity. Pure Land Buddhists reconcile theory and practice by means of the *Trikāya* doctrine. In this respect, the place of this teaching within Nori's tradition is similar to that of the doctrine of the Trinity within my own. The doctrine of the Trinity holds together Christian witness to the Father, Son, and Holy Spirit in the economy of salvation with the demands of Jewish monotheism and neo-Platonic metaphysics.

Of course, the *Trikāya* teaching is based on Mahayana Buddhist presuppositions. Therefore, before looking at the *Trikāya* doctrine itself, I will need to mention teachings basic to early Buddhism and their subsequent elaboration in Mahayana Buddhism.

**Early Buddhist teachings**

Buddhism in all its forms aims at attaining freedom (*nirvāna*) from the suffering (*duhkha*) that arises from attachments to things that are in fact fleeting and insubstantial. We cling to things (our health and wealth, our national sovereignty and military might, our prestige and social standing) as if they were permanent and enduring, when in fact they are ephemeral and transient. Since there is nothing at all that is eternal, attachment in all its forms produces suffering. The interface of our multiple attachments serves to create a deep-seated illusion: the "false view" that we are an eternal, enduring self (*ātman*), when in fact, no enduring self is to be found (*anātman*). The doctrine of no-self is related to the early Buddhist metaphysics of causality, "dependent co-arising" (*pratītya samutpāda*). Nothing at all exists as its own cause; rather, all things cause all other things to exist. Thus, everything is contingent and there is nothing that is self-subsistent (*swabhāva*). Everything arises, endures for a time, and then ceases, depending on conditions. This means that to live in what the Lotus Sutra calls "this burning house" in terms of attachment leads inevitably to suffering. This is because nothing endures. The doctrine of dependent co-arising also means that complete liberation from suffering is possible by following the path of non-attachment. In keeping with the law of causality, Buddhists teach that all things are "empty" (*śūnya*) and without substance. This claim is not to be taken in a negative and certainly not in a nihilistic way.

The emptiness (*śūnyatā*) of all phenomena does not mean that things are not real, only that they are caused, conditioned, and thus impermanent. An unenlightened person has a "false view" of things, looking on them as enduring substances to which one might cling for refuge from suffering. The enlightened person sees the emptiness of all things and does not cling. Therefore liberation (*nirvāna*), properly understood, is not an escape from this world of suffering (*samsāra*) into a transcendent world beyond. Rather it is to see all things as they really are, no longer objectified by attachments to illusory substances.

### Mahayana Buddhism

Around the time of Christ, the Mahayana movement in India (spreading later into East Asia) promoted the rise of a new spiritual and ethical ideal for Buddhism: the bodhisattva. Before this time, the goal of Buddhist practice was to cultivate non-attachment to the world in the quest for *nirvāna*. Bodhisattva practice holds up a radical understanding of non-attachment. The goal of practice is to cultivate non-attachment not only to *samsāra*, but to *nirvāna* as well. Non-attachment to *nirvāna* takes the form of the bodhisattva's vow to renounce final liberation from suffering and to abide within *samsāra* in order to act for the benefit of all sentient beings. Therefore, if the cultivation of wisdom (*prajñā*) leads one to practice non-attachment to *samsāra* in the pursuit of *nirvāna*, then the bodhisattva's perfection of wisdom (*prajñā pāramitā*) requires the cultivation of non-attachment even to *nirvāna*. In this way, the bodhisattva realizes not only the emptiness of *samsāra*, but the emptiness of *nirvāna* as well. *Nirvāna*, to the extent that the mind-of-ignorance constructs *nirvāna* as an object of attachment that stands in opposition to *samsāra*, is an illusion thoroughly without substance. Attachment to this objectified *nirvāna* leads to suffering. Thus, in the perfection of wisdom, the bodhisattva realizes the truth that *nirvāna* is not an eternal realm that transcends *samsāra* into which one escapes. But somewhat paradoxically, in realizing this truth, the bodhisattva is enlightened by having overcome all attachments. Mahayana Buddhists refer to this practice as entering the "gate of non-duality" (*funimon*). Thus the bodhisattva confronts us with a truth that is both paradoxical and profoundly ethical: enlightenment means renouncing our attachment to *nirvāna*, at least to the extent that *nirvāna* is constructed as enlightenment for one's own benefit.

The metaphysical structure of the bodhisattva's insight into the non-duality of *nirvāna* and *samsāra* is captured in the famous words of the Heart Sutra: "form is emptiness; emptiness is form." The many forms which arise within the world of objectified attachment (*samsāra*) are in fact utterly empty of all enduring substance. There is nothing at all that is self-subsistent. The renunciation of attachment to *samsāra*, therefore, is wisdom. But the temptation to make the emptiness of all things into an ultimate metaphysical substance, the ground of reality, must also be renounced if the wisdom of non-attachment is to be perfected. Therefore emptiness is nothing other than form and has no existence apart from the world of forms. Ethically, the bodhisattva's realization of the emptiness of everything, even *nirvāna*, takes the form of wisdom-compassion (*jibi*). When even attachment to one's own liberation is overcome, the bodhisattva is purified of even the faintest tincture of egocentricity. Thus in this perfection of wisdom lies the perfection of compassion.

### The doctrine of the three bodies

From the beginnings of the Buddhist movement, the status of Siddhartha Gautama during his earthly life and after has been a subject of debate among Buddhists. Is the Buddha merely the greatest of all teachers? A human being who discovered the way of liberation and nothing more? Or, in becoming enlightened, has the Buddha become a kind of deity? These questions were given urgency by the fact that the Buddha quickly became an object of devotion for both monks and laity. Mahayana Buddhists embraced these devotional practices and thus, more than other Buddhist groups, needed a theology of Buddhahood to explain how "faith" in the Buddha was compatible with the practice of non-attachment. Herein lies the origin of the doctrine of the "three bodies of the Buddha" (*Trikāya*). I wish to present the basics of this teaching from the perspective of the Pure Land School of Mahayana Buddhism.[6]

According to this teaching, Buddhahood is present in three different "bodies." The first is the *Dharmakāya*, the body (*kāya*) of ultimate reality (dharma). *Dharmakāya* is the ultimate emptiness of all things beyond the illusion of self-subsistent substances. Since the dharma-body is completely formless, "body" is predicated of the Buddha as ultimate reality only in a highly metaphoric sense. The *Dharmakāya* is a body, but not a form that can be perceived as existing within the world. As such, the dharma-body is inconceivable, unimaginable, and unknowable. Since it is the emptiness of all things, the *Dharmakāya* must be associated with the dependent co-arising of phenomena. In this regard, Japanese Buddhists speak of *Dharmakāya* as the "unhindered interpenetration of all things" (*jiji muge*) by means of which all things arise according to the principle of dependent co-arising. Finally, *Dharmakāya* is the purest realization of wisdom-compassion (*jibi*). To "see" the dharma-body of the Buddha is to "see" the emptiness of all things. This is wisdom. Likewise, to "see" the *Dharmakāya* is to have renounced all attachment to illusory selfhood in realizing a radical selflessness in which there are no longer any hindrances (*muge*) between "self and other" (*jiji*).

The second of the three bodies of the Buddha is the *Nirmānakāya*, the "appearance body" of the Buddha. This is the body of Siddhartha Gautama and other Buddhas who have appeared within space and time. According to an early Buddhist scripture, the historical Buddha once said, "Those who see me, see the Dharma; those who see the Dharma, see me." *Nirmānakāya* is the sensible form of the formless *Dharmakāya* within time and space, an intra-mundane appearance of the dharma-body of the Buddha. The *Dharmakāya* takes form within time and space for the benefit of sentient beings who need to be taught the dharma.

The third body of the Buddha is the *Sambhogakāya* or "bliss-body." Mahayana Buddhists embraced devotions to multiple "savior Buddhas," who have been liberated from the illusions of *samsāra* and become the *Dharmakāya* by awakening to the emptiness of all things. Perhaps the best-known of these savior Buddhas is Guan-yin, the one who "hears the cry of suffering arising from the earth" and responds with an outpouring of compassion. The religious practice of Pure Land Buddhists is focused exclusively on Amida Buddha in his Pure Land. Like Guan-yin, Amida is an example of a *Sambhogakāya*. Like the *Nirmānakāya*, the bliss-body is an embodiment of the *Dharmakāya*, a perceptible form capable of interacting with sentient beings, but not a physical body appearing within time and space. The *Sambhogakāya* is celestial.

I wish to make several observations about the *Trikāya* teaching. First, Buddhists teach that the *Nirmānakāya* and *Sambhogakāya* are the "skillful means" (*hōben*) employed by the *Dharmakāya* to meet the needs and limitations of sentient beings. *Dharmakāya*'s freedom from substance (egocentricity) means that it is pure compassion – meaning that egocentricity has been fully overcome. For this same reason, the *Dharmakāya* is able to be infinitely "skillful" in the means it employs to connect with sentient beings that are blinded by their own attachments. Thus the *Trikāya* theory provides for a kind of "high Christology" in regard to the historical Buddha. Siddhartha Gautama was a historical form skillfully assumed by the *Dharmakāya* so that the dharma could be preached in a way accessible to ignorant human beings. The *Nirmānakāya* is the skillful means of the infinitely compassionate *Dharmakāya*. Similarly, the Bodhisattva Guan-yin (an example of *Sambhogakāya*) is a celestial form assumed by the *Dharmakāya* with infinite skill in order to accommodate itself to the needs of sentient beings. Like wisdom-compassion, the notion of *Dharmakāya* as skillful means is also governed by the Mahayana logic of the perfection of wisdom and the spiritual practice of the bodhisattva. As perfect non-attachment, the *Dharmakāya* does not cling even to its liberation from form (*samsāra*), but renounces its formlessness (*nirvāna*) in order to take on form for our benefit. The *Dharmakāya* does this with skillful means because it is free of the illusion of being a self-subsistent substance.

Second, the *Dharmakāya* is not only the formless "embodiment" of the emptiness of all things. The *Dharmakāya* itself is empty of substance. Here again, the logic of the perfection of wisdom and the spiritual dynamics of the bodhisattva can be seen. "Form is emptiness," according to the Heart Sutra. But emptiness is nothing other than form and must not be hypostasized into a substance that forms an eternal, unchanging ground out of which appearances arise. The *Dharmakāya* is emptiness only in a highly dialectical way – the emptiness of emptiness itself. This means that the *Dharmakāya* brings with it a significant contrast with certain prominent elements within the Greek tradition of metaphysical thinking. For example, the *Dharmakāya* cannot be equated with Aristotle's *hypokeimenon*. It is not a "substratum" that provides a metaphysical ground for the world of appearances. The Dharma-body is not an *archē*, at least if this be understood as origin or source. Neither is the *Dharmakāya* the one (*monas*) from which the many emanate as in Plotinus, for the dharma-body is not the "emitter" (*proboleus*) from which the world of appearances emanates.

Third, Pure Land Buddhists interpret the *Dharmakāya* in conjunction with the sacred narrative of Amida Buddha and his vow to save all sentient beings. In Pure Land Buddhism, therefore, the *Dharmakāya* is recognized as the "Primordial Vow" (*hongan*). This is a significant element in the Pure Land school's appropriation of the *Trikāya* teaching as a way to reconcile theory (emptiness and non-attachment) with practice (faith in Amida's vow to save). In the complete emptiness of the *Dharmakāya*, wisdom is continuously perfected by taking on form, namely, the skillful, compassionate means of Amida who vows to save all sentient beings who entrust themselves in faith. Thus, in Pure Land teaching, the ultimate reality of all things is "Vow." The sacred narrative of Amida and his vow is but a skillful means employed by the *Dharmakāya* as it takes form in order to become accessible to sentient beings. As the skillful means of the *Dharmakāya*, Amida's vow is the form of the formless "Vow" which is the ultimate reality. In their dialogue with Pure Land Buddhists, therefore, Christians come face to face with a metaphysically articulated religious affirmation that ultimate reality is not indifferent to the suffering of sentient beings. The *Dharmakāya* is "for us" in every respect because it is entirely emptying itself in order to take on form.

Therefore, Christians should look upon the *Trikāya* teaching as a "theology." This is my fourth point. Christians should look on this teaching as a Buddhist example of "faith seeking understanding." The Mahayana community needs to reconcile its religious practice (faith in savior Buddhas like Amida and Guan-yin) with its religious theory (non-theism, non-attachment, emptiness). In the case of the Pure Land community within the Mahayana movement, the work of theology is accomplished in two movements. First, for Pure Land Buddhists like Nori, the *Trikāya* teaching is a *lex credendi*. Faith in Amida Buddha must comply with the demands of Mahayana teachings regarding emptiness and non-attachment. Pure Land faith, therefore, cannot fashion an eternal, transcendent deity out of Amida. As *Sambhogakāya*, Amida is nothing more than the skillful means of the *Dharmakāya*. Faith in Amida's vow, therefore, is not attachment to the illusion of a transcendent deity, but rather the legitimate Buddhist practice of self-surrender to the ultimate emptiness of all things working as compassion. In this sense, Pure Land faith is an "awakening" (*kaku*): the realization of our own selflessness. Doctrine regulates religious practice. The appropriation of the *Trikāya* teaching by Pure Land Buddhists, however, is also a *lex orandi*. The Mahayana teachings of emptiness and non-attachment must be understood in a way that supports the Pure Land practice of faith as trusting in the Primordial Vow (*shinjin*).

## THE WORK OF COMPARISON

As a theology analogous to the doctrine of the Holy Trinity, the *Trikāya* doctrine responds to the need of the Buddhist community to reconcile theory and practice. I selected this doctrine for consideration precisely because it constitutes a *quaerens*. How does this Buddhist vision of the embodiment of wisdom-compassion assist Christians in thinking in new ways about their Christian faith? To answer this question, I recommend that the soteriological preoccupations of the "theology of religions" be put aside. Instead, I propose that Christians enter into a kind of solidarity with Buddhists in which the mutual recognition of similarity and difference becomes the basis of a shared quest for theological understanding. The nature of the *Trikāya* teaching as a Buddhist *quaerens* recommends it as an entry point for this kind of dialogue. Noriaki Ito, my Buddhist friend, is helping me to think in new ways about the Holy Trinity. An initial step toward establishing solidarity with Buddhists would be for Christians to receive the *Trikāya* teaching as a gift.

What would it mean for Christians to think of God not as substance, but as emptiness as in the Mahayana Buddhist tradition? Of course, I do not mean "emptiness" in the atheistic or nihilistic sense that this word has come to retain in the modern West. In the *Trikāya* teaching, the *Dharmakāya* can be recognized as empty only "for the benefit of sentient beings," not in any nihilistic sense. Reconfiguring our understanding of God with a metaphysics of emptiness would have to pass this same test. Neither do I mean to suggest that only our knowledge of God is empty. The notion that the soul's *itinerarium ad Deum* is propelled by abandoning every understanding of God as preliminary has a long history in Christian tradition. My dialogues with Nori, however, have required me to go far beyond the *via negativa* of apophatic theology. Instead, I mean that divinity itself (*theotēs*) is empty of substance. Only if the *theotēs* is empty of substance can the God of Christian faith be the perfection of self-communicating love. In effect, I want to imagine the Trinity as "Primordial Vow," Nori's metaphor for the ultimate meaning of reality as compassion.

Associating divinity with emptiness is hardly unknown to Christian faith. Even before Paul wrote his letter to the church at Philippi, Christians were singing of the kenosis of the Son: "though he was in the form of God, he did not regard equality with God something to be grasped. Rather, he emptied himself, taking the form of a slave" (Phil 2:6–7). For one of my Buddhist teachers, Masao Abe, this is "one of the most impressive and touching passages in the Bible."[7] In the incarnation of the Word, the Son empties himself in an act of non-attachment to "God." In this self-emptying, God becomes God-for-us by taking form – the "form of a slave." I think, however, that the dialogue with Buddhism invites us to a more radical understanding of the divine kenosis. The dynamics of self-emptying love cannot be restricted to the hypostasis of the Son. If God is the perfection of love, divinity itself must be kenotically self-communicating. Karl Rahner seems aware of this issue when, in his discussion of the incarnation, he alludes to the "self-emptying of God," not merely the *hypostasis* of the Son, as "the primary phenomenon given by faith."[8] Pure Land Buddhists like Nori affirm the ultimate benevolence of reality by recognizing the emptiness of the *Dharmakāya* as it continuously takes form for our benefit. Only as such can the *Dharmakāya* be affirmed as Vow. So also in receiving the *Trikāya* teaching as a gift, let Christians affirm the ultimate benevolence of reality by witnessing to the complete self-emptying of the Godhead into an economy of salvation. This means that, before affirming God as "sovereign Lord" (as with Barth) or as "Absolute Mystery" (as with Rahner), Christians must affirm God as self-communicating love, emptied out into the world of suffering for our benefit. Before all else, the transcendent Godhead continuously renounces all attachment to un-dialectical transcendence by taking on form in an economy of salvation.

Taking this approach brings with it several implications for our understanding of the Trinity. First, receiving the *Trikāya* teaching as a gift would mean that the three divine *hypostases* can be construed as "form" in contrast to the formless Godhead. The lyrics of the *Carmen Christi* (Phil 2:6–11), of course, speak of the Son as the "form of God." I want to extend this interpretation to the Father and the Spirit as well. All three divine *hypostases*, in their particularity (*idiotēs*), constitute the form of the formless Godhead. Divinity has taken form as Jesus' Abba, as the incarnate Messiah, and as the fiery Paraclete. Moreover, the three divine *hypostases* – the unbegotten Father, the only-begotten Son, and the Spirit that proceeds – are forms into which the formless Godhead empties itself out of love. This also means that the three bodies of the Buddha, *Dharmakāya*, *Sambhogakāya*, and *Nirmānakāya*, do not correspond to the three *hypostases*, the Father, Son, and Holy Spirit. Rather, the relationship between *Dharmakāya* and the other two bodies offers a model for understanding the relationship between the Godhead and the three *hypostases*.

Of course, as form, the three divine persons are not three individual substances. Form is emptiness, not substance. The three divine persons are continuously realizing themselves as persons by emptying themselves into one another in a *perichōrēsis* of "unhindered interpenetration," analogous to the Buddhist principle of *jiji muge*.[9] This Buddhist way of imagining the divine *perichōrēsis* closely tracks the intuition of the Cappadocians, who violated the canons of the Council of Nicaea by distinguishing *hypostasis* from *ousia*. A *hypostasis* could not be a substance, for this would lead Christian faith into tritheism. A *hypostasis* is a person, not a substance. And a "person," according to Nori, is a form that is emptied of substance. The *hypostases* are persons because they are emptying themselves of aseity in a *perichōrēsis* of forms.

Second, as form of the formless, the *Trikāya* doctrine helps us to recognize that the three divine persons are the "skillful means" of the Godhead, which is completely "God-for-us." The *Dharmakāya* is constantly empyting itself into form (*Sambhogakāya* and *Nirmānakāya*) that is adapted to the needs and limitations of sentient beings. Otherwise, it would not be pure wisdom-compassion. So also, the formless *theotēs* continuously empties itself into form (Father, Son, and Holy Spirit). And this is accomplished with what Nori calls "skill" – there is nothing about the Godhead that is not "God-for-us." As the *Dharmakāya* is the perfection of wisdom-compassion only if it is completely emptied out into a form accessible to sentient beings, so also the God of Christian faith can be recognized as the perfection of love only if the formless Godhead is completely revealed as Emmanuel, that is, as a form accessible to human beings.

This leads to a third implication. The immanent Trinity is completely revealed to us. Quite as much as the economic Trinity, the immanent Trinity is the form of the formless Godhead. The notion of the immanent Trinity as a *deus absconditus* in contrast to the economic Trinity as a *deus revelatus* can no longer be held. In other words, the "immanent Trinity," and not only the economic Trinity, is the "skillful means" employed by the Godhead for our salvation. Formless divinity not only takes on the form of the historical Jesus for our benefit. The Godhead is constantly renouncing aseity by taking form as Father, Son and Holy Spirit. How, then, can Christians continue to speak about the immanent Trinity apart from the economic Trinity? Perhaps one course of action would be to abandon the distinction and say that there is no immanent Trinity, if "immanent" should mean that there is a part of God that has not been emptied into revealed form. To claim such would mean that there is an aspect of God that is eternally withdrawn into itself and therefore not for our benefit. This leads to a blasphemy, namely the conclusion that it is *God* that has "fallen" from full personhood into what Kierkegaard called "shut-up-ness" and what Augustine called *curvatus in se*, which are analogous to what Nori calls the "false view of self-existence." This conclusion would imply that there is a depth within God which is eternally denied to the creature by retaining for itself an un-dialectical transcendence of un-emptied, unrelated, unrevealed formlessness (from a Buddhist perspective) or substance (from a Greek perspective). The *Trikāya* doctrine allows us to revisit Rahner's famous claim that the immanent Trinity can be nothing other than the economic Trinity.

This leads to a fourth implication, an issue that was not fully explored by Rahner. If there is no difference between the immanent and the economic Trinities, should we continue to speak of the intra-trinitarian relations and their economy of creating, redeeming, and sanctifying as two different things? The *perichōrēsis* of the persons and their *oikonomia* must in fact be the same activity, namely the skillful means of the Godhead emptying itself into form for the benefit of all. This is because there is but one divine "working" in which the formless takes on form. "Working" is my translation of what Nori calls *hataraki*. My intuition is that this term, at least in the technical sense employed by my friend, helps to illuminate what Christian theology refers to as *oikonomia*. The one skillful "working" of the Godhead overcomes the duality of immanent and economic by subsuming the immanent Trinity into the economic. The formless Godhead continuously realizes itself as love by taking on form in one, seamless, *hataraki*. In this one "working," the traditional distinction between the intra-divine *perichōrēsis* of the three hypostases and their *oikonomia* of creating, redeeming, and sanctifying no longer holds. The living God of Christian faith is not the immanent Trinity first and the economic Trinity only subsequently. The one divine Mystery continuously takes hypostatic form in a *perichōrēsis* which is simultaneously the *oikonomia* and has no meaning apart from this *oikonomia*. The one "working" of the Godhead is to empty itself into form – Father, Son, and Holy Spirit who create, redeem, and sanctify – for our benefit. The *perichōrēsis* of the "immanent Trinity," quite as much as the *oikonomia* of the economic Trinity, is God-for-us.

Fifth, receiving the *Trikāya* teaching as a gift also suggests new ways to think about the very old problem that modalism presents to Christian tradition. What William Hill calls the "neo-modal Trinitarianism"[10] of Barth and Rahner can be traced back to the inability of the Cappadocians to work out a full speculative solution to the problem of the unity of the three divine persons. As mentioned above, Catherine LaCugna argued that the root of their failure lay in their lack of an "ontology of relation" which would have provided an alternative to the Greek metaphysics of substance. The Cappadocians embraced personhood (the *treis hypostaseis*) as a relational category, but could not extricate themselves from the notion of substance (the *mia ousia*). As noted above, sometimes they reluctantly argued that the one divine substance functioned like a kind of Platonic universal, in which the three *hypostases* were "modes" (*tropoi*) of a *theotēs* which somehow is not a pre-personal ground of the *perichōrēsis*.

The logic of the *Trikāya* teaching suggests another approach. Pure Land Buddhists teach that the *Dharmakāya* is the emptiness of all phenomena, but not "emptiness itself" taken as a substance that transcends appearances. The *Dharmakāya* has no existence apart from the unhindered interrelatedness of all things (*jiji muge*). Analogously, Christians can say that the *theotēs* has no existence apart from the perfectly unhindered *perichōrēsis* of the three *hypostases* as they empty themselves into one another. The Godhead, in other words, is not a pre-personal substance that is ontologically prior to the *perichōrēsis* of the three *hypostases*. There is no *divinitas* apart from the kenotic *perichōrēsis* of the three *hypostases*. Neither is there a Godhead that functions as a metaphysical substratum (*hypokeimenon*) for the three *hypostases*. The Buddhist ontology of relation allows us to confirm what the Cappadocians intuited and struggled to explain: the Godhead is not a neo-Platonic *monas* from which the three *hypostases* have emanated. Therefore Christians, in resisting modalism, should not look on the Godhead as the substantial "source" (*pēgēs*), "cause" (*aitia*), or "principle" (*archē*) of the three divine persons. Within the divine *perichōrēsis*, causality is mutual: the three *hypostases* arise in accordance with the principle of dependent co-arising. There is no eternal substance that is ontologically prior to them. Therefore the *theotēs* need not be construed as a Platonic universal. But then neither is the Godhead the one sovereign subject, which is the root of Barth's and Rahner's neo-modal trinitarianism. As in the *Trikāya* teaching, the formless Godhead has no existence apart from its actual instantiation in form. And yet the Godhead is a "body" in the highly metaphoric sense with which Pure Land Buddhists use this word in regard to the formless *Dharmakāya*. The Godhead is real; in fact, it is the one ultimate reality. But its ultimacy lies in what Mahayana Buddhists see as the perfection of wisdom (*prajñā pāramitā*): the Godhead is the emptiness of the three *hypostases*, but not "emptiness itself." The Godhead realizes its divinity by eternally renouncing all attachment to self-subsistence by taking form as the three hypostases. Therefore, the *hypostases* are not "modes" of a pre-personal divine substance. Form is emptiness, and emptiness is nothing other than form.

Sixth, I also want to offer a brief reflection on the considerably more difficult problem of the monarchy of the Father. This issue is more complicated for several reasons, including the fact that it brings us to the traditional affirmation of the Father as unbegotten and that it figures within the dialogue between the Western and Orthodox churches. In attempting to work out the relationship between the three *hypostases* and the one divine substance, the Cappadocians not only appealed to a

Godhead that, somehow, does not transcend the divine *perichōrēsis* as a pre-personal substance. The Cappadocians also taught that the *hypostasis* of the Father is the one source (*monas archē*) of the Trinity. Thus the unity of the three *hypostases* is to be found in the *monarchia* of the Father. Gregory of Nazianzus, for example, wrote that "The three have one nature . . . the ground of unity being the Father, out of whom and toward whom the subsequent persons are reckoned."[11] Basil held that "the Father is the one who has given the beginning of being (*archē tou einai*) to the others . . . the Son is the one who has had the beginning of his being (*archē tou enai*) by birth from the other."[12]

John Zizioulas has mounted an impressive defense of this principle. The monarchy of the Father, he argues, is necessary in order to insure that the trinitarian life of God remains a matter of personal will and freedom and does not decay into a mere metaphysical necessity. Against modalism, in its various forms, Zizioulas insists that the Trinity is not derived as an emanation from an impersonal substance that is ontologically prior to it.[13] Instead, the cause of the other two *hypostases* is the personhood of the Father. The Father wills that there be an other (the Son and then the Holy Spirit). Citing Gregory of Nazianzus, Zizioulas is quick to note that this causation is "out of time"[14] and therefore cannot be understood in a way that might suggest subordinationism. The Father, in other words, is not the efficient cause of the Son and the Holy Spirit, but rather their eternal *archē*. Therefore, among the *hypostases*, causality is about the relatedness of persons (the personal will of the unbegotten leading to the begotten and spirated), not efficiency. The Trinity, therefore, is the result of the personal freedom of the Father, not of metaphysical necessity in which the three persons emanate from a pre-personal Godhead.

I do not see how the Buddhist-inspired trinitarian theology being developed in this chapter can be reconciled with the view that the *archē* of God must be identified with only one of the three *hypostases*. The notion that the Father is the cause of the Trinity in a way that is not true of the Son and Holy Spirit would seem to stand in stark contrast with the Buddhist principle of dependent co-arising (*pratītya samutpāda*) in which causality is mutual, all things being the cause of all things. In fact, Zizioulas would almost seem to have Buddhism in mind when he writes that the three persons do not "co-emerge and co-exist simultaneously and automatically."[15] In contrast to the Buddhist notion of mutual causality, the Son and the Holy Spirit take their eternal origin from the Father by means of what Zizioulas calls an "ontological derivation."[16] Any interpretation that would replace the personal agency of the Father with an "ontological co-emergence" or "co-inherence" in which "the one God is not the Father" but rather "the unity of Father, Son and Spirit in their co-inherence or interrelatedness" must be ruled out.[17] I can only presume that this would include the understanding of the trinitarian relations I have sketched with the help of the Buddhist ontology of relation. On the other hand, if the three divine persons are mutually caused in keeping with the principle of dependent co-arising, we cannot single out one of the three as *monas archē*. The monarchy of the Father, hardly a marginal aspect of Christian tradition, stands in sharp contrast with teachings that go to the core of Buddhist faith.

In light of what seems to be insurmountable difference, let me say that the purpose of interreligious dialogue is not to arrive at consensus on doctrinal matters. Noting similarity is helpful, especially in the initial stages of dialogue. The appreciation of difference, however, can be a sign that the dialogue is deepening. Sometimes the recognition of difference has the salutary effect of helping dialogue partners to honor the specificity of each religious tradition. The Buddhist religious vision cannot be reduced to a paler shade of Christianity's coat of many colors. The differences that distinguish Buddhist and Christian teachings are not merely apparent. Buddhism and Christianity are not alternative interpretations of the same "religious experience." Resisting the temptation to marginalize difference sometimes has the salutary effect of allowing Christians to recognize unresolved tensions within their own tradition. In the case at hand, the clash between the Buddhist ontology of relation and the monarchy of the Father reveals an *aporia* within Christian trinitarian theology itself. If Christians reject the notion that the divine persons "co-emerge and co-exist simultaneously and automatically," as Zizioulas insists they must, and embrace the notion of the Father's *monarchia*, then I must ask, what does it mean to teach that the Father is "unbegotten" (*agennētos*)? Does this traditional affirmation not imply that the Father is self-subsistent in a way that requires that the Father be ontologically distinguished from the Son and the Holy Spirit? Does it mean that the Father exists first and then is related to the Son and Holy Spirit only subsequently or externally? Does the unbegotten-ness (*agennēsia*) of the Father not require us to recognize that the Son and Holy Spirit are derivative, as would seem to be implied in Zizioulas' phrase "ontological derivation"[18]? How can the *archē* of the Father not be hierarchical, and thus subordinationist, even if the begetting and spirating take place "outside of time" as Zizioulas holds? These questions indicate that the doctrine of the Father's monarchy poses problems not only for my experiment with the *Trikāya* teaching;

they indicate that there are basic, unresolved questions within Christian theology itself.

For the present, let me only testify to my experience that difference, not only similarity, provides a basis for the solidarity with Buddhists. In a preliminary way, this can be seen in the very fact that the dialogue has served to allow Christians to recognize that an ancient teaching (the unbegotten-ness of the Father) is in fact part of an unresolved tension within Christian tradition which can be traced back to the inability of the Cappadocians to resolve the problem of the unity of the three divine persons with a metaphysics of substance. The solidarity I seek with Buddhists, however, is more extensive than this preliminary recognition. In the future, I hope to reflect on the problem of the unbegotten-ness of the Father by joining together with my Buddhist friends in asking a question that is basic to both Buddhism and Christianity. What is a person? And how does the meaning of personhood shape our understanding of the Trinity? This leads to my last reflection.

The meaning of personhood has been crucial for Christian reflection on the Trinity ever since the Cappadocians first appealed to this concept as an alternative to *ousia* in understanding the three *hypostases*. Personhood, however, is not a traditional category for Buddhists. Instead, the Buddhist tradition has focused on the overcoming of the illusion of a substantial self (*ātman*). As one would expect of a Pure Land Buddhist, Nori is not comfortable with speculation about a "true self" or a "higher self." I know this to be the case because I have begun to share my thoughts with him about what I am calling "original personhood." As I imagine it, original personhood is what is obscured by the illusion of a substantial self. It is "original" in the sense that Christians speak of the pre-lapsarian personhood of Adam with the term "original innocence." Original personhood, therefore, is what human beings have in common with the divine persons: *originally*, to be a person is to be the *imago Dei*.

This is a rather Buddhist way of talking to Nori about the admittedly un-Buddhist category of personhood. Zen Buddhists, for example, like to talk about our "original face" (*honrai no menboku*). Even so, Nori is much more comfortable talking about the Pure Land practice of "faith" (*shinjin*) than about personhood. *Shinjin* means entrusting oneself to the compassionate working of the Primordial Vow. The Chinese ideographs combine "entrusting" with the character for "mind" or "heart." *Shinjin* arises when the illusion of selfhood and all its ego-generated "calculating" (*hakarai*) is abandoned and the mind of illusion is entrusted to the compassionate mind of Amida. Therefore, Pure Land "faith" is the wisdom-compassion of the *Dharmakāya* renouncing its formlessness and taking form as a human person.

In the future, I want to ask Nori to reflect with me about faith as a "form" that arises within *samsāra*. How is *shinjin* as "form of the formless" to be differentiated from what Pure Land Buddhists and Christians agree is an illusory, sinful self? I am confident that Nori's reflections on this matter will be another gift to me as I reflect on the notion of our original personhood that is the image and likeness of divine personhood. I have a gift to give to Nori as well. I want to tell him the story of Moses and his encounter with God at the foot of Mount Sinai (Ex 3). When Moses expressed his fear of returning to Egypt to face Pharaoh, God responded to his human frailty with a vow: "I shall be with you." In my view, this vow to Moses is the real meaning of the name of God given two verses later. At least this is what I will tell Nori. I will be very pleased if, in some small way, this little gift is of some benefit to my Buddhist friend.

## Notes

1. Karl Rahner, *The Trinity*, trans. Joseph Donceel, introduction, index, and glossary by Catherine LaCugna (New York: Crossroad, 1997; original 1969), 10–11.
2. Catherine Mowry LaCugna, *God for Us: The Trinity and Christian Life* (San Francisco: Harper-San Francisco, 1991), 8 and *passim*.
3. Ibid., 210.
4. Ibid., 246–47.
5. Jaroslav Pelikan, *The Emergence of the Catholic Tradition (100–600)* (Chicago: University of Chicago Press, 1971), 220–23.
6. For the best comprehensive overview of the *Trikāya* teaching from a Pure Land perspective, see Dennis Hirota and Yoshifumi Ueda, *Shinran: An Introduction to his Thought* (Kyoto: Hongwanji International Center, 1989), 108–22.
7. See Masao Abe's essay "Kenotic God and Dynamic Sunyata," in Masao Abe and Christopher Ives, eds., *The Emptying God: A Buddhist–Jewish–Christian Conversation* (Maryknoll, NY: Orbis, 1990), 9.
8. Karl Rahner, *Foundations of Christian Faith: An Introduction to the Idea of Christianity*, trans. William V. Dych (New York: Seabury, 1978), 222.
9. Pan-Chiu Lai, "The Doctrines of Trinity and Christology and Hua-yen Buddhism," *Ching Feng*, 5:2 (2004), 203–25.
10. William J. Hill, *The Three-Personed God: The Trinity as Mystery of Salvation* (Washington, DC: Catholic University of America Press, 1982), 111–47.

11. Gregory of Nazianzus, *Orations* 42:15, cited in John Zizioulas, *Communion and Otherness: Further Studies in Personhood and the Church*, ed. Paul McPartlan (London: T. & T. Clark, 2006), 118.
12. Basil, *C. Eun.* 2:22, cited in Zizioulas, *Communion and Otherness*, 132.
13. Zizioulas, *Communion and Otherness*, 133.
14. Gregory of Nazianzus, *Orations* 42:15, cited in Zizioulas, *Communion and Otherness*, 119; ibid., 120.
15. Zizioulas, *Communion and Otherness*, 135.
16. Ibid., 134–35.
17. Here, Zizioulas cites A. J. Torrance's *Persons in Communion: An Essay on Trinitarian Description and Human Participation* (Edinburgh: T. & T. Clark, 1996), 293 ff.
18. Zizioulas, *Communion and Otherness*, 134–35.

## Further reading


Abe, Masao, and Christopher Ives, eds., *The Emptying God: A Buddhist–Jewish–Christian Conversation* (Maryknoll, NY: Orbis, 1990). See especially Abe's seminal essay, "Kenotic God and Dynamic Sunyata," 3–65.

Clooney, Francis X., *Seeing through Texts: Doing Theology among the Srivaisnavas of South India* (Albany, NY: State University of New York Press, 1996).

Cook, Francis, *Hua-yen Buddhism: The Jewel Net of Indra* (University Park, PA: Pennsylvania State University Press, 1977).

Fredericks, James L., *Buddhists and Christians: Through Comparative Theology to Solidarity* (Maryknoll, NY: Orbis, 2004).

*Faith among Faiths: Christian Theology and the Non-Christian Religions* (Mahwah, NJ: Paulist, 1999).

Habito, Ruben, "The Trikaya Doctrine in Buddhism," *Buddhist–Christian Studies*, 6 (1986), 52–62.

Hirota, Dennis, and Yoshifumi Ueda, *Shinran: An Introduction to his Thought* (Kyoto: Hongwanji International Center, 1989).

Lai, Pan-Chiu, "The Doctrines of Trinity and Christology and Hua-yen Buddhism," *Ching Feng*, 5:2 (2004), 203–25.

Lopez, Donald, *Elaborations on Emptiness: Uses of the Heart Sutra* (Princeton University Press, 1996).

Rahula, Walpola, *What the Buddha Taught* (New York: Grove, 1974).

Williams, Paul, *Mahayana Buddhism: The Doctrinal Foundations* (New York: Routledge, 1989).

# 20 Trinity in Judaism and Islam

DAVID B. BURRELL

> For the soul, home is where prayer is, and a soul without prayer is a soul without a home.
>
> Abraham Joshua Heschel

> Like living stones let yourselves be built on Christ as a spiritual house in the Spirit.
>
> 1 Peter 2:5

> Faith in divine unity [*tawhîd*] brings about insight [while] the state of trust in divine providence [*tawakkul*] will only be perfected by confidence in the trustworthy One.
>
> Abu Hamîd al-Ghazâli

Comparative theology is a fledgling discipline, taking its cue from *Nostra aetate*, its impetus from Karl Rahner's celebrated "world church" essay of 1979, and its form from recent practitioners like Frank Clooney. As a result, those who have been formed in traditional theology curricula, most of which bear the stamp of some form of "Christendom," tend to see exercises in comparative theology as addenda to the "real thing," a modish appendix to proper theology. The aim of this chapter is not so much to bring such critics up to date as to remind them how pervasive comparative efforts have been in shaping Christian theological tradition from the outset. What has altered radically has been the attitude that Christians take toward other faiths, as nearly all forms of Christianity have responded to the cue of *Nostra aetate*. It then becomes my task, in a volume dedicated to the uniquely Christian doctrine of "the Trinity," to translate that profound change in attitude into a *locus theologicus*, a "clearing" in which we can delineate how alterations in attitude can inaugurate a fresh stage in the development of Christian theology, yet one quite continuous with its tradition. The theologian axial to this endeavor will be Bernard Lonergan, SJ, whose manner of displaying theological inquiry as "faith seeking understanding" will provide us with tools to carry out Rahner's impetus to theological renewal from "other faiths." Often identified as "a theologian's theologian," Lonergan devoted himself before, during, and after Vatican Council II to shaping a mode of thinking which could bring the *ressourcement* elaborated by the *nouvelle théologie* to a systematic focus, thereby showing us how to let theological attitudes disseminated in that council bear fruit in genuine developments in theology. Yet given the relentlessly philosophical quality of the inquiry he stimulated, his "influence" was inevitably more subterranean than evident, so one can understand his absence from the theologians treated in this volume, yet also welcome the opportunity an interfaith perspective provides to reclaim his signal role in trinitarian theology.[1] All of this should help show how "comparative theology" can contribute to genuine development in Christian theology itself, perhaps because of the staunchly philosophical strategies it must employ to bridge between apparently fixed traditions, notably by showing how they have always been fluid, so that fixing them will betray them as traditions.

To anchor our comparative inquiry in recent Catholic theology, let us recall Karl Rahner's prescient thesis in his 1979 article entitled "Towards a Fundamental Interpretation of Vatican II," where "fundamental" in Germanic parlance tends to mean "what has always already been going on."[2] The burden of this seminal lecture at Boston College had been to focus on a Christian tradition now facing other major religions, much as Jewish Christians of the first century had been faced with pagans wishing to affirm Jesus. That comparison allowed him to offer 70 and 1970 as symbolic dates, so bracketing together nineteen centuries of Western European Christianity and helping us to recognize that we stand on the threshold of a "world church," as his proposal soon came to be called. The parallel was striking to me at the time, involved as we were in Jewish–Christian understanding, yet becomes even more so today, as Islam takes its place as the late yet now inevitable "third" among the Abrahamic faiths. Rahner's precise point is that revelational communities are sometimes called upon to make decisions regarding matters for which the community itself has not yet been able to muster the appropriate categories to offer reasons appropriate to those decisions. In short, they have to "wing it." The example he gives illustrates how the emergence of a distinct community of Jewish and Gentile believers in Jesus from what was to become "Judaism" (itself a reaction to the emergence of the new community) creates the conundrum that Paul trenchantly articulates: should pagans responding to the invitation to follow Jesus first be circumcised in order to be initiated properly into this community of largely Jewish believers in Jesus? One could certainly have argued that "ontogeny recapitulates phylogeny," so the practice of circumcision could have served as a fitting catechesis, showing how one cannot even speak of Jesus without invoking the entire context of the scriptures which he treasured, with his community, and which he had brought to an incisive focus.[3] Yet Paul insisted on a clean break: there was no need for them to be circumcised, yet he was unable to give a rationale, so in part helping to cinch the "parting of the ways."

In 1979 Rahner could only remind us how unprepared was Christian theology to negotiate interfaith issues.[4] Beyond a few intrepid pioneers, like Jules Isaac for Judaism, Louis Massignon for Islam, and Jules Monchanin for Hinduism, there had been little sustained consideration of "other faiths" as a theological issue, thereby reinforcing his selection of 1970 as a symbolic date inaugurating such an inquiry. Five years after the council had ended, we could then begin to see what novel steps *Nostra aetate* had initiated, making it a landmark document from Vatican II; *Nostra aetate* shared with *Dignitatis humanae* the distinction of being the only two documents which really broke new ground, the rest of them having largely disseminated the *nouvelle théologie* to a wider church. In fact, the argument of this very chapter would not have been invited or entertained until quite recently. But let us now elicit Bernard Lonergan's help to move us beyond Rahner's programmatic proposals.

The heart of Lonergan's trinitarian theology lies in his dissection of Nicaea.[5] Offered as part of the standard tract on Christology during his years teaching at the Gregorian University in Rome before and during Vatican Council II, his way of proceeding reflected philosophical strategies he had just developed in *Insight*.[6] Everything turns, of course, on the way we interpret the "way to Nicaea," the tortuous path, three centuries long and not without rancor and bloodshed, culminating in the introduction of a non-biblical Greek term of art, *homoousion*, into the Christian creed. In the wake of virulent objections of nineteenth-century Protestant critics against such a "Hellenization" of the community of followers of Jesus, Lonergan reached for a deeper dynamic, locating it in the human desire to understand and to make sense out of what was delivered to us in revelation and handed on by subsequent practice. That very quest for understanding which turns doctrine (or received teaching) into theology, as "faith seeking understanding," requires astute interpretation of what has now been delivered to us as the community's consensus in conciliar documents. At a time when *hermeneutics* was the rage,

Lonergan formulated its central strategy succinctly: if the statements of Nicaea (and other councils) are presented to us as *answers*, it is incumbent upon us (if we are to understand how they are answers) to come to know the *questions* which they are proposed to answer. Once we learn to inquire into our tradition in this way, we can allow ourselves to be instructed by the strategies developed, and so begin to gain the intellectual skills required to do theology, rather than simply be asked to imbibe it. Introducing students into theology as a mode of inquiry, whereby faith is constantly seeking understanding, also allows us to participate in what makes a tradition live, or, better, what differentiates *tradition* from *ideology*, namely, its self-critical *ethos*. So Lonergan's philosophical approach moves beyond a purportedly "critical" reading of "the past," which animated "revisionist" thinking, to offer a critical appropriation of a tradition, while displaying the continuing vitality of that tradition. It will also help us see how that same tradition can respond creatively to challenges posed by both Judaism and Islam.

To delineate this potential, we should move on to Chalcedon, assisted now by Thomas Weinandy's illuminating rendition of the four centuries that it took to reach some consensus on the ontological constitution of Jesus.[7] Indeed, the verve with which Weinandy delineates the conflicts involved reflects a philosophical acumen close to Lonergan's, showing how most of the logical possibilities regarding understanding the person of Jesus were canvassed as they were disputed. So what was going on? While the discussion may often have borrowed terms from Hellenic philosophy, the issues were starkly biblical: how can this community of believers in Jesus pray to Jesus without making him "something alongside God"? For if our prayer to Jesus were to entail that, we would be idolaters to Jews, and (later on) infidels to Muslims, engaging in *shirk*, associating a creature with the creator. The sticking point is the central tenet of Judaism: "hear, O Israel: the Lord our God is one Lord" (Deut 6:4). The insistence that our God is one – an insistence shared from the outset with Jews and later with Muslims – handily explains what otherwise sounds scandalous: that it took the community of Christians four centuries to clarify the central tenet of their faith: the reality of Jesus. So we can hardly speak blithely about "the doctrine of the Trinity," as though it were anything less than an arduous endeavor on the part of a worshiping community – remember Arius and the extent of Arian Christianity. Yet as it turns out, the torturous path to that "doctrine" will provide a salient opening, inviting us to show how current interfaith reflection may extend our rich theological tradition, once we realize that such exchange has never been absent from it. Moreover, the fact that the formulation which Weinandy shows to be so remarkable an achievement failed to be accepted by the entire community of Christian believers testifies to yet other factors which continue to muddy intellectual exchange now, as they did then.[8] Yet as the crucible in which were forged what we now call doctrines, the patristic period will prove to be instructive in approaching Judaism and Islam, and so may help us to distinguish salient from adventitious developments in comparative theological inquiry, with a view to ascertaining how that inquiry can enrich our tradition today. Yet we should first resume the explicitly interfaith medieval discussion of creation before returning to some of the neuralgic issues surrounding redemption. However, we should never forget that patristic reflection on these two mysteries – creation and redemption – always regarded them as twins: to mention one was to refer implicitly to the other.[9]

## CREATION OR ORIGINATION?

The primordial act of faith relevant here avers a free and intentional act of origination that orders the universe. The lineaments of the articulated response of Muslim, Jewish, and Christian thinkers can be traced from al-Ghazzālī (d. 1111) through Moses Maimonides (d. 1204) to Thomas Aquinas (d. 1274).[10] The standing alternative to the biblical and Qur'anic revelation of a free creator, confronting each tradition, was Plotinus' appropriation of Hellenic philosophy into the seamless garment, adapted by al-Farabi into a scheme of necessary emanation from "the First." The philosophical cachet of this unifying scheme was reinforced by its appeal, notably in Ibn Sina (Avicenna), to Aristotle's presumption that the universe always existed, bolstered by his arguments that a temporal beginning made no sense. Both al-Ghazzālī and Maimonides found it necessary to identify the alternative their revelations offered with a beginning of the universe coincident with the beginning of time itself (a "temporal beginning"), whereas Aquinas' rendition of free creation found it intellectually compatible with an everlasting universe, though in fact the strategy he inherited from Maimonides legitimized believers in accepting a temporal beginning, since neither could ever be proved.

Yet given these shared conceptual strategies for introducing a free creator into the Hellenic scheme, what kind of knowing does talk of such a creator presume? Briefly, that the "distinction" between creator and creatures be *sui generis*.[11] That is, the act of creation brings the universe into being while allowing the *distinction* to obtain, yet the unique character of this action, with its correlative "distinction," should also keep us from conceiving of the creator as "over against" the universe. In traditional theological parlance, the creator must be at once transcendent and immanent to its creation. If, as Aquinas insists in the *Summa theologiae* (*The Summa of Theology*), the "proper effect of creation is the very to-be of things" (1, q. 45, a. 5), then the to-be of each existing thing participates in the divine to-be: to be created is to participate; to create is to be participated. So a creature's to-be is to-be-to-the-creator: *esse creaturae est esse ad creatorem* (cf. 1, q. 45, a. 3). It is worth recalling Aristotle's trenchant critique of Plato: "participation" is but a metaphor (*Metaphysics* 1); yet "emanation" (or "overflow") is equally metaphorical. Indeed, this "distinction" can never be articulated in terms proper to characterizing relations among things in the world; as Robert Sokolowski reminds us, this "distinction is glimpsed on the margin of reason . . . at the intersection of reason and faith."[12]

As a result, customary ways of expressing the creator's activity, like the "intervention" of creator in creation (as in the giving of the Torah to Moses, the incarnation of the Word of God in Jesus, or the "coming down" of the Qur'an to Muhammad), will prove intrinsically misleading. For how can the creator-of-all, the one in whom our very being participates, be said to "intervene" in creation? Unless, that is, we had improperly thought of the creator as one thing and the universe as another. Indeed, Sara Grant has argued for adapting Shankara's arresting term "nonduality" to render the "non-reciprocal relation of dependence" which Aquinas insists creation must be.[13] So we see how a proper grasp of the act of creating must be a proper ingredient of the act of self-revealing, as well as a proper grasp of the act of covenanting and a proper grasp of the act of incarnating. Indeed, only a creator could unite with created nature without contradiction, since creator and creature are not two separate things to start with. Indeed, it is illustrative to note how the Qur'an proposes, pairwise, the resurrection of the body as "proof" of creation, and creation as "proof" of the resurrection: that is, accepting one in faith stands or falls with accepting the other.

So the upshot of each of these revelations is to move their faithful into new ways of speaking and thinking: about the universe of which we are a part, and of our part in it. About the universe,

> by the introduction of a new distinction, the distinction between the world understood as possibly not having existed [recall Aristotle's presumption that the universe always was] and God understood as possibly being all there is, with no diminution

> of goodness or greatness. It is not the case that God and the world are each separately understood in this new way, and only subsequently related to each other; they are determined in the distinction, not each apart from the other.[14]

So "God is understood not only to have created the world, but to have permitted the distinction between himself and the world to occur."[15] With regard to our part as intentional microcosms of the universe, our very being entails the task of learning how, in whatever we do, to be returning everything to the one from whom we received everything – by Torah-observance for Jews, by following Jesus for Christians, and by "Islam" for Muslims. So our life becomes our own, and our actions become free when we so respond to the invitation divinely proffered. The only authentic freedom lies in a servant's response to God's call. Yet this issues from an act of faith in a free creator, given distinctive voice in each Abrahamic tradition.

## FREE CREATION THROUGH THE WORD

Now the precise sense in which the one God is free to create must indeed escape us, as Aquinas implicitly affirms in insisting – employing another sense of "necessary" – that knowledge of divine triunity is "'necessary' for us to have the right idea of creation, to wit, that God did not produce things of necessity, [for] when we say that in God there is a procession of love, we show that God produced creatures not out of need, nor for any other extrinsic reason, but on account of the love of God's own goodness" (*Summa theologiae* I, q. 32, a. 1 ad 3). God's freedom in creation lies not even in the intrinsic reason of "God's own goodness," but in God's love for that very goodness, where the reduplication gestures at an interpersonal life within the one which quite escapes philosophy. So the right idea of creation will elude reason operating unilluminated by revelation – expressly, by the Christian revelation – since reason itself could never conclude to the divine triunity which we need to direct our thinking about intentional origination. And by a similar reasoning, the precise sense in which God's creating can be said to be free escapes us as well. For if we were unable confidently to affirm it without having been informed of the divine triunity, which itself escapes our comprehension, then so will the freedom which that triunity announces and protects.[16] We have, of course, moved well beyond logical necessity here, yet the generation of the Son (Word) with the procession of the Holy Spirit (Love) in God, which in

Aquinas' thought alone secure the freedom of creation, cannot itself be a free act of God, but is presented as God's own revelation displaying to creatures the inner life (or complete "nature") of the creator.[17] Once that life is revealed, then, it will be *necessary* that such a one act freely, out of love, yet the manner whereby that loving free consent to the divine goodness allows it to overflow into creation will utterly escape us. Just how God is free in creating is not for us to know.

So an adequate account of God's freedom in creating will escape us in principle; hence Aquinas' prescient reference to a dimension of divinity which we could never reason to ourselves, but could only be revealed to us. What proves significant here is the way in which this presumption is shared by Jewish and Muslim thinkers as well. Without the benefit of an explicitly trinitarian revelation, both Moses Maimonides and al-Ghazzālī perceive clearly how the issue of free creation implies and is implied by the unanticipated and undeserved bestowal of the Torah and of the Qur'an respectively. Indeed, it belongs to the ethos of Islam to insist that humankind needs to be alerted to the traces (*ayât*) of divine wisdom in the world by pondering the verses (*ayât*) of the Qur'an. One might indeed reason to the universe's origination, after the fashion of the Muslim *falâsifa* and in the spirit of Plotinus, but to see all that is as the "best possible" effect of divine wisdom requires God's revelatory initiative.[18] Yet once averred, the word of divine creative wisdom assumes center stage in creation. Here the testimony of revelation, as in the Qur'an's repeated avowal "God said 'be' and it is" (6:73), confirms the inference from metaphysics that creation involves no change at all (Aquinas, *Summa theologiae* 1, q. 45, a. 2). In literary terms shared by both Bible and Qur'an, everything is accomplished by God's merely speaking the creative word, the Word which is made Arabic in the Qur'an and human in Jesus. And that same Word, "by whom the universe is made" (Jn 1:10), structures the very order of the universe, which discloses traces of divine wisdom to those attuned to it.

Here is where the metaphysical theorem enunciating creation by identifying created *esse* as a participation in the *esse subsistens* of God joins the intentional discourse of *word* and *wisdom* to remind us just how elusive is the relation of creation to its creator. Kathryn Tanner has elaborated a set of semantic rules to articulate properly what she calls a "non-contrastive" relation of creatures to their intentional creator.[19] The effort dovetails with Sokolowski's "distinction," as each reminds us that the creator cannot be "other than" creatures in the way in which one creature is other than another. Sara Grant carries this mode of thought a step further to make a highly suggestive connection with Sankara's Advaita, proposing that we read Aquinas' determination that creation consists in a "non-reciprocal relation of dependence" in creatures as a Western attempt to articulate what Sankara calls "non-duality."[20] For is that not what the "non-contrastive" relation between creator and creatures comes to, in our terms: neither *other* nor the *same*? What has long been regarded as sharply differentiating Western from Eastern thought turns out to be a conceptual illusion on our part: we seemed to think that we could adequately distinguish God from creatures, so readily accused Hindu thought of failing to do so. Charges of "monism" used to abound, but can they be sustained? We must also revise, as I have suggested, any sharp difference between emanation properly understood (that is, as no longer identified with its model of logical inference) and free creation, perhaps coming to regard these two schemes as complementary ways of articulating what defies proper conceptualization. Here a study of Aquinas' dicta would best be complemented by an examination of Meister Eckhart's assertions regarding these matters, allowing for a signal difference in the genre of their writings as well as the goal of their respective inquiries. Aquinas' goal was to show how and in what respect *theologia* could be a *scientia* (where both terms become ambiguous for modern readers when translated), while Eckhart, presuming that work had been accomplished, could focus on plumbing the implications of the teaching itself.[21] Indeed, a recent study by Robert Dobie comparing Meister Eckhart and Ibn al-Arabi perfectly complements the approach we have been proposing, showing how the works of these authors dovetail, notably in their understandings of the ineffable relation of creature to creator.[22]

It may seem redundant to have elaborated the issue of free creation so extensively, since *Nostra aetate* assures us that Jews, Christians, and Muslims agree on this fundamental tenet. Yet for our purpose of showing how comparative theology can appropriately contribute to extending the Christian theological tradition in the new circumstances so nicely limned by Rahner, the elaboration makes two salient points: first, that collaboration has long existed with respect to a major doctrine, indeed to the point where the recognized masterwork of Christian theology, Aquinas' *Summa theologiae*, may already be regarded as an intercultural, interreligious document, and second, that the notion of *creation* at issue cannot be a "merely philosophical" assertion of origination, but rather an asseveration of God's freely creating the universe, indeed, *ex nihilo* and *de novo*; and it is this properly theological tenet which each Abrahamic faith believes and teaches. Finally, while medieval expositions of creation on the part of each community could presume a shared set of philosophical strategies, the current task of addressing the theme of redemption may not be able to do so. Yet we may nonetheless borrow some medieval strategies to ease the transition.

## WHERE TRADITIONS DIVERGE, HOW MAY WE EXPLOIT DIVERGENCE WITHOUT ENFORCING SIMILARITY?

Those who work in interfaith contexts will inevitably become more attuned to analogous discourse than other theologians, even though any *bona fide* exercise of philosophical theology will have to display analogical reasoning in its exposition of truths of faith, or risk falling into idolatry: that is, treating the creator as a subset of creation. That is the rule which Sokolowski's "distinction" imposes on theological discourse by showing this intellectual demand is already imbedded in Christian life and practice, and which (I argue) can be extended analogously to Jewish and Muslim thought *in divinis*.[23] Yet these grammatical rules will become even more salient as we discuss matters often seen as downright contradictions among Abrahamic faiths. Comparison will often turn to contrast, with Christian revelation on the one side and Judaism and Islam together on the other. Yet we shall see that differences may be even more revealing of each faith than apparent similarities, though outright contradictions can hardly be countenanced. It is in treating apparent contradictions that strategies employed by medieval thinkers in assessing clashes between faith and reason will prove helpful. Yet we must recall the profound differences between our situation and theirs with regard both to *reason* and to interfaith *attitudes*. While medievals could aver that human reason is able to find truth, whatever its context or starting point, they were far less accepting than we have become – again, since *Nostra aetate* – of other faiths as genuine paths to God. Christian doctrine had to accept the veracity of the revelation of God to Moses, of course, and even reaffirm it in the face of Marcion, but Christian attitudes left little room for accepting the authenticity of the life and worship of contemporary Jews. Hence *Nostra aetate*'s elevating Paul's insistence that "the gifts and call of God are irrevocable" (Rom 11:29) represented a sea-change in relation to contemporary Judaism, offering a paradigm case of a community's rank-ordering scriptural statements, much as Muslim tradition has determined that certain verses of the Qur'an abrogate others. For there are contrary New Testament claims, notably in the letter to the Hebrews, which uses Jeremiah 31:31–34 to conclude that "in speaking of a new covenant he treats the first as obsolete. And what is becoming obsolete and growing old is ready to vanish away" (Heb 8:13). Now in fact this attitude toward Jews proved far more representative of Christian life and practice than the view which *Nostra aetate* espoused and reaffirmed as authentic Christian teaching.

When it comes to neuralgic points of doctrine, both Jews and Muslims more readily balk at the incarnation than at trinitarian teaching, since the Word's becoming human represents a direct broaching of "the distinction" between creator and creatures, whereas trinitarian claims are far less clear and tend – as Christians themselves know so well – to be rendered in abstruse language. Again, this can prove instructive to Christians, for we have seen how early conciliar statements focused on Jesus, whereas more explicit assertions regarding the divinity of the Holy Spirit would derive from those regarding the Son's "being of one substance with the Father" (Nicaea). (John Milbank refers to this development as introducing a "second difference."[24]) Yet in fact, however offensive "the incarnation" may prove to Muslims, they can rest far more easily with Jesus than can Jews, for two obvious reasons. First, Jesus was a Jew, and as a Jew intended to bring the Hebrew scriptures to an unprecedented focus – the Christian trope is "to fulfill them" – so, in his person and teaching, Jesus represents a challenge to Jews, so much so that rabbinic "Judaism" developed largely in reaction to the Jesus movement among Jews, and so appeared chronologically later than "Christianity." Second, the Qur'an recognizes Jesus as a prophet, whose miraculous birth from the Virgin Mary was a portent of God's continuing revelation confirmed in the Qur'anic account. Yet of course this prophet Jesus can hardly be the one whom Christians worship, so irenic conciliation around Jesus proves misleading, especially as it can lead to putative comparisons between Jesus and the Prophet, Muhammad.[25] In fact – and this is utterly crucial to comparative work between Islam and Christianity – the salient comparison is rather between Jesus and the Qur'an! These parallel formulae offer the prime example of the similarity-cum-difference which will structure our comparison, demanding that it always be analogous: Christians believe that Jesus is the Word of God made human, while Muslims believe the Qur'an to be the Word of God made "book."[26]

Parsing these parallel formulae will elucidate similarities and differences in such a way as to deconstruct misunderstanding from the outset. The manifest differences allow Christians to underscore what makes their revelation distinctive among the Abrahamic faiths: that it resides primarily in a person. So while it is understandable that Muslims will understand Christian revelation according to the pattern established by the Prophet's receiving the Qur'an from God, to honor them as "people of the book," that honorific distorts the revelation in Jesus as effectively as some evangelical Protestants do, in locating Christian revelation primarily in the New Testament rather than in the person of Jesus.[27] Moreover, once we identify Jesus and the Qur'an as the salient points of contact and comparison, we will be better able to resist comparing Bible and Qur'an, which leads Christians to query: when will Muslims countenance "historical-critical" approaches to their revelatory books, as we have with ours? – a lightly veiled criticism of Islam as being "pre-enlightenment," and a presumption that Muslim claims about the manner of divine relation in the Qur'an lead them inescapably to being "fundamentalist." But what if Bible and Qur'an represented different modes of revelation, quite different forms of "book"? Moreover, even if the form of "book" which Muslims believe the Qur'an to be were resistant to some varieties of "source criticism," it would hardly follow that orthodox Muslims are "fundamentalist," since Islam is replete with a commentary tradition (not unlike Judaism) whose proliferation allows orthodox (and educated) Muslims to deplore "fundamentalist" uses of the Qur'an. So concentrating on the parallel between "Qur'an" and "Jesus" will help us avoid conceptual confusions and entangled misunderstandings so rife today, and at the same time open us to fruitful comparisons in theory and in practice which can move dialogue forward rather than divert it from the outset. A related consideration between Christians and Jews lies in distinguishing "Hebrew scriptures" from "Old Testament," to call attention to the way in which Jewish scriptures have an integrity of their own, despite the ways in which Christians have colonized them to vindicate their faith in Jesus. Yet however Jews may resent that Christian impulse, it is at root anti-Marcion, affirming a continuous single covenant, rather than claiming the New Testament to represent the radical break suggested in the letter to the Hebrews.

Yet despite the fact that "Jesus" can be less contentious for Muslims than for Jews, there remains a sharp conflict between Islam and Christianity regarding Christian claims about Jesus, which stems from the Qur'an itself, turning on claims that he is the "Son of God." In fact the Qur'anic passages on this point are overwhelmingly polemical in tone, and sound so utterly opposed to Christian teaching that an observer as astute as Paul Griffiths could use them to illustrate an outright contradiction between the respective teachings of Christianity and Islam on this matter.[28] Here is where medieval reflection of the putative contradictions between faith and reason can come to our aid, but first to the relevant passages in the Qur'an, to let the context itself help us determine what is being affirmed and what denied regarding God and "a son."[29]

> The very Creator of the heavens and of the earth, how could there be a "son" to Him, there never having been a "spouse" to Him – He who created everything and who is omniscient over all things?
>
> (6:101)

> They have ascribed invisible beings as partners to God, though He created them, and in their total ignorance they have attributed to Him sons and daughters.
>
> (6:100)

> He whose is the kingdom of the heavens and the earth. He has adopted to himself no progeny. In his sovereignty He has no associate. He created everything and established the order within which everything exists.
>
> (25:2)

> Had God willed to adopt a son He could have chosen as He wished from His creation.
>
> (39:3)

> God has adopted no son and there is no god with Him. For in that event each god would certainly have taken up his own creation and some would have gotten the better over others. Glory be to God immune from all they attribute...
>
> (23:91)

> They say: "the Merciful has adopted a son." It is an appalling assertion they have made! The heavens would almost break up and the earth disintegrate at it, and the mountains collapse into ruin – they are claiming a son to the Merciful!
>
> (19:88–91)

> The Jews affirm that 'Uzair is the son of God while Christians affirm that the Christ is the son of God. Such is the talk of their mouths: it is the kind of thing that unbelievers have alleged in earlier times.
>
> (9:30)

A simple perusal of these Qur'anic passages should dispel any suspicion of contradiction between what Christians claim and what the Qur'an asserts about God.

In fact, the Qur'an protects itself by reporting hearsay: "they say." Moreover, it is clear that "son" here has all the carnal qualities which attend ordinary human sonship, notably a "spouse." Finally, there is confusion between begetting and adopting a son, betraying some unclarity about what "they say." *En bloc*, we might note that the consternation of the Qur'an over what it presumes that Christians claim offers a neat set of reasons why it took Christianity four centuries to formulate its central teaching about the ontological constitution of Jesus as "the Christ." For those claims cannot constitute a return to polytheism or any suspicion that there be more than one God. So the very objections of the Qur'an can be found to have guided – *avant la lettre* – the torturous path to Chalcedon! In a more systematic way, Aquinas can come to our aid here. Following the lead of a Jewish thinker, Moses Maimonides, he was more concerned with contradictions between faith and reason than with conflicting formulations from differing religious traditions, since Jews, Christians, and Muslims in his time seemed to presume their traditions to be starkly incompatible on key issues. (Yet we shall see how the logic remains the same, even if a host of attitudes today regarding "other religions" differ significantly from those of Aquinas' day.) His strategy is simple: if a point of "sacred doctrine" appears to contradict a point that has been rationally demonstrated, then either we have miscast the doctrinal teaching or we have failed to demonstrate properly. In other words, the proper deliverances of faith and reason cannot possibly be at odds, since the free creator of the universe is the ultimate author of both. So we must have made some mistake in formulation. Indeed, it hardly behooves us to presume that we can always "get it right" in these matters, and so common sense, together with the divine source of revelation, cannot but elicit a strong dose of intellectual humility. Indeed, all of the Abrahamic thinkers in medieval times were prone to use this critical strategy to defuse conflicts between faith and reason, as they sought to illustrate their shared conviction that all truth derives from a free creator. So all we need to do is to extend it, as they were not inclined to do, to conflicts between formulations of different faiths in one God, when those formulations appear to be outright contradictory. Has each reader not already done that with this set of Qur'anic verses?

But what about "trinity" itself? Do not Muslims oppose it in the name of God's unalterable unity, *tawhîd*? Of course, but this very volume should disabuse us from thinking there is something called "trinity," something about which all Christians are clear! Beyond that initial step of sophistication, however, there is a clear discrepancy between

Muslims beginning their prayer with *b'ism Allah ar-Rahman ar-Rahim* and Christians "in the name of the Father, the Son and the Holy Ghost." Indeed, but does even this stark difference amount to a contradiction? Not overtly, for again, the difficulties which the early Christians had in formulating anything like a "trinitarian doctrine" all turned on respecting the *shema*: "God our God is one!" So what Christians really claim is that God's revelation in the person of Jesus opened his followers to a view of the inner life of the one God, a view which challenges theologians to a proper articulation, and which leads believers, "like living stones . . . into a spiritual house, to be a holy priesthood to offer spiritual sacrifices acceptable to God though Jesus Christ" (1 Pet 2:5). If Jews are God's own people by virtue of the covenant established by him, with the temple in Jerusalem the very icon of that covenant, Peter reminds Christians that they have been grafted onto this people to become that temple themselves: "a chosen race, a royal priesthood, a holy nation, God's own people, that you may declare the wonderful deeds of him who called you out of darkness into his marvelous light" (1 Pet 2:9). So "the trinity" becomes a God-given way of relating to God and to one another, as it offered for Aquinas a way of understanding the creator's activity in granting the primordial gift of existence as the first "grace," so orienting us to a life of thanksgiving, outlined for Muslims in the Qur'an: a "straight path" leading intentional creatures to return everything to the one from whom we received everything. For the Qur'an, as Daniel Madigan reminds us, has always been more than a "book," rather expressing "the divine–human interaction that takes place in the encounter between the Prophet and his listeners, both believers and opponents."[30]

## SOME CONCLUDING REMARKS AND SUGGESTIONS

To take this a final step further, one needs to recall how one strand of early Islamic thought – the Mu'tazilite – had insisted that the Qur'an had to be created, following the lead of the Qur'an's own polemic regarding what "Christians say" about Jesus: only God can be uncreated; all else must be creatures of God. Such is the import of a radical belief in divine unity, *tawhîd*, the very basis of Islam. But before long, Muslims wondered whether this one God could be mute, so adopted what became the orthodox position: that the Qur'an itself is the uncreated Word of God, while the Qur'ans we use for prayer are obviously created exemplars. So Muslims would be comfortable with the opening words of John's gospel: "In the beginning was the Word, and the Word was with

God, and the Word was God" (1:1). For the Word of God could hardly be "other than God" without being "associated with God" – the same dilemma faced by early Christians in following John to try to articulate Jesus as God's Word. Now clearly Jesus is not the Qur'an, nor do Muslims have a "doctrine of 'the trinity,'" but these analogies have been offered to suggest how comparative theological inquiry can illuminate each other's faith traditions, bringing us to better understanding of ourselves as well as of one another. For "mutual illumination," as the goal of comparative theological inquiry, is consonant with the goal of theology itself as "faith seeking understanding," where the watchword is *understanding*. Claims to truth can be made by the community in other ways, most effectively by a witness that cannot be gainsaid. Would that such witness were patent from each of the Abrahamic faiths! Yet what we can find, anywhere and at all times, are believers who embody the revelations which they espouse, showing by their lives and comportment how effectively their traditions have formed them. These potential and actual "partners in dialogue" may then become friends as well, and when that happens, comparative theology will be experienced as a lived practice, whereby each one leads the other to a richer appreciation of both traditions as they wend their way together toward becoming "friends of God."

## Notes

1. Frederick Christian Bauerschmidt offers inadvertent testimony to my contention in his review of Fergus Kerr's *Twentieth Century Theologians* in *Modern Theology*, 23 (2007), where he questions the inclusion of Bernard Lonergan among the authors featured, seeing it "more as a result of Kerr's predilection for philosophical theology than for their long-term significance for Catholic theology. For example, while Lonergan is an interesting thinker, when we consider the influence of his theology he pales in comparison with his fellow North American Jesuit John Courtney Murray" (651). I am grateful to Fritz for illustrating my point by what Lonergan would call an "inverse insight," thereby suggesting the tack taken in this chapter. For the generation directly inspired by Lonergan's mode of inquiry would know that John Courtney Murray constantly deferred to him as his mentor in matters theological, so my sustained argument here will try to show that it is precisely thinkers trained in philosophical theology who have a better chance of "long-term significance for Catholic theology," as their mode of inquiry will prove more apt to inform developments unforeseen by their own inquiries. If I am successful, then it will appear condescending to reduce Lonergan to the category of "the interesting," as Kierkegaard regularly castigated liberal Christian theologians for doing to Jesus!

2. Karl Rahner, "Towards a Fundamental Interpretation of Vatican II," *Theological Studies*, 40 (1979), 716–27.
3. This fact, encapsulated in Paul's insistence to the pagans of Rome that "you, a wild olive shoot, were grafted in [the Jews'] place to share in the richness of the olive tree" (Rom 11:17), received spontaneous testimony in a 1975 visit to Mbarara, celebrating seventy-five years of Catholic Christianity in Uganda. Stunned at how recent this had been, I turned to some "White Fathers" (members of the Missionary Society of Africa), asking them how their community described the initial contact. How could they simply say: "I want to tell you about Jesus," for there would be no effective context for such an introduction? The response was telling; as they had gleaned it, the pioneers in this endeavor listened to the people's stories, responding that "we have stories like that: there was this man Abraham . . ." thereby corroborating Paul's point as well as receiving good marks as missionaries: they learned the language and they listened!
4. Although Jewish–Christian exchange had begun soon after the publication of *Nostra aetate* in 1965, a gathering of Jews, Christians, and Muslims at the Tantur Ecumenical Institute in Jerusalem (1975), under the inspiration of Sister Marie Goldstein, RSHM, was utterly unprecedented. As John Esposito has testified, it would take another ten years for Islam to be recognized as even a potential third partner.
5. Bernard Lonergan, *The Way to Nicea*, trans. Conn O'Donovan (Philadelphia: Westminster, 1976).
6. Bernard Lonergan, *Insight: A Study of Human Understanding*, 5th edn., rev. and augmented, ed. Frederick E. Crowe and Robert M. Doran (University of Toronto Press, 1992; originally London: Longmans Green and Co., 1957).
7. Thomas Weinandy, *Does God Change? The Word's Becoming in the Incarnation* (Still River, MA: St. Bede's Publications, 1985).
8. When I asked a Latin priest in Amman (in 2004) why so many Latin clergy had come from his village in Jordan, he told me that his grandfather had become angry with the Orthodox priest and led the village community to Rome. Knowing how clergy can foment such conflicts, I showed little surprise at that reaction. Yet he moved smoothly across fourteen centuries to go on to inform me: "And when those people came from the Arabian peninsula we knew nothing about Islam; we just knew they were not Greeks!" So much for the fate of astute formulations, in the face of overwhelming power.
9. See David Burrell and Elena Malits, *Original Peace: Restoring God's Creations*, with Elena Malits (New York: Paulist, 1997), for a discussion of patristic propensity to treat creation and redemption as twin foci of an elliptical inquiry.
10. David Burrell, *Knowing the Unknowable God: Ibn-Sina, Maimonides, Aquinas* (University of Notre Dame Press, 1986); David Burrell, *Freedom and Creation in Three Traditions* (University of Notre Dame Press, 1993).

11. Robert Sokolowski, *The God of Faith and Reason* (University of Notre Dame Press, 1982; reprinted Washington, DC: Catholic University of America Press, 1995).
12. Ibid., 39.
13. *Sara Grant, Towards an Alternative Theology* (University of Notre Dame Press, 2002), 40.
14. Sokolowski, *The God of Faith and Reason*, 23.
15. Ibid., 33.
16. Norman Kretzmann's struggles with this issue, in "A General Problem of Creation: Why would God Create Anything at All?," in Scott MacDonald, ed., *Being and Goodness* (Ithaca, NY: Cornell University Press, 1991), offer oblique testimony to Aquinas' point; while James Ross' attempts to offer a positive characterization help to confirm ours, in "Real Freedom," in Jeff Jordan and Daniel Howard-Snyder, eds., *Faith, Freedom and Rationality: Philosophy of Religion Today* (New York: Rowman and Littlefield, 1996) 89–117.
17. For a constructive treatment, see Gilles Emery's magisterial study of Aquinas' commentary on Lombard's *Sentences: La Trinité créatrice* (Paris: J. Vrin, 1995).
18. Eric Ormsby, *Theodicy in Islamic Thought: The Dispute over al-Ghazâlî's "Best of All Possible Worlds"* (Princeton University Press, 1984), amplified and clarified in "Creation in Time in Islamic Thought with Special Reference to al-Ghazâlî," in David Burrell and Bernard McGinn, eds., *God and Creation* (University of Notre Dame Press, 1990), 246–64.
19. Kathryn Tanner, *God and the Doctrine of Creation* (Oxford: Blackwell, 1988).
20. Grant, *Towards an Alternative Theology.*
21. I am indebted to a conversation with Stacey Wendlinder, formerly a doctoral candidate at the University of Notre Dame working on Eckhart, for proposing this way of suggesting the difference between them.
22. Robert Dobie, *Mythos and Logos: Ibn 'Arabi, Meister Eckhart and the Analogical Imagination* (Washington, DC: Catholic University of America Press, 2008).
23. David Burrell, "The Christian Distinction Celebrated and Expanded," in John Drummond and James Hart, eds., *The Truthful and the Good* (Dordrecht: Kluwer Academic Publishers, 1996), 191–206.
24. John Milbank, "The Second Difference," in *The Word Made Strange* (Oxford: Blackwell, 2003), 171–93.
25. See Roger Arnaldez, *Three Messengers for One God* (University of Notre Dame Press, 1995) for a distinguished Catholic Islamicist's valedictory comparative work, despite the misleading title.
26. Wilfred Cantwell Smith first introduced me to this salient comparison, which Daniel Madigan has amply developed in "God's Word and the World: Jesus and the Qur'an, Incarnation and Recitation," in Terrence Merrigan and Frederik Glorieux, eds., *Godhead Here in Hiding: Incarnation and the Mystery of Human Suffering* (Leuven: Peters, 2008).

27. The controversial Vatican document *Dominus Jesus* (2002) would have been better advised to make this point about the distinctiveness of the Christian revelation, rather than rely on the historically contentious claim (in paragraph 2) that Christianity had "in fact" always given testimony to Jesus!
28. Paul Griffiths, *Problems of Religious Diversity* (Malden, MA, and Oxford: Blackwell, 2001).
29. The translation I use is the one which can best introduce Christians to the Qur'an: Kenneth Cragg's *Readings in the Qur'an* (San Francisco: Collins, 1988). His grasp of Islam and of Arabic allows him to render the verve of the Arabic into a corresponding English, and while his re-configuration of the verses of the "book" into thematic sections is nontraditional, the order of chapters [*sura*] and verses [*aya*] is not divinely given, and the result for Jews and Christians, used to a more narrative scripture, is salutary.
30. Daniel Madigan, "The Limits of Self-Referentiality in the Qur'an," in Stefan Wild, ed., *Self-Referentiality in the Qur'an*, Diskurs der Arabistik, 11 (Wiesbaden: Otto Harrassowitz, 2006), 60. See also Madigan's extended discussion: *The Qur'an's Self-Image: Writing and Authority in Islam's Scripture* (Princeton University Press, 2001).

## Further reading

Armstrong, Karen, *God is One: Fundamentalism in Judaism, Christianity and Islam* (New York: HarperCollins, 2001).

Burrell, David, *Freedom and Creation in Three Traditions* (University of Notre Dame Press, 1993).

*Knowing the Unknowable God: Ibn-Sina, Maimonides, Aquinas* (University of Notre Dame Press, 1986).

Ess, J. van, *The Flowering of Muslim Theology* (Cambridge, MA: Harvard University Press, 2006).

Michel, Thomas, and Michael Fitzgerald, eds., *Recognizing the Spiritual Bonds that Unite Us: Sixteen Years of Christian – Muslim Dialogue* (Vatican City: Vatican Press, 1994).

Wolfson, Harry Austryn, "The Muslim Attributes and the Christian Trinity," in *The Philosophy of the Kalam* (Cambridge, MA: Harvard University Press, 1976), 112–32.

Zebiri, Kate, *Muslims and Christians Face to Face* (Oxford: Oneworld, 1997).

# Part VI

*Systematic connections*

# 21 Trinity, Christology, and pneumatology

ANNE HUNT

In the opening verses of his first letter to the Thessalonian community, among the very earliest texts of the New Testament,[1] the Apostle Paul refers to three *dramatis personae*, God and Father, our Lord Jesus Christ, and the Holy Spirit:

> Paul, Silvanus, and Timothy, To the church of the Thessalonians in God the Father and the Lord Jesus Christ: Grace to you and peace. We always give thanks to God for all of you and mention you in our prayers, constantly remembering before our God and Father your work of faith and labor of love and steadfastness of hope in our Lord Jesus Christ. For we know, brothers and sisters beloved by God, that he has chosen you, because our message of the gospel came to you not in word only, but also in power and in the Holy Spirit and with full conviction.
>
> (1 Thess 1:1–5)

What is remarkable is that, even at this early stage, the community is clearly well acquainted with this triadic pattern. No explanation is offered; evidently none is necessary. The pattern is apparently already well established as the distinctively and typically Christian way of speaking of God.[2]

This text, along with many others in the New Testament, clearly attests to the lived experience of the Three in the early Christian community. Now, there is no question that this is trinitarian doctrine. It would not be for some centuries that doctrine *per se* would be formally defined. But what is very evident, here in our earliest sources, is a distinctly triadic-shaped faith, a faith that was given expression in prayer and worship. It is this lived experience of these Three that would eventually blossom in the doctrine of the Trinity and the theological specializations that we now call trinitarian theology, Christology, and pneumatology.

It is the connection between Trinity, Christ, and Spirit, and therefore between trinitarian theology, Christology, and pneumatology that is the focus of attention in this chapter. Now, one might well presume that, of all the doctrines in the Christian tradition, Christology and pneumatology are inconceivable outside of an expressly trinitarian context. Here, one would surely expect that the interconnection of the mysteries (the *nexus mysteriorum* to which Vatican Council I referred[3]) would be most obvious and developed. Yet, following in the direction established in the prior development of trinitarian doctrine, classical Christological doctrine, while undoubtedly grounded in Christian faith in the Triune God and designed to protect the realism of Christian faith in Jesus' full humanity and divinity, took a strongly metaphysical turn that left it strangely remote from its trinitarian bearings and, moreover, from the mystery as revealed in and through Jesus' life, death, and resurrection. Similarly, pneumatology, the theology of that most "implicit" of the three divine persons, the Holy Spirit, came to be largely confined to reflection on the indwelling of the Holy Spirit in the human person and the spiritual gifts thereby bestowed. Pneumatology subsequently languished in the abstractions of the scholastic theology of grace. In the process, it was effectively privatized and disconnected from ecclesiology, to the impoverishment of both. As a consequence, these three areas of theology – Trinity, Christology, and pneumatology – were not obviously interconnected in the scholastic theological manuals of the nineteenth and twentieth centuries that were standard seminary fare at that time. Nor did they function as the framework within which the whole suite of Christian doctrine finds its most vital source of reference. The explicit interconnection of the theologies of Trinity, Christ, and the Holy Spirit is in fact by no means to be presumed.

In this survey of their interconnection, we shall begin with a brief consideration of various perspectives on their interrelatedness. We shall proceed to an overview of the classical expression of their interconnectedness. We will then move to a brief overview of contemporary approaches and highlight some areas of genuine advance and promise in contemporary trinitarian scholarship.

## TRINITY, CHRISTOLOGY, PNEUMATOLOGY: PERSPECTIVES ON THEIR INTERRELATEDNESS

There is first the empirical data of revelation. The very basis for the interconnection of these mysteries is given, first and foremost, phenomenologically, in the New Testament, which witnesses strongly to a profound sense in the early Christian community of the threefold structure and dynamism of God's self-revelation and the interrelatedness of the roles of these three *dramatis personae*. While the full threefold reference can rarely be found in single passages, there are many texts that refer to two of the Three and which combine to reinforce the threefold pattern and rhythm. In some respects, those various references reach a crescendo in the concluding verses of Matthew's gospel with the baptismal formula: "Go therefore and make disciples of all nations, baptizing them in the name of the Father and of the Son and of the Holy Spirit" (Mt 28:19).

The inherent interrelationship of the Three emerges clearly in the New Testament. The Father–Son relationship, for example, is strongly depicted. "He is the image of the invisible God" (Col 1:15). Jesus' relationship to the Father is unlike any other. "He who has seen me has seen the Father" (Jn 14:9). With astonishing intimacy, Jesus invokes the Father as Abba (Mk 14:36).[4] The Son–Spirit relationship is also strongly depicted. Jesus is conceived by the power of the Holy Spirit (Mt 1:18, Lk 1:35). The Spirit is communicated at Jesus' baptism (Mk 1:8, Mt 3:11, Lk 3:16, 22), after which the Spirit leads Jesus into the desert (Mk 1:12). The Spirit accompanies and guides Jesus through his life and his death. Finally, Jesus is raised in the Spirit. Ascending to the Father, the Son sends the Spirit from the Father to the community (Jn 15:26, 16:7, 20:22). The Father sends the Spirit in the name of the Son (Jn 14:26). He is the Spirit of the one who raised Jesus from the dead (Rom 8:11). The Spirit is the spirit of the Father (Jn 14:16, Lk 11:13, Mt 10:20) and of the Son (Rom 8:9, Gal 4:6, Phil 1:19). The Spirit is the one who identifies and confirms Jesus' identity. "No one can say 'Jesus is Lord,' except by the Holy Spirit" (1 Cor 12:3). The Spirit's mission is to mediate the presence of the risen Christ, to interiorize the redemption wrought by Christ, and to animate the ecclesial structures established by Christ. It is to complete what was established by Christ. Ultimately, the Spirit's mission is the incorporation of all humanity, and indeed the whole cosmos, in Christ and, through Christ, to the Father (1 Cor 15:28, Eph 1:10, Col 1:19–20).

In the New Testament narrative, from the moment of Jesus' conception by the Spirit in Mary's womb, there is a reciprocity and mutuality between the missions of the Son and Spirit. Each has a distinct mission, a mission given by the Father, but those missions are inextricably interrelated. Both missions come from the Father and lead back to the Father, as source and goal of all. Thus Irenaeus could speak of the Son and Spirit, Word and Wisdom, as the two hands of God,[5] a description reminiscent of the Pauline teaching of the two sendings, the two missions: "When the time had fully come, God sent forth his Son, born of woman, born under the law, to redeem those who were under the law, so that we might receive adoption as sons. And because you are sons, God has sent the Spirit of his Son into our hearts, crying 'Abba, Father'" (Gal 4:4–6). Phenomenologically, then, each implies the others.

This phenomenological interconnection grounds their hermeneutical interconnection. Hermeneutically, they connect in a circle or spiral of interpretation. As Yves Congar, one of the foremost ecclesiologists of the twentieth century, noted: "there can be no Christology without pneumatology and no pneumatology without Christology."[6] Christology must be pneumatologically shaped, taking into account the vital role that the Spirit plays in the life, death, resurrection, and mission of Jesus. Similarly, pneumatology must take into account the relationship between the mission of the Spirit and that of the Son. Just as Son and Spirit co-inhere in the one trinitarian mystery, each is present and active and implicated in the mission of the other. They simply cannot be interpreted or understood except in relationship to each other.

Congar is surely right to insist on the interrelatedness of Christology and pneumatology. But we could press further and call for an expressly *trinitarian* Christology and a *trinitarian* pneumatology.[7] The interrelatedness of the three divine persons in the one perichoretic mystery of the Trinity necessitates a determinedly *trinitarian* strategy of interrelatedness in our hermeneutics, in other words, a circle or spiral of interpretation that takes due account of their interconnection. Andrei Rublov's exquisite trinitarian icon *The Hospitality of Abraham* captures visually the other-directedness which characterizes their interconnection and which should characterize a fully integrated theology of Trinity, Christology, and pneumatology.

Alongside the biblical witness to their phenomenological interrelatedness is the liturgical witness which indicates that Christian worship, from very early times, is also fashioned along distinctly triadic lines. Justin Martyr, around 150, describes a Eucharistic prayer: "the [presider] taking [the bread and wine], sends up praise and glory to the Father of all the universe through the name of the Son and of the Holy Spirit, and offers thanksgiving at some length that we have been deemed worthy to receive these things from him."[8] The *Apostolic Tradition*, traditionally attributed to Hippolytus, provides another early example of a Eucharistic prayer, attesting to a celebration that is expressed in the light of the mystery of the Three: "We render thanks to you, O God, through your beloved child Jesus Christ, whom in the last times you sent to us as a saviour and redeemer and angel of your will . . . he was made flesh and was manifested as your Son being born of the Holy Spirit and the Virgin."[9] Similarly, Hilary of Poitiers, in the fourth century, writes of the mystery of the Eucharistic communion and its link with the Trinity.[10]

Two thousand years later, the Eucharistic anaphora maintains a profoundly trinitarian structure and rhythm. The entire Eucharistic liturgy is encompassed in a Eucharistic-trinitarian *inclusio*, with the trinitarian invitation – "In the name of the Father, and of the Son, and of the Holy Spirit" – at the outset, and the trinitarian blessing – "May almighty God bless you, the Father, the Son and the Holy Spirit" – at the conclusion. The triumphant hymn of praise, the *Gloria*, takes up the opening trinitarian note and rises to a trinitarian hymn of praise. The liturgy of the Word prepares for the liturgy of the Eucharist, where the eucharistic prayer, celebrating the history of salvation, is fashioned along explicitly trinitarian lines in three stages: (1) *Eucharistia* (thanksgiving to the Father), (2) *Anamnesis* (remembrance, the calling to mind of the Son), and (3) *Epiclesis* (invocation of the Spirit). While the Eucharistic prayer is essentially addressed to the Father, as the one to whom the church addresses its thanksgiving, it unfolds with strong Christological and pneumatological tones, each echoing the other.[11] The whole liturgy is a celebration of the Trinity, in which the uniqueness and specificity of the divine persons are articulated and celebrated, and the Three worshiped and glorified.

As the biblical and liturgical witness demonstrates, Christian faith in the mystery of the Three was first expressed in prayer and worship, long before it was to find expression in dogma. Indeed, as Prosper of Aquitaine recognized, worship serves to express the *lex orandi* (the law of praying) of the Christian community, and as such effectively functions as a guide in, and criterion for, the discernment of the *lex credendi* (the law of believing) of the church, as has been demonstrated at a number of crucial points in the development of Christian doctrine.[12] For example, in the fourth-century debates concerning the question of the divinity of the Holy Spirit, Basil of Caesarea (Basil the Great) insisted on the co-equal divinity of the Spirit in the Triune Godhead on the basis of the *Gloria Patri* prayer (Glory be to the Father . . . ), arguing that "the Spirit is spoken of together with the Lord in precisely the same manner in which the Son is spoken of with the Father."[13] Gregory of Nazianzus argued along similar lines: "If He [the Holy Spirit] is not to be worshipped, how can He deify me by Baptism? but if He is to be worshipped, surely He is an Object of adoration, and if an Object of adoration He must be God."[14] In other words, the fact that the Holy Spirit was being invoked, on equal terms with the Father and the Son, in baptism, in doxology, and in liturgy, served as irrefutable proof of the Holy Spirit's full and co-equal divinity, on which the Council of Constantinople I (381) duly elaborated. The *lex orandi* thus informed and determined the formulation of the *lex credendi*.

It is this ontological interconnection that fundamentally grounds the interrelatedness of Trinity, Christology, and pneumatology from these phenomenological, hermeneutical, and liturgical perspectives. The Trinity *in se* is the original and ultimate mystery, from which everything else derives and in which everything else is located. It is from the Father, the font of divinity, the *archē*, that Son and Spirit proceed in the intra-trinitarian mystery of the Trinity, God *ad intra*. It is from the Father that Son and Spirit receive their missions *ad extra*, missions which are distinct but inseparable. Given that God has truly revealed Godself, the economic Trinity *is* the immanent Trinity. Herein lies the ontological foundation of the interconnection.

In terms of our actual experience of the Trinity in salvation history, the Trinity *ad extra*, it is the Spirit whom we first encounter, the Spirit who is given to us: "God's love has been poured into our hearts through the Holy Spirit who has been given to us" (Rom 5:5). It is the Holy Spirit who leads us to recognize, and incorporates us into, the mystery of Christ, in and through whom we are made sons and daughters of the Father. Thus, *quoad nos*, the Spirit is first, leading us to Jesus the Christ, and through him to the Trinity; but, *in se*, the Trinity is the originating mystery, the ontological ground of the interconnection of Trinity, Christology, and pneumatology.

It was inevitable that the ontological question of the relationship between Father, Son, and Spirit would eventually arise in the development of Christian doctrine and demand resolution. The radical claim, from within a conscious and determined monotheism, that Jesus is Lord and God eventually demanded clarification and definition. Such was the case when the so-called Arian crisis eventually erupted in the fourth century, with the question sharply focused on the status of the Son in relation to that of the Father. Once the question was catapulted to prominence, there would be no avoiding it. Even the Roman Emperor Constantine recognized the significance and the danger inherent in the moment, for the controversy threatened not only the unity of the church, but the stability of the newly united empire.

It would take decades to resolve the Arian controversy. The Council of Nicaea (325) provided a definitive endorsement of the full divinity of the Son: he is of one being, the same being (*homoousios*) with the Father, begotten, not created. The statement was all the more astonishing, given the council's use of the problematic and by no means respectable provenance of that non-biblical term. But the Arian argument was not so easily dispelled. Questions concerning the Spirit, about whom Nicaea said so little, prompted new variations on the Arian subordinationist theme. Then, as ever since, subordinationism offered in many ways a more plausible account of the interrelatedness of the Three. But, building on the theological contributions of the Cappadocians, and such principles as the *lex orandi, lex credendi*, the Council of Constantinople I defined that the Holy Spirit is truly really and fully God. While avoiding use of the vexatious *homoousios*, it proclaimed the divinity of the Spirit in no uncertain terms. The Holy Spirit, it proclaimed, is "the Lord and Giver of life, who proceeds from the Father, who together with the Father and the Son is worshiped and glorified, who has spoken through the prophets."[15] The council then added a series of affirmations, which effectively parallel the affirmations, stated in the earlier articles of the creed, of the work in salvation history of the Father (creation) and the Son (redemption), pronouncing: "[And we believe] in one Holy Catholic and apostolic church. We acknowledge one baptism for the forgiveness of sins. We expect the resurrection of the dead and the life of the world to come." As Jaroslav Pelikan has noted, these affirmations highlight the Spirit's role in the church, sustaining its structures, animating its life, inspiring its ministries.[16]

## THE CLASSICAL EXPRESSION OF THE INTERCONNECTION

The articulation of doctrine is one thing; the exploration and mediation of its meaning another. It is the task of theology, of faith seeking understanding, to tease out the meaning of doctrine and to mediate meaning within the intellectual framework of a given culture. Augustine of Hippo made a monumental contribution to the development in the West of an understanding of the mystery of the Trinity. Augustine brought two particularly significant and influential insights to trinitarian theology: (1) the clarification of the relationship between mission *ad extra* and procession *ad intra*, with the recognition that the mission *is* the prolongation, in time, of procession and, as such, a revelation of the eternal mystery of the procession; and (2) the exploration of what is now called the psychological analogy, as a means to deepen an understanding of the mystery of the intra-trinitarian processions.

The insight that the missions reveal the processions, as prolongations *ad extra* of the *ad intra* processions, crystallized a notion that is utterly critical to trinitarian theology, effectively connecting our knowledge of God *ad extra* with our knowledge of God *ad intra* (described in contemporary theology as the economic and immanent Trinity). Here is the intrinsic connection between the immanent and economic Trinity. It is through knowledge of the missions *ad extra*, revealed in the life and especially the paschal mystery of Jesus Christ, that we glean, if but dimly, the mystery of the processions *ad intra*. So what is revealed *ad extra* – that is, the relationship between Son, Spirit and Father, and the interrelatedness of the missions of Son and Spirit – constitutes the basis for our appreciation, albeit ever so limited, of the mystery of the Trinity *ad intra*, and the interrelatedness of Father, Son, and Spirit *in se*.

Focusing on the image of the Trinity in the very constitution of the human person, Augustine's exploration of analogies for the Trinity in the unity of the Godhead was to have profound influence on the development of trinitarian thinking in the West. Augustine explored numerous variations on this one theme: the analogy of memory, understanding, will, and the mental activities or operations of understanding and loving. This psychological analogy was later taken up and transposed into a highly refined Aristotelian metaphysical framework by Thomas Aquinas. The point of the analogy is that, here, in human consciousness, are three inherently interrelated operations or faculties, dynamically coinhering in the one being. It was, moreover, an image, an analogy, that was closely aligned with biblical witness to the missions of the Son and Spirit as Word and Love. This intra-subjective psychological analogy, as described by Augustine and refined by Thomas Aquinas, then served for centuries, right through to the twentieth century, as the explication *par excellence* of the mystery of the Trinity, with its two intra-trinitarian processions and the missions of the Word and Spirit in salvation history.

## RECENT ADVANCES: *ECONOMIA*-FASHIONED THEOLOGIES

Despite its elegance and refinement, the classical Thomistic explication of the mystery of the Trinity by way of the psychological analogy is no longer persuasive and effective in mediating meaning in the very different cultural milieu of the twenty-first century. The metaphysical framework which Thomas exploited to such effect is no longer presumed. It is neither surprising nor unwelcome that, in this very different cultural milieu, modern theologians look for new ways in which to explore and expound the mysteries of faith.

Most prominent in the renewal of trinitarian theology in the recent years has been the emergence of what might be called *economia*-fashioned trinitarian theologies. Karl Rahner provided singular impetus to take up an economic approach to the mystery of the Trinity, as revealed to us precisely in and through the person of Jesus Christ. For God is known, Rahner insisted, where God has revealed Godself, and that is precisely as manifest in the life of the Word incarnate, the Word existing as man, Jesus Christ. God's self-communication is truly a real *self*-communication. Karl Rahner rightly insisted, in the now oft-quoted "Rahner's Rule," that the economic Trinity *is* the immanent Trinity.[17] These *economia*-fashioned trinitarian theologies thus insist on beginning with what has been revealed in the economy of salvation and proceeding thence to an exploration of the mystery of the Trinity.[18]

Christology and pneumatology have similarly been re-fashioned from a determinedly economic perspective. In a *Christology from below*, the focus is not on Jesus' heavenly origins, nor even on his identity as the divine Logos, but on his life among us, his teaching, his miracles, his concern for the poor and oppressed, his suffering and death. A Christology from below starts with the Jesus of Nazareth in Galilee, the testimonies of those who knew him, their experience of life transformed through him, and their experience of his death and resurrection. In this kind of Christology, the focus is not on the descent of the Son from his Father in the heavens, but on the Word incarnate himself, in person, dwelling among us, sharing our humanity.[19]

Others have sought to fashion Christology along explicitly pneumatological lines. In a *Spirit Christology*, the primary concern is to articulate a Christology that is firmly grounded in the missions of Son and Spirit and their interconnection. After all, the hypostatic union of the human and the divine in the person of Jesus Christ is realized through the Holy Spirit and, indeed, it is made accessible to us through the Holy Spirit. We thus find a firm emphasis on the role of the Spirit in Jesus' life and mission, from his incarnation, in his baptism, through his life and ministry, to his death and resurrection. The crucial role which the Spirit plays in Jesus' life is thus highlighted, and a distinctly pneumatologically fashioned Christology results.[20] Some have pressed further and sought a determinedly trinitarian Christology, which attends not only to the role of the Spirit but also the role of the Father in Jesus' life, death, and resurrection.[21]

The flourishing of trinitarian theology and the new efforts in Christology have also provided impetus for new efforts in pneumatology, and in particular a distinctly *Christ-shaped pneumatology*.[22] Liberation theology, for example, whatever its particular perspective, be it Latin American, feminist, or ecological or whatever, focuses on the good news of liberation which characterizes Jesus' life and teaching and on the Spirit who accompanied, inspired, and motivated him. Liberation theologies recognize the tangible presence and power of the Christ-like Spirit everywhere at work in the quest for liberation in the world.[23]

One of the most significant of all the advances in trinitarian theology in recent decades is the *economia*-fashioned exploration of the mystery of the Trinity as revealed in the paschal mystery of Jesus Christ. Jürgen Moltmann and Hans Urs von Balthasar are pre-eminent pioneers of this nexus (interconnection) of the Trinity and the paschal mystery. For Moltmann, the cross is constitutive of God's triune being and the beginning of the trinitarian history of God. God is *this* trinitarian event, the event of the cross: the Father who delivers up his Son, the Son who is abandoned, the Holy Spirit who is the bond of union between them. For Balthasar, on the other hand, the separation of Father and Son in the cross is eternally allowed for, included and exceeded in the eternal supra-temporal drama of trinitarian life wherein the Father begets the Son. It is not that divine being is rent asunder in the event of the crucifixion, as Moltmann would suggest, but rather that, in the cross event, the Triune God of love, who in love allows for the radical separation and differentiation of freedom, enters the very hiatus of our death and draws creation into God's own life. While coming from such different perspectives, Moltmann through an eschatological origination and Balthasar through a primordial origination, both grapple with the reality of God's genuine engagement in the life, the struggle and the suffering of the world, and the problem of evil that afflicts us. In retrospect, it is perhaps not so surprising that such concerted and dramatic theological attempts to tackle the problem of evil surfaced in the wake of the horrors of two world wars, which threw into even sharper relief the arid abstractions of post-Tridentine scholastic theology and the inadequacy of the textbook approach of the manuals. The effort to construct a trinitarian theology in the clear light of Jesus' paschal mystery also sought to engage with and respond to the protest atheism that flourished in post-war Europe.[24]

What all of these theological approaches share is a concern to ground their explorations in the divine self-communication enacted in Jesus Christ. For that reason and in the process, more traditional ontological or metaphysical questions concerning the mystery of the Trinity are either deferred or dismissed as existentially irrelevant. Despite this invigorating soteriological emphasis, however, there are problems. When the starting point is the divine Three, as revealed in salvation history, there emerges a vitally refreshed perception of their distinctiveness and proper roles. The interplay of the three *dramatis personae* comes to the fore, with less consideration given to their unity – and hence, a special difficulty, somewhat similar to that which the Cappadocians faced and which provoked Gregory of Nazianzus' treatise *On Not Three Gods*. The *economia*-fashioned approaches typically yield a socially conceived Trinity, often designated as "the social model" of the Trinity. With a strong emphasis on the relational and social aspects of personhood, this approach has proved generally persuasive and appealing in the contemporary milieu.[25] In such constructions, questions of terminological and conceptual rigor are muted in favour of more existentially compelling accounts of faith's mysteries and meaning. The technicalities demanded by the cognitive function and the theoretical realm of meaning of trinitarian faith tend to take second place.[26] What count most are the effective function of meaning and the practical ramifications of trinitarian faith for Christian life and conduct in the world. When and if the ontological question of the unity of the Three is raised, it is addressed by appealing to the patristic notion of the divine *perichōrēsis*, the dynamic mutual indwelling.[27]

## CONTINUING EXPLORATIONS

In the current theological arena, there are, I suggest, two particularly noteworthy areas of potentially very fruitful exploration of the mystery of the Trinity and its interconnection with Christology and pneumatology.

### Trinitarian soteriology

The development of an expressly trinitarian soteriology allows a much more inclusive approach to the question of the salvation of non-Christians and to the world religions to which they belong. An explicitly *trinitarian* approach to this range of questions has the potential to mitigate problems associated with the classical Christomonist approach. It affords Christian faith the possibility not only of an enriched theology of religions, but also of a deeper appreciation of the trinitarian mystery in its Christological, pneumatological, and indeed patrological dimensions.

Raimon Panikkar has made a significant contribution here that is still to be fully appreciated. Admittedly, Panikkar's thought is complex and continues to evolve in a highly creative way that is uniquely his own. But, to summarize very briefly, Panikkar suggests that the realm of spiritual experience and spirituality is a more fruitful avenue of approach to interfaith dialogue, rather than creeds and doctrinal formulations. Let us start, he suggests, "by defining any given spirituality, pragmatically and even phenomenologically, as being one typical way of handling the human condition. Next let us put this in *more* religious terms by saying that it represents man's basic attitude *vis-à-vis* his ultimate end."[28] On the basis of his own experience of the world religions in the religiously rich context of Asia, Panikkar recognizes three essentially different forms of spirituality in the world religions. He relates this to three concepts of the divine: (1) a silent self-emptying apophatic dimension of spirituality, such as is found in the Buddhist experience of *nirvāna*; (2) a personalistic dimension, as is expressed in the spirituality of the person of the Son in Christianity, which has its history in Judaism and Yahweh's revelation to the Jews; and (3) an immanent dimension, which is found in Hinduism and its spirituality of nonduality of the self and the Absolute, and of undifferentiated union with the Absolute. Panikkar then brings an explicitly trinitarian approach to the phenomenon of a plurality of world religions, by relating these three different spiritual understandings and spiritualities that he perceives in the world religions to the Christian experience of the three persons of the Trinity. His intention is not to expound the doctrine of the Trinity, but to show how these three forms of spirituality can be reconciled in the light of the mystery of the Trinity.

Panikkar firstly relates the Christian understanding of the person of the Father, *ho theos*, in the Trinity with the Hindu sense of the Absolute. Panikkar thus relates Buddhism and its apophatic silence to the Christian experience and understanding of the Father – who himself is silent, who dwells in inaccessible light, and expresses himself only through the Son. Panikkar then relates Judaism, Islam, and Christianity, as religions which claim personal divine revelation of the Word of God, to the Christian experience of the person of the Son, who mediates between God and humankind and through whom all creation has been made and has its being. While transcendence characterizes the Father, immanence characterizes the Spirit. Here Panikkar makes the connection between the immanent dimension of the spirituality of Advaitan Hinduism with the Christian understanding of Spirit. Panikkar can thus summarize the spiritualities of the world religions in terms of apophaticism, personalism, and divine immanence – and so identifies these three essential dimensions of spirituality with the three persons of the Trinity: Father, Son, and Holy Spirit. In Panikkar's approach, the Trinity emerges as the junction where the spiritualities manifest in the world religions meet.

Indeed, the very existence of religious pluralism is grounded ontologically in the mystery of the Trinity. There is undoubtedly much more work to be done in the area of trinitarian soteriology, but Panikkar's insights point the way to promising possibilities for development in this area.

### Retrievals and transpositions of the classical approach

The classic psychological analogy has fallen seriously out of favour in much contemporary theology, Catholic as well as Protestant. This is no doubt due in large part to the refined – but now obsolete and, for most, inaccessible – metaphysical framework in which it found its classical Thomistic expression. Interpersonal relations have now risen to the fore and captured the theological imagination, perhaps reflecting a crisis of interpersonal relationships within the wider culture. Nevertheless, there are signs of the emergence of a renewed appreciation of Aquinas' contribution. Current developments in historical theology are recovering the authentic contribution of Aquinas. As a result, later accretions deriving more from later commentators, such as Cajetan and Suarez, and post-Tridentine scholasticism, have been identified more clearly, and the attenuated Thomism of the post-Tridentine manuals corrected.[29]

Secondly, there are the efforts of a reinvigorated systematic theology to retrieve the psychological analogy itself, and to appreciate and exploit its explicative power in new ways. This has meant setting aside the metaphysical wrappings in which the analogy is classically expressed, and transposing it into a framework informed by contemporary understandings of the human person.[30] Here, Bernard Lonergan's magisterial contribution has proved seminal, with his analysis of human interiority and the fundamental dynamism of human intentionality manifest in the self-transcending dynamics of questioning, thinking, judging, in the restless search for the good, the true, the beautiful, and the holy.[31] Lonergan's followers have carried forward his effort, incorporating contemporary social sciences and modern psychology, and demonstrating that the psychological analogy, appropriately transposed for contemporary discourse, can continue fruitfully to serve theology's endeavour to mediate the meaning of the trinitarian mystery in the contemporary cultural and social context.[32]

## CONCLUSION

In our necessarily brief overview, we have surveyed contemporary developments in the area of the interconnection of Trinity, Christology, and pneumatology. What is very clear is that the old theological divisions are not working effectively and persuasively in the new situation of contemporary culture, as is evident in the burgeoning of new approaches. A new systematics of interconnections is coming to light, albeit under a variety of guises and in response to various exigencies.[33] Some exciting and potentially very fruitful new areas of interconnection are emerging. Some gaps are also becoming evident, calling for further exploration. One cannot but note, for example, that mainstream Christian theology is still predominantly Western in style and conceptuality. We eagerly await the flowering of non-Western, non-Eurocentric theologies of Trinity, Christology, and pneumatology – Asian, African, indigenous – and their warm reception in the service of the universal church and its mission.

## Notes

1. Earl J. Richard, *First and Second Thessalonians*, Sacra Pagina (Collegeville, MN: Liturgical Press, 1995), against more common views that date 1 Thess around 50 or 51, argues for dating the Thessalonian correspondence to the 40s, and for the composite character of 1 Thess, with 2:13–4:2 an earlier missive and 1:1–2:12 and 4:3–5:28 a later one.
2. Larry Hurtado traces the early emergence of devotion to Jesus, within monotheism, in *Lord Jesus Christ: Devotion to Jesus in Earliest Christianity* (Grand Rapids, MI, and Cambridge, UK: Eerdmans, 2003).
3. Vatican I, *Constitution on Divine Revelation, Dei Filius*. See J. Neuner and J. Dupuis, eds., *The Christian Faith in the Doctrinal Documents of the Catholic Church*, 6th rev. and enlarged edn. (New York: Alba House, 1996), §132, or H. Denziger and A. Schönmetzer, eds., *Enchiridion symbolorum: Definitionum et declarationum de rubus fidei et morum*, 36th edn. (Freiburg: Herder, 1976), §3016.
4. See Joachim Jeremias' classic study *The Prayers of Jesus*, Studies in Biblical Theology, Second Series, 6 (London: SCM Press, 1967). See also, in regard to Jesus' use of the name Abba, Wolfhart Pannenberg, *Systematic Theology*, trans. Geoffrey W. Bromiley, 3 vols. (Grand Rapids, MI: Eerdmans, 1991–98), I, 260.
5. Irenaeus, "Against Heresies," 4.19.2, 4.20.1–2, 5.1.3, and 5.6.1, in *The Ante-Nicene Fathers*, I, ed. A. Roberts and J. Donaldson (Grand Rapids, MI: Eerdmans, 1975), 487–88, 527, 531.
6. Yves Congar, *The Word and the Spirit*, trans. David Smith (London: Geoffrey Chapman; San Francisco: Harper & Row, 1986), I; see also Yves Congar, *I Believe in the Holy Spirit*, trans. David Smith (New York: Seabury; London: Geoffrey Chapman, 1983), II, 35.
7. Of all contemporary theologians, it is Wolfhart Pannenberg who has achieved a systematic theology which is most thoroughly trinitarian. See Pannenberg's three-volumed *Systematic Theology*.

8. Justin Martyr, *First Apology* 65, in Cyril C. Richardson, ed., *Early Christian Fathers* (New York: Macmillan, 1970), 286.
9. Hippolytus, *Apostolic Tradition*, 4. See Geoffrey J. Cuming, *Hippolytus: A Text for Students, with Introduction, Translation, Commentary, and Notes* (Bramcote: Grove Books, 1976). See R. C. D. Jasper and G. J. Cumin, eds., *Prayers of the Eucharist: Early and Reformed*, 3rd edn. (New York: Pueblo, 1987), 35. See also John F. Baldovin, "Hippolytus and the Apostolic Tradition: Recent Research and Commentary," *Theological Studies*, 63 (2003), 520–42.
10. See Hilary of Poitiers, "The Trinity" VIII.13–17, in *Nicene and Post-Nicene Fathers*, Second Series, IX, ed. W. Sanday, trans. E. W. Watson, L. Pullan, and others (Grand Rapids, MI: Eerdmans, 1976), 141–12.
11. For detailed discussion of the history and structure of the Eucharist, see Enrico Mazza, *The Celebration of the Eucharist: The Origin of the Rite and the Development of its Interpretation*, trans. Matthew J. O'Connell (Collegeville, MN: Liturgical Press, 1999).
12. For use of the *lex orandi, lex credendi* principle, see Jaroslav Pelikan, *Credo: Historical and Theological Guide to Creeds and Confessions of Faith in the Christian Tradition* (New Haven and London: Yale University Press, 2003), 166–78.
13. Basil of Caesarea, *On the Holy Spirit* 17.43, in *Nicene and Post-Nicene Fathers*, Second Series, VIII, ed. P. Schaff and H. Wace (Grand Rapids, MI: Eerdmans, 1975), 27.
14. Gregory of Nazianzus, *Fifth Theological Oration: On the Holy Spirit, Oratio* 32, 28, in *Nicene and Post-Nicene Fathers*, VII, ed. P. Schaff and H. Wace, trans. C. G. Browne and J. E. Swallour (Grand Rapids, MI: Eerdmans, 1974), 327.
15. Note that the phrase "and the Son" (Latin: *filioque*) is not included in this Creed. Its later unilateral inclusion in the Western church contributed in large measure to the continuing division between the East and West. Note also, however, that the creed does not say that the Holy Spirit proceeds from the Father *alone*.
16. Pelikan, *Credo*, 25.
17. Karl Rahner, *The Trinity*, trans. Joseph Donceel, introduction, index, and glossary by Catherine LaCugna (New York: Crossroad, 1997; original London: Burns and Oates, 1969), 21–24.
18. A notable pioneer in the construction of *economia*-fashioned theology of Trinity, Christology, and pneumatology, albeit in the field of biblical theology, is François-Xavier Durrwell.
19. For examples, see the Christologies of Edward Schillebeeckx and Jon Sobrino.
20. See, for example, David Coffey's theology.
21. See the theology of Wolfhart Pannenberg and Jürgen Moltmann, who have consistently attempted an expressly *trinitarian* approach in their theologies. See especially Pannenberg's *Systematic Theology*.
22. For a monumental contemporary attempt in pneumatology, see Congar, *I Believe in the Holy Spirit*.

23. See, for example, the Latin American liberation theology of Leonardo Boff, the feminist liberation theology of Elizabeth A. Johnson, and the ecotheology of Denis Edwards.
24. For a discussion of the nexus of the Trinity and the paschal mystery of Moltmann and von Balthasar in this regard, see Anne Hunt, *The Trinity and the Paschal Mystery* (Collegeville, MN: Liturgical Press, 1997), 164–71.
25. Consider, for example, the use of the social model of the Trinity in the theologies of Jürgen Moltmann, John Zizioulas, and Catherine LaCugna.
26. For a discussion of the different functions and realms of meaning, see Bernard Lonergan, *Method in Theology* (New York: Seabury, 1972), 76–85.
27. Gary D. Badcock, *Light of Truth and Fire of Love: A Theology of the Holy Spirit* (Grand Rapids, MI, and Cambridge: Eerdmans, 1997), 212 ff., also notes the difficulties associated with constructing a systematic trinitarian conception on the basis of the economy of salvation, due to the sheer diversity of paradigms given in the economic data provided by the New Testament.
28. Raimando Panikkar, *The Trinity and the Religious Experience of Man: Icon-Person-Mystery* (Maryknoll, NY: Orbis; London: Darton, Longman & Todd, 1973), 9.
29. See, for example, the work of Jean-Pierre Torrell and Gilles Emery.
30. Anthony Kelly, "The 'Horrible Wrappers' of Aquinas' God," *Pacifica*, 9 (1996), 185–203.
31. See, for example, Bernard Lonergan, *Collected Works of Bernard Lonergan*, XII: *The Triune God: Systematics*, ed. Robert M. Doran and H. Daniel Monsour (University of Toronto Press, 2007).
32. See, for example, the work of Frederick Crowe, Robert Doran, Anthony Kelly, and Neil Ormerod.
33. See Anne Hunt, *Trinity: Nexus of the Mysteries of Christian Faith* (Maryknoll, NY: Orbis, 2005).

## Further reading

Congar, Yves, *I Believe in the Holy Spirit*, trans. David Smith, 3 vols. (New York: Seabury; London: Geoffrey Chapman, 1983).

*The Word and the Spirit*, trans. David Smith (London: Geoffrey Chapman; San Francisco: Harper & Row, 1986).

Hunt, Anne, *The Trinity and the Paschal Mystery* (Collegeville, MN: Liturgical Press, 1997).

*Trinity: Nexus of the Mysteries of Christian Faith* (Maryknoll, NY: Orbis, 2005).

*Trinity: Insights from the Mystics* (Collegeville, MN: Liturgical Press, 2010).

Pannenberg, Wolfhart, *Systematic Theology*, trans. Geoffrey W. Bromiley, 3 vols. (Grand Rapids, MI: Eerdmans, 1991–98).

# 22 The Trinity in the liturgy, sacraments, and mysticism

SUSAN K. WOOD

The role of the Trinity in both liturgical prayer and mystical prayer, as different as these prayer forms might seem, must be understood within the economy of salvation, that is, in God's action to reconcile the world to himself. This involves a trinitarian dynamic, which one might call the "grammar of Christian life."[1] Christians are reconciled to the Father through Christ in the power of the Spirit. The relationship of Christ to the Father and to the Spirit is strikingly evident in his baptism and in his death, where his orientation to the Father and the reception and gift of the Spirit occur in what can only be called a trinitarian tableau at the beginning and end of his life. This chapter examines how the larger pattern of all liturgical action incorporates this trinitarian pattern, as do the individual sacramental rites and a number of examples of mystical prayer. That mysticism should reflect this dynamic is not surprising since the spirituality of the mystics is formed by their immersion in scripture and the liturgical life of the church.

Although there is no explicit doctrine of the Trinity in the scriptures, the life of Jesus is framed by two iconic images of the Trinity: Jesus' baptism in the Jordan and his death on the cross.[2] At Jesus' baptism in the Jordan, when Jesus came up from the water, the heavens were opened and the Spirit of God descended like a dove upon him. A voice from heaven said, "This is my Son, the Beloved, with whom I am well pleased" (Mt 3:17). This theophany of Father, Son, and Spirit reveals Jesus as the Christ, the anointed one, and the beloved Son of the Father.

At the end of his life, in Matthew's and Mark's gospels, Jesus' only words on the cross are the cry of the righteous person abandoned by God: "My God, my God, why have you forsaken me?" (Mk 15:34; Mt 27:46; Ps 22:1). In Luke, Jesus' words are the prayers of a righteous person surrendering to God: "Father, into your hands I commend my spirit" (Lk 23:46; Ps 31:5). In John's gospel Jesus bows his head and gives up his spirit (Jn 19:30). In his last words, Jesus remains oriented to the Father and, in his death, gives his spirit, identified with his very breath (Lk 23:46). This last moment is a recapitulation of his whole life oriented to the Father.

This reference to spirit in Luke's account of Jesus' death is consistent with the emphasis on spirit in the rest of Luke's gospel, where Jesus' identity and the mission flowing from that identity are indissociable from the Spirit. In his baptism in the Jordan, the Holy Spirit descends upon him in bodily form like a dove (Lk 3:22). Luke also carefully notes that filled with the Spirit, Jesus returns from the Jordan and is led by the Spirit into the wilderness to be tempted (4:1), and again "filled with the power of the Holy Spirit" begins his public ministry in Galilee by reading the text of the prophet Isaiah, "The Spirit of the Lord is upon me, because he has anointed me to bring good news to the poor" (4:18) and by announcing that "Today this scripture has been fulfilled in your hearing" (4:21). Jesus' mission of salvation and redemption is thus clearly accomplished in the Spirit.

Jesus' intimate relationship with his Father is captured in his prayer to the Father, addressing him as "Abba" (Mk 14:36), in teaching his disciples to pray by addressing God as Father (Lk 11:2), and in following this instruction on prayer by the example of repeated and insistent prayer with the conclusion: "If you then, who are evil, know how to give good gifts to your children, how much more will the heavenly Father give the Holy Spirit to those who ask him" (Lk 11:13). Prayer is directed to the Father, and the greatest answer to prayer is the gift of the Spirit. Therefore we see that although the scriptures do not contain an explicit doctrine of the Trinity as such, the dynamic of Jesus' life and death, as well as the dynamic in which he instructs his disciples, is trinitarian in structure: Christ, the Son of God, is the exemplar of the Christian life, oriented to the Father and empowered by the Spirit.

Christ is not just an external exemplar of Christian living. In the sacraments Christians are joined to Christ in the power of the Spirit and actually participate in his paschal mystery of dying and rising. Christ's trinitarian pattern of life becomes theirs. The relations between Father, Son, and Spirit become the grammar or form of Christian living. For example, according to Ephesians 2:18 we have access to the Father through Christ and in one Spirit. The Trinity is the central doctrinal explication of what we do in the public prayer of the church in liturgy: praise and glorify the Father through the Son in the power of the Holy Spirit. Conversely, the liturgy also functions as the source and context of trinitarian theology.[3] The patterns of the liturgy disclose the trinitarian dynamic of Christian living: everything comes from God the Father through Christ, in the Spirit, and everything returns to God the Father, through Christ, in the Spirit (Eph 1:3–14).[4]

The larger pattern of liturgical action is trinitarian and reflects this "grammar" of the Christian economy. In the liturgy there is both a descending movement, comprising God's saving action directed toward us, and an ascending movement, of our praise and thanksgiving, directed toward God.[5] Thus liturgy is dialogic, comprised of a divine word and a human answer. Liturgy is also doxological: we give thanks and praise to the Father, we remember the Son, and we invoke the Holy Spirit. The twofold purpose of liturgy is the sanctification of women and men and the worship of God.

The movement of God's saving action and our response are related to two essential liturgical elements, anamnesis and epiclesis. Anamnesis, translated as "memorial," "commemoration," or "remembrance," actually has the much stronger meaning of making present an event or person from the past. Anamnesis asks God to remember his saving work in Jesus Christ in order that the benefits of Christ's sacrifice may be made present to the faithful here and now. These deeds are actually made present in the liturgy in the anamnesis, not as a repetition of his saving deeds or as a mere recollection of them, but as an actualization of them within the modality of sacramental sign. The anamnesis is accomplished through the work of the Spirit, who "awakens the memory of the Church then inspires thanksgiving and praise."[6]

The epiclesis is a calling on the Spirit to transform the material of creation and make it salvific in its sacramental use. Sacraments are effective because they are Christ's action, made present through the power of the Spirit. Although we may think of the epiclesis primarily in terms of the Eucharist, most of the sacraments, as we shall see, have an epicletic moment. The Holy Spirit brings us into communion with Christ, effects our spiritual transformation into the image of Christ, both individually and corporately, and constitutes Christ's ecclesial body, the *corpus mysticum*. Thus the Spirit is the bond of unity in the church and the source of empowerment for service and mission.

The Father as the source and end of all blessings of creation and salvation is the source and goal of the liturgy, which reveals and communicates the divine blessing.[7] We receive these blessings through the incarnate Word of the Father, who, in turn, pours out the gift of the Spirit. The liturgy offers adoration, praise, and thanksgiving to the Father by offering to the Father his own gifts, especially the gift of his Son. The Spirit "recalls and makes Christ manifest to the faith of the assembly," "makes Christ present here and now," and "unites the Church to the life and mission of Christ."[8]

The end or purpose of all the sacraments is reconciliation with the Father and the Father's glorification (Eph 1:12; 2 Cor 3:18; Jn 17). The Latin word for sacrament, *sacramentum*, is a translation of the Greek word *mysterion*, which refers to God's plan for salvation (Col 1:26–27). This plan is the Father's plan "to reconcile to himself all things through Christ, in whom the fullness of God was pleased to dwell, who made peace through the blood of his cross" (Col 1:19–20). The paschal mystery is the keystone of the Christian mystery. All the liturgical feasts and sacraments are referenced to the event of Christ's dying and rising and to this great pattern of reconciliation with the Father through Christ in the power of the Spirit. Thus the liturgical year is not simply a memesis or imitation of Christ's life. Christmas is primarily about God's Word becoming flesh and dwelling among human beings in order to bring salvation. Sacraments are not just seven anthropological markers of lifetime passages such as birth, puberty, sickness, and marriage, but relate to the two fundamental sacraments, baptism and Eucharist, in their functions of reconciliation and building up the church as a messianic saving community.[9] Sacraments give access to participation in this plan of salvation, anamnesis (memorial) and epiclesis being essential to each of them. Anamnesis recalls the saving event of Jesus' death and resurrection so that it is actually present today, and epiclesis makes it effective through the power of the Spirit. As Louis-Marie Chauvet has noted, "The sacraments appear not as the somehow static prolongations of the incarnation as such but as the major expression, in our own history, of the embodiment (historical/eschatological) of the risen One in the world through the Spirit, embodiment whose 'fundamental sacrament' is the church visibly born at Pentecost."[10]

## BAPTISM

In Matthew's gospel the dominical command to baptize is in the name of the Trinity: "Go therefore and make disciples of all nations, baptizing them in the name of the Father and of the Son and of the Holy Spirit" (Mt 28:19). Scripture scholars are generally agreed that this represents a later development of the text and clearly reflects a liturgical tradition already in place in the Matthean community. The other scripture passage which puts a reference to baptism on the lips of Jesus, Mark 16:16, belongs to the later addition to the gospel and dates from the second century. Vorgrimler concludes that we cannot attribute the practice of baptism to the direct institution by Jesus, even though it is certain that early Christian communities baptized from an early date.[11]

Thus the trinitarian relationship to Christian baptism is not simply to be found in a biblical proof text about baptism. This is further substantiated by the fact that there is evidence that the earliest baptisms were not in the triune name, but in the name of Jesus (Acts 2:38, 8:16, 10:48, 19:5). Later baptism in the triune name represents a Christological development in terms of Jesus' identity as Son of the Father and giver of the Spirit. A better place to find the trinitarian foundation of Christian baptism is in the revelatory scene of Jesus' baptism in the Jordan, which manifests Jesus' identity as the beloved Son of God anointed by the Spirit as well as in the overall trinitarian economy of salvation.

The rite of baptism actually contains three reiterations of this trinitarian economy of salvation: the blessing of the baptismal water, the most extended and explicit explication of this economy, the threefold profession of faith, and the trinitarian formula of baptism. With each reiteration, the trinitarian reference becomes shorter as if a sort of shorthand for the former.

The structure of the prayer over the water is that of a Eucharistic anaphora: anamnesis, epiclesis, and a concluding doxology. In replicating the structure of Eucharistic prayer, the prayer evokes the grammar and purpose of liturgical prayer. We give thanks and praise to the Father, we remember the Son, and we invoke the Holy Spirit. The sacrament is given for the glorification of God through Christ's self-gift to the Father and through our transformation into Christ and incorporation in that same self-gift.

The baptismal prayer explicitly identifies water as the Father's gift, a symbol of the grace of the sacrament. The anamnesis begins with the remembrance of all the ways in which water has figured in the history of salvation: the Spirit breathing on the waters at the dawn of creation, making them the "wellspring of all holiness"; the waters of the great flood, a sign of baptism that makes an end of sin and a new beginning of goodness; the waters of the Red Sea through which the Israelites passed to safety; the waters of the Jordan in which the Son was baptized by John and anointed with the Spirit; and, finally, the water and blood which flowed from the side of Christ on the cross. The epiclesis asks the Father to give to the water the grace of his Son by the power of the Holy Spirit so that in the sacrament of baptism all those whom the Father has created in his likeness may be cleansed from sin and arise to a new birth of innocence by water and the Holy Spirit. In addition, the epiclesis asks that the Holy Spirit may be sent upon the waters of the font that all who are buried with Christ in the death of baptism may rise also with Christ to newness of life. The *exitus* is a departure from sin and death, and the *reditus* is resurrection in newness of life with Christ. In baptism Christians are sanctified and give glory to God.

In the threefold profession of faith the candidate is asked:

> Do you believe in God, the Father Almighty, creator of heaven and earth?
>
> Do you believe in Jesus Christ, his only Son, our Lord who was born of the virgin Mary, was crucified, died, and was buried, rose from the dead, and is now seated at the right hand of the Father?
>
> Do you believe in the Holy Spirit, the holy Catholic Church, the communion of saints, the forgiveness of sins, the resurrection of the body, and life everlasting?

This interrogatory form of the Apostles' creed identifies the work of the Father as creation, names the paschal mystery of the Son, and identifies the work of the Spirit as the bond of unity of the church, the forgiveness of sin, and the instrument of final resurrection and eternal life.

Finally, the celebrant either immerses the candidate or pours water three times on the candidate's head saying, "I baptize you in the name of the Father, and of the Son and of the Holy Spirit." With these words the new Christian is initiated into a trinitarian way of life. The mission of the Trinity is the Father sending the Son to give the Spirit in order that all may be reconciled to him. The Christian is called to participate in that same mission. This entails a life that is oriented to the other rather than the self, a self-donation in love arising out of freedom. It implies a life lived in communion with others since God's very being is a communion of relations. Human love, human family, and community become iconic of God.

A Christian enters the church through the waters of baptism. The church, trinitarian in its identity as the people of God constituted as temple of the Spirit and Body of Christ, is an effective sign – and thus a sort of sacrament – of intimate union with God, and of the unity of all humankind.[12] The church is an instrument of communion through which Christians are inserted into these trinitarian relationships in the economy of salvation, and both model with their lives communion with God and work to promote the unity of all humankind.

## THE EUCHARIST

The trinitarian dynamic of the economy of salvation is perhaps most evident in the celebration of the Eucharist, which commemorates the great *exitus-reditus* wherein we recognize the Father as the creator and giver of gifts which are transformed in the power of the Holy Spirit into the Body of Christ and returned in offering to the Father. The Eucharistic prayers are structured according to this trinitarian pattern: giving thanks to the Father, remembering the saving deeds of the Son, and calling on the Spirit. The Eucharistic prayers end with the great doxology: "Through him, with him, in him, in the unity of the Holy Spirit, all glory and honor is yours, Almighty Father, both now and forever." The Eucharist is given for the glorification of God through Christ's self-gift to the Father and through our transformation into Christ and incorporation in that same self-gift. Participants in the liturgy actually participate in Jesus' paschal mystery and his present glory through the mediation of the Eucharist.

The saving deeds of the Son and his death, resurrection, and anticipated return at the end of time are remembered in the liturgical anamnesis. The church invokes the Holy Spirit's transforming power in the epiclesis. The first epiclesis calls on God the Father to send the Holy Spirit to transform the gifts of bread and wine into the sacramental body and blood of Jesus. A second epiclesis prays that the assembly may be transformed into Christ's body, effecting the ecclesial body of Christ and the unity of the church.

The Eucharist in its anamnesis remembers the paschal mystery of Jesus Christ in his life, death, resurrection, and exaltation. In recalling this paschal event, the church offers to God Christ's one sacrifice now sacramentally present as the bread of life and the cup of eternal salvation.

This paschal mystery of salvation is not only Christological: it is trinitarian, for the Father sends the Son who lives, dies, rises, and sends the Spirit that we, too, may ascend to the Father through Christ in the power of the Holy Spirit. The anamnesis is not merely remembering in the sense of recalling or bringing to mind something long past and perhaps forgotten, but renders that event present and active.

## CONFIRMATION

The close association of confirmation with baptism is observed in the rite through a renewal of baptismal promises, which includes the threefold interrogatory profession of faith. The profession of faith in the

Holy Spirit is expanded to include a reference to Pentecost and the belief that on this day the Spirit is given sacramentally to the confirmand. Although rich in allusions to the Holy Spirit, as in all liturgical prayer, the prayer of confirmation is directed to the Father. Just before the anointing with chrism, the bishop and the priests who will minister the sacrament with him extend their hands over the candidates. The bishop prays for the gift of the Spirit, which equips the confirmands with the qualities needed for their prophetic role in the church lived out primarily by being a living witness to Christ.

The blessing at the end of Mass is trinitarian in form:

> God our Father
> made you his children by water and the Holy Spirit:
> may he bless you and watch over you with his fatherly love.
> R/. Amen.
> Jesus Christ the Son of God
> promised that the Spirit of truth
> would be with his Church for ever:
> may he bless you and give you courage
> in professing the true faith.
> R/. Amen.
> The Holy Spirit
> came down upon the disciples
> and set their hearts on fire with love:
> may he bless you,
> keep you one in faith and love
> and bring you to the joy of God's kingdom.
> R/. Amen.
> May almighty God bless you,
> the Father, and the Son, and the Holy Spirit.
> R/. Amen.

Even though this blessing is trinitarian in form, it retains an emphasis on the Spirit, who is referenced in all three main sections. This blessing links confirmation to baptism in the allusion to water and the Holy Spirit, references the prophetic office in the mention of the Spirit of truth, and alludes to the role of the Spirit in creating unity where it speaks of setting the hearts of the disciples on fire with love.

## THE RITE OF PENANCE

In the rite for individual confession and absolution the prayer of absolution is pronounced while the priest extends at least his right hand over the penitent's head, an epicletic gesture. The form of the prayer is trinitarian, announcing God's reconciliation of the world to himself through the death and resurrection of the Son and the mission of the Holy Spirit for the forgiveness of sins. It ends in a brief doxology.

The longer form of absolution, in the rite for reconciliation of several penitents with general confession and absolution, offers a richer and much more expanded trinitarian theology:

> God the Father does not wish the sinner to die
> But to turn back to him and live.
> He loved us first and sent his Son into the world to be its Savior.
> May he show you his merciful love and give you peace.
> R/. Amen.
> Our Lord Jesus Christ was given up to death for our sins,
> and rose again for our justification.
> He sent the Holy Spirit on his apostles
> and gave them power to forgive sins.
> Through the ministry entrusted to me
> may he deliver you from evil
> and fill you with his Holy Spirit.
> R/. Amen.
> The Spirit, the Comforter, was given to us for the forgiveness of sins.
> In him we approach the Father.
> May he cleanse your hearts and clothe you in his glory,
> so that you may proclaim the mighty acts of God
> who has called you out of darkness into the splendor of his light.
> R/. Amen.
> And I absolve you from your sins
> in the name of the Father, and of the Son,
> and of the Holy Spirit.
> R/. Amen.

In the sacrament of penance, the penitent is reconciled to the Father through the saving death and resurrection of the Son in the power of the Spirit.

## THE ANOINTING OF THE SICK

The introductory part of the thanksgiving over the blessed oil in the rite of the anointing of the sick and in the prayer for blessing the oil during the rite is trinitarian in form:

Praise to you, God, the almighty Father.
You sent your Son to live among us
and bring us salvation.
Response: Blessed be God who heals us in Christ.
Praise to you, God, the only-begotten Son.
You humbled yourself to share in our humanity
and you heal our infirmities.
Response: Blessed be God who heals us in Christ.
Praise to you, God, the Holy Spirit, the Consoler.
Your unfailing power gives us strength
in our bodily weakness.
Response: Blessed be God who heals us in Christ.

The prayer highlights the mission of the Father in sending the Son to bring salvation, the curative power of the Son, and the consoling function of the Spirit. The trinitarian references are specifically fitted to health, for the root meaning of "salvation" is *salus*, health.

## THE SACRAMENT OF ORDER

The prayers of ordination for the bishop, presbyter, and deacon are trinitarian in form and situate ministry within a trinitarian context. In the prayer for a presbyter, for example, the prayer is directed to the Father, who by the power of the Holy Spirit provides various forms of ministry within the church of Christ, the Son. The anamnesis of the prayer recalls how, in an earlier covenant, the Father set Moses and Aaron over the people to govern and sanctify them and how men next in rank and dignity were chosen to accompany them and assist them in their task. The prayer also recalls how the spirit of Moses was implanted in the hearts of seventy wise men to assist him and how an abundant share of their father's plenty was poured upon the sons of Aaron so that the number of the priests prescribed by the Law might be sufficient for the sacrifices of the tabernacle. Finally, in a second trinitarian dynamic, the prayer recalls that Jesus, God's Son, is the Apostle and High Priest who offered himself through the Holy Spirit to the Father as a spotless victim. Jesus made the Apostles sharers in his mission who, in turn, also had companions in their work of salvation. The purpose of this anamnesis is to remind the Father that he has always provided ministers and helpers to form a priestly people, in order to beseech that he may do so again this day through the ordination of presbyters who will be co-workers with the bishops.

The gift of the Holy Spirit for the office of presbyter is conferred by the laying-on of hands and the prayer of ordination. The central epicletic moment is the prayer to the Holy Spirit at the moment of the imposition of hands in silence just before the prayer of ordination. The laying-on of hands is always an epicletic gesture and is also used in confirmation, penance, and the anointing of the sick. The epiclesis within the prayer of ordination asks for the Spirit of holiness so that the priests may instill good conduct through their manner of life. It is through the Spirit that the gospel bears fruit in human hearts even to the ends of the earth. The final trinitarian reference is the concluding doxology.

## MARRIAGE

The rite of marriage perhaps has the least developed trinitarian theology and prayer texts of all the sacraments. The rite contains references to marriage "in Christ" and allusions to the marriage of Christ and his church, but references to the Spirit are almost absent. The exchange of rings, a comparatively minor moment in the marriage rite, includes a doxology: "N., take this ring as a sign of my love and fidelity. In the name of the Father, and of the Son, and of his Holy Spirit."

One would expect to find a rich trinitarian theology in the nuptial blessing that sends the couple forth to embark on their new life. Although the blessing concludes with a doxology, as do all blessings, it does not have the threefold trinitarian structure common in the extended blessings of the sacramental matter of the other rites. The blessing is addressed to the Father and includes references to the "peace of Christ," the example of Christ's love for the church as a model for the husband's love of his wife, and a prayer that the couple may be witnesses of Christ to others, but an explicit prayer to the Holy Spirit is conspicuously absent. An opportunity to invoke the Holy Spirit as the bond of unity in the couple's relationship as the domestic church analogous to the Spirit's role in the ecclesial church would strengthen the comparisons between Christ's relationship to the church and the relationship between husband and wife in Ephesians 5 and also complete the Christological allusions with a necessary pneumatological dimension.

## TRINITARIAN MYSTICISM

Karl Rahner has commented on how little impact the Trinity has on contemporary piety, saying that most Christians are practical and spiritual monotheists. He speculates that were the doctrine of the Trinity to disappear, the major part of religious literature would remain unchanged.[13] Although in mysticism one at times encounters the mystical worship of the primordial one, an anonymous God, some Christian mysticism exhibits a strong trinitarian dimension. This is particularly true of Bonaventure, Ruusbroec, John of the Cross, Marie de l'Incarnation, and Elizabeth of the Trinity.

Just as the trinitarian dimension of the liturgy and the sacraments finds its source in the economy of salvation, so does trinitarian mysticism. Trinitarian mysticism follows the law of the economy of salvation that we ascend to the Father through the Son in the Spirit. Trinitarian spirituality is one in which the persons of God are experienced as distinct, the economic Trinity as manifested in history revealing the immanent Trinity.

Identity and union with God are possible because human beings are made in the image of God and thus bear the vestiges of the Trinity within the soul. Not merely an external resemblance, this image is the very indwelling of the Triune God. Mysticism is essentially the awareness of the presence of the Word within the soul, itself the image and identity of the Father, and, through the experience of the Word, participation in the life of the Father. Through the image the soul ascends to that which is beyond image, namely the Father, in what can be an imageless experience of darkness and silence. Yet, as Ruusbroec testifies, God continues to speak his Word out of this silence, and in the darkness we see the divine light.[14] In this participation, the soul is transformed into that which it seeks, a union with the divine image in love.

Some examples of the dynamism of trinitarian mysticism excerpted from the writings of John of the Cross, Teresa of Avila, and Elizabeth of the Trinity illustrate these relationships. The purpose is not to present the trinitarian theology of the mystic, but rather to examine how the Trinity is manifested in the mystic's experience of God.

## TERESA OF AVILA (1515–1582)

Teresa writes of her experience of three persons in her soul: "The presence of the three Persons is so impossible to doubt that it seems one experiences what St. John says, that they will make their abode in the soul. God does this not only by grace but also by His presence, because He wants to give the experience of this presence."[15] The distinction between grace and presence along with the emphasis on experience gives Teresa certitude of God's abiding within her. In another testimony, she writes of the Father receiving within her soul the body of Christ when she receives communion, and of her experience of the presence of the divine persons there.[16]

## JOHN OF THE CROSS (1542–1591)

In stanza 38 of the *Spiritual Canticle,* John of the Cross describes the state of spiritual marriage of the soul:

> The breathing of the air,
> The song of the sweet nightingale,
> The grove and its living beauty
> In the serene night,
> With a flame that is consuming and painless.[17]

Although this stanza does not appear on a first reading to be trinitarian, in John's commentary on this stanza, the "breathing of the air" is the breath or spiration of the Holy Spirit from God to the soul and from the soul to God. The flame indicates the love of the Holy Spirit. He explains that the Holy Spirit elevates the soul, making it capable of breathing in God the same spiration of love that the Father breathes in the Son and the Son in the Father, which is the Holy Spirit itself.[18] This breathing out to the soul transforms the soul into God by participation and union with the divine Trinity: "for the soul united and transformed in God breathes out in God to God the very divine spiration which God – she being transformed in Him – breathes out in Himself to her."[19] John of the Cross wrote of mystical union that "it would not be a true and total transformation if the soul were not transformed into the three Persons of the Most Holy Trinity."[20]

In John's mysticism, access to the trinitarian life is primarily pneumatological. God is the bridegroom, the soul is the bride, and union is accomplished through the Holy Spirit. In spite of multiple references to the Trinity, there is no explicit reference to Christ in this depiction of spiritual marriage. The aspects of the Trinity emphasized here are mutual union and mutual spiration.

## ELIZABETH OF THE TRINITY (1880–1906)

Elizabeth of the Trinity's trinitarian mysticism differentiates clearly the work and presence of Father, Son, and Spirit, as in her spiritual treatise *Heaven on Earth,* where she describes a mystical death as

> plunging into the Furnace of love burning within them which is none other than the Holy Spirit, the same Love which in the Trinity is the bond between the Father and His Word . . . They live, in St. John's expression, in "communion" with the Three adorable Persons, "sharing their life," and this is "the contemplative life"; this contemplation "leads to possession."[21]

Union with God occurs through a return to the center of the soul, made a dwelling of the Trinity through baptism.

The following prayer to the Trinity was found without a title in her notes. It bears some similarity to both Thérèse of Lisieux's *Act of Oblation* and St. Catherine of Siena's *O Eternal Trinity*, both of which were known to Elizabeth:[22]

> O my God, Trinity whom I adore, let me forget myself entirely that I may be established in you as still and as peaceful as if my soul were already in eternity. May nothing disturb my peace or make me leave you, O my Unchanging One, but may each minute carry me further into the depths of Your Mystery. Give peace to my soul; make it your heaven, Your beloved dwelling and your resting place. May I never leave You there alone but be wholly present, my faith wholly vigilant, wholly adoring, and wholly surrendered to Your creative Action.
>
> O my beloved Christ, crucified by love, I wish to be a bride for your heart; I wish to cover You with glory; I wish to love You . . . even unto death! But I feel my weakness, and I ask You to "clothe me with Yourself," to identify my soul with all the movements of Your Soul, to overwhelm me, to possess me, substitute Yourself for me that my life may be but a radiance of Your Life. Come into me as Adorer, as Restorer, as Savior. O Eternal Word, Word of my God, I want to spend my life in listening to You, to become wholly teachable that I may learn all from You. Then, through all nights, all voids, all helplessness, I want to gaze on You always and remain in Your great light. O my Beloved Star, so fascinate me so that I may not withdraw from Your radiance.
>
> O consuming Fire, Spirit of Love, "come upon me," and create in my soul a kind of incarnation of the Word: that I may be another humanity for Him in which He can renew His whole Mystery. And You, O Father, bend lovingly over Your little creature; cover her with Your shadow, seeing in her only the "Beloved in whom You are well pleased."

> O my Three, my All, my Beatitude, infinite Solitude, Immensity in which I lose myself, I surrender myself to You as Your prey. Bury Yourself in me that I may bury myself in You until I depart to contemplate in Your light the abyss of your greatness.[23]
>
> November 21, 1904

This prayer contains themes present in Elizabeth's other spiritual writings: the soul as heaven on earth, Elizabeth's identity as *Laudem Gloriae* (Praise of Glory), spiritual marriage with Christ, and the displacement of self so that God may become the life of the mystic. It distinguishes the three persons according to their specific characteristic: immutability of the Father, the Son as Word and redeemer, and the Spirit as fire of Love. Through this experience Elizabeth identifies with the role of Christ as another incarnation of the Word whom the Father can also call "Beloved."

Although the liturgy and the sacraments with their external ritual may at first seem far removed from the interiority, silence, and imagelessness of mysticism, the role of the Trinity in each shows a striking resemblance once the "grammar" of salvation is grasped in terms of the economic Trinity. The Father comes to us through the Son in the power of the Spirit, and we ascend to the Father through the Son in the power of the Spirit. This grammar of salvation is both the grammar of the liturgy and the grammar of mystical prayer.

## Notes

1. See Catherine Mowry LaCugna, *God for Us: The Trinity and Christian Life* (San Francisco: HarperSanFrancisco, 1991), esp. chs. 9 and 10; Michael Downey, *Altogether Gift: A Trinitarian Spirituality* (Maryknoll, NY: Orbis, 2000), ch. 2.
2. For Jürgen Moltmann, the cross is at the center of the Trinity: *The Trinity and the Kingdom of God: The Doctrine of God*, trans. Margaret Kohl (San Francisco: Harper & Row; London: SCM Press, 1981), 83.
3. Catherine Mowry LaCugna, "Trinity and Liturgy," in Peter E. Fink, ed., *The New Dictionary of Sacramental Worship* (Collegeville, MN: Liturgical Press, 1990), 1293.
4. Ibid.
5. A. Verheul, *Introduction to the Liturgy: Towards a Theology of Worship* (Collegeville, MN: Liturgical Press, 1968), 18.
6. *Catechism of the Catholic Church* (Collegeville, MN: Liturgical Press, 1994), §1103.
7. Ibid., §1082.
8. Ibid., §1092.

9. Susan K. Wood, "The Paschal Mystery: The Intersection of Ecclesiology and Sacramental Theology in the Care of the Sick," in Genevieve Glen, ed., *Recovering the Riches of Anointing: A Study of the Sacrament of the Sick* (Collegeville, MN: Liturgical Press, 1989), 1–19.
10. Louis-Marie Chauvet, *The Sacraments: The Word of God at the Mercy of the Body* (Collegeville, MN: Liturgical Press, 2001), 160.
11. Herbert Vorgrimler, *Sacramental Theology* (Collegeville, MN: Liturgical Press, 1992), 102; see also Alasdair I. C. Heron, ed., *The Forgotten Trinity*, I: *The Report of the BCC Study Commission on Trinitarian Doctrine Today* (London: BCC/CCBI, 1989), 7.
12. *Lumen gentium*, 1.
13. Karl Rahner, *The Trinity*, trans. Joseph Donceel, introduction, index, and glossary by Catherine LaCugna (New York: Crossroad, 1997; original 1969), 10–11.
14. As reported by Louis Dupré, *The Common Life: The Origins of Trinitarian Mysticism and its Development by Jan Ruusbroec* (New York: Crossroad, 1984), 28.
15. Teresa of Avila, "Spiritual Testimonies," in *The Collected Works of St. Teresa of Avila*, I (Washington, DC: ICA Publications, 1976), §65.9.
16. Ibid., I, §52.
17. John of the Cross, *The Collected Works of St. John of the Cross*, trans. Kieran Kavanaugh and Otilio Rodriguez, with introduction by Kieran Kavanaugh (Washington, DC: ICS Publications, Institute of Carmelite Studies, 1973), 557. The entire poem is reproduced in ibid., 712–17, where the stanza in question occurs on p. 717, but is listed as stanza 39, a discrepancy when compared with John of the Cross' commentary, which identifies it as stanza 38.
18. John of the Cross, *The Collected Works of St. John of the Cross*, trans. Kieran Kavanaugh and Otilio Rodriguez (Washington, DC: ICS Publications, Institute of Carmelite Studies, 1964), 558.
19. Ibid., 558.
20. John of the Cross, *Spiritual Canticle*, stanza 38.3, in *Collected Works*, 558.
21. Elizabeth of the Trinity, *Heaven on Earth*, in *The Complete Works*, I: *General Introduction: Major Spiritual Writings* (Washington, DC: ICS, 1984), 98.
22. Elizabeth of the Trinity, *The Complete Works*, I, 185.
23. Ibid., I, 183–84.

## Further reading

Chauvet, Louis-Marie, *The Sacraments: The Word of God at the Mercy of the Body* (Collegeville, MN: Liturgical Press, 2001).

Downey, Michael, *Altogether Gift: A Trinitarian Spirituality* (Maryknoll, NY: Orbis, 2000).

Dupré, Louis, *The Common Life: The Origins of Trinitarian Mysticism and its Development by Jan Ruusbroec* (New York: Crossroad, 1984).

Elizabeth of the Trinity, *The Complete Works*, I: *General Introduction: Major Spiritual Writings* (Washington, DC: ICS, 1984).

Heron, Alasdair I. C., ed., *The Forgotten Trinity*, I: *The Report of the BCC Study Commission on Trinitarian Doctrine Today* (London: BCC/CCBI, 1989).

LaCugna, Catherine Mowry, *God for Us: The Trinity and Christian Life* (San Francisco: HarperSanFrancisco, 1991), esp. chs. 9 and 10.

'Trinity and Liturgy," in Peter E. Fink, ed., *The New Dictionary of Sacramental Worship* (Collegeville, MN: Liturgical Press, 1990), 1293.

Maloney, George A., *Invaded by God: Mysticism and the Indwelling Trinity* (Denville, NJ: Dimension, 1979).

Teresa of Avila, "Spiritual Testimonies," in *The Collected Works of St. Teresa of Avila* (Washington, DC: ICA, 1976), I.

Verheul, A., *Introduction to the Liturgy: Towards a Theology of Worship* (Collegeville, MN: Liturgical Press, 1968).

# 23 The Trinity and socio-political ethics

DALE T. IRVIN

The Trinity is the foundation and framework for everything else that Christianity teaches regarding belief and practice. It is not in the first instance an abstract argument or philosophical puzzle, but an expression of who God is and how God lives. For the majority of Christians through the ages, God has been understood to be a living communion of Three-in-One.[1] Christian identity is grounded in this divine reality. The vast majority of Christians worldwide have literally been baptized into the name of the Father, Son, and Holy Spirit as they entered the Christian community, the church.[2] In worship the vast majority of Christians pray to the Father, Son, and Holy Spirit, or to the Father through the Son in the Holy Spirit.

The doctrine of the Trinity emerged as theologians of the ancient church sought to reflect upon the experience and expression of the divine Three-in-One in life and worship. Worship in particular has been important through the ages for articulating Christian identity, for it is the primary work that the Christian community as a whole undertakes to perform, the service that it offers to God. Christian worship not only gives expression to the trinitarian mystery. To a degree it reflects this mystery in its performance, and in the manner that it models many being together as one. At the heart of worship is a joyous celebration of the experience of communion. Through the centuries trinitarian theology has continuously been nourished, replenished, and articulated afresh through the ongoing experiences and expressions of this communion with God in ever new contexts. Communion is but another way to name the Trinity.[3]

Christian life and worship have from the beginning and in every branch of the tradition been grounded in the life and ministry of Jesus of Nazareth, as witnessed by his first followers. This life was fully one of communion, first and foremost with the One he called his Father (*Abba* in Aramaic), but also with others, including the poor and outcasts, and his disciples. The New Testament is the primary authoritative source of information regarding Jesus of Nazareth and his earliest followers, and is thus the primary source of information regarding the Trinity. While the word "Trinity" does not itself appear in the New Testament, the experience of God in communion that it names is everywhere present in those pages.

At the center of this communion are Jesus, who is called the only-begotten Son; the One whom Jesus called Father; and the Spirit who came from the Father and rested upon, empowered, and raised from the dead the only-begotten Son. There is not a book in the New Testament that does not hold with absolute certainty that the One about whom Jesus preached and to whom Jesus prayed is the God who was known and worshiped in Israel, the God of Abraham, Isaac, and Jacob. The New Testament both assumes and proclaims that the identity of this one true God is closely tied to the history and people of Israel.[4] Jesus was understood by the apostolic writers not to be displacing that history, but through the power of the Spirit of God to be extending it in a new direction by revealing a dimension that had long been hidden, namely how the Gentiles would be brought into this communion. This is an important point to note, for the New Testament depends upon and assumes much in terms of socio-political life that was derived from the Hebrew scriptures regarding God's divine rule and eventual triumph in history.[5]

To his followers Jesus revealed in a new way the One who was eternally unseen, doing so through the power of the Spirit that was upon him. The communion that he had with the Father, to which the New Testament bears witness, became for Christians definitive of who God is. God is not a solitary figure but one who from all eternity has been in communion, the gospel of John in particular says. Throughout the pages of the New Testament one catches glimpses of the communion of the Son with the Father in and through the Spirit, even as the fullness of that communion remains a mystery beyond human understanding. The inner life of this communion of Father, Son, and Spirit transcends the historical circumstances and conditions of its appearing, but it does not eradicate them.

The capacity human beings have in their created nature not only to believe in One who transcends their comprehension, but to experience something of the transcending communion that is revealed, can itself be attributed to their being a reflection of the image or the nature of this same God who created them.[6] Being made in the image of God means that human beings are made to be in communion. As Thomas Hopko has noted:

> Like the God in whose image they are made, human beings are not intended to be separate individuals in relationship with one another in an external manner. Neither are they called to exist as a "collective" without personal "standing" or integrity. They are rather, like their Creator, made to be persons in community, distinct hypostases in an identity of nature, called to a perfect – and, according to Gregory of Nyssa, ever more perfect – union of being and action in fulfillment of all virtues, the greatest of which is love.[7]

This union of being and action in fulfillment of virtue, manifested as friendship or love, is another way to describe salvation. Salvation comes about by being joined to this inner life of communion of God who is Father, Son, and Spirit. It means being friends with God and with others, or experiencing in a direct manner the love of God and love of neighbor.[8] In historical terms salvation means joining the community that was formed by the revelation of this three-in-oneness. In other words, salvation entails being joined to the church.

The Trinity is thus revealed from the pages of the New Testament not to be a communion closed in upon itself, but to be a communion open to the world. One manner of this opening takes concrete form as the church. The church has from its conception understood itself to have received a universal calling. Humanity as a whole is invited ultimately to enter into its ranks, and thereby to enter into a new and deeper communion with God who is Three-in-One. This is not to say that the church is the only place where such communion is or can be experienced. Jesus himself said that the Spirit blows where it will. Furthermore, Jesus invited those within his hearing to join him in expectation of the imminent revelation or consummation of what he called the "kingdom of God," when love and justice would be finally fully realized in history. While the church in all of its history can be seen as an anticipation of such an event, the fact is that history still continues and the reign of God has not yet been fully realized.

Few in the long history of Christian theology have argued for a full revelation of the Trinity outside the church and its scriptures. By far the majority of theologians and churches have held that the Trinity is revealed most fully through the scriptures and teachings of the church and its theological traditions. Some, perhaps most notably Augustine of Hippo, have argued that signs, traces, or marks of the Trinity (*vestigia Trinitatis*) can be found throughout the creation, especially in the human person. The vestiges of the Trinity that are found in creation are a reflection of the trinitarian nature of God who is the creator, the mark of the maker imprinted upon nature much as the nature of a craftsperson can be found in the object that she or he creates.[9] Few have argued that such vestiges of the Trinity are in and of themselves an adequate source of revelation. More often they have been employed as analogies or metaphors to aid in understanding the trinitarian mystery that is revealed fully only within the life of the church, through its scriptures.

There have been some who have found in other religions elements of trinitarian truth, or reflections of the trinitarian life. So the doctrine of the Buddha's Three Bodies and the so-called "trinity" of Brahma, Shiva, and Vishnu in Hinduism have been offered as examples of a more general religious propensity toward trinitarian truth.[10] Such efforts have the effect, however, even if unintended, of minimizing the integrity of other religious traditions and reducing the experience and teachings of other religions to being poorer forms of the universal Christian truth. Ironically they are ways of theological comparison that do not fit the trinitarian pattern itself. A more trinitarian model, as S. Mark Heim has argued, allows for a diversity of religious ends and multiple modes of representations of the divine.[11]

This is not to say that the doctrine of the Trinity has nothing to do with life beyond the walls of a church, or outside the circle of the community of those who have been baptized. The Trinity does have much to say to the wider world, but what is said to the wider world is communicated most clearly through the life and witness of a particular church. Jesus invited his followers to join him in a new mode of community that anticipated the reign of God by participating in its realization. How those followers treated both one another and those who remained outside their community, especially those whom Jesus called "the least," was to be a sign that anticipated the values of love and justice that would one day be fully realized in the presence of God.[12] Through the centuries Christians have continued to work upon their assignment to treat one another and those outside the church in ways that are congruent with being made in the image of the Trinity. Such work is carried out by promoting efforts to help those inside and outside the church become more loving and just. At the same time, any effort to assess the relationship between the Trinity and the wider circle of social and political experience must pass through the church. In every instance trinitarian ethics are (or should be) ecclesial ethics as well.[13]

Here one must be cautious not to speak to simplistically about "the church" as if this were a monolithic institutional reality. The Christian movement from its earliest days has been characterized by considerable diversity in the cultural and theological forms of its collective expressions and practices. Yet even if we were to speak in the plural about "the churches," the fact remains that there were and are enough commonalities to make it possible to draw some general conclusions regarding the Trinity and social life in the church.

To begin, all churches, no matter what their cultural or theological identity, have through the ages, as was noted above, been organized primarily around the practices of worship. In worship the supreme moment of communing with God who is Three-in-One takes place. Entrance into the liturgical spaces of such communion entails ritual, moral, psychological, and even physical acts of preparatory cleansing. The reason is that those who enter the divine presence must become more like the divine, who is holy and "other." In the presence of the divine the everyday appears to be not only less than ultimate, but sinful and broken. Making things whole and making them holy are two sides of the same complex reality that the concept of holiness entails.

Wholeness and holiness take concrete expression in Christian moral life as love and mutuality. Here the trinitarian connection between Christian worship and Christian life is forged in particularly expressive ways. One is expected to be in the world a living representative of God, acting in ways that befit the divine character. To do so one must live a life of love and mutuality, for these are the central moral categories or attributes expressed in God. The Trinity is a community of divine love and mutual self-giving. Each member not only loves the other, but acts for the well-being of the other in an effective manner. Those who would enter into the divine communion are expected to engage in ethical practices of love and mutuality, in the church as well as in the wider world. This is not to say that all who call themselves Christian will ever fully realize these ethical ideals. Few, if any, are capable of attaining the ethical fullness of the trinitarian confession of faith. The Trinity remains a reality that lies beyond human realization, ethically as well as ontologically. Yet through the ages the understanding of virtually all branches of the Christian tradition has been that the more closely one enters into the trinitarian life of communion with God through Christ in the Spirit, the more one's life can be expected to reflect these divine attributes.

Life in the church across the ages in its diverse cultural and theological streams has hardly ever been a democratic affair. Churches have rarely been egalitarian in their structures and functioning. The vast majority of churches globally through the ages have been and continue to be hierarchical in structure.[14] Many would say this is by divine design, for there is a certain hierarchical structuring intrinsic to the Trinity, even if such is understood to be without subordination or subjugation. The Trinity is both One and Many. So the church – any church – can be characterized as being both one and many. But the Many of the Trinity are not of the same rank, order, or authority, even if they are of the same substance. The Father, according to the ancient tradition, is the *monarche* or "one origin" of the Trinity. Both the Son and the Spirit derive their divinity from the Father, such derivation being understood to take place not in time but in eternity. Not an ordering of time, but an ordering of love, manifested concretely in the obedience of the Son to the will of the Father, characterizes the trinitarian relations in this model.

One hears repeatedly in the works of theologians through the ages the assertion that the Son and the Spirit are not subordinate to the Father. The reason for the assertion is that such subordination would undermine the claim that the Son and the Spirit are of the same substance as the Father, and therefore are not two lesser deities. Yet precisely because the Father is understood to be the One who is the source of all divinity, and thus of all divine attributes, the ordering that is found in the ancient understanding of the Trinity can easily slip into subordinating. The alternative manner of comprehending the Trinity as three persons sharing a common divine substance that thus transcends each of them lessens somewhat the subordinationist tendency. Yet even for those who conceptualize the Trinity in such a way, the fact that the Father remains the One who is without beginning, the Son is begotten by the Father, and the Spirit is breathed forth by the Father lends itself to a hierarchical understanding of power and authority.

The three persons of the Trinity are distinct, even though they are related, asserted the ancient definitions of faith. So persons in communion are distinct, though related. Furthermore the three persons occupy different offices. So in the church there are understood to be offices, and not all are of the same order. The exercise of mutuality within the Trinity has rarely been portrayed as being symmetrical. Within the Trinity the Son obeys the Father and seeks to do the will of the Father. Likewise the Spirit, who rested on the Son, now goes obediently where the Son sends. Obedience to one in authority, even when such authority appears to be arbitrary, has been a central tenet of Christian spiritual life through the centuries. One is to obey a superior authority as Christ was obedient to the will of the Father, but at the same time the one holding authority is to exercise this charge with love and concern only for the well-being of the others over whom she or he holds power.

Yet even in the most authoritarian expressions of trinitarian ethics, hierarchy has not been the last word, for in the end ranking and order do not define the relations between the three persons. Love and mutuality do. The Son does not glorify himself, but the Father; and the Spirit does not glorify herself, but the Son and the Father. The Father glorifies the Son, and the glory is the Spirit. The Son emptied himself in love in obedience to the Father, but the Father also sent the Son and breathed forth the Spirit in love. In the end the Father does not even hold on to his own, but turns over his kingdom to the Son, who occupies the throne. This constant drama of one emptying into the other and glorifying the other portrays what is often called *perichōrēsis*, a mode of being in which each indwells the other and each moves within and around the other in love. The communion that is God is ultimately characterized by other-centeredness, mutuality, justice, and love. These are, or ought to be, characteristic of any community that claims the trinitarian communion to be its own.[15]

The inherently hierarchical character of traditional representations of the Trinity was explicitly challenged by some in the past, but their numbers have increased dramatically in the last century. At issue is the question of whether hierarchical representations are not intrinsically contradictory to the central attributes of love and mutuality. Hierarchy, according to this perspective, is inherently and essentially unequal and thus ultimately incompatible with a trinitarian vision of true mutuality and love. One set of challenges to hierarchical thinking have tended to focus trinitarian reflection upon the self-giving life of Jesus of Nazareth as emblematic for the whole of the divine reality. They have tended to be especially attentive to the ministry of Jesus and the lowly social status on the margins that he occupied. Jesus called his followers to begin relating to others in ways that embodied a radical equality. The mighty of the Magnificat (Lk 1:52) have been brought down and the lowly lifted up, not so that they may exchange their historic positions and continue a social order of inequality, but so that they may become equals, thereby ending inequality. Seen through the life and ministry of Jesus of Nazareth, the Trinity does not offer a model of revolutionary action that simply inverts the existing structures of oppressor and oppressed, but calls for a new way of structuring that achieves the liberation of all through mutuality, reconciliation, justice, and love.[16]

An alternative non-hierarchical model of trinitarian ethics has been offered in the life of the Spirit, who empowers agency and raises up the lowly to overcome imbalances in history. The church is the household of God in which the Spirit, sent upon it by the risen Christ, continues to dwell. Inclusion within this household entails women and men living as equals. The Spirit elevates to leadership ones who possess no innate abilities that have been previously recognized. Charismatic structures take the place of hierarchical ordering.[17] The Spirit falls upon whom the Spirit wills and gives gifts as she sees fit. The fruit of the Spirit, according to Galatians 5:22–23, "is love, joy, peace, patience, kindness, generosity, faithfulness, gentleness, and self-control." Those practices are inconsistent with social inequality and injustice. They flow from and lead to a different society.

In such theologies as these, themes of the hiddenness and vulnerability of God have often been more pronounced. The One whom Jesus addressed as his Father is a mystery and remains hidden, while the Son becomes vulnerable and the Spirit empowers those who have been marginalized, beginning with Jesus Christ, whom the Spirit raised from the dead. The Trinity is associated here not with power but with powerlessness in history. It is radically incarnational and relational, emphasizing the economic Trinity more than the immanent Trinity.[18]

Closely related to the non-hierarchical criticisms of traditional Trinitarian theology have been criticisms of the patriarchal and gender-exclusive character of traditional representations of trinitarian life. God as Father, Son, and Spirit has left little, if any room, for representing the divine image in feminine gendered form. The implication of gender-exclusive language, in English-speaking contexts at least, is that God is male.[19] The problem stems in part from the reduction of gender to sexual identity, for in English only things having sexual life are assigned gender. In languages where non-sexual objects are also assigned gender, gender is not so tied to sexuality. The reduction of the masculine gender to male sexual identity in language relating to God is particularly problematic in that it may seem to be saying that God is male. Some on both sides of the gender-exclusive debate in recent years have argued that the traditional Christian doctrine does indeed understand God to be ontologically male.[20] This is a position that the majority of Christian theologies past and present have explicitly rejected. To name God "Father" is not to speak of the divine substance, but to name a relation within the divinity. Furthermore while Jesus was born a male, the image of God that was reflected in him who was the Logos in human flesh is diminished only if it is reduced to having a sexually exclusive identity.

Over the centuries there have been a number of instances of more inclusive gender imaging of the Trinity, many of them recognized as fully orthodox, that can be helpful in addressing this issue today. In early Syriac liturgies the Holy Spirit is often represented in the feminine gender. Few have questioned the historical fact that Jesus was biologically male, yet there is a long tradition of representing the risen Christ as both male and female. Julian of Norwich in the fourteenth century wrote in this vein of Jesus as Mother. The Third Council of Toledo in 589 spoke of Jesus as being born from the "womb of the Father," an image that explicitly challenges the attribution of an exclusive sexual identity to the first person of the Trinity. Reflecting in part on this image, Jürgen Moltmann has noted the need to expand the gender categories in order to represent God more adequately. Thus he writes of God as a "fatherly mother" and a "motherly father."[21]

The model of human social experience that trinitarian theology has most often used to name the divine relationality through centuries is the familiar image of parent and child. God is revealed through the generational tropes of Father and Son. Use of gendered relationships often associated with reproduction, of male and female or husband and wife, is not entirely absent from the trinitarian vocabulary. Humanity, in its two-gendered form as male and female, bears the image of God. But such gendered images associated with husband and wife are far more often used to depict the relationship of God to humanity. It is important to note here that even within the ancient tradition the Trinity was never entirely confined to such familiar images. One finds the Spirit in particular escaping such familiarly defined roles. One can find the Trinity conceptualized through a variety of models, not all of them even necessarily human. But one finds that all forms of conceptualization tend to point back to renewal of community, renewal of human life, coaxing one to move beyond the narrow boundaries and definitions of current social and political options.[22]

Efforts to represent God in ways that are non-hierarchical and gender-inclusive recognize an inherent connection between theological images and social life. The relationship between them can move in either direction. Non-hierarchical and inclusive images of the Trinity can be seen as both the product of and the means to a more non-hierarchical and inclusive social life. It might seem in this regard that the entire discussion of non-hierarchical and gender-inclusive imaging of God is little more than the result of modern social concepts creeping into theology. While one cannot discount the impact of modern social ideologies upon Christian representations of God, a cursory glance at the long history of alternative trinitarian images, however much in the minority they may have been in the past, suggests this is not entirely the case. On the other hand one sometimes hears the argument that these modern, and often Western, social and political ideals are themselves products of a long Western history of Christian culture. The driving force of intrinsic Christian values, such as the inherent worth of all individuals that is derived in no small part from the doctrine of the Trinity, is said to have resulted in many of our modern social and political values. While there may be truth in such arguments, the very controversy that the argument engenders among Christians suggests that one should not too quickly accept that the reduction of modern political values is the product of only Western Christian culture.[23]

One of the areas in social life that has occupied considerable Christian attention concerns the organization and distribution of power known as politics. As with Christian responses to other areas of social life, there has been considerable diversity in the political options that Christians have embraced through the ages. One can find both royalists and populists, or imperialists and anti-imperialists, in churches over the past two millennia. There are those who have supported political efforts that favor the accumulation of wealth, limit the accumulation of wealth, and redistribute the already accumulated wealth. Over the past century socialist, liberal-democratic, revolutionary, and anti-revolutionary options have all been given Christian support. One finds no clear correlation that would allow for a particular political position to be said without reserve to represent best the trinitarian theological perspective. The best that can be said in this regard is that virtually all are agreed that justice and love are ultimate commitments, even if there is considerable disagreement regarding which particular political pathway is most effective in achieving them.

Where there is broad Christian consensus today concerning trinitarian political ethics is in the widespread rejection of traditional monarchical models of rule. Traditional trinitarian theologies often depicted both the Father and Son, if not as emperor or king, then in ways congruent with the image of an emperor or king. God the Father ruled his creation the same way an earthly king ruled his kingdom, and in fact in many cases the image of God the Father as king undergirded kings' claims to divine right to rule. In traditional trinitarian theology, the kingdom of God refers first and foremost to the Trinity itself, where the Father exercises his monarchical will and the Son and Spirit obey him. God in the traditional trinitarian formulations is not just the king, but the kingdom, leaving considerable cognitive dissonance when seeking to relate this image to modern rulers and the nation-states in which they exercise their rule.

Kings and emperors represent a particular way of organizing political power from the social top. Sovereignty is understood in this model to reside at the top of the political order, and to be handed on through lineages of birth. The New Testament writers drew freely upon their surrounding dominant political experiences to describe the manner in which the risen Christ would exercise power and authority. God, who had long been understood in Israel through the figure of the king, in the book of Revelation shares rule with his son, Jesus Christ. The Lamb who was slain now sits alongside the Father on the throne, while God's glory, in the figure of the Holy Spirit, extends throughout the world.

The glory of a king or emperor (for example Caesar) in the form of an image on coins represented well the manner in which rulers were perceived to be immanent in day-to-day material transactions of their realm in the ancient world. The figure of the king or emperor reached deeply into the marketplaces and temple courtyards (see Mt 22:15–22). The notion that the divine is immanent in the world politically through such structures and practices allows for an alternative image of political rule to emerge. Alongside ancient notions of kingship one finds in almost all locations in ancient cultures a corresponding idea of citizenship or membership in the public body. In the ancient world those individuals who shared in the benefits and privileges of political life, as opposed to resident aliens and slaves, were citizens. Kings continued to rule for only so long as sufficient numbers of citizens, including those who exercised influence in the military, supported them. Citizenship in the first-century Mediterranean world was understood not so much to be a function of language or culture as to entail an identity that allowed one a direct relationship of access to the king or emperor who ruled in a particular region. The Apostle Paul has such an understanding in view when he writes in Philippians 3:20a, "But our citizenship is in heaven."

The notion of citizenship allows for an alternative trinitarian politics to emerge more clearly, at the same time opening up options for greater engagement in non-monarchical political situations today. Sovereignty within the Trinity does not reside at the top in this view, but in fact is derived from the whole of the Trinity, from the nexus of relationships among the Three. Once again the ancient doctrine of *perichōrēsis*, of the mutual indwelling of one with the other, proves to be an effective trinitarian concept. In the same way as the Father is by definition related to another in order to be named as such, for one is a father only if there is a son or daughter, so the *monarche* ("one origin") of the Trinity is only such in relation to those who proceed from this One. Participation and responsiveness characterize the political life of the Trinity in this model, and ought to guide the efforts of those in human history who seek to live out the trinitarian faith. Whether or not the modern liberal-democratic state, coupled as it is with a free market economy that is increasingly consumer-driven, is the best means of embodying the trinitarian values of *perichōrēsis* and mutual self-giving is an open question. What is important is that the fuller trinitarian values of life in community be attended to.

Whatever the precise relationship between the doctrine of the Trinity and any particular historical, social, and political formation may be, theologians are generally in agreement that there should be some such relationship. The doctrine of the Trinity in the end cannot be confined to the life of the church, for the church is in the world and participates in the social and political realities around it. Even when they are seeking most adamantly to withdraw from the world, Christians end up participating in it, precisely through their effort to withdraw from it. No church exists apart from the wider social and political world from which Christians draw their financial sustenance and in which they learn their primary language and engage in the exercise of political power.

While a church can never be totally apart from the wider social world in which it exists, it is nevertheless able to be distinguished from it. No church, even at the height of Western Christendom, was ever totally congruent with a wider social world. By the same token, while aspects of the social and cultural world are always integrated into the life of any particular church, no church can be reduced to its surrounding social world or context. There is always something of an excess in the life of a church, something that connects it with other Christians in other times and social locations. The fact that a distinction can thus be made in any situation between a particular church, or the church, and the social, political and cultural context in which it lives is important for understanding trinitarian social ethics. The Trinity is always related to human society in complex ways that in the end go beyond it.

Leonardo Boff has pointed out that the global renewal in trinitarian theology that has been taking place over the last century is not unconnected to the currents of social and political renewal that have been taking place in multiple global contexts. He writes:

> There is a renewal of trinitarian thought taking place now on the basis of reflection, still in its infancy, but very serious, on the links that bind women and men together in community and society – links that also involve the Persons of the Trinity. Society is not just the sum total of the individuals that make it up, but has its own being woven out of the threads of

> relationships among individuals, functions and institutions, which together make up the social and political community. Cooperation and collaboration among all produce the common good; within a multiplicity of social and political mediations and instruments and manifestations of community life, a unity in the social process can be discerned. So human society is a pointer on the road to the mystery of the Trinity, while the mystery of the Trinity, as we know it from revelation, is a pointer toward social life and its archetype.[24]

The heart of the matter is that God is communion. To be in communion means to be responsive, capable of responding to the other, grounded in the other. It is relational and participatory, more conscious of the other than of the self. In more abstract theological terms, God is three distinct yet never separate *hypostasis*. God is a communion in which each person's identity is found in relation to the other two. In the West greater emphasis was traditionally placed on the oneness of this reality. The One God is known as Father and Son who live in a relation of love, which is Spirit. In the Eastern Christian world the emphasis fell more on the threefold nature of God and the communion in which the Three live. God is *koinōnia*, whose unity is preserved by the *monarche* of the Father.

For either branch of the ancient tradition, creation is the work of one who lives in communion and thus bears the reflection of the divine nature. Creation itself is thus fundamentally relational, for it bears the image of the one who made it. This means that the ultimate character of the universe is not impersonal but personal. Even the atheist in our midst strains to find life elsewhere in the universe. Stars and endless light-years of empty space reflect the glory of a living God whose beauty and majesty compel us toward an ultimate destiny. Humanity bears the image of this God who lives in communion. Human society is to be an expression of this God, a communion in which the other is received and embraced. Thus one finds the ultimate social and political meaning of the Trinity not in itself alone but in its relation to humanity and the whole creation.

## Notes

1. Since the end of the fourth century the Nicene creed has served as the standard of trinitarian orthodoxy. During the fourth century many of the Germanic tribes along the borders of the Roman Empire converted to Arian Christianity, which denied the full divinity of the Son,

but they too confessed a version of the trinitarian doctrine, and during the fifth and sixth centuries most of these converted to Catholic teaching. Over the centuries there have been occasional non-trinitarian movements within the Christian churches, but they have not been significant in number. During the last century one wing of the modern Pentecostal movement, known as "Jesus Only" or "Oneness," has rejected the Nicene understanding of the Trinity without abandoning the notion that God has been revealed in the three different dispensations of history as Father, Son, and Spirit. Oneness Pentecostalism resembles in this way the ancient teaching that was known as Modalism, embracing the economic understanding of the Trinity but not an immanent understanding of the Trinity.

2. It should be noted here that Oneness Pentecostals do not baptize in the threefold formula as found in Matthew 28. Oneness Pentecostals believe that the Apostles baptized in the name of Jesus, as seen in the book of Acts, and that this remains normative for Christian practice.
3. John D. Zizioulas, *Being as Communion: Studies in Personhood and the Church* (Crestwood, NY: St. Vladimir's Seminary Press, 1985) is the most influential theologian to make this connection in recent years.
4. See Robert W. Jenson, *The Triune Identity: God According to the Gospel* (Philadelphia: Fortress, 1982).
5. J. Christiaan Beker, in *Paul the Apostle: The Triumph of God in Life and Thought* (Philadelphia: Fortress, 1980) writes in the "Preface to the First Paperback Edition," xiv: "Paul's apocalyptic with its Jewish and Old Testament roots is able to secure the abiding importance of Old Testament themes for Christian theology. Contrary to our common conception of a *Christocentric* promise-fulfillment scheme, Paul refuses to spiritualize the Old Testament promises. His hope in a transformed creation makes his christological thought subservient to the God who is faithful to his promises, that is, to the theocentric fulcrum of Paul's thought which centers on the question of the public manifestation of God's sovereignty."
6. See Stanley J. Grenz, "The Social God and the Relational Self: Toward a Trinitarian Theology of the *Imago Dei*," in Paul Louis Metzger, ed., *Trinitarian Soundings in Systematic Theology* (London and New York: T. & T. Clark, 2005), 87–100.
7. Thomas Hopko, "The Trinity in the Cappadocians," in Bernard McGinn and John Meyendorff in collaboration with Jean Leclerq, eds., *Christian Spirituality: Origins to the Twelfth Century* (New York: Crossroad, 1989), 273.
8. See Miroslav Volf, "Being as God Is: Trinity and Generosity," in Miroslav Volf and Michael Welker, eds., *God's Life in Trinity* (Minneapolis: Fortress, 2006), 3–12.
9. *Saint Augustine*: *The Trinity*, trans. Edmund Hill (Brooklyn, NY: New City Press, 1991), explores a number of these traces or marks (*vestigia Trinitatis*) in books VII–XV. See also David Cunningham, *These Three are One: The Practice of Trinitarian Theology* (Malden, MA, and Oxford: Blackwell, 1998), 90–107.

10. See for instance Raimundo Panikkar, *The Trinity and the Religious Experience of Man: Icon-Person-Mystery* (Maryknoll, NY: Orbis; London: Darton, Longman & Todd, 1973).
11. S. Mark Heim, *The Depth of the Riches: A Trinitarian Theology of Religious Ends* (Grand Rapids, MI: Eerdmans, 2001).
12. See Ian A. McFarland, *Listening to the Least: Doing Theology from the Outside In* (Cleveland: Pilgrim, 1998).
13. Ruth C. Duck and Patricia Wilson-Kastner, *Praising God: The Trinity in Christian Worship* (Louisville, KY: Westminster John Knox, 1999), esp. ch. 7, "Living the Trinitarian Life: Ethics and Worship," 120–135.
14. The Vatican II document *Lumen gentium*, or "The Dogmatic Constitution on the Church," states explicitly in ch. 3 that the church is hierarchical in structure, and was established as such by Christ.
15. See Brian M. Doyle, "Social Doctrine of the Trinity and Communion Ecclesiology in Leonardo Boff and Gisbert Greshake," *Horizons*, 33:2 (2006), 239–55.
16. This is the direction that Leonardo Boff takes in *Trinity and Society*, trans. Paul Burns (Maryknoll, NY: Orbis, 1988).
17. This point is made by Edward Schillebeeckx, *The Church with a Human Face: A New and Expanded Theology of Ministry* (New York: Crossroad, 1987), 120–21: "The development of ministry in the early Christian churches was not so much, as is sometimes claimed, a historical shift from charisma to institution but a shift from the charisma of many to a specialized charisma of just a few . . . Specialization by individuals of what belongs communally to everyone is from a sociological perspective and, in the case of a church group, from an ecclesial perspective, an obvious development in any group formation . . . The danger of such a development is, however, that the particularized ministerial charisma of the Spirit, which also blows elsewhere in the community, begins to be swallowed up and so 'the Spirit quenched' (I Thess. 5.19) in the community. The charismatic and pneumatic ecclesial dimension cannot be derived from the ministerial church, but this last must be understood as rooted in the baptism in the Spirit of all Christians. If that is not the case, then the believers become the sheer object of ministerial or priestly concern, and not the subject of faith and expressions of faith."
18. See Catherine Mowry LaCugna, *God for Us: The Trinity and Christian Life* (San Francisco: HarperSanFrancisco, 1991).
19. See Ruth Duck, *Gender and the Name of God: The Trinitarian Baptismal Formula* (Cleveland: Pilgrim, 1991).
20. Mary Daly, *Beyond God the Father: Toward a Philosophy of Women's Liberation* (Boston: Beacon, 1973), 19, formulates the classic feminist theological statement of this when she writes: "If God is male, then the male is God." On the other side, while they do not exactly argue for ontological maleness, a number of the essays in Alvin F. Kimel, Jr., ed., *Speaking The Christian God: The Holy Trinity and the Challenge of Feminism* (Grand Rapids, MI: Eerdmans, 1992) come close to doing so by arguing for the ontological nature of the relationship between Father and Son in the Trinity.

21. See Sarah A. Coakley, "The Trinity and Gender Reconsidered," in Volf and Welker, eds., *God's Life in Trinity*, 133–42; Jürgen Moltmann, *The Trinity and the Kingdom of God: The Doctrine of God*, trans. Margaret Kohl (San Francisco: Harper & Row; London: SCM Press, 1981), 164.
22. In this vein Mercy Amba Oduyoye, *Hearing and Knowing: Theological Reflections on Christianity in Africa* (Maryknoll, NY: Orbis, 1986), 145, writes: "Our baptism into the name of the Trinity means that we should stand not for monarchies and hierarchies but rather for participation."
23. See Oduyoye's extended reflections, ibid., 140–45, where in a few deft paragraphs she relates the traditional doctrine of the Trinity, in both its classical Greek and Latin formulations, to traditional African life and conceptions of community.
24. Boff, *Trinity and Society*, 119.

## Further reading

Baker-Fletcher, Karen, *Dancing with God: The Trinity from a Womanist Perspective* (St. Louis, KY: Chalice, 2006).

Boff, Leonardo, *Trinity and Society*, trans. Paul Burns (Maryknoll, NY: Orbis, 1988).

Duck, Ruth C., and Patricia Wilson-Kastner, *Praising God: The Trinity in Christian Worship* (Louisville, KY: Westminster John Knox, 1999).

Grenz, Stanley J., *Rediscovering the Triune God: The Trinity in Contemporary Theology* (Minneapolis: Fortress, 2004).

Heim, S. Mark, *The Depth of the Riches: A Trinitarian Theology of Religious Ends* (Grand Rapids, MI: Eerdmans, 2001).

Jenson, Robert W., *The Triune Identity: God According to the Gospel* (Philadelphia: Fortress, 1982).

LaCugna, Catherine Mowry, *God for Us: The Trinity and Christian Life* (San Francisco: HarperSanFrancisco, 1991).

Moltmann, Jürgen, *The Trinity and the Kingdom of God: The Doctrine of God*, trans. Margaret Kohl (San Francisco: Harper & Row; London: SCM Press, 1981).

Volf, Miroslav, and Michael Welker, eds., *God's Life in Trinity* (Minneapolis: Fortress, 2006).

Zizioulas, John D., *Being as Communion: Studies in Personhood and the Church* (Crestwood, NY: St. Vladimir's Seminary Press, 1985).

# Index